The Mass Media Declaration of UNESCO

COMMUNICATION AND INFORMATION SCIENCE

A series of monographs, treatises, and texts
Edited by
MELVIN J. VOIGT
University of California, San Diego

William C. Adams•Television Coverage of the Middle East
William C. Adams•Television Coverage of International Affairs
William C. Adams•Television Coverage of the 1980 Presidential Campaign
Mary B. Cassata and Thomas Skill•Life on Daytime Television
Hewitt D. Crane•The New Social Marketplace
Rhonda J. Crane•The Politics of International Standards
Herbert S. Dordick, Helen G. Bradley, and Burt Nanus•The Emerging Network
    Marketplace
Glen Fisher•American Communication in a Global Society
Oscar H. Gandy, Jr.•Beyond Agenda Setting
Oscar H. Gandy, Jr., Paul Espinosa, and Janusz A. Ordover•Proceedings from the
    Tenth Annual Telecommunications Policy Research Conference
Edmund Glenn•Man and Mankind: Conflict and Communication Between Cultures
Bradley S. Greenberg•Life on Television: Content Analyses of U.S. TV Drama
Bradley S. Greenberg, Michael Burgoon, Judee K. Burgoon, and Felipe
    Korzenny•Mexican Americans and the Mass Media
Cees J. Hamelink•Finance and Information: A Study of Converging Interests
Robert Landau, James H. Bair, and Jean H. Siegman•Emerging Office Systems
John S. Lawrence and Bernard M. Timberg•Fair Use and Free Inquiry
Robert G. Meadow•Politics as Communication
William H. Melody, Liora R. Salter, and Paul Heyer•Culture, Communication, and
    Dependency
Vincent Mosco•Broadcasting in the United States
Vincent Mosco•Pushbutton Fantasies
Kaarle Nordenstreng and Herbert Schiller•National Sovereignty and International
    Communication
Ithiel de Sola Pool•Forecasting the Telephone
Dan Schiller•Telematics and Government
Herbert I. Schiller•Who Knows: Information in the Age of the Fortune 500
Indu B. Singh•Telecommunications in the Year 2000
Jennifer Daryl Slack•Communication Technologies and Society
Dallas W. Smythe•Dependency Road
Janet Wasko•Movies and Money

In Preparation:

Alan Baughcum and Gerald Faulhaber•Telecommunications and Public Policy
Gerald Goldhaber, Harry S. Dennis III, Gary M. Richetto and Osmo A.
    Wiio•Information Strategies
Heather Hudson•Telecommunications and Development
Armand Mattelart and Hector Schmucler•Communication and Information
    Technologies
Vincent Mosco•Proceedings from the Eleventh Annual Telecommunications
    Policy Research Conference
Keith R. Stamm•Communication and Community
Sari Thomas•Studies in Communication Volumes 1–2
Tran Van Dinh•Independence, Liberation, Revolution
Georgette Wang and Wimal Dissanayake•Continuity and Change in
    Communication Systems

The Mass Media Declaration of UNESCO

Kaarle Nordenstreng
University of Tampere, Finland

with
Lauri Hannikainen

ABLEX PUBLISHING CORPORATION
NORWOOD, NEW JERSEY 07648

Copyright © 1984 by Ablex Publishing Corporation

Printed in the United States of America.

Library of Congress Cataloging in Publication Data

Nordenstreng, Kaarle.
  The mass media declaration of UNESCO.

  (Communication and information science)
  Includes the text of the Declaration on fundamental
principles concerning the contribution of the mass media
to strengthening peace and international understanding,
to the promotion of human rights, and to countering
racialism, apartheid and incitement to war.
  Includes indexes.
  1. Declaration on fundamental principles concerning
the contribution of the mass media to strengthening
peace and international understanding, to the promotion
of human rights, and to countering racialism, apartheid
and incitement to war.   2. Freedom of the press.
3. Mass media—Law and legislation.   4. Journalistic
ethics.   I. Hannikainen, Lauri.   II. Declaration on
fundamental principles concerning the contribution of
the mass media to strengthening peace and international
understanding, to the promotion of human rights, and to
countering racialism, apartheid and incitement to war.
III. Title.   IV. Series.
K3255.A41978N67   1984   341.7'577   83-25818
ISBN 0-89391-077-5

Ablex Publishing Corporation
355 Chestnut Street
Norwood, New Jersey 07648

Contents

Preface... xi

PART I. THE DECLARATION.................................   1

1. **The Context: A Movement Towards a New
   International Information Order.**....................   3
   Strategies in the 1970s: Forces in Confrontation....   7
   Truce: Process Through Compromise................ 27
   The 1980s: Contradictions Continued............... 57
   The Concept of NIIO................................. 68

2. **The Shaping: A History of the Preparation.**........ 79
   The Quiet Beginning................................ 80
   The Outburst of Controversies..................... 94
   The Search for Reconciliation...................... 113
   The Outcome Appreciated........................... 128

3. **The Contents: An Examination of the Text.**........ 133
   The Preamble...................................... 133
   The Articles...................................... 135
   The Significance of the Text...................... 138

PART II. INTERNATIONAL LAW AND THE MASS MEDIA......... 139

4. **International Law as a Regulator of
   International Standards.**........................... 141
   Subjects of International Law...................... 142
   Basic Principles of Contemporary International
   Law... 143
   Sources of International Law...................... 148

5. **International Instruments Setting Standards
   for the Mass Media.**.............................. 153
   An Inventory of International Instruments.......... 154

The Responsibility of States for Observing
International Standards. 161

6. **Prohibition of War Propaganda**. 167
International Legal Instruments. 167
The Prohibition of War Propaganda in
International and Domestic Law. 172
Legal and Illegal Use of Force. 174
Who Should Be Punished?. 178
Questions of Responsibility. 178

7. **Contribution to Peaceful Coexistence Among
Nations**. 183
Disarmament. 183
Detente. 185
Peace and Security. 187
Friendship and Cooperation. 189
Quality and Responsibility. 192
Subversive Propaganda. 195
Decolonization and the New International
Economic Order. 197

8. **Standards at the National Level**. 201
Racial Discrimination. 202
Genocide. 205
National Order and the Rights of Individuals. 206

PART III. **FROM INTERNATIONAL LAW TO PROFESSIONAL
ETHICS**. 211

9. **Codes of Ethics: An Inventory**. 215
Comparison with International Instruments. 215
Suggestion to Foster International
Responsibility. 222

10. **Journalism as a Profession: A Discussion**. 251
The Declaration of Talloires. 251
New Professional Ethics. 257
From Contradictions to Challenge. 261

APPENDICES. 269

Appendix 1. 271
Declaration on Fundamental Principles concerning the
Contribution of the Mass Media to Strengthening Peace and
International Understanding, to the Promotion of Human

Rights and to Countering Racialism, Apartheid and Incitement
to War (final text adopted at the 20th session of the General
Conference in November 1978)

Appendix 2 . . . . **276**
Statement of Amadou-Mahtar M'Bow, Director-General of
Unesco (from speech at the close of the 20th session of the
General Conference in November 1978)

Appendix 3 . . . . **278**
Report of Existing Legislation and Measures Taken by Member
States to Encourage the Use of Mass Media Against
Propaganda on Behalf of War, Racialism and Hatred Among
Nations (presented to the 17th session of the General
Conference in 1972)

Appendix 4 . . . . **289**
Draft Declaration of Fundamental Principles Governing the Use
of the Mass Media (first draft prepared by Hilding Eek in
January 1974)

Appendix 5 . . . . **292**
Draft Declaration of Fundamental Principles concerning the
Strengthening of Peace and International Understanding by
the Mass Media (prepared by meeting of experts in March
1974)

Appendix 6 . . . . **296**
Draft Declaration of Fundamental Principles on the Role of
the Mass Media in Strengthening Peace and International
Understanding and in Combating War Propaganda, Racism
and Apartheid (presented to the 18th session of the General
Conference in 1974)

Appendix 7 . . . . **300**
Letter from the Delegation of the United States (at
intergovernmental meeting of experts in December 1975)

Appendix 8 . . . . **301**
Draft Declaration on Fundamental Principles Governing the
Use of the Mass Media in Strengthening Peace and
International Understanding and in Combating War
Propaganda, Racism and Apartheid (prepared by
intergovernmental meeting of experts in December 1975 and
presented to the 19th session of the General Conference in
1976)

Appendix 9 . . . . **306**
Summary of Interventions Made in Programme Commission III
(at the 19th session of the General Conference in November
1976)

Appendix 10. . . . . **341**

Draft Declaration of Fundamental Principles on the Role of the Mass Media in Strengthening Peace and International Understanding and in Combating War Propaganda, Racism and Apartheid (prepared by Gunnar Garbo for the Drafting and Negotiating Group of the 19th session of the General Conference in November 1976)

Appendix 11. . . . . **347**

Draft Declaration on Fundamental Principles Governing the Use of the Mass Media in Strengthening of Peace and International Understanding and in Combating War Propaganda, Racism and Apartheid (prepared by consultants in July–September 1977; with Aide Memoire)

Appendix 12. . . . . **360**

Draft Declaration on Fundamental Principles concerning the Contribution of the Mass Media to Strengthening Peace and International Understanding and to Combating War Propaganda, Racism and Apartheid (prepared by consultants in December 1977)

Appendix 13. . . . . **371**

Report of the Director-General and Resolution by the Executive Board concerning a Final Draft Declaration (at the 104th session of the Executive Board in April–June 1978)

Appendix 14. . . . . **375**

Draft Declaration on Fundamental Principles Governing the Contribution of the Mass Media to Strengthening Peace and International Understanding and to Combating War Propaganda, Racialism and Apartheid (presented to the 20th session of the General Conference in 1978; with explanatory notes)

Appendix 15. . . . . **382**

Letter from the Union of Journalists in Finland with proposal for a "Professional Alternative" text of the Declaration (presented to international and regional organizations of journalists in September 1978; with explanatory notes)

Appendix 16. . . . . **391**

Proposal for a "Western Alternative" text of the Declaration (presented to the 20th session of the General Conference in November 1978)

Appendix 17. . . . . **396**

Proposal for a "Socialist Alternative" text of the Declaration (presented to the 20th session of the General Conference in November 1978)

Appendix 18. . . . . **399**
Proposal for a "Non-Aligned Alternative" text of the
Declaration (presented to the 20th session of the General
Conference in November 1978)

Appendix 19. . . . . **404**
Coverage of the debate on the Declaration in *Time* magazine
(before and after its adoption in November 1978)

Appendix 20. . . . . **408**
Selected interventions in Programme Commission IV (at the
20th session of the General Conference in November 1978)

Appendix 21. . . . . **438**
"Unesco Declaration—Best of Bad Alternatives" (evaluation by
L. R. Sussman, USA)

Appendix 22. . . . . **441**
"Declaration and Its Falsifiers" (evaluation by Y. Kashlev, USSR)

Appendix 23. . . . . **444**
"All's Well That Ends Well" (evaluation by D. R. Mankekar,
India)

Appendix 24. . . . . **449**
International Instruments concerning Journalism and Mass
Communication

Appendix 25. . . . . **454**
Mexico Declaration (adopted by representatives of
international and regional organizations of journalists in April
1980)

Appendix 26. . . . . **458**
The Declaration of Talloires (adopted by leaders of
independent news organizations in May 1981)

Appendix 27. . . . . **461**
Major Events, Statements, and Resolutions of a Worldwide
Debate Until 1978

Name Index. **467**

Subject Index. **471**

Preface

On 22 November, 1978 the United Nations Educational, Scientific and Cultural Organization, Unesco, made up of virtually all independent states in the world, adopted by acclamation a document called *Declaration on Fundamental Principles concerning the Contribution of the Mass Media to Strengthening Peace and International Understanding, to the Promotion of Human Rights and to Countering Racialism, Apartheid and Incitement to War.* The consensus grew out of a decade-long professional and political debate on the role of the mass media in society and the world at large—a debate which has since continued as a controversy around the concept of a "new international information order."

The Mass Media Declaration constitutes a landmark in the history of journalism and mass communication, demonstrating the unprecedented political attention which mass media issues gained throughout the world in the 1970s. Moreover, the Declaration can be seen, in the words of Amadou-Mahtar M'Bow, the Director-General of Unesco, as "a new set of principles which all creators and distributors of information would be able to endorse," since "for the first time, the international community has at its disposal a body of principles and ideals such as can provide guidance for the action and practice of all those whose hearts are set on justice and peace."

It is indeed remarkable that an agreement could be found upon such a "body of principles and ideals" at a time when ideological confrontations, rather than harmony, became characteristic of the international community. As M'Bow put it, the outcome was "an example of the triumph of patient efforts to achieve conciliation," with "the pre-eminence which should be given to the worldwide approach which, while still taking account of specific circumstances, gives pride of place to the common interests of mankind."

Politically, it was a triumph of "détente," peaceful coexistence between different social systems—so-called East and West, North and South.

Professionally, it was a reminder of the fact that journalism and mass communication, however ideological in nature, has a common ground of universal values on which an international code of ethics can be constructed.

Since November 1978, these optimistic perspectives of universal humanism have been challenged increasingly by political developments towards greater, rather than reduced, use of force in settling international disputes, and towards more, rather than less, power to the ruthless market forces in determining the relations between rich and poor. "The law of the Jungle is returning," said President Nyerere of Tanzania in receiving the 1981 Third World Prize in New Delhi in February 1982—after meeting with President Reagan in the "North-South Summit" in Cancun. Indeed, by the middle of 1982 the world has turned more into an uncivilized jungle, with military force instead of reason and negotiations determining the cause of events in the Malvinas-Falkland Islands and in Lebanon. At the diplomatic level, the United States refused to join the most comprehensive collective exercise in setting mutually beneficial rules for the international community, the Law of the Sea Treaty. At the United Nations, the Second Special Session on Disarmament—meeting during Israel's raiding of the Palestinians in Lebanon—failed to agree on anything substantial about the greatest global problem facing mankind.

In the field of journalism and mass communication, the same development was reflected in a vote at the United Nations General Assembly in December 1981, when the U.S., together with Israel, broke the consensus which had prevailed ever since the adoption of the Mass Media Declaration. Since the beginning of 1981, the U.S. government, in alliance with private enterprise spokesmen from journalistic and academic communities throughout the Western hemisphere, has waged a campaign against the movement, which, after bringing about the Mass Media Declaration, promoted a number of other projects towards a "new order."

A central theme in this campaign has been "the efforts by the Soviet Union and some Third World governments to legitimize, under the rubric of 'New International Information Order,' government controls over the collection, transmission and publication of news by the press and other mass media," as the concern was expressed in a study on the United States Policy toward the United Nations, issued in early 1982 by a U.S. group of prominent international affairs experts (including former Secretaries of State Dean Rusk, Cyrus Vance, and Edmund Muskie). Corporate-sponsored advertisements of the campaign warned against "Danger at the UN," where both "press freedoms and economic freedoms are under attack." "The defenders of economic freedoms, led by President Reagan in Cancun," were urged to fight back, and it was recommended that "the United States should not feel compelled to continue its generosity toward UN agencies that remain relentlessly hostile to freedom of information and other fundamental principles of democracy."

The evidence provided by this volume sharply contradicts such an understanding of the situation, which appears to be a flagrant fabrication rather than an adequate reflection of reality. Certainly, there is a great deal of ignorance involved in this campaign, but it is also obvious that to accuse Unesco of promoting governmental controls is, in many cases, only an excuse to defend the *status quo*—the old order with its built-in bias against the very principles of the Mass Media Declaration: to strengthen peace and international understanding, to promote human rights, to counter racialism, apartheid, and war propaganda. Whereas it is not fashionable to refrain from supporting these noble ideals of the international community—at least from paying lip service to them—it is a virtue to defend "freedom" against "censorship."

All the same, the campaign falls short of both truthfulness and honesty. The new Secretary-General of the UN, Javier Perez de Cuellar, made this a point of his first speech on communication in June 1982 (addressing the UN Committee on Information in New York):

> Unfortunately, influential sections of the mass media, in a number of countries, seem to have been alarmed by the adoption of the Declaration, and by the debates which have subsequently occurred on this subject, and their presentation of it to the public has reflected certain unfounded fears. The nature and intention of the Mass Media Declaration has, in the process, been considerably misperceived. The Declaration, though a formal and solemn instrument, is not in any way binding upon States, nor, of course, upon the media. Its articles, whether directed to the mass media or to States, do not purport to be anything but advisory. What then is the use of such a document, it might be asked. The answer is that its use lies in stating a generally acceptable approach on a matter of critical importance to the international community. The Declaration refers to the Universal Declaration of Human Rights and to the 1966 Covenant on Civil and Political Rights—and thus, by implication, to the legal obligations of States to assist the mass media to implement its moral and professional obligations.
>
> Critics of the Declaration, who express concern that national public authorities have been given an instrument to limit freedom of the press, are mistaken. Such a concept was not and could never be the intention of any United Nations deliberative body, in which free and open debate always prevails.

Perez de Cuellar also emphasized that "our thoughts and actions are daily affected by the nature and quality of the information directed to us" and that "[t]he structures of world peace are often built in the minds of ordinary people, based on feelings of security and confidence in a just and rational world."

Indeed, considering the deterioration of the international situation since the adoption of the Declaration, it can be said that its importance has become the greater, the more the world has been pushed toward the law of the jungle. The emerging universal ethics in journalism reflect the same contradictions as are manifested in the new peace movement demanding a freeze on all nuclear weapons; both are inspired by an intellectual and moral realization that the world is heading towards a disaster unless the course of development is drastically changed.

The fundamental nature of the Mass Media Declaration, its prehistory and significance, makes it an indispensable part of the basic knowledge of all professional communicators—journalists and other producers of mass media content—as well as those responsible for the management of mass media enterprises and for the training of their creative personnel. Beyond that, the message of this book is intended for those diplomats and other decision makers in international relations who shape the normative and political framework within which the mass media operate.

The book is divided into three parts. The first focuses on the diplomatic process of formulating the Declaration in the context of a "new international information order." The second part reviews the international law applicable to the field of journalism and mass communication; it is an introduction to an emerging area of study which has been greatly enhanced by the Declaration. The third part covers another area which, along with the Unesco debate in the 1970s, has become more and more central for professional communicators: the social ethics and the philosophical foundations of mass communication.

Throughout, the book has been written as a scientific contribution to a debate which has been predominantly political and polemical in nature, even in the academic community. This has necessitated many (and lengthy) quotes in the text and the extensive appendices at the end.

In systematic studies of mass communication, the present book fits best in a unit on international communication, together with other basic readings such as *National Sovereignty and International Communication* (Ablex, 1979) and *Many Voices, One World* (the "MacBride Report," Unesco, 1980). For those interested in further study, much relevant material is listed in the footnotes.

The author wishes to acknowledge the cooperation of the Unesco Secretariat for furnishing documentation and advice. Professor Hilding Eek (Sweden), Mr. Gunnar Garbo (Norway), and Mr. Gunnar Naesselund (Denmark), who were centrally involved in the preparation of the Declaration, were kind enough to review various drafts of Chapter 2. Collegial cooperation from outside Unesco and Scandinavia in writing the history of the Declaration include contributions from Mr. Clement Jones (UK), Mr. German Carnero Roque (Peru), Mr. D. R. Mankekar (India), and Dr. Valeri Anichtchouk (Byelorussia). Professor Leo Gross (USA) and Dr. Yuri Kolossov (USSR) gave valuable comments on the draft chapters of Part 2. Special acknowledgement is due, of course, to the collaboration of Mr. Lauri Hannikainen, Licenciate of Law from the University of Helsinki (and former student of Prof. Gross at the Fletcher School of Law and Diplomacy). The staff of Ablex and the Series Editor Mel Voigt deserve compliments for smooth processing of a project which was not only politically sensitive but also technically burdensome.

Finally, the author owes thanks to the professional and human environment of those places where he operated while preparing this book: the University of Tampere, Finland; Southern Illinois University at Carbondale, USA (April 1981 and February 1982); and Tanzania School of Journalism, Dar es Salaam (through 1981 until mid-1982).

Kaarle Nordenstreng

I

The Declaration

"Declaration on Fundamental Principles concerning the Contribution of the Mass Media to Strengthening Peace and International Understanding, to the Promotion of Human Rights and to Countering Racialism, Apartheid and Incitement to War" is perhaps the most thoroughfully negotiated text about journalism and mass communication which ever has been produced. The text itself, reproduced as Appendix 1 to this volume, is hardly revolutionary. In fact, at first glance it may appear as a piece of obscure political rhetoric, written in "Unescese," not particularly appealing to mass media professionals. A closer look shows, however, that the Declaration constitutes a significant case—not so much because of its manifest content, but rather due to its political and professional implications. These can be "read" in the six-year long history of preparing the Declaration—a history which makes up a central chapter in a global movement towards a "new international information order." Therefore the adoption of the Declaration at the General Conference of Unesco* in November 1978, without dissenting votes from any of Unesco's 146 Member States at the time, was not just another event of routine diplomacy but indeed a historical move.

By adopting the Mass Media Declaration, the international community had determined for the first time overall guidelines for the mass media—comprehensive, albeit vague—and, furthermore, this had happened without a divisive vote, by consensus. It is a diplomatic miracle that such an outcome was possible in a case which had caused more controversy in Unesco and, in general, among those involved with the mass media, than perhaps any other single issue had previously. That the case had become politically "hot," is only natural, since at issue were not only matters of the mass media, but, ultimately, the fundamental values of different socio-economic-political systems.

Not without reason, then, was the passing of this Declaration seen to be an outstanding achievement for Unesco and a personal victory for its

---

*The form "Unesco" (without capitalizing) is used throughout this book, in conformity with the documents of the Organization itself.

Director-General, Amadou Mahtar M'Bow. (M'Bow's own assessment of the significance of the consensus reached at Unesco is reproduced as Appendix 2.)

Yet the Declaration is not only a landmark of diplomacy, but also a significant case for the professional field of journalism and mass communication. The debate throughout the process of its drafting had not only been political, but also professional, extending from problems of everyday practice, such as the working conditions of journalists, to philosophical foundations of the profession, such as the role and tasks of the mass media in society. And there is little doubt that the result is subscribed to by the majority of working journalists in the world. A demonstration of this support can be found in the "Mexico Declaration," which was issued on 3 April 1980 by five international and regional organizations of journalists, representing together some 300,000 professionals in all parts of the world (see Appendix 25).

Therefore, a study of this Declaration is of importance in the education of journalists, both for professional training and life-long education. The three chapters in Part 1 are intended to help in introducing the Declaration into the programs of journalism training and in retaining it on the permanent agenda of professional debate. Chapter 1 outlines the international-political context out of which the Declaration emerged and within which its adventurous formulation occurred in the 1970s. This Chapter also provides a review of relevant developments after the adoption of the Declaration until early 1982 by which time the movement towards a new international information order had entered another stage of confrontation. Chapter 2 provides concrete historical evidence related to various stages of the drafting process of the Declaration, with special emphasis on what took place behind the doors of diplomatic meetings. Chapter 3 provides a brief analysis of the final text itself from the point of view of professional standards of journalism.

Article VIII of the Declaration makes a direct appeal that "people who participate in the professional training of journalists . . . and who assist them in performing their functions in a responsible manner should attach special importance to the principles of this Declaration when drawing up and ensuring application of their codes of ethics." In fact, it is impossible to look at the Declaration in isolation from the general normative framework provided by so-called "international law" on the one hand, and from the nature and ethics of the profession of journalism on the other. Therefore, Part 1 of this book should be seen as an introduction—in terms of the concrete history of the Declaration—to the topics dealt with in Parts 2 and 3.

1

The Context: A Movement Towards a New International Information Order

"The media have not escaped a world in turmoil." These opening words in one of the by now innumerable publications on the "great debate"[1] are symptomatic. Something threatening is happening in the world which is inviting trouble in the field of journalism and mass communication. Surely this is a partisan view, determined by a "war between free press and controlled press philosophies," as the problem is defined from a typically Western perspective. The perspective of the developing countries, as well as that of the socialist countries of Eastern Europe, is not nearly as gloomy; rather it presents a promising view of a world that can be changed for the better. Nevertheless there is "a world in turmoil," and it is generally agreed that, worldwide, the field of journalism and mass communication is in a state of crisis.

This crisis surfaced during the 1970s. An unforseen intensity of activities— professional and scientific, as well as diplomatic—involve matters of communication in general and of international communication in particular. One of the reviews of this worldwide debate is illustrative of major events, statements, and resolutions. It is reproduced in Appendix 27.[2]

Yet it is evident that the recent, almost explosive, attention to matters of (international) communication has a long history, extending at least to the origin of the United Nations (as well illustrated by the chart in Appendix 27).

---

[1]*The Media Crisis . . .* , World Press Freedom Committee, 1980 (quote from George Beebe's Introduction, p. vii). A concise overview of the beginning of this "great debate" is provided in the Autumn 1978 issue of *Journal of Communication* (Philadelphia). Included in this overview is a summary of Jonathan F. Gunter's report "United States and the Debate on the World 'information order'," made for the U.S. International Communication Agency in the Academy for Education Development, Inc., 1978. See also J. Richstad & M. H. Anderson (Eds.), *Crisis in International News: Policies and Prospects,* New York: Columbia University Press, 1981.

[2]*Toward a New World Information Order: Consequences for Development Policy,* Bonn: Institut für internationale Begegnungen and Friedrich Ebert Stiftung, 1979. The publication reports an international seminar organized in Bonn in late 1978, and the appendix chart is based on a paper by Dietrich Berwanger from West Berlin. Appendix 27 is reproduced here with the permission of the Institute for International Relations (Bonn).

In fact, it can be argued that the debate of the 1970s concerning a new international information order provides little that is genuinely new.[3]

For example, the problem of global imbalance of information structures and flows was recognized by the United Nations (UN) long before any "great debate." The UN's Economic and Social Council, ECOSOC, addressed the problem in 1961 (see item 5 in Appendix 27). One year later, the UN General Assembly expressed its concern over the fact that "70 percent of the population of the world lack adequate information facilities and are thus denied effective enjoyment of the right to information," and invited the governments of developed countries "to cooperate with less developed countries with a view to meeting the urgent needs of the less developed countries in connexion with this programme for the development of independent national information media, with due regard for the culture of each country."[4] Moreover, as early as 1952 a UN General Assembly resolution considered that "it is essential for a proper development of public opinion in under-developed countries that independent domestic information enterprises should be given facilities and assistance in order that they may be enabled to contribute to the spread of information, to the development of national culture and to international understanding," and continued that "the time has arrived for the elaboration of a concrete programme and plan of action in this respect."[5]

It is interesting—if not even ironic—that it took nearly thirty years before the UN system, through Unesco, reacted to this appeal by mobilizing a major international program for the development of communication (IPDC, to be discussed later in this Chapter). Why did it take such a long time before major action was taken on a problem which had been recognized for decades? The review of developments in and around Unesco which follows provides an answer in two parts.

First, there has been a gradual but fundamental *change in the relations of social, economic, and political forces in the world,* beginning with the establishment of the "socialist" countries (the Soviet Union and the rest of the "Second World") and ending with the process of decolonization, which created the "developing" countries of the "Third World." In this situation the "capitalist" countries of the "First World" (dominated by the United States) have gone on the defensive, faced with an overall challenge which was articulated in demands for a new order—in the field of

---

[3]This point was made by the present author in a paper ("Defining the New International Information Order: Parameters, Principles and Terminology with Regards to International Relations") presented to the conference "World Communications: Decisions for the Eighties" at The Annenberg School of Communications, University of Pennsylvania, Philadelphia, 12–14 May 1980. To be published in G. Gerbner & M. Siefert (Eds.), *World Communications Handbook,* New York: Longman (in press).

[4]Resolution 1778 (XVII) of the 17th session of the UN General Assembly (7 December 1962).

[5]Resolution 633 (VII) of the 7th session of the UN General Assembly (16 December 1952).

international communications as well as in the world economy. Thus, the new international information order became an issue not so much because of the emergence of some drastically new phenomena (such as communications technology), but fundamentally because a sufficiently strong coalition of social forces had accumulated to enforce a new order—at least as a political program, even if not as an immediate reality. Thus, the struggle around a new international information order— and the Mass Media Declaration of Unesco as an integral part of it—no longer appears as a distinct case, but rather as a reflection of conflicting socio-economico-political forces on a world scale. The media debate is indeed an integral part of "a world in turmoil."

Second, the setting-up of the IPDC in 1980, as a manifestation of the new information order, was an outcome of political tactics on the part of the U.S. and other Western powers. *Material support for media facilities in the developing countries was supposed to reduce the force of the political demands for a new order*. The leading Western powers did not oppose such a transfer of resources to the underdeveloped world; on the contrary, they advocated it, since it was considered to be an effective means of diverting the demands for a new order. As put by the Western strategists themselves, its intention was "trading ideology against cooperation."[6] And certainly the main source of inspiration for this "trade-off" was the Mass Media Declaration, supported by the Soviet-led front of socialist and developing countries and perceived in the West as the most notorious of "their proposals for a 'better' information order, promoted in lofty dimensions, [which] often prove to be cleverly disguised strategies to gain further control and regulation of the flow of news."[7]

Consequently, we are dealing with a complex problem combining long-term historical developments on a worldwide scale with political maneuvering at a UN organization, Unesco. In both respects, the Mass Media Declaration has played a central role: as a manifestation of a new power constellation in international relations, whereby a "Third-World Socialist" offensive has pushed the Western side into positions of reaction and retreat. Not surprisingly, the new information order appears to those who have vested interests in the old order as "a bad idea that refuses to die."[8] Equally logical is the enthusiasm with which the same idea is being entertained among those whose interests are at odds with the old order. This position, held typically by advocates of the developing and socialist countries, has been well expressed by Unesco's Director General, for

[6]R. Righter, "Lessons From Belgrade . . . The Bankruptcy of Consensus," in *Voices of Freedom* (Working Papers of a Conference held in Talloires, France, 15–17 May 1981), Medford, Mass.: The Edward R. Murrow Center of Public Diplomacy in cooperation with the World Press Freedom Committee, 1981, p. 20.

[7]G. Beebe, op. cit. in note 1 above.

[8]Op. cit. in note 1 (quote from the title of an article by Leonard H. Marks, p. 29).

whom the new order is "an idea whose time is near." In his review, the Mass Media Declaration comprises "a contribution of the highest importance to preparing people for the advent of a new information order."[9]

In order to properly appreciate this situation, it is necessary to keep in mind the fact that the foundation of Unesco was an outcome of predominantly Western activity in 1945, and that it was the United States that stressed "the paramount importance of the media in spreading knowledge and common understanding for security."[10] After having introduced the communication component into the Constitution, the U.S. proposed, at the first session of the General Conference (Unesco's highest decision-making body), that Unesco should establish a worldwide communication system worth some $250 million. This proposal was turned down, largely due to resistance by the British, who feared that the U.S. would use Unesco "to blitz the world with American ideas."[11] However, as Joseph Mehan showed in his review of the U.S.-Unesco history:

> The U.S. continued pursuing this approach, producing material for Unesco radio programs that even friendly editorial comment in Western Europe called "American propaganda." The Polish delegate at the 1947 General Conference introduced a resolution urging Unesco to take legal measures "to put mass information at the sole disposal of friendly international cooperation," which would "render impossible any activity hostile to such cooperation." The Polish initiative, however, did not succeed after Senator Benton rose to denounce it.
>
> The same situation prevailed into the 1950s. When the Korean War began, the United States stepped up its efforts to have its viewpoints promoted in all Unesco communications media. U.S. newspapers supported this effort, with headlines such as "US looks to Unesco to Tell Korea Truth" and "Unesco's Aid Sought Along the Propaganda Front." In response, the *London News Chronicle* editorialized, "American insistence that Unesco enter the Cold War by spreading pro-Western, anti-Communist propaganda is producing a crisis which may wreck the Organization." While Unesco's activities were criticized frequently by the world press as reflecting too strongly U.S. foreign policy and ideologies, an Associated Press story at that time quoted senator Benton denouncing Unesco's "aloofness" and demanding that it recognize "its role as a political instrument of the Cold War."[12]

[9]Amadou-Mahtar M'Bow, "Unesco and Communications in the Modern World," speech at the University of Bujumbura (Burundi), 5 February 1980. Reprinted in op. cit. in note 1 (quote on p. 19).

[10]J. A. Mehan, "Unesco and the U.S.: Action and Reaction," *Journal of Communication*, Autumn 1981, p. 159.

[11]Ibid., p. 160.

[12]Ibid., p. 160.

The U.S. action did not succeed in turning Unesco to a political instrument of the Cold War. Yet, by the early 1960s the world organization was "extremely popular in the U.S., particularly among intellectuals and the media," as Mehan put it. But "in the turbulent decade of the sixties, when some 70 former colonies gained their independence, the relationship between the United States and Unesco cooled considerably."[13]

Obviously, the changes in the global relations of socio-political forces that caused the "turbulence" of the 1960s also determined the shift of official U.S. policy towards Unesco from action to reaction. And one should not forget that these changes were not only a consequence of the decolonization of the "Third World," but also of the fact that the socialist "Second World" was consolidated and became more active in the international arena. Thus, as shown by Wolfgang Kleinwaechter, the Soviet Union's entry into Unesco in 1954 was reflected, by 1956, at the 9th session of the General Conference in New Delhi, where a resolution was passed inviting Member States to direct the mass media toward the cause of peace and international understanding.[14] In 1960, the 11th session of the General Conference in Paris even demanded that steps be taken against war propaganda and in support of the UN efforts towards disarmament. On the other hand, at the 15th session of the General Conference in Paris in 1968, the USSR did not succeed in having a convention introduced to the effect of prohibiting the use of the mass media for propagating "militarism, revanchism, hatred among peoples and racial discrimination."[15]

We now focus on the specific developments which make up the movement towards a new international information order in the 1970s.

STRATEGIES IN THE 1970S: FORCES IN CONFRONTATION

At least three different, although partly overlapping, "strategic designs" or stages can be discerned in the development of the global relation of forces during the 1970s—in the field of communication policies as well as in the grand designs of world political strategies.[16] The first, occupying

---

[13]Ibid., pp. 160–161.

[14]W. Kleinwaechter, "Die Tätigkeit der Unesco auf dem Gebiet der Information (1. Teil: 1946–1970)" (The Activity of Unesco in the Field of Information, in German), *Theorie und Praxis des sozialistischen Journalismus* (Journal of the faculty of Journalism at Karl-Marx-University, Leipzig), No. 3, 1977, p. 76.

[15]Ibid., p. 78.

[16]This division, and the bulk of the present passage, is based on the author's article "Struggle around 'New International Information Order'," *Communicator* (Journal of the Indian Institute of Mass Communication, New Delhi), No. 4, October 1979, pp. 24–29. As indicated in the article, the present author prefers using the phrasing "new international information order," whereas the phrase "Third World" is considered too vague to be taken at face value in a scholarly text.

the early 1970s until 1976, is dominated by an *offensive on the part of developing countries against the industrialized West*. The second stage might be characterized as a *Western counterattack of a self-defensive nature,* which peaked around 1976–1977. The third strategic situation emerged soon after the second and was highlighted on a number of occasions in 1978, including the adoption of the Mass Media Declaration. It might be described as a stage of *tactical maneuvering in a spirit of compromise.*

Naturally, such an outline cannot do justice to all aspects of reality. In particular, one should not forget that this history does not begin and end with these stages, but that they constitute only small cycles in a broader transition of long-term processes.

Decolonization Offensive

The first of these three stages was a logical continuation of the decolonization process, which accelerated in the 1960s. Herbert I. Schiller has characterized the emergence of this situation in these apt words:

> The idyllic picture of a world coming together culturally and economically under the benign auspices of American capitalism began to blister and crack in the late 1960s. A combination of developments focused attention on what the conditions actually were behind the glossy images that were circulated by the powerful Western communications machinery. Many new nations found that their economies remained as feeble and dependent as ever. The victorious but devastating wars of national liberation by the peoples of Korea, Algeria, Cuba, Indo-China, Angola, and Mozambique revealed the extent to which imperialists would go to hold on to their privileged positions.
>
> Finally, the appearance of a new, powerful communications technology, satellite communications, provided instantaneous, worldwide transmission. This potential, taken together with the experience that had been accumulated from 25 years' exposure to United States media outputs, set off an alarm signal across the oceans. What might be expected from an American, corporate-controlled communications satellite system, free to beam its transmissions into any spot or home across the globe.[17]

By the early 1970s, the developing countries had accumulated a great deal of political power and economic potential, with the assistance of such organizations as the Movement of Non-Aligned Countries and OPEC. All this created a new relation of forces in the world arena, al-

---

[17]H. I. Schiller, "Cultural Domination Adjusts to the Growing Demand for a New International Information Order," paper presented at the seminar organized by the Latin American Institute of Transnational Studies (ILET) in Amsterdam, September 1977, Mexico City: ILET, 1977.

ready under pressure from the socialist part of the world, leading to such manifestations as the oil crisis and the UN declaration on the New International Economic Order—all of which worked against the vested interests of the Western world order. Another corollary to this offensive of the "underdog" against the West was a polarization of the Arab-Israeli conflict, reflected, not only in a war between the parties, but also in the UN resolution by which the majority of the international community defined zionism as a form of racism.

In this situation, it appeared that a new chapter in world history was in the making, and it was not by chance that the phrase "new order" became popular. After all, it implies a *radical analysis of the world*; the concept of "order" points at a global structure not far from Lenin's theory of imperialism. Beyond this, it suggests a *radical program to change the world*; the notion of "new" may well be interpreted as a call for war against the "old order." Consequently, the basic pattern was that *the West was on the defensive and the developing countries, supported by the socialist countries, were on the offensive.*

As a political program and an intellectual concept, decolonization was well established by the early seventies (legitimized by the authority of the UN). But before 1973, the idea of decolonization was not applied in an articulated and authoritative manner to the sphere of information and culture. This occurred at the *Fourth Conference of Heads of State or Government of the Non-Aligned Countries in Algiers* (Algeria), attended by 75 members of the Non-Aligned Movement. The political declaration of the Conference made the point that "the activities of imperialism are not confined solely to the political and economic fields, but also cover the cultural and social fields," and demanded "concerted action in the fields of mass communication" as a part of the Action Program for Economic Cooperation.[18]

The initiative launched in Algiers was carried forward in 1975 at the *Ministerial Conference of the Non-Aligned Countries in Lima* (Peru), where the attending 81 Foreign Ministers adopted a special resolution on "Cooperation in the Field of Diffusion of Information and Mass Communications Media."[19] In the same year, a *Pool of Press Agencies of the Non-Aligned Countries* started its operation under the coordination of the Yugoslavian news agency Tanjug.[20]

---

[18]Tran Van Dinh, "Nonalignment and Cultural Imperialism," in K. Nordenstreng & H. I. Schiller (Eds.), *National Sovereignty and International Communication*, Norwood, New Jersey: Ablex, 1979, pp. 265–266.
[19]Ibid., p. 266-267.
[20]See e.g., A. Spasic, "News Agencies Pool of the Non-Aligned Countries," *The Democratic Journalist*, (Journal of the International Organization of Journalists, Prague), No. 5, 1977 (pp. 5–8); reprinted in O. Bures (Ed.), *Towards a New World Information Order*, Prague: International Organization of Journalists, 1977.

The real breakthrough of the ideas of "information decolonization" took place in 1976. In March, the *Non-Aligned Symposium of Information* in Tunis (Tunisia), attended by 38 Member States and 13 observers, laid down a political framework for the "emancipation" of the developing countries from the "structures of imperialist power."[21] The phrase "new international order" was first applied to information there:

> Since information in the world shows a disequilibrium favouring some and ignoring others, it is the duty of the non-aligned countries and the other developing countries to change this situation and obtain the decolonization of information and initiate a new international order in information.[22]

In July 1976, the *Conference on Press Agencies Pool of the Non-Aligned Countries* met in New Delhi (India), "for the first time at the high political level of ministers of information."[23] The ministers from 59 Non-Aligned countries prepared the Constitution for the Pool and issued a landmark statement, the *New Delhi Declaration,* which contains a sharp analysis of the existing international order as a justification of demands for a new order:

> 1. The present global information flows are marked by a serious inadequacy and imbalance. The means of communicating information are concentrated in a few countries. The great majority of countries are reduced to being passive recipients of information which is disseminated from a few centres.
> 2. This situation perpetuates the colonial era of dependence and domination. It confines judgements and decisions on what should be known, and how it should be made known, into the hands of a few.
> 3. The dissemination of information rests at present in the hands of a few agencies located in a few developed countries, and the rest of the peoples of the world are forced to see each other, and even themselves, through the medium of these agencies.
> 4. Just as political and economic dependence are legacies of the era of colonialism, so is the case of dependence in the field of information, which in turn retards the achievement of political and economic growth.
> 5. In a situation where the means of information are dominated and monopolized by a few, freedom of information really comes to mean the freedom of these few to propagate information in the

---

[21]"Information in the Non-Aligned Countries; Vol. 1: Final Resolutions, Speeches and Messages, Working Papers," Secretariat of State for Information, Tunis, 1976 (mimeo), p. 30 (paragraph 26 of the resolution of the first commission).

[22]Ibid., (paragraph 27).

[23]*Communicator,* No. 2–3, April-July 1976, p. 20.

manner of their choosing and the virtual denial to the rest of the right to inform and be informed objectively and accurately.

6. Non-Aligned countries have, in particular, been the victims of this phenomenon. Their endeavours, individual or collective, for world peace, justice, and for the establishment of an equitable international economic order, have been under-played or misrepresented by international news media. Their unity has sought to be eroded. Their efforts to safeguard their political and economic independence and stability have been denigrated . . .[24]

This Declaration was endorsed by the highest authority of the Non-Aligned Movement, the *Fifth Conference of Heads of State or Government of the Non-Aligned Countries,* which met in Colombo (Sri Lanka) in August 1976, with the participation of 87 members of the Non-Aligned Movement.[25] The Colombo summit also legitimized the demands for a new order:

> A new international order in the fields of information and mass communications is as vital as a new international economic order.
>
> Non-Aligned countries noted with concern the vast and ever-growing gap between communication capacities in non-aligned countries and in the advanced countries which is a legacy of their colonial past. This has created a situation of dependence and domination in which the majority of countries are reduced to being passive recipients of biased, inadequate and distorted information. The fuller identification and affirmation of their national and cultural identity thus required them to rectify this serious imbalance and to take urgent steps to provide greater momentum in this new area of mutual cooperation.
>
> The emancipation and development of national information media is an integral part of the overall struggle for political, economic and social independence for a large majority of the peoples of the world who should not be denied the right to inform and to be informed objectively and correctly . . . .[26]

New Professional Perspectives

Related to this overall political development was a gradual change in perspective, which could be noticed beginning in the late 1960s, in the *academic community of communication scholars,* not only in the developing countries, but above all in the West. It was a reorientation of theoretical

[24]Ibid., pp. 20–22.

[25]The proceedings of the Colombo summit have been published in *Review of International Affairs* (Belgrade), No. 634, 1976 (5 September 1976).

[26]Ibid., pp. 30–31 (paragraphs 160–162 of the Political Declaration).

approaches, beginning with self-critical awareness of how "non-political" research had in fact promoted conservative mass media policies, and ending with fundamental reappraisal of the scientific world outlook or paradigm which had dominated the tradition of communication research in the West. Since this tradition was mainly "made in USA," the emerging critical school of thought alienated scholars from American authorities who, until the late 1960s, had enjoyed virtual hegemony in this field of study all over the world, with the exception of socialist countries with their Marxist-Leninist approach. And the more the critical orientation departed from the U.S. mainstream, the more versatile became the field of study, where some Marxist scholars also found a legitimate place.[27]

The new orientations in the political as well as the academic sphere were brought together by Unesco at the *Meeting of Experts on Mass Communication and Society* convened in Montreal (Canada) in June 1969.[28] The meeting, attended not only by "radical" advocates of a new academic approach, but also by well-known authorities of the established American tradition, ended up with a fairly critical assessment of the "state of the art," challenging, among other things, the doctrine of the "free flow of information" and urging communication scholars to adopt a more committed policy orientation in favor of democratic mass media structures under conditions of cultural identity and national sovereignty. On the basis of the Montreal meeting, the General Conference of Unesco launched a program for studies on the effects of communication on society in 1970 (cf., Chapter 2), leading in 1971 to the *Proposals for an International Programme of Communication Research.*[29] As far as communication policies are concerned, Unesco produced the *Report of the Meeting of Experts on Communication Policies and Planning*, a conceptual document which "underlines the importance of research in the formulation of policies and the development of planning strategies to produce communication systems which are functional and fulfill the 'communication needs of society'."[30] Among the several projects which

[27]The present author has elaborated these academic tendencies in an article, "Communication Research in the United States: A Critical Perspective," *Gazette* (Amsterdam), No. 3, 1968 (pp. 207-216); in a collection of essays, *Informational Mass Communication*, Helsinki: Tammi Publishers 1973; and in a chapter, "From Mass Media to Mass Consciousness," in G. Gerbner (Ed.), *Mass Media Policies in Changing Cultures*, New York: Wiley, 1977 (pp. 269–283).

[28]*Mass Media in Society: The Need of Research*, Paris: Unesco Reports and Papers on Mass Communication, No. 59, 1970. (Includes a working paper prepared by Professor James D. Halloran from the University of Leicester, U.K., and the final report of the meeting.) A prelude to this meeting was a symposium on "Mass Media and International Understanding," organized in Ljubljana (Yugoslavia) in September 1968 (proceedings published by the Department of Journalism, School of Sociology, Political Science and Journalism, University of Ljubljana, 1969).

[29]Unesco document COM/MD/20 (Paris, 10 September 1971).

[30]Unesco document COM/MD/24 (Paris, 1 December 1972).

followed these Unesco exercises was a worldwide study of television program structures and flows, as well as a symposium to digest the findings
of this inventory, organized at the University of Tampere (Finland).[31]

Accordingly, *Unesco served as a central forum* for the articulation and
mobilization of a new policy-oriented generation of communication research. But it would be misleading to understand the new perspectives as
a creation of Unesco; all that Unesco did was to facilitate the expression
of certain political and intellectual tendencies of the day. Thus, accusations that the Unesco Secretariat was infiltrated by anti-Western elements
who then instigated a radical line in the organization's communication
program are ill-founded. An objective analysis of the geographic and political backgrounds and of the professional performance of the staff in
the Secretariat will show that, if anything, it was biased towards an overall
Western approach—which, in fact, has given rise to the concept of an
"Anglo-Saxon Mafia" operating within Unesco.

However, a new professional philosophy was gradually introduced
at Unesco, which, until the late 1960s, had faithfully followed the dominant Western tradition. Matters of general political concern (colonialism,
neo-colonialism, racism, peace and war, etc.) were admitted as more natural and primary concerns for communication research and policy than
had been the case before. This merging of political and professional concerns brought mass media policies and philosophies, including principles
of operation and guidelines for media contents, to professional attention,
whereas before they had been typically seen as exclusively "political" matters to be dealt with in the higher spheres of diplomacy. In this—and only
this—sense it is correct to say that the new orientation meant a *politization
of Unesco's involvement* in the field of communication.

In a historical perspective, the new orientation around and within
Unesco reflected not only emerging political and intellectual trends, but
also revived projects which had been introduced at the *UN Conference on
Freedom of Information,* held in Geneva in 1948, but which were then paralyzed by the Cold War. Before the early 1950s the UN General Assembly
and ECOSOC had considered such questions as freedom of information,
standards for professional conduct (including an international code of
ethics for journalists), and right of reply—highly political items.[32] However, the international politics of the time did not allow for their elaboration, and ECOSOC's *Subcommission on Freedom of Information and of the*

---

[31]*Television Traffic—A One-Way Street? A Survey and Analysis of the International Flow of Television Programme
Material* (by K. Nordenstreng and T. Varis), Paris: Unesco Reports and Papers on Mass Communication
No. 70, 1974. Among the contributions to this Tampere symposium was an address by Dr. Urho
Kekkonen, President of Finland.

[32]See e.g. H. Eek, "Principles Governing the Use of the Mass Media as Defined by the United Nations
and UNESCO," in Nordenstreng & Schiller op. cit., pp. 173–194.

Press "failed to reach agreement on anything of consequence and disappeared leaving hardly a trace in history."[33]

First, Unesco was not involved in these unsuccessful attempts, but was instead "pursuing its merry way in projects that were largely devoid of conflict."[34] Indeed the UN and Unesco had an unspoken division of labor, whereby the former operated at the "political" and the latter at the "technical" level. Unesco's achievements in the "technical" field included international agreements on the importation of educational, scientific, and cultural materials, programs for the promotion of books, and support for the setting up of national news agencies, particularly in the developing countries. But later, Unesco was bound to be "politicized," as described by Julian Behrstock, former director of Unesco's Division of Free Flow of Information:

> The beginning of the end of the Unesco's ivory tower was not to become manifest until the mid-1960s. It was the advent of space communication with its capacity for instantaneous worldwide transmissions that put Unesco itself into orbit. A space communication conference held in 1965 produced a report that was published by Unesco with the prefatory comment that the time had come to move beyond the techniques of communication to "a common concern with the content of what is transmitted." More than that: "It is evident that in enhancing the power of the mass media to reach and influence vast audience, space communication imposes a commensurate responsibility for the media to be used for the benefit of all."[35]

It was in this situation that the Mass Media Declaration was introduced on Unesco's agenda in 1972. In fact, the *Declaration came to serve as a symbol and catalyst for conflict between the forces of the new order and its adversaries.* No wonder, then, that this document became controversial; it stood not only for what was written in its text, but came to symbolize the struggle between conflicting forces in the world arena as well. In December 1975—when the so-called Nairobi version, including Article XII on "State responsibility," was prepared in the intergovernmental meeting in Paris—the developing and socialist countries seemed to form a broad front, pressing the West into positions of retreat and even despair, as demonstrated by the vote concerning the above-mentioned UN "zionism-racism resolution," which caused a walk-out of the Western bloc (for details, see Chapter 2).

---

[33]J. Behrstock, "News, Politics and Unesco's Wrong Turn," *International Herald Tribune,* 7 November 1978.
[34]Ibid.
[35]Ibid.

Western Counterattack

At this time a counterattack was mobilized in the West with the aid of old and new mass media lobbies and the publicity provided by the international news agencies and the commercial media themselves. The Draft Declaration served as an early warning device, as the UN and Unesco resolutions on direct broadcasting satellites had done a few years before.[36] However, the most alarming developments for Western eyes were the events in the Non-Aligned Movement reviewed above.

No doubt, such developments gave rise to Western concerns and counterattacks, which in the absence of direct diplomatic participation took the form of a *journalistic campaign over the Western mass media*. Targets of attack were the news agency Pool and other manifestations of the information struggle in the Non-Aligned Movement. But this mobilization of reaction did not neglect Unesco. An attack was launched against the first regional conference on communication policies, organized in San José (Costa Rica) in July 1976:

> The San José conference opened in a tense setting. The IAPA's officers, headed by George Beebe and Germán E. Ornes, established an opposition command post across the street from the Unesco conference. They held meeting with the press and effectually established an opposition presence. Mr. M'Bow invited the IAPA leadership to discuss the news media issues. There seemed to be some convergence of views but that did not persist once the sessions began. The IAPA adamantly foresaw the undermining of freedom of expression if "communications policies" were approved. "The press of the Americas," said the IAPA, "is before one of the most unusual threats it has ever faced in all its turbulent history."[37]

In October-November 1976, attention was concentrated on Nairobi (Kenya), where the General Conference of Unesco met at its 19th session and where, according to Western media coverage, the life or death of press freedom was to be determined by the Draft Declaration. (For studies of this media campaign, see notes 39 and 52 in Chapter 2.)

The seriousness of this counteroffensive in the mass media field is indicated by the fact that it was not only a campaign waged through daily

---

[36]See e.g. E. Ploman, "Satellite Broadcasting, National Sovereignty, and Free Flow of Information," in Nordenstreng & Schiller, op. cit., pp. 154–165.

[37]L. R. Sussman, *Mass News Media and the Third World Challenge*, Washington, D.C.: Center for Strategic and International Studies, Georgetown University, and Beverly Hills/London: Sage Publications, 1977; reprinted in D. B. Fascell (Ed.), *International News*, Washington, D.C.: Center for Strategic and International Studies, Georgetown University, and Beverly Hills/London: Sage Publications, 1980 (quote on p. 122).

and weekly press coverage but strongly supported by *committed lobby organizations* such as the International Press Institute (IPI) and the Inter-American Press Association (IAPA). Furthermore, more or less academic *studies and books* also began to appear in support of this counteroffensive.[38] However, these conservative voices by no means dominated the community of communication research; the bulk of scholars in this field either remained uncommitted (and quite ignorant of the issues involved) or went along with the academic reorientation towards new perspectives discussed above.

This counteroffensive from the West, like the previous strategic stage when the Western powers were generally on the defensive, was by no means a matter of communication politics only, but fundamentally a question of overall international politics. At this stage, the dominant Western line also became harder in a number of other issues, where its interests were at stake—from world economy (UNCTAD and so-called North-South dialogue) to ideology (East-West relations). In particular, Soviet-American relations deteriorated from the relaxed state of "détente" which had dominated the first half of the 1970s, with such historical achievements as the Strategic Arms Limitation Treaty (signed in 1972 in Moscow by President Nixon and Secretary-General Brezhnev) and the Final Act of the Conference on Security and Cooperation in Europe (signed in 1975 in Helsinki by 35 heads of state, including Presidents Ford and Brezhnev). It may also be significant in this respect that towards the end of the 1970s the U.S. Administration adopted a strategy of "trilateralism" whereby the Western world (USA, Western Europe, and Japan) was being mobilized to be stronger and more coherent in defending its interests.

Tactical Shift from "Stick" to "Carrot"

At this time, around 1976-1977, the *U.S. Senate Committee on Foreign Relations* began to prepare special reports and organize hearings on the topic.[39] To be precise, these activities were no longer typical manifestations of the second counterattack stage. While certainly motivated by the same fundamental interests, they advocated a new and more flexible approach—a strategy of selective accommodation to, and active

---

[38]See e.g. Sussman, op. cit., and R. Righter: *Whose News? Politics, the Press and the Third World*, London: Burnett Books and IPI, 1978.

[39]See in particular *The Role and Control of International Communications and Information*, Report to the Subcommittee on International Operations of the Committee on Foreign Relations, United States Senate, 95th Congress, First Session, June, 1977, Washington, D.C.: U.S. Government Printing Office, 1977; and *The New World Information Order*, A Report by George Kroloff and Scott Cohen to the Committee on Foreign Relations, United States Senate, November 1977 (mimeo).

partnership with, the forces confronting the West. Especially outspoken in this respect is the U.S. *Kroloff & Cohen report,* which begins by observing: "Whether we like it or not, there will be a 'New World Information Order'," and continues:

> Worldwide the "New World Information Order" could be good or bad. As the situation now stands, the United States has more to lose than any other nation as the "Order" becomes a fact. It should be noted, however, that the United States need not be a loser if appropriate actions are taken.[40]

Indeed, the third stage of strategic designs of the 1970s was shaped very soon after the second one, but for some time it was largely masked by the loud propaganda of the second stage. In fact, before and during the *19th session of the General Conference of Unesco in Nairobi in 1976*—while the Western press and private broadcsting interests kept campaigning against Unesco—Western diplomats were busy suggesting deals to the developing countries. The political purpose was to play down the Draft Declaration, which by that time had become a symbol for a consideration of the principles and contents of the mass media within an anti-Western context. To this effect, leading Western governments offered material help for the mass media infrastructures in the developing countries. The obvious intention in the West was to buy the "Third World" out of espousing a militant line by offering a few hundred thousand dollars; it was simply "trading ideology against cooperation" (as later put by Rosemary Righter). Such a frank statement confirms what is substantiated by the historical facts to be reviewed in greater detail in Chapter 2—in 1976, new strategy was developed in the West, although not all coming from the Western hemisphere agreed to follow it (notable exceptions were the voices of Finland and Norway).

By and large, the new strategy followed the old formula: "If you cannot beat them, join them!" Also, the formula of "divide and rule" was employed in response to the fact that it had been precisely the united front of the developing countries, backed by the socialist countries, which had brought about the political defeats for the West during the first stage. To quote Schiller again:

> To prevent the approval of the resolution aimed at establishing criteria for the content of international information flows—a recommendation viewed by U.S. media and government as a direct and dangerous thrust against the system of private ownership of the media—the U.S. delegation supported a compromise proposal which

---

[40]Kroloff & Cohen, op. cit., p. 1.

called for a study on ways to rectify imbalances in the flow of news. Indirectly this gave endorsement to the recently-organized Third World News Pool as well as legitimising the concept of "balance" in the flow of news. Up to this time, both of these conceptions/structures had been adamantly opposed by the United States . . .

The admission at Nairobi that poor nations have legitimate grievances in the information sector is an acknowledgement, long overdue, of reality. But it would be delusionary to regard this admission as evidence of a new United States international information policy. The accommodation of Nairobi represented a tactical shift. It prevented an immediate and damaging thrust against the vitals of American global communications power. It also afforded a breathing space for U.S. decision-makers to work out effective policies to frustrate attacks.[41]

And the time proved to be opportune for this Western initiative—in general, as well as in the field of communication. For a number of reasons the developing countries no longer appeared to be committed to their earlier militant stand—at least not at a high price or against lucrative offers for "help" and "cooperation." Consequently, the initiative shifted largely to the Western side, which generated various formulas for accommodation, particularly with the so-called "moderate" developing countries. It is worth recalling in this connection what *President Jimmy Carter* said in his Notre Dame address in May 1977:

> We will cooperate more closely with the newly influential countries in Latin America, Africa and Asia. We need their friendship and co-operation in a common effort as the structure of the world power changes.[42]

Such a strategic line was well elaborated by the time of the *20th session of the General Conference of Unesco in Paris in 1978.* An outspoken statement of this strategy was given by the head of the U.S. delegation, *Ambassador John E. Reinhardt,* who in his contribution to the general policy debate contrasted "restrictive declarations" against "positive cooperation" and made a call for "a more effective program of action," including "American assistance, both public and private, to suitably identified regional centers of professional education and training in broadcasting and journalism in the developing world," as well as "a major effort to apply the benefits of advanced communications technology, specifically communications satellites, to economic and social needs in the ru-

---

[41]Schiller, op. cit.

[42]Jimmy Carter, "Address at Commencement exercises at the University. University of Notre Dame, 22 May 1977," in *Public Papers of the Presidents of the United States,* Jimmy Carter, 1977:1, Washington 1977, p. 961.

ral areas of developing nations."[43] There was little new in the elements of this program, but its launching at Unesco as a kind of political demonstration gave rise to the concept of a "Marshall Plan of Telecommunications," muted by those developing world representatives who were not quite convinced of the sincerity of U.S. intentions.

Obviously the U.S. "carrot" was designed to play down—if not bury—the Mass Media Declaration, as well as other "political" manifestations of the new order. However, the fact that the Declaration was finally adopted, only three weeks after launching this "Marshall Plan," shows that the Western strategy did not succeed in producing the intended outcome. It did not stop the developing countries, with the help of socialist countries, from pushing "restrictive declarations." It helped the Western side only as a leverage in the bargaining process with the developing countries over the formulations of the Declaration. At this period of accommodation, the United States did not deploy its "stick"—for example, by threatening to withdraw from Unesco, as it had done two years before in approaching Nairobi. Consequently, it had no alternative but to live with what it considered as negative "politization" of the communication field, and to keep struggling for what it called "positive cooperation."

A major effort in this struggle, waged according to the latest strategy of flexible accommodation and partnership, was in parallel to the Mass Media Declaration at the same 20th session of the Unesco General Conference. The U.S. delegates, accompanied by representatives of Australia and France, joined some outstanding advocates of the developing countries (notably from "moderate" Sri Lanka, Tunisia, and Venezuela) in order to find a compromise between the "Marshall Plan" project and another idea put forward by the developing countries to set up a special fund at Unesco for helping these countries in the development of their media infrastructures. The compromise reached was not far from the U.S. approach, whereby the new order is reduced to a relatively simple transfer of know-how and technology from the "information rich" to the "information poor," within an overall "free flow" context. The joint resolution, which then was unanimously adopted by the General Conference, among other things:

> *Requests* the Director-General to intensify the encouragement of communications development and to hold consultations designed to lead to the provision to developing countries of technological and other means for promoting a free flow and a wider and better balanced exchange of information of all kinds;

[43]Reinhardt's address in Paris on 5 November 1978 was issued by the U.S. delegation as a press release and reproduced in *Records of the General Conference, Twentieth Session* (Paris, 24 October to 28 November 1978), Volume 3: Proceedings, Paris: Unesco, 1978, pp. 648–653 (quotes from pp. 649, 651, 652)

> *Invites* the Director-General for this purpose, to convene as early
> as possible after the conclusion of this twentieth session of the General
> Conference a planning meeting of representatives of governments, to
> develop a proposal for institutional arrangements to systematize col-
> laborative consultation on communications development activities,
> needs and plans . . .[44]

It was this resolution that two years later led to the establishment of
the *International Programme for the Development of Communication (IPDC)* at
the 21st session of the General Conference in Belgrade, on the basis of
consensus reached in a planning meeting held at Unesco in April 1980.[45]
As things turned out later, the shaping of the IPDC did not quite follow
the U.S. formula, beginning with the fact that an invitation to hold the
planning meeting in Washington was politely turned down by the
Director-General, who welcomed only a minor pre-planning meeting to
be hosted by the U.S.[46] However, at the time of the 20th session of the
General Conference in Paris, the U.S. strategy appeared to work with
considerable success. At least it was perceived so by the U.S. Administration, as indicated by the self-congratulatory tone of statements, such as
given soon after Paris by Roland Homet, in which the final outcome of
the Mass Media Declaration was "hailed as a vindication of free information flows, and also as a diplomatic triumph for the West."[47]

Another resolution, prepared on the same "U.S.-Third World" ba-
sis and adopted by consensus at the 20th session, concerned the
*International Commission for the Study of Communication Problems ("MacBride
Commission")*, which had been established in 1977 to help in overcoming
the controversies accumulated around the Draft Declaration in
1975-1976. This resolution appreciated the interim report which the
Commission had prepared for the General Conference, and invited the
Director-General, among other things:

> to request the members of the International Commission for
> the Study of Communication Problems to address themselves, in the
> course of preparing their final report, to the analysis and proposal of
> concrete and practical measures leading to the establishment of a
> more just and effective world information order . . . .[48]

[44]From Resolution 4/9.4/2; see *Records of the General Conference, Twentieth Session,* Volume 1: Resolutions,
Unesco: Paris, 1979, p. 105.

[45]For proceedings of the intergovernmental planning meeting, see Unesco document CC/MD/45
(1980).

[46]For report of the planning meeting, see Unesco document CC/79/CONF. 622/3 (1979).

[47]R. Homet, "Goals and Contradictions in a World Information Order," *Intermedia* (Journal of the
International Institute of Communications, London), No. 2, March 1979, p. 14.

[48]From Resolution 4/9.1/3; see op. cit. in note 44 above, p. 100.

Although this resolution did not contain explicit "free flow" references, it obviously met the Western interest in alluring the developing countries to turn their attention away from fundamental principles and content considerations (such as the Draft Declaration) to practical cooperation (such as the "Marshall Plan"). Significant in this respect was the very *phrasing of the new order,* hammered out as a compromise in intensive negotiations between diplomats from the West (mainly U.S.A.) and the developing countries (mainly Tunisia). The phrase used both in the resolution on the MacBride Commission and in the final version of the Mass Media Declaration speaks about "[a new,] more just and more effective world information and communication order."

Those who take the Western approach certainly find this formulation less disturbing than the original phrase "a new international information order"—sometimes even with the definite article and capital letters (often referred to as "NIIO").[49] The compromise formulation no longer suggests such a close connection to the New International Economic Order ("NIEO") and no longer gives an impression of a fixed program based on a set of principles hostile to an unconditional "free flow" position. Rather, what is left, according to typically Western thinking, is only a general recognition of the need for reform, or to be sure, a particular kind of reform which will not violate fundamental Western interests—it must be "just" not only for the developing countries but also for the West, and it must be "effective," calling for delicate dependence on Western technology and ideology. At least the official U.S. understanding of "more just and more effective" was "to denote an evolutionary process building on the present order rather than breaking radically from it."[50]

As to "world," instead of "international," it implies (although probably not recognized by most users of this language) a theory of "interdependent world" which, like the McLuhanian "global village," undermines national sovereignty as well as class-based division between socialist and capitalist countries. Finally, "information and communication" (or sometimes just the latter) is problematic, since at least in the Anglo-American linguistic context it may be taken to emphasize the technical and formal aspects of communication, at the expense of the media content which is more clearly referred to by the term "information."

The U.S. and its Western allies, since the 20th session of Unesco General Conference, have generally used the phrase "new world information and communication order," which they regarded as a negotiated

---

[49]The present author prefers using the original phrase, or simply referring to "the new order," so as to keep in line with the authentic ideas of the Non-Aligned Movement.

[50]Prepared Statement of John E. Reinhardt (Director of the U.S. International Communication Agency) at Hearing before the Subcommittee on International Organizations of the Committee on Foreign Affairs, House of Representatives, 96th Congress, First Session, 19 July 1969; in *Unesco and Freedom of Information*, Washington, D.C.: U.S. Government Printing Office, 1979, p. 5.

compromise not only in semantics, but in substance as well. The other parties agreed to the phrasing and it is this formulation that has appeared since November 1978 in most Unesco and UN documents relating to the new order. However, it soon became evident that an agreement on the phrasing was no guarantee of consensus on the political substance. The original advocates of the new order continued to understand the matter in terms of a fundamental change which would hardly compromise anything but the "cosmetics" of phrasing.

Uncompromised Positions Behind Semantic Agreement

Thus the consensus at the 20th session of the General Conference was far from complete, even if a spirit of accommodation helped to reach a mutually acceptable compromise on the Mass Media Declaration and a number of other resolutions. As stated by the present author in early 1979, "behind consensus emerges a new debate and test of forces around the substance and even wording of the New International Information Order."[51]

There was, in fact, one notable exception to the consensus: *a resolution specifically devoted to the new order* was adopted by an overwhelming majority, but without the support of the U.S. and other leading Western powers.[52] Its final "operative part":

> 1. *Endorses* efforts to establish a new, more just and more balanced world information and communication order;
>
> 2. *Invites* the Director-General . . . to continue his efforts with a view to the establishment of this new order, entailing in particular the promotion of national systems in developing countries and the establishment of a new equilibrium and greater reciprocity in the flow of information.

Until the last moment, this resolution was intended to become another landmark of consensus, and therefore its tone is quite modest as compared to the militant positions typically put forward from the ranks of the Non-Aligned Movement. (The very phrasing of the new order follows the formula negotiated with the West, although "effective" has been replaced by "balanced.") It advocates a fairly vague concept of a new or-

---

[51]K. Nordenstreng, "Behind the Semantics—A Strategic Design," *Journal of Communication*, Spring 1979, p. 196.

[52]Resolution 4/9.1/2; see op. cit., in note 44 above, p. 99. The *Records of the General Conference, Twentieth Session*, Volume 2: Reports, indicate that the resolution was adopted at the Programme Commission "by a vote of 46 to none with 12 abstentions" (paragraph 517, p. 151). Those abstaining were the U.S., Canada, Australia, New Zealand and most West European countries (except France and the Nordic countries).

der, with reference to "free flow" (something that was insisted on by the Western countries as a condition for their endorsement), but neither was it explicit in terms of standards for the contents of the media.

As such, this resolution might appear to represent the "center" of various political orientations which met each other in that Unesco forum. However, in the reality of international politics it came to stand for the original aspirations of the Non-Aligned Movement, known to be far from welcome to the dominant Western interests. Furthermore, it was the first resolution ever passed in a UN forum which is exclusively devoted to the question of the new information order. Thus it was the spirit rather than the letter of this resolution that kept the spokesmen of the West from endorsing it. Their abstention is a significant indication of the disagreements which were buried under formal consensus.

The Western hesitation at the time was certainly fed by documents prepared for the MacBride Commission by two of its members, *Mustapha Masmoudi* of Tunisia and *Bogdan Osolnik* of Yugoslavia.[53] Their outlines for the new order were appendiced to the interim report of the Commission submitted to the General Conference. The documents aimed at giving both conceptual and practical shape to the idea of the new order as advocated by the Non-Aligned Movement. While by no means extremist in their approach, they laid down uncompromised positions.

> The present situation in the field of information and mass media is the legacy of the inequitable development of mankind and especially of the colonial past . . . Both under conditions of "laissez-faire" and of monopolistic capitalism the inexorable logic of the law of the market encouraged progress primarily in the direction of economic rationalization and the satisfaction of commercial interests, with a tendency to subordinate all other areas of human life to this expansion.[54]
>
> This situation of imbalance has naturally prompted the wish for a radical overhaul of the present international information system and highlighted the need to establish a new world order for information. While representing one of the many aspects of the required transformation of the world situation, its primary purpose must be to initiate further reforms and to establish other new international orders, more just and more beneficial to the whole community of mankind.—In calling for this new world information order, the developing coun-

---

[53]M. Masmoudi (Secretary of State for Information, Tunisia), "The New World Information Order," document No. 31 of the International Commission for the Study of Communication Problems (July 1978). Osolnik (Member of the Federal Parliament, Yugoslavia), "Aims and Approaches to a New International Communication Order," document No. 32 (July 1978). An abridged version of Masmoudi's document is published in *Journal of Communication*, Spring 1979; and in Richstad & Anderson, op. cit. in note 1 above.

[54]Osolnik, op. cit., p. 3.

tries are doing no more than invoking the rights solemnly proclaimed by the present-day international community in such important texts as Article 19 of the Universal Declaration of Human Rights, Article 19 of the International Covenants on civil and political rights and on economic and social and cultural rights, and the relevant resolutions adopted by the United Nations General Assembly.[55]

... there is growing recognition of the fact that peaceful coexistence and the common advancement of all mankind can only be achieved if in the field of international communication too, principles are accepted, which will in time become part of international law or at least unwritten norms of international relations and the professional ethics of all those who work in this area.[56]

Especially Masmoudi, who covered the topic from the political, legal, and technico-financial viewpoints, hit several explosive issues. For example:

> The problem of allocating the frequency spectrum, which is a universal but limited natural resource, arises today with particular urgency. The developing countries are in fact more determined than ever to challenge vigorously the rights that the developed countries have arrogated to themselves in the use of the frequency spectrum. They are also determined to secure an equitable sharing out of this spectrum.—It is common knowledge that almost 90% of the source of the spectrum is controlled by a few developed countries, and that the developing countries, although covering far more extensive areas, possess fewer channels than the developed countries. The power density per square kilometre is four times less in the developing countries than in the developed.[57]

Not surprisingly, Masmoudi's document was singled out by the opponents of the new order as a warning. The Board of Trustees of *Freedom House,* an authoritative U.S. lobby, addressed Secretary of State Cyrus Vance on the eve of the General Conference in October 1978, expressing concern about both the Declaration and the Tunisian document, which was considered "in some respects, more ominous than the draft declaration," since it "would disestablish Western communication systems."[58] The executive director of Freedom House, Leonard Sussman, specified:

> Potentially the most crucial battleground of the media struggle will be the World Administrative Radio Conference (WARC) of the

[55]Masmoudi, op. cit., p. 2 (paragraphs 4–5).

[56]Osolnik, op. cit., p. 10.

[57]Masmoudi, op. cit., p. 9 (paragraph 31).

[58]*Freedom at Issue* (Journal of the Freedom House, New York), No. 48, November-December 1978, p. 11.

International Telecommunications Union (ITU) which opens in October 1979 in Geneva.—Nearly every nation will participate at WARC. The stakes are high. For the first time in twenty years the entire electronic spectrum will be put on the block. The WARC decides which countries may use specific broadcast frequencies. This affects domestic and international communications, radar, satellites; and scores of personal, corporate, political, intelligence and military services . . . [59]

It is worth noting that the issue of the new order was brought into the focus of Western concerns at the time the documents by Masmoudi and Osolnik were issued.[60] The significance of their documents was understood by all; not only did they speak for the political majority of the international community, but they also reflected the search for new perspectives, which continued within the academic community.[61] By 1979, the new information order had become a widely recognized concept, serving as a framework for scientific symposiums and publications—not only among those engaged in polemics against the new order, but above all for those who were seriously interested in changing the world in conformity with the ideals of peace, democracy, and social justice in general, and of the objectives of the Non-Aligned Movement in particular.[62]

In this situation, it goes without saying that, when the developing countries were eager to seek for consensus, it did not mean that they simply would have sold short their principles and subscribed to a U.S.-designed position. On the other hand, neither did they turn down a historical opportunity to obtain material support for the setting-up and maintenance of their media infrastructures—if not yet in terms of open cheques, at least in authoritative promises. As Osolnik, who was a Yugoslavian delegate to the 20th session of the General Conference, has put it, those advocating the new order "feel that various types of assistance are

---

[59]L. R. Sussman, "A New World Information Order?" ibid., p. 2.

[60]For example, in early 1978 Sussman reviewed "Third World/West Open Media Dialogue, As Unesco 'Radicalization' Proceeds," without displaying the concept of the new order as a central issue; see *Freedom at Issue*, No. 44, January-February 1978, pp. 20–28.

[61]For reasons of casting political doubts on Masmoudi's document, Sussman among other Western commentators "disclosed" that the document had in fact been written on Unesco's account by Cuban, Vietnamese and East German experts. While this was simply propagandistic misinformation, it is true that a team of scholars from some Non-Aligned countries (however excluding those "radicals" mentioned) did help Masmoudi in preparing the document.

[62]An illustrative example was an international scientific symposium on "The Role of the Mass Media in Maintaining and Strengthening Peace," organized in Orivesi (Finland) in November 1978. Its three topics covered "Perspectives for the new international order, Peaceful coexistence and the mass media, Codifying the new international information order." The proceedings of the symposium are published in *Peace and the Sciences* (Quarterly of the International Institute for Peace, Vienna), No. 1, 1978, pp. 1–92. Note also that *Journal of Communication* published a special symposium entitled "International Information: A New Order? Third World News and Views" in its Spring 1979 issue. Included were articles by the present author and Masmoudi, as well as contributions by Rosemary Righter (U.K.), and Elena Androunas and Yassen Zassoursky (USSR), among others.

not enough and that what is needed is a fundamental restructuring of relationships, the elimination of all forms of inequality and foreign domination through the powerful media of contemporary communications."[63] Or, to quote the general policy statement of another
Non-Aligned European country, Finland, whose government, in the
words of its Minister of Culture:

> . . . wishes to stress the fact that this particular new order is not
> only an action programme for the correction of imbalances of a tech-
> nical nature, but also and above all a programme of principle, in-
> tended to create mass media structures and policies which would pro-
> vide the public with accurate information about objective realities, at
> the national and international levels alike.[64]

Obviously, then, there were different interpretations of what is
meant by a new information order, and the differences imply quite
contradictory approaches to the role and tasks of the mass media. For
most of those coming from the developing and socialist countries it has
been an approach of *fundamental strategic nature*, whereas for most coming
from typically Western countries (and standing for such alliances as
NATO and the European Common Market, EEC) it has been an approach of *tactical nature,* intended to neutralize the "Third World offensive." Such differences in approch were not eliminated with the
accommodating spirit of the third strategic stage of the 1970s; it only
helped to produce formulations which are vague and diluted enough to
leave room for different interpretations. In fact, the fundamental
contradictions involved were exposed in the statements made on behalf
of various countries at Unesco on 22 November 1978, on the very occasion of adopting, by acclamation, the Mass Media Declaration (see Appendix 20). Likewise the relief, and even euphoria, which was felt among
most Western diplomatic circles as a response to the compromise reached
in Paris, was accompanied by uneasiness and even bitter criticism in the
first press reactions to the compromise (see Chapter 2).

In such a situation, it was natural that the compromise, which
emerged in Nairobi (1976) and helped to bring about the consensus in
Paris (1978), was only a fragile construct, far from a permanent design of
historical significance. What is significant, rather, are *the uncompromised
positions, usually masked by diplomatic concessions but ultimately based on the conflicting forces which direct the historical cause of development in the global arena.*
It is not difficult to see that these uncompromised positions boil down to

[63]B. Osolnik, "Unesco: The Mass Media Declaration," *Review of International Affairs*, No. 690, 1979 (5
January 1979), p. 26.

[64]The address by Kalevi Kivistö, the Finnish Minister of Culture, is reproduced in op. cit. in note 43
above (quote from p. 411).

no more than two basic standpoints—those corresponding to the advocates and opponents of the process that brought about the Mass Media Declaration and gradually gave shape to the idea of a new international information order.

In an overall analysis, the historical process is one—the drafting of the Mass Media Declaration and the struggle around the new order are two themes of a single story. When the Draft Declaration was first introduced on Unesco's agenda in 1972, there was not yet talk about a new order, but, as is shown in Chapter 2, all the essential elements of the forthcoming concept were present in this early debate. Although the Declaration was never intended to constitute a prelude in a movement towards a comprehensive new order, the process of its drafting helped to articulate the arguments about the new order—both in favor and against. And by the time of the compromise in 1978, *the Declaration had become an integral part of a delicate political construct which all parties conceived in terms of a process towards a new order,* however different the approaches to this order held by each party.

On the other hand, the story of the Declaration did not come to an end in Paris on 22 November 1978. The controversial case continued its political life as part and parcel of the overall compromise around the new order. And since this compromise was a dynamic process rather than an agreed-upon set of ideas and programs, the story continued as a struggle around the new international information order. A review of the developments after the balance of the 20th session of the General Conference will help us in placing the Declaration in perspective and grasping its true nature and significance.

TRUCE: PROGRESS THROUGH COMPROMISE

Although the positions were divided, the compromise reached in Paris in late 1978 continued to provide a framework for dialogue and even further agreements between the parties concerned. The first time the outcome of the 20th session of the General Conference was put to a diplomatic test was the adoption of a resolution on questions of information at the 33rd session of the *General Assembly of the United Nations* in New York, only three weeks after the compromise was sealed at Unesco. The political significance of Resolution 33/115, adopted by consensus, was that the Paris formula was now endorsed by the highest authority of the international community. Under the title "International Relations in the Sphere of Information and Mass Communications," the General Assembly not only "recalled" the Mass Media Declaration and other relevant decisions of Unesco's General Conference, but also referred to the UN resolutions concerning the New Internationl Economic Order, as well as to the decisions and recommendations on information of the Non-Aligned Movement. In this political framework the resolution:

> *Taking into account* the widespread hopes . . . to establish a new, more just and better balanced world information and communciation order,
>
> 1. *Affirms* the need to establish a new, more just and more effective world information and communication order, intended to strengthen international peace and understanding and based on the free circulation and wider and better-balanced dissemination of information;
>
> 2. *Approves* the efforts being made to establish this new world order, which should reflect in particular the concerns and legitimate aspirations of the developing countries and the views expressed at the twentieth session of the General Conference of the United Nations Educational, Scientific and Cultural Organization . . . [65]

Since this resolution of December 1978, the UN General Assembly has adopted a resolution every year on questions of information, mainly endorsing the developments at Unesco and suggesting practical measures to promote the "public information" activities of the UN itself (through UN Informtion Centres, publications, radio programs, etc.). These resolutions have been prepared in the framework of a special working group, institutionalized in 1979 to a permanent *UN Committee on Information* (with members from 67 countries).[66] However, neither this Committee nor its parent body, the General Assembly, has, at least until the early 1980s, performed a particularly innovative role in the process towards a new international information order. The main UN forum has only endorsed the agreements reached at Unesco, but thus it has helped to legitimize the work of this specialized UN agency, which, as admitted by the General Assembly, has a "central and important role" in fulfilling the mandate of the UN in the field of information, while the General Assembly iteslf has a "primary role in elaborating, co-ordinating and harmonizing United Nations policies and activities in the field of information."[67]

Although the "primary role" of the General Assembly has proved to be passive, it is significant that at this level the questions of information are treated as a natural part of overall UN politics. Typical in this respect are the linkages made in the resolutions on information to a number of the other highly political preoccupations, for example:

---

[65]Resolution 33/115 of the 33rd session of the UN General Assembly, adopted on 18 December 1978, section B.

[66]Resolution 34/182 of the 34th session of the UN General Assembly, adopted by consensus on 15 December 1979.

[67]Ibid.

Mindful of the fundamental contribution that the information media and mass communications can make to the establishment of the new international economic order, the strengthening of peace and international understanding, the realization of the goal of general and complete disarmament under effective international control, the promotion of universal respect for human rights and the struggle against racism, apartheid and colonialism . . . [68]

Political Level

At Unesco, the first landmark after the Paris compromise was in Kuala Lumpur (Malaysia), where the *Intergovernmental Conference on Communication Policies in Asia and Oceania* (the second regional conference after San José) met in Feburary 1979.[69] There the Paris formula was confirmed with the participation of not only 18 developing countries (some with quite different political orientations—from Pakistan and Indonesia to Afghanistan and Vietnam) but also three Western industrialized countries (Japan, Australia, and New Zealand—the USA attended only as an observer) as well as the Soviet Union and China. Moreover, this conference took a position considerably closer to the political line of the Non-Aligned Movement than that of the 20th session of the General Conference a few months before. In other words, the "Third World," supported by the Soviet Union, took another step, whereas the West yielded another step of retreat (although especially Japan did its best to defend a "free flow" position).

The main political document of this conference, the *Kuala Lumpur Declaration,* went beyond the customary reference to "imbalances," by specifying the problem in terms of colonialism and neo-colonialism: ". . . the developing countries of our region are still suffering from a dependence upon colonial legacies which have resulted in imbalances in communication structures and information flows."[70] Furthermore, the document contained some fundamental positions which were either absent or implicit in earlier compromises, including the Mass Media Declaration:

We, the representatives of the governments of the States of Asia and Oceania . . . hereby declare that:

People and individuals have the right to acquire an objective picture of reality by means of accurate and comprehensive informtion through a diversity of sources and means of information available to them, as well as to express themselves through various means of culture and communication . . . .

[68]Ibid.

[69]The Final Report has been published as Unesco document CC/MD/42 (Paris, September 1979).

[70]Ibid., p. 33 (from section VII of the Kuala Lumpur Declaration).

Consequently, since each nation has the right to determine its own communication policies, we call for the elaboration, by States and citizens together, of comprehensive national policies and programmes based on a global vision of communication and on the goals of economic and social development. Countries planning the implementation of these policies and programmes should do it as an integral part of overall national planning . . . .

The mass media of the developing countries bear a responsibility for contributing to the common task of nation-building and to the further development of the cultural identity of peoples and ethnic minorities, so ensuring national cohesion and creating abilities to derive the utmost benefit from enriching influences coming from outside . . . .

In the world of today the maintenance of world peace and security, the strengthening of international co-operation, the assurance of social progress, the raising of living and educational standards, the promotion of human rights and freedom of thought, and the establishment of a new economic order are among the prerequisites for effective communication.

At the same time, within the national communication systems freedom of expression and freedom of information are also prerequisites for effective communication between peoples and individuals.[71]

This text suggests a departure from the way in which communication has been typically conceived in earlier Unesco resolutions. The human right advocated by the Kuala Lumpur Declaration stands not only for unconditional freedom of information but for fulfilling the human potential to rationally grasp reality and to creatively participate in social and cultural life. Freedom, instead of being understood as an isolated and abstract value of highest degree, is given more concrete meaning in terms of international relations, socio-economic progress, and the interests of the people—thus stressing not only the professional autonomy, but, above all, the social responsibility of those who run the media.

This overall approach to the nature of communication and the role of the mass media was confirmed by the next regional Unesco conference, the *Intergovernmental Conference on Communication Policies in Africa,* which met in Yaoundé (Cameroon), in July 1980.[72] The *Yaoundé Declaration,* signed by the representatives of 28 African states, went just as far as the one in Kuala Lumpur:

---

[71]Ibid., pp. 31–32 (from sections I, II and IV of the Kuala Lumpur Declaration).
[72]The Final Report has been published as Unesco document CC/MD/46 (Paris , January 1981).

In Africa, in the communication field more perhaps than in any other, the prevailing situation is the direct result of the heritage of colonization. Political independence has not always been followed by a decolonization of cultural life or by the elimination of many alienating factors imposed by the colonial system. Communication structures often still conform to the old colonial patterns and not to the needs and aspirations of the African peoples. We are resolved to decolonize them in their turn. We are also determined to extend the opportunities for social communication to the various social, cultural, political and economic groups that currently make up African societies . . .

We consider that, if information organs are systematically used to strengthen national unity, mobilize energies for development and greater participation by popular masses in communication and reinforce African solidarity and combat all that divides the African continent and prevents it from asserting itself in all its dignity, this will be a means of liberation and an expression of our peoples' freedom.

The Declaration on fundamental principles concerning the contribution of the mass media to strengthening peace and international understanding, to promotion of human rights and to countering racialism, apartheid and incitement to war, which the General Conference of Unesco adopted at its twentieth session, highlights the responsibility of the mass media in combating the great scourges of mankind and in achieving its most noble ideals. Large-scale action by the mass media and the news agencies, both public and private, can facilitate positive mobilization of the creativity of the rural and urban masses and make it possible for them to give full expression to their aspirations and to the vision they have of their nation's future evolution. In this national effort, which presupposes a qualitatively new role for communication, free access to information is a factor that stimulates development. We need a new conception of freedom of information such as will truly enfranchise men and society instead of subjecting them to the conditioning of those who control the powerful communication media; such as will contribute to the democratization of communication and recognize the rights of individuals and peoples to be informed, to inform and freely to express themselves.[73]

In addition to outlining the political and philosophical framework, the Yaoundé Declaration focused on problems of cultural heritage as well as on the shortage of human and material resources for modern means of mass communication in this underdeveloped continent. Also, the "internal obstacles" were mentioned, although no concrete political solutions can be found in this document to implement the professed objective of "democratization" (not surprising, given the participation of

[73]Ibid., pp. 23–24 (from sections I and II of the Yaoundé Declaration).

countries such as Zaire). While singling out "the gross disproportion in communication capacity as between the industrialized and the developing countries, and the grip of the multinationals on world communication," the Yaoundé Declaration confirms the position of the Non-Aligned countries, whereby "the solution of communication problems cannot be reduced simply to the transfer of technology or to more redistribution of resources, although both for Africa and for the world these measures are an essential part of a new information and communication order."[74]

In understanding the outcome of Yaoundé, it is important to note that neither the "American West" nor the "Soviet East" were parties to this Declaration (USA, USSR, and some European countries attended only as observers). On the other hand, both Western and socialist ideas had their supporters among the African participants—from Morocco and Ivory Coast to Tanzania and Ethiopia. Thus Yaoundé can be taken as a fairly representative sample of the political forces which constitute the Non-Aligned Movement at large. As such, the message is clear: a comprehensive approach to the new order, understood as a component in the process of decolonization, national liberation, and socio-economic development, including both assistance to the media facilities in the developing world and universal standards for the performance of the mass media as prescribed by the Mass Media Declaration. Politically speaking, it was a fairly balanced approach, not simply a repetition of the original positions of the Non-Aligned Movement. As far as the issue of freedom is concerned, the Western ideology of "free flow" was rejected—but it was not replaced by another advocating government control.

In other words, Yaoundé (1980) confirmed the compromise reached in Paris (1978)—without proceeding beyond the balance achieved in Kuala Lumpur (1979). The same overall political reading is indicated, not only by the UN General Assembly resolutions discussed above, but also by another universally representative forum of global forces, the *Inter-Parliamentary Union* (IPU). At its 66th conference in Caracas (Venezuela) in September 1979, the parliamentarians of 82 countries adopted a resolution unanimously on "Ways and means of promoting international understanding, co-operation and peace in the areas of education, information and communication."[75]

The IPU resolution demonstrates that the political elites of the world were quite satisfied with the Mass Media Declaration of Unesco one year after its adoption. The Declaration was "recalled" in the beginning of the resolution, together with the Universal Declaration of Human

[74]Ibid., p. 25 (from section V of the Yaoundé Declaration).
[75]See *Proceedings of the LXVIth Inter-Parliamentary Conference*, Geneva: IPU, 1980 (pp. 701–705).

Rights and other central UN instruments of human rights and peace. The importance of the Declaration was stressed with a recommendation to "Parliaments and Governments to work for the implementation of and respect for the fundamental elements of this document within the framework of national legislation." Likewise, it was recommended that Parliaments and Governments "utilize the achievements of technological progress effected in this sphere, with the goal of encouraging in every possible way the mass media to contribute to the promotion of peaceful cooperation, democratic development and general progress in the international community, in conformity with the 1978 Unesco Declaration on the mass media."

As to the global distribution of communication resources and flows, the IPU resolution goes beyond the consensus formulations of Unesco, "nothing with concern . . . the continuing imbalance in the contents and flow of information and the possibility that circumstances may arise in which developing nations can become 'passive recipients of biased, inadequate and distorted information' from abroad, as stated by the Non-Aligned Summit Conference in 1976." The recommendations given to Parliaments and Governments include the provision of assistance to the developing countries "at their request . . . in conformity with the needs of each individual country."

In addition to this, the Caracas resolution of IPU makes a special point regarding journalists:

> *Urges* National Groups to take action within their Parliaments and through their Governments so as to guarantee to journalists, communicators and others involved in the information process such protection as will ensure the best possible conditions for the performance of their work in a responsible, objective and lawful manner;
> *Views with concern* any efforts to protect journalists and other agents of the information media by Governments and Parliaments that would involve any restrictive or discriminatory practices against them.[76]

The idea of protecting journalists against arbitrary measures of the governments—but not against democratically established national and international legislation—was incorporated in the Paris compromise through the Mass Media Declaration, which contains special paragraphs on the matter. The point made by the IPU resolution is in conformity with the Declaration on the protection of journalists, but the resolution is more outspoken than the Articles of the Declaration. Of particular interest is the latter paragraph quoted above, which spells out Western con-

---

[76]Ibid., p. 705 (paragraphs 6–7).

cerns about misusing protection as a pretext for guidance, or even censorship.

Such concerns had grown after the adoption of the Declaration, when attempts were made at Unesco to transform the idea of protecting journalists into a set of institutional arrangements. Studies and proposals were generated on this matter during the biennium 1979-80, first under the auspices of the MacBride Commission and then as part of Unesco's regular activities in the field of journalism and mass communication.[77] None of the resulting documents advocated such a distortion of the idea of protection; on the contrary, the deliberations at Unesco meant that the initiative was shifted from the UN (intergovernmental level) to the professional organizations of working journalists (non-governmental level). Nevertheless, the uninterrupted campaign against the new order, waged in the Western press, accused Unesco of eroding press freedom and legitimizing state control under the pretext of protecting journalists. This campaign turned the theme of protection into such a "high profile" issue that it was gradually perceived as a central element in the new order controversy, not only in the eyes of the general public but also of political decision makers such as parliamentarians.

Non-Governmental Level

With public campaigning, however, the movement towards a new order continued to gather momentum, to win wider support, and to become clarified. One of the landmarks of this progress was established on the territory of non-govenmental professional interest groups at the meeting of *international and regional organizations of journalists* in Mexico City in April 1980.[78] This meeting could speak in the name of nearly 300,000 professional journalists from all continents, i.e., an overwhelming majority of the organized journalists of the world, extending from bourgeois liberals to communists and from Catholics to Moslems. The *Mexico Declaration,* which was issued by this historical forum, not only demonstrated support for Unesco and its Mass Media Declaration, but also proposed ten principles for an international code of journalistic ethics (for details, see Chapter 9 and Appendix 25). In articulating this set of principles, the professional journalists associated themselves with the positions of the Non-Aligned Movement even more clearly than had been done by government representatives in Kuala Lumpur and Yaoundé, or by parliamentarians in Caracas.

[77]See document No. 90 of the International Commission for the Study of Communication Problems (Sean MacBride, "The Protection of Journalists") and *Protection of Journalists,* Paris: Unesco series New Communication Order, No. 4, 1980.

[78]See *Journalists' Affairs* (bulletin of the International Organization of Journalists, Prague), special issue, May 1980; and *Newsletter of IOJ, special issue, October 1980.*

The fact that the International Catholic Union of the Press was among the signatories of the Mexico Declaration is a significant indication of the support which the new order had gained amoung *Christian churches*. The Pope himself appealed in June 1980 that "a new order of international relations be established on the basis of an ethics of justice, respect for the human person, recognition of the sovereignty of every nation, and solidarity."[79] The Catholic as well as the Protestant churches regarded the ethics of communication as a particular extension of Christian ethics in general. And it so happened that the original demands for a new order closely coincided with overall Christian aspirations:

> Information and communication are much more than "commodities" or "consumer goods," a concept promoted by the West. They are essential needs for person-in-community and communities-of-persons. All people want and need to enrich their lives by sharing information and ideas with other people and societies. Both content and form of communications must therefore respond to genuine communication needs of the people in a society.[80]

> But before reflecting on the responsibility of churches and Christians for a new communication order, we must become conscious of what our present order is. For it is in the context of present realities that Christians are being called upon to make changes for a better future. In particular, changes will have to be made in favour of the poor, the powerless, the rejected and the oppressed. We do not consider the bias towards the poor merely an obligation of justice or charity, but we are convinced that God speaks to each generation primarily through the poor and oppressed. It is they who will have to show us the way in which a new communication order can truly become a sign of the coming of His Kingdom. . . . The new order of information and communication which Unesco proposes . . . is a logical consequence of the process of political decolonization which started after the Second World War, and which was followed by new thinking about economic decolonization. The third stage is informational and communication decolonization, i.e., that sharing and transfer of information and communication power which will enable Third World countries to develop their own resources, express their own values and control their own destinies.

---

[79]From the address given by Pope John Paul II in Paris to representatives of International Catholic Organizations accredited to Unesco; see e.g. *UCIP Information* (quarterly bulletin of the International Catholic Union of the Press, Geneva), No. 3, 1980, p. 2.

[80]"Towards a New International Information order (NIIO)," Editorial in *Media Development*, (Journal of the World Association for Christian Communication, London), No. 4, 1980, p. 1.

[81]"Communication in a new world order: A Christian appraisal of the NIIO," a joint staff paper of the World Association for Christian Communication, January 1981 (mimeo).

MacBride Report

Given such wide support to the primary ideas of the new order, it is not surprising that the MacBride Commission also ended up with a report promoting the overall approach "towards a new, more just and more efficient world information and communication order," to use the words of its subtitle.[82] The composition of the Commission—16 experts from different geographical and political parts of the world—made it a fairly representative forum for suggesting what might be an enlightened world opinion in matters of communication. In this respect it is significant that while the MacBride Report confirms the need for a comprehensive approach to communication problems, whereby technology and infrastructures are closely linked with socio-economic policies and political principles, and whereby freedom and responsibility are understood as indivisible, the concept of a new information order remains vague and indeed undefined. A closer look shows that crucial differences of opinion existed among the commissioners on such fundamental issues as the concept of a new order, and, therefore, the Report was bound bo be "more a negotiated document than an academic presentation."[83]

Sean MacBride writes in his preface to *Many Voices, One World* that the "resulting distillation . . . is a consensus of how the Commission sees the present communication order and foresees a new one," and that "with good will governing future dialogues, a new order benefitting all humanity can be constructed."[84] Less promising perspectives are opened by the reservations which were attached to the main Report, notably by four commissioners. *Sergei Losev* (USSR) regrets that "the very notion of the New International Information Order has been eroded in the process of compiling the Report."[85] *Mustapha Masmoudi* again "would have wished that the Commission had further advanced its reflection by proposing to the Director-General the text for a declaration and draft charter" for a new order, to be placed on the agenda of Unesco and the UN.[86] *Cabriel Marques* and *Juan Somavia* (from Colombia and Chile but living in exile), made, among others, the following point:

> The insistence on the need to develop communication infrastructures in the third world countries is correct and necessary, but it should not be overstated. It is not possible to solve contemporary communication problems through money and training alone.

[82]*Many Voices, One World; Communication and Society, Today and Tomorrow,* Paris: Unesco, 1980.
[83]Ibid., p. 281 (from statement of Marquez and Somavia).
[84]Ibid., p. xx.
[85]Ibid., pp. 279–280.
[86]Ibid., pp. 280–281.

The idea of a "Marshall Plan" for the development of third world communications is inappropriate and will tend to reproduce western values and transnational interests in third world societies. Actions in this field should be carefully selected so as not to reinforce minority power structures within third world countries or serve as a vehicle for cultural domination.[87]

No less critical remrks came from the scholarly community, as demonstrated by a reader published only some months after the MacBride Report itself.[88] For example, *Oswaldo Capriles* (Venezuela) showed that the Report does little to help us go beyond the existing confusion about the new international information order (NIIO), in reference to the subtitle of the Report:

> In fact, this typical compromise formula indicates that though the point of departure for the Report may have been a challenging of the "old order" dominated by the western transnational corporations, throughout the writing of the Report an accommodation was achieved that is strikingly western in its bias. The core question of the NIIO—and the related question of the national communication policies—has been dealt with in such obscure and fragmented manner that the Report does not contribute to our better understanding.[89]

Cees Hamelink (Netherlands) pointed out that such a vague compromise "could very well be the world order of the transnational corporations (the 'corporate village' with international political blessing)" and warned:

> This "cosmetic response" (Phil Harris) to Third World demands could very well turn out to be the major obstacle to achieving a fundamental re-ordering of informational relations in the world. This may be so because it obscures the intrinsic relation between a new information and a new economic order and—more importantly—it leads away from a radical interpretation of these concepts.[90]

Accordingly, not only were the ideas of the new order promoted during this period of compromise, but there was also *growing concern among academic circles* (as such, sympathetic to the concerns of the developing countries) that the forces of the new order might become subject to

---

[87]Ibid., p. 281.

[88]C. Hamelink (Ed.), *Communication in the Eighties: A Reader on the "MacBride Report,"* Rome: IDOC International, 1980.

[89]Ibid., p. 32.

[90]C. Hamelink, "The NIIO: The Recognition of Many Different Worlds," op. cit. in note 80, p. 4.

deceptive cooption by "powerful interests vested in the old information order."[91] As the present author put it:

> It is indeed vital that the new order continues to be a programme for radical analysis at the level of theory and conceptualisation, while at the same time various means are found to turn it into a professional practice. Too much attention to the practical, however, is precisely what is intended by the defenders of the old order: instead of principles and content of information (such as the Unesco Declaration on mass media), attention is being turned to action programmes on how to build infrastructures and how to train communicators.
>
> What's more, at present stage of the debate, there is another and more subtle trap waiting for the advocates of the new order. This is caused by insufficient understanding of the problems involved whereby the supposedly radical analysis remains superficial and is replaced by more or less radical *rhetoric* only. A warning example in this respect is the final report of the MacBride Commission as I indicated in my contribution to some critical reflections on the report . . . Therefore it is crucially important always to keep the new order in broad and deep perspective, without letting the advocates of the old order dictate the terms of debate with their ideologically one-sided and intellectually apologetic arguments.[92]

It goes without saying that those who criticized the MacBride Report (and indirectly the Unesco Secretariat) for deceptive compromises that might coopt the new order movement to Western interests were fundamentally opposed to those other critics who attacked the Report and Unesco on the well-known grounds of Western "free flow." In fact, apart from *scientific considerations,* the *political significance* of the MacBride Report has been that it was generally welcomed by leftist circles, as indicated by an overview of *Jörg Becker* on the situation in the Federal Republic of Germany (FRG):

> The Report will be able to advance its arguments against the highly vehement activities of the conservative forces on the sphere of international media policy, since, interestingly enough, this over-all topic has been dealt with far more carefully and as far more important by conservative forces in the Federal Republic than by the Social Democrats. Within the Social Democratic Party the Report can and must serve to support the socialist wing which has turned its close attention in the past two years to questions of the democratization and decommercialization of the media within the FRG (i.e., cable TV, me-

---

[91] Ibid., p. 6. The same point is made in Hamelink's paper to the MacBride Commission (No. 34, 1979).
[92] K. Nordenstreng, "A Call for More Democratic Structures in Communication," op. cit. in note 80, p. 12.

dia growth, viewdata), but has scarcely realized the international dimensions.[93]

As far as the Western positions in general are concerned, the MacBride Report was received with mixed feelings. Hardly anyone found it particularly exciting, since it offered little new, politically or substantially, beyond pooling various earlier ideas and proposals. But the very fact that the Report constituted such an eclectic reservoir created uneasy reactions among liberals as well as conservatives. Those who had adopted a flexible policy of accommodation towards the new order movement were troubled by the continuing coexistence of normative and practical considerations in the debate; in fact, the long list of proposals all but reinforced a "Marshall Plan" approach to communication problems. Those conservatives, who from the beginning had adopted a rejectionist position towards the new order, again became more confident in their belief that it was all part of a grand design to destabilize the "free world."

An illuminating example of the Western concerns, both liberal and conservative, is provided by the U.S. member of the MacBride Commission, *Elie Abel,* who had produced his position paper in 1978 to balance the new order documents of Masmoudi and Osolnik.[94] Abel suggested to his fellow commissioners that in the light of the 1978 resolution on the Commission (quoted above) they should "eschew political sloganeering and undertake an honest search for steps that can lead to action in the world as it is, pluralistic yet increasingly interdependent," and that "the Commission would be well advised to separate the more intractable political and philosophical issues from those relatively value-free, on which consensus is possible and even likely."[95] The latter, in his paper, included telecommunication tariffs, access to satellite services, technology transfer, and financial and training assistance, whereas the "issues of political sensitivity" were right of access, licensing of journalists, the right of rectification, codes of ethics, and access to the frequency spectrum. Obviously Abel's position paper was motivated particularly by Masmoudi's document, which, as Abel later openly admitted, was perceived as a really dangerous package:

> If adopted, this version of the new world information order would have serious consequences for the United States. As Senator George McGovern once observed, "One way to attack a nation such as

[93]J. Becker, "The Scientific and Political Significance in the Federal Republic of Germany," op. cit. in note 88, p. 45.

[94]E. Abel, "Communication for an Interdependent, Pluralistic World," document of the International Commission for the Study of Communication Problems, No. 33 (1979). Reproduced in Richstad & Anderson, op. cit. in note 1.

[95]Ibid., pp. i, 14.

the United States which depends heavily on information and communciations is to restrain the flow of information." Adopting Masmoudi's proposal would mean accepting the idea of state control (i.e., censorship) over all news or information crossing a nation's borders. It could reduce greatly the amount of news about the world available to Americans and their Government. It might provide justification for countries to exclude from their markets American movies, television programs and advertising. It might even produce the extraordinary result of nationalizing information throughout the world, thereby enabling governments to tax or even prohibit computer conversations via satellites.[96]

And what was the outcome of the MacBride Commission? Certainly not an endorsement of either Masmoudi's or Abel's proposals. Not one of the "issues of political sensitivity" were placed side as Abel had advised, and although the collective opinion of the Commission was understandably mild and vague, the political framework admitted by the Report (with the consent of Abel among others) was not far from that advocated by the Non-Aligned Movement. Also, despite Losev's critical remarks, he and *Yassen Zassoursky* expressed the Soviet appreciation of the MacBride Report in terms of "a serious contribution to the cause of placing information in the service of peace and progress."[97] No doubt this created concern in the West about future developments, especially when recalling the somewhat bitter experience at the time of adopting the Mass Media Declaration:

> The result was regarded in the West as a great victory for freedom of the press. The old Article XII, condoning state control of the news media, had been eliminated. Press freedom and access by journalists to all news sources, including those in opposition to the government, were endorsed. The idea of a mandatory right of reply to supposedly inaccurate news stories was softened.
>
> But as the celebration champagne flowed, the price that Masmoudi and the non-aligned group had exacted became clear: In exchange for Unesco endorsement on press freedom, the West would be expected to support a new world information order, to be obtained largely through Unesco.[98]

---

[96]P. H. Power & E. Abel, "Third World vs. The Media," *The New York Times Magazine,* 22 September 1980.

[97]Y. Zassoursky & S. Losev, "Information in the Service of Progress," *Journal of Communicaion,* Autumn 1981, p. 121. (First published in Russian in *Pravda* on 5 May 1980).

[98]Power & Abel, op. cit.

The U.S. Position

Since Paris 1978, the destiny of the new information order became more and more of a central problem for U.S. foreign policy. This is clearly shown by a hearing on "Unesco and freedom of information," held in the House of Representatives, Committee on Foreign Relations (Subcommittee on International Organizations), on 19 July 1979. In this forum, *Reinhardt* made another outspoken statement, this time as the Director of the U.S. International Communication Agency. Addressing the question, "Where is the new order going to take us?" he told the House, among other things:

> There have been some preliminary definitions issuing from the Non-Aligned Movement that, frankly, we find unacceptable. They would entail such things as a wholesale withdrawal of radio frequencies from current users, and a possible abolition of international copyright for published works entering the Third World. Here again we resist.
>
> But this resistance can and must be contained within a broader posture of creative engagement in the elaboration of the "New Order" idea. That is not simply because the idea has now been accepted by UN consensus. It is because the momentum behind the effort to redress neocolonial status in the world, to remedy historic disparities and dependencies as they are called, is in any event irresistible. Our own history and sense of mission are favorably inclined to this evolution. We might have been able to divert or defer the evolutionary pressure for a while, but eventually it would break through. And we are in far better condition to shape the future course of the "New Order" as co-architects than we would be if we were following a policy of detachment . . . .
>
> The struggle between conflicting tendencies is already there within and among the societies of the world. It seems more likely that we can influence the outcome through creative engagement than through a kind of passive disengagement. Although Americans are properly skeptical of sweeping and ill-defined new policy directions, we have learned that when a large number of countries join their energies behind such proposals the sound defense of our national interests counsels engagement. And we are better off moving in early rather than late.
>
> There is a tendency on the part of the Non-Aligned "Information Order" proponents to urge steps in parallel with the development of the "New International Economic Order" (NIEO). Thus we have already been approached to support the creation of an International Fund for communications and information—modeled

after the troublesome NIEO Common Fund. The International Fund would be financed by increased dues or voluntary payments going to Unesco, a centralizing drain on available resources. This time, however, we have a creative alternative for systematic bilateral collaboration—with which to counter the (in our judgement) unrealistic International Fund proposal . . . .

The major U.S. initiative at the last Unesco General Conference was a proposal for creation of a Communications Development Consultative Group, as a forum where developed and developing countries alike could draw together communication needs and available resources in a systematic and coherent fashion. The initiative would also engage the powerful creative energies of private information industries, whose participation is essential to the realization of any just and effective new order.[99]

Thus Reinhardt still believed that it was worthwhile "to make the New World Information Order resemble as much as possible the order prevailing in our own 'new world'—the United States of America."[100] It was logical, then, that three months after this statement Reinhardt admitted that the adoption of the December 1978 resolution at the UN General Assembly had made the USA and other Western countries parties to a common effort to define the new order:

But although it was not radical, the adoption of the UN resolution did mark a significant new departure in the approach of the industrialized democracies. Hitherto we had tended to downplay conceptual rhetoric and to focus instead on the adoption of concrete and practical measures that would move in the direction of equalizing information relationships among societies. Those measures are still very important . . . But after the UN resolution, I would submit that they are no logner sufficient. The world information and communication order has yet to be defined with any particularity in a way that can command widespread consent. It is incumbent on us in the developed world to introduce our own theoretical formulation, faithful to libertarian traditions but also responsive to the needs and interests of the developing world.[101]

By and large, such a line of cooperation and accommodation continued in official U.S. policy until the end of the Carter Administration (Jan-

---

[99]Op. cit. in note 50 pp. 4–5.

[100]Ibid., p. 5.

[101]J. Reinhardt, "Towards an Acceptable Concept of the New World Information Order," address to the U.S.-Japanese symposium "International Communications: New Challenges & Responsibilities" at the Fletcher School of Law and Diplomacy, Tufts University, Medford, Mass., 11–14 October 1979. Released by USICA and reproduced in Occasional Papers of the Edward R. Murrow Center of Public Diplomacy, Tufts University, 1979 (quote from pp. 2–3).

uary 1981). It was probably supported by the outcome of the significant *World Administrative Radio Conference* (WARC 79) of the international Telecommunication Union (ITU) which met in Geneva from September to December 1979. WARC 79 was perceived in advance to pose to the United States a heavy "new order challenge" (cf. Sussman, above), but "after some give-and-take, the U.S. came away largely satisfied," as *Business Week* put it.[102] Indeed, WARC constitutes a vital component of the new information order developments—both as a threat to the technologically advanced West (with its hegemony in the use of the radio spectrum, the world's common resource) and as a promise to the developing countries (with their great needs for future use of radio waves). In this case, the socialist countries of Easten Europe do not constitute such a "natural ally" of the developing countries as they do in most other questions of the new order debate, because these "advanced socialist countries" have also acquired a relatively large share of the common global resource of the radio spectrum over the years, and thus have their vested interests as well. (A concise review of WARC, especially WARC 79, is provided by Thomas McPhail.[103])

If the liberals went along with the new order movement—more or less reluctantly—the conservatives for their part became more and more vocal in their displeasure with the whole idea. As expressed by Congressman *Dante B. Fascell* in 1980, a "threat has emerged in international forums over the last few years as communist ideologues have combined with many Third World leaders in a concerted effort to frame what has been termed as a 'New World Information Order'."[104] *Time* magazine let it be understood that "a First Amendment war is shaping up on a global scale," since the new order, "as some Third World zealots would define it, directly threatens press freedom as Americans and Europeans conceive it."[105]

Moreover, there was a growing disillusionment over the feasibility of what might be called the "Reinhardt strategy," in which Unesco occupies a central position as a forum of constructive bargaining and cooperation. The most outspoken criticism of the strategy of flexible accommodation came from the British Managing Director of Reuters, *Gerald Long*, who delivered an illuminating speech in New York in May 1980:

---

[102]"The Third World Lays a Claim on the Airwaves," *Business Week*, 3 March 1980, p. 32 B-1.

[103]See especially Chapter 6: "The Medium: International Telecommunication Union and the World Administrative Radio Conference," in McPhail's *Electronic Colonialism: The Future of International Broadcasting and Communication*, Beverly Hills and London: Sage Publications, 1981 (pp. 149–170).

[104]D. B. Fascell: "Introduction," op. cit. in note 37, p. 12.

[105]C. Prendergast: "The Global First Amendment War," *Time*, 6 October 1980, p. 24.

Unesco's aims are clear: it seeks money from those countries that have developed the technology of media communications, and which are for the most part committed to the view that information is an essential component of freedom, and makes plans to use that money to transfer media technology to the countries that do not have it, while encouraging them to use the technology to control information for the purposes of government. We are being asked to put up the money and provide the technical, human and operational resources to spread throughout the world that very view of information that is most repugnant to us. The fact that such a programme has not already been rejected out of hand shows that we would be wrong to underestimate the political skill of Unesco.[106]

IPDC

Such hard-line conservative positions were voiced, particularly after the representatives from 85 Member States of Unesco had gathered in Paris in April 1980 at the *Intergovernmental Conference for Co-operation on Activities, Needs and Programmes for Communication Development.*[107] This Conference recommended, by consensus, "a project for the establishment, within the framework of Unesco, of an International Programme for the Development of Communication."

The outcome of this diplomatic exercise was clearly closer to the "international fund" idea put forward by the Non-Aligned Movement (and not opposed by the USSR and other socialist countries) than to the "consultative group" proposal pushed by the United States. Yet the IPDC was a compromise which could be seen to meet the Western interest "to de-emphasize normative prescriptions for information flows and to stress structural solutions for information imbalances—thereby promoting improved equality through conditions of freedom," as Reinhardt has characterized the U.S. negotiating strategy in matters of the new order.[108] After all, the compromise demoted the IPDC to become largely clearing house, instead of promoting it as funding agency—an accommodation in view of the Western refusal to let Unesco decide, with its developing and socialist world majority, how to distribute the resources originating mainly from the West.

On the other hand, the consensus recommendation of the IPDC begins with a clearly political statement along the lines of a UN resolution, certainly not to Western liking, in which the Conference says it is:

[106]G. Long, Speech at a Reuter dinner for media representatives at the Plaza Hotel on 13 May 1980 (mimeo).

[107]Report of the intergovernmental conference has been published as Unesco document CC/MD/45 (Paris, 15 September 1980).

[108]Op. cit. in note 50, p. 5.

1. *Conscious* of the increasing role of communication among peoples and nations in promoting political, economic, social, scientific, educational and cultural progress, as well as in improving mutual understanding, strengthening international peace and safeguarding national sovereignty and cultural identity,

2. *Conscious* of the close relationship linking the concepts, objectives, and results of the overall development of each country and of all countries with the systems, practices, means and infrastructures of social communication,

3. *Noting* the deplorable situations of dependence and the significant inequalities of a technological, professional, material and financial nature which exist between developed countries and developing countries in most fields of communication, and further noting calls for larger participation in, and democratization of, international relations in the field of information and for the overcoming of vestiges of colonialism . . . .

8. *Considering* that international co-operation in the field of communication development should take place on the basis of equality, justice, mutual advantage and the principles of international law, and mindful of the fundamental contribution that the information media and mass communications can make to the establishment of a new international economic order, the strengthening of peace and international understanding, the realization of the goal of general and complete disarmament under effective international control, the promotion of universal respect for human rights and the struggle against racism, apartheid and colonialism,

9. *Considering* that assistance to developing countries should not be politically tied and that favourable conditions should be enhanced to facilitate better access to modern communication technology for developing countries . . . .[109]

The statement also "recalled" the Mass Media Declaration and "underlined" the need to establish a new information order, as indicated in the relevant resolutions of the 20th session of the General Conference (including that adopted without full Western support).

All this was endorsed by the *21st session of the General Conference in Belgrade in October 1980,* additionally "taking note of the declarations and recommendations of the Intergovenmental Conferences on Communication Policies held at San José in July 1976, Kuala Lumpur in February 1979, and Yaoundé in July 1980," as well as "stressing that this international programme, aiming to increase co-operation and assistance for the development of communication infrastructures and to reduce the gap between various countries in the communication field, must form

[109]Op. cit. in note 45. Also published in *Records of the General Conference, Twenty-First Session* (Belgrade, 23 September to 28 October 1980), Volume 1: Resolutions, Paris: Unesco, 1980 (Resolution 4/21, Annex 1, quote from pp. 74–75).

part of the efforts for the establishment of a new, more just and more effective world information and communication order."[110]

By the same decision, the General Conference in Belgrade adopted Statutes for the IPDC, whereby the Programme remains within Unesco under the direct control of the General Conference which appoints its governing body, the Intergovernmental Council, with 35 Member States (i.e., government representatives) from different regions of the world. This means that the Western countries remained in the minority and did not manage to guarantee a special status for those "donors" who financially contribute to the Programme. Likewise, the Belgrade decision meant a defeat of persistent attempts by the U.S. government to have the private sector (national and transnational corporations, etc.) recognized as more or less equal partners with the Member States in the management of the Programme.

It is remarkable indeed that the United States and other leading Western powers went along with the IPDC as finally formulated. After all, the outcome gave substantial ammunition to those opposing Unesco from a conservative point of view. However, seen in a historical perspective, the West could hardly do anything but join the consensus, given its five-year old strategy of flexible accommodation in favor of a technical assistance approach. Moreover, the whole project was inspired by a U.S. initiative (the "Marshall Plan"). As the U.S. delegation put it in the Belgrade debate: "We see the IPDC as a potentially useful vehicle for channeling Unesco and other available resources and energies into issues of communication development and away from non-productive or ideological approaches."[111]

The Belgrade decision on the IPDC was given additional weight by a resolution adopted, again by consensus, by the 35th session of the *UN General Assembly* in New York in December 1980. This resolution from the highest UN body "expresses its satisfaction" at the establishment of the IPDC, "which constitutes an important step in the establishment of a new world information and communication order. . . ."[112]

General Conference in Belgrade 1980

The 21st session of the Unesco General Conference was historical, not only because it formally established the IPDC, but also because it brought together all aspects of the "great debate" of the 1970s, including its most

---

[110]Resolution 4/21, in op. cit. above (quotes from p. 72).

[111]From intervention of William Harley, member of the U.S. delegation in Belgrade, 21 October 1980, released by USICA. A more elaborated and significantly more reserved appreciation of the IPDC by Harley was presented as a working paper to the "Voices of Freedom" conference in May 1981 (see op. cit. in note 6; reproduced in *Journal of Communication*, Autumn 1981).

[112]Resolution 35/765 of the 35th session of the UN General Assembly, adopted on 16 December 1980.

controversial elements concerning the conceptual and political substance of the new order.

First, as a kind of reminder, a resolution was passed on the *application of the Mass Media Declaration.*[113] In this resolution the General Conference:

1. *Calls upon* Member States to take all necessary steps to ensure that public opinion, journalists and others working in the mass media in their countries become even more conversant with the aforesaid Declaration, and to publish it in as many languages as possible, if they have not already done so;

2. *Calls upon* Member States, intergovernmental and non-governmental organizations, journalists and other professionals working in the mass media, as well as their professional associations, to contribute actively to the implementation of the aforesaid Declaration of Unesco;

3. *Calls upon* Member States, in accordance with their constitutional provisions, and governmental and non-governmental organizations having co-operative relations with Unesco to provide the Director-General with any information at their disposal concerning the way in which the principles set forth in the aforesaid Declaration have been put into effect;

4. *Invites* the Director-General:

a) to have the 1978 Declaration concerning the mass media circulated as widely as possible and in as many languages as possible;

b) to ensure that Unesco's programmes in the field of communication are based upon the fundamental principles stated therein;

c) to convene in 1983, on the occasion of the fifth anniversary of the adoption of the Declaration, an international congress (Category IV), to be financed from extra-budgetary funds, to further the application of the Declaration;

5. *Invites* the Director-General to prepare, on the basis of data collected and any other information in his possession, a comprehensive study on the implementation of the principles set forth in the Declaration and to include that study in the report on the activities of the Organisation which he will submit to the General Conference for consideration at its twenty-second session.

This resolution was not passed by consensus in the Programme Commission but by a vote of 68 in favor (most developing countries and all socialist countries except China), one against (Switzerland), and 27

---

[113]Resolution 4/20, op. cit. in note 109 (pp. 71–72).

abstensions (most Western countries).[114] The two years since the adoption of the Declaration had thus eroded the consensus which had been one of the most carefully constructed compromises within the UN system. Obviously, in 1980 the Declaration was no longer perceived by the U.S. government as "a vindication of free information flows, and also as a diplomatic triumph for the West" (as Homet put it in 1978). Yet it was decided in Belgrade that the Declaration continues to occupy a central place on Unesco's agenda—as a well-established element in the movement towards a new order.

Two other resolutions, specifically related to the issue of a new information order, were passed in Belgrade. One of these was a long document based *on the MacBride Report* and on comments on it by the Director-General and by the General Conference at large.[115] Patient and painful negotiations between and within various geographic-political groupings led to consensus around this resolution, which no doubt is politically the most significant outcome of Belgrade. It begins with a paragraph whereby the General Conference reaffirms its attachment to the principles of the UN Charter, of the main instruments of human, civil, and political rights, as well as of the Constitution of Unesco and the Mass Media Declaration. Accordingly, the Declaration was classified as an exceptionally significant set of universal principles, comparable to the UN Charter and the Universal Declaration of Human Rights. It is interesting to note that this was done without any dissent from those who withheld their support from the resolution on the application of the Mass Media Declaration.

It is also significant that in the preamble of the consensus resolution on the MacBride Report an explicit reference is made to "the Movement of Non-Aligned Countries which, in the Declaration of Colombo Summit (1976), stated that 'a new international order in the fields of information and mass communications is as vital as a new international economic order' and, in the Declaration of the Havana Summit (1979), noting progress in the development of national information media, stressed that 'cooperation in the field of information is an integral part of the struggle for the creation of new international relations in general and a new international information order in particular'."

Among several points, the resolution invited the Director-General "to undertake or sponsor, in particular, the studies and analyses necessary for the formulation of specific and practical proposals on the establishment of a new world information and communication or-

---

[114]*Records of the General Conference, Twenty-First Session,* Volume 2: Reports, Paris: Unesco, 1981, p. 189 (paragraph 564).

[115]Resolution 4/19, op. cit. in note 109 (pp. 68–71).

der . . . ." The concluding part (VI) of the resolution presents an outline of the new order under two paragraphs:

(a) this new world information and communication order could be based, among other considerations, on:

(i) elimination of the imbalances and inequalities which characterize the present situation;

(ii) elimination of the negative effects of certain monopolies, public or private, and excessive concentrations;

(iii) removal of the internal and external obstacles to a free flow and wider and better balanced dissemination of information and ideas;

(iv) plurality of sources and channels of information;

(v) freedom of the press and information;

(vi) the freedom of journalists and all professionals in the communication media, a freedom inseparable from responsibility;

(vii) the capacity of developing countries to achieve improvement of their own situations, notably by providing their own equipment, by training their personnel, by improving their infrastructures and by making their information and communications media suitable to their needs and aspirations;

(viii) the sincere will of developed countries to help them attain these objectives;

(ix) respect for each people's cultural identity and the right of each nation to inform the world public about its interests, its aspirations and its social and cultural values;

(x) respect for the right of all peoples to participate in international exchanges of information on the basis of equality, justice and mutual benefit;

(xi) respect for the right of the public, of ethnic and social groups and of individuals to have access to information sources and to participate actively in the communication process;

(b) this new world information and communication order should be based on the fundamental principles of international law as laid down in the Charter of the United Nations . . . .

It is not difficult to see that, under (a), a great deal of diplomatic trading has resulted in favoring the Western "free flow" position. However, all of these 11 points are merely "among other considerations" on which the new order *could* be based. Under (b), on the other hand, is a brief but crucial statement on which the new order *should* be based. As is shown in Part 2 of this book (especially Chapter 4), the fundamental principles of international law constitute a clearly defined basis for all international relations, including those in the field of journalism and mass communication. Accordingly, not only did all the Member States (including USA) approve the idea of defining the new order, but its over-all orientation was fixed to the UN principles of international relations. This may not appear, at first sight, as a particularly significant position, but on closer examination it can be seen as a central part of the demands by the Non-Aligned Movement, as well as by the socialist countries.

By and large, the resolution was tilted towards the positions of the advocates of the new order—perhaps more so than the MacBride Report itself had been. Thus it was not surprising to witness a sharp political debate within the Western group of countries about whether or not the resolution was worth supporting at all. The most reluctant to go along with the compromise was the United Kingdom, which made it known that "it would be wrong for anyone to assume that avoidance of a vote is necessarily the same thing as total agreement," and specified that most of its concern was caused by Part VI, regarding the definition of the new order.[116]

The other resolution concerning the new order, proposed in Belgrade somewhat unexpectedly by Venezuela, was on "measures to initiate studies necessary for the elaboration of principles related to a New World Information and Communication Order."[117] This short document, which came to be known as the *Venezuelan resolution,* begins by "recalling" the Mass Media Declaration, the recommendations of the three regional Intergovernmental Conferences, as well as other relevant resolutions of Unesco and the UN since 1978, and makes the point that "it would be desirable and beneficial for all sectors concerned if a clear and practical definition were drawn up of the principles and aims underlying the concept of a New World Information and Communication Order, as already expressed in various forums such as Unesco and the Non-Aligned Movement and in meetings of professional organizations." Its operative part:

> *Invites* the Director-General to take immediate steps to initiate studies with a view to drawing up the fundamental principles underlying a new world information and communication order and exploring the possibility and desirability of such studies serving as a basis for a Declaration on the Establishment of a New World Information and Communication Order.

[116]From intervention of the U.K. delegation in Belgrade on 25 October 1980.

[117]Unesco document 21C/DR.264 (17 October 1980 and thereafter amended orally in Programme Commission IV).

Hardly revolutionary, but still the resolution met strong opposition among the Western delegations, which obviously were afraid of another unpleasant history such as the Mass Media Declaration. Yet this "time bomb" was adopted in the Programme Commission by 51 votes in favor, 6 against, with 26 abstentions—by and large with the same cleavages as emerged in the case of the resolution on the Mass Media Declaration (those voting against were USA, Canada, U.K., Switzerland, Japan, and New Zealand).[118]

Like the resolution on the IPDC, the other resolutions concerning information that were adopted in Belgrade were welcomed by the *UN General Assembly* a few months later.[119] The UN after "recalling," among other things, the Mass Media Declaration of Unesco, "as well as the relevant resolutions on information and mass communications adopted by the General Conferences at its nineteenth, twentieth and twenty-first sessions," expressed its "satisfaction" with the Belgrade resolutions, in particular the resolution on the MacBride Report. It also singled out the resolution on studies concerning the new order, but instead of "express-ing its satisfaction" with this more divisive decision of Belgrade, it merely "takes note of" it.

In addition to the four resolutions on major information issues (IPDC, Declaration, MacBride, new order), the Belgrade Conference adopted *Unesco's regular program and budget* for the period 1981-1983, authorizing the Director-General to carry out a number of projects in the field of information and communication.[120] The program contains both practical-technical and normative-conceptual elements, and thus repre-sents the same comprehensive approach to communication problems ad-vocated by the MacBride Report. Its overall profile follows the pattern which had emerged in the early 1970s (cf., Chapter 2) and which had been unanimously confirmed by the General Conference at its sessions throughout the decade. In this perspective, it is significant that in Belgrade the communication program was not adopted unanimously, but that several proposed projects were opposed by the U.S., Denmark, Sweden, and some other Western countries.[121]

It is interesting to note that most of the controversial projects were more or less academic studies (on the impact of advertising, on transnational corporations, on the right of reply and rectification, on the

---

[118]Op. cit. in note 114, p. 167 (paragraph 347 [d]).

[119]See note 112.

[120]Unesco document 21C/5 Approved, pp. 459–466 (paragraphs 4373–4429).

[121]A U.S. resolution to this effect (document 21C/DR.397) was rejected in a vote with 3 for, 56 against, and 13 abstentions. Another, similar, resolution by Denmark and Sweden was rejected with 12 for, 50 against, and 10 abstentions. See op. cit. in note 114, p. 168 (paragraph 349).

relationship between NIEO and NIIO, on the relations between the concepts of freedom and responsibility, etc.)—an area which in earlier Unesco debates and programs had been considered quite uncontroversial compared to outright normative projects such as the Mass Media Declaration. It can be concluded that communication research had been politicized, not only by "radical" scholars at odds with the established (Western) order but now, above all, by Western politicians obviously afraid of the new intellectual perspectives challenging Western interests.

Beyond the resolutions and program covering Unesco's sector of Culture and Communication, the information issue was incorporated in some "general resolutions" relating to all fields of Unesco's activity. One of these was on the *new international economic order,* adopted by consensus (with U.S. reservations), which among other things "considers" that the new economic order "necessarily presupposes" a new information order, and which invites the Member States "to develop national infrastructures that could, among other things, help to promote ideas conducive to the establishment of a new international economic order."[122] Another such general resolution was devoted to *Unesco's contribution to peace,* adopted with the U.S., Canada, and Switzerland abstaining, in which the Member States are invited "to encourage educators, scholars, information specialists and all persons engaged in the preservation and advancement of culture to assist, in their fields, in preparing societies for life in peace and to support Unesco's efforts to this end."[123] This resolution also invited the Director-General, among other things, to encourage "efforts by the mass media to spread the ideas of peace, friendship among peoples, human rights and international understanding."

By and large, the *balance of Belgrade* (1980) repeated the main characteristics of Paris (1978): a fragile compromise with notable exceptions, surrounded by a good deal of public controversy. This time the coverage of Unesco proceedings in the Western mass media was indeed quite heated and biased.[124] In fact, the public response to Belgrade reflected divisions deeper than those exposed after Paris, comparable only to the fierce campaign before and during Nairobi (1976). And now the central point of controversy was the new order, as well indicated by an editorial on Unesco, the "International Big Brother," published in *The Washington Post* while the General Conference was still meeting in Belgrade:

---

[122] Resolution 9, op. cit. in note 109, pp. 101–104.

[123] Resolution 10.2, op. cit. in note 109, pp. 107–109.

[124] Studies of the press coverage of Belgrade, including one carried out by the U.S. National News Council, are reported in *Journal of Communication,* Autumn 1981, pp. 164–187. Introducing the topic, the *Journal* observed (p. 103): "Judging by the studies offered here, it might well be asked whether the treatment of the MacBride Report and the Belgrade conference exemplify the very problems that prompted the Report."

Last month, when Unesco opened a big meeting in Belgrade with an item on the international media at the top of its agenda, we warned of the risks of setting up an International Big Brother in terms that some of our readers found intemperate. We plead guilty as charged: we were intemperate. The trouble is, we perhaps were not intemperate enough. For the Unesco conference has since charged ahead in a way that confirms the darkest apprehensions of those who feared that the Communist—Third World bloc and the Unesco secretariat would do everything they could to institutionalize restraints on a free press. What is happening at Belgrade could turn out to be even worse than the pessimists anticipated.

The Unesco general conference, according to news reports, is proceeding to put into place as much of the "new world information and communication order" as it can muster the votes for. This "order" does to ideas roughly what the "new international economic order" does to the global economy: It asserts that ideas and information are a political commodity properly subject to the definition, redistribution and manipulation of a one-nation one-vote legislative process. . . .[125]

At the Conference itself, a neoconservative line was put on record by the Chairman of the IPI, *Cushrow Irani* (an editor and publisher from India), who did not welcome even the IPDC and repeated the reasoning of Long of Reuters by warning that "the anxieties of a free press everywhere will increase."[126] The address of Irani—obviously reflecting the opinion of the 1,900 editors throughout the "free world" who are members of the IPI—did not hesitate to put it bluntly that "I believe the time has come to say categorically that Unesco is, or ought to be concerned with education, science and culture and with nothing else."

In other words, the Western mass media management interests represented by the IPI had evidently come to the end of their faith in Unesco as a forum to debate and compromise on matters of journalism and mass communication. Irani was immediately given a reply by the Assistant Director-General for Culture and Communication, *Makaminam Makagiansar* (from Indonesia), who reminded the Conference that communciation was written in Unesco's Constitution in 1945 as one of the central fields of operation through which this UN Organization was to contribute to international peace, security, and human understanding. Obviously such an explanation did not satisfy the IPI and like-minded interests; if anything, the concerns were only increased among those who were afraid of the involvement of governments and intergovernmental organizations in mass media affairs. Immediately after the session, *the IPI*

---

[125]*The Washington Post*, 20 October 1980. Reprinted in *International Herald Tribune*, 21 October 1980.
[126]From address of C. Irani in Belgrade on 7 October 1980, released by IPI.

Report signalled that "Belgrade paves the way for . . . information to order":

> Most Western countries came to Belgrade in the belief that they had put to rest the irreconcilable conflict over the role of the press. But the net result of the conference is to give Unesco the go-ahead and the tools to work out the political framework . . . .
>
> The United States, Britain, West Germany and several other Western delegations made clear that they disagreed with the phrases in the resolutions that the Third World and the Soviet bloc interpret as giving Unesco the right to police news organisations. The Third World and the Soviet bloc also interpret these phrases as an acknowledgement that news is a political commodity that governments should control.
>
> Nevertheless, they have already shown their determination to start moving towards the kind of radical new information order they favour, despite Western reservations.
>
> The west could cetainly have achieved more if they had entered the debate more fully briefed. Those countries that pride themselves on a free press should now fight to put forward a coherent policy to meet real Third World needs.
>
> They must use the next three years before the next annual assembly of Unesco takes place, to see that their governments will be kept fully informed as to the dangerous developments we may have to face.[127]

Those closer to *U.S. government* (Carter Administration) did not express an equally sceptical view of Belgrade. For example, *Sarah Goddard Power,* Deputy Assistant Secretary for Human Rights and Social Affairs, made it known soon after Belgrade that "we were able to continue the process of turning Unesco away from Soviet-inspired ideological approaches to communications questions and to establish a communications development clearinghouse which institutionalizes, for the first time, our practical, non-ideological approach."[128] She admitted that "we were not entirely satisfied with the resolution on the MacBride Commission Report," and that the U.S. would never accept the concept of the new order "as a specific program of action, especially one which is written in a committee of 150," and continued:

> We have succeeded, however, in isolating the Soviets on this issue for two reasons, I believe.

[127]*IPI Report,* (monthly bulletin of IPI, London), No. 5, November 1980, p. 1.

[128]Address of S. G. Power before the Economic Club of Detroit on 5 December 1980. Released by the U.S. Department of State, Bureau of Public Affairs, Washington, D.C.: Current Policy No. 254, "The Communications Revolution," 5 December 1980 (quote from p. 3).

First, we have acknowledged that the developing countries do, in fact, have legitimate aspirations to tell their own story in their own way. We have offered them something in place of the empty and dangerous rhetoric of the Soviets by taking the lead in improving the ability of the international community to respond to their communications development needs . . . .

Second, we have not been put off by the rhetorical excesses of the debate. We have fought back and stayed in the game when some observers would have had us abandon Unesco . . . .

We are now in a stronger position to pursue U.S. communications interests not only in Unesco but throughout the UN system, drawing support from our traditional allies and also from Third World moderates who see us as a leader which is willing to listen.[129]

These remarks it is important to note, were made in the context of "U.S.-based multinational corporations engaged in the gathering, processing and dissemination of data across national frontiers . . . . The information industry—now the second largest export enterprise in the United States—made approximately $75 billion in foreign sales last year."[130] Indeed, one of the distinctive features of the Belgrade session, as compared to the Paris one two years earlier, was the recognition that at issue were not "small potatoes" and that "restrictions on the free flow of images, sounds, and symbols across national borders would have profound implications for the U.S. economy and for our democratic society."[131]

An official U.S. optimism concerning the political balance of the information issues at Belgrade also was made known in a special assessment report prepared in the Department of State under Power's direction. This report concludes:

The U.S. can take satisfaction in an overall positive assessment of the 21st General Conference: the recommendations of the MacBride Report were not endorsed or rushed into implementation; the IPDC was established in a form which meets our criteria of offering concrete development opportunities while defusing ideological rhetoric; and the Soviet-inspired resolution on implementing the Mass Media Declaration was drastically watered down, leaving only a call for a meeting at which, if it is ever held, we should be able to offset Soviet propaganda with an exposé of Soviet censorship . . . .

However, it is essential that we remain closely engaged with the issues in Unesco, as well as increasingly responsive to legitimate

---

[129]Ibid.
[130]Ibid., p. 2.
[131] Ibid.

Third World communications development aspirations, if we are to retain these new links with Third World moderates. Having won a bridgehead in hard fighting in three successive General Conferences (Nairobi 1976; Paris 1978; Belgrade 1980), were are in a good position to make further gains. With close public/private sector cooperation, we should be able to exploit our advantage . . . .[132]

The *Soviet assessment* of the outcome of Belgrade was, as might be expected, diametrically opposed to the American point of view. *Yuri Kashlev,* executive secretary of the USSR Commission for Unesco, summarized the situation in these terms:

Two viewpoints clashed on practically every question discussed at the conference: one upheld by the socialist and most of the developing countries, and the other upheld by a group of capitalist countries led by the United States.

The Soviet delegation held that the Belgrade session should make the 1978 Declaration on mass media central to Unesco activity and ensure the practical implementation of this document, that the report of the MacBride Commission should find a broad response in the world and help to rebuild international relations in the field of information on a democratic basis, and that the session should encourage Unesco to give practical assistance to the developing nations in this field . . . .

Despite the opposition of the imperialist forces, the Belgrade session did adopt some useful decisions on mass information. This was a major victory for the socialist and developing countries. The offensive against the positions of imperialism in a highly important field of ideological struggle continues.[133]

That this evaluation spoke not only for the Soviet Union, but reflected a wider perspective shared to a great extent by the Non-Aligned Movement, is demonstrated in a *Yugoslavian review* on the 21st session of the General Conference. *Ivo Margan,* Vice-President of the Federal Executive Council, and Head of the Yugoslavian delegation to the Conference, argued that the decisions in Belgrade "rounded off ten years of work of the non-aligned movement in the struggle for the democratization of international relations, particularly in the field of information."[134] In his analysis, the General Conference marked "a vic-

---

[132]"The U.S. View of Belgrade, prepared under the direction of Sarah Goddard Power," *Journal of Communication,* Autumn 1981, pp. 148–149.

[133] Y. Kashlev, "The World, Information and Unesco," *New Times* (Moscow), No. 48, November 1980, pp. 21–22.

[134]I. Margan, "The XXI General Conference of Unesco," *Review of International Affairs,* No. 738, 1981, (5 January 1981), p. 8.

tory of the progressive and, it may be said, revolutionary approach, and the struggle of the non-aligned movement, publicly to assert in this sphere of international life the rights of individual states, as opposed to the monopoly held by a number of agencies of the advanced countries . . . effecting a form of 'information imperialism'."

THE 1980s: CONTRADICTIONS CONTINUED

If the balance of Belgrade appears to be somewhat confused in the light of the first reactions, the pictue took a more definite shape during the next few months. First, the socialist and Non-Aligned positions, such as those quoted above, by and large remained as the final reading of that side's view on promoting the new order. The political reaction of the leading Western powers seems to have shifted towards a neoconservative approach, such as that advocated by the IPI in Belgrade. It turned out that the words of Irani, the British delegation, and other "hardliners" at the Conference were warning signals of a new confrontation to replace the uneasy spirit of compromise.

A penetrating analysis from the conservative point of view was offered soon after Belgrade by *Rosemary Righter,* a journalist with *The Sunday Times* of London and an adviser of the IPI:

Increased state intervention in the gathering and dissemination of news will be a reality of the 1980s. A larger role for governments is implicit in the concept of a "new world information order," already accepted in principle by all Unesco member states. That role will be further developed through the formulation of government policies mobilising the media in the service of national unity, cultural sovereignty and political goals. News-as-instrument is coming of age . . . .

After Belgrade, Unesco enters the decade with Western blessing for its "major role" in the shaping of international communications, symbolized by the creation of a new international programme through which Unesco is to coordinate, encourage and finance governments which want to create comprehensive communications policies. It has also been invited to define the new world information and communication order . . . with a view to drawing up a declaration on it. The result is bound to be even more controversial and more consequential than the organization's long-contested 1978 Declaration on the Media . . . .

The important point is that all governments have accepted a document that says firmly that it is possible to define the new world order of information and communication. An explicit corollary is that governments are the proper formulators of guidelines for news.[135]

Righter regretted the strategy of accommodation, which had placed Western countries "on the defensive, again trying to buy time." But she saw signs that "the events at Belgrade, in the aftermath, may finally provoke Western realization that it must stop this slow erosion of the freedom of the press and of the flow of news and ideas." Her conclusion:

> If a common Western strategy were to emerge from Belgrade, it would possibly throw in question Western participation in Unesco's communications programme in all its aspects. For it was finally clear that cooperation, promised or performed, would not take the edge off the ideological challenge to the very concept of a free press.[136]

The reaction was made even more serious by the fact that "Western news organizations will no longer be perceived as fighting alone in the name of press freedom and democracy" but that how "they will be allied with powerful businesses whose interests in maintaining the status quo are unabashedly materialistic."[137] Moreover, the self-criticism exercised in the West exposed the true nature of the demands for a new order:

> The West had failed to understand fully that the demands were part of a broad drive to increase the developing countries' share of *all* resources. They seek a new economic order that would rewrite the rules of international trade and finance in their favor, the West fears. "It's not about information. It's about politics, high politics," said Peter Blaker, the British Minister for United Nations affairs.[138]

Such reactions soon escalated into a new campaign where "gloves come off in the struggle with Unesco." And this time, it was not only a propaganda campaign in support of diplomatic bargaining. What happened was, rather, a *fundamental change in the Western strategy—from accommodation back to confrontation.* It was a historical reappraisal, because ever since Nairobi (1976), and, in particular, after the Kroloff & Cohen report (1977), the official Western approach (vacillation notwithstanding), as recorded at Unesco and the UN, remained fairly consistent until the end of 1980. This approach had been an integral part of the foreign policy of the Carter Administration.

---

[135]R. Righter, "Unesco Strengthens Its Programme for the Press," *Intermedia* (Journal of the International Institute of Communication, London), No. 6, November 1980, Special Report on the 21st General Conference in Belgrade, p. iii.

[136]Ibid., p. v.

[137] P. Lewis, "Western Press Fights Back; Gloves Come Off in Struggle With Unesco," *The New York Times,* 24 May 1981.

[138]Ibid.

The fact that Reagan took over from Carter at this stage obviously gave encouragement to a radical change in strategy—from a flexible liberal line to a hard conservative one. However, it would be too simplistic to explain the reorientation of the Western approach in terms of the change in the U.S. Administration alone. After all, the Western strategy had never been particularly coherent and united, even within the U.S. community of mass media experts. Rather the change was due to a longstanding discord and disillusionment, which by this time had accumulated to the degree of enforcing a new offensive approach to the international information arena.

The Talloires Offensive

A prelude to a new stage of confrontation was displayed at Unesco in February 1981. On that occasion, the international and regional organizations of professional journalists (those behind the Mexico Declaration) were supposed to establish an international commission for the protection of journalists. The idea dates back to an initiative of the International Federation of Editors-in-Chief from 1957, and since 1970 it was promoted especially by the IPI as a response to the disappearance of 17 foreign correspondents in Cambodia.[139] However, the *Consultative Meeting on the Protection of Journalists,* as well as a working paper prepared for it,[140] came under heavy attack by the IPI, IAPA, the International Federation of Newspaper Publishers (FIEJ), and the World Press Freedom Committee, supported by the government representatives of leading Western powers, particularly those from the United States. An intensive diplomatic and public campaign resulted in the admission of the "gang of four" (as the Western press organizations came to be known) in the Consultative Meeting, which then could not agree even on a modest communique at the end of divisive debate.[141]

---

[139]See H. Topuz, "Introduction: Why, From Whom and From What Should Journalists Be Protected?" and "First Proposals by Professional Organizations," in *Protection of Journalists,* Paris: Unesco series, New Communication Order No. 4, 1980, pp. 1–6 and 30–41.

[140]P. Gaborit (Professor of Political Science, University of Paris-Nord), "Project for the Establishment of an International Commission and a Periodical International Conference for the Protection of Journalists," Unesco document CC-80/WS/53 (Paris, 17 November 1980, mimeo).

[141] Although the meeting was convened on the legitimate basis of Unesco's Programme and Budget for 1981-83 (document 21C/5, approved in Belgrade), the campaign turned it into such a controversy that no consensus was possible. That the Western behavior was indeed designed to torpedo the project has since been disclosed by the representatives of the "gang of four" as well as of the U.S. government. For example, Sarah G. Power—now as former Deputy Assistant Secretary of State—testified in March 1981 before the Committee on Foreign Affairs of the House of Representatives that " . . . instead of a precooked outcome, the meeting broke up without a consensus. We are now going to build on this outcome in order to demonstrate the protection of journalists and other work inconsistent with our first amendment principles can cause the organization more harm than good." See *Review of U.S. Participation*

Three months later—half a year after Belgrade—63 delegates from 21 countries gathered in Talloire (France) at the *Voices of Freedom Conference of Independent News Media*, organized by the Tufts University's Fletcher School of Law and Diplomacy in cooperation with the World Press Freedom Committee.[142] Well prepared by a set of working papers,[143] the conferees had an ambitious task:

> For seven years a debate has been conducted in the councils of Unesco and other international organizations over the media and proposed curbs of press freedom. Those who advocate these controls have pressed for the creation of a so-called New World Information Order which is as yet undefined.
>
> In response the free world media decided to take initiative and to announce the principles to which a free press subscribes . . .
>
> At this session for the first time Western and other free newspapers, magazines and broadcasters took a united stand against the campaign by the Soviet bloc and some Third World countries to give Unesco the authority to chart the media's future course.[144]

Accordingly, as put by Rosemary Righter, who wrote one of the working papers and also participated in the conference in Talloires, "after 10 years of losing ground in this long-simmering controversy, western governments are at last formulating a common strategy to reverse the trend towards state interference in the exchange of news and information and its content."[145] And Talloires turned out to be some-

---

in Unesco (Hearing and Markup Before the Subcommittees on International Operations and on Human Rights and International Organizations, 97th Congress, 1st Session), Washington, D.C.: U.S. Government Printing Office, 1982, p. 21. Typical of the public campaigning that accompanied diplomacy is the editorial in *The New York Times* reprinted in *International Herald Tribune* on the last day of the meeting (18 February 1981). Entitled "'Ethical' Censors at Unesco," it concluded: "The latest idea is to give safe-conduct passes to reporters who comply with 'generally accepted' ethics of journalism. But Americans, among others, 'generally accept' none of the ethics of many of their would-be judges, including the Russians and such Third World nations as Libya. It is impossible to compromise Western standards of free expression with the censorship of states that monopolize information. Americans should have no part in such compromises, and if Unesco won't drop this enterprise they should simply quit."

[142]Although the first-mentioned organizer was the Fletcher School and the meeting place was its European center at Talloires, it seems evident that the true force behind the conference was the World Press Freedom Committee and that Tufts University was there mainly to give academic prestige or "window dressing" for a fundamentally political affair. Otherwise it could not have happened that perhaps the best known authority of the international law of communications at the Fletcher School, Professor Leo Gross, was not involved in the conference or even consulted in preparing "The Declaration of Talloires" (personal communication between Gross and the author in Feburary 1982).

[143]Op. cit. in note 6 above.

[144] From introduction to The Declaration of Talloires ("Why Was a Conference Held at Talloires?") in a printed booklet published by the World Press Freedom Committee's Rex Rand Fund, Leonard Marks, Treasurer (1981).

[145]R. Righter, "West to Fight Back on Press Freedom," *The Sunday Times*, 24 May 1981.

thing that has been described as "the Magna Carta of the free press." [146] In the West this was widely perceived as a relief—in the context of an understanding, perpetuated by influential Western lobbies and media, that the new order would be "a step toward Big Brother control over human lives similar to that pictured in George Orwell's frightening novel."[147] We shall examine the *Declaration of Talloires* (see Appendix 26) in greater detail in Chapter 10.

The next steps in an escalating confrontation were taken within the U.S. government. Hearings were organized by the *Committee on Foreign Affairs of the U.S. House of Representatives*.[148] There, a Senator testified that "the new world information order remains a very real and present danger,"[149] and a broadcasting executive urged "you to continue your efforts to make clear to Unesco and to the world that American people believe that the New World Information Order is an attack on free press principles . . . "[150] The Assistant Secretary of State, *Elliott Abrams*, had this to say:

> We oppose interpretations of a New World Information Order which seek to make governments the arbiters of media content. We oppose interpretations which seek to place blame for current communications imbalances on the policies of Western governments and media. We oppose interpretations which seek to translate biases against the free market and free press into restrictions on Western news agencies, advertisers and journalists. Attempts to justify such restrictions as a necessary adjunct of the development process are spurious. The potential can be achieved only with freedom of choice in the information field. We reject any linkage of a New World Information Order with the New International Economic Order and the radical restructuring of the international economic system which it includes.[151]

[146]L. H. Marks, of the World Press Freedom Committee, at the hearings before the Committee on Foreign Affairs, see op. cit. in note 141 above, p. 164.

[147]M. Stone, "A 'Big Brother' Threat," *U.S. News & World Report*, 15 June 1981, p. 84.

[148]In fact, the first hearing on the U.S. participation in Unesco had already taken place on 10 March 1981 (soon after the February meeting on protection). The hearings after Talloires took place on 9 and 16 July 1981, and involved 12 persons who testified, with a lot of material submitted for the record; see op. cit. in note 141 above.

[149]From prepared statement of Hon. Dan Quayle, U.S. Senator from the State of Indiana, ibid., p. 41. According to this witness, the new information order is basically "an attempt to control the flow of information and facts across international borders" (ibid., p. 37).

[150]From prepared statement of William J. Small, President of NBC News (ibid., p. 62).

[151]From prepared statement of Hon. Elliott Abrams, Assistant Secretary of State for International Organization Affairs (ibid., p. 94). This statement, like those by Small and Quayle, is typical of the "sense of the House" which prevailed in the hearings around Unesco. Only one witness, Professor Hamid Mowlana (American University, Washington, D.C.) defended the idea of a new information order and denied the charges that Unesco was moving to license journalists or to regulate the press (ibid., p. 201).

The debate in the House of Representatives produced a resolution to the effect of withdrawing the U.S. contribution to Unesco's budget (about 25% of total) "if that organization implements any policy or procedure the effects of which is to license journalists or their publications, to censor or otherwise restrict the free flow of information within or among countries, or to impose mandatory codes of journalistic practice or ethics."[152] This move received an unusually high-level of support from the President of the United States. In a letter, 17 September 1981, addressed to the Speaker of the House of Representatives, *President Ronald Reagan* wrote:

> We recognize the concerns of certain developing countries regarding imbalances in the present international flow of information and ideas. But we believe that the way to resolve these concerns does not lie in silencing voices nor restricting access to the means of communication, but in encouraging a broad and rich diversity of opinion. Efforts to impose restrictions on the activities of journalists in the name of issuing licenses to "protect" them, and other restrictions of this sort that have been proposed by certain members of Unesco, are unacceptable to the United States. We strongly support—and commend to the attention of all nations—the declaration issued by independent media leaders of twenty-one nations at the Voices of Freedom Conference, which met at Talloires, France, in May of this year. We do not feel we can continue to support a Unesco that turns its back on the high purposes this organization was originally intended to serve.[153]

The fact that this pressure against the movement towards a new order was not only generated in the U.S. but had a wider Western basis, is demonstrated by an article published in late 1981 in *Nato Review*. Writing on "Freedom of the Press and the Threat of State Intervention," *Douglas Hurd,* the British Minister of State at the Foreign and Commonwealth Office in London, warns the members of NATO that they "must recognize the seriousness of the menace, and act together to meet it."[154]

Another statement by an academic expert, Professor Seth Spaulding (University of Pittsburgh), appendiced to the proceedings, said that the Talloires meeting—the springboard for the House hearings—"was full of misconceptions of how Unesco operates and of what the various concerns are surrounding the international debate" (ibid., p. 286). Among the members of the Committee that held the hearings, there appears to have been only one prominent opponent to the prevailing anti-Unesco and pro-Talloires orientation. Representative George W. Crockett, who in reference to Unesco and the result of Belgrade, had "difficulty pinpointing a single portion of that basic resolution that I would interpret as an attempt to regulate news content and to formulate rules and regulations for the operation of the world press" (Ibid., p. 201).

[152] For this "Beard amendment," see e.g. L. Sussman, "Oh, Brave New Order!" *Freedom at Issue,* No. 64, January-February 1982, p. 41.

[153] Text released by USICA.

[154] *NATO Review,* No. 6, December 1981, p. 10.

However, by December 1981 the new offensive of the Western powers had not changed the behavior of NATO countries, other than the U.S. An accurate reading of the political positions of various parties is provided by the annual *resolution on "Questions Relating to Information," adopted by the UN General Assembly* on 16 December 1981.[155] This resolution, which once more "recalls" the Unesco and Non-Aligned conferences (this time also international seminars "such as that which took place at Tashkent in September 1979"), as well as various decisions reached in those forums, including the Mass Media Declaration, supports the IPDC and a number of UN-related activities in line with the "establishment of a new, more just and more effective world information and communication order, intended to strengthen peace and international understanding and based on the free circulation and wider and better balanced dissemination of information."[156] The resolution was adopted, not by consensus as had been the case every year since 1978, but after a vote in which 147 countries were in favor, two against, with no abstentions. Those voting against were Israel and the United States.

The U.S. explained its vote at the General Assembly in terms of "financial implications" (proposed increase of the budget for the UN Department of Public Information), and even indicated that it had accepted "unwarranted reference to various 'new orders' and to one-sided language in many paragraphs."[157] However, it was widely understood that the true motivation behind the U.S. move was a general reluctance to support UN in areas which seem to counter the U.S. interests. Also the U.K. expressed strong reservations but went along with the majority. Even so, the outcome of the UN vote is a significant indication of the end of consensus—at least at the stage of international politics that emerged in the early 1980s.

[155]Resolution 36/149 of the 36th session of the UN General Assembly. The resolution was prepared by the Special Political Committee of the General Assembly on the basis of reports of the permanent UN Committee on Information, of the UN Secretary-General and of the Director-General of Unesco.

[156] The resolution is composed of two parts (A and B), the first mainly focusing on the IPDC, while the second is devoted to both general aspects of the new order and to specific activities of the UN Department of Public Information.

[157] UN document A/36/PV.100 (provisional verbatim records of the General Assembly), p. 71. The explanation relates to Part B of the resolution, and also the vote was on this second part, while Part A was adopted by consensus. Since the United States also adopted Part A, endorsing the IPDC, it can be concluded that the Reagan Administration continued to support this particular approach to the new order, despite an obvious turn towards confrontation in the UN and Unesco. Yet this support was little more than symbolic, as shown by the fact that in January 1982, when the IPDC Council met in Acapulco to launch the Programme, the U.S. promised only "aid in the form of expert services" worth $100,000—a contribution comparable to that of the GDR (East Germany) and less than one-tenth of what the Soviet Union contributed to this category of expert services. Several countries, including Canada, China, France, Indonesia and Venezuela, announced their decision to give notable subventions in cash to the IPDC fund—the Soviet Union alone some $300,000, plus more in rubles. Even developing countries such as Bangladesh, Benin and Tunisia gave symbolic cash contributions of a few thousand dollars, while the U.S. failed to give a single dollar as direct and unconditional funding to be used by the decision of the IPDC Council.

The same neoconservative tendency that was reflected in the UN vote was signalled by a campaign waged in influential U.S. media in February 1982 as paid advertisements warning about "Danger at the UN."[158] The tone of this campaign—displayed as a scientific commentary—was so openly hard-line that it deserves to be quoted as another landmark statement in the struggle towards a new international information order.

> Imagine Franklin Roosevelt and Harry Truman, the UN's true godfathers, discovering a Unesco-sponsored coalition of tyrannies and their accomplices hatching elaborate plots to muzzle free world news media, all in the name of correcting alleged "omissions" and "imbalances" in coverage . . .
>
> Recognizing that the New World Information Order imperils freedom, 63 leaders of independent news organizations from 21 countries met last May in Talloires, France. The Talloires delegates accurately described the goal of their adversaries as essentially, a *New World Propaganda Order* . . .
>
> Since Talloires, the defenders of global press freedom have adopted a shrewd carrot-and-stick strategy. Whenever the subject had arisen at the UN, Western and moderate Third World representatives have answered new order advocates with efforts to implement information measures outside of Unesco's control. These include training programs and communications technology sharing schemes designed to strengthen resistance to government pressures by independent journalists in LDCs (Less Developed Countries) . . .
>
> The lessons seem obvious. With Western technical aid, we should concentrate on strengthening the media in societies that show some resolve to resist state domination of communications . . .
>
> The defenders of economic freedom, led by President Reagan at Cancun, also have begun to fight back. They have rejected LDC extortion as a method for negotiating over resources with developed societies.
>
> The LDCs, to be sure, possess valuable raw materials and important markets. But the developed countries hold coveted technologies and vital capital, as well as their own natural resources and *indispensable* markets.
>
> By selectively offering and withholding our markets, skills and capital, we can convince the often unstable regimes of poor countries that neither stability nor prosperity can be obtained through bureaucratic coercion . . .

[158] A four-page supplement, sponsored by the SmithKline Corporation (a "high-technology company" active in manufacturing and marketing of medicine, medical instruments, etc. in 120 countries), appeared in the *Time* magazine issue of 1 February 1982 (pp. 39–42, including the center opening of the issue) and in the *Newsweek* issue of 8 February 1982 (pp. 85–88). The message was obviously directed to the U.S. audience since the supplement did not appear in the international editions of these news magazines.

The free world press had paid scant attention to the parallels between Unesco's regulatory plans for journalists and efforts by other UN agencies to sponsor both the New International Economic Order and a host of additional restrictions upon private investment and trade in developing countries.

Yet both press and business should recognize the clear convergence of their interests in halting two comparably dangerous schemes. Unfortunately, all too many journalists and corporate heads (and union leaders) hesitate to act upon a self-evident truth: political and economic freedoms flourish or wither in tandem, whatever the society . . .[159]

The Uncompromised New Order Position

The new offensive launched under the name of Talloires, was met by the advocates of a new order—information as well as economic order—with less spectacular presentations but without any notable compromising. The first reaction from the *Non-Aligned Movement* came only a few days after the "Voices of Freedom" had been raised in Talloires. The Intergovernmental Council for the Coordination of Information among Non-Aligned Countries (a ministerial body first appointed by the Colombo summit in 1976 and enlarged by the Havana summit in 1979) happened to meet in Georgetown (Guyana) in May 1981, on which occasion the Council expressed "its full support for the activities of Unesco concerning the promotion of the New International Information Order" and by the same token, "rejected the simultaneous campaign of destabilization launched by Transnational Power Centers against the International Organization since the end of 1980, in the understanding that these global attacks by the big news agencies and corporate enterprises are truly aimed at preventing the implementation of the New International Information Order and its fundamental principles, as stated in the V and VI Summit Conferences of the Non-Aligned countries in Colombo and Havana respectively."[160]

---

[159]Excerpts from the text by Professor Allen Weinstein (Georgetown University, Center for Strategic and International Studies, Washington, D.C.). The text of this "SmithKline Forum" is entitled: "Press freedoms and economic freedoms are under attack in the U.N. The defenders of each must now unite, argues historian Allen Weinstein."

[160]Final Report of the Fourth Meeting of the Intergovernmental Council for the Coordination of Information among Non-Aligned Countries, Georgetown, 20–21 May 1981 (mimeo, pp. 4–5, paragraph 13). Three months earlier (9–13 February 1981), the Foreign Ministers of Non-Aligned Countries "affirmed their determination to strengthen mutual co-operation in this field and for the creation of a new international information order as conceived at the Colombo Summit in 1976 and proclaimed by the Sixth Summit Conference at Havana." (From Political Declaration of the Ministerial Conference, paragraph 14; in *Review of International Affairs*, No. 741, 20 February 1981, p. 22).

The *socialist countries of Eastern Europe* were equally vocal in denouncing Talloires and expressing support to Unesco. Reflecting the uncompromised non-aligned position, a Yugoslavian comment called the Declaration of Talloires "at best surprising and an anachronism for these times . . . openly for the first time against the new international information order being sought by the non-aligned and developing countries and the immense majority of mankind they encompass." [161] Soviet reactions displayed a more dramatic picture of "information war" declared in Tallories—with its originators "often been caught red-handed in collaboration with the CIA."[162]

In an authoritative article in *Pravda,* entitled "For a New International Information Order," the Soviet representative at the IPDC Council, *Anatoli Krasikov,* recalled that the Western powers had "stubbornly resisted" the drafting of the Mass Media Declaration of Unesco and went along "only when faced with the threat of isolation and with a united front of the socialist and a majority of developing countries."[163] This official Soviet position admitted that "having signed the document . . . the Western powers, however, have not changed their policies in the field of information" but were engaged in "an unbridled propaganda of animosity and violence" and "fantastic allegations about a 'Soviet military threat'." After demonstrating Soviet support to the IPDC, *Pravda* concluded that "the newly independent nations can rest assured that the Soviet Union and other countries of the socialist community will remain active as their allies in the struggle for the establishment of a new international order in the field of information."[164]

In fact, the new stage of confrontation gave further evidence to the conclusion which cannot be escaped in any objective analysis of the struggle around the new information order: *there exists a kind of "natural alliance" between the socialist and the developing countries, based on parallel, if not identical interests, with regards to the existing Western order.* To split and divide this coalition was a central aim of the Talloires offensive—just as had been intended before by the "Marshall Plan of Telecommunications." Thus it was vital to capitalize on "moderate Third World representatives" (Weinstein in the SmithKline Forum), as well as to show that "there is no Third World viewpoint" and that "many of them are tired of this rhetoric."[165] However, such a perspective is rather a reflection of Western

---

[161]Č. Vučković, "Equality and the News and Information Monopoly," *Review of International Affairs,* No. 760, 1981 (5 December 1981), p. 25.

[162]A. Grachov, "'Information War'against Unesco," *Moscow News,* No. 28, 1981, p. 7.

[163]*Pravda,* 5 October 1981.

[164]Ibid. The same point was made by President Leonid Brezhnev two years earlier in his message to the Tashkent seminar; see note 170 below.

wishful thinking than a valid statement of objective reality. While there naturally are many individuals to be found in the developing countries who for one reason or another take a Western position, it remains a fact that by far the most representative opinion of the developing countries has continued to be determined and united in its support of the new order.

The unity and uncompromised stand of the developing countries have not only been demonstrated by the official positions of the Non-Aligned Movement but also by *professional journalists*. For example, the editor of *South* magazine (London-based monthly representing a "Third World" point of view) wrote in August 1981:

> It is absurd to suggest that for developing countries to regulate the present uninterrupted flow of news from the North amounts to a denial of press freedom. (Free press is essentially a national concept, whereas the free flow of information is part of international commerce.) Developed countries set up formidable tariff and non-tariff barriers to regulate the flow of leather goods, textiles and jute manufactures from the developing countries and they are not embarrassed or deterred by the commitment to free trade . . . .
>
> The *Washington Post* (30 May 1981) commenting on the Talloires Declaration expressed the hope that it might "become the first line of international defence." Against whom? The Third World is not fighting against the principle of free press. The people in the developing countries are engaged in a relentless struggle for the establishment of a free press in their own countries. What they want is freedom to develop an independent press of their own, secure from domestic control as from foreign inundation. They face a dual challenge, one from authoritarian regimes in their own countries and the other from rapacious commercial media managers of the North; the two acting in collusion is not a wholly unfamiliar phenomenon. Their determination to preserve their creative freedom and cultural identity is no threat to press freedom, it is a refusal to allow western news agencies to exploit the information market wholly for their own purpose and profit.[166]

[165]From statement of Leonard Marks at the hearings before the Committee on Foreign Affairs, in op. cit. in note 141 above, p. 161. Marks elaborated: "At Talloires there were 21 countries represented. They included many Third World countries, some large, some small, some poverty stricken, some pretty well along the way. They didn't reflect any single viewpoint in favor of control, but they all seek private industry, an enterprise that they can participate in, a free press."

[166]Altaf Gauhar, "Free Press vs. Free Flow," *South*, August 1981, p. 10. The November 1981 issue of *South* published an interview with Unesco's Director-General M'Bow, who on this rare occasion rectified accusations that Unesco was encouraging state control over the press: "M'Bow said he made no distinction between foreign domination and internal domination. He would act always in support of democracy and the freedom of the press . . . " (p. 11).

A widely representative position of mass media professionals was articulated by the consultative meeting among interntional and regional organizations of journalists in Baghdad (Iraq) in February 1982 (two years after they had met in Mexico City).[167] This opinion, in the name of over 300,000 journalists around the world, reconfirmed the "Mexico Declaration" of 1980 (see Appendix 25) and exposed the "campaigns orchestrated by industrial, political and military monopolies" against the new order. The "Baghdad Declaration" also specified that, while the new order is based on the respect for international law and the UN Charter, it does not mean the establishment of "government censorship" or "licensing of journalists," as the Western campaign accused.

Consequently, by 1982 the decade-long movement towards a new international information order had gained *support among an overwhelming majority of the international community*—both at the political-governmental level and at the non-governmental level of mass media professionals. The Talloires offensive seems to have caused little real setback in this historical course. The new confrontation has just ensured that the field of mass media continues to be a controversial arena for politicians as well as for professional journalists and scholars of communication.

THE CONCEPT OF NIIO

This review of the historical "movement" towards a new international information order (NIIO) has presented the main ideas and positions of different parties with regards to the concept. But throughout this "great debate" the concept of NIIO (and even its terminology) has remained somewhat obscure—not so uncommon with political slogans that capture vital aspects of social reality but fail to provide a comprehensive definition of the issues involved. Clearly, NIIO has been an evolving concept, and thus far it has not been defined in a scientifically rigorous manner. There is no lack of fruitful starting points for a theoretical elaboration of NIIO. They have been provided by a number of authors who, either from the ranks of the Non-Aligned Movement or as empathetic observ-

[167]The meeting in Baghdad on 22-24 February 1982 was attended by leading representatives of International Organization of Journalists, International Federation of Journalists, International Catholic Union of the Press, Federation of Latin American Journalists and Federation of Arab Journalists, as well as observers from Unesco and some Arab and Asian organizations. The meeting adopted "The Declaration of Baghdad." See e.g. 10J Newsletter, March 1982.

ers from outside, have contributed to the "great debate" with works which go beyond partisan polemics and simple documentation.[168]

However poorly defined the concept remains in the early 1980s, its main "political profile" seems to be consolidated enough to account for an analytical summary on the basis of authoritative sources from the three main "camps" of the "great debate": the Movement of Non-Aligned Countries, the Soviet Union with its socialist allies, and the United States with its Western allies.

The Non-Aligned Movement—the original promoter of NIIO—articulated its understanding of the concept in concise and formal terms in a resolution adopted at the fourth meeting of the Inter-Governmental Coordinating Council for Information of Non-Aligned Countries in Baghdad in June 1980.[169] The preamble of this resolution begins by "recalling" the relevant decisions of the Summit Conferences in Algiers (1973), Colombo (1976), and Havana (1979), the UN decisions concerning a new international economic order, disarmament, and information, as well as the Mass Media Declaration and other relevant decisions of Unesco (using phrasing more or less identical with the UN and Unesco resolutions since 1978). The last few paragraphs of this extensive preamble and the first operative part of the resolution read as follows:

> *Noting with concern* that the sphere of information and mass communications is still characterized by injustice and inequality, colonial and neo-colonial dependence and usurped privileges, linked with the dominance of transnational corporations in international information activities,
>
> *Noting furthermore* that the same fundamental problems apply to new forms of electronically processing and transmitting all kinds of data thus extending the concern over the New Interntional Information Order widely beyond the traditional sphere of the mass media and transmission of news,

---

[168]See e.g. contributions by Hamelink, Kleinwaechter, Masmoudi, Osolnik, Schiller and Tran Van Dinh referred to above. Another indispensable source concerning NIIO is the Latin American Institute for Transnational Studies (ILET, based in Mexico City, with Juan Somavía as its Director); see *Development Dialogue* (journal of the Dag Hammarskjöld Foundation, Uppsala), No. 2, 1981. Books by activists in the NIIO movement include D. R. Mankekar, *Whose Freedom? Whose Order? A Plea for a New International Information Order by Third World*, Delhi: Clarion Books, 1981, and B. Oslonik, *The New International Information and Communication Order*, Beograd: Jugoslovenska Stvarnost, 1980. For a perspective from a liberal Western viewpoint, see e.g. A. Smith, *The Geopolitics of Information*, London and Boston: Faber & Faber, 1980.

[169]The four-page resolution on NIIO has been reproduced in *EPD-Entwicklungspolitik-Materialen* (information bulletin of the Evangelical Press Service, Frankfurt am Main), No. VI, 1980. For an extensive quote, see also op. cit. in note 88 above.

Believing that the development of truly independent and democratic national systems of information and mass communication, supported by the decolonization and democratization of international relations in the field of information, is an essential prerequisite for the establishment of a new international information order,

1. *Considers* that the New International Information Order is based on:

(a) the fundamental principles of international law, notably self-determination of peoples, sovereign equality of states and non-interference in internal affairs of other states,

(b) the right of every nation to develop its own independent information system and to protect its national sovereignty and cultural identity, in particular by regulating the activities of the transnational corporations,

(c) the right of people and individuals to acquire an objective picture of reality by means of accurate and comprehensive information as well as to express themselves freely through various media of culture and communication,

(d) the right of every nation to use its means of information to make known worldwide its interests, its aspirations and its political, moral and cultural values,

(e) the right of every nation to participate, on the governmental and non-governmental level, in the interntional exchange of information under favourable conditions in a sense of equality, justice and mutual advantage,

(f) the responsibility of various actors in the process of information for its truthfulness and objectivity as well as for the particular social objectives to which the information activities are dedicated.

2. *Considers further* that the New International Information Order is intended to contribute in particular to:

(a) the establishment of the New International Economic Order;

(b) the fight against imperialism, colonialism, neocolonialism, *apartheid*, racism including zionism and all forms of foreign aggression, occupation, domination and interference;

(c) the promotion of human rights through intensified efforts to consolidate social, economic and cultural development and to combat hunger, disease, illiteracy and unemployment;

(d) strengthening peace and international understanding, in particular through the goal of general and complete disarmament under effective international control.

The Soviet version of NIIO was characterized in a working paper presented by the United Nations Association of the USSR to the seminar "New World Information and Communication Order," organized by the World Federation of UN Associations in Geneva in October 1981.[170] After opening with the thesis that "mass information of today serves as an important instrument of moulding the public opinion that, in its turn, is generating a considerable impact upon home and foreign policies of nations," the paper spells out the essence of the Soviet concept of NIIO in the following two paragraphs:

> The growing awareness of the importance of moral and ideological decolonization on the part of developing nations has brought to life the problem of a new international information order. It implies the cessation of using the international mass information as a political weapon for enslaving nations, the elimination of domination by Western information monopolies in the sphere of moulding the public opinion, the imparting of equitable and mutually advantageous nature to international information exchanges, the ensuring of balanced flows of information between countries, the exclusion of biased and slanted pieces of information, the prohibition of using the mass information as a weapon for psychological warfare.
>
> The process of establishing the new international information order has to be based upon the combination of strict observance of generally accepted basic principles of international law in the field of international information activity, elaboration and adoption of special principles and rules of international mass information, elimination of inequality in developing the national mass media systems. The content of the principles of new international information order may be of general democratic nature, aimed at achieving social progress and maintaining relations of peaceful coexistence among all nations.

Furthermore, it is worth noting that the Soviet policy at Unesco is to push the Organization in the 1980s, as far as the sector of communication is concerned, to concentrate "primarily on matters relating to the content of information and on developing equitable and democratic standards as regards international information exchanges with a view to making a more effective use of the mass media for strengthening international peace and cooperation, for deepening détente, and for the struggle against militarism, hegemonism, colonialism and apartheid."[171] In prac-

---

[170] Working-paper No. 12 of the Seminar (mimeo, 4 pp.).

[171] From "Proposals and Recommendations of the USSR Concerning Unesco's Medium-Term Plan for 1984-1989" (document of the National Commission of the USSR, submitted to Unesco's Director-General on 29 June 1981), in *Commission of the USSR for Unesco Bulletin*, No. 3-4 (45–46), 1981, p. 46.

tical terms, the USSR advocates "a profound scientific elaboration of the NIIO concept, with the subsequent establishment in a clear-cut manner of its purposes and principles in international law, above all the principles of sovereign equality of states, non-interference in their internal affairs, and others."

Comparing the Non-Aligned and Soviet versions of NIIO, it is evident that by and large they coincide, even to the extent of using mostly identical terminology. There is only one notable difference: the Soviet concept does not give priority to the New International Economic Order. Also the emphasis given to the notion of contents of communication, as well as to the objective of international peace and détente, is obviously greater in the Soviet concept than in the Non-Aligned version of it. The Non-Aligned concept, for its part, is more specific in terms of spelling out the principles and objectives of NIIO. However, there is little doubt that all of the points listed in the Baghdad resolution (inter alia, NIEO and "racism including zionism") would well suit a Soviet list, if such were constructed in greater detail.

As a demonstration of the similarity, or even identity, of views held in the Non-Aligned Movement, on the one hand, and in the socialist countries of Soviet orientation, on the other, we may point to the internationl seminar of journalists and mass media experts in Tashkent (Uzbekistan SSR) in September 1979. This seminar was attended by participants coming from 46 countries of all continents, including leading experts from the socialist camp as well as several outstanding representatives of the Non-Aligned Movement.[172] The final statement of the Tashkent seminar can be seen as an easy synthesis of the two parallel concepts:

> The participants expressed their agreement about the vital role
> of communication in the *internal life* of every society, stressing espe-

[172]The seminar was organized by the USSR Commission for Unesco and the Union of Journalists of the USSR, with the support of Unesco. Attending were, among others Yuri Kashlev and Yassen Zassoursky from the Soviet Union, Jadwiga Pastecka from Poland (cf. Chapter 2), D. R. Mankekar from India (Chairman of the Pool of Non-Aligned News Agencies), James Halloran from the U.K. (President of the International Association for Mass Communication Research), and Cees Hamelink from the Netherlands. The present author attended as President of the International Organization of Journalists. The opening of the Seminr was addressed by Amadou-Mahtar M'Bow, Unesco's Director-General, and the main paper to the Seminar ("The Mass Media in the Struggle for Peace and Social Progress") was presented by Sharif Rashidov, Alternate Member of the Politbureau of the Soviet Communist Party and First Secretary of the Communist Party of Uzbekistan. Leonid Brezhnev sent to the participants of the Seminar his greetings, including the following: "Soviet people view with understanding and sympathy the desire of the peoples of Asia, Africa and Latin America to create their information bodies, to protect themselves from the ideological expansion of imperialism and to put an end to the 'spiritual colonialism.' It is clear that a stubborn struggle is ahead and the extent of its success will depend on the coordinated action of the developing countries and their friends and allies—the countries of the socialist community. In this just cause progressive journalists of the world may count upon our sincere assistance." (*International Seminar of Journalists in Tashkent,* Moscow: Novosti Press Agency Publishing House, 1980, p. 10).

cially the significance of the mass media as an instrument for achieving economic and social progress. It was their conviction that economic and political independence cannot be complete without independence of the communication and information field as well.

The participants recognized that revolutionary changes in the *international life* over the last few decades also apply to the sphere of information and communication. This sphere is governed by the same norms and principles of international law that are valid for other fields. Its main objective is to serve the goals and causes set forth by the international community, above all the preservation of peace and security, safeguarding and fostering of cultural identity and at the same time strengthening of mutual understanding and cooperation among peoples, promotion of human rights as well as the struggle against propaganda for war, arms race, colonialism, neocolonialism, racism, apartheid—thus improving the moral and political climate of the world. To this end, the participants affirmed their support to the Mass Media Declaration of Unesco adopted by the General Conference in 1978 and urged its full implementation by all States, mass media and professional organizations. The participants also welcomed the Declaration on the Preparation of Societies for Life in Peace, adopted by the General Assembly of the United Nations in 1978, and exhorted the UN to work out proper steps for its implementation.

The participants voiced their awareness of the need for fresh efforts to stimulate the process of making the sphere of information more compatible with the just social and economic requirements and needs of the developing countries, and to eliminate all kinds of colonialism and usurped privileges still existing in the field of information. They expressed their strong support to the demand for the establishment of a new international information order aimed at the decolonization and democratization of this field in terms of both content and distribution of messages.

In view of the participants, this new order, understood as an integral part of the new international economic order, should be based on the generally recognized principles of international law, in particular on respect for national sovereignty and non-interference in internal affairs of other States. Nationally this new order requires democratic social structures, on the basis of which an independent and endogenous national system of information and communication may be built, thus enabling them an effective participation in the international exchange of information as full-fledged members of the international community . . . .[173]

---

[173]The eight-page statement by the Seminar was published in the proceedings referred to above and in *Journalists' Affairs,* No. 21-22, 1979, pp. 12–19.

The U.S. version of NIIO is found in the U.S. working paper to the above-mentioned UN Associations' seminar in Geneva.[174] The point of departure is strikingly similar to the corresponding Soviet position. According to the U.S. view, the call for a new order "reflects growing awareness of the central role that communications play in the functioning of the international system." But then the U.S. position moves in a different direction: "In international commerce, information and communication are commodities, whose value is rising as the recognition of their importance grows."

To be sure, such a statement might well have originated from a Marxist source, at this time of transnational corporations, and it is not difficult to imagine the Soviets endorsing it. But there is a crucial difference in perspective: while the Soviet concept is based on reasoning about "public opinion," i.e., the ideological role of the mass media, the U.S. concern is focused on "international commerce," i.e., economic implications of transnational information flow. Even more striking is the contradiction between the U.S. and the Non-Aligned concepts of information and communication; what is advocated by one ("commodities") is explicitly denied by another: "Information must be understood as a social good and cultural product, and not as a material commodity or merchandise."[175]

The essence of the U.S. concept of NIIO is contained in the following two paragraphs:

> Through the veil of rhetoric and contention, two fundamental themes that are neither incompatible nor unrealistic have emerged. First is the strong conviction, voiced principally but not solely by the Western democracies, that the international flow of information should not be restricted by governmental actions. Second is the demand by many developing countries for aid in building their own capabilities for compiling and disseminating information in order to reduce their dependence on western organizations and technology. Taken together, these themes may well suggest a reasonable basis for achieving a global compromise on a range of issues of legitimate concern to all countries.
>
> Advocates of a "new order" should recognize that their larger objectives can only be harmed by further proposals aimed at silencing or censuring the media. Attempts to restrict international news organizations cannot possibly reverse the North-South imbalance in communications capabilities, which can only be rectified by positive steps to enlarge the communications

---

[174] Working-paper No. 7 of the Seminar (mimeo, 4 pp.).

[175] Masmoudi, op. cit. in note 53, p. 15.

infrastructures within developing countries. Such efforts are likely instead to alienate the potential sources for much-needed technical and financial assistance.

The two "fundamental themes"—against restricting the information flows, and for assisting the developing countries—are, as such, by and large compatible with the concept of NIIO as advocated by the Non-Aligned and socialist camps. After all, no one has "aimed at silencing and censuring the media"; on the contrary, the documents of Baghdad and Tashkent clearly stand for a greater worldwide variety of information than is provided by the existing order. As the Director-General of Unesco put it in Talloires, the developing countries have "no other aim in view but the application of a universally recognized right," bringing us closer to the day "when the free flow of ideas and knowledge will no longer be the good fortune of some but the common asset of all."[176]

However, viewed as a whole, and considering the historical context reviewed above, it is obvious that the Western concept of NIIO has little in common with the concept of Non-Aligned and socialist countries. As well pointed out by the above-quoted statement of Abrams, the U.S. concept is mainly composed of elements *rejected*. Indeed, in this respect it may not be fair to call it a "concept," because in comparison to the *positive approach* of its Non-Aligned and socialist counterparts, the U.S. version represents a negative, *apologetic approach*.

In the U.S. version of NIIO there is no positive room for the *New International Economic Order,* for the *democratization* of communication at the *national level,* for the *contents* of communication and its *responsibility,* for *international law* other than the aspect of free flow—all central constituents of NIIO as conceived by its advocates. The only common element is *transfer of technology,* but even this has been appreciated in different ways by the two contradictory approaches. The most divisive question is obviously *government-media relations;* one approach being based on "abstract" notions of freedom and government which are seen to stand in sharp contrast to each other, whereas the other approach is based on "concrete" socio-economic interests as represented by the media as well as governments. It should be noted that these two positions are not diametrically opposite; the "Third World-Soviet" version does not advocate a universal system whereby the mass media are under governmental control and journalists "licensed." Such accusations are based on either a lack of understanding of the issues involved or on deliberate distortion for political purposes.

[176]The address of Amadou-Mahtar M'Bow at the "Voices of Freedom" conference is reproduced as appendix to the Committee on Foreign Relations hearings, op. cit. in note 141 above, pp. 260–261.

Common Ground for Universal Interest

However marked the contradictions, the situation does not set up a simple battlefield of opposing camps. In fact, outstanding advocates of NIIO insist that a new order is not only in the interest of the developing and socialist countries but ultimately a matter of universal interest. As put by Osolnik, from the Non-Aligned point of view:

> The problems involved are not exclusively of developing countries. They can take even more striking form in advanced industrial societies. The new international order must therefore include the democratization of the news and information functions as a prerequisite for the realization of human rights and democratic social development in every country and for the participation of all in peaceful international cooperation.[177]

The same point was made by Hamid Mowlana (a U.S.-Iranian expert in international communication) in his testimony to the U.S. House of Representatives:

> In my opinion, correcting the present imbalance of communication and information exchange in the world not only will benefit the Third World, but also will be in the national interest of the United States and will contribute to the security and peace of the world. It simply means that if the Third World is to be enabled to participate fairly in the international exchange, a certain amount of restructuring of international communication becomes inevitable and, for some, this poses honest concerns.
>
> Viewing such a controversial north-south issue in east-west zero-sum terms, as some of the previous witnesses have done, undoubtedly restricts analysis and the search for solutions . . . .
>
> Mr. Chairman, the views, values and interests of more than two-thirds of mankind in the less developed world cannot be ignored without risking international security and peace. The New World Information Order can only be brought about if the world community gets together and decides to make possible equitable distribution of technical facilities, provide all nations capabilities and raw materials, encourage all nations to set up comprehensive communication policies, and finally, respect and recognize the diversity in human resources and values. This, of course, requires international cooperation and solution.[178]

[177]Op. cit. in note 159 above, pp. 49–50.
[178]Op. cit. in note 141 above, pp. 209–210.

After reviewing the movement towards a new international information order—a history of continuing contradictions—it is indeed important to remember that *the international community has a limited but significant common ground* for coping with problems of communication. This ground is to be found in the universally recognized human and social values as elaborated by the international community in such instruments as the UN Charter and generally in international law. An important reconfirmation and even further development of this common ground was the Final Act of the Conference on Security and Co-operation in Europe (so-called "Helsinki Accords") adopted in 1975—at a time when the new order movement was taking momentum. In 1978, the adoption of the Mass Media Declaration constituted a similar step—emphasizing that there is to be found a universal interest in the middle of an ideological struggle. As will be documented in Parts 2 and 3 of this book, this universal interest is not only made up of political considerations, but also contains a lot of juridical, ethical and professional substance.

2
The Shaping: A History of the Preparation

The "official" history of the Declaration can be traced through a number of Unesco meetings and many related documents. It began in the fall of 1970 with a resolution at the 16th biannual session of the General Conference (the highest decision-making body of the Organization attended by government delegations from all Member States) and ended in November 1978 at the 20th session of the General Conference, which adopted the final "consensus text" of the Declaration by acclamation. The most significant manifestations of this official history are some dozen documents and the following eight occasions:

1. Sixteenth session of the General Conference, Paris, November 1970 (resolution 4.301)
2. Seventeenth session of the General Conference, Paris, November 1972 (resolution 4.113)
3. Meeting of experts, Paris, March 1974 (working paper, including the first draft by Professor Eek, and report of the meeting, including an amended draft)
4. Eighteenth session of the General Conference, Paris, November 1974 (document 18C/35, including a further amended draft, and resolution 4.111)
5. Intergovernmental meeting of experts, Paris, December 1975 (report of the meeting, including a new draft)
6. Nineteenth session of the General Conference, Nairobi, November 1976 (document 19C/91, including the preceding draft, and resolution 4.143)
7. Hundred-and-fourth session of the Executive Board, Paris, June 1978 (document 104 EX/28 and decision 5.5.4)
8. Twentieth session of the General Conference, Paris, November 1978 (document 20C/20, including a new draft, and adoption of the final text 20C/20 Rev.)

The final Declaration and brief account of this history have been published for wide distribution in a Unesco pamphlet.[1] Another Unesco publication includes comprehensive documentation of the steps noted above, including full texts of the resolutions and reports (with the exception of those related to the 104th session of the Executive Board).[2] The present Chapter, with all the documents in the appendices, complements these Unesco publications by including numerous historical facts and the full text of a number of intermediary drafts of the Declaration, which are not immediately apparent in the official history. Given the eight-year-long history of preparation involving a number of episodes and maneuvers (often less official in nature), this Chapter is necessarily rather extensive.

THE QUIET BEGINNING

The first step in 1970, while it constituted the political beginning of the long process of preparing the Declaration, did not envision a specific Unesco declaration. Resolution number 4.301, passed by the 16th session of the General Conference, merely reaffirmed a number of Unesco and UN resolutions on the promotion of peace and international understanding and on the elimination of colonialism and racism. It made the point "that propaganda on behalf of war, racialism and hatred among nations by means of information media is incompatible with the purposes and principles of the United Nations Charter and the Constitution of Unesco."[3] The final operative part of this resolution drove home this point by speaking about *"the inadmissibility of using information media for propaganda on behalf of war, racialism and hatred among nations"* and by *inviting "all States to take necessary steps, including legislative measures, to encourage the use of information media"* against such propaganda. The resolution furthermore invited the States to "provide Unesco with information on the subject" and asked the Director-General of Unesco to submit a report based on such information to the next session of the General Conference.

This resolution was submitted by the Byelorussian SSR to the Commission dealing with communication issues, under the chapter "Public information and promotion of international understanding." The records of the General Conference describe the proceedings as follows:

[1] *Declaration on Fundamental Principles concerning the contribution of the Mass Media to Strengthening Peace and International Understanding, to the Promotion of Human Rights and to Countering Racialism, Apartheid and Incitement to War,* Paris: Unesco, 1979.

[2] *Historical Background of the Mass Media Declaration,* Paris: Unesco series New Communication Order, No. 9, 1982.

[3] *Records of the General Conference, Sixteenth Session* (Paris, 12 October to 14 November 1970), Volume 1: Resolutions, Paris: Unesco, 1971, p. 60. This as well as all subsequent quotes from relevant resolutions are reproduced in the publication referred to in note 2 above.

Thirteen delegates spoke in favour of the resolution as drafted, two opposed it although expressing disapproval of the media's use for propaganda of the kind mentioned, on the grounds that prohibitory legislation would not be possible under their systems. One of these delegates added that government control of the media is in direct opposition to the "freedom of information" which is cherished by many Member States. Two other delegates expressed reservations as to the wording of the resolution and the Byelorussian delegate proposed amendments which were accepted.

The Commission recommended by 43 votes to 5, with 10 abstentions, that the General Conference adopt resolution 4.301 (draft resolution 16C/DR.101, amended).[4]

Thus the fundamental contradictions discussed in Chapter 1 were clearly present at the first step. However, the situation did not turn into a heated controversy at this stage; neither was it accompanied by wide publicity. This "low profile" is not surprising, given the nature of Resolution 4.301, which, its strong wording notwithstanding, did not suggest anything essentially beyond what was already a legitimate international line established by a number of resolutions at the UN and Unesco. Furthermore, no "time bomb" was involved, since Unesco was invited to act only as a "post office" for informing the Member States on relevant national legislation.

Thus it was considered by most as another routine resolution without far-reaching significance. However, because crucial contradictions of a principal nature were involved, it would have provided a natural springboard for an ideological clash—had there been a need for that. But potential political forces as well as relevant professional circles remained relatively silent, and the debate at this session of the General Conference took place in a business-like atmosphere—perhaps encouraged by emerging détente.

It is worth noting that the same Programme Commission debated *research and studies in mass communication*, welcoming, among other things, an international program for studies of the effects of communication on society, as well as another new program on the definition of *communication policies*. The records of the debate reveal that the delegates unanimously felt that "it was high time that the notion of communication as a public service be generally recognized, and that, as a consequence, communication planning and the formulation of communication policies be included in overall development planning."[5] Furthermore, the topic of *codes of ethics in journalism* was placed on Unesco's agenda at that same session:

[4]*Records of the General Conference, Sixteenth Session*, Volume 2: Reports, Paris: Unesco, 1971. p. 115 (paragraphs 1305–1306).
[5]Ibid., p. 113 (paragraph 1272).

Several delegates referred to the importance of establishing professional codes of ethics for the mass media, with regard both to national and to international communication. They emphasized the need to associate the professionals themselves in the elaboration of such codes, and recommended that Unesco should compile and analyze codes which have already been adopted, with a view to establishing a common basis.[6]

The records do not suggest that there was any controversy involved in this debate. The same business-like atmosphere is reflected in the response of Unesco's Member States to Resolution 4.301; few of the 57 replies received by the Director-General made a big issue of the contradictions involved, and none gave an outright polemical response (not even United Kingdom, which appeared most reluctant towards the resolution). The report prepared by the Director-General on the basis of these replies in September 1972 for the forthcoming 17th session of the General Conference is reproduced in Appendix 3.

The *"Report on existing legislation and measures taken by Member States to encourage the use of mass media against propaganda on behalf of war, racialism and hatred among nations"* did not receive notable attention in the diplomacy of the General Conference, any more than in the public debate on the mass media. Yet the report provides quite relevant material for the debate on the tasks and role of the media, demonstrating that socialist and developing countries as well as many Western (capitalist) countries were bound by legislation along the lines advocated by the resolution. (Obviously there have been many changes in national legislation during the 1970s, but the basic situation has changed very little, as proved by a recent overview of national legislation prepared for the MacBride Commission.[7])

General Conference 1972

No further action was taken on this report, which was merely noted by the 17th session of the General Conference in Fall 1972. Instead, the focus of attention was turned to a new proposal, submitted by the Byelorussian SSR and the USSR, to prepare *"a draft declaration concerning the fundamental principles governing the use of the mass information media with a view to strengthening peace and international understanding and combating war propaganda, racialism and apartheid."* This proposal was a logical follow-up to the 1970 resolution. The political profile of the new proposal was almost the

[6]Ibid., p. 113 (paragraph 1270).

[7]"Survey of national legislation (1): Constitutional provisions," document no. 23 prepared for the International Commission for the Study of Communication Problems, Paris: Unesco, 1980.

same as the earlier one, with, perhaps, further emphasis on détente. The difference was in the operative part of the new resolution, which not only repeated the main point of the 1970 resolution and took note of the report on existing legislation and the measures taken by the Member States, but also requested the Director-General to prepare and to submit a draft declaration as phrased above to the General Conference at its 18th session.

The records of the Programme Committee on Communication at the 17th session of the General Conference provide an illuminating summary of the debate in which some twenty delegates participated:

> Most of the speakers supported the proposal. They pointed out that such a declaration would be fully in accord with the principles of Unesco as set forth in the Constitution and in many other declarations and resolutions of the General Conference. The present debate had shown the widespread concern with the role of mass media in influencing the attitudes and values of the public and it would, in short, be most desirable to bring many of these considerations together in a considered text which might best be embodied in a formal declaration.
>
> Other speakers, while subscribing to the objective of strengthening peace and international understanding, expressed strong reservations about the method proposed. They felt that the contents of mass media was primarily a matter for professional responsibility on the part of journalists and broadcasters, rather than an appropriate subject for legislative guidance. In some countries there is a fundamental contradiction with principles enshrined in national legislation respecting the right to freedom of information and expression.[8]

Furthermore, the records of the debate reveal that the *Secretariat of Unesco* was far from enthusiastic about this new initiative. The Deputy Director-General (an American by nationality) told the delegates that the relevant division of the Secretariat was already engaged in a substantial program "involving, for example, satellites, codes of ethics, and assistance in the establishment of news agencies." His comments were hardly encouraging; indeed, it may be said that the Draft Declaration was placed on Unesco's agenda *despite* rather than *because of* the activity of the Secretariat. The driving force was pressure from Member States, "from the floor."

It seems that at that time the Secretariat followed the line that Unesco was supposed to carry out pragmatic missions in the field of communication, without "politicizing" the field by normative instru-

[8]*Records of the General Conference, Seventeenth Session* (Paris, 17 October to 21 November 1972), Volume 2: Reports, Paris: Unesco, 1974, p. 122 (paragraphs 158–159).

ments touching upon the contents of communication. As was shown above in Chapter 1, this typically Western orientation had espoused a kind of division of labor between the UN and Unesco, whereby the so-called political aspects of information were left to the UN, "while Unesco's domain was to be the more technical work involved in attempting to ease the flow of information across frontiers," as the former Director-General René Maheu is quoted as having defined it in the late 1940s.[9] In the early 1970s, the bulk of Unesco's communication program was in harmony with this division of labor, although, after the 16th session of the General Conference, there had been an increasing tendency to understand Unesco's task of promoting "the free flow of information and international exchanges" in a way that was essentially broader than the traditional Western approach would suggest.[10] In any case, it was only natural that the Unesco Secretariat felt somewhat frustrated when confronted with what many saw as a futile attempt to reconcile the Western and Eastern approaches to information, its freedom and responsibility.

By and large, the introduction of the Draft Declaration as well as its predecessor, Resolution 4.301 of 1970—both relating directly to the "political" contents of the mass media—mark a notable departure from an orientation which had been established over the years and which was operating in the ultimate interest of the Western countries. However, it should be noted that this Western orientation itself represented a departure from the original Unesco mandate, as determined in its Constitution and confirmed in a number of General Conference resolutions, setting out its mission in the field of information in highly "political" terms. In this respect, the 1970 resolution and the 1972 proposal for a draft declaration represented a return to a constitutional track.

This reversal included a strategic reorientation, not only isolated political moves. This conclusion is supported by another, parallel, development in Unesco's program on codes of ethics for the mass media. The 17th session of the General Conference also debated a new project in this area, under the topic *"Professional standards in the field of the mass media,"* as summarized by the records:

[9]Behrstock, "News, Politics and Unesco's Wrong Turn," *International Herald Tribune*, 7 November 1978.
[10]Indications of this tendency can be found e.g. in "Suggestions to Member States on measures to promote the free flow of information and international exchanges," prepared in accordance with the decisions of the 17th session of the General Conference and first published in 1974 for the 18th session (18C/90) which decided to have them dispatched to Member States (this was done by letter CL/2434 of the Director-General, 23 May 1975). These suggestions might have been directed against the normative approach represented by the Draft Declaration, but in fact the document presents a fairly balanced view; it devotes one of its five sections to "the content of what is published and broadcast as well as the effects of the mass media on audiences," while another section "covers the national policies and plans required for the effective use of communication to further social and economic progress and individual well-being" (CL/2434 Annex, paragraph 6).

There was unanimous agreement that such codes would be valuable and that, if they were to be effective, they must be worked out in the closest co-operation with the professionals of press, film, radio and television. A number of speakers called, however, for immediate attention to the drafting of guiding principles on an international level, leaving national codes to national authorities. Other speakers maintained that the best sequence for the programme would be first to study national codes and to encourage more States to adopt such statements of principle. Once this had been done, it would be time to turn to international guidelines. . .

A speaker expressed strong reservations; in his view an international code of ethics might go counter to the very principles of cultural diversity and the free flow of information for which the Organization stood. Several other delegates also called for a prudent approach to the problem of codes of ethics. Nevertheless, they felt it would be useful to study existing national codes to see what common denominators existed. It was suggested that this might lead to a model code to which professional organizations in Member States might subscribe. Another speaker felt that Unesco should limit its programme to stimulation and support, since codes were a matter for the professionals to consider in a national context. Another noted that codes could not be separated from the differing institutional structures in Member States, which would require preliminary examination.

While accepting the importance of national codes, several delegates emphasized that they were primarily interested in codes of ethics that would cover international reporting; in other words, a code for foreign correspondents.

They pointed out that national codes were within national competence and that satisfactory arrangements existed, or were being formulated, in many Member States. On the other hand, there was at present no international code, and only Unesco could take the lead in trying to meet the need for one. A delegate suggested that such a code might concern itself not only with the rights and responsibilities of foreign correspondents but also with the obligations of the host country towards them.[11]

Members voted to support a project designed to promote codes of ethics (by a vote of 50 for, 6 against, with 9 abstentions), thus demonstrating an overwhelming majority in favor of an increased commitment to journalistic responsibility in mass media content.[12] As far as the Byelorussian-USSR draft resolution for the preparation of the Mass Media Declaration is concerned, it was also adopted by a majority, al-

[11]*Records of the General Conference, Seventeeth Session,* Volume 2: Reports, Paris: Unesco, 1974, pp. 112–113 (paragraphs 32–35).

[12]Ibid., p. 113 (paragraph 37).

though not so overwhelmingly. Resolution 4.113, as it was numbered in the proceedings of the 17th session of the General Conference, was adopted—after the sponsors of the original draft resolution had introduced amendments in the light of the debate—by the following vote:

- *for*, 32 including East European socialist countries, a number of developing countries, and Greece;
- *against*, 15 including the USA, Federal Republic of Germany, Switzerland, Denmark, Norway, and Sweden;
- *abstention*, 13 including France, Finland, Ethiopia, and Somalia.[13]

After this vote in the Programme Commission, the resolution passed a plenary session of the General Conference with a much broader margin: 68 in favor, 16 against, with 6 abstentions. This notwithstanding, there is no doubt that members were deeply divided over the issues involved. Yet the resolution—like the question concerning the "use" of the mass media in general—did not occupy a particularly central place on the political agenda of Unesco at that time. Most of the professional and political attention in the communication field at this session of the General Conference was captured by another declaration, that on *direct broadcasting over satellites*, including the issue of the so-called "prior consent principle."[14] At the next (18th) session of the General Conference in 1974, the Draft Declaration on the Mass Media received considerable attention. It did not, however, become the dominating issue in the communication sector, let alone in the whole session, as was clearly the case in 1976, in Nairobi, at the 19th session of the General Conference.

Preparations in 1974

The Draft Declaration debated at the 18th session of the General Conference was preceded by two drafts prepared in 1974. Both of these were proposed by outside consultants, invited in the name of the Director-General to assist in the implementation of Resolution 4.113. This is a normal practice at Unesco: the Secretariat performing the role of a modera-

[13]Ibid., p. 122 (paragraph 162). The official records of the General Conference report the distribution of the votes only in terms of numbers, since no roll-call vote was taken on this point, whereas information about which countries were included in each category is based on the internal report of the delegation of Finland (the author had access to these reports in his capacity of a member of the Finnish National Commission for Unesco, Section for Communication). Unless otherwise indicated, the same unofficial source has also been used below when disclosing information which is not apparent in the official records or other published materials. Concerning Resolution 4.113, it was "cosponsored" before the vote by Ukrainan SSR, Bulgaria, Czechoslovakia, Mongolia, Hungary, Poland, Chile, Peru, Cuba, Dahome and Cameroon (personal communication by V. Anichtchouk who represented Byelorussia at the session).

[14]See e.g. "Part 2—Direct Satellite Broadcasting: Exemplar of the Challenge to National Sovereignty," in K. Nordenstreng & H. I. Schiller (Eds.), *National Sovereignty and International Communication*, Norwood, N.J.: Ablex, 1979, pp. 115–165.

tor, with the substantive matters being dealt with by well-known experts representing various socio-political and regional interests.

The groundwork was prepared by *Hilding Eek*, a Swedish expert in international law and a specialist in the legal aspects of freedom of information.[15] His proposed text, submitted to the Secretariat in January 1974, was the first Draft Declaration put on paper. (This text is reproduced in Appendix 4.) Being a legal expert, Eek wrote his draft to faithfully reflect the political mandate of Resolution 4.113 and, furthermore, to keep it in line with relevant principles of international law. Typical in this respect is his Article I:

> Each State is internationally responsible for the conduct of its governmental information services and their activities beyond its own borders as well as for its national legislation relating to the performance of mass media within its own territory. International responsibility is based on the principles and rules of international law, in particular the Charter of the United Nations.[16]

This is merely a factual statement of state responsibility over the media. Indeed, most of Eek's draft simply paraphrased relevant passages of already valid international conventions, declarations, and resolutions. Thus it would be fundamentally wrong to interpret this draft as a blueprint of sinister forces advocating state control of the media—after all, the author was a liberal internationalist. On the other hand, it was also evident that Eek did not subscribe to the "libertarian theory" on the role and functions of the mass media in society, as it is usually understood in the private sector, but that he rather represented the "social responsibility theory."[17] This was demonstrated by his Article IX:

> Professional organizations in the field of the mass media contribute to awareness of journalistic responsibility. Efforts should be made to encourage high ethical standards and to improve the professional training of media personnel both on the national and international level to encourage the use of the media to spread ideas of peace, friendship and mutual understanding among nations.

---

[15]Hilding Eek is Professor Emeritus of International Law at the University of Stockholm and resided in the 1970s in Brandon, Vermont (USA). In 1948–1952 he was Chief of Section for Freedom of Information at the UN Secretariat in New York, and among his contributions at Unesco is also the first draft for the 1972 Declaration on direct satellite broadcasting. For Eek's publications, see note 1 in Chapter 5.

[16]Unesco document COM-74/CONF.616/3, p. 2. This as well as all subsequent quotes from the official draft texts are reproduced in the publication referred to in note 2 above.

[17]For a general, albeit somewhat outdated presentation of these doctrines, see F. Siebert, T. Peterson, & W. Schramm, *Four Theories of the Press*, Urbana: Illinois University Press, 1956.

The framework of the Eek draft remains in most of the subsequent drafts, although the formulations may differ substantially in detail. The second version of the text was based directly on the Eek draft but was reformulated by a *meeting of experts* in March 1974 to provide a balanced package which would accommodate various political interests and reservations.

Twelve experts, nominated by their respective National Commissions for Unesco (USA, Canada, UK, France, Mexico, Argentina, Senegal, Kenya, Lebanon, India, Poland, and USSR) attended the March 1974 meeting.[18] The choice of the countries was up to the Secretariat, and those selected include all regions of the world, but with an obvious overrepresentation from the West (four NATO members, against two Warsaw Pact countries). However, the experts participated in a personal capacity and not as representatives of their governments (although five of them were in fact government functionaries). No vote is taken in this type of Unesco meeting. Also attending as observers were four international non-governmental organizations, covering various regional and political interests among professional journalists and broadcasters. The experts used the Eek draft and comments on the draft by two other consultants, chosen in advance by the Secretariat: a Swiss newspaper manager and former President of the International Association for Mass Communication Research, Jacques Bourquin, and a Yugoslavian university professor and parliamentarian, Bogdan Osolnik. Another consultant, a French professor of the law of the press, Ferdinand Terrou, instead of providing his written comments, attended the meeting, as did Eek. By and large, the meeting was well prepared and representative, in terms of both professional qualifications and ideological orientations.

The text produced by the meeting (reproduced in Appendix 5) was bound to be softened somewhat, and can be characterized as a diluted and ambiguous version of the Eek draft. This is indicated immediately by a change in the title. "Fundamental principles governing the use of the mass media" (Eek) was replaced by "fundamental principles concerning the strengthening of peace and international understandiang by the mass media" (meeting of experts). In regard to state responsibility, the meeting of experts replaced Article I of the Eek draft by a general statement, listed as Article X:

> The responsibility of a State in the international sphere for the activities of mass media under its jurisdiction is governed by customary international law and relevant international agreements.

---

[18]Unesco document COM-74/CONF.616/5 (Report of the Meeting of Experts on Draft Declaration concerning the Use of the Mass Media, Unesco House, Paris, 11–15 March 1974). This document is also reproduced in the publication referred to in note 2 above.

This formulation was determined by a typically Western approach. Thus one should not even refer to state responsibility for legislation relating to media performance. The meeting of experts contemplated—with the participation of both American and Soviet experts—that "the declaration refers only to customary international law, which concededly limits State responsibility for the operation of independent media organizations very severely."[19] It is ironic that this very Article (in a reworded version) was later to come under concerted attack from the West.

The text, which was published in July 1974 for the 18th session of the General Conference in the name of the Director-General as *document 18C/35* (see Appendix 6), is practically the same as the draft prepared at the meeting in March. However, a number of minor reformulations were introduced by the Secretariat—most of them significantly in favor of a Western approach. Thus the title was rephrased, using the term "the role of the mass media," so that, from a libertarian point of view, there would be little doubt about the harmless nature of the instrument. Similarly, for example, Article IV was changed to read: "It is a responsibility of the mass media to promote. . . " instead of "Mass media should promote. . . " Reformulations of this kind brought the text as close to the Western positions as was possible, given the guidelines of Resolution 4.113. Strictly speaking, the Secretariat had already stepped beyond the limits determined by the General Conference, for example, by replacing the word "use" in the title by the word "role."

Indeed, the outcome (18C/35) did not contain anything that would have stirred up notable opposition among professional mass media circles— in the West any more than elsewhere. A convincing test of this was a Scandinavian expert seminar, convened in August 1974 by the Finnish National Commission for Unesco, which recommended, after thoroughly studying the fresh draft (18C/35), that the Nordic delegations at the 18th session of the General Conference should take a positive approach towards the adoption of the Draft Declaration.[20] The seminar also recommended that the respective Nordic delegations should support the project on guidelines for national codes of ethics, as drafted by the Secretariat (practically the same formulation which was adopted in para-

[19]Ibid., p. 6 (paragraph 29).

[20]In addition to a number of Finnish experts representing various mass media and political organizations, the seminar was attended by a representative of the National Commissions for Unesco (Section for Communication) in Sweden, Norway, and Denmark plus the Rector of the Stockholm School of Journalism and the Chairman of the Norwegian Union of Journalists as invited speakers. The Secretariat of Unesco was represented by Gunnar Naesselund, Director of the Department of Free Flow of Information and Development of Communication (also of Scandinavian origin), who addressed the meetings on the topic "Activities undertaken by Unesco in the field of code of ethics." An unpublished report (in Swedish and English), "Kommunikationsseminarium den 2.–3. augusti 1974," is available from the Finnish National Commission for Unesco, Ministry of Education, Helsinki.

graph (b) (i) of Resolution 4.111), without going further by inviting Unesco to prepare an international code for journalists.

General Conference 1974

The 18th session of the General Conference in Fall 1974 was faced with the text *18C/35 as well as 11 draft resolutions proposed by the Member States to amend the text* submitted by the Director-General.[21] Nine of these proposals came from the socialist countries (the USSR and its allies), introducing elements, which, in a Western framework, were perceived as dangerous tendencies towards state control of the mass media. Therefore, the General Conference debate in 1974 was perhaps more heated than any before that time on matters dealing with communication (except for the 1972 Declaration on direct satellite broadcasting).

The report of the Programme Commission stated that "a very large number of delegates" touched upon the Draft Declaration, and that "all speakers felt this was a very important issue":

> Many of them underlined the moral and ethical standards which should govern the use of the mass media. In the view of a large number of delegations there was a need for such a declaration of fundamental principles governing the flow of information and ideas.
>
> From the general comments made on the scope and objectives of the declaration there appeared a difficulty in striking an appropriate balance between, on the one hand, the concept of freedom of information and, on the other, the need for a sense of responsibility to prevent abuses of this freedom. The vast and growing importance of the mass media in ensuring the preservation of peace and mutual understanding between peoples was emphasized and many speakers observed that the power of the mass media made it imperative to avoid misuse.
>
> Speakers from developing countries particularly stressed the need for a multidirectional flow of information. They felt that the cultural integrity of their countries required freedom from undue influence of large foreign media organizations serving private interests and often monopolistic in character. They considered that the principle of free flow of information was not being practiced when countries lacked the production capacity to participate in such a flow on an equal basis.
>
> Another cause for concern among certain delegates was that the mass media in some countries sometimes sowed seeds of national hatred, offended national feelings and waged intolerant campaigns

---

[21]The 11 proposals were distributed as Unesco documents 18C/COM/DR.1–11 and are reproduced in the publication referred to in note 2 above.

against national minorities. They felt also that the mass media in some countries were not contributing to international understanding and mutual respect of other countries and that they failed to understand and report the legitimate concerns and aspirations of other countries and nations. Some delegates felt that countries should have the right to take measures to protect themselves against mass media that do not act responsibly. It was also stated that the rapid development of the mass media made it necessary to underline the responsibility of States in this field. One delegate observed that this responsibility should be defined in the text of the declaration and that the role of Unesco should also be specified there. Another delegate expressed the view that the real problem for the developing countries was that the establishment and strengthening of mass media infrastructures was not dealt with by the Draft Declaration. Still another was of the opinion that national control of the mass media was needed and that the ownership of the mass media should be transferred to the social sectors concerned.

Other delegates considered that no amendment to the Draft Declaration should be made in the direction of limiting freedom of information. They felt that government intervention was not the way to encourage mass media to respect ethical standards and act responsibly. One speaker felt that one should not lose sight of the diversities which Unesco should preserve and indicated that he could not subscribe to any text that would limit the free flow of information. This delegate made the proposal, which was supported by other speakers, that the Declaration should be deleted and the funds thus saved be used for concrete activities in developing countries.

One delegate noted that constitutional protections of freedom of information would preclude certain countries from enacting legislation requiring mass media within their jurisdiction to comply with the Declaration. Other speakers felt that it would not be sufficient to simply draft a declaration and make it known but that its principles should be implemented and the results achieved reported on.[22]

The controversies escalated but had not reached the point of confrontation. The Western strategy was clearly exposed by a proposal to abandon the whole project and transfer the limited funds available for "concrete activities in developing countries."

The parallel debate on *codes of ethics* also became more heated in 1974 than it had two years earlier, mainly because there now were stronger voices to speak against the project and even against any involvement of Unesco in this field. The records of the Programme Commission show that in the debate on codes of ethics it was proposed, among other

---

[22]*Records of the General Conference, Eighteenth Session* (Paris, 17 October to 23 November 1974), Volume 2: Reports, Paris: Unesco, 1976, p. 127 (paragraphs 40–45).

things, that these activities be suppressed and that the funds foreseen for them be transferred for "developmental activities in the African region."[23] However, this proposal was defeated by a vote of 32 against, 26 in favor, with 8 abstentions.[24] Subsequently the General Conference authorized the Director-General:

> . . .(b) in order to further the observance of adequate professional standards in the use of the mass media:
>
> (i) to prepare, with a view to strengthening international understanding and world peace, guidelines for national codes of ehtics designed to promote the sense of responsibility which should accompany the full exercise of freedom of information, including those principles of democratization in the use of the media of mass communication that ensure this, and to encourage their application by national media councils.[25]

The same resolution, number 4.111 under the 1975-1976 program and budget for the area of "Free flow of information and international exchanges," specified that the *preparation of the Draft Declaration was to be continued as a parallel project to the codes of ethics in order to promote "the observance of adequate professional standards in the use of the mass media"*:

> (ii) to convene an intergovernmental meeting of experts (category II) to prepare, in the light of the draft text contained in document 18C/35 and the proposed amendments to it, a draft declaration on fundamental principles governing the use of the mass media in strengthening peace and international understanding and in combating war propaganda, racism and apartheid, for submission to the General Conference at its nineteenth session.

This was the final outcome of the debate noted above. It was a compromise formula, based on a proposal submitted by Belgium in the name of members of the Council of Europe (a West European coalition), with the following vote in the Programme Commission:

[23]Ibid., pp. 126–127 (paragraph 36).

[24]Ibid., p. 127 (paragraph 38).

[25]Note that the mandate concerns *national* codes of ethics only, leaving aside the question of international codes. As seen above, both national and international codes had had their place in the debates of the General Conference since 1970, and in each case there were arguments both for and against Unesco's involvement. Obviously, international codes were finally left outside this project because of the fact that the Draft Declaration had created suspicion in the West on the role of this intergovernmental Organization in relation to press freedom. The scope of the project was further limited by the authorization only to prepare *guidelines*. On the other hand, references to democratization of the media and the national media councils extended the project to major questions communication policies. By and large, it was a balanced project (as shown by the position of the Nordic experts in their seminar in Finland), later providing also a good basis for implementing the Helsinki Accords among professional journalists (the author made a concrete proposal to this effect in the article referred to in note 3 in Chapter 7).

- *for*, 40 including most West European and Latin American countries;
- *against*, 5 including India and France;
- *abstension*, 17 including Finland.[26]

The U.S. delegation did not properly belong in any of the categories, because it wanted to remove the entire item of the Draft Declaration from the Unesco agenda. Neither did the vote follow the immediate interests of the USSR and other East European countries, which wanted to have the Draft Declaration passed at that session, preferably including their own proposals to "improve" the text (18C/35). India was an outspoken advocate of those developing countries that insisted on immediate adoption of the Declaration. China, for its part, opposed the very procedure of debating and deciding the matter in that session of the General Conference.

As far as the political substance of the compromise formula contained by Resolution 4.111 is concerned, it should be noted that, while the postponement of the Declaration clearly meant a concession in favor of Western interests, the mandate of the General Conference for further preparation of a document did not imply any compromise in terms of the nature of the instrument to be drafted. It was to continue to be a declaration on the "use" of the mass media, and its political substance would not differ essentially from that contained already in Resolution 4.301 of 1970, especially since further preparation was to be "in light of document 18C/35 and the proposed amendments to it"— most of the latter being less acceptable to the Western delegations than the draft text of 18C/35 had been. Furthermore, the compromise formula clearly pooled together the definition of fundamental principles for the contents of the mass media and the promotion of professional codes of ethics in journalism—two projects which had been appearing separately on Unesco's agenda since 1970 and were both meeting stronger Western resistance.

As in 1972, the *Unesco Secretariat* remained noncommittal in 1974. At the 18th session of the General Conference, the Director-General— both the retiring René Maheu of France and the newly elected Amadou Mahtar M'Bow of Senegal—remained aloof from the growing controversy, observing the struggling political forces "on the floor." However, at this stage the Secretariat, and ultimately the Director-General, had a greater formal stake in the matter than they had had two years earlier. Whereas, at the 17th session, the debate had been on a draft resolution submitted by two Member States, at issue at the 18th session was a draft text submitted by the Director-General. Document 18C/35 was prepared

---

[26]*Records of the General Conference, Eighteenth Session*, Volume 2: Reports, Paris: Unesco, 1976, p. 128 (paragraph 127).

by the Secretariat in accordance with Resolution 4.113 of 1972, and contained the first draft text of the Declaration to be considered by the General Conference. Nevertheless, it was understood that this Draft Declaration did not represent the position of the Secretariat, but was intended to do no more than to accommodate the various contradictory views expressed during the preceding stages. Even those who were totally against the project (notably the USA and China) did not accuse Unesco of advocating a position, but rather objected to the political forces behind the project (notably the USSR).

As far as the international community of mass media experts (including national and international organizations of journalists) was concerned, more or less silent support was given to the preparation of the Draft Declaration, until the 18th session of the General Conference in late 1974. Thus, the failure of the text 18C/35 to pass was due to political causes rather than to any notable opposition from professional circles. It remains an academic question whether a Mass Media Declaration would have been adopted in 1974, against the will of a Western minority, if the USSR and its allies had followed a less "maximalist" line, quickly accepting the compromise formulation of 18C/35. In any case, what followed after the period of "silent beginning," 1970-1974, was a growing controversy around mass media issues in general and the Draft Declaration in particular. And in such a situation the outcome in 1978 was bound to be influenced by a Western pressure—more than 18C/35 had been.

THE OUTBURST OF CONTROVERSIES

The next stage of shaping the declaration is marked by two occasions (listed as steps 5 and 6 at the beginning of this Chapter). This was a period of polarization, if not confrontation, in the overall relations between the developing countries and the Western industrialized world. As far as East-West relations were concerned, it remained a relatively relaxed period, with the landmark of détente being the Final Act of the Conference on Security and Co-operation in Europe, or the so-called Helsinki Accords, signed in August 1975. However, there is no doubt that the controversy around the Draft Declaration stemmed not only from a "North-South" problem but also continued to be, perhaps above all, a matter of "East-West" relations.

Intergovernmental Meeting of Experts 1975

In category II Unesco meetings, all Member States are invited to attend and to choose their governmental representatives (a delegation of one or more experts). All international organizations (governmental and non-governmental) that have consultative status with Unesco are invited as observers. (The March 1974 meeting of experts was at a lower category, with the choice of participants and observers up to the Secretariat.) Thus, in this December 1975 event, the permanent apparatus of Unesco was formally involved only in providing technical facilities for the meeting. All discussions, political activity, and conclusions were among the delegations. The Director-General remained aside, not even addressing the meeting. (The opening address was given by his deputy.)

The meeting was attended by 85 Member States with the right to vote— an exceptionally high attendance for this category of meeting. Five more governmental delegations and the PLO participated as observers, as did some dozen UN, intergovernmental, and non-governmental organizations.[27] Most of the "governmental experts" were diplomats, but there were also many academic and other professional experts among the delegations (e.g. from European countries, USA, and USSR).[28]

The meeting had before it the "testament" of the 18th session of the General Conference (18C/35, plus 11 proposed amendments) as well as a background report describing the work done over the years by the UN and Unesco on issues relating to the Draft Declaration.[29] Furthermore, at the beginning of the meeting various delegations formally submitted 26 new proposals for formulations of the Draft Declaration.[30]

The general discussion for the first days of the meeting, as recorded in the official report,[31] was along broad lines, a repetition of what had been said in earlier debates of the General Conference on the Draft Declaration. A new element in the discussion was a widely expressed desire

[27]Unesco document 19C/91, Annex II–Appendix 2. Like other reports of relevant meetings, this document is reproduced in the publication referred to in note 2 above. As to the number of participants, it should be noted that only some fifty delegations were present at the beginning of the meeting, while the rest of the 85 entered at a later state—obviously alerted by the controversy which had accumulated during the first three days of the meeting. Among those countries which do not appear on the list of participants are Brazil, India, and China; one may only wonder why they did not send their representatives to the meeting, especially India, which showed exceptional interest in the project during the 18th session of the General Conference.

[28]The U.S. delegation included the Dean of the School of Journalism at the University of Missouri (Roy M. Fischer), and the Soviet delegation included the Dean of the Faculty of Journalism at Moscow University (Yassen Zassoursky). The present author (Kaarle Nordenstreng) participated as a member of the Finnish delegation, representing both academic expertise and the National Commission for Unesco, in which he chaired the Section for Communication.

[29]The background report (Unesco document COM-75/CONF.201/4) was prepared with the help of Eek. An edited version of it, "Principles Governing the Use of the Mass Media as Defined by the United Nations and UNESCO," is published in Nordenstreng & Schiller, *op. cit.* (pp. 173–194) and in another reader *Professional Codes in Journalism*, edited by L. Bruun, Prague: International Organization of Journalists, 1979 (pp. 112–125).

[30]The proposals were distributed as COM-75/CONF.201/DR.1-26 and are reproduced in the publication referred to in note 2 above.

[31]Unesco document 19C/91 (cf. note 27 above), pp. 2–4 (paragraphs 14–26).

for *consensus*, "although it was recognized by some that a consensus might be difficult to obtain."[32] Also, new in the December 1975 meeting was a reference to "Zionist propaganda which, the observer from the Palestine Liberation Organization considered, was designed to efface the Palestinian collectivity from the map; deny its rights to the land of Palestine and refuse it the right of speech, thus reducing it to the status of a subversive group as had been done with African and Asian liberation movements."[33] In this connection, several speakers referred to *UN Resolution 3379*, adopted on 10 November 1975 by the 30th session of the General Assembly, defining zionism as a form of racism.[34]

The atmosphere at the beginning of the meeting was somewhat more heated than it had been in earlier Unesco debates on the matter. However, practically all delegations took it for granted that a Draft Declaration would be prepared, which could then reach final adoption at the 19th session of the General Conference in one year's time. Only a few voices were raised against the basic idea of having a Unesco Declaration on the Mass Media, and even the U.S.—which a year earlier had been busily working against the whole project—indicated its constructive approach by submitting several proposals for reformulating the text of 18C/35. One of the amendments proposed by the U.S. was to Article IV, showing that the sponsor was not afraid of having a Unesco declaration with direct obligations to the mass media:

> The mass media should avoid any encouragement of the evils of war, violence, apartheid, disrespect for human rights, and other forms of hatred.[35]

It soon became evident in the lobbies, during the meeting, that the largest political obstacle was whether or not the Draft Declaration should include a reference to UN Resolution 3379. The Arab countries, encouraged by their success at the UN General Assembly, obviously hoped to make the Declaration an instrument to promote an anti-zionist line. More moderate forces in the Movement of Non-Aligned Countries,

---

[32]Ibid., p. 3 (paragraph 16).

[33]Ibid., p. 4 (paragraph 25).

[34]This resolution, after recalling earlier relevant UN resolutions (notably 1904, unanimously proclaiming the Declaration on the Elimination of All Forms of Racial Discrimination, and 3151, condemning inter alia "the unholy alliance between South African racism and zionism,") and after taking note of recent decisions of the Organization of African Unity as well as of the Non-Aligned Movement, contains only one operative paragraph: "Determines that zionism is a form of racism and racial discrimination." Resolution 3379 (XXX) was adopted by 72 votes in favor, 35 against, with 32 abstentions. Among those who voted against were all West European countries, Israel, USA, Canada, Australia, New Zealand, and a number of Central American countries.

[35]Unesco document COM-75/CONF.201/DR.5.

recognizing the highly explosive and divisive nature of Resolution 3379 for the Western countries, looked for a delicate way to incorporate this new aspect of the concept of racialism. The Yugoslavian delegate (Osolnik, who had been involved in the preparation for the March 1974 meeting of experts) made great efforts to persuade all parties to accept a compromise formula, to be inserted as a new paragraph in the preamble:

> Recalling all the resolutions of the United Nations General Assembly, and more particularly resolutions 1904, 3151 and 3379 on the elimination of all forms of racialism and racial discrimination.[36]

This formula was reluctantly accepted by the Arab delegations and supported by the socialist countries and most of the non-aligned countries. But the Western delegations were not prepared to compromise on this point; they refused to have any reference to the UN Resolution, against which they had just voted at the General Assembly, included. In this situation, the question was whether or not the Western minority would succeed in isolating this controversial issue from the rest of the proceedings by postponing a final stand on it. These countries expected that the issue of Resolution 3379 would remain open at least until a working party, established by the meeting to amalgamate various proposed amendments or to sort them out as alternative formulations, had completed its task.

However, when discussing the proposals paragraph by paragraph before passing them on for processing by the working party, the plenary session of the meeting adopted the Yugoslavian amendment, thus taking a firm stand before the drafting of details had properly started. The surprise move to vote on this issue immediately was made by the delegate of Algeria, whose militant intervention, supported by a number of other developing countries, made it clear that the meeting was faced with a crucial conflict between the so-called South and the West. The USSR and its allies—the original sponsors of the Draft Declaration — were not prominent in this clash. Thus it would be wrong to say that this was an East-West confrontation; rather it was a typical case of what may be characterized as "natural alliance" between the socialist and the developing countries.

The Yugoslavian amendment was adopted on the third day of the meeting (December 17), after a hot debate in which 20 delegates participated, with 36 votes in favor, 22 against, and 7 abstentions.[37] Half of the negative votes were cast by countries belonging to NATO and EEC (the European Economic Community), while the rest were neutral West Euro-

[36]Unesco document 19C/91, Annex II, p. 5 (paragraph 33).

[37]Ibid., p. 6 (paragraph 35). As the total of this vote makes 65, 20 delegations registered as participants in the meeting must have been absent at this stage (cf. note 27 above).

pean countries, Israel, Australia, and some developing countries known for their pro-Western orientation. After the vote, the French delegation moved to suspend the meeting, but this proposal was defeated.

At this stage, 13 of the delegations that had voted against the Yugoslavian amendment made an exceptional countermove; they walked out of the meeting, or, as diplomatically expressed in the report of the meeting, "they had decided to refrain from further participation in the meeting."[38] These delegations were the EEC countries, USA, Canada, Israel, and Australia. It appeared that the initiative for such a protest came from the EEC (not least the Federal Republic of Germany) rather than from NATO (USA jumped on the bandwagon rather than acting as a prime mover). All of those who walked out explained their behavior in letters to the Chairman of the meeting. (The letter of the U.S. delegation is reproduced as Appendix 7.) None of the developing countries which had voted against the amendment walked out. Neither did Austria, Finland, Sweden, or Switzerland join the hard-line demonstration, although they also had voted against the amendment. Austria and Sweden, however, demonstrated their displeasure by discontinuing in active participation in the meeting (by withdrawing proposals for amendments and abstaining in all subsequent votes).

The vote on the Yugoslavian amendment and the subsequent Western walkout marked a landmark in the history of the Draft Declaration. Now at last, it became clear that it was not only an instrument to govern the professional operation of the mass media that was at issue, but also a *vital act of international politics*. The Draft Declaration was over-politicized. This was clearly reflected also in the *press coverage*. For the first time, the Draft Declaration reached the headlines of *International Herald Tribune* and other Western opinion-forming media. This controversy also marked a historical turn as far as the press coverage of Unesco is concerned, since on this occasion the Western media began to devote more than reasonable attention to the mass media issues at Unesco (compared to all other fields of Unesco's activity). At the same time, they began to adopt a predominantly negative framework in portraying Unesco (measured by customary journalistic standards of balance, objectivity, etc.).[39]

After the explosion, the meeting went on preparing the Draft Declaration, and, given the absence of those who always had been least enthusiastic about the project, the atmosphere was quite constructive and

[38] Ibid., p. 6 (paragraph 38).

[39] There is no systematic statistical evidence to substantiate this generalization; it is based on an overall monitoring of the Western press and is supported by case studies by R. Salinas (see note 48 below), by P. Harris (see note 52 below), and by R. Heacock ("Unesco and the media," in Etudes et Traveux, No. 15, Geneva: Graduate Institute of International Studies, 1977).

business-like. At the same time, it was understood that the minority was only temporarily silent and that the political obstacles were by no means removed. The working party of the meeting produced a new text, which was formally adopted in the final plenary session (on 22 December).

The new text, which was later published in the General Conference document 19C/91 (see Appendix 8), clearly went further towards the demands of the socialist and developing countries than had the previous one (18C/35). It contained not only the Yugoslavian amendment, but also most of the proposals (in more or less similar wording) made before the 18th session of the General Conference in 1974 to "improve" the text of 18C/35.

The issue of *state responsibility* (Article I of the Eek draft, Article X of the draft by the March 1974 meeting of experts as well as of the draft 18C/35) received the following formulation (as Article XII):

> States are responsible for the activities in the international sphere of all mass media under their jurisdiction.

This wording follows that of an amendment proposed by Mongolia before the 18th session of the General Conference.[40] At the intergovernmental meeting of experts, the delegation of the USSR had submitted proposal[41] to formulate this Article with wording closer to that of 18C/35, but in the course of the drafting process this proposal was merged with the Mongolian formulation. The Soviet delegation explained that the brief wording which was finally adopted is a statement of fact, its meaning being essentially the same as all formulations beginning with the Eek draft. Eek, who attended the meeting as a consultant, when asked his opinion, agreed that a fair reading of the new Article XII does not necessarily suggest a closer control relationship between the state and the media than is implied by customary international law, but he still would have preferred a less ambiguous formulation, such as the Soviet proposal. However, despite such assurances, as many as 12 delegations (not including those who had left the meeting) would have preferred to drop this Article from the new text; but they were defeated by a majority of 19 votes (the rest either abstaining or being absent).

On the other hand, the new text (19C/91) was by no means a "maximalist" formulation of an ultra-radical nature. In fact, the Soviet delegation made it known that for them it was a compromise, "a modest formu-

[40]Unesco document 18C.COM/DR.8 (cf. note 21 above).

[41]Unesco document COM-75/CONF.201/DR.13. The proposed Soviet amendment for Article X reads: "States shall bear responsibility for the activities of the mass media in territories under their jurisdiction, in accordance with international law."

lation, the least minimum we can accept," a view similar to that of the most outspoken delegations from the non-aligned countries, such as Algeria and Peru. A careful reading of the text shows that, indeed, most of it is in harmony with a universal approach, including the Western positions. For example, Article V can hardly be understood as more "hard line" than the U.S. proposal quoted earlier:

> It is a responsibility of the mass media to avoid any justification or encouragement of the evils of war, violence, apartheid and other forms of national, racial or religious hatred.

An indication of the generally acceptable nature of the text is the fact that the delegation of Finland (which participated fully throughout the meeting and, in the abnormal situation that existed, took a demonstratively Western approach) voted in the final plenary session against only three preambular paragraphs out of the total of 17 (one of them being the Yugoslavian amendment) and against two and a half Articles out of 12 (one of them being Article XII on state responsibility). It is reasonable to expect that, in a normal atmosphere, it would have been easy to reach consensus among all the delegations, including those who walked out, on something like two thirds of the text.

However, given the stumbling blocks, there could not be a consensus on the text as a whole—even among those who participated until the end of the meeting. In the final vote, after the text had been processed paragraph by paragraph, the new Draft Declaration was adopted with 41 votes in favor, 8 against, and 3 abstentions[42] (the rest of 85 being absent). The delegations which voted against were from Austria, Ecuador, Finland, Ivory Coast, Sweden, Switzerland, Uruguay, and Venezuela—all countries that had voted against the Yugoslavian amendment (except for Ivory Coast, which had not participated in the earlier vote).

Consequently, the text of 19C/91 was adopted with the expressed consent of 41 governmental expert delegations, against the expressed opinion of 21 delegations (including those who had walked out of the meeting). As only three delegations abstained in the final vote, appapproximately 20 of the delegations remaining in the meeting did not take part in the final vote. Most of these were from small developing countries, unable or unwilling (due to political or practical obstacles) to take a quick stand in such a controversial situation.

Thus the mandate of Resolution 4.111 of the 18th session of the General Conference was fulfilled: an intergovernmental meeting of experts had prepared, "in the light of the draft text contained in document

---

[42]Unesco document 19c/91, Annex II, P. 11 (paragraph 68).

18C/35 and the proposed amendments to it, a draft declaration. . . for submission to the General Conference at its nineteenth session." In terms of formal proceedings, everything was normal, except for the walkout by a number of delegations. Politically speaking, however, the meeting had worsened the controversies, rather than helped to overcome them. It should be recalled that Resolution 4.111 was a compromise proposed by the West European countries, and now this compromise formula had turned the situation even more strongly against the interests of the Western governments than it had been at the 18th session of the General Conference.

In this connection, it is worth observing that the other part of Resolution 4.111, inviting the Director-General to prepare guidelines for national codes of ethics, was practically forgotten after the 17th session of the General Conference. The Secretariat did little to implement it[43] neither was it followed up by any notable diplomatic pressures on Unesco. And yet, formally speaking, this was a parallel project to the Draft Declaration, although the Director-General was neither specifically requested to hold a meeting on the matter of professional codes nor was he obliged to report on this project to the next session of the General Conference. This is an instructive example of how two formally equal paragraphs in a Unesco program resolution may lead to quite different consequences, depending on the amount of political steam that accumulates behind each project, and also depending on the ability of the Secretariat to find appropriate ways and means to implement each project.

Towards Nairobi 1976

After the December 1975 meeting, the next formal step was the 19th session of the General Conference in Fall 1976, held in Nairobi—for the first time in the history of the Organization in Africa, on "Third World" soil. But before the Nairobi General Conference began to deal with the matter, a number of vital developments had taken place, all related to the movement towards a new international information order, on the one hand, and to the reaction created by this movement on the other (cf. Chapter 1). For the proceedings in Nairobi, the following five developments were of crucial importance:

---

[43]A study was commissioned to the International Federation of Journalists (uniting national organizations of professional journalists mainly in Western Europe and North America) but this report (1975) was never published. Another study was commissioned to J. Clement Jones, a distinguished British journalist and Chairman of Press Freedom and Ethics Committee of the Commonwealth Press Union, and his report was published as *Mass Media Codes of Ethics and Councils: A Comparative International Study on Professional Standards*, Paris: Unesco, Reports and Papers on Mass Communication 76 (Special Issue), 1980.

First, Unesco organized, in San José (Costa Rica) in July 1976, the *Intergovernmental Conference on Communication Policies in Latin America and the Carribean.*[44] While this high-level, regional conference did not take a direct stand on the Draft Declaration, it is obvious that the overall approach of the conference was in the same direction aimed at by those who, since the early 1970s, had promoted the idea of a Unesco Declaration on the use of the media. Let us recall two paragraphs of the main political document of the conference, the Declaration of San José:

> That all the members of a society are responsible for ensuring the peaceful and beneficial use of communication media.
>
> That communication policies should contribute to knowledge, understanding, friendship, co-operation and integration of peoples through a process of indentification of common goals and needs, respecting national sovereignties and the international legal principle of non-intervention in the affairs of States as well as the cultural and political plurality of societies and individuals, with a view to achieving world solidarity and peace.

Second, the *Movement of Non-Aligned Countries* introduced their new program in the field of information, as articulated in the Non-Aligned Symposium on Information (Tunis, March 1976)[45] and in the Ministerial Conference on Press Agencies Pool (New Delhi, July 1976)[46] and as finally ratified at the highest level in the Fifth Conference of Heads of State or Government of the Non-Aligned Countries (Colombo, August 1976). This program was not only in harmony with the move which had promoted the project for a Mass Media Declaration at Unesco, but contained an explicit, although not quite specific, reference to the project:

> . . .non-aligned countries should coordinate their activities in the United Nations and other international forums to enable the adoption at an early date of a proper declaration of fundamental principles on the role of mass media in strengthening peace, promoting international understanding and co-operation contributing to the early establishment of an international economic and social order based on equality and justice and in combating rac-

---

[44] The proceedings of this conference are published in its *Final Report*, Unesco document COM/MD/38, Paris, 1976.

[45] The proceedings of this meeting have been published as a mimeographed report, "Information in the Non-Aligned Countries," (Vol. I: Final resolutions, speeches and messages, working papers) by the Tunisian Secretariat of State for information, Tunis (1976). The present author participated as the representative of Finland, who attended the meeting in the capacity of an invited guest.

[46] For proceedings of this conference, see *Communicator* (Journal of the Indian Institute of Mass Communication, New Delhi), No. 2–3, April–July 1976.

ism, racial discrimination, apartheid, zionism, neo-colonialism and all other forms of oppression. Non-aligned countries should ensure that such declaration could also be an effective instrument for reducing their dependence in the information field in keeping with the objectives incorporated in this Declaration.[47]

However, it should be recalled (cf. Chapter 1) that the non-aligned program was by no means limited to attacks on Western "media imperialism" and to concern about the political content of the mass media. It was also a concerted program for establishing the technical and practical means for communication in and among the developing countries. Thus, the non-aligned program for a new information order *both* came into conflict with the traditional Western approach on the values and principles involved *and* was in harmony with the tactical moves that had been made by some Western delegations at the General Conferences since 1972 aimed at turning attention away from normative consideration of media contents to technical consideration of media infrastructures.

Third, alerted by the December 1975 meeting at Unesco, and further influenced by the San José conference as well as the series of non-aligned events, private press publishers, commercial broadcasters, and other Western mass media-related circles representing private enterprise interests mobilized a *campaign against Unesco* and the Movement of Non-Aligned Countries. Especially active in this campaign was the Inter-American Press Association (IAPA), and as a consequence, for example, the press coverage of the San José conference was far from fair and objective.[48] Given the dominance of U.S.-based news agencies and syndicated services in the world newspaper market, and thanks to the ideological "networking" of most publishers and editors throughout the Western hemisphere (by such organizations as the International Press Institute, IPI), the mobilization of a reaction was both rapid and visible. By Fall 1976 the campaign had reached, in one way or another, at least the "seri-

[47]From the main political resolution of the Ministerial conference, the "New Delhi Declaration," adopted unanimously on 12 July (published in *Communicator* referred to above). The paragraph on a UN declaration is included in the operative part of the resolution in which the conference lists five points as "decided."

[48]As was shown in Chapter 1, the campaign "participated" in the conference, and it obviously affected those in charge. This can be seen even in the address by the Foreign Minister of the host country Costa Rica on his election as President of the Conference: a chapter is devoted to "the attracks of the IAPA" (see *Final Report*, p. 59). For a content analysis of how the conference itself was covered, see Raquel Salinas Bascur, "News Agencies and the New Information Order: The Associated Press Coverage of the Intergovernmental Conference on Communication Policies on Latin America and the Caribbean held in Costa Rica, July 1976," in T. Varis, R. Salinas, & R. Jokelin, "International News and the New Information Order," Reports from the Institute of Journalism and Mass Communication, University of Tampere, 39/1977, pp. 29–88.

ous" papers, both conservative and liberal.[49] Furthermore, the reaction not only stimulated momentum among publishers, editors, and the lobbies representing these leading circles of Western private media, but several working media professionals, went along with this reaction, due either to ignorance and manipulation or through deliberate choice.[50]

Fourth, there was a *coordinated effort of diplomacy* by Unesco representatives from Western countries to prevent the Draft Declaration (19C/91) from being adopted, or even from being seriously considered, in Nairobi. This effort was centralized in an informal group including government representatives at Unesco from the countries of West Europe, North America, Japan, Australia, and New Zealand. This "information group" met several times just before Nairobi to consider the question of the Draft Declaration, indicating that the matter had by now become top priority on the political agenda of the General Conference. Both the U.S. and the Federal Republic of Germany had prepared alternative texts for the Draft Declaration, and by early October these were merged into a single Western alternative (based largely on the first U.S. draft, which went farther away from the official text of 19C/91 than the German first draft had).

Since the Western group was almost unanimous in its objective to postpone the adoption of a Mass Media Declaration of any kind at Nairobi, the U.S./West German alternative text was not intended as a serious base for discussing the matter in substance, but rather as a tactical instrument to show how far the official Draft Declaration prepared in December 1975 was from a genuine Western position. At the same time, however, it was believed that it would be useful to have a concrete text available in Nairobi in order to prove to the developing countries that the Western side was really aiming at a better text and not just maneuvering to win more time (although this was precisely the motive of at least the leading Western countries). In this respect the "liberals" of the Western

---

[49]For example, the *International Herald Tribune* pointed out on 31 July 1976 that "large parts of the third world are moving towards the Russian position," and on 6 September *Newsweek* already spoke about "Orwellian mind control on a continental scale." In Finland the leading daily, liberal *Helsingin Sanomat*, carried an editorial on 8 August 1976 entitled "Unesco and freedom of speech," voicing concern that Unesco was abandoning the idelas of freedom of information as expressed in the Universal Declaration of Human Rights in favor of new information models which legitimize party and government control of the media. When the organ of the Finnish Social Democratic Party, *Demari*, responded (10 August) by referring to the broader progressive changes in the international order which are quite naturally reflected in the field of information, *Helsingin Sanomat* argued (11 August) that there is no room for a new information order, since at issue are the relations between governments and citizens, and the paper demagogically suggested that a "new order" would only introduce well-known "ministries of truth" and "thought police."

[50]Such a "bandwagon effect" was both reflected and further enforced by the International Federation of Journalists (cf. note 43 above), which at its congress in Vienna in May 1976 took a demonstratively negative stand towards the Draft Declaration (see IFJ bulletin "Direct Line," May 1976).

group (the Scandinavian countries in particular) were critical of the Western alternative, since it was not attractive enough to persuade the developing countries to wait for another two years. The "hard-liners" responded that, if the Western text were brought closer to the official base, the risk of a real redrafting process would increase. Consequently, the Western group went to Nairobi with a more or less shared strategy but without agreed-on tactics.

Another proposal for a Western tactical move was an idea for a resolution which would establish that developments since December 1975 among the Movement of Non-Aligned Countries, and also at the UN, had, in fact, made the Draft Declaration largely obsolete, thus calling for a fresh approach to the normative work of Unesco, as well as for increased contributions by Unesco to support building up the media infrastructures of the developing countries. This idea obviously originated within the Unesco Secretariat from those in charge of "Free Flow of Information and Development of Communication" (officers with predominantly Western background), and it was promoted in particular by the representatives of the Scandinavian countries, including the Nordic member of Unesco's Executive Board, Gunnar Garbo of Norway. On the other hand, the Scandinavian countries did not commit themselves to a Western hard line opposing the adoption of any Draft Declaration at Nairobi. At least Finland and Norway were open to a debate on the substance of a text, and even for adoption, provided a text could be developed that would be acceptable to them as well as to others (i.e. a consensus text).

On the eve of the Nairobi meeting, this idea took the shape of a draft "talking paper," which recommended to the General Conference that the Director-General be authorized (a) to analyze the outcome of relevant recent meetings and initiatives of the developing countries, (b) to revise the Unesco program for 1977-1978 in this light, "with a view to achieve a more relevant, just and effective sharing of information at the international level and to overcome the gap between information poverty and information affluences within societies and among nations," (c) to find new funds for such a revised program "estimated at a total increase of 750,000 dollars," (d) to undertake "renewed studies and consultations. . .concerning normative actions aimed at inspiring media professions and institutions to be guided by the goals of Unesco. . ." (five more points were listed).

The motivation for this move was not only the tactical interest in having the Draft Declaration postponed and the normative issues turned back to a new process of preparation (although this certainly gave the decisive push for the initiative), but also a genuine strategic interest in countering the acknowledged information imbalance in the world. Thus the idea reflects *both* an intention to "buy" the developing countries to the side of a more moderate political line (the "price" being $750,000) *and* a determination to make real investments in the setting up and mainte-nance of information resources in the developing countries (on terms de-fined by these countries themselves).

Furthermore, the initiative was motivated by a growing concern (felt strongly by Garbo among others) that the case of the Draft Declara-tion threatened not only to paralyze Unesco's communication program but to distract from the rest of Unesco activities as well. The idea was to save Unesco from a destructive clash, and, instead, to put it on a new track which would be "pro-Third World" but not "anti-West."

Fifth, the Unesco Secretariat not only helped such activists as Garbo to prepare "compromises," but even the *Director-General became personally involved* in reconciling the controversies which accumulated around the Draft Declaration—the first time that top management of the Organiza-tion personally entered into the drafting process. What is generally known about the moves of the Director-General at this stage is that he pushed for the establishment of a semi-formal organ of the General Con-ference, the Drafting and Negotiating Group, to deal with politically dif-ficult matters. Also it is understood that M'Bow was active in lobbying among the African and Arab countries to reduce their ambitions related to the Draft Declaration, and no doubt his arguments carried great weight by hinting at the possibility of a serious explosion at Unesco—if not *of* Unesco—on African soil, under the leadership of an African Director-General. This was an even greater possibility, since, on the eve of Nairobi, top officials of the State Department had stated that the U.S. had set two conditions for remaining in Unesco (it had already frozen the payment of its membership dues): a reasonable policy towards Israel, which had become a target of increasingly severe sanctions at Unesco, and an uncontroversial outcome in the case of the Draft Declaration, which, under the circumstances, could hardly mean anything less than a postponement of the matter.

By and large, this was the situation at the beginning of the Nairobi General Conference. It is worth noting that no special action on the Draft Declaration seems to have taken place in the socialist camp, led by the USSR, in view of preparing for Nairobi.

General Conference

There is no doubt that the Draft Declaration and related issues of infor-mation and communication occupied prime attention at the 19th session of the General Conference. This "high profile" was true of the main speeches delivered by heads of delegations in the general policy debate[51] and of the mass media coverage of the conference.[52]

The formal processing of the matter was placed on the agenda of *Programme Commission III*, which first debated it for more than two days (from the night of 4 November until 6 November), and then forwarded it to the Drafting and Negotiating Group for "further study." This debate was not limited to procedure (as the Western delegations had intended), but turned into a historic stock-taking of not only the Draft Declaration but also of communication problems in general. A summary record of the interventions made by more than 50 delegations is reproduced as Appendix 9.[53]

The debate produced three proposals: (1) to send it to the Drafting and Negotiating Group (based on a Brazilian amendment), (2) to appoint a working group of the Programme Committee itself to modify the text (interventions of Yugoslavia and Egypt), and (3) to postpone the matter another two years (intervention of Colombia). Based on the interventions, it became clear that a definite majority supported the first alternative, which, as hinted at by points made by the Director-General and the Assistant Director-General, strongly suggested that the final outcome in fact might be the third alternative. The opposition to 19C/91 did not come only from the West—those who had left the December 1975 meeting it also appeared that most of those countries whose government experts had voted for the text in December 1975 were now, in less than a year's time, no longer prepared to support it and, moreover, were unwilling to enter a normal process of accommodating divergent positions (i.e. to do redrafting within the Programme Commission).

[51]The positions presented in these major political speeches were not essentially different from what had been stated on communication at Unesco since 1970. However, now the Western side clearly gave greater emphasis on the need to assist developing countries in setting up their media facilities. The head of the U.S. delegation (Ambassador Reinhardt), in fact, put forward in Nairobi the ideas of what two years later became known as a "Marshall Plan of Telecommunications" (cf. Chapter 1). Other Western speakers did not hide the fact that this increased willingness was linked with a particular stand on the Draft Declaration. For example, the Netherlands stressed "a complete freedom of expression which we consider a cornerstone of a free and democratic society and a necessary precondition for a real two-way flow of information between developed and developing countries. Therefore, we have to reject the principles behind the draft declaration governing the use of mass media proposed to this Conference, but at the same time we are of the opinion that the developing countries ought to be supported, by Unesco or otherwise, in the shaping of their mass-media infrastructure." (From verbation record issued in Nairobi.)

[52]See e.g. Phil Harris, "News Dependence: the Case for a New World Information Order" (Final Report to Unesco of a Study of the Internal News Media), Centre for Mass Communication Research, University of Leicester, November 1977. In a content analysis of the news agency coverage of the Conference, Harris shows that the Draft Declaration was the top story in the wires of AP, UPI, Reuters, and AFP, and that the mass media questions in general accounted for some 40% of total coverage of Nairobi.

[53]This document was prepared by the Unesco Secretariat (dated in Paris, April 1977) but has never been published; neither were customary records of the Programme Commissions published from the 19th session of the General Conference.

Obviously, the Director-General had been successful in persuading most African, Latin American, and Asian delegations to play down the matter in the interest of the integrity of the Organization. But beyond this, it can be said that the U.S. and other Western countries were successful in putting aside the Draft Declaration, at least in the first round in Nairobi. It seems that this "success" was based more on their uncompromising hard line (sometimes reaching the point of outright blackmail on the part of the USA), supported by the wide publicity of the Western-dominated mass media, than as a result of "buying" the developing countries with subventions for their media infrastructures.

As a matter of fact, the Western initiative to channel more material aid for the mass media to the developing countries, at the expense of normative projects such as the Draft Declaration, was not particularly successful. The Nordic "talking paper" did not attract enough political momentum or promises for financing (even from the Scandinavian countries) to become a central factor in the diplomatic struggle of Nairobi. Instead, a draft resolution prepared by Tunisia[54] became the vehicle that turned Unesco toward meeting, more than before, the material needs of the developing countries, and resulted in Unesco operating as an important follow-up agency for relevant recommendations of the Movement of Non-Aligned Countries.

The *Tunisian resolution,* while concentrating on "supporting the efforts of the developing countries which are seeking to establish and strengthen their own information and communication systems in line with their needs," did not take an explicit stand on the burning question of "normative actions." Yet, one can conclude that the resolution supports statements such as that quoted above from the New Delhi Declaration, since the Director-General was invited "to pay very special attention to the activities of the bodies. . .responsible for co-ordinating and implementing the information programme of the non-aligned countries. . ." and "to give priority to such Regular Programme activities as are consistent with these recommendations." No wonder, then, that the U.S. and some other countries (including Chile and Uruguay), suspicious of the "non-aligned trend," abstained when voting on the points quoted above. In the end, no one voted against the Tunisian resolution, although during the debate on the Regular Programme (treated separately from the Draft Declaration) it was made clear by the Western side that support of

---

[54]The draft resolution was circulated as Unesco document 19C/DR.19. As adopted it became Resolution 4.142 in the proceedings of the 19th session of the General Conference. The "Tunisian resolution" was prepared in wide negotiations which began in March 1976 in the Tunis symposium of the non-aligned countries, where Naesselund (with the assistance of Nordenstreng among others) pooled together various proposals, inviting Unesco's participation in the realization of the non-aligned program on information.

concrete activities in the development of communication systems was intended as an alternative to, and not as an extension of, such normative activities as the Draft Declaration.

As to the Draft Declaration, the USSR, together with Bulgaria, Czechoslovakia, and other socialist countries, clearly indicated readiness to find a new and more acceptable wording for the "state responsibility" Article XII. (Note also that the USSR repeated its earlier "mild" interpretation of this Article.) Similarly, Arab countries appeared quite moderate in comparison to their stand at the December 1975 meeting, and, although Jordan and Iraq, for example, did refer to the controversial UN Resolution 3379, it became clear that these countries were prepared to compromise (Iraq even to the point of "ironing out" the zionism paragraph).

Consequently, the substance of the Draft Declaration should no longer have been an unsurmountable problem— had there been political will to seriously seek a solution in a business-like atmosphere. For example, when the Draft Declaration 19C/91 was examined carefully before Nairobi by the Finnish National Commission for Unesco (representing different political orientations, including commercial newspaper publishers), the recommendation was for the Finnish delegation to accept the text if the two major stumbling blocks (Article XII and the Preambular paragraph 5) were removed and few other points were edited to eliminate a tendency for "state control."[55]

However, the matter had become too politicized to allow for a cool and analytical approach at Nairobi. Thus the delegates, especially those from the Western hemisphere, but also most of those from the developing countries, took a predominantly political and tactical stand on the matter. If they brought any balanced expert recommendations for further drafting of the text, these were of little value in the heated atmosphere in Nairobi, which was fed daily by aggressive reporting of the international news agencies and even by the newspapers of the host coun-

---

[55]Such a professional approach was also expressed in the address of the International Organization of Journalists (uniting national organizations and groups of journalists mainly in the socialist and developing countries, altogether some 150,000 journalists from 110 countries in all continents), delivered in the plenary debate on 6 November (by its President, Kaarle Nordenstreng): "As a professional organization representing journalists from various socio-economic and ideological conditions, we find it difficult to perceive this Draft Declaration as controversial as it has been indicated to be by many distinguished speakers in this Plenary. My Organization is standing for a broad concept of freedom of information, and we read little in the present Draft Declaration that might violate the fundamental principles, subscribed by most journalists in all hemispheres, according to which the citizens should be provided by objective information in order that they may form an accurate and comprehensive picture of their own society as well as the world at large. . . And what is also significant—if not alarming—in this connection, we are led to ask whether Unesco is yielding under the pressures exercised by some lobbies running a media campaign against it. As a professional organization we regret tha the media coverage of Unesco and its communication programme has often been far from the journalistic objectives of accuracy and comprehensiveness. . . ."

try.[56] In such a situation, and considering the determination of the Director-General to do his utmost to avoid an open confrontation, it was natural that the debate in Programme Commission III was bound to lead to the prearranged "smooth" outcome, i.e. leaving the matter for the Drafting and Negotiating Group. This decision was supported by an overwhelming majority of 78 votes, while 15 delegations (mostly socialist countries) voted against and 6 abstained.

The *Drafting and Negotiating Group,* chaired by the Ambassador of Bénin (Boissier-Palun, a friend of M'Bow), carried out its task for "further study" by appointing a working group under the chairmanship of the Ambassador of India (Parthasarathi). The group, after a debate for several days, asked its Nordic member, *Gunnar Garbo,* to undertake the task of preparing a new text for the Draft Declaration in the light of the present situation. Thus, the socialist countries and many developing countries pressed the Western countries to proceed with the redrafting, although few may have had serious expectations from the Garbo "emergency project." Evidently, Garbo himself took the task conscientiously; after all, the Nordic position did not exclude the option of having a "mild" Declaration prepared and adopted in Nairobi. After working for several days, he presented a new draft to the working group (dated 16 November 1976 and distributed as General Conference document 19C/INF.21).

The "Garbo text" (reproduced as Appendix 10) was based on the draft 19C/91, but altered it considerably by reintroducing several formulations of the earlier draft 18C/35, as well as by adding new elements emphasizing the needs of the developing countries for adequate mass media structures (see Preambular section II and Article II of his draft—the sources of his changes are indicated in parentheses, and formulations of his own are italicized). At the same time Garbo had deleted the "zionism paragraph" from the preamble and the "State responsibility Article" from the main text. By and large, it may be said that in his draft Garbo succeeded in encapsulating the "spirit of Nairobi" as far as the substance of communication problems is concerned. This means, among other things, that the normative-political and the operative-practical were interlinked; Garbo had obviously abandoned the Western attempt to present these as alternatives.

But the *"spirit of Nairobi"* was not determined by professional substance, dealt with in a business-like atmosphere, but rather by highly political considerations ultimately stemming from the uncompromising line pursued by leading Western powers, in particular the U.S. and the Federal Republic of Germany. Thus the service provided by such intermediaries as Garbo was not much appreciated. Neither was the flexible atti-

---

[56]For example, the journalistic catchword used by the local English-speaking papers in referring to the Draft Declaration was "the curb"—suggesting an instrument to control press freedom.

tude of the USSR and other socialist countries of help: the Western side simply refused any compromise other than postponement of the matter to the next session of the General Conference. In such a situation, the majority of the Member States and the Director-General had little choice but to follow this "master's voice." Consequently, the "spirit of Nairobi" came to mean that the "Third World" was yielding—paradoxically, on its own ground in Africa. Some observers in the corridors of the Kenyatta conference center went even further by commenting, "Americans have bought Africa." This, however, was a premature judgement, since the "pure" Western formula of eliminating the normative and concentrating on the operative did not pass in Nairobi. In this respect the "spirit of Nairobi" really meant a compromise.[57]

In terms of formal proceedings, the Drafting and Negotiating Group produced a *consensus draft resolution* which was adopted without vote by the plenary of the General Conference on 29 November, only one day before the session was closed. This Resolution 4.143 of the 19th session of the General Conference, after first referring to the important "role" (note the term) of the mass media "in furthering peace, promoting international understanding and combating war propaganda, racialism and apartheid," and after recalling relevant resolutions of the 17th and 18th sessions, and after taking into account the proceedings of the 19th session:

> 1. Invites the Director-General to hold further broad consultations with experts with a view to preparing a final Draft Declaration on "Fundamental Principles Governing the Use of the Mass Media in Strengthening Peace and International Understanding and in Combating War Propaganda, Racialism and Apartheid," which could meet with the largest possible measure of agreement, as well as to proposing any other action which may be called for in the light of these consultations;
>
> 2. Requests the Director-General to submit such a Draft Declaration to Member States at the end of 1977 or early in 1978, as well as any other proposal he might formulate;
>
> 3. Decides to include this item in the agenda of its twentieth session.

It is not difficult to see that this compromise is made up of two main elements. First, no Draft Declaration was adopted in Nairobi; the issue was "shelved" for two years. Second, a "final Draft Declaration" was due in those two years, based on a mandate not far from the original Soviet-Byelorussian moves from 1970 to 1972.

[57]Yet it remains a fact that the USA got both of its overall political conditions fulfilled in Nairobi: the Draft Declaration was postponed and also the question of Israel was solved by including it in the European group, although two other resolutions were passed against the U.S. vote, among others, condemning Israel for its activities in the occupied Arab territories.

After this solution the Director-General could express relief— certainly reflecting a sentiment of most delegations—by referring to

> . . .a controversy in which the clash of seemingly irreconcilable points of view threatened to lead the international community, divided against itself, into a conflict of the kind that paralyses its action to the detriment of all. But wisdom prevailed once again, and this nineteenth session of the General Conference may be given credit for having made notable progress in the search for a genuine dialogue designed to lead to the determination of a common course which everyone admits to be necessary. . .
>
> The adoption, by consensus, of the resolution on the draft declaration shows that your States hold similar views on two important principles. To begin with, this international instrument, the value of which will be primarily of an ethical nature, cannot be operative unless it is the subject of the broadest possible agreement throughout the world. Secondly, the declaration should not restrict itself to the statement of great moral principles. It must also lay down specific courses of action for Unesco. . .
>
> You have, indeed, asked the Secretariat to take action but you have also asked it to inquire more deeply into the role, aims and conditions of communication. As I had occasion to state earlier during the discussion on this item, I intend, within the framework of the mandate you have laid upon me, to undertake wide-ranging consultations in support of the work we have been asked to do, making use, if necessary, of a discussion group, so that at its twentieth session the General Conference may be presented with a comprehensive study on the problems of communication in the modern world.[58]

The end of this quote refers to the idea which grew out of the debates in Nairobi to set up a "reflexion group of wise men" to undertake a *penetrating study of communication problems,* in contrast to the over-politicized diplomacy which had dominated the proceedings of the General Conference. This idea was supported by all parties—not least by the U.S. delegation—and thus it cannot be understood as a simple "price" for the deals made in Nairobi. Rather, it reflects the positive side of the "spirit of Nairobi," whereby, despite bitter controversies, all parties were prepared to get down to a serious study of the problems involved. At the same time, however, the idea was so vague that it did accommodate different and even contradictory interests, such as, on the one hand, the intention of many communication scholars (the present author among them) to achieve an uncompromised scientific analysis of the theoretical-

---

[58]Address by Amadou-Mahtar M'Bow at the closing meeting of the 19th session of the General Conference on 30 November 1976, Unesco document 19C/INF.23, pp. 6–7.

conceptual as well as the practical-political problems involved, and, on the other hand, the intention of many experts inside and outside the Unesco Secretariat to bring the debate back "down to the earth" and get to the practical instead of the normative. Thus the seeds of the controversy around the McBride Commission were sown already at its birth.

THE SEARCH FOR RECONCILIATION

After Nairobi, the fundamental positions of the different parties remained as they had been during the battling at the General Conference. But as far as tactics are concerned, Nairobi was a lesson for all: that there was a limit set by the Western side beyond which one could not compromise the "free flow" position, and that there was another borderline, determined by the *de facto* coalition between the developing and socialist countries, beyond which one could not proceed to compromise the "new order" position. Given this lesson, the overall atmosphere around Unesco in general, and the further drafting of the Mass Media Declaration in particular, was relatively calm and was favorable for a realistic continuation of the process. On the other hand, Western mass media lobbies did not turn passive—on the contrary, instead of a predominantly propagandistic line, they now launched more comprehensive programs to meet the challenge posed by Unesco and the Movement of Non-Aligned Countries.[59]

Consultations 1977

The Unesco Secretariat entered the post-Nairobi stage in Spring 1977 by recruiting consultants for advice in preparing a new draft. The matter was handled by Gunnar Naesselund (who at the time was Deputy Assistant Director-General in charge of communication), who suggested a *three-man team of experts* to represent various geographic-political orientations.[60] One of those chosen was J. Clement Jones (from England), who had participated in the March 1974 meeting of experts and who was also working for Unesco's project on the codes of ethics (see note 43). Another consultant chosen by Naesselund was the present author (Nordenstreng), who had served as consultant to Unesco since 1969 on various projects on communication research and policies and who had been elected President of the International Organization of Journalists in September

---

[59]See e.g. "The Unesco Debate" (at IPI's general assembly in Oslo in June 1977), *IPI report*, May–June, pp. 7–20, and "Unesco: Follow-up of the Nairobi General Conference" (at FIEJ's congress in May 1977), *FIEJ-Bulletin*, July 1977, pp. 13–18.

[60]Personal communication from Gunnar Naesselund who, upon his retirement from Unesco in the middle of 1977, worked at the Nordic Council in Stockholm.

1976.[61] The third person who captured the attention of Naesselund and his superiors was Germán Carnero Roqué (from Peru), until 1977 the Peruvian press attaché in Europe, in which capacity he had represented Peru at the December 1975 government expert meeting and in the 1976 Non-Aligned Symposium on Information in Tunis.[62] The matter was dealt with in a confidential manner, and in May 1977 the choice of the consultants was known at the Unesco Secretariat only by Naesselund, his superior Makaminan Makagiansar (from Indonesia; 1976–1981 the Assistant Director-General for Culture and Communication), the Director-General, and his deputy.

The three-man team met in Paris for one week in July 1977, working intensively, together with Naesselund and his colleague Ahmed Kettani (an expert in communication law at the Secretariat). Before getting to the text itself, they attended a closed meeting, chaired by Makagiansar, with representatives of various relevant divisions of the Secretariat,[63] in order to consider the nature and objectives of the Draft Declaration. Although there appeared to be somewhat differing opinions as to the feasibility and probability of having a Declaration adopted, all agreed that the draft must be similar to the one drafted before Nairobi and must focus on the points enumerated in its title (as phrased in Resolution 4.143) without aiming at a broader Declaration on the New International Information Order. Starting with the texts drafted thus far,[64] the approach was to edit them with a view to avoiding obstacles—whether on principles of freedom of information or over the state responsibility of the media. Such a modest and pragmatic approach was then followed by the team, which, after a thorough consideration of the text, arrived at a consensus on how the Draft Declaration might read to "meet with the largest possible measure of agreement."

This first, post-Nairobi drafting process was finalized in early September 1977 in a further meeting between the consultants and some

[61]The proposal was made to the present author by Naesselund in May 1977 in New York, where both of them attended a conference "Third World and Press Freedom," sponsored by The Fletcher School of Law and Diplomacy, Tufts University (see P. Horton (Ed.), *The Third World and Press Freedom*, New York: Praeger, 1978.) At that time Nordenstreng was Visiting Professor at the University of California, San Diego. As the consultants were supposed to work in a private capacity and not as representatives of any organizations, the proposal was accepted without seeking advice from any outsiders.

[62]In mid-1977 Carnero was also being recruited as Unesco's regional adviser on communication in Latin America (posted in Quito, Ecuador), but the consultant's task on the Draft Declaration was considered separate from this full-time engagement.

[63]Division of Human Rights, Office of Public Information, etc. Also, among these officers from the Secretariat was Asher Deleon (from Yugoslavia), whom the Director-General had appointed in June 1977 to serve as the Executive Secretary of the International Commission for the Study of Communication Problems (the Chairman and the members of this "MacBride Commission" had not been chosen in July 1977).

[64]A working document had been prepared in the Secretariat, reviewing in detail the texts prepared so far.

members of the Secretariat.[65] The outcome was "Proposal for a revised text of the Draft Declaration. . ." (the title reading as in 19C/91 and Resolution 4.143), accompanied by an "Aide Memoire" which explained the draft's general features and specific formulations in relation to the earlier drafts.[66] Both documents making up the *"September 1977 draft"* are reproduced as Appendix 11.

While the revised text was welcomed by those few in the Secretariat who had access to it and by the Director-General, who was said to have read it with enthusiasm, it was understood by all that it was not only the substance of the text that was important, but also the way in which the new Draft Declaration was to be presented to the Member States and to professional circles. In this respect, it was considered best to proceed with a "low key" approach, by first carrying out a *round of confidential consultations* among a number of governmental and non-governmental representatives of various regional and political interests. The revised text was to be presented as a draft prepared by the Secretariat, with the help of a small group of consultants, and considered by the Director-General to be sufficiently advanced to provide the basis for the broad consultations called for in Resolution 4.143. A list of some 50 persons to be consulted was compiled, including the members of the Drafting and Negotiating Group at Nairobi, as well as leading representatives of international mass-media related organizations. Of these, about one third were from the West (either Western diplomats or representatives of Western mass-media interests). Only half a dozen were from the socialist countries of Eastern Europe, while about half were from the non-aligned, developing countries.

These persons were sent a confidential letter in September 1977, signed by Makagiansar, along with the "Proposal for a revised text." In the next few weeks they were contacted by a Unesco "emissary," who provided more information (Aide Memoire, etc.) and collected their comments. The personal part of the consultations was carried out by the original three-man team (Jones in Western Europe and the USA, Nordenstreng in Eastern Europe and the Arab World, Carnero in Latin America and the Caribbean) as well as by Unesco's regional adviser on communication in Africa (Alex Quarmyne, stationed in Nairobi, Kenya), by a distinguished Asian diplomat (Roeslan Abdulgani from Indonesia), and by two senior officers from the Unesco Secretariat (Kandil and Pierre Navaux, the Chief of Division of Development of Communication Sys-

---

[65]Meanwhile, Naesselund had retired from Unesco, and the main responsibility for the project at the Secretariat was borne by Makangiansar, with the assistance of Hamdy Kandil (from Egypt), the newly appointed Chief of the Division of Free Flow of Information and Communication Policies.

[66]The bulk of the "Aide Memoire" was prepared by Nordenstreng.

tems). The total number of persons contacted in this round of consultations grew close to one hundred, but the reports of the "emissaries" contained specific comments from 56 persons. Of these, 17 were from the West, 6 from the "socialist East," and 33 from the non-aligned countries in Africa, Asia, and Latin America.

The overall reaction to the revised Draft Declaration was positive in 40 of the 56 cases, negative in 14, and noncommital (neither negative nor positive) in two. All of the responses from the developing countries and from the socialist part of the world were positive, although there were many proposals for further editing of details. All of the negative reactions came from the West, but also several Western responses were either positive or neutral. Of the negative reactions, 9 were strongly negative—along the lines of the campaign before Nairobi—but even these individuals were quite cooperative in the consultations, for example, by offering concrete suggestions for further editing of the text.

Thus, there was a high degree of agreement on the revised text. In fact, the "emissaries" themselves were pleasantly surprised by the overall reaction. As far as the negative responses were concerned, everyone understood that either they were based on a fundamental position which would refuse any Unesco Declaration of the sort intended, or they came from interest groups that had vested so much in an adversary position in the past that it would have been unnatural for them to suddenly adopt a positive or even a neutral approach to the Draft Declaration. In view of the past controversies, the consultations were encouraging, for they indicated that now the opponents were at least prepared to get down to the substance and constructively cooperate in the final drafting.

These conclusions were brought by the "emissaries" to a meeting at Unesco headquarters in December 1977. On this occasion, a special one-day consultation was held with the representatives of the International Federation of Journalists and the International Organization of Journalists.[67] With all the responses, comments, and proposals for further

---

[67]This joint consultation produced a comprehensive set of comments and proposals both from the point of view of those who were "not fully convinced that there is a need for such a Delcaration" (IFJ) and those who thought that a Unesco Declaration was "useful, even necessary to remind journalists of existing international principles and to show the way towards a new order" (IOJ). There was no serious disagreement between the two organizations about the issues of state responsibility and Zionism (both welcomed the deletion of earlier references to these points), whereas the main separating issue appeared to be whether or not "political and ideological" should be added to the qualifiers of discrimination (in Articles II, III and VIII of the "September 1977 draft"). The IFJ was trying to turn the Declaration into an instrument which would not only provide support to those struggling against colonialism, racisim, etc., but which would become a weapon also in the hands of the dissidents in the socialist countries. As to the Article (X) specifically concerning journalists and their organizations, the formulation of the "September 1977 draft" left a lot to be clarified, although both IFJ and IOJ welcomed the intention behind this Article to render support to autonomous journalists' bodies against undue pressures from both the private employers and the states.

drafting, the next task was to prepare a new revised text, which would take these consultations into account as much as possible. This task was carried out mainly by those "emissaries" who were not working at the Secretariat (Jones, Nordenstreng, Carnero, Quarmyne, and Abdulgani), along with Jadwiga Pastecka, a Polish expert who had attended the March 1974 and December 1975 meetings, and who joined the team as the first and only consultant from the socialist countries. This *special working group* arrived at a consensus text without major difficulties. An indication of the consultants' effort to remove obstacles from what they now felt was a final draft, was the change of the title. Instead of the controversial ". . .governing the use of the mass media. . .," it was now a Draft Declaration ". . .concerning the contribution of the mass media. . .".[68] The *"December 1977 draft"* is reproduced as Appendix 12.

In addition to polishing the text in the light of the consultations, the group again joined Makagiansar and some of his colleagues from the Secretariat to review the overall situation—still in a "low key" manner, secretly and confidentially.[69] It was noted that a successful round of consultations had helped to further revise the text and that, according to the Nairobi mandate, the Director-General was obliged to present a new Draft Declaration in late 1977 or early 1978. The consultants took it for granted that the "December 1977 text" was to be the new Draft Declaration to be sent to the Member States as well as to relevant non-governmental organizations for their consideration before the 20th session of the General Conference in Fall 1978. But this optimistic review was not shared by all those involved from the Secretariat. Navaux suggested that the consultations might not have been sufficiently broad, and Deleon warned against thinking that the "Third World" would simply support the draft, whereas the "First World" would oppose it, and that the friends and enemies of Unesco would be defined in the same divisive terms. Deleon (who meanwhile had begun substantial work with the MacBride Commission) was seemingly reluctant to accept the very idea of this particular Draft Declaration, and he recommended instead a "fresh

---

[68]The term "contribution" was proposed by Nordenstreng after it had become obvious that the word "use" was obsolete in the title at this stage, when it was removed from the text itself (with the exception of the Preambular paragraph quoting Unesco's own Constitution, according to which the states are agreed and determined to "employ" the means of mass communication). Moreover, the team agreed that the title as phrased in 19C/91 and Resolution 4.143 only provided an unnecessary excuse for the opponents of the Draft Declaration.

[69]The Secretariat officers included, in addition to Kandil, Navaux, and Deleon from the Communication Sector, the Chief of the Legal Division and a senior member of Office of Public Information (this journalist, an American by nationality, also participated actively in the redrafting process with the consultants). Despite the secrecy around the matter, some investigating journalists had spotted the consultations by December 1977; for example, Rosemary Righter of the *Sunday Times* (and the IPI) tried to chase the consultants for an interview while they met in Paris.

look" at the matter—including the possibility of waiting until the MacBride Commission had prepared its report.

Diplomacy 1978

After the consultants left Paris, before Christmas 1977, the matter was left in the hands of the Unesco officers involved, who took care of briefing the Director-General. Either because of their advice (not least considering the position of Deleon) or own hesitation, the Director-General did not make any official, public move "at the end of 1977 or early in 1978" as he had been invited to do by the Nairobi mandate. Obviously the Director-General and his closet advisors paid greater attention to the influential Western circles, known to be against the Draft Declaration, than to the "silent majority" to be found in the socialist and developing countries. Also, it seems that the briefing of the Director-General had been somewhat ill-advised regarding the controversies which remained after the 1977 consultations, and the actual position of the Movement of Non-Aligned Countries.[70] Furthermore, the overall international situation continued to deteriorate in early 1978, and the Director-General, emphasizing the principle of consensus in international organizations such as Unesco, and recollecting the "spirit of Nairobi," believed that one should not go forward without regard for the will of minorities.[71]

All of this made the Director-General hesitate and finally seek the advice of the Executive Board, the "Parliament" of Unesco which functions as the highest decision-making body between the sessions of the General Conference. *The report of the Director-General to the Executive Board* was submitted to the 104th session of the Board in mid-April 1978 (see Appendix 13). The essence of this document is a summary of the points of view expressed in the 1977 round of consultations. The document was prepared in the Sector for Communication—evidently on the basis of views held especially by Deleon.

The report displayed the outcome of the consultations as far more problematic than were seen by the consultants themselves. While certainly not "failing to reflect the originality of the points of view expressed," the five categories into which the reactions were grouped could be misleading, since there was no indication of how many and which kinds of persons consulted held each opinion. In fact, of the some 100

---

[70]For example, the Coordination Committee of the Non-Aligned Countries' Press Agencies Pool was reported having recommended in its April 1977 meeting in Djakarta that Unesco should prepare an essentially new kind of Declaration.

[71]See "Le consensus dans les organisations internationales," address by Amadou Mahtar M'Bow at l'Academie diplomatique internationale; Unesco Press release No. 22, Paris, March 1978.

persons consulted, nearly 90 fell into the first two categories, accepting the "September 1977 draft" either as such or in principle, but with specific modifications. And as shown above, even many of those who thought that any Unesco Declaration would be useless were not absolute in their rejection but cooperated in finding formulations which would better meet their interests.

These critical remarks on the report were brought to the attention of the Director-General in a joint personal message from two of the 1977 consultants, Jones and Nordenstreng.[72] They also pointed out that the "December 1977 draft" was desgined to be as close to consensus as possible, given all the evidence available, and they advised the Director-General to take a firm stand in favor of this latest text. On the other hand, they pointed out that, while this text had every chance of approval by an overwhelming majority, a complete consensus in this matter, or on many questions relating to communication, was hardly possible—in the present world situation or later.

In addition to this consultants' message, M'Bow received a letter from D. R. Mankekar, the Indian Chairman of the Coordination Committee of the Non-Aligned Countries' Press Agencies Pool, who also recommended, on the basis of decisions of the Committee, that the Director-General should take a "firm stand" on the matter and without further hesitation introduce the revised Draft Declaration for adoption at the 20th session of the General Conference.[73] Another, politically still more significant message, came from Havana, where the Intergovernmental Council for the Coordination of Information of the Non-aligned Countries (appointed by the Colombo summit in 1976) held its second meeting in April 1978. It proposed, among other things, that the Mass Media Declaration be supported as an expression of the interests of the non-aligned countries, and that the Director-General should submit the Draft Declaration to Member States and put it to a vote at the forthcoming 20th session of the General Conference, in line with Resolution 4.143.[74]

Accordingly, by the time the Executive Board began to consider the matter (at the end of May 1978), new evidence had accumulated showing that the political momentum around the Draft Declaration was not, after all, quite as discouraging as suggested by the Director-General's report. However, despite the signals coming from the Movement of Non-Aligned Countries, intended to encourage the Director-General to proceed as determined by the Nairobi mandate, M'Bow continued to hesitate

[72]Telex sent from Stockholm on 27 April 1978 (while attending an international seminar on news transmission organized by the MacBride Commission).

[73]Letter dated May 10, 1978, sent by Mankekar for information of the present author.

[74]Resolution on the Intergovernmental Council's Cooperation with Unesco.

and did not distribute the "December 1977 draft," even to the Executive Board, although, unofficially, the text had been circulating for some time in the lobbies inside and outside Unesco. It was understood that he did not object to having the Draft Declaration sent to the MacBride Commission, rather than having it once more become an obstacle at the General Conference. The same view was held by many African representatives on the Executive Board. No doubt most of the Western diplomats also welcomed the possibility of once more postpoining the Declaration; indeed, it had been a delicate part of Western tactics in Nairobi to create a "reflexion group" to provide a graveyard for such unpleasant projects as the Draft Declaration.[75] On the other hand, the MacBride Commission was not welcomed by all of the Western delegates as a pleasant alternative to the Declaration, for by 1977 this group of "wise men" was increasingly disliked among those who opposed the "politization" of Unesco.

However, the situation in Paris in May-June 1978 was not the same as in Nairobi in October-November 1976. The controversy was no longer so heated, and there was no public campaign on the matter—thanks, probably, to the round of consultations in 1977 which had helped in the pursuit of quiet diplomacy. It also appeared that, by and large, the Executive Board took a moderate approach to the matter—not hiding nor dramatizing the controversies involved, thus reflecting the delicate balance of political forces which prevailed. A definite majority of the Board expressed the wish to find consensus on the basis of Resolution 4.143, which meant submitting a final Draft Declaration to the 20th session of the General Conference.

The Executive Board appointed a working group under the chairmanship of the Ambassador of Mexico (Luis Echeverria, former President of Mexico) to prepare the Board's position, and this group arrived at a draft resolution without major difficulties (see Appendix 13). This was unanimously adopted by the Executive Board. The *resolution of the Executive Board* clearly showed a preference for "the possibility of drafting a final Declaration" to be forwarded to Member States before the 20th session of the General Conference, but it left the Director-General with an option to fail in his efforts to elaborate a final draft "which could reflect the largest possible measure of agreement and thus constitute a step towards the establishment of a new international order of information." It should be noted that this resolution, in creating the link between the Draft Declaration and the idea of a "new order," constitutes a significant step in legitimizing the position of the Movement of Non-Aligned Coun-

---

[75]Such a position was not held by the Scandinavian representative on the Executive Board, Garbo, who supported the submission of a Draft Declaration to the 20th session, in accordance with what was agreed in Nairobi.

tries (although the Western side refused an explicit reference to the Havana resolution of April 1978 see note 74).

The Director-General now lost no time in moving forward. He decided to take a "firm stand" and prepared a new Draft Declaration, on the basis of the 1977 consultations, mainly with the advice of his personal acquaintance, René Lefort, a French freelance journalist (with *Le Monde*). The result was published in September 1978 as a General Conference *document 20C/20* (reproduced as Appendix 14). The title and the preamble of this text was practically the same as in the "December 1977 draft," with some editing in which only one element had been deleted altogether: the paragraph on détente. This was an interesting indication of the changing mood of the time. (Note that the phrasing of this paragraph had changed already from September to December 1977 by the deletion of qualifier "positive.") As far as the "operative part" listing the Articles was concerned, it was also based on the "December 1977 draft," with the explanatory notes which accompany the new text largely taken from the "Aide Memoire" of the consultants. However, the actual phrasing of the Articles in 20C/20 revealed several details where the final drafting had departed from the "testament" of the 1977 consultants.

Obviously the authors of 20C/20 had seriously intended a text which would have minimized the controversies and helped in facilitating the largest possible measure of agreement, "given the goodwill in the search for a common ground," as advised by the Executive Board. The result, however, did not quite succeed in fulfilling these intentions it gave rise to the same kind of controversies that had troubled the project in Nairobi and before. For example, the IPI responded with detailed notes on the text 20C/20, regretting that despite "some welcome acknowledgements" (human rights, diverse sources, etc.) the overall tone and the basic clauses of the new text leaned heavily towards "the concept of a controlled press."[76] The IPI response also referred to the "December 1977 draft," which, even if not published, is ". . .widely known, and it could be argued that it represents—much more truly than the present published Draft—the consensus which the Director-General was asked to seek."

Critical comments on the text 20C/20 accumulated. Not surprisingly, U.S. diplomacy made it clear to the Director-General that the text invited by the Nairobi mandate was "not yet before us," but by the same token it was indicated that the U.S. was prepared to collaborate in trying to work out a broadly acceptable text. What was new in this wave of criticism were voices from the socialist countries regretting that the text had

---

[76]"Notes on 20C: Draft Declaration on the Media", mimeo of the International Press Institute marked RR/jw/9.78 (obviously prepared by Rosemary Righter).

gone too far towards the "free flow" position. Paradoxically, these social-ist comments coincided with the IPI opinion that the "December 1977 draft" would have been more acceptable than the text now endorsed by the Director-General. Indeed, it seemed as if some of the formulations of the text 20C/20 had created unnecessary complications for all parties in-volved. For example, Article XI again generated the controversy on state responsibility, which was delicately avoided in the corresponding Article X of the "December 1977 draft."

The Union of Journalists in Finland, a nationally representative or-ganization of professional journalists, made an attempt to provide a *"Pro-fessional Alternative"* to 20C/20 by editing it with the help of the "December 1977 draft."[77] This proposal for an alternative text (with accompanying explanatory notes) was sent to the international and regional organiza-tions of journalists with a view towards getting them to present such a "professional alternative" jointly, as a solution to a diplomatic stalemate (see Appendix 15). The IOJ and IFJ, in fact, followed up on this idea. Their representatives met at Unesco on the eve of the General Confer-ence. Although they could not agree on a single alternative text, they pro-vided the Director-General with a number of concrete proposals for al-ternative formulations, assuring that the professional journalists' organizations were not far from consensus in support of his Draft Decla-ration with specific modifications.

General Conference 1978

As things developed on the eve of the 20th session of the General Confer-ence, such a "professional approach" did not stand much of a chance; the Draft Declaration had become overpoliticized, as it had been in Nairobi two years earlier. The "Nairobi syndrome" reappeared in Western press coverage of the General Conference, which focussed on the Draft Decla-ration, creating a dramatized and predominantly negative public image.[78]

---

[77]The redrafting was done by Lars Bruun, a Finnish mass media lawyer and secretary of the legal sub-committee of the Nordic Federation of Journalists, in collaboration with the present author (as a Finnish professor and an ex-consultant to Unesco on the matter).

[78]No systematic content analysis was made of the press coverage of the 20th session of the General Con-ference in Paris, but there is no doubt about a striking similarity with the treatment of Nairobi, although the tone now seemed to be somewhat less aggressive than two years earlier. For example, *Helsingin Sanomat* in Finland (obviously mobilized by the IPI) published a long editorial on 1 October 1978 about "Unesco Declaration," recognizing the improvements of the new proposed text but alerting the Finnish delegates at the General Conference that the press will not tolerate compromising basic issues of freedom of information. As another preparation for the 20th session, *Helsingin Sanomat,* like most other Western "quality papers," had published several articles relating to the MacBride Commission, among them a large overview by Indian Crusow Irani (Editor of *The Statesman* in Calcutta and later Chairman of the IPI)

Diplomacy continued in such an electrified atmosphere. Once more the Western "information group" became active in coordinating the efforts to play down the Draft Declaration. But unlike the time before Nairobi, there was little support for a totally rejectionist position, because now it was understood that the project had proceeded too far (with the support of the Executive Board) to allow a radical turn back. Only British diplomats took an inflexibly hard line, in which no compromise was possible and the text 20C/20 was considered "garbage." At the other extreme was the French position, insisting that the text submitted by the Director-General must be accepted as the basis for negotiations or the whole atmosphere of the General Conference would be spoiled. Also, the U.S. approach was flexible as indicated above. However, all Western diplomats at Unesco agreed that the text 20C/20 was not acceptable as such, although "there is a certain improvement in the new draft declaration," because it "manifests a state control of the media, which is not in political and legal conformity with relations between the media and the state in most of the Western countries."[79] Therefore detailed proposals to amend the text were produced and brought to the attention of the Director-General. Thus the Western side (or most of it) was now prepared to negotiate the substance of the text—unlike Nairobi, where efforts had been concentrated on postponing the matter.

On the other hand, in October 1978 there were those who though that it would be possible to "push" the Draft Declaration to the MacBride Commission (this position was held especially by Australia and Canada). Furthermore, all Western diplomats were busy in using the "infrastructure card." They showed off the willingness of the Western governments to render material support to the developing countries and

which "analyzed" the situation by warning that the developing countries had a crucial choice between a "professional line" in support of Western-type press freedom, and a "Soviet line" legitimizing government control of the mass media. On the eve of the General Conference, *Newsweek* (2 October 1978) provided a page for Leonard Sussman, the executive director of the U.S. Freedom House, warning that "Third World countries at Unesco's general conference in Paris will try later this month to change the kind of foreign news you read, hear, and see. Because most nations do not permit a free press, international forums increasingly threaten to make governmental control of the news media the model for a New World Information Order." But Sussman also had a "constructive" proposal: "By aligning ourselves with the moderates, we will undercut Marxist efforts to exploit Third World dissatisfaction. In 1976, the Soviets proposed that the world press should be controlled. The moderates understand that passing such a declaration will not improve Western news coverage. Indeed, condoning news-media controls could reduce coverage."

[79]The permanent delegates of the EEC countries at Unesco produced a memorandum regretting also the use of expressions like "objective," "accurate," "free and balanced," "reciprocal," "impartial," "complete," etc.—which ironically belong to the traditional arsenal of Western journalism. These first EEC comments accepted most of the preamble of 20C/20, rejecting some paragraphs (including No. 14, which was still seen to contain reference to the UN Resolution 3379), but suggested more or less fundamental changes in virtually all Articles of the main text.

thus tried to soften the "Third World."[80] Thus the "Nairobi syndrome" was repeated and was solidified in an idea proposed by Tunisia, Sri Lanka, and other non-aligned countries to establish a special fund at Unesco for financing media infrastructures, training, etc. in the developing countries. However, it soon became evident that the non-aligned countries (and the Director-General) were not prepared to "sell out" the Declaration for lucrative "help." The two could not be taken as alternative projects, but rather as bargaining elements. The unity of the "new order" idea—however poorly defined at this stage—was preserved, and the normative and the operative continued to coexist at Unesco, as shown in Chapter 1.

The formal processing again took place in the relevant *Programme Commission IV*. But this time there was no need for a great debate (such as had occurred in Nairobi, reported in Appendix 9), and the struggle continued primarily in the lobbies of the General Conference, accompanied by some public statements made in the general policy debate (e.g. the U.S. position by Reinhardt quoted in Chapter 1), and surrounded by intensive press coverage. The Director-General himself was now fully engaged—both personally and through an unofficial intermediary, Boissier-Palun (former delegate of Benin, now an independent lawyer-consultant in Paris), whom M'Bow had invited to help in the negotiations. At the Programme Commission level, its Chairman, the Ambassador of Peru (Alberto Wagner de Reyna), formed a small working party composed of representatives from the three "Worlds." Finally, *the Western, the Eastern-Socialist, and the Non-Aligned groups* held intensive internal meetings. It followed from the politics involved that the Chairman of the Non-Aligned "Group 77," the Ambassador of Tunisia (Mustapha Masmoudi), occupied a particularly central position in the negotiations between the three groups. In fact, the working group within the framework of the Commission was soon superseded, as all essential negotiations were held directly among the three groups and, at the final stage, through the Director-General.

Despite the predominantly behind-the-scene diplomacy, each of the three groups put on record one official document: a draft resolution proposing amendments to 20C/20, each from their political point of view. The first to officially present its position was the Western group, which offered a considerably modified text. In fact, as expressed by its title, a new kind of Declaration was proposed, covering not only peace, international understandiang, racialism, and apartheid (war propaganda being altogether deleted), but, stressing foremost, human rights and, in

---

[80]For example, all Scandinavian countries announced in their addresses in the general policy debate (delivered by respective Ministers) that they had made donations to a Unesco "fund in trust" for the training of communicators in Africa.

particular, freedom of information. While formally based on 20C/20, it was a "maxi-version" of the stereotyped Western position, obviously designed to leave room for bargaining. This *"Western Alternative,"* reproduced as Appendix 16, was submitted by 10 Western countries, including the U.S., Canada, and the Federal Republic of Germany, but excluding a number of NATO-EEC-Western countries, thus reducing its credibility. The most important sponsor missing from this group was the *United Kingdom,* which had submitted a parallel draft resolution separately, proposing "to defer until a later session of the General Conference its further consideration of the Draft Declaration," and inviting the Director-General, "in the light of the final report of the MacBride Commission and of the views expressed by the Member States," to prepare a further paper on the matter, and, finally, inviting the Member States to assist the developing countries in strengthening their media "by means of technical assistance, training and equipment."[81] It is obvious that this position was presented as a tactical move. At a later stage of the negotations it was withdrawn to pave the way for consensus.

Two days after the Western group had submitted its alternative text, the socialist countries of Eastern Europe (excluding Romania and Yugoslavia) and the socialist-oriented developing countries Viet Nam, Afghanistan, Mozambique, and Ethopia (but not Cuba) submitted their *"Socialist Alternative,"* reproduced as Appendix 17. This could not be compared with the "Western Alternative" as a socialist "maxi-version," because it did not return to the earlier texts, such as 19C/91, but rather kept close to the Director-General's text by redrafting only parts of 20C/20 (mainly on the basis of the alternative of the Non-Aligned group and the "December 1977 draft"). The third draft resolution submitted by the Non-Aligned group (including Cuba and Yugoslavia) was similar in its revisions. This *"Non-Aligned Alternative"* is reproduced as Appendix 18.

Such were the positions which the Director-General brought together in an intensive round of negotations between 18 and 20 November 1978. The situation was described authentically, but from a typically American point of view, in the 1978 November 20 issue of *Time* magazine (reproduced as Appendix 19).

Most of the diplomatic dealings were with the Western and the Non-Aligned groups, and between the two. At one time it seemed as if the Socialist group would be isolated. However, since by and large the Non-Aligned and the Socialist groups shared the same overall approach, which was not far from the Director-General's position (as expressed in 20C/20), and whereas the Western view drastically departed from these, it was only natural that the main problem was between the Western group

---

[81]Unesco document 20C/PRG.IV/DR.6 (17 November 1978).

and the other groups. Furthermore, tactically speaking, the Non-Aligned countries held a key position, because they held not only an absolute majority of the votes but also expected something from the Western countries as a price for compromising. Also, the Western countries knew that by bargaining with the Non-Aligned group they could get further politically than by dealing with the Socialist group. The final outcome of this bargaining was obviously closer to the Western position than it would have been, given only two parties, East and West. On the other hand, the Director-General also consulted with the socialist countries in the final negotiations. Although these countries had to move quite far from their original positions, nothing in the final text ran counter to their basic line—at least as they themselves read the text. The same was true of the other two groups as well.

On 21 November 1978 the *document 20C/20 Rev.* was issued with the title "Compromise text proposed by the Director-General with a view to consensus." The introduction reads as follows:

> Since it was issued on 6 September, the Draft Declaration in document 20C/20 has aroused keen interest and generated much discussion, which the importance of the subject fully justifies.
>
> Not only were statements concerning the text of the Draft Declaration made by most of the heads of delegation in the General Policy Debate; its content was also extensively discussed during the numerous discussions which the Director-General held with the heads of delegation of Member States and with the observers attending the General Conference.
>
> In the light of these statements and consultations and of the discussions which he has held in particular with the different regional groups, the Director-General has felt able to submit to the General Conference a new text which is in his view likely to command the broad agreement which the General Conference deemed desirable at its nineteenth session.
>
> As its title indicates, this new text is a compromise text. The result of lengthy and patient negotiations, it takes into account the ideas underlying the proposed amendments, and its wording is designed to dispel the misgivings generated by certain misunderstandings.
>
> The Director-General submits this revised text in the firm hope that it will be possible for it to be adopted by consensus by the General Conference.

The text attached to this introduction (Appendix 1) was characterized by the Director-General in his presentation to the Programme Commission on 22 November 1978 as something moderate, so that ". . .nobody can expect to find in it, word by word, the exact draft he would like to see. On the other hand, nobody can say that it runs counter, in any pro-found sense, to the principles to which he is deeply attached."[82] The pro-ceedings of the General Conference give the following report of what happened after the Director-General had presented his compromise text:

> The President then put to the vote the Draft Declaration as set forth in document 20C/20 Rev., which was approved by acclamation. The President addressed the meeting briefly, saying that 22 November 1978 was a historic day for Unesco.
>
> The Director-General expressed his gratitude to the Commis-sion and voiced his satisfaction that determination to reach a success-ful outcome within Unesco had prevailed over the diversity of Mem-ber States' views.
>
> The delegates of 58 States and observers from three non-governmental organizations then took the floor to explain their vote and to comment upon the adoption of the Declaration. They were unanimous in congratulating the Director-General, the Secre-tariat and certain delegates on the role which they had played in achieving this consensus and acknowledged the importance of the Declaration.
>
> Some delegates nevertheless expressed reservations concerning certain parts of the text or expressions used in it, and stressed that they had approved the draft in so far as it preserved freedom of in-formation and its free flow. Many delegates pointed out that the adoption of the Declaration constituted a major step forward in the establishment of a new, more just and more effective world order of information and communication, while regretting that the responsi-bilities and duties of journalists and the media were not more explic-itly set out in it. In general, stress was also placed on the example which Unesco had given to the world in its concern to reach a consen-sus on one of the most difficult problems of cultural policy of our time.[83]

Politically speaking, this "successful outcome" was reached in the Programme Commission (IV) on Culture and Communication on that "historic day for Unesco," 22 November 1978. However, this was not the final decision; the Declaration was forwarded to a plenary session of the General Conference where its adoption was finally sealed, purely as a for-mality, "on this twenty-eight day of November 1978," as expressed in the last paragraph of the preamble (see Appendix 1). At that time Unesco had 146 Member States (after Zimbabwe was admitted at that session),

[82]*Records of the General Conference, Twentieth Session* (Paris 24 October to 28 November 1978), Volume 2: Reports, Paris 1979, p. 153 (paragraph 559).
[83]Ibid., p. 154 (paragraphs 562–565).

but actually the number of governments attending the 20th session in Paris was 140.

THE OUTCOME APPRECIATED

The statements made by the *delegates and observers* after the adoption of the declaration were included in full in the proceedings of the General Conference.[84] The bulk of this revealing debate, including the speeches of the delegates of the U.S., U.K., and USSR, as well as of the observers of the journalists' organizations, is reproduced in Appendix 20.

The *press reaction* to the adoption of the Declaration was, by and large, less euphoric than the speeches at Unesco.[85] The Western press, which over the years had built up a major (negative) image of the Declaration, either noted the event of its adoption without particular attention— even as a kind of anti-climax after a dramatic "conflict" (see the *Time* article of 4 December in Appendix 19)— or the Declaration was appreciated as a doubtful if not dangerous instrument compromising press freedom. An example of the latter reaction is the editorial of *The Washington Post* of 27 November (reprinted in the *International Herald Tribune* of 28 November):

> The outcome of Unesco's yearlong debate on the mass media has to trouble deeply all those truly interested in advancinag the organization's chartered purpose of enchancing the "free flow" of information and ideas. True, the members removed from the final text most of the language explictly authorizing any state's control over the operations of its own news media or that of other nations' working within its borders. This took a lot of scrapping by the Western delegations and it put some of them in a somewhat self-congratulatory frame of mind after the declaration was shouted through unanimously in Paris the other day.
>
> We don't wish to seem ungracious for official efforts undertaken in our, that is to say, the Western media's, behalf. It is evident, however, that by helping to write and by approving even a moderate declaration like this one, the Western delegations condoned the idea that it is within the proper province of governments to call the media tune. That this particular tune—this time around—is less dirge than walk-on music is nice but essentially irrelevant. Why else, after all, would it be supported by all the totalitarian states, both the Communist ones, which practice media control systematically as a matter of ideology, and the Third World states, which practice it more casually as a matter of political convenience.

[84]Unesco document 20C/135. All the speeches are reproduced (in an English translation, with the exception of those delivered in French) in the publication referred to in note 2 above.

[85] A number of studies were commissioned in 1979 by Unesco to provide documentation and analysis of the way in which the Declaration has been portrayed in the press of different regions of the world. These studies have not been published by Unesco (by the end of 1981).

Indeed, in a field so contentious, how can something acceptable to, let us say, the Soviet Union or Nigeria, be also acceptable to the West? One answer is, of course, that the declaration is a compromise, carrying everyone's ideological baggage on level shoulders. But to the extent that this is so, it indicates how far from the principles of its charter Unesco has moved. A second answer is that the declaration is only hortatory, not enforceable. Quite true, but in that case how can any comfort or reassurance be taken from the declaration's pledges to protect journalists and assure their "freedom to report," to allow deprived parties the right of reply, to give a voice to those "who are unable to make their voices heard within their own territories"?

You will perhaps pardon us for suspecting that the parts of the declaration most likely to be honored—in the places where the media are constrained—are the parts reinforcing state policies, such as "the strengthening of peace" and "the countering of incitement to war."

As for the United States' pledges to offer technical and material help to the media of underdeveloped countries, that would have been a sensible proposal even without a Unesco conference. Though it evidently was not possible to say so at Paris, we trust such aid will go only to countries that are ready to let their media move in the direction of the Unesco charter.

From the viewpoint of U.S. diplomacy, no doubt the Paris outcome reflected a certain success. The United States found itself aligned with Third World members and other states on an issue on which it and its Western friends had previously been isolated from them. From the viewpoint of the U.S. news media, however, the result represented a clear erosion of the favor and protection they were accorded three decades ago by the Unesco charter. And that is what worries us now.

It is interesting to compare this appreciation of the outcome with the *official U.S. position* as expressed in "Report of the Secretary of State to the President on International Journalistic Freedom":[86]

      . . .The product of the negotiations was a text not only stripped of language implying state authority over the mass media, but which also included positive language on freedom of information. Instead of imposing duties and responsibilities upon journalists, as various drafts attempted, it proclaimed that they must have freedom to report and the fullest possible facilities of access to information and be assured of protection guaranteeing them the best conditions for the exercise of their profession. . .

[86] The report, dated January 15, 1979, was submitted to the Congress to describe "U.S. Government efforts internationally to safeguard the rights of journalists" whereby the principal focus "was our preparation for and participation in the recent Unesco General Conference which adopted by consensus a mass media declaration. . . ." The unpublished but widely circulated report has 7 mimeo pages (plus annex); quotes from pp. 4–5.

While technically the Unesco Declaration is a statement of principle and not a document binding on member states, it is significant that it was adopted by all 146 Unesco members by consensus. It thus represents a consensus among virtually the entire world community. The fact that the Declaration specifically points out the necessity for governments to respect the rights of journalists makes it an excellent vehicle for conveying US concerns over conditions in a number of countries which restrict the full exercise of journalism, both for domestic and foreign journalists.

Based on the Declaration, the State Department dispatched a circular cable to all posts, specifying representations to be made based on the Unesco Declaration. This had, in addition to voicing our strong objections to mistreatment and/or restriction of foreign journalists, the added benefit of (a) approving the global application of the principles in the Unesco Declaration and (b) reiterating the long-standing US commitment to press freedom.

Another American appreciation worth noting here came from *Freedom House,* a non-profit organization defending the traditional U.S. concept of civil liberties and since 1976 focussing aggressive attention on developments at Unesco and the Movement Non-Aligned Countries. Its executive director, Leonard Sussman, considered the final text as the "best of bad alternatives" and even wrote: "The solution was a honorable one." (For a comprehensive evaluation by Sussman, see Appendix 21.) Thus, a hard line "free flow" advocate, known as an activist in such lobbies as the Inter-American Press Association and the World Press Freedom Committee, took a position which is clearly less critical of the final Declaration than the opinion of leading organs of the U.S. journalistic community, and which in fact is joining the official line of the U.S. government in defense of the Declaration as a kind of human rights instrument.

If the reaction to the Declaration took different lines within the same libertarian approach, it is not surprising that the appreciation of the outcome as viewed in the USSR and other socialist countries was in radical contrast to most of what was presented in the U.S.—to the extent that one could hardly any longer recognize the same Declaration behind the different reviews. An outspoken *Soviet evaluation* is provided by the executive secretary of the USSR Commission for Unesco, Yuri Kashlev, who paraphrased the USSR statement in the Programme Commission on 22 November (see Appendix 20) by characterizing the Declaration as "the first instrument in the history of international relations which clearly and directly draws the attention of the mass media to their responsibilities for peace and friendship and the independence of peoples." (Kashlev's review of the Declaration and some of its press polemics is reproduced in full as Appendix 22.)

As far as the *"Third World" advocates* are concerned, their appreciation took yet another approach, which, in conformity with how things developed during the drafting process, was closer to the overall approach of the socialist countries than that of the West. A typical example of this orientation can be found in the writings of D. R. Mankekar of India, the Chairman of the Coordination Committee of the Press Agencies of Non-Aligned Countries in 1977–1979 (in which capacity he participated in the diplomacy in 1978, as noted above). In a review of the final drafting stage and its outcome (reproduced as Appendix 23) Mankekar concluded: "By adopting the Declaration on media at Unesco, the world has laid the foundations and ground rules for orderly international operations of the media in consonance with modern conditions created by the electronic revolution. The world has thus taken a big step towards the establishment of the New World Information Order for which the developing countries have been agitating, and given recognition to the latter's grievances and demands in the sphere of media."

Consequently, in its final consensus form, the Declaration contained such a variety of material, put together in such a loose manner and in so vague a compromise language, that it was possible to use the instrument for defending and justifying even diametrically opposed political positions. Yet the text of the Declaration, if taken conscientiously and not just as a reservoir of tactical elements for arbitrary use, does constitute a definite orientation. We shall have a closer look into this orientation in Chapter 3, and the remaining chapters—in fact, the present book as a whole attempts at exposing the largely implicit message of the Declaration.

The story of the shaping of the Declaration can best be concluded by pointing out the most obvious lessons which emerge from the history of its preparation.

First, at various stages of its drafting the Declaration has been at least as much a *symptom of overall socio-economic-political tendencies* as it has been an instrument relating to the mass media. Thus the controversies that accumulated stemmed not only from irreconcilable conflicts between different schools of thought about the press but equally or even more from the general contradictions in so-called East-West and North-South problems, i.e. *global problems*.

Second, it can be said that the adoption of the Declaration in 1978, after such a troublesome history, was a remarkable demonstration of the fact that *international cooperation and even détente continued as a significant force* in overcoming political and ideological divisions and in directing the international community according to some *universally shared values*.

Third, this overall perspective notwithstanding, the case of the Declaration provides a convincing illustration of the fact that *information in general, and the mass media in particular, have played a more and more important role in international relations.* Information issues occupy an increasingly central place in social processes, national and international.

Fourth, within the limits determined by such "general laws," *much depends on chance and other specific factors* which enter the process, such as the choice of persons to represent countries or to advise the Director-General. Even simple timing of events may have crucial consequences. For example, the history of the Declaration could have been quite different had the "zionism-racism" resolution not been adopted by the UN General Assembly just before the government expert meeting at Unesco.

Fifth, *Unesco has operated as a catalyst only,* by mainly reflecting, in a passive way, the above-mentioned socio-economic forces. Moreover, the Secretariat of Unesco has more often than not influenced the process of the preparation in favor of a Western strategy by doing away with normative consideration of the contents of the mass media. Thus it would be both groundless and misleading to characterize Unesco as a source and base for revolutionary tendencies challenging Western positions.

Finally, the *role of the press and its professional organizations has been parasitic,* far from how a vigilant and independent "watchdog of democracy" is supposed to behave according to Western journalistic ideals. Professional attention was drawn to the issues of international media policies only after they had been politicizedthe professionals were coopted by a political mobilization and used as instruments in an ideological struggle. The press coverage, particularly in the West, of the preparation of the Declaration provides an illuminating example of how the supposedly independent mass media in fact operate as extensions of certain political forces.

3

The Contents:
An Examination
of the Text

The text of the Declaration (reproduced in Appendix 1) is composed of two parts, as is customary for such instruments: an introductory "preamble", and the "operative" articles. In most declarations and conventions the preamble is no more than a short formality, introducing the main, operative part. However, in this Declaration the two parts are approximately the same length.

THE PREAMBLE

The preamble of the Mass Media Declaration is particularly important. It lists many other international instruments and thus creates linkages between the Declaration and the existing framework of international law and politics. Furthermore, all parts of a declaration, as with a normal resolution, have equal legal weight. Only in internationally binding treaties do the articles carry more legal significance. Consequently, it is essential that the preamble be included with the text when the Declaration is reprinted for any purpose, including bringing it to the attention of journalists.

It is indeed no surprise that, during the negotiations, discussion of the preamble resulted in almost as many problems as did the articles of the text. In the 1975–1976 draft preamble, reference was made to the UN resolution concerning zionism as a form of racism, and this became one of the primary causes of the large scale international controversy to which the Declaration gave rise. Another indication of the importance of this particular preamble is that, in the final text, explicit references to the new information order have been placed in the preamble and not in the operative part.

It is significant not only which international instruments are listed in the preamble and how their contents are characterized, but also which international instruments relating to information have been "forgotten" in the preamble. Both of the conventions which were adopted exclusively with a view to international sphere of mass communication are missing: the 1936 convention on broadcasting and the 1952 convention on the international right of correction. (A closer examination of these documents will be made in Part 2.) It is obvious that these have been deleted because, on the one hand, they are not very well known among professionals in the mass media, and, on the other, because they have not been particularly welcomed in Western political circles, as the obligations contained in these conventions are rather straightforward.

Neither can one find in the final list of instruments the 1972 Unesco Declaration on direct satellite broadcasting. This instrument, which in the early 1970s was understood as a victory for the developing and socialist countries which were challenging the Western "free flow" position, was now, half a decade later, no longer insisted upon by any significant group. The reason for a decline of interest in this Declaration was the fact that the UN Outer Space Committee had at the same time progressed in its drafting of an international convention on direct satellite transmissions, bringing it to a stage where the earlier Unesco Declaration was considered politically outdated—especially as far as compromises surrounding the free flow of information were concerned.

From the viewpoint of the freedom of information issue, it is significant in this context that, along with the 1948 Universal Declaration of Human Rights, the 1966 International Covenant on Civil and Political Rights was included. In fact, the latter (convention) receives greater weight than the former (declaration), especially because the Covenant introduces essential specifications to the freedom of information concept as understood in the Universal Declaration (see Part 2). The same parallel listing of the two instruments is repeated in Article XI, which indicates again that one of the significant compromises relating to the Declaration was the combining of the somewhat Western-biased 1948 Universal Declaration with the politically more balanced 1966 Covenant.

The first two paragraphs of the preamble "recall" the Constitution of Unesco. These quotations from the Constitution are significant, not only because they form an introduction to the Declaration and because they are taken from Unesco's most fundamental instrument (drafted and adopted in 1945 by a predominantly Western group of nations), but, above all, because the Constitution contains several principles relating directly to the mass media. First, it is made clear that the overriding purpose of Unesco is to "contribute to peace and security," the well-known phrase "free flow of ideas by word and image" being subordinated to this purpose. Second, the sixth preambular paragraph of the Constitution reminds us that the Member States not only believe "in the free exchange of ideas and knowledge" (note that the phrase "free flow" is not used here), but "are agreed and determined. . .to employ" the means of mass communication for the purposes cited. One may wonder why it was so difficult for some (who presumably subscribe to Unesco's Constitution) to accept the phrase "use of the mass media" in earlier drafts—even without reference to the States. Third, the Constitution advocates an informational role for the mass media, whereby they should further "mutual understanding" between peoples and "a truer and more perfect knowledge of each other's lives." This, together with a dedication to "objective truth," makes it clear that it is perfectly in line with the letter and spirit of Unesco to set normative standards for the contents of the mass media, provided that such standards are in harmony with the humanistic line advocated by the Constitution.

THE ARTICLES

In the articles, the *traditional libertarian concept of freedom of information* is strongly evident. For example, Articles I and II contain the idea that communication, free of all restrictions and obligations, as such, contributes to "the strengthening of peace and international understanding" (see more on this relationship in Chapter 7). It is true that the wording of Article I, paragraph 1, is ambiguous. The term "vital factor" does not necessarily mean the same as *condition* or *prerequisite;* rather it can be understood as *positive effect,* which is a quite balanced way to examine the relationship between communication and peace.

The same two articles also embody the idea of value pluralism in speaking of "the extent that the information reflects different aspects of the subject dealt with" and the "diversity of the sources and the means of information." On the other hand, the concepts of accuracy and objectivity are also presented, which is in itself significant for, despite their attempts to do so, the Western nations were not able to exclude completely these provisions specifying the nature of information. Here, however, the demand for objectivity lies more upon the receiver of information than upon those shaping and transmitting it.

The veracity of information and, in general, the principal questions of journalism, have been handled much more boldly in other instruments than in this Declaration. In this respect the Declaration is clearly slanted towards the West. In the same way, the Declaration can be said to be leaning one-sidedly towards the West on many of the points which speak directly of journalists (Articles II and IX). On the basis of this Declaration, journalists are guaranteed freedom of information, even special protection. These sections do not directly express obligations for journalists, but obliquely make clear that the prerequisite for this freedom and protection is to act in accordance with the principles and in the spirit of the Declaration.

On the other hand, it should be noted that the title of the very Declaration expressly sets out *obligations concerning the content of the mass media,* and thus directs the Declaration politically along the lines promoted by the socialist and developing countries. Although journalists are not specifically mentioned in all of the sections of the Declaration, it is clear that obligations relating to the content of the mass media (e.g., Article II, paragraph 3, and Article III, paragraph 1) are intended for them as well. If, in the above, there is cause to view the wording relating to journalists as leaning slightly to the West, here we can note a similar slant to the East.

An interesting detail in respect to communication policy is contained in Article II, paragraph 2, the final sentence of which proposes that "peoples and individuals" participate more actively in the production of the mass media. In other words, a position is taken supporting the kinds of *democratization of mass communication,* such as "open channel" programs and "worker correspondent" reports, that include the perspective of the common man.

All in all, the Declaration is *carefully balanced* between different political, professional, and even philosophical views. Thus, the result does not necessarily represent the entire viewpoint of any single orientation, and in details it may shift, not only into obscure and meaningless phrases, but also into precarious positions. One example of this is contained in Article III, paragraph 2, which states that racism and apartheid are *"inter alia* spawned by prejudice and ignorance." Taken literally, this is undoubtedly true; psychology does have a part in the genesis of these extreme forms of discrimination. But when, in the same connection, no mention is made of the social structures (particularly in South Africa) which maintain racism and apartheid, and when one considers how severely condemned under international law the phenomenon in question is, one cannot avoid concluding that, in this case, the developing countries have abandoned their principles.

In the same way it can be said that the socialist countries have abandoned their principles in Article I, in which the freedom of information can be understood as a prerequisite for strengthening peace and the prohibition of war propaganda. It is difficult, however, to find a point in the articles which can be said, in the same way, to be a rejection of principles deeply held by Western nations. Thus the articles do not set out obligations for the mass media and journalists directly, and urge them to strengthen peace, etc. Instead, several of the sections speak of the positive influence of the mass media, while, in fact, recognizing only a certain connection between the mass media and the content objectives in question.

But in this respect the Declaration is delicately balanced. For example, in Article III, paragraph 3, the positive influence of the mass media is subordinated in a way to the objectives expressed in the title, because this influence is exercised "with a view to these objectives." In Article III, paragraph 2, the mass media do not only "contribute to" certain objectives, but are also involved in "promoting the formulation by States of the policies best able to promote the reduction of international tension and the peaceful and equitable settlement of international disputes." Although this is again more of a recognition of a state of affairs than the setting of a standard, such a linkage of the mass media to the basic structure of international relations is very significant.

The strongest formulations setting standards for the content of the mass media are found in connection with the education of young people (Article IV), the right of reply (Article V), and a new kind of international economic order (Article VII; note that here this matter is not presented as concisely as in paragraph 7 of the preamble). It is also true that Article X, paragraph 1, contains a rather forceful obligation "to create and maintain throughout the world the conditions which make it possible for the organizations and persons professionally involved in the dissemination of information to achieve the objectives of this Declaration."

If by "the objectives of this Declaration" is meant the strivings expressed in the title—and this is the only logical conclusion—a corresponding obligation for professionals in the information field and their organizations is entailed. Although the point is vaguely put by speaking of the creation of favorable conditions and their maintenance, the basic idea remains; the achievement of the objectives of the Declaration is the task of organizations and individuals professionally involved in the dissemination of information. The obligation thus extends to journalists, but not to them alone. It is also the responsibility of those not specifically named, who create and maintain such conditions.

In addition to setting overall principles relating to the content of the mass media (as expressed in the title), the Declaration also spells out (in Article VIII) special obligations for the mass media and those who participate in the professional training of journalists—the Declaration is intended to be reflected in professional codes of ethics. This subject is dealt with in more detail in Part 3.

Article VIII contains the only passage which directly addresses the responsibility of communicators. In earlier drafts, the word "responsibility" appeared frequently, but in the final stage of the negotiations it was removed from many passages because of pressure from the Western countries. It can be concluded that the official West was not prepared to endorse what is known as the social responsibility theory of the press, a doctrine which, in fact, was born out of the libertarian tradition. Rather, the West preferred to hold fast to a conservative tradition. Yet it was not possible to push this line through in a pure state, as speaking simply of the content of journalism violated the principles of libertarianism, at least in its extreme form.

Although reading the Declaration in close detail reveals many interesting matters, it can hardly be considered especially beneficial in terms of practical journalism. As will be shown below in Part 2, many of the subjects expressed in such a twisted and ambivalent manner in this text are to be found in other international instruments in a form more satisfying to mass media professionals. For example, another declaration approved at the same Unesco General Conference in 1978 deals much more clearly and in more detail with the dissemination of information on the race questions. Also, the Unesco recommendation of 1974 on international education serves as an excellent guide to journalism, and is in many respects more outspoken than the Declaration on the Mass Media.

We may conclude that the Declaration, as such, serves the development of journalism and the mass media *more as a general means of arousing the observance of obligations under international law than as a finished guideline.* Therefore, it is particularly important to follow up a study of the Declaration by examining international law and professional ethics along the lines proposed in Part 2 and 3.

THE SIGNIFICANCE OF THE TEXT

Politically, legally, and philosophically, it is significant that the Declaration is the first document authorized by the UN system which not only touches upon a particular aspect of communication but which broadly defines the tasks, rights, and responsibilities of the mass media, linking them into a composite whole—including *duties and responsibilities.* It not only lays down general and abstract principles for mass media activities and functions, but also sets *standards for media content*—something that has been almost taboo within the Western libertarian tradition, but which is central to the demands of developing and socialist countries. A vital aspect of the Declaration is that it places the mass media—their contents, rights, and responsibilities—within a general *framework of interstate relations and international law.* The preambular paragraphs preceding the Articles are of crucial importance in this respect.

Consequently, the Declaration was a political "victory" for developing countries and socialist countries, a step forward for them, although a small step compared to what was once intended. Correspondingly, for the Western world it meant a withdrawal—although, for them, just a small step backward.

These are the conclusions which can be drawn from an examination of the Declaration from an overall *political* perspective. If the examination is done from a *professional* perspective, it is difficult or impossible to say which side has "won." Yet, it can be said that the Declaration constitutes a qualitatively new step in the regulation of communication under international law, and this also holds true for the profession of journalism.

II

International Law
and the Mass Media

One of the most significant consequences of the Mass Media Declaration of Unesco will probably be the development of what can be called "international law of communications." This "law," expressing relationships between communications, including journalism, on the one hand, and the principles and rules of international law on the other, has to a large extent been discovered and inspired by the Unesco Declaration. Paradoxically, such a general perspective is far from the issues spelled out by the Declaration and those debated throughout its drafting. Yet the perspective of international law may turn out to be revolutionary in the long run because of the influence it can have on fundamental thinking on the role of journalism—a much greater influence than over-politicized controversies can have.

Thus far, the international law of communications remains an emerging and poorly articulated field of study; indeed, the scientific and professional communities might be accused of neglecting the consideration of communications in terms of international law. Therefore, it is not possible to give as clear-cut answers as would be desirable to questions that must be posed in considering the relationship between communications and international law. What follows—indeed, in large part, this entire book—should be considered as a contribution to a much needed field of study.

Naturally, there are a number of aspects of the international law of communications, such as post and telecommunication; transfer of educational, scientific, and cultural materials; freedom of information; and the content of communication. The approach of the following five chapters focuses on the last of these, international standards concerned with the performance of the mass media and, therefore, with their contents. Thus, it is not our intent to discuss the entire field of the international law of communications. For example, it is not our ambition to solve the ever-present problem of freedom of information. On the other hand, this general field of study is so poorly developed that even such an inventory-type overview of internationally determined standards for the mass media as is contained in these chapters cannot be found elsewhere, at least not in international literature addressed to journalists and students of journalism.

The following chapters, first drafted in Finnish, in 1979, for a textbook prepared for students at the University of Tampere, was the result of cooperation between the author of this book, representing journalism (Nordenstreng), and a colleague from international law, who also has an interest in journalism (Hannikainen). In fact, this cooperation was initiated by the Unesco Declaration. The colleagues were first brought together by the national debate on the Declaration, which stimulated this interdisciplinary approach to the international law of communications. Chapters 4 and 6 were written by Hannikainen, in consultation with Nordenstreng. Chapters 5, 7, and 8 were written by Nordenstreng, in consultation with Hannikainen.

After a discussion of international law as a regulator of international relations (Chapter 4) and an overall inventory of standards relating to the contents of the mass media (Chapter 5), we single out so-called "war propaganda" (Chapter 6) as a particularly controversial area, which, however, has a well established tradition in terms of internationally recognized regulation. It should be noted that incitement to aggressive war is at the very center of international relations. Finally, Chapters 7 and 8 consider a number of other standards, both at the international and national level, that are especially important in relation to the Declaration.

4

International Law
as a Regulator of
International Relations*

International law, in its present sense, is the result of a relatively late development. Christian states in Europe began to apply the present-type of international law in their relations during the latter part of the Middle Ages. Hugo Grotius, a Dutch theologian and statesman, has been called "the founder of international law." His book, *De jure belli ac pacis,* dealing mostly with war, was published in 1625. At that time there were so many states in Europe that the need for international law had become evident, and at the end of the 18th century the European states considered themselves to be bound by international law.[1]

According to Grotius, the fundamental principles of international law were eternal, unchanging, and independent of the will of states. Their basis was the divine order and the harmony of nature; the result was *natural law.* Grotius did not, however, limit himself to natural law but thought that there were also international rules, which were established by states and were dependent on their will. In this sense he differed from most of his predecessors who relied emphatically on natural law.

The natural law doctrine, based on the divine order, was predominant throughout the Middle Ages. In opposition to natural law, *a school of positivist legal thought* emerged in the 17th century. Its leading principle was the decisive importance of the practice of states.

The positivist doctrine acquired predominance in the 19th century and superseded the natural law doctrine. The rise of the nationalist ideology and the birth of national states created favorable circumstances for the advancement of the positivist doctrine. The emphasis on the omnipotence of national sovereignty often led to extremes. Not even the legal interest of other states could do much to restrict a sovereign state's rights. Only such rules as were consented to by states could be international legal rules. The positivist doctrine has retained its predominance in the 20th century, but its extremes have been ground away.

* This chapter was written by Lauri Hannikainen.

[1]For the history of international law, see, for example, the following:
A. Nussbaum, *A Concise History of the Law of Nations,* New York: Macmillan, 1954.
W.E. Hall, *A Treatise on International Law,* 7th ed., Oxford: Clarendon Press, 1917 (or the 6th, 1909, or 8th, 1924, ed.)
R.P. Anand, *New States and International Law,* New Delhi: Vikas Publishing House, 1972.

The greatest weakness of 19th century international law was the lack of the prohibition of aggressive war. This lack, together with the oppression of the peoples in colonies contributed to the weakness of international law. Among the accomplishments of 19th century international law were the regulation of international sea areas, the suppression of slave trade and slavery, as well as the limitation of the most horrifying means of warfare.

The 19th century international order broke down in World War I. After the war the League of Nations was established as a framework for the international community. The purpose was to establish a central international organization to be responsible for the maintenance of peace and to regulate the organized conduct of international relations. The efforts of the League were seriously weakened by the rise of aggressive fascism in Europe in the 1930s. The United Nations (UN), organized after the Second World War, has been much more successful than was the League of Nations.

SUBJECTS OF INTERNATIONAL LAW

The main objective of international law is to *regulate interstate relations*. Traditionally, *states* have been subjects of international law, i.e., bearers of international rights and obligations—between whom international law is applied.[2] Also, during the latter half of this century, *international governmental organizations* have assumed many functions which belong to the subject of international law. To some extent *national liberation movements* and other insurgent organizations, which have been recognized as belligerent parties, have been acknowledged as bearers of certain international rights and obligations.

Individuals (and non-governmental organizations, corporations, etc.), as such, are not proper subjects of international law; they have only a very limited international legal personality. International law has established direct obligations for individuals by placing responsibilities on those guilty of international crimes as defined by international instruments and customs. International law has also established rights for the benefit of individuals, but usually individuals lack procedural capacity to bring claims before international tribunals. Only under certain treaties, such as human rights conventions, have persons living in the ratifying states the right to legal proceedings in international bodies.

One of the basic principles in international law is that of *sovereign equality* of states. The concept of *sovereignty* means that states have an ex-

---

[2]On the subjects of international law, see, for example the following treatises: G. von Glahn, *Law Among Nations*, 3rd ed., New York: Macmillan, 1976; M. Sorensen (Ed.), *Manual of Public International Law*, New York: St. Martin's Press, 1968.

clusive jurisdiction within their territory and that, usually, a state is bound only by those norms to which it has given its consent. In fact, a central aim of international law is to determine the jurisdiction of states so that they can look after their international interests adequately without injuring the rights of other states. As far as *equality* is concerned, it presupposes that, in principle, all states have the same rights and obligations and that each state must respect the rights of other states.

International law is different from *domestic (internal) law.* In the latter there are organs of legislation, execution, and jurisdiction, and an effective system of sanctions controls the observance of domestic laws. International law does not have a similar division of organs or a similarly effective system of sanctions, although various means of control and of sanction may be applied with the UN acting as a supreme coordinator. Many international conventions provide control systems and procedures for the settlement of disputes.

Among sanctions we may note the enforcement measures vested in the UN Security Council—including the use of armed force, expulsion of a state from international organizations, economic blockade, interruption of traffic and communication, etc. States may independently apply sanctions (to a limited extent) against a state, which has injured their rights, although the practice has evolved towards the concentration of enforcement measures at the United Nations and other international organizations.

Contemporary international law has been called international law of *peaceful coexistence.* Basic principles of international law, to be discussed below, have established for minimum obligations of peaceful coexistence for every state. States are not allowed to deviate from the basic principles, except in a positive direction, i.e., towards greater peaceful international cooperation.

BASIC PRINCIPLES OF CONTEMPORARY INTERNATIONAL LAW

The basic principles of international law are principles of a general character establishing *obligations and rights for all states.* They incorporate the main purposes placed upon international law by the international community, and/or express the basic features of the structure of international law. Even though these principles are general in character, they, nevertheless, establish basic legal obligations upon states. The basic principles constitute the fundamental foundations for the conduct of states; they must be observed in all domains of interstate relations—including international communications. The leading sources of the basic principles are the UN Charter, other multilateral conventions, international custom, and declarations of the UN General Assembly.

The basic principles of contemporary international law as summarized from various sources can be listed as follows:[3]

Principles Relating to Sovereign Equality of States and Self-determination of Peoples

Respect for Sovereign Equality of States. According to the domestic and territorial elements of this principle, a state has exclusive jurisdiction within its territory and has the right, without outside interference, to choose and develop its socio-political system and decide upon its laws. This principle also includes an international dimension whereby a state has the right to equal communications across national boundaries. The general rule is that a state is only bound by those rules of international law to which it has given its consent. (However, the basic principles and peremptory norms—*jus cogens*—of international law are binding on all states, including both existing and new-born states.) States must respect the territory and the rights of other states.

Respect of Self-Determination of Peoples. According to this principle, the peoples have the right, without alien interference, to determine their political status and to pursue, as they wish, their political, economic, social, and cultural development.

A forceful extinction of the right of self-determination through alien occupation or colonial domination, or through a minority regime which exerts racial oppression against the majority of the population, is a crime under international law. Such an oppressed people has the right to pursue its self-determination by all means and to receive external assistance to this effect. After gaining its independence, a people has the right to determine its own socio-political system.

Obligation of Each State to Refrain from Interference in the Internal Affairs of Other States. Neither the UN nor other states have the right to intervene in matters which are essentially within the domestic jurisdiction of a state. Yet, this does not prejudice the application of enforcement measures sanctioned by the UN Security Council in compliance with the Charter.

---

[3]See, for example:

G. Herczegh, *General Principles of Law and the International Legal Order,* Budapest: Akadémiai Kiadó, 1969.

B.G. zu Dohna, *Die Grundprinzipien des Völkerrechts über die freundschaftlichen Beziehungen und die Zusammenarbeit zwischen den Staaten,* West-Berlin: Duncker and Humblot, 1973.

M.K. Nawatz (Ed.), *Essays on International Law in Honour of K. Krishna Rao,* Leyden: A.W. Sijthoff, 1976.

M. Sahovic (Ed.), *Principles of International Law Concerning Friendly Relations and Cooperation among States,* Belgrade: 1972. (Published also by Oceana Publications, Dobbs Ferry, New York, 1972.)

G. Tunkin (Ed.), *Contemporary International Law,* Moscow: Progress Publishers, 1969.

The solid foundations of the domestic jurisdiction of states are the sovereign equality of states and the self-determination of peoples. By virtue of these principles, inter alia, the foundations of the political, economic, cultural, administrative, and legal systems, as well as the system of basic civil rights, fall within the domain of domestic jurisdiction, unless a state has entered into specific obligations towards some other state.

States must refrain from all measures which could be considered as attempts to pressure another state to a certain type of decision in matters which are within its domestic jurisdiction. This rule is not meant, however, to prevent the normal conduct of relations between states. Also, more general statements about the inadequacies of a special socio-political system do not constitute intervention as long as they are not directed in an accusing form against some specific state.

Principles Relating to Maintenance of International Peace and Security

Obligation of States to Refrain from the Threat or Use of Force against Another State. In compliance with this principle, states shall refrain from the threat or use of force against the territorial integrity or political independence of any state. This principle is one of the cornerstones of international law. This principle and the related prohibition of war propaganda is discussed in the chapter on war propaganda.

Obligation of States to Settle Their International Disputes through Peaceful Means. In pursuance of this principle, states must settle their international disputes through peaceful means in such a manner that international peace and security and justice will not be endangered. States must not resort to any measures which might aggravate the situation or endanger international peace. The UN Security Council has the right to take measures for the settlement of a dispute which threatens international peace. This principle does not oblige states to eliminate their political differences. States only have the obligation to live in peaceful co-existence, so as not to let their differences endanger international peace and security.

The Right of States to Self-Defence against Armed Aggression. Pursuant to this principle, the right of states for self-defence against an armed agression entitles a state and the states which come to its assistance to armed counter-measures even outside their territory, until the Security Council of the UN has taken adequate measures. In the exercise of their right of self-defence, states shall not violate the rights of third countries. In the absence of an armed aggression a state may not resort to acts of armed self-defence outside of its own territory.

Principles Relating to Respect for Human Rights

Respect for Human Rights. In accordance with this principle, each state has a general obligation to respect human rights in its territory and to cooperate internationally for the promotion of human rights. The application of this principle is hampered by the uncertainty of the contents of several human rights that are considered universal. However, the minimum obligations of the states are known in most cases. The principle has limits also because the implementation of human rights falls mainly within the domestic jurisdiction of states. The strict obligation of every state not to commit crimes against humanity, and other flagrant and massive violations of human rights, gives more concrete content to the principle.

Respect for Humanitarian Law in Wars and Armed Conflicts. In compliance with this principle the parties to an armed conflict may not resort to any means for the purpose of injuring the enemy but are restricted by the rules of humanitarian law concerning the physical protection of individuals and basic human rights. These rules were originally established to regulate international conflicts, but today many of them are applicable also in armed conflicts not of an international character.

Principles Relating to Freedom and Use of Common Benefit of International Maritime Areas and of Space

Freedom and Use for Common Benefit of Maritime Areas and of Space Beyond the Jurisdiction of States. In accordance with the principle of the freedom of the high seas and of the air space above it, no parts of these areas are subjects to national appropriation by a claim of sovereignty of any state. Ships of all states may make use of the high seas for navigation and their aircraft may use the air space for their passage. All states have the right to exercise fishing on the high seas and to lay submarine cables, pipelines, etc.

All states have an equal right to use and explore the sea-bed. The deep-sea bed constitutes a common heritage of mankind; its natural resources shall be used for the common benefit of mankind, particularly for the benefit of the developing countries.

Each state has the right to explore and exploit outer space, but states may not occupy any part of it. Space must be used in such a way that is in harmony with the maintenance of international peace and security. States may not place weapons of mass destruction in outer space, on celestial bodies, or on the sea bed. States bear the responsibility for the acts committed in space by both governmental and non-governmental bodies under their jurisdiction.

Principles Relating to Protection of Environment and to Rational Use of Natural Resources

Obligation of States for Protection of Environment and for Rational Use of Natural Resources. The origins of this principle are the principles of the sovereign equality of states and of the use for common benefit of international areas. According to this principle it is the obligation of each state to insure that no damage is inflicted within its jurisdiction upon the environment of other states or of international areas.

Principles Relating to Development of Cooperation between States

The Right of Each State to Take Part in International Cooperation and the Obligation of Each State to International Cooperation for the Settlement of International Problems. In accordance with the principle of cooperation each state has the right to take part in international intercourse and cooperation. Every state has the obligation to cooperate in the implementation of the basic principles of international law, in the promotion of disarmament, and in the furtherance of economic and social progress in the developing countries. The principle of equal sovereignty must be observed in this cooperation. States have the obligation to refrain from acts which obviously would impede the attainment of the objectives of cooperation.

Principles Relating to the Basic Features of the Structure of International Law

Several of the foregoing principles are of critical importance from the viewpoint of the structure of international law—especially the principle of sovereign equality. One principle has thus far not been touched upon; a principle which in many important instruments has been regarded as being one of the basic principles.

Obligation of Each State to Fulfill its Commitments. The Final Act of the Conference on Security and Cooperation in Europe (1975) gives a pertinent definition of the principle: " . . .states will fulfill in good faith their obligations under international law, both those obligations arising from the generally recognized principles and rules of international law and those obligations arising from treaties or other agreements, in conformity with international law, to which they are parties . . ."

SOURCES OF INTERNATIONAL LAW

In accordance with Article 38 of the Statute of the International Court of Justice, the main sources of international law are international treaties, international customary law, and the general principles of law recognized by civilized nations.[4] According to the same article, the subsidiary sources are "judicial decisions and the teachings of the most highly qualified publicists of the various nations."

There are different types of international *treaties*.[5] There are well-nigh universal treaties, such as the Charter of the UN and the charters of several specialized organizations of the UN; covenants and conventions which have been ratified by a majority of states; and regional or bilateral agreements.

A state usually becomes a party to a treaty by ratifying it. The signing, which is done prior to ratification, does not mean that the state has obligated itself to observe the treaty. A state must observe treaties to which it is a party in good faith. The consequence of a transgression of a treaty brings about the responsibility for the breach and the obligation of reparation. In general, a state cannot withdraw from its treaty obligations except with the consent of the other parties to the treaty.

International law had traditionally been *customary law*. The customs have developed and assumed an obligatory character over a long period of time. In 1927, judge Negulesco of the Permanent Court of International Justice stated in Jurisdiction of the European Commission of the Danube case that a custom presupposes the existence of an immemorial practice.

The coming into being of a custom presumes two conditions:[6] 1) that a uniform or nearly uniform inter-state practice has evolved, and 2) that states feel that they have a legal obligation to observe such a practice (opinio juris). A custom is often said to have evolved through an inter-

---

[4]General analyses on the sources of international law can be found, for example, in the following treatises:

I. Brownlie, *Principles of Public International Law*, Oxford: Clarendon Press, 1979.

M. Sørensen (Ed.), Manual of Public International Law, New York: St. Martin's Press, 1968.

G. Tunkin, *Theory of International Law*, Cambridge: Harvard University Press, 1974.

H. Waldock, "General Course of International Law," *Recueil des Cours*, Académie de Droit International, 1962, Vol. II.

[5]On the law of treaties, see: I.M. Sinclair, *The Vienna Convention on the Law of Treaties*, Dobbs Ferry, New York: Oceana Publications, 1973.

[6]On customary law, see: H.W.A. Thirlway, *International Customary Law and Codification*, Leyden: A.W. Sijthoff, 1972.

state *tacit agreement;* a practice begins to develop, it is not explicitly opposed, and as time passes it comes to be considered binding. If any state from time to time lets it be known that it does not consider a custom in the process of formation to be binding on it, this custom, in general, does not bind the state concerned.

A good example of a silent agreement is provided by foreign radio broadcasting; rules have developed in practice without treaties. A different example is provided by broadcasting of television programs over satellites; there is a great need of regulation by a multilateral treaty, because states have not reached silent agreement through practice.

In contemporary international law the formation of a custom has been considerably expedited. States take part in the work of international organizations and in various treaty negotiations, etc. The statements and measures of states in themselves constitute a part of international practice and bear evidence of the existence of opinio juris. In 1969, the International Court of Justice made a statement in the North Sea Continental Shelf case that a customary rule may come into being quickly if the state practice is extensive and virtually uniform and reveals a general recognition that a rule of law or legal obligation is involved. In the domain of space law, e.g., customary law developed rapidly in the 1960s when the need for it was pressing.

Only some rules of customary law are universal. Other customs are generally, regionally or locally binding.

Even if treaties have gained additional importance at the expense of custom, customary law still has significance. Universal international law, binding on all states, comes into existence through the process of customary law. There are no completely universal treaties, even if the Charter of the UN is almost universal. States, which are not parties to a treaty, may become bound through custom by the main rules included in the treaty. Today most rules of universal international law evolve through the interaction of treaty and custom.

The general principles of law recognized by the civilized nations have remained in a secondary position. In the present context they are understood as principles which are applied in all of the most important types of domestic legal systems and which can be applied in international law as well. The International Court of Justice has been cautious in applying them and has not used them as a basis for decision. Some of them may contain elements of natural law, and, as far as international relations are concerned, are inapplicable unless they have the consent of states.

The Statute of the International Court of Justice does not include the *declarations and resolutions adopted by international organizations* as a source of international law, although they have proven to be important for the development of international law. Formally, the declarations and resolutions adopted by the General Assembly of the UN or of its specialized agencies (including Unesco) are not legally binding on states, they are merely recommendations. The following points, nevertheless, render them of considerable juridical significance:

- if a declaration or a resolution has been adopted unanimously, and
- if the text deals with rules of international law or with the basic principles in a certain domain, and has been worded in a legally obligatory form (words like "states shall refrain from" are used), or
- if a declaration or a resolution is intended to interpret or clarify a stipulation of the UN Charter or of another multi-lateral convention, one can speak of a unanimously adopted clarification of an existing rule, and
- if states subsequently refer to a declaration or to a resolution as an important and binding instrument, and generally observe it.[7]

Thus a declaration or resolution may become a part of state practice and may express the conviction of states of an existing or evolving rule of customary law. In this way declarations and resolutions have accelerated the evolution of the rules of customary law and the universalization of their obligatory force.

The 1970 UN General Assembly Declaration on Principles of International Law concerning Friendly Relations and Cooperation among States in accordance with the Charter of the United Nations (GA Res. 2625, (XXV)) is a good example of this process. First, it was adopted without opposition, second, it gives a more explicit definition of the seven basic legal principles of the UN Charter, third, its text has been written in a binding form, fourth, it states that it constitutes a milestone in the development of international law, and fifth, it declares that the defined seven principles are basic principles in international law. Likewise, the 1960 Decolonization Declaration (GA Res. 1514 (XV)) and the 1974 Definition of Aggression (GA Res. 3314 (XXIX)) are remarkable instruments pertaining to international law.

On the other hand, the Universal Declaration of Human Rights of 1948, which has been strongly advocated, deals with aspirations and moral obligations rather than with legal obligations. Hence, the central role in the international development of human rights has been allotted to two extensive UN human rights convenants (both adopted in 1966); one concerning economic, social and cultural rights, another concerning

[7]On the legal significance of declarations and resolutions of international organizations, see, for example:
O.Y. Asamoah, *The Legal Significance of the Declarations of the General Assembly of the United Nations*, The Hague: M. Nijhoff, 1966.
J. Castaneda, *Legal Effects of the United Nations Resolutions*, New York: Columbia University Press, 1969.

civil and political rights. Their definitions are more juridical and more specific than those found in the Universal Declaration.

Declarations are resolutions, by which states formulate principles of special importance; but formally they are no more obligatory than ordinary resolutions. Ordinary resolutions may also contain legally important stipulations.

5

International Instruments
Setting Standards
for the Mass Media

How does international law relate specifically to the mass media? This question has been addressed from various viewpoints in a number of academic works concerning freedom of information, foreign propaganda, and the so-called "ideological struggle." Perhaps the most outstanding authority on this question is Hilding Eek, Emeritus Professor of International Law at the University of Stockholm. In the early 1950s Eek worked as a UN expert on freedom of information, and in the middle of 1970 he served as a prime consultant to Unesco during the first steps of the preparation of the Mass Media Declaration.[1] Other academic contributions to this problem include works by the U. S. experts Leo Gross, John Whitton, Arthur Larson, James Martin, and Phillip Davison,[2] as well as works by the Soviet experts Georgi Arbatov and Yuri Kolossov,[3] and GDR expert Wolfgang Kleinwaechter.[4] Further

[1] See H. Eek, "Principles Governing the Use of the Mass Media as Defined by the United Nations and Unesco," in K. Nordenstreng & H.I. Schiller (Eds.), *National Sovereignty and International Communication,* Norwood, New Jersey: Ablex Publishing Corporation, 1979; and an earlier work, *Freedom of Information as a Project of International Legislation,* Uppsala Universities Arsskrift 1953:6, Acta Universitatis Upsaliensis, 1953. Eek has also contributed to the Unesco report *Historical Background of the Mass Media Declaration,* New Communication Order, No. 9, Paris, 1982.

[2] See L. Gross, "Some International Law Aspects of the Freedom of Information and the Right to Communicate" (1977), and J. B. Whitton, "Hostile International Propaganda and International Law" (1971), both published in Nordenstreng & Schiller, *op. cit.* in note 1 above. See also J. B. Whitton & A. Larson, *Propaganda—Towards Disarmament in the War of Words,* Dobbs Ferry, New York: Oceana Publications, 1964; L. J. Martin, *International Propaganda, Its Legal and Diplomatic Control,* Minneapolis, Minnesota: University of Minnesota Press, 1958; and W. P. Davison, *Mass Communication and Conflict Resolution: The Role of Information Media in the Advancement of International Understanding,* New York: Praeger, 1974.

[3] See G. Arbatov, *The War of Ideas in Contemporary International Relations; The Imperialist Doctrine, Methods and Organization of Foreign Political Propaganda,* Moscow: Progress Publishers, 1973; Y. Kolossov, "The Mass Media and International Law," *International Affairs* (Moscow), July 1973, pp. 53–58. A comprehensive presentation by Kolossov is to be found in his book *Massova informazija i mezduarodnoje pravo* (Mass Media and International Law, in Russian), Moscow: International Relations, 1974; translation into German, in *Theorie und Praxis des socialistischen Journalismus* (Leipzig), *2,* pp. 71–105; *5,* pp. 84–118, 1976.

[4] See W. Kleinwaechter, "International Legal Aspects of Direct TV Transmissions from Satellites," *The Democratic Journalist* (Prague), *7–8,* pp. 11–16, 1978; "Massenmedien und internationale Beziehungen" (Mass Media and International Relations, in German), *Deutsche Aussenpolitik 10,* pp. 78–92, 1977; "Journalismus und Verantwortung in International Relations" (Journalism and Responsibility in International Relations, in German), *Theorie und Praxis des socialistischen Journalismus 3,* pp. 208–218, 1980.

relevant material on the question is provided by the MacBride Commission.[5]

Such studies of law and political science provide a framework to approach the relationship between international law and the mass media. We shall discuss this conceptual framework later in Chapter 10, and will focus in the present Chapter directly on the question that is most relevant to the practice of journalism: What precisely are the normative standards relating to the mass media in general and their contents in particular, as stated by various sources of international law?

AN INVENTORY OF INTERNATIONAL INSTRUMENTS

Our point of departure is a study based on a simple inventory of all so-called "international instruments" of a more or less legally binding nature which are relevant to the *performance* of the mass media.[6] "Mass media" is defined here in general terms, covering all media of mass communication, printed and electronic, as well as all types of information transmitted (news, documentaries, fiction, entertainment, etc.). "Propaganda," a term that will be used frequently, constitutes a particular form of mass media material with a systematic and intensive character and, typically, is aimed at a wide audience, thus having a potential for great social impact.

Altogether 49 such instruments were adopted between 1936 and 1978 by international law-making bodies, such as UN and Unesco. These are listed in Appendix 24. Included are those *standard-setting instruments* that make direct or indirect reference to the performance of the mass media, as well as those that constitute a basis for such mass-media related instruments, even though they do not refer directly to information.

Instruments of a technical or administrative nature are not included, notably the International Telecommunication Convention, the copyright conventions, and Unesco's agreements concerning the movement of educational, scientific and cultural materials (the so-called Beirut and Florence agreements). Also omitted is the 1923 Geneva convention

---

[5] Besides the final report *Many Voices, One World*, Paris: Unesco, 1980, the following background documents prepared for the Commission are especially relevant: "'List of International Instruments Concerning Different Aspects of Communication" (No. 21); "Communication: Extracts from International Instruments" (No. 22); and "Responsibility and Obstacles in Journalism" (No. 53), all issued by Unesco in Paris in 1979 and 1980.

[6] See Appendix 24 for the inventory. The study was made in 1979 at the Department of Journalism and Mass Communication, University of Tampere, under the guidance of Nordenstreng and Hannikainen. Antti Alanen acted as research assistant and reported the most important conclusions in a thesis (in Finnish), comparing standards of international law with codes of journalistic ethics. (The latter part of this study is summarized in Chapter 9.)

on the prevention of the dissemination of and commerce in pornographic publications. Although this instrument touches directly upon the contents of mass media, it has a somewhat special character, and is not relevant to the main problems being discussed here. On the other hand, the present list is more comprehensive with regard to the contribution of the mass media to *international relations* than those compiled by Eek and the MacBride Commission, since it includes such instruments as the Charter of the Nuremberg Tribunal of 1945 (Item 3), and UN declarations on the Granting of Independence to Colonial Countries and Peoples (15), on the Principles of International Law Concerning Friendly Relations and Co-operation among States (19), on the Strengthening of International Security (20), and on the Preparation of Societies for Life in Peace (28), as well as two relevant documents on disarmament (16 and 25). The list also contains significant instruments of regional scope on human rights in American and European hemisphere (12, 13, and 30) and the Final Act of the Conference on Security and Co-operation in Europe (31). Also included because of their significance are two documents on freedom of information (11, 29) which are in draft form and have not been adopted as proper instruments.[7]

The list is intended to be exhaustive as far as proper treaties (conventions and charters) and legally less binding declarations are concerned.

There are a dozen relevant *treaties* (plus an important draft convention), including the UN Charter (the latter does not contain any reference to the mass media, or even to information in general, but it occupies a central position among "proper" information instruments). Of these dozen instruments, only two are exclusively devoted to the mass media: The International Convention Concerning the Use of Broadcasting in the Cause of Peace (1), adopted by the League of Nations in 1936 and still in force under the UN; and the Convention on the International Right of Correction (6), adopted by the UN in 1952. Five other treaties contain sections relating directly and explicitly to the mass media, while the rest contain more general references to "information", "propaganda", "public opinion", etc., and thus constitute indirect standards for the performance of the mass media.

---

[7] Another draft instrument, which also has a great value of principle but which still is at its formative stage and thus is not included here, is the draft Convention on direct television broadcasting by means of satellites, under preparation in the UN Outer Space Committee. The list does not include the four Geneva Conventions on Humanitarian Warfare (1949), whereby states have committed themselves to disseminate the text of the convention as widely as possible. Also not included are the two Protocols to the Geneva Conventions (1977), in which the protection of journalists is regulated. Another convention not listed is the Convention on the High Seas (1958), which includes a regulation on the incitement to piracy (Art. 15), an indirect standard for the performance of the mass media.

Seventeen *declarations* and one draft declaration are included in the listing (14 to 31), four of which do not contain direct or indirect references to the mass media, but which constitute a basis for other subsequent instruments. There are only two universal documents wholly devoted to the mass media, both adopted by Unesco: the Declaration on direct satellite broadcasting of 1972 (21), and the Mass Media Declaration of 1978 (27). On the other hand, there are six instruments which contain some parts with direct and explicit reference to the mass media, beginning with the Universal Declaration of Human Rights of 1948 (14) and ending thirty years later with the Declaration on the Preparation of Societies for Life in Peace (28).

The list of *resolutions* (32 to 49) is not intended to be complete. It includes only such instruments that have attained an important position under international law and/or which can be considered significant from the point of view of principles involved. Even so the present list includes eighteen resolutions adopted by the UN General Assembly or the General Conference of Unesco. Of these, eleven are devoted entirely to questions of information, as they set standards for the performance of the mass media, i.e., their contents. A good number of other UN and Unesco resolutions also set such standards, either directly (in explicit terms) or indirectly (implicitly), but in the context of a broader topic, such as decolonization or disarmament. In fact, there are many more resolutions of this latter kind than those listed in the present inventory; for example, since 1971 the UN General Assembly has passed a resolution devoted to the dissemination of information on decolonization in virtually every annual session, but the list includes only the first of this succession of fairly uniform resolutions (40). Furthermore, resolutions that concentrate on media infrastructures rather than media contents have not been included.[8]

Those instruments included in the present list which contain direct or indirect reference to the mass media (44 documents, when instruments with no reference to information are omitted) have been subjected to a crude content analysis by listing for each instrument the topics for which standards are set. The broad topics used in this inventory which emerge as dominant themes in the substance matter of the instruments are:

1. peace and security,
2. war propaganda,
3. friendship, international understanding, and cooperation,
4. objectivity, veracity and honesty of information,

---

[8] There are a number of UN (ECOSOC) and Unesco resolutions on the development of the mass media facilities as quoted in Chapter 1 (see notes 4 and 5).

5. racial equality/discrimination,
6. other duties and responsibilities concerning contents, and
7. free flow of information.

The first four themes represent standards concerned with *international relations*, while the next two pertain to standards relevant primarily at the *national level* (the subdivision of "other duties" in theme 6 is specified below). Strictly speaking, the last theme is not concerned with standards for the performance of the mass media in the same sense as the other themes. In fact, *free flow of information* is usually defined as having no relation to the contents of communication. It has been included for the sake of comparison and covers all customarily considered aspects of freedom of information (including working conditons of journalists).[9]

Table 1 provides a summary of this content analysis of international instruments on simple counts of the presence (direct or indirect) or absence of the seven themes as they relate to the mass media in the 44 instruments under study.

The table shows clearly that international law sets significant standards for the performance of the mass media, not least in matters directly concerning international relations: the promotion of international peace and security and, in general, of friendly relations between states and peoples, on the one hand, and the prevention of propaganda for war, on the other (themes 1–4). In each content category there are direct references to the mass media from all levels of international instruments, including proper vehicles of international law (conventions and charters). A similarly significant set of standards focuses on matters concerning primarily the national level: the promotion of racial equality, other human rights, socio-economic progress, etc., on the one hand, and the prevention of propaganda for racial or other discrimination, or for colonialism, etc., on the other (themes 5–6).

Furthermore, the table shows that free flow of information (theme 7) has not been determined in international law to be more central than standards relating to various aspects of mass media content. More specifically, in the view of international law the idea of unconditional freedom of information is to be seen as subordinated to such obligations as the promotion of peace and security and the prevention of propaganda for war or racism. What is more, the table indicates that five conventions out of twelve not only provide standards for the performance of the mass media but also touch upon such fundamental issues of the journalistic pro-

---

[9] The problems of "free flow" are not discussed in this connection here. For a review on the history of the "free flow" issue, see H. I. Schiller, *Communication and Cultural Domination*, White Plains, New York: International Arts and Sciences Press, 1976.

Table I
Content Analysis of International Instruments

Content Categories	Treaties (12)			Declarations (14)			Resolutions (18)			All Instruments (44)		
	D	I	N	D	I	N	D	I	N	D	I	N
1. Peace and security	3	1	8	7	4	3	9	4	5	19	9	16
2. War propaganda	3	5	4	1	6	7	1	2	15	5	13	26
3. **Friendship**	5	1	6	6	4	4	10	5	3	21	10	13
4. **Objectivity**	5	0	7	6	2	6	6	0	12	17	2	25
5. **Racial propaganda**	1	7	4	5	1	8	3	0	15	9	8	27
6. Other duties	5	3	4	9	2	5	12	2	4	26	5	13
7. Free flow	5	3	4	7	2	5	8	0	10	20	5	19

D = direct references to the mass media
I = indirect references to the mass media
N = no reference to the mass media

fession as truthfulness and objectivity of information, honesty, and freedom from prejudice of communicators (theme 4).

Although, in most cases, the sources of standards consist of conventions and declarations as well as individual resolutions, it becomes clear from the table how information concerning peace and international friendship—a positive obligation—is not more strongly bound under international law than the rather strictly defined prohibition of propaganda for war of aggression or for racial discrimination. This situation reflects the fact that, to a great extent, the international community has formulated codes of conduct for itself by specifying certain prohibitions.

On the other hand, over the years, the positive obligations of an international code of conduct—such as the strengthening of peace and human rights—have been specified and have also risen in political priority, as manifested, for example, by the mid-1970s declarations on the New International Economic Order and on Security and Co-operation in Europe (22 and 31).

Moreover, it should be noted that a state has an *obligation* under international law to work for information standards that promote peaceful and friendly *international relations*—however loose the formulation of these standards may be—whereas in most matters at the *national level* a state has no mandatory obligation under international law, but only a *right* to establish standards on the contents of communication. (On racial discrimination, however, states are bound by an obligation.)

To be precise, a clear distinction between matters of national and of international concern is somewhat problematic and is, in some respects, even a controversial issue. For example, in cases of racial or religious hatred, national problems often extend to international relations. Moreover, human rights are typically considered within a national sphere, while at the same time they have been recognized as an integral part of international relations.

A closer look at both the international and national levels will be made in the next three chapters. Chapter 6 is devoted to the "classic" standards designed to promote international peace and security through negative measures countering propaganda for war. A separate chapter is devoted to this theme, not only because it is included in so many international instruments, but above all because it represents directly the fundamental principles of international law, as pointed out in Chapter 4. Chapter 7 provides a review of other standards in support of peaceful and friendly international relations, both through positive measures whereby information is put to serve these objectives, and also through negative measures, for example, by countering false and distorted reports harmful to these objectives. Chapter 8 looks at standards relating primarily to the national level.

The basis of the above-discussed Table 1 is given in Table 2 in which the individual instruments are listed (according to Appendix 24; note that the five instruments that do not include standards concerning information are missing from the table). Table 2 displays the presence or absence of direct (o) and indirect (x) references to the mass media within each of the seven themes. A more detailed breakdown is given in Appendix 24 where a separate table is to be found for each of the themes (except theme 7, freedom of information), with 8–10 specific topic categories displaying the presence or absence of direct and indirect references to the mass media. Table 2 has been constructed on the basis of these "primary data" given in Appendix 24 by noting (o) and (x) whenever there is at least one corresponding case to be found in the respective specific topic categories.

Table 2 shows that the only instrument which contains direct references to the mass media in all the seven themes considered in the present inventory is the Mass Media Declaration of Unesco. In this respect the Unesco Declaration can be seen as a unique international instrument. But on the other hand, it is equally clear that this Declaration contains little that goes beyond the rich material provided by all the international instruments which had been adopted by 1978. Thus the present inventory confirms the thesis that the significance of the Unesco Declaration is not to be found in great innovations, but rather in the fact that it brings a pool of standards into the focus of professional and political attention, standards which had been set in a number of disparate international in-

Table 2
Summary of Standards in Instruments

o = direct reference to the mass media
x = indirect reference to the mass media

		Peace and Security	War Propaganda	Friendship	Objectivity	Racial Propaganda	Other Duties	Free Flow
1	Broadcasting 1936/38	o	o	o	o			
3	Nuremberg 1945		x			x	o	
4	Unesco 1945	x	x	o	o	x	x	o
5	Genocide 1948/51					x	x	
6	Correction 1952/62	o	o	o	o		o	o
7	Discrimination 1965/69		x			x		x
8	Civil & political 1966/76		x			x	x	x
9	Outer space 1967		x					
10	Apartheid 1973/76		o			x		x
11	Draft conv 1959/61	o		o	o	o	o	o
12	Council of Eur 1950						o	o
13	San José 1969		x	o	o	x	o	o
14	Human rights 1948						o	o
16	Disarmament 1962	o	x	x				
17	Youth 1965	x	x					x
18	Cultural coop 1966	x		x	x		o	x
19	Friendly rel 1970		x					
21	Satellite 1972	o	x	o	o		o	o
23	Education 1974	x		o		o	o	
25	10th special 1978	o			x			
26	Race 1978	x	x	x	o	o		o
27	Mass media 1978	o	o	o	o	o	o	o
28	Peace 1978	o	x	o		o	o	
29	Draft decl 1960	o		o	o	o	o	o
30	Council of Eur 1970				o		o	o
31	CSCE 1975	o	x	o	o	x	o	o
32	GA Res 59 (I)	o		o	o		o	o
33	GA Res 110 (II)	o	x	x			o	o
34	GA Res 127 (II)			o	o		o	
35	GA Res 424 (V)	o		o	o		o	o
36	GA Res 634 (VII)			o	o			o
37	GA Res 1313 (XIII)	o		o	o			o
38	GA Res 2621 (XXV)						o	
39	Unesco 4.301/70	o	x	o		o	o	
40	GA Res 2879 (XXVI)						o	
41	GA Res 2916 (XXVII)	o		o			o	o
42	Unesco 4.113/72	o	o	o		o	o	
43	Unesco 5.61/72	x		x			x	
44	Unesco 13.1/76	x						
45	Unesco 12.1/76	x		x				o
46	GA Res 32/154			o	o		o	
47	Unesco 11.1/78	o		x			x	
48	Unesco 4/0.1/78	x		x			o	o
49	GA Res 33/115	o		o		o	o	

struments, and that it thus introduces a general approach to the international law of communications.

The standards for the performance of the mass media, set by international law—whether direct or indirect, national or international in character—are imposed in the first place upon the states and their official bodies, i.e., upon the subjects of international law. Normally, the standards for the mass media and for communicators working for them come into being through the domestic laws and regulations of individual countries. It is only in cases involving the most strongly prohibited types of communication—such as incitement to racial discrimination and to mass destruction—that the norms under international law impose *direct obligations* upon individual mass media and their communicators. However, all the norms of international law do create strong *moral obligations* for the media and communicators. Therefore, all communicators, and journalists in particular, should include an understanding of international communication law as provided in Chapters 6, 7, and 8 as an integral part of their professional knowledge.

THE RESPONSIBILITY OF STATES FOR OBSERVING INTERNATIONAL STANDARDS

Before looking at the standards for the mass media in greater detail, we shall first discuss briefly the problem of state responsibility with respect to the performance of the mass media under international law.[10] It is not our intent to raise the general question of state-media relationship, and we shall address this question only as far as it concerns *international relations,* i.e., with respect to the contribution of the mass media to international relations as prescribed by the standards of international law.

It is generally accepted in the theory of international law that the mass media can violate international rules and principles. For example, an American expert on international propaganda, O'Brien, writes:

> Obviously, all states are obliged to prevent within their jurisdiction such activities, that are threatening the territorial integrity and political independence of sovereign states with which they have friendly relations . . .In view of the well known importance of propaganda in present-day international relations it is contrary to law for a

---

[10] This section is based on a corresponding chapter in the Unesco document "Responsibility and Obstacles in Journalism" (see note 5). It relies heavily on collaboration with Dr. Wolfgang Kleinwaechter.

state to tolerate or to promote diversion and war propaganda and in some cases defamatory propaganda.[11]

In a "Dictionary of International Law" it is stated: "According to practice of states and the almost unanimous theory hostile propaganda towards foreign countries acts contrary to international customary law . . .Foreign propaganda against the existence or the constitutional order of other states violates the national sovereignty rights."[12]

The question of state responsibility has been under discussion in the UN International Law Commission (ILC) for over a decade. A draft article (19) defines the notion "international crime by a state." Under it an international crime may result, for example, from a serious breach of an international obligation of essential importance for:

(a) the maintenance of international peace and security, such as the prohibition of aggression;

(b) . . .safeguarding the right of self-determination of peoples, such as that prohibiting the establishment or maintenance by force of colonial domination;

(c) . . .safeguarding the human being, such as those prohibiting slavery, genocide, apartheid;

(d) . . .safeguarding the preservation of human environment, such as those prohibiting massive pollution of the atmosphere or the seas.[13]

It is quite clear that the mass media can contribute to such a breach of an international obligation and that they can even produce such a violation.

As is well known, the mass media are organized in different ways in different countries. There are news agencies, radio and TV stations, and even newspapers and journals which are indeed organs of a state, acting in fact on behalf of the state. In other cases, the mass media are private or so-called "public" institutions, clearly separated from the state. Therefore, the problem of state responsibility with respect to the activities of mass media in international relations leads to a distinction between the mass media (1) as state organs, and (2) as a private or public institution, and these must be discussed separately.

---

[11] W. V. O'Brien, "International Propaganda and Minimum World Public Order," in C. C. Havighurst (Ed.), *International Control of Propaganda*, Dobbs Ferry, New York: Oceana Publications, 1967, p. 155.

[12] K. Strupp & H. Schlochauer, *Wörterbuch des Völkerrechts*, (West) Berlin: De Gruyter, 1961, p. 808.

[13] UN Doc. A/31/10, 1976, 31st session, General Assembly, Supplement 10, p. 171.

The Responsibility of States for the Conduct of the Mass Media Acting in Fact on Behalf of the State

In this case the state is responsible for all activities of the mass media which are under its control. This control means not only the direct subordination of a news agency, radio, or TV station to any state organization. The state is responsible as well for the conduct of a mass medium, if the government or another state organization directly determines its policies and financially supports it.

The Special Rapporteur of the ILC for the question of state responsibility has written in his 4th report: "Where it can be seen that the Government encourages and even promotes the organization of such groups, that it provides them with financial assistance, training, and weapons, and coordinates their activities with those of its own forces . . ., the groups in question cease to be individuals from the standpoint of international law."[14]

In this context it is obvious that, for example, the stations Radio Liberty and Radio Free Europe, which are financed by the U.S. government and which operate on the basis of an US-FRG-Treaty on the territory of the Federal Republic of Germany, are not private institutions, and that the USA and the FRG are responsible for the conduct of these stations.[15] On the other hand, not all mass media in the socialist countries are state media in this respect. In fact, it is an exception rather than a rule when the national media are directly controlled or financed by the state; usually they are operated by various popular organizations.

It goes without saying that the state is responsible for the conduct of its proper international information agencies, official radio stations included. All major nations have such agencies for foreign propaganda, or, in more sophisticated words, for international information.

When the new U.S. International Communication Agency (ICA) was established, President Carter touched upon the status of the Voice of America. He stressed "that the charter of the VOA provides that VOA news will be accurate, objective, and comprehensive and the VOA will present U.S. policy clearly and effectively. . . .VOA will be solely responsible for the content of news."[16] Surely, the VOA can decide for itself within certain limits what news will be distributed through its network.

---

[14] R. Ago, "4th Report on State Responsibility," in *Yearbook of the International Law Commission,* 1972, Part II, p. 108.

[15] See B. Graefrath, E. Oeser, & P. A. Steininger, *Völkerrechtliche Verantwortlichkeit der Staaten,* Berlin: Staatsverlag der Deutsche Demokratische Republik, 1977, p. 104; or M. Sørensen (Ed.), *Manual of Public International Law,* New York: St. Martin's Press, 1968, pp. 316, 540, 560.

[16] *U.S. Department of State Bulletin,* 1977, Vol. LXXXV, No. 2003, p. 684.

But if, for instance, this news distribution constitutes interference in internal affairs of other states, the U.S. government is responsible for the activities of the VOA, because the VOA is an integral part of the international information system of a state, financed by the government, and is thus acting on behalf of the state.

The Responsibility of States with Respect to the Conduct of Private or Public Mass Media

It is generally accepted that the state is not responsible for the conduct of private or public institutions that are not acting on behalf of the state. On the other hand, the state is not only responsible for an activity of its own organs, but also for an omission. Article 3 of the above-mentioned ILC-draft reads as follows: "There is an internationally wrongful act of a state when conduct consisting of an action or omission is attributable to the state under international law."[17]

In the theory of international law it is recognized that the state can become responsible, not *for*, but, *with respect to*, the conduct of private or public persons in international relations. The Austrian lawyer Dahn writes: "The state can be held responsible for the fact that its organs cause, promote or—contrary to duty—do not prevent the activities of private persons that are contrary to law."[18] The British lawyer McNair uses the term "secondary liability" in this connection.[19]

International law obliges the state to undertake appropriate measures. Especially within its jurisdiction, the state has to guarantee the respect of the peremptory (*jus cogens*) principles of international law, laid down in the UN Charter and more precisely defined by the UN Declaration on Principles of International Law (1970), by private or public persons. For instance, the principle of non-interference in internal affairs contains special duties for the state: "No state shall organize, assist, foment, finance, incite, or tolerate subversive, terrorist or armed activities directed towards the violent overthrow of the regime of another state, or interfere in civil strife in another state."[20] Thus, if a state tolerates such conduct of the mass media directed at interference in the internal affairs of other states, it is responsible for an omission of its organization.

[17] UN Doc. A/31/10, op. cit., 1976, p. 170.
[18] G. Dahn, *Völkerrecht*, Band III, Stuttgart: Kohlhammer, 1961, p. 196.
[19] A. D. McNair, *International Law Opinions*, Vol. II, Cambridge: University Press, 1956, p. 288.
[20] UN Resolution 2625 (XXV), 25 October 1970.

Consequently, whenever a state has accepted special duties in an international instrument, it has no free choice. Which measures the state in fact undertakes in guaranteeing its international obligations is its internal affair and not a matter of international discussion; only the measures have to be effective.

In this context, the relation between international and internal law naturally becomes a problem. Especially in the U.S., it is often argued that the Congress cannot pass any law in this field against the background of the First Amendment. This argument is not valid; international obligations have special consequences for domestic law.

In the Convention on the Law of Treaties, Article 27 stipulates: "A party may not invoke the provisions of its internal law as justification for its failure to perform a treaty."[21] The ILC-Draft also states: "An act of a State may only be characterized as internationally wrongful by international law. Such characterization cannot be affected by the characterization of the same act as lawful by internal law." [22]

In recent years the discussion about the First Amendment in the United States has shown that many experts now recognize that freedom of information and the corresponding duties and responsibilities constitute a unity under the obligations of the First Amendment. For example, James Barron has pointed out that the state can and has to undertake measures also in the information field.[23] Another US expert, Phillip Davison, has made clear that the state has many possibilities to influence the media in the sense of peace and understanding and to fulfill its obligations in this field.[24]

In summary, it becomes clear that there is an obligation for the state to create conditions within its own jurisdiction so that private or public media do not act against the principles of international law and the international obligations of the state. This does not mean interference by the state in the affairs of the media themselves or a special form of censorship; it only means that the state has to undertake activities to accomplish its international obligations.

Not only is the state responsible for a failure of a mass medium in this negative sense. It can and it must also play a positive and constructive role in the information field, above all by promoting the production and distribution of information furthering peace, mutual understanding, détente, disarmament, and cooperation. Cooperation, promoted by the

---

[21] UN Doc. A/Conf. 39/27, 23 May 1969.

[22] UN Doc. A/31/10, op. cit. 1976, p. 170.

[23] See J. Barron, "Access to the Press: A New Concept of the First Amendment", *Harvard Law Review*, June 1967; and *Freedom of the Press for Whom?*, Bloomington, Indiana: Indiana University Press, 1973.

[24] Op cit. in note 2.

state, can encourage a freer, wider, and better balanced flow of accurate, comprehensive, and objective information in the area of international relations. The state can also promote the elaboration of principles governing the work of journalists and the activities of private or public mass media. Also in this connection, the formulation of codes of ethics can play an important role.

Thus, a codification of state responsibility with respect to the conduct of mass media in international relations should not be understood as an action against the international exchange and distribution of information, but as an action designed to promote the international flow of information on the base of equality and principles of international law, and to create more legal security in this field.

Regarding Unesco activities in this direction, in particular recalling the issue of state responsibility in the debate related to the Mass Media Declaration, it is very interesting to note that in the discussion in the UN Committee on Outer Space concerning an instrument on direct satellite broadcasting, important progress has been made in the question of state responsibility. An already widely accepted draft article states: "States should bear international responsibility for activities in the field of direct television broadcasting by means of artificial earth satellites carried out by them or under their jurisdiction, and for the conformity of any such activities with the principles set forth in this document."[25]

---

[25] UN Doc., A/AC.105/171, Annex II, p. 2, 28 May 1976.

6

Prohibition of War Propaganda*

The prohibition of the use of aggressive force in state relations has evolved since the 1920s into one of the most important rules of international law. The UN Charter numbers the maintenance of international peace and security as the first and most important among its four basic purposes. In the era of nuclear weapons, interstate violence constitutes a threat to even the very existence of mankind.

In their domestic laws, states prohibit acts that contravene the basic values of the society. Also, each state has subjected communication to prohibitory rules. In a similar manner, the international community is expected to prohibit forms of mass communication which would endanger peace and security. Among the most detrimental forms of international communication is *propaganda for war, i.e., incitement of a state to acts of armed aggression against another state.*

In the internal systems of all states, incitement to crime has been made punishable. It would seem logical that this principle would be applied in international law as well. Whereas, in many cases, international law does not follow the patterns of domestic law, but constitutes an independent legal system of its own, the prohibition of war propaganda under international law must be justified through ways other than mere analogical reference to the generally accepted principles of domestic law.

INTERNATIONAL LEGAL INSTRUMENTS

The fundamental instruments on the prohibition of the use of force are the so-called *Kellogg-Briand Pact* of 1928 and the *UN Charter* of 1945. According to article 2 (4) of the Charter, member states shall refrain from the threat or use of force against the territorial integrity or political independence of any state, or in any other manner inconsistent with the purposes of the Charter. Over 150 states have obligated themselves to observe the provisions of the Charter as members of the UN. There appears to be no opposition to the basic principles of the Charter within the inter-

*This chapter was written by Lauri Hannikainen.

national community; the few non-member states have accepted them as rules of customary law.[1]

The UN Charter says nothing about the banishment of war propaganda, but the maintenance of international peace and security as well as the development of friendly international relations are among its basic purposes. Inasmuch as the prohibition of the use of force is one of the most important juridical principles of the UN Charter, we may draw the conclusion that *propaganda for war is against the purposes and principles of the UN Charter*.

With a world war becoming ever more imminent, the League of Nations, in 1936, drew up *The International Convention Concerning the Use of Broadcasting in the Cause of Peace*. In compliance with Article 2 of the Convention, the contracting parties committed themselves to ensure that the broadcasting from their territories does not contain expressions inciting to war against any contracting party. The Convention remains in force under the auspices of the UN and has been ratified by 23 countries.

The Statute of the Nuremberg International Military Tribunal, concluded by the four leading victorious nations in 1945 and acceded to by 19 nations, declared that crimes against peace and against humanity, as well as war crimes, are international crimes for which there shall be individual criminal responsibility. The Statute defined, as crimes against peace, the preparation, instigation, and waging of a war prohibited by international law, as well as participation in a common plan for launching a war. Also, according to the Statute, the instigators participating in a common plan to launch a war were to be condemned as criminals. The Nuremberg Tribunal pronounced several defendants guilty, inter alia, of exercising propaganda. Julius Streicher was sentenced to death for incitement to crimes against humanity, even though he was not involved in the execution of the crimes. Rudolf Hess was charged with psychological preparation for an aggressive war, the Tribunal establishing that Hess actively supported the launching of a war of aggression in his public speeches. Those sentenced by the Nuremberg Tribunal were leaders of Nazi Germany; they were not condemned in the capacity of private persons but in the capacity of leaders of a governmental plan of crimes.[2]

---

[1] This was emphasized by the International Law Commission of the UN in 1976; see General Assembly, Official Records A/31/10, p. 250.

[2] The Charter and the Judgment of the Nuremberg Military Tribunal can be found, for example, in L. Friedman (Ed.), *The Law of War*, I–II, New York: Random House, 1972, pp. 883–893, 922–1026. This work also contains the documents of the Tokyo Military Tribunal (1948), which followed the principles on international crimes of the Nuremberg Tribunal.

The General Assembly of the UN unanimously accepted the Nuremberg principles in 1946 (GA Res. 95 [I]).

Murty, an American legal expert, interprets the rulings of the Nuremberg and other trials arising from the Second World War and their approval by the international community of states in such a way that, in future international trials concerning crimes against peace, legal proceedings can be undertaken not only for acts of aggression, but also for the intensive ideological and psychological preparation for such acts.[3]

In 1947 the *UN General Assembly unanimously adopted a resolution condemning all forms of propaganda which are designed to provoke or encourage any threat to the peace, breach of the peace, or act of aggression* (GA Res. 110 [II]). In 1950 the General Assembly reinforced this view.

The objective of freedom of information dominated in the 1950s. Hence, problems relating to prohibited information were set aside. However, the Draft Convention on Freedom of Information, which has not lent itself to becoming a valid convention, stated that freedom of information does not prevent, inter alia, the prohibition of incitement to war.[4]

In 1962, the *18-nation Disarmament Committee* reached an agreement in Geneva on a declaration which stipulated that *appeals for war and for the settlement of disputes between states by the use of force, and also statements to the effect that war is indispensable or inevitable, must be condemned.* War propaganda was considered to be contrary to the UN Charter.[5]

In 1966 the UN opened the *International Covenant on Civil and Political Rights* for ratification, which became effective in 1976. Its article 20 (1) stipulates that all *propaganda for war shall be prohibited by law.* Sixty-nine states had ratified the Covenant at the end of 1981. Ten Western countries have made a reservation to article 20 (1); thus, they consider that they are not bound to the stipulation. The states are Australia, Denmark, Finland, France, Iceland, New Zealand, the Netherlands, Norway, Sweden, and the United Kingdom. They have referred to the importance of freedom of speech and to the vagueness of the ban of war propaganda.

Seven other Western countries have, however, found it possible to enact a ban on war propaganda in their internal legislation. These states are Austria, Canada, the Federal Republic of Germany, Italy, Japan,

---

[3] B. S. Murty, *Propaganda and World Order*, New Haven: Yale University Press, 1968, p. 241.

[4] H. Eek explains the draft convention in a section on the freedom of information in his "Principles Governing the use of the Mass Media as Defined by the United Nations and UNESCO," in K. Nordenstreng & H. I. Schiller (Eds.), *National Sovereignty and International Communication*, Norwood, New Jersey: Ablex Publishing Corporation, 1979, pp. 179–183.

[5] The text can be found in J. B. Whitton & A. Larson, *Propaganda—Towards Disarmament in the War of Words*, Dobbs Ferry, New York: Oceana Publications, 1964, pp. 234–235.

Portugal, and Spain. Of the 69 ratifying countries, 59 have agreed to include the prohibition of war propaganda in their legislation. The view on the predominance of the freedom of speech held by the ten states noted above has remained that of a small minority.

In 1967 the UN adopted the so-called *Outer Space Treaty*, which has been adopted by about 80 nations. It does not specifically deal with communication save in the preambular paragraphs, according to which the UN General Assembly resolution 110 (II) that condemns propaganda in threat of peace or in instigation of war is applicable also to outer space. Thus, the ratifying states *must refrain from war propaganda in satellite transmissions from outer space.*

The *American Convention on Human Rights* of 1969 is very clearcut. Article 13 stipulates that any propaganda for war constitutes an offense punishable by law. The United States at the first stage proposed the abolishment of this provision, on the ground that it would infringe on freedom of information, but eventually consented to this compromise wording, which it itself drafted. Seventeen nations had ratified the Convention at the end of 1981. The United States has announced that if it ever ratifies the Convention it will make a reservation to the provision on war propaganda. It has given a similar notification regarding the Covenant on Civil and Political Rights. (USA has not, by 1981, ratified this Covenant.)

In 1970 the General Assembly of the UN adopted, without opposition, the *Declaration of Principles of International Law Concerning Friendly Relations and Co-operation among States in Accordance with the Charter of the United Nations* (GA Res. 2625 [XXXV]). The Declaration defines seven basic legal principles of the UN Charter. The principles are, in the words of the Declaration, "basic principles of international law." The principle of prohibition of the use of force includes a provision that, *in accordance with the purposes and principles of the United Nations, states have the duty to refrain from propaganda for wars of aggression.*

In 1974 the General Assembly of the UN adopted the *Definition of Aggression* (GA Res. 3314 [XXIX]); only the People's Republic of China opposed it. (China wanted a more detailed definition.) The definition, which concentrates on the concept of armed aggression, lends itself to a determination of the border between legal and illegal use of force under international law. The contents of the definition are discussed below.

Under chapter 1 (b) of the "first basket" of the Final Act *of the Conference on Security and Co-operation in Europe (CSCE)*, some rules of conduct are listed for the purpose of giving effect to the Declaration of Principles Guiding Relations between Participating States. According to a provision in chapter 1 (b), *the participating states of the CSCE consider it their duty to re-*

frain from propaganda for wars of aggression or for any threat or use of force against another participating state. Also, 35 participating states promise to conduct their relations with the states outside the CSCE in the spirit of the Declaration of Principles.

There are also two documents from the year 1978. First, the *Mass Media Declaration of Unesco* proclaims that *among the most important contributions of the mass media is countering incitement to (aggressive) war.* Second, the UN General Assembly *Declaration on the Preparation of Societies for Life in Peace* (GA Res. 33/78), which was adopted by 138 votes in favor, with only Israel and the USA abstaining from the vote, states that each nation and each individual has the right to live in peace. According to the Declaration *all states have the obligation to refrain from propaganda for wars of aggression, and they must—with due regard for their system of fundamental rights— prohibit, inter alia, incitement to hatred against other nations, to violence, and to war.*

In conclusion, numerous instruments of international law condemn propaganda for war. Besides the UN Charter, several other conventions establish obligations for states to refrain from war propaganda. In accordance with the view of the Nuremberg Military Tribunal, instigators to crimes against international law must be punished under the authorization of international law. The international community confirmed, at the United Nations, the justness of the Nuremberg verdicts. In compliance with the Covenant on Civil and Political Rights, nearly 60 states have bound themselves to ban war propaganda in their territories. The numerous declarations and resolutions of the UN General Assembly and of the Unesco General Conference, unanimously adopted and worded in obligatory form, constitute a proof of state practice and of the contemporary view of states against propaganda for war. These factors are of primary importance in the verification of the existence of a norm of universal customary law.

Hence, it s indisputable that, in accordance with international law, states must refrain from war propaganda. As far as war propaganda exercised by state officials is concerned, responsibility for it falls, *under international law,* both upon the state and upon the officials themselves. On the other hand, a closer study is needed to clarify whether and how far a state has an obligation to suppress war propaganda that is made in its territory by non-governmental organizations, the mass media, or individuals—and what the responsibility of that state is in those cases. This question is discussed below.

The unlawfulness of war propaganda is confirmed by legal experts, including Quincy Wright, John Whitton, Arthur Larson, and William O'Brien from the United States; Grigory Tunkin from the Soviet Union;

Konstantin Obradović from Yugoslavia; Bogumil Sujka from Poland and Allan Rosas from Finland.[6]

THE PROHIBITION OF WAR PROPAGANDA IN INTERNATIONAL AND DOMESTIC LAW

The rule of international law on the prohibition of war propaganda endeavours to prevent intensive and/or outspoken public advocation of armed aggression capable of influencing public opinion. Thus, in our opinion, war propaganda is in violation of international law when constituted by large scale public propaganda activities or communications which:

    1. incite the domestic or a foreign government to armed aggression;

    2. endeavour to persuade public opinion to assume an approving stand towards a committed or an imminent act of aggression;

    3. endeavour to mould public opinion towards the idea of aggression against another state; or

    4. idealize armed aggression as a means for settling international disputes.

The sphere of application of the rule is not confined to the country of the propagandist. The rule prohibits war propaganda, be it directed to one's own country or to another country. It covers armed aggression all over the world.

The international community of states should see to it that those who are guilty of war propaganda are brought to trial for conviction. This is what happened in the aftermath of World War II, the Nuremberg trial being the most notable example. But, in most cases, international law lacks the means of implementation. The decision to bring a law-suit against war propagandists is often left in the hands of those states which are able to apprehend the propagandists.

---

[6] Q. Wright's article on war propaganda in *American Journal of International Law*, 1948, especially pp. 131, 134.

J. B. Whitton & A. Larson, *op. cit.*, pp. 65–72, 82; see also Whitton's article on war propaganda in Nordenstreng & Schiller, *op. cit.*, pp. 217–229.

W. V. O'Brien's article on propaganda in C. C. Havighurst (Ed.), *International Control of Propaganda*, Dobbs Ferry, New York: Oceana Publications, 1967, p. 155.

G. Tunkin, *Theory of International Law*, Cambridge: Harvard University Press, 1974, pp. 83–86.

K. Obradović's article on the prohibition of force in M. Sahović (Ed.), *Principles of International Law Concerning Friendly Relations and Cooperation*, Belgrade 1972, p. 120 (also published by Oceana Publications, Dobbs Ferry, New York, 1972).

B. Sujka's article on international propaganda and information activity in *Studies on International Relations* (Warsaw), 3/1974, pp. 19–37.

A. Rosas in *Oikeus* (Helsinki), No. 4, 1981, pp. 225–225.

Even though international law prohibits states from committing, or from permitting in their territories the commission of, a number of acts which would disturb the international community, international law has been able in only a few cases to place an obligation on states to punish the offenders. The establishment of such obligations has been possible only through multilateral conventions; and such conventions bind only the parties to them. There is no universal obligation of punishment, e.g., in cases of the ban on the use of aggressive force or on the exercise of war propaganda. Finnish law, for example, does not declare the launching of a war of aggression or the exercise of war propaganda to be crimes.

Within the UN, states can be pressured to enact laws in fulfillment of the endeavours of the international community. Consequently, each state should, in its legislation, forbid both the launching of armed aggression against another state and propaganda to this effect. It does not suffice that a state and the guilty individuals are declared responsible under international law. There is a need for interaction between international and domestic law. The contribution of internal legal systems towards the punishment of war propagandists is of great value. In the international legal system, punishment is confined to certain major cases—when the aggression has been committed. Internal legal systems have the capacity to prevent war propaganda at earlier stages.

At least 60 states have forbidden propaganda for war. Inter alia, almost all socialist countries, as well as the Federal Republic of Germany and Italy, have enacted laws which declare war propaganda criminal. However, the prohibitive rule is not found in the legislation of the United States, the United Kingdom, or China. In the following we give examples of the laws in some countries.

In accordance with 80 § of the Criminal Code of the Federal Republic of Germany, anyone who publicly incites to a war of aggression will be sentenced to prison for a minimum of three months. According to 6 § of the Constitution of the German Democratic Republic, any one who foments militarism or war or hatred against other races and nationalities shall be punished. The Soviet Law on Safeguards of Peace states that propaganda for war—no matter in what form it appears—is a severe crime against humanity; the transgressors shall be tried in the courts as dangerous criminals. In compliance with Article 6 of the Mexican Constitution, citizens enjoy freedom of speech, provided that they do not endanger peace.

The following are guidelines for the drafting of national prohibitory rules regarding war propaganda.

The aim of war propaganda is to influence public opinion. As far as *non-governmental propaganda* is concerned, the prohibition should be directed against outspoken war propaganda which takes place on a wide scale. A single act of public incitement is not sufficient to constitute non-governmental war propaganda. On the other hand, the precondition of punishment is not that the propagaged aggression actually takes place. The purpose of the prohibition is to prevent public war propaganda which influences public opinion.

As far as *governmental propaganda* is concerned, even individual instances of propaganda can influence public opinion. A single public speech by the highest governmental leaders can have a considerable effect on public opinion, because of the wide publicity it receives and the respectability of the responsible leader. Such a speech may be punishable as war propaganda. If a public speech by the highest of government officials contains an outspoken *threat* of aggressive force against another state, it is punishable in such capacity. In general, states should prohibit any war propaganda activities by their officials.

Because the definition of war propaganda is not very precisely laid out in international law, states have some freedom in the formulation of their laws. States where public opinion is very concerned with the preservation of peace will want to enact a strict law. Many socialist states are among these. States which put special weight on the freedom of information may be inclined to punish only for systematic and exceptionally dangerous propaganda. They may be motivated by the fact that communicators, representatives of non-governmental organizations, etc., are not very familiar with international law and do not know the exact borderline between the legal and illegal use of force.

LEGAL AND ILLEGAL USE OF FORCE

The UN Charter contains provisions relating to two forms of legal use of armed force. (1) According to Article 51, states have the right to self-defence against an armed attack. (2) Under Chapter VII, the Security Council may authorize or prescribe the use of force for the maintenance or restoration of international peace and security.

The Definition of Aggression adopted by the UN General Assembly in 1974 states in the preamble that armed aggression is the most dangerous form of the illegal use of force. Under Article 1, aggression is defined as the use of armed force by a state against the sovereignty, territorial integrity, or political independence of another state, or in any other manner inconsistent with the Charter of the UN. The first to use armed force is the aggressor unless the Security Council determines otherwise.

Article 3 enumerates the acts which constitute armed aggression. They include various direct armed invasions and attacks against the territory of another state, the bombardment of its territory, the blockade of its ports or coasts, and the sending of armed bands or guerillas in substantial numbers to commit acts of force. The list is not exhaustive, but the Security Council may determine that other acts also constitute aggression.

According to Article 5, a war of aggression is a crime against international peace, and aggression gives rise to international responsibility.

Article 7 states that nothing in the Definition can in any way prejudice the right to self-determination and independence of peoples under colonial or alien domination, nor their right to struggle to that end and to receive support in their struggle in accordance with the principles of the Charter. Thus, the use of force by a people against their colonial or alien masters for the attainment of self-determination is the third form of legal use of force in the international arena.

All acts of armed aggression under the Definition are *illegal*. But are they also *criminal*? Article 5 states that a war of aggression is a crime. The word "war" means the use of armed force on a large scale. The Definition is not confined to armed aggression on a large scale, but also covers lesser acts.

It is well documented that wars of aggression are crimes under international law. This has been stated by the Charter of the Nuremberg Tribunal and by the Nuremberg judgment, as well as by several unanimous declarations and resolutions of the UN General Assembly. At the UN, a large majority of states have been ready to declare all acts of aggression as crimes under international law, but a number of Western states have been reluctant to agree.

Clearly, the development of international law has led in the direction of declaring all acts of armed aggression as criminal. The major task of the UN is the maintenance of international peace and security. The Charter regards the use of aggressive force as the most serious threat to international peace and security. If, according to Article 39 (in Chapter VII), the Security Council determines that there exists a threat to the peace, or that a breach of the peace or an act of aggression has taken place, it may prescribe sanctions, even armed sanctions, against the aggressor state. Under the Charter, all members are under the obligation to obey such decisions. Under Article 2 (6), the UN shall ensure that nonmembers do not endanger international peace and security. Thus, the decisions of the Security Council under Chapter VII can create very weighty obligations for all States: present international law does not provide any stronger sanctions than those by the Security Council under

Chapter VII; Chapter VII does not speak of a war of aggression but of an act of aggression.

The approach of the UN Charter is realistic. In today's world, any act of armed aggression in state relations may be a threat to international peace and security. Under the Charter, acts of aggression are grave offences; it is possible to regard them as crimes.

In summary, it is not fully clear whether, under international law, all acts of armed aggression are crimes, or whether only acts of a relatively large scale are crimes.[7] This leaves states some freedom in determining what degree of advocacy of the use of aggressive force they will prescribe as punishable under their law. The states should keep in mind that all acts of armed aggression form a threat to international peace and constitute a violation of international law. It is not advisable to permit outspoken propaganda for any kind of aggressive force.

Actually, the development of international law makes the term "war propaganda" somewhat obsolete. The decisive element involved is not the existence of a declared war. The most accurate term would be "propaganda for armed aggression." However, the term "war propaganda" has been retained here, as it is in general use, because of its brevity.

The Definition of Aggression covers most forms of the illegal use of armed force, but leaves out certain problematic forms. An exaggeration of the right of self-defence, or the involvement of the armed forces of an outside state in a civil war, may constitute armed aggression.

No state is permitted to exaggerate its right of self-defence by resorting to armed force outside its territory, unless it has been attacked by armed force. A border clash does not justify large scale military operations. The exaggeration of the right of self-defence may constitute armed aggression.

Civil wars or other ongoing armed conflicts inside a state should be evaluated on the following premises:

- In general, international law does not take a stand on the internal use of force. Its concern is with the participation of other states in a civil war or in an armed conflict in another state.
- Should any state participate with its armed forces in an ongoing domestic armed conflict in another state, with the purpose of conquering a territory or imposing domination, for example in order to

---

[7] Brownlie says that action undertaken in good faith and with the limited intention of saving the lives of nationals in another state, or of preventing massacre of a racial or other minority on the territory of another state, probably cannot be regarded as criminal, even assuming that such action is no longer justified in general international law. I. Brownlie, *International Law and the Use of Force by States,* Oxford: Clarendon Press, 1963, p. 213.

set up a puppet régime, it is guilty of armed aggression. In such cases, a state cannot plead the invitation of a party to the conflict.

• A ruling government has traditionally had the right to invite outside help to quell a rebellion (and also for other purposes). This right has not been abolished, save in certain cases where international law regards the government as illegal. Illegal governments in this respect are: a colonial or alien régime, a minority régime that practises gross racial discriminations, and, in individual cases, other régimes which intensively suppress the right of self-determination of a people.

• An outsider state does not, as a rule, have the right to render assistance to insurgents. Support, in the form of armed force to the insurgents, constitutes armed aggression against the target state. However, if the UN has recognized a national liberation movement as the genuine representative of a violently suppressed people's aspirations to self-determination, assistance to it is considered permissible.

• Armed involvement, which is based on an invitation by either party and which does not strive for domination, should, in unclear cases, be considered from the viewpoint of the principle of non-interference and not from the viewpoint of armed aggression. In compliance with the principle of non-interference, a state is not permitted to interfere in affairs within the domestic jurisdiction of another state. An act may violate the non-interference principle without constituting armed aggression; the advocacy of such an act is not war propaganda.

• Should the government of a state be guilty of genocide, outside armed support to the liberation movement should probably be evaluated in accordance with the criteria of legal or illegal interference.

The conclusion is that, despite difficulties and marginal cases, *international law has created adequate rules* for the definition of the illegal use of armed force. Outspoken public advocacy for such armed force, on a scale larger than border clashes or other small scale acts of aggression, is war propaganda. On the other hand, public advocacy of the legal use of armed force is fully legitimate and permissible.

In international practice there have appeared, and probably will continue to appear, cases which present difficulties for the determination of legal or illegal use of force. If needed, the views of the principal UN organs can be used in the interpretation. Should a court come to the conclusion that, in a given case, the citizens, other than governmental officials, cannot reasonably be expected to be able to estimate the legality or illegality of the use of armed force, it should acquit the defendant. The objective of international law is met to the extent that all states prevent propaganda for such armed force which can reasonably be verified as illegal.

WHO SHOULD BE PUNISHED?

According to international law the guilty offenders may be *heads of state, political leaders, governmental (state) officials, communicators, representatives of civil organisations, or private individuals.* Should any of these be released from responsibility, the prohibition of war propaganda would be considerably weakened. The international trials in the aftermath of World War II confirmed the responsibility of the individual for crimes against international law. There are practically no divergent views of the validity of this principle.

Article 15 of the Covenant on Civil and Political Rights states that no one shall be held guilty of any criminal offence which "did not constitute a criminal offence, under national or international law, at the time when it was committed." The Article goes on, stating that nothing shall "prejudice the trial and punishment of any person for any act or omission which, at the time when it was committed, was criminal according to the general principles of law recognized by the community of nations."

QUESTIONS OF RESPONSIBILITY

The preparation of the Mass Media Declaration of Unesco showed that Western countries were reluctant to tackle questions of responsibility. Explicit rules of responsibility concerning international mass communication have not evolved in international instruments. However, this is no serious disadvantage, because the general rules of international law on the responsibility of states and individuals are relatively clearcut. They are applicable also in the field of international communication.

A state is responsible for all acts of its organs and officials which violate the rights of other states or international law. The responsible officials may face criminal responsibility directly under international law if they are guilty of an international crime. Not even legislation of their homeland, permitting the crime, nor the command of a superior, releases them from this responsibility. This was confirmed by the Nuremberg Tribunal and by Article 15 of the Covenant on Civil and Political Rights.

Also, individuals who do not have any official functions may face direct criminal responsibility under international law for their propaganda.

The American experts Whitton and Larson submit that war propaganda by individuals should be considered an offence under international law for which they are individually responsible.[8]

Is a state responsible for activities against other states committed by non-governmental organizations or associations or by private individuals within its territory? The answer is affirmative on the following grounds:

- According to a generally accepted principle of international law, the territory of a state must not be used in a manner detrimental to other states.[9] This principle is a part of the principle of sovereign equality of states.
- Whereas states possess full jurisdiction within their own territory under international law, a state is expected to be capable of maintaining order and hence to prevent all injurious acts from its territory against other states. Tammes points out that international practice confirms the responsibility of each state for insuring that the non-governmental organizations, etc. and private persons under its jurisdiction do not make use of its territory for acts injuring the rights of other states.[10]

The responsibility of states for acts of non-governmental persons does not, in general, mean a direct responsibility for an illegal act, but its foundation is in the omission of the obligation of supervision.[11] A state may not appeal to the provisions of its domestic law as a basis for the neglect of its obligation of supervision, because *the international obligations of a state have, under international law, a precedence over its domestic legislation.* Article 27 of the Vienna Convention on the Law of Treaties (1969) stipulates that a party to a treaty may not invoke its domestic law as justification for its failure to observe a treaty.

Several significant international law cases confirm the rule of the responsibility of a state with respect to the acts of non-governmental persons within its territory. The International Court of Justice stated in the Corfu Channel case in 1949 that it is "every State's obligation not to allow knowingly its territory to be used for acts contrary to the rights of other States." The court considered that Albania had neglected her responsibil-

---

[8] Whitton & Larson, p. 173.

[9] See the chapter by M. Sahović & W. W. Bishop on the authority of the state in M. Sørensen (Ed.), *Manual of Public International Law*, New York: St. Martin's Press, 1968, p. 316.

[10] See A. J. Tammes' article on the binding force of international obligations of states for persons under their jurisdiction in R. J. Akkerman, P. J. van Krieken, & C. O. Pannenborg (Eds.), *Declarations on Principles*, Leyden: A. W. Sijthoff, 1977, pp. 61–63.

[11] See "Responsibility and Obstacles in Journalism," *op. cit.* in notes 5 and 10 of Chapter 5 above.

ity of supervision.[12] The arbitration court set up by the United States and Canada stated in the Trail Smelter case, in 1935, that in compliance with the principles of international law "no State has the right to use or permit the use of its territory in such a manner as to cause injury by fumes in or to the territory of another.[13] Whitton and Larson say that "it is not much of a step from harmful fumes to harmful words carried by electronic impulses across national boundaries."[14] In both the Caroline and the Alabama cases, the arbitration courts held the state concerned to be responsible with respect to private armed entities operating from its territory in the territory of another state.[15]

The 1967 Outer Space Treaty is of special importance. In accordance with its Article 6, states bear the responsibility for all national activities in outer space carried out by both governmental and nongovernmental entities. Hence, the state bears the direct responsibility for the satellite communications of broadcasting institutions (both governmental and non-governmental) which operate in its territory. This principle is included separately in a draft treaty, under preparation in the UN Outer Space Committee, concerning the use of satellites in direct television broadcasting to the public at large.

Notwithstanding the clearcut general rules of international law, scholars are not entirely unanimous on the supervision responsibility of the state with respect to private propaganda which is directed from its territory to other countries. Some Western scholars have held that private entities and individuals have the freedom of speech, which the state shall not touch and with respect to which it therefore bears no responsibility. The American expert Martin is of the opinion that the majority of scholars favor the acknowledgement of the responsibility of states.[16] This view seems to have gained in strength in international law during the 1960s and 1970s. The Outer Space Treaty is one indication of this. Another expert, Garcia-Mora, notes that states have, in the name of international peace and security, the responsibility to prevent hostile propaganda launched by private persons against other states.[17] Whitton and Larson are not certain about the existence of such a universal responsibility, but they consider that this responsibility would cover the supervision

---

[12] *International Court of Justice, Reports of Judgments, Advisory Opinions and Orders*, 1949, p. 22.

[13] See "Trail Smelter Arbitral Tribunal," prepared by Jan Hostie, Charles Warren & R. A. E. Greenshields for the *American Journal of International Law*, 1941, pp. 684, 716.

[14] Whitton & Larson, *op. cit.*, p. 132.

[15] Tammes explains these cases briefly, *op cit.*, pp. 61–62.

[16] L. J. Martin, *International Propaganda—Its Legal and Diplomatic Control*, Minneapolis, Minnesota: University of Minnesota Press, 1958, pp. 58–60.

[17] M. R. Garcia-Mora, *International Responsibility for Hostile Acts of Private Persons against Foreign States*, The Hague: M. Nijhoff, 1962, p. 108.

of broadcasting, due to the universal, relatively great degree of control of governments in this field.[18]

The appeal to freedom of information as abolishing the responsibility of states is based on a misunderstanding of international law. *Freedom of information does not hold such an important standing in international law that it could abolish the fundamental responsibilities of the state towards other states or towards the whole international community.*

---

[18] Whitton & Larson, *op. cit.*, pp. 160, 166. Their study was published prior to the conclusion of the Outer Space Treaty.

7

Contribution to Peaceful Coexistence among Nations

Moving from war propaganda to perspectives of peaceful relations between nations, we must first note that international law does not only prohibit propaganda for armed aggression but that also *propaganda for the use of such destructive weapons that are banned by international conventions must be considered forbidden.* As put by the U.S. expert Morris Greenspan: "It would be wrong to incite illegal acts of warfare, as for example the use of poison or poisonous weapons, and killing and wounding by treachery."[1]

Moreover, a logical extension of the prohibition of propaganda for war and/or for the use of illegal weapons is the obligation to refrain from *propaganda for the first use of weapons of mass destruction.* To be precise, this is not as solid a case of "positive law" as in the prohibition of war propaganda, since the use of nuclear weapons has not, thus far, been unqualifiedly forbidden. Nevertheless, a ban on the use of weapons of mass destruction, particularly their first use, seems to be winning increasing support in the international community—despite contradictory tendencies in contemporary international politics.

DISARMAMENT

Another standard, also as an extension to the prohibition of war propaganda, consists of a positive alternative to violence—information for disarmament. The issue of disarmament and its relation to public opinion appeared in a significant international instrument for the first time in 1962, when the *18-nation Disarmament Conference in Geneva* declared that the participating states:

> . . . undertake to promote by every means at their disposal the widest possible circulation of news, ideas and opinions conducive to the strengthening of peace and friendship among peoples, and to extend cultural, scientific and educational relations with a view to better dissemination of the ideas of peaceful and friendly cooperation among states, and general and complete disarmament. . .[2]

[1] M. Greenspan, *The Modern Law of Land Warfare,* Berkeley: University of California Press, 1959, p. 324.
[2] The text of this declaration is reproduced in J. B. Whitton & A. Larson, *Propaganda—Towards Disarmament in the War of Words,* Dobbs Ferry, New York: Oceana Publications, 1964, pp. 234–235. The other instruments quoted below are to be found in respective proceedings of the UN and Unesco conferences.

In recent years, obligations on disarmament information have been raised to a new level. *The Tenth Special Session of the UN General Assembly on Disarmament,* held in the summer of 1978, made an inclusion of the following passage in its Final Document (adopted unanimously):

> 15. It is essential that not only Governments but also the peoples of the world recognize and understand the dangers in the present situation. In order that an international conscience may develop and that world public opinion may exercise a positive influence, the United Nations should increase the dissemination of information on the armaments race and disarmament with the full cooperation of Member States.

In the program of action adopted by this Special Session, a separate section (paragraphs 99 to 105) is devoted to the dissemination of information "in order to mobilize world public opinion on behalf of disarmament." A number of specific measures are "designed to increase the dissemination of information about the armaments race and the efforts to halt and reverse it." The last of these paragraphs reads:

> 105. Member States should be encouraged to ensure a better flow of information with regard to the various aspects of disarmament to avoid dissemination of false and tendentious information concerning armaments, and to concentrate on the danger of escalation of the armaments race and on the need for general and complete disarmament under effective international control.

The subsequent *33rd regular session of the UN General Assembly* in the autumn of 1978 reviewed the implementation of the recommendations and decisions adopted by the Tenth Special Session on Disarmament. The resulting resolution (33/71, adopted on 14 December 1978) devotes a distinct section to "Dissemination of Information on the Arms Race and Disarmament" in which the General Assembly reconfirms the above-quoted position:

> *Convinced* that it is essential that both the Governments and the peoples of the world should be better informed of the dangers of the arms race, particularly the nuclear arms race, and of the efforts made to contain it,
>
> *Recalling* that, in paragraph 99 of the Final Document of the Tenth Special Session, it recognized that, in order to mobilize world public opinion in favour of disarmament, concrete measures must be taken to increase the dissemination of information on the arms race and disarmament,
>
> 1. Urges Member States, the specialized agencies and the International Atomic Energy Agency, as well as non-governmental organi-

zations and concerned research institutes, to promote education and information programmes relating to the arms race and disarmament. . . .

In addition, the resolution adopted by the *20th session of the General Conference of Unesco* in the autumn of 1978, concerning the "Role of Unesco in generating a climate of public opinion conducive to the halting of the arms race and transition to disarmament," reminds us of the importance and timeliness of this obligation. The resolution invites the Member States:

> . . .to pay particular attention to the role which information, including the mass media, can play in generating a climate of confidence and understanding between nations and countries as well as in increasing public awareness of ideas, objectives and action in the field of disarmament, as proposed in the Final Document of the Special Session.

DÉTENTE

The standards discussed thus far (war propaganda, weapons of mass destruction, disarmament) all represent the *military* facet of international relations. The *political* side of international relations also suggests several standards concerning information. In general terms, they might be characterized as obligations of political détente or *peaceful coexistence,* since they aim at the maintenance and strengthening of peace, security, and international understanding, especially with a view toward so-called East-West relations, i.e., nations with different socio-political systems.

Thus the international community, along with the prohibition of war propaganda, has developed a significant, although general, set of norms in support of peaceful and friendly relations among nations. Furthermore, international law has evolved a rather balanced set of both military and political standards.

The best known contemporary instrument for political détente, i.e., relaxation of international tensions, is the *Final Act of the Conference on Security and Co-operation in Europe* (CSCE) of 1975.[3] But the same guiding principles have been nurtured in the UN since its establishment. Especially important in this respect are the UN declarations of 1970 on Principles of International Law Concerning Friendly Relations and Co-operation among States, and on Strengthening of International Security. Likewise, the two conventions devoted specifically to the dissemination of information (broadcasting of 1936, and correction of 1952) can be seen as universal expressions of the striving towards détente.

[3] See the chapter "Helsinki: The New Equation", by K. Nordenstreng & H. I. Schiller in their *National Sovereignty and International Communication*, Norwood, New Jersey: Ablex Publishing Corporation, 1969, pp. 238–243.

Yet the idea of détente—like that of peace and security in general—has not always been attached to communication in the form of a special standard. As a matter of fact, information is often thought of as an abstract category, in the sense of unrestrained *free flow*. As such, it is understood to be a factor which, without any contentious considerations, will promote peace and détente, or which is an integral part of peaceful international relations. (E.g., the 1960 Draft Declaration on Freedom of Information, and Resolution 59 (I) of 1946.) The wording of the 1958 *UN Resolution 1313 (XIII)* on Freedom of Information is typical in this respect:

> *Recognizing further* that greater freedom of communications would lessen international tension and promote mutual understanding and confidence, thereby allowing countries and peoples more easily to understand and compose their differences. . . .

It is evident that this kind of linkage between information and peaceful international relations does not mean the same as a clearcut obligation placed on the contents of communication. A typical example of the latter is the 1947 *UN Resolution 110 (II),* which urges the Governments of Member States to take appropriate steps, within their constitutional limits:

> a) to promote, by all means of publicity and propaganda available to them, friendly relations among nations based upon the purposes and principles of the Charter;
>
> b) to encourage the dissemination of all information designed to give expression to the undoubted desire of all peoples for peace. . . .

In the same spirit, but worded even more clearly, the *Declaration of the Principles of International Cultural Cooperation,* adopted unanimously by the General Conference of Unesco in 1966, states (article VII, paragraph 2):

> In cultural co-operation, stress shall be laid on ideas and values conducive to the creation of a climate of friendship and peace. Any mark of hostility in attitudes and in expression of opinion shall be avoided. Every effort shall be made, in presenting and disseminating information, to ensure its authenticity.

In fact, the political objective may turn against itself, depending on how the relationship between communication and peace has been established.[4] Therefore, the meaning and the context of the concepts used are

[4] Ibid., p. 239, and Nordenstreng, "Détente and Exchange of Information Between East and West", in *Yearbook of Finnish Foreign Policy 1975,* Helsinki: The Finnish Institute of International Affairs, 1976, pp. 57–65.

just as important as is the fact, whether or not a theme (in this case, détente) occurs in connection with information. Consequently, we must be careful in reading inventories such as that presented in Chapter 5, because two identically marked instruments may in fact contain opposite patterns of thinking.

In any case, we may say that a quite clearcut principle can be derived from international law, according to which *the dissemination of information should promote détente and international understanding that in turn promote peace and cooperation among nations.* The doctrine that any communication and propaganda, as such, is regarded as an element in peaceful international relations, is alien to this general principle. That doctrine dominated the international community in the 1940s and 1950s, but by now it has lost much of its legitimacy, due to the challenges of the socialist and developing parts of the international community. On the other hand, in many instruments—including the the Mass Media Declaration of Unesco —the objectives of peace, security, détente, etc., have been linked with mass communications in such a loose manner that may give rise to conflicting interpretations.[5]

Contradictory and evasive formulations do not, however, reduce the importance of the general principle. In a closer look we may single out the following standards:

1. communication in support of peace and security in general;
2. communication, particularly in support of friendly relations between states and of international cooperation, including the obligation to refrain from defamatory propaganda;
3. refrain from false and distorted reports, i.e., standards for the truthfulness and objectivity of information;
4. refrain from information supporting subversive activities in another country.

PEACE AND SECURITY

The obligation placed on communication in promoting international peace and security can be understood in general terms as an objective which also includes the aforementioned three "military standards." The theme of peace and security is used here in a narrower sense: to advocate *the cause of peace and security through communication by making use of various positive means,* such as objective descriptions of the historical develop-

---

[5] The Constitution of Unesco, if recalled as a whole and not only in terms of the "free flow" phrase, provides a linkage between peace and information in a clear and evident manner, as indicated above in Chapter 3. See also K. Nordenstreng, "IOJ President Denies Moves at Unesco Assembly Had State Control of Media as Their Target," *IPI Report,* February 1977 (Vol. 26., No. 2), pp. 10–11.

ments of nations and their present social conditions, and by providing information on the reasons behind international conflicts and on peaceful means for their settlement. Similarly, explanations of the foundations of the international system and of international law are positive means available in disseminating information for the promotion of the cause of peace and security. As early as 1936, the *International Convention on Broadcasting* stated (in its Article 5):

> Each of the High Contracting Parties undertakes to place at the disposal of the other High Contracting Parties, should they request, any information that, in his opinion, is of such a character as to facilitate the broadcasting, by the various broadcasting services, of items calculated to promote a better knowledge of the civilisation and the conditions of life of his own country as well as of the essential features of the development of his relations with other peoples and of his contribution to the organisation of peace.

Whereas the maintenance of international peace and security has been recognized as one of the fundamental objectives of the international community, it is obvious that this objective creates obligations on communication to ward off information that directly threatens peace and security, and, conversely, to support this objective actively and by positive means. Thus, participation in, and support of, peace movements should be understood not merely as free civil activities or fashionable political undertakings, but as obligations on states, derived from international law, to be taken seriously by the mass media and by journalists.

How this obligation can be adhered to and translated into practice is well exemplified by the 1974 *Unesco Recommendation Concerning Education for International Understanding, Cooperation and Peace and Education relating to Human Rights and Fundamental Freedoms.* This instrument, with recommendations that the mass media promote its objectives, proposes:

> 14. Education should include critical analysis of the historical and contemporary factors of an economic and political nature underlying the contradictions and tensions between countries, together with study of ways of overcoming these contradictions, which are the real impediments to understanding, true international cooperation and the development of world peace.
>
> 15. Education should emphasize the true interests of peoples and their incompatibility with the interests of monopolistic groups holding economic and political power, which practise exploitation and foment war.
>
> 18. Education should be directed both towards the eradication of conditions which perpetuate and aggravate major problems affect-

ing human survival and well-being—inequality, injustice, international relations based on the use of force—and towards measures of international cooperation likely to help solve them. Education which in this respect must necessarily be of an interdisciplinary nature should relate to such problems as:

a) equality of rights of peoples, and the right of peoples to self-determination;

b) the maintenance of peace; different types of war and their causes and effects; disarmament; the inadmissibility of using science and technology for warlike purposes and their use for the purposes of peace and progress; the nature and effect of economic, cultural and political relations between countries and the importance of international law for these relations, particularly for the maintenance of peace. . . .

FRIENDSHIP AND COOPERATION

A special aspect of the obligation concerning peace and security is the obligation regarding the dissemination of information to promote friendly relations between states, as well as international cooperation. In many instruments of international law the two obligations appear together, as may be noted in the above quotations (see particularly the Geneva declaration of 1962). The *UN Resolution 32/154* of 1977 is typical in this respect. (It concerns the implementation of the 1970 Declaration on the Strengthening of International Security.) Its preambular section contains the following phrase:

[General Assembly] *Recognizing* the need for objective dissemination of information about developments in the political, social, economic, cultural and other fields and the role and responsibility of the mass media in this respect, thus contributing to the growth of trust and friendly relations among States.

It is noteworthy that here the idea and, to some extent, even the wording is the same as in a Finnish-Soviet communiqué issued at the conclusion of the 25th anniversary celebration of the Treaty of Friendship, Cooperation and Mutual Assistance in April 1973, stating, inter-alia, that the mass media of the two countries have:

. . . a significant task in serving the further strengthening of friendship and trust between the Finnish and Soviet peoples with the sense of responsibility and with the objectiveness that this important matter requires, without jeopardising the favourable development of friendly relations between both countries.[6]

Consequently, although the standard for friendship and cooperation is inseparable, in a way, from the standard for peace and security, friendship and cooperation can also be understood as a separate issue. The same distinction can be found in the fundamental principles of international law; the maintenance of peace and security and the striving for international cooperation both have their place as basic principles.

Moreover, there is a special standard that pertains to friendly relations among states: *to refrain from defamatory propaganda about other states, their leaders and people.* Whitton, for example, lists this type of propaganda (defamatory propaganda) as one of the three categories of "hostile international propaganda" put under sanctions by international law, the other types being war propaganda and subversive propaganda.[7] The fact that this standard has been generally recognized can be explained by the basic principles of international law; one consequence of the equal sovereignty of states is that states must respect the rights of other states.

The standard for friendly international relations was put into clear language for the first time towards the end of the 1930s in the League of Nations Convention Concerning the Use of Broadcasting in the Cause of Peace quoted earlier. Its Article 3 reads:

> The High Contracting Parties mutually undertake to prohibit and, if occasion arises, to stop without delay within their respective territories any transmission likely to harm good international understanding by statements the incorrectness of which is or ought to be known to the persons responsible for the broadcast. They further mutually undertake to ensure that any transmission likely to harm good international understanding by incorrect statements shall be rectified at the earliest possible moment by the most effective means, even if the incorrectness has become apparent only after the broadcast has taken place.

After the war, the same standard was stated soon after the establishment of the new world organization. In 1947 the *UN General Assembly Resolution 127 (II)* invited the Governments of Members States:

---

[6] The relevant part of this communiqué has been reproduced in Nordenstreng's article referred to in note 4 above, p. 63.

[7] J. B. Whitton, "Hostile International Propaganda and International Law," in Nordenstreng & Schiller, *op. cit.*, pp. 217–229.

. . .to study such measures as might with advantage be taken on the national plane to combat, within the limits of constitutional procedures, the diffusion of false or distorted reports likely to injure friendly relations between States. . . .

Later on, this standard appears in several contexts, as, for example, in the 1950 *UN Resolution 424 (V),* dealing with interference with radio signals in external broadcasting (by condemning such interference as contrary to the objective of freedom of information, as was customary under the conditions of the Cold War):

4. Invites all governments to refrain from radio broadcasts that would mean unfair attacks or slanders against other peoples anywhere and in so doing to conform strictly to an ethical conduct in the interest of world peace by reporting facts truly and objectively.

The latest pronouncement of the international community to this effect can be found in the *UN Declaration on the Preparation of Societies for Life in Peace,* adopted in December 1978:

Every state has the duty to discourage advocacy of hatred and prejudice against other peoples as contrary to the principles of peaceful coexistence and friendly co-operation.

We may note that this Declaration does not specify inadmissible information by definitions such as "false or distorted," but that it speaks in general terms about hostile and prejudiced information, i.e., also including information that may be true. It can be concluded that the international community is more and more prepared to accept this principle, if not yet always in practice, to work in favor of friendly relations between states and peoples, or, as it is concisely called, international understanding.

The prohibition of defamatory propaganda obliges states to prevent the practice of such mass communication within their respective territories. On the other hand, the prohibitive standard does not confer an obligation upon a communicator to refrain from criticism or even from accusations against a foreign country and its leaders; it only presupposes *the avoidance of hostile campaigns of broad dimensions and with obvious defamatory intent.* Furthermore, if the international community, under the leadership of the UN, has declared the government of a state criminal and unlawful, it can hardly be thought that the prohibition of defamatory propaganda is any longer applicable in such a case.

QUALITY AND RESPONSIBILITY

The standards relating to friendly relations among states are of particular interest because they provide quite *specific definitions of the character and nature of disseminated information,* and even of the journalistic principles governing the acquisition and elaboration of information. Most of the instruments quoted earlier concerning this standard specify, in one way or another, the requirements for the quality of information ("objective," "false or distorted reports," etc.).

Besides the specific quality of information, these international instruments also stress the *responsibility of the mass media and communicators.* The 1952 *Convention on the International Right of Correction* is particularly explicit in this respect, as it states (Article II):

> 1. Recognizing that the professional responsibility of correspondents and information agencies requires them to report facts without discrimination and in their proper context and thereby to promote respect for human rights and fundamental freedoms, to further international understanding and cooperation and to contribute to the maintenance of international peace and security.

In some instruments, the question of the specific quality—most important, that of veracity—has been elaborated in a separate standard, which is not presented simply as a means of promoting friendly international relations, but as a *professional norm* pertaining to mass communication in general. The quest for truth is a typical norm of this kind. Such journalistic-type definitions conferred upon the contents of communication do not, however, constitute a separate category of standards under international law. It remains a general rule that international instruments qualify the contents of information through certain political obligations, such as peace, friendship, etc.

However, there is one aspect relating to the quality of information from the journalistic point of view which has been repeated in international instruments with such a degree of consistency that it can be accepted as a distinct standard: *the purposeful dissemination of false information.* It is typically related to problems of friendly international relations, whereby this form of communication is defined as impermissible ("the dissemination of false or distorted reports is likely to injure friendly relations among states"), but it has also been associated with standards concerning other themes, though often implicitly. The above-mentioned Final Document of the UN Special Session on Disarmament is particularly clearcut. It urges Member States "to avoid dissemination of false and tendentious information concerning armaments."

In principle, it is significant that the requirement to refrain from dissemination of false information, and thus to maintain truthfulness and objectivity, has been presented as a condition in many international instruments, which specifies, and, in that respect, limits, the principle of freedom of information. Hence, the 1958 UN Resolution (1313 [XIII]), for example, while it suggests that freedom of information as such alleviates international tensions and promotes mutual understanding, likewise defines freedom of information in an essentially different manner from Article 19 of the Universal Declaration on Human Rights (which does not confer any requirements upon the contents of information):

> [General Assembly] *Reiterating* its belief in the free flow of undistorted news and information within countries and across national frontiers as an essential basis for an accurate and undistorted understanding of events and situations. . . .

In the same way, the principle of freedom of information was qualified in the years 1959 to 1961 by the *Draft Convention on Freedom of Information,* adopted by the Third Committee of the UN General Assembly. In its preamble the States Parties to this Convention:

> *Considering* that the free interchange of accurate, objective and comprehensive information and of opinions, both in the national and in the international spheres, is essential to the causes of democracy and peace and for the achievement of political, social, cultural and economic progress,
> *Considering* that freedom of information implies respect for the right of everyone to form an opinion through the fullest possible knowledge of the facts. . . .

Article 2 of the Draft Convention enumerates a number of items which entitle to limitation of freedom of information by law. These limitations include "systematic dissemination of false reports harmful to friendly relations among nations."

The same idea had been expressed earlier, in the 1952 Convention on the International Right of Correction, the preamble of which deserves being quoted in entirety:

> *The Contracting States,*
> *Desiring* to implement the right of their peoples to be fully and reliably informed,
> *Desiring* to improve understanding between their peoples through the free flow of information and opinion,

Desiring thereby to protect mankind from the scourge of war, to prevent the recurrence of aggression from any source, and to combat all propaganda which is either designed or likely to provoke or encourage any threat to the peace, breach of the peace, or act of aggression,

Considering the danger to the maintenance of friendly relations between peoples and to the preservation of peace, arising from the publication of inaccurate reports,

Considering that at its second regular session the General Assembly of the United Nations recommended the adoption of measures designed to combat the dissemination of false or distorted reports likely to injure friendly relations between States,

Considering, however, that it is not at present practicable to institute, on the international level, a procedure for verifying the accuracy of a report which might lead to the imposition of penalties for the publication of false or distorted reports,

Considering, moreover, that to prevent the publication of reports of this nature or to reduce their pernicious effects, it is above all necessary to promote a wide circulation of news and to heighten the sense of responsibility of those regularly engaged in the dissemination of news,

Considering that an effective means to these ends is to give States directly affected by a report, which they consider false or distorted and which is disseminated by an information agency, the possibility of securing commensurate publicity for their corrections,

Considering that the legislation of certain States does not provide for a right of correction of which foreign governments may avail themselves, and that it is therefore desirable to institute such a right on the international level, and

Having resolved to conclude a Convention for these purposes,

Have agreed as follows:

Accordingly, there is in the international community an orientation towards a balanced understanding of freedom of information—a *concept of freedom in which the truthfulness of information constitutes an integral part.* Such an orientation means, as a matter of fact, a return to the concepts that had a legitimate status before the Cold War period; for example, in addition to the free flow of information, the Charter of Unesco speaks in 1945 about the "pursuit of objective truth."

Manifestations from the 1970s in support of the new balanced concept of freedom can be found in the Final Act of the CSCE, and in the 1970 *Declaration on the Mass Communication Media and Human Rights, adopted by the Council of Europe.* (The major member states of the Council of Europe belong to NATO and undoubtedly represent a "Western" viewpoint.) This Declaration, besides underlining the right of the mass media to a free acquisition and diffusion of information, sets forth an obligation, associated with this right, which means that the mass media "must diffuse complete and general information on public affairs." Specifically pertaining to information about foreign countries, the Declaration states:

> Special measures are necessary to ensure the freedom of foreign correspondents, including the staff of international press agencies, in order to permit the public to receive accurate information from abroad. These measures should cover the status, duties and privileges of foreign correspondents and should include protection from arbitrary expulsion. They impose a corresponding duty of accurate reporting.

Incidentally, this declaration by the Council of Europe is the only major international instrument that makes a distinction between news and commentary; in general, the instruments speak only about "reports," "information," etc. However, the distinction between news and commentary is not of central importance in this declaration; it only mentions "the clear distinction between reported information and comments" as one question among many others that the professional code of ethics for journalists ought to cover.

Concerning the principles of communication, we should repeat in this context what was said earlier about propaganda for war; freedom of information must not be used for dissemination of information contrary to international law, including information likely to jeopardize international cooperation and friendly relations between states and peoples. Moreover, these conditions, conferred upon the dissemination of information and determined by international law, specify the concept of freedom of information; freedom must not be allowed to be used for a purported deviation from the facts, nor from an over-all picture founded on these facts. We may say here that *objectivity of information*—in the sense of the fullest possible truthfulness or veracity as they are understood in the modern theory of journalistic objectivity[8]—is a principle strongly supported by international law, although it has not yet been elaborated into a specific international standard.

SUBVERSIVE PROPAGANDA

Subversive propaganda directed against another state can be understood as the opposite of all the positive aspirations dealt with above concerning peace and security on the one hand and friendship and cooperation on the other. In a way this kind of propaganda may be regarded as being

---

[8] See P. Hemánus, "Objectivity in Mass Communication," *The Democratic Journalist*, 10/1979, pp. 7–11.

parallel to the propaganda for war. The prohibition of subversive propaganda has long been a rule of international law and, as Whitton states, "of all categories of hostile propaganda, this has been the most frequent, the most deeply feared and resented, and the greatest cause of friction and retaliation—from diplomatic protest to actual warfare."[9] That this aspect of limiting freedom of information is indeed appreciated by distinguished experts of international law is demonstrated by Ian Brownlie, professor of international law at the Oxford University in England:

> . . .States need not submit to subversion. . .but may take all possible counter-measures on their territory and commit acts of lawful reprisal. . .Thus jamming of propaganda broadcasts would be a lawful reprisal.[10]

It is logical, then, that the 1936 Convention Concerning the Use of Broadcasting in the Cause of Peace begins with a provision on this very aspect (Article 1):

> The High Contracting Parties mutually undertake to prohibit and, if occasion arises, to stop without delay the broadcasting within their respective territories of any transmission which to the detriment of good international understanding is of such a character as to incite the population of any territory to acts incompatible with the internal order or the security of a territory of a High Contracting Party.

Subversive propaganda has not been dealt with very extensively in international instruments, but in scholarly theories it has been defined quite precisely. It has become customary to make a distinction between three kinds of subversive propaganda. First, there is propaganda aimed at creating such confusion in a foreign state as to weaken its position in relation to one's own state. The second category is made up of propaganda which is directed to an ethnic, racial, or religious segment of the population in a foreign country, with the purpose of provoking that part of the population to resistance against their government. Third, there is direct, full-scale propaganda aimed at promoting revolution in a foreign country.

Here, as in the case of defamatory propaganda, it must be noted that propaganda against a foreign government may be permissible in a situation in which the government in question has been declared criminal

---

[9] Whitton's article referred to in note 6 above, p. 218.

[10] I. Brownlie: *International Law and the Use of Force by States*, Oxford, U.K: Oxford University Press, 1963, p. 435. Also Brownlie's predecessor O'Connell has pointed out: "There is no duty on a State not to resort to *jamming of radio* broadcasts from other States." See D. P. O'Connell, *International Law, Volume One*, Dobbs Ferry, New York: Oceana Publications, 1965, p. 331.

and unlawful by the UN-led international community. Yet the prohibition of subversive propaganda is the general rule. Normally this kind of propaganda is an infringement of two leading principles of international law, state sovereignty and the principle of non-intervention in the internal affairs of another state.

DECOLONIZATION AND THE NEW INTERNATIONAL ECONOMIC ORDER

A contemporary inventory of international standards for the mass media remains incomplete if it does not include standards for the promotion of decolonization and the New International Economic Order, as defined by the UN. To be precise, this theme—unlike war propaganda, subversive or defamatory propaganda, and information in the service of friendly international relations—has not yet reached the level of undisputed "positive law." Thus far it reflects only political pressures prevailing in the international community due to the emergence of the developing countries and their organizations, such as the Movement of Non-aligned Countries and OPEC.

This pressure, however, is so considerable and has already been expressed in so many instruments, relevant from the viewpoint of international law, that standards in support of the struggle against neocolonialism, as well as for the implementation of the New International Economic Order, deserve their place in a listing of international standards concerning the mass media. In this respect, the theme can be compared with standards for disarmament information, which also represents an emerging theme without legally established international rules, but with strong political pressure behind it.

The UN program of action for the full implementation of the 1960 Declaration on the Granting of Independence to Colonial Countries and Peoples, adopted in 1970, includes the following:

> [The General Assembly] *Considering* that, by arousing world public opinion and promoting practical action for the speedy liquidation of colonialism in all its forms and manifestations, the Declaration has played and will continue to play an important role in assisting the peoples under colonial domination in their struggle for freedom and independence. . .
>
> 7. All States shall undertake measures aimed at enhancing public awareness of the need for active assistance in the achievement of complete decolonization and, in particular, creating satisfactory conditions for activities by national and international non-governmental organizations in support of the peoples under colonial domination.

8. The United Nations as well as all States shall intensify their efforts in the field of public information in the area of decolonization through all media, including publications, radio and television. Of special importance will be programmes relating to United Nations activities on decolonization, the situation in colonial Territories and the struggle being waged by colonial peoples and the national liberation movements.

In its recent (annual) *resolution on Dissemination of Information on Decolonization* (34/95 of 13 December 1979) the UN General Assembly, inter alia:

2. *Reaffirms* the importance of effecting the widest possible dissemination of information on the evils and dangers of colonialism, on the determined efforts of the colonial peoples to achieve self-determination, freedom and independence and on the assistance being provided by the international community towards the elimination of the remaining vestiges of colonialism in all its forms;

3. *Requests* the Secretary-General, having regard to the suggestions of the Special Committee, to continue to take concrete measures through all the media at his disposal, including publications, radio and television, to give widespread and continuous publicity to the work of the United Nations in the field of decolonization. . .

4. *Invites* all States, the specialized agencies and other organizations within the United Nations system and non-governmental organizations having a special interest in the field of decolonization to undertake or intensify, in co-operation with the Secretary-General and within their respective spheres of competence, the large-scale dissemination of the information referred to in paragraph 2 above.

Also, the above-mentioned Declaration on the Preparation of Societies for Life in Peace, adopted by UN General Assembly in 1978, includes a strong appeal for decolonization:

7. Every State has the duty to discourage all manifestations and practices of colonialism, as well as racism, racial discrimination and *apartheid*, as contrary to the right of peoples to self-determination and to other human rights and fundamental freedoms.

That this duty is relevant also to the mass media is made clear by a subsequent passage in which all states are called upon, in order to implement the principles of the Declaration, inter alia:

To ensure that their policies relevant to the implementation of the present Declaration, including educational processes and teaching methods as well as media information activities, incorporate contents compatible with the task of the preparation for life in peace of entire societies and, in particular, the young generations.

As with standards for peace discussed above, it should be noted here as well that what is involved is not only a principle emerging from changes in international political conditions, but also the implementation of the basic principles of international law, particularly of the self-determination of peoples. Consequently, the mass media should be interested in "Third World problems" not only because they provide politically and economically important material for news and reports, but also, and above all, because this interest is based on principles of international law.

Moreover, it becomes clear from contemporary instruments, such as the Declaration on the Preparation of Societies for Life in Peace, that the objectives of decolonization and of the New International Economic Order are closely related to the overall objective of international peace and security. This is explicitly stated in a resolution (34/100), adopted by the UN General Assembly in 1979, where a preambular paragraph states:

> *Reaffirming* the close link existing between the strengthening of international peace and security, disarmament, decolonization and development, and stressing the urgent need for concerted action to achieve progress in the implementation of the decisions and recommendations adopted at the sixth and seventh special sessions of the United Nations General Assembly concerning the establishment of a new international economic order, decisions and recommendations adopted at the tenth special session of the General Assembly devoted to disarmament, and the Declaration on the Preparation of Societies for Life in Peace contained in General Assembly resolution 33/73.

8

Standards at the National Level

International standards relating to the contents of communication on matters primarily at the national level are not as diversified and stratified as those regulating information activities at the international level. Indeed, regulation of the national level is concisely expressed in one single UN instrument, the 1966 *International Covenant on Civil and Political Rights*. Its Article 20, prohibiting by law any propaganda for war (an obligation at the international level discussed in Chapter 6), also sets a standard which typically represents the regulation of communication at the national level. Paragraph 2 of this Article reads as follows:

> Any advocacy of national, racial or religious hatred that constitutes incitement to discrimination, hostility or violence shall be prohibited by law.

Moreover, Article 19, on the freedom of opinion and expression, provides:

> 1. Everyone shall have the right to hold opinions without interference.
>
> 2. Everyone shall have the right to freedom of expression; this right shall include freedom to seek, receive and impart information and ideas of all kinds, regardless of frontiers, either orally, in writing or in print, in the form of art, or through any other media of his choice.
>
> 3. The exercise of the rights provided for in paragraph 2 of this article carries with it special duties and responsibilities. It may therefore be subject to certain restrictions, but these shall only be such as are provided by law and are necessary:
>
> a) For respect of the rights or reputations of others;
>
> b) For the protection of national security or of public order (*ordre public*), or of public health or morals.

This provision of the Covenant defines certain grounds on which states have a *right* to restrict the freedom of communication. On the other hand, this Article does not impose international legal *duties* upon states concerning the contents of communication in the same way as, for example, Article 20 does. Article 19(3) involves more general regulation, which, however, must be noted here because of the essential manner in which it relates to the contents of communication.

As a real obligation on the contents of communication pertaining to domestic matters, the Covenant, in conformity with international law in general (cf., the prohibition of propaganda for war), defines a certain prohibition: *prohibiting the advocating such hostile propaganda against some national group, race, or religious community as amounts to incitement to discrimination or violence.* It is no coincidence that discrimination and violence are expressly mentioned in this definition of prohibited propaganda. The prohibition of various forms of violence and discrimination—including those carried out by means of information—has become binding international law, as demonstrated, for example, by the UN Charter and the documents of the Nuremberg trials.

Thus, the obligation to refrain from propaganda which incites to discrimination and violence for national, racial, or religious reasons is, from the viewpoint of international law, more important than the right, defined by the Covenant, to restrict the freedom of information in the name of national security, public order, and morals, or for reasons connected with the rights and reputation of the individual. It is another matter that, apparently, the last-mentioned right is applied more often, and more broadly, than is the obligation to refrain from propaganda supporting discrimination and violence.

The general applicability of this standard is well illustrated by the *American Convention of Human Rights,* concluded in 1969. Article 13 of this instrument contains the following provision (drafted with the cooperation of the USA):

> 5. Any propaganda for war and any advocacy of national, racial or religious hatred that constitute incitements to lawless violence or to any other similar illegal action against any person or group of persons on any grounds including those of race, color, religion, language, or national origin shall be considered as offenses punishable by law.

RACIAL DISCRIMINATION

The *International Convention on the Elimination of All Forms of Racial Discrimination,* adopted in 1965, contains the following provisions:

> *Article 4*
> States Parties condemn all propaganda and all organizations which are based on ideas or theories of superiority of one race or

group of persons of one colour or ethnic origin, or which attempt to justify or promote racial hatred and discrimination in any form, and undertake to adopt immediate and positive measures designed to eradicate all incitement to, or acts of, such discrimination and, to this end, with due regard to the principles embodied in the Universal Declaration of Human Rights and the rights expressly set forth in article 5 of this Convention, *inter alia*:

(*a*) Shall declare an offence punishable by law all dissemination of ideas based on racial superiority or hatred, incitement to racial discrimination, as well as all acts of violence or incitement to such acts against any race or group of persons of another colour or ethnic origin, and also the provision of any assistance to racist activities, including the financing thereof;

(*b*) Shall declare illegal and prohibit organizations, and also organized and all other propaganda activities, which promote and incite racial discrimination, and shall recognize participation in such organization or activities as an offence punishable by law;

(*c*) Shall not permit public authorities or public institutions, national or local, to promote or incite racial discrimination.

Article 7

States Parties undertake to adopt immediate and effective measures, particularly in the fields of teaching, education, culture and information, with a view to combating prejudices which lead to racial discrimination and to promoting understanding, tolerance and friendship among nations and racial or ethnical groups, as well as to propagating the purposes and principles of the Charter of the United Nations, the Universal Declaration of Human Rights, the United Nations Declaration on the Elimination of All Forms of Racial Discrimination, and this Convention.

In Article 5, this Convention further obligates states to guarantee to everyone, "without distinction as to race, colour or national or ethnic origin," among other rights, the right to freedom of opinion and expression. This provision emphasizing the freedom of information is intended to afford protection against discrimination, and in no case can it annul the obligations placed on communication by the provisions cited above. The communication aspect is expressed in a similar way in the *International Convention on the Suppression and Punishment of the Crime of Apartheid*, adopted in 1973. The crime of apartheid is defined so as to include the deprivation of the freedom of opinion and of expression on the basis of racial discrimination.

It should be noted that Article 7 of the Convention on Racial Discrimination covers, besides racial discrimination, friendly relations among nations in general. Thus it contains, in addition to standards concerning national communication, for the abolition of discrimination, the standard, discussed in Chapter 7, for promoting friendly relations among countries and peoples.

It is also noteworthy that all the Nordic Countries, among others, have accepted these obligations concerning communication without reservations. Some Western countries, including England, Italy, Austria, France, and the U.S., have made a reservation in this respect (to Article 4). On the other hand, it is interesting to note that, only a few years later, most of these countries no longer considered it necessary to make a reservation to the corresponding provision in the International Covenant on Civil and Political Rights. As for the U.S., the question is open, because thus far it has not ratified the Covenant—the most significant human rights instrument.

The spirit of these conventions suggests an obligation to eliminate from communication even manifestations of propaganda not amounting to direct and consistent instigation. This kind of interpretation of relevant international legal rules is supported by the recent *Unesco Declaration on Race and Racial Prejudice,* unanimously adopted by the General Conference in 1978. Article 5 of this Declaration contains a specific provision on the mass media:

> The mass media and those who control or serve them, as well as all organized groups within national communities, are urged—with due regard to the principles embodied in the Universal Declaration of Human Rights, particularly the principle of freedom of expression—to promote understanding, tolerance and friendship among individuals and groups and to contribute to the eradication of racism, racial discrimination and racial prejudice, in particular by refraining from presenting a stereotyped, partial, unilateral or tendentious picture of individuals and of various human groups. Communication between racial and ethnic groups must be a reciprocal process, enabling them to express themselves and to be fully heard without let or hindrance. The mass media should therefore be freely receptive to ideas of individuals and groups which facilitate such communication.

In Article 7, the same Declaration states:

> In addition to political, economic and social measures, law is one of the principal means of ensuring equality in dignity and rights among individuals, and of curbing any propaganda, any form of organization or any practice which is based on ideas or theories referring to the alleged superiority of racial or ethnic groups or which seeks to justify or encourage racial hatred and discrimination in any form. States should adopt such legislation as is appropriate to

this end and see that it is given effect and applied by all their services, with due regard to the principles embodied in the Universal Declaration of Human Rights. Such legislation should form part of a political, economic and social framework conducive to its implementation. Individuals and other legal entities, both public and private, must conform with such legislation and use all appropriate means to help the population as a whole to understand and apply it.

Also, the Unesco Recommendation Concerning Education for International Understandiang, etc., cited in Chapter 7, contains some useful material relevant to the present topic:

> 39. Member States should promote appropriate measures to ensure that educational aids, especially textbooks, are free from elements liable to give rise to misunderstanding, mistrust, racialist reactions, contempt or hatred with regard to other groups or peoples. Materials should provide a broad background of knowledge which will help learners to evaluate information and ideas disseminated through the mass media that seem to run counter to the aims of this recommendation.

GENOCIDE

The crime of genocide can be understood as the gravest form of discrimination. In international law it has been defined by a special *Convention on the Prevention and Punishment of the Crime of Genocide,* adopted in 1948 stating inter alia:

> *Article II*
> In the present Convention, genocide means any of the following acts committed with intent to destroy, in whole or in part, a national, ethnical, racial or religious group, as such:
> (*a*) Killing members of the group;
> (*b*) Causing serious bodily or mental harm to members of the group;
> (*c*) Deliberately inflicting on the group conditions of life calculated to bring about its physical destruction in whole or in part;
> (*d*) Imposing measures intended to prevent births within the group;
> (*e*) Forcibly transferring children of the group to another group.
>
> *Article III*
> The following acts shall be punishable:
> (*a*) Genocide;

(b) Conspiracy to commit genocide;

(c) *Direct and public incitement to commit genocide;*

(d) Attempt to commit genocide;

(e) Complicity in genocide.

(Emphasis added)

The Genocide Convention is one of the relatively few important international legal instruments[1] to contain an indisputable standard concerning communication, although in this case the obligation is indirect ("public incitement"), in so far as the mass media is not explicitly mentioned. On the other hand, in many countries this convention is of no current interest. Yet in some countries, genocide is anything but a theoretical concept, as evidenced by what has happened, for example, in Kampuchea, East-Timor (Indonesia), and Uganda in the 1970s.

NATIONAL ORDER AND THE RIGHTS OF INDIVIDUALS

International law does not set other clearly defined standards for the performance of the mass media at the national level than those dealt with above. On the other hand, under the Covenant on Civil and Political Rights, states have a certain right to restrict freedom of information to the extent that it endangers interests connected with national order or rights of individuals. The same restrictions are included in the 1950 (West-) European Convention on Human Rights and in the American Convention on Human Rights. Thus, information concerning these questions is subject to regulation by international law, even though no direct standards are imposed with regard to these matters at the national level.

Here the concept of "national order" is understood to cover the *protection of national security, public order, public health, or morals.* The sphere of limitations discussed here has been defined by these words in Article 19 of the International Covenant on Civil and Political Rights. At the same time, the Article means that national laws restricting this kind of communication are not in conflict with the principle of freedom of information. The list contained in the above-mentioned European Convention on Human Rights is somewhat longer and more detailed. Even more extensive is the enumeration of possible limitations in the UN Draft Convention on Freedom of Information which, as was noted earlier, includes in its cata-

---

[1] The Convention was in fact the first UN treaty on human rights; it was unanimously adopted, and by 1980 has been ratified by nearly 90 states, not including the United States. An interesting discussion in this respect is provided by W. Korey in an article, "Sin of Omission," *Foreign Policy*, 39/1980, disclosing among other things: "The American failure to ratify the genocide treaty is a profound embarrassment to U.S. representatives in international forums." (p. 173)

log the systematic dissemination of incorrect reports which jeopardize friendly international relations. Furthermore, in the relevant provision (Art. 2), the Draft Convention also mentions incitement to violence and crime and includes attacks against the founders of religions.

It is well known that all of these concepts are rather vague—especially as far as limitations on information are concerned. Thus, the protection of morals against pornography is dependent on what kind of performances the prevailing moral and juridical views regard as "obscenity". These views have changed considerably since the adoption of the Geneva Convention, but the changes have not always been the same, even within a single country, not to speak of differences between societies. There is often disagreement on the subject, and sometimes it is not even possible to find a clear majority opinion.

State security is also a most problematic concept, and it is apparent that many countries—especially rightist dictatorships—tend to resort to it far beyond what is necessary, i.e., as a means of protecting the political group in power, rather than in maintaining proper national security. An instructive example is provided by Iran—both under the Shah's monarchy and under the Islamic Republic of Khomeini.

The International Covenant on Civil and Political Rights recognizes that, if the existence of the nation is threatened, the enjoyment of most human rights may be temporarily restricted. In Article 4, it is stated that in times of public emergency which threaten the life of the nation, and when the existence of such an emergency has been officially proclaimed, a contracting state may take measures derogating from its obligations under the Covenant to the extent required by the situation. These measures, however, may not be inconsistent with the state's other obligations under international law and may not involve discrimination against some part of the population. A state applying this emergency provision must immediately inform the UN Secretary General of this measure. A further communication is required when the state ceases to apply the restrictions. There are many rights concerning personal inviolability, legal personality of the individual, and fair trial from which no derogations are permitted even in time of public emergency, but, according to the Covenant, freedom of information does not belong to these strongly protected human rights. Consequently, *in times of public emergency which threaten the life of the nation, states are allowed to impose temporary limitations upon communication.*

There is another relevant provision in contemporary international law relating to state security which would justify restrictions in the field of information. This is to be found in the *Convention on the Law of the Sea*, the largest and most comprehensive codification project ever pursued by the international community. The Convention was completed by the Third

UN Conference on the Law of the Sea in 1982, whereby it was signed by as many as 117 states (not including the USA). Article 19 of this Convention deals with the innocent passage of foreign ships in the territorial sea of the coastal states: in the interest of navigation, foreign ships have the right to pass "innocently" through the territorial sea of any state. The Article also discusses activities which do not constitute such innocent passage:

> Passage of the foreign ship shall be considered to be prejudicial to the peace, good order or security of the coastal state, if in the territorial sea it engages in. . .
> (d) Any act of propaganda aimed at affecting the defence or security of the coastal state.[2]

Moreover, it is not only national security that justifies certain limitations to information, but a more general principle of state sovereignty is also involved. As stated by Leo Gross:

> The principle of freedom of outer space like the freedom of the high seas has its limits. Just as the freedom of the high seas ends where the territorial sea begins, so freedom of outer space ends where the territorial air space begins. But whereas there is a right of innocent passage through the territorial sea there is no such right through territorial air space. The right of innocent passage does not include, apart from some exceptions, the right for ships to enter ports without the consent of the territorial State. Similarly the use of outer space for satellite broadcasting does not include the right to enter the territorial air space or the territory of the subjacent State. If it is conceded, as in the present submission it must be, that a State may exclude radio transmissions, then it must also be conceded that it may exclude television broadcasts. It is always open to States to negotiate agreements for opening up access to their territories for radio and for television broadcasts.[3]

One of the essential elements of the national order is the concept of *public order*. In the 1966 Covenant (and in the Draft Convention on Freedom of Information) its contents have been made more precise by adding the French expression "ordre public" in parenthesis. In fact, this concept must be understood as being a synonym for *public policy,* as shown by the U.S. lawyer T. Buergenthal:

> The public policy of a state is reflected in its political, cultural, educational, social, and economic policies. Laws deemed necessary to

[2] UN document A/CONF.62/WP. 122 (7 October 1982).

[3] L. Gross. "Some International Law Aspects of the Freedom of Information and the Right to Communicate," in K. Nordenstreng & H. I. Schiller (Eds.), *National Sovereignity and International Communication,* Norwood, N.J.: Ablex, 1979, p. 211.

protect the "public order" could consequently encompass legislation prohibiting or restricting radio and television advertisements, requiring the licensing of all or certain communications media, promulgating programming standards, regulating the importation of foreign cultural and information products, and so on. . . . Clearly, the public policy limitation can be interpreted very broadly indeed and is the clause most likely to be invoked to legitimate restrictive governmental measures designed to guard against "cultural imperialism."[4]

The concept of public order is mentioned as grounds for limitation, not only in the human rights conventions referred to above but also in those *Unesco agreements which regulate the importation and international circulation of educational, scientific, and cultural materials.* These agreements do not affect "the rights of contracting States to take measures, in conformity with their legislation, to prohibit or limit the importation, or the circulation after importation, of articles on grounds relating directly to national security, public order or public morals" (as stated in Article V of the Florence Agreement). Moreover, in the *International Telecommunication Convention* (Montreaux, 1965, and Torremolinos, 1973) it is also stated that public order (in addition to national security) is a legitimate reason for states to restrict telecommunication. This Convention is the basis of organized broadcasting and other telecommunication at the world-wide level, and is also the legal basis of the ITU, the UN specialized agency in charge of the technical-administrative aspects of these activities.

On the basis of public order and, more broadly, on the basis of national self-determination, it is possible to elaborate on what is meant by the protection of national culture—for example, by restrictions concerning the importation and ciruclation of international "mass culture." It is the view of international law that this and other corresponding explicitly-recognized rights of states to impose restrictions at the national level must be respected by other states, regardless of whether these restrictions happen to be in accordance with the views of other states. The international community should not, however, accept such restrictions when they are based on a clear exaggeration of the public order concept. Consequently, grounds entitling a state to impose limitations at the national level must not be applied in a manner to annul other parts of human rights conventions and the principle of freedom of information defined in them.

In addition to factors connected with public order, *the rights or reputations of others* are also accepted as grounds justifying limitations with regard to communication at the national level. The emphasized words can

---

[4] T. Buergenthal., "The Right to Receive Information Across National Boundaries," in *Control of Direct Broadcast Satellites: Values in Conflict,* Palo Alto, California: The Aspen Institute for Humanistic Studies, 1976, pp. 78–80.

be found in Article 19 of the International Covenant on Civil and Political Rights, in which respect for individuals is mentioned as one ground, in addition to the protection of public order, in a kind of catalog of the reasons justifying restrictions on freedom of information. This being the case, dissemination of information through the mass media which jeopardizes the "respect of the rights and reputations of others" may be subjected to restrictions provided by law, with no international legal rules on freedom of information being violated thereby.

The offence of *libel* has been traditionally a part of the criminal legislation of most countries. For instance, in Finland it was recently supplemented by a provision on the *right to privacy*. (This happened after commercial magazines had excessively exploited the private affairs of individuals.) These rules, as well as those legislative reforms which aim at securing the secrecy of computer registers containing personal data, are, therefore, in complete accordance with the international regulation of communication and do not, as such, contravene the principle of freedom of information.

Copyright must also be regarded as one of the rights of individuals under consideration here. Not only the Universal Declaration of Human Rights (Art. 27) but also the *International Covenant on Economic, Social and Cultural Rights* of 1966 (which is parallel to the International Covenant on Civil and Political Rights) mentions copyright. In Article 15 it is stated that the states parties to the Covenant recognize the right of everyone

> . . .to benefit from the protection of the moral and material interests resulting from any scientific, literary or artistic production of which he is the author.

Here, as in the context of national order, the (West-) European Covention on Human rights and the UN Draft Convention on Freedom of Information specify and, as it were, broaden the sphere of matters accepted as being subject to restrictions, at least if this sphere is compared with the narrow formulations included in the Covenant on Civil and Political Rights. In the two conventions the list has been extended by a reference to the *impartiality of the judiciary*, which, in effect, means limitations upon communication with respect to the reporting on trials, disclosure of names of those convicted, etc. The Council of Europe Declaration on Mass Communication Media and Human Rights of 1970 mentions this principle of impartiality of the judiciary as one of the questions which should be dealt with in journalistic-ethical rules. This declaration, moreover, contains an entire section of detailed recommendations on the right to privacy.

III

From International Law to Professional Ethics

The preceding survey of standard-setting instruments has revealed a large number of international documents relating to the mass media. In fact, the collection would be even larger if we included the bilateral and multilateral treaties which states have agreed on outside the UN forums, but in conformity with the principles of international law (to end wars, to establish regional economic communities, to agree on mutual friendship and cooperation, etc.). Many of these "geopolitical" instruments contain indirect, if not direct, obligations for the mass media, and thus add further standards to those deriving from the "universal will" (of the substantial majority) of the international community.

As noted in Chapter 5, international standards are usually not aimed directly at the mass media, but rather at states as subjects of international law. In fact, there is only one instrument of international law proper that is clearly addressed to journalists: the Convention on the International Right of Correction (cf., Chapter 7). In recognizing "the professional responsibility of correspondents and information agencies" for factual reporting in the interest of universal values, such as peace and international understanding, this instrument clearly states that journalists may be understood to be subject to international law. However, since the Convention has not won wide acceptance in the international community, this acknowledgement cannot be considered as an international principle. Those conventions of a more universal nature which prohibit incitement to war, racial discrimination, apartheid, and genocide also carry obvious obligations for the mass media, but it is understood that a state entering into such conventions will introduce the necessary regulations within its own jurisdiction.

Consequently, journalists and other "gatekeepers" of the content of the mass media, while they are expected to know the relevant standards of international law, are not simply subordinated to an array of international instruments. It is the domestic jurisdiction that provides the immediate legal and political framework for the mass media, including the journalists, of each country. Thus the state (national legislation) can be seen as an intermediary between the international community (international law) and the mass media (journalists). This leads us to consider the relationship between the media (whatever their form of ownership and control) and the state (whatever its political system), not only in terms of the rights and obligations of the media in each society, but also in terms of the standards set by the international community. In this respect, it is only natural to say that "States are responsible for the activities in the international sphere of all mass media under their jurisdiction," as the controversial Article XII of the "Nairobi draft" reads (cf., Chapter 2).

This "State responsibility" for the mass media under international law is a matter of fact, regardless of the form of ownership and system of control of the mass media in a country—whether by the state, parties, trade unions, churches, private corporations, or individuals. International instruments, including the Mass Media Declaration (and the drafts that preceded it), do not prescribe any particular form of media system, for example "state control" or "government censorship," as has been claimed by those opposed to the movement towards a new international information order, and to the Mass Media Declaration as its manifestation. It is up to each country to define the rules and regulations by which the international obligations are enforced upon relevant institutions.

It is a well-known fact that the Western "libertarian" system of state-media relationship lays great emphasis on the professional competence and responsibility of those in charge of the mass media, in particular journalists, as a substitute for legal or other types of official control of the content of communication. As is well illustrated by the history of the Mass Media Declaration, Western countries are reluctant to apply the standard-setting international instruments at the national level by means of binding laws and state decrees. Such official regulation is seen as a dangerous—if not unconstitutional—step towards "government control" away from the "freedom of the press." Instead, the "self-regulation" of the mass media is viewed as an appropriate mechanism for fulfilling the obligations placed on the media by society as well as by the international community. It is logical, then, that "social responsibility" and "professional ethics" have become concepts of strategic importance.

But we are led to study professionalism and its manifestations, such as codes of ethics, not only because of the Western tradition. As noted in

Chapter 5, the standards provided by relevant international instruments, even if not directly binding on the media legally, do create strong moral obligations for those in charge of the performance of the media, in particular journalists. In brief, international law is to be seen as an essential source of professional ethics in journalism. This is not only an analytic conclusion but also an obvious reflection of the fact that, in addition to what is determined by the Convention on the International Right of Correction, the International Covenant on Civil and Political Rights—an important authoritative instrument of international law—sets a strong obligation to use the freedom of information in a responsible way (cf., Chapter 8).

The remaining two chapters focus on these perspectives of professionalism. Chapter 9 reviews various codes of journalistic ethics which have been adopted or suggested for professional self-regulation. An inventory of the topics covered in these instruments proves that international standards are poorly, if at all, represented in them. Journalistic ethics seem to be underdeveloped in terms of international affairs. Yet the rich material provided by the instruments of international law and politics serve as an excellent source for extending the codes of ethics—and at the same time the whole philosophy of professionalism in journalism—to the sphere of international relations.

Together with the preceding parts of the book, Chapter 9 is a contribution to the long-term project of modernizing professional codes by bringing them from a narrow-minded, technocratic and parochial approach to a genuinely ethical one, in conformity with what may be called "universal values"—a project advocated both by the international community (the Mass Media Declaration) and the profession itself (the Mexico Declaration). An appeal to the same effect is made in Chapter 10—after an examination of the arguments of those who in the "Talloires offensive" have argued against, not only Unesco and the new order, but also the internationalization of professional ethics.

9

Codes of Ethics: An Inventory

Professional codes in journalism have many faces and several functions, as shown by surveys on their development throughout the world.[1] In the light of these surveys, it is evident that a consideration of international obligations as defined by various instruments has not been a central factor in the process of introducing and updating these formalized manifestations of professional ethics. However, there are good reasons to believe that the Mass Media Declaration constitutes a turning point in the history of journalism, in that, since the end of the 1970s, the ethics and codes of the profession will pay more and more attention to the international arena. The present Chapter provides material for such a reconstruction of professional ethics by pooling together internationally relevant elements of the codes written or proposed by the early 1980s.

COMPARISON WITH INTERNATIONAL INSTRUMENTS

Our point of departure is a crude content analysis of 50 codes of ethics, using the same overall classifications used in analyzing the international instruments (see Chapter 5 and Appendix 24). Since the codes in question include most national and international codes of journalistic ethics known to Unesco in the late 1970s,[2] it can be said that we are *comparing manifestations of professional ethics in journalism around the world with the standards set by the international community.* The results of this exercise[3] can be summarized by noting how many codes, on the one hand, and international instruments, on the other, deal with each of the seven themes in question:

[1]For contemporary surveys with historical perspectives, see L. Bruun (Ed.), *Professional Codes in Journalism,* Prague: International Organization of Journalists, 1979; and J. C. Jones, *Mass Media Codes of Ethics and Councils: A Comparative International Study on Professional Standards,* Paris: Unesco Reports and Papers on Mass Communication, 1980.

[2]The bulk of the material under study was received from Unesco in 1976 when the Secretariat was involved in collecting copies of professional codes from the Member States (based on Resolution 4.111 of the 18th session of the General Conference in 1974, cf., Chapter 2). Some of these are reproduced in full in the two above mentioned surveys (Bruun, op. cit., and Jones, op. cit.). For a number of U.S. codes, see W. L. Rivers, W. Schramm & C. G. Christians, *Responsibility in Mass Communication* (Third Edition), New York: Harper & Row, 1980.

[3]As a matter of fact, this is part of the study on international instruments reported in Chapter 5 (see note 6 therein). The results of the "codes part" of the study were reported also in the author's contribution to *Protection of Journalists,* Paris: Unesco series New Communication Order, No. 4, 1980 (pp. 108–128).

	Codes (total 50)	Instruments (total 44)
1. Peace and security	14	28
2. War propaganda	5 (3 int.)	18
3. Friendship and cooperation	12	31
4. Objectivity, veracity, honesty	49 (4 int.)	19
5. Racial equality/discrimination	18	17
6. Other obligations	47 (9 int.)	31
7. Free flow of information	34 (4 int.)	25

Thus, 14 out of 50 codes, or just over one-fourth, cover in one way or another professional responsibilities related to peace and security. The same theme is included in 28 instruments out of 44, or well over half (note that the figures for instruments are based on those presented in Table 1, Chapter 5). War propaganda is included in only five codes, one tenth of the total, and even that number is high, because two of the codes speak about domestic or unspecified violence and security, leaving only three codes with a specifically international approach to the theme. The same distinction between a *general obligation* and a specifically *international obligation* is made for the topics of objectivity, other obligations, and free flow—all salient features in the codes as *general qualifiers,* but poorly reflected as *international standards.* Disregarding general references to truth, freedom, etc. (which do not specifically mention international reporting), and also disregarding here the theme of race (which, although regulated by international law, concerns primarily national affairs), we may conclude that *three codes out of five fail completely to cover international questions.*

To the extent that these codes do consider the international level, the best represented is the obligation to promote peace and security, typically combined with the standard of friendship and cooperation. On the other hand, standards concerning war propaganda and the nature of information disseminated (truthfulness, objectivity, honesty, etc.) as a factor in international relations are practically absent from the professional codes of journalists, with some notable exceptions to be discussed below. A code-by-code display of the presence and absence of the seven themes in question, both as general standards and as specifically international obligations, is presented in Table 3.[4]

---

[4]For convenience, names of countries are used to denote various codes, which does not imply that professional codes represent a state position. The titles, dates, and forums of adoption, etc. of the codes are not reported here. Most of this information can be obtained from the two surveys referred to in note 1 above. However, it should be noted that there is no comprehensive and unambiguous register of all national codes—on the contrary, there is much confusion about the status and significance of various codes.

Table 3
General (X) and International (O) Standards in Professional Codes of Ethics

	Peace and Security	War Propaganda	Friendship etc.	Objectivity etc.	Racial Equality	Other Duties	Free Flow
1. Australia				X		X	
2. Austria				X	X	O	O
3. Belgium	O		O	X		O	
4. Burma				X	X	X	X
5. Canada				X		X	
6. Chile	O			X	X	X	X
7. Corea (S) I				X	X	X	X
8. Corea (S) II				X		X	X
9. Cuba	O		O	X		O	
10. Egypt	O		O	X		O	O
11. England				X	X	X	X
12. Finland				X	X	X	X
13. France				X		X	X
14. Germany FRG I		O	O		X	X	
15. Germany FRG II				X	X	X	X
16. Germany GDR	O		O	X		O	
17. Greece				O		X	
18. Hungary			O	X		O	X
19. Ireland				X		X	X
20. Israel				X	X	X	X
21. Italy				X		X	X
22. Jamaica	O	X		X	X	X	
23. Japan	O			X		X	X
24. Mali				X		X	X
25. Mexico				X		X	X
26. Nigeria I	O	X		X	X	X	
27. Nigeria II				X		X	
28. Norway				X	X	X	X
29. Pakistan				X		X	X
30. Poland				X	X	X	
31. Portugal	O		O	X	X	X	X
32. S-Africa I			O	X		X	X
33. S-Africa II				X	X	X	X
34. Sri Lanka				X		X	X
35. Sweden				X	X	X	X
36. Switzerland				X		X	X
37. Turkey				X		X	
38. USA I (Soc.)				X		X	X
39. USA II (Guild)				X	X	X	
40. USA III (Sigma)				X		X	X
41. USSR	O		O	X		O	
42. Venezuela	O		O	X		X	X
43. IUPA 1936	O	O	O	O			X
44. IFJ 1939				X		X	
45. America 1942				X		O	
46. America 1950				X			
47. UN Draft 1952	O			O		X	O
48. IFJ 1954				X		X	X
49. EEC 1971				X		X	X
50. FELAP 1979	O	O	O	O	X	O	O

Among the codes which pay no or little attention to international obligations are those from most Western countries and from a number of developing countries. On the other hand, all codes in the socialist countries cover at least some international aspects. For example, the Soviet code (from the statutes of the USSR Union of Journalists) covers three international themes, whereas none of the three U.S. codes included in this inventory contain any reference to international obligations. As stated by John Whitton and Arthur Larson, in their examination of the "Canons of Journalism" of the American Society of Newspaper Editors, "the absence of a precise treatment of the type of news and editorial writing bearing on international tensions, particularly when defamation, subversion and war-mongering dangerous to international peace are involved, is greatly to be regretted."[5]

Yet we cannot conclude that the tendency to disregard international aspects of professional ethics would be a simple reflection of the sociopolitical systems involved. After all, codes with a strong emphasis on international relations can be found in both of the Germanies (East and West), in Austria and Belgium, as well as in Cuba and Egypt.

It is interesting to note that the only national code which explicitly condemns *war propaganda* ("glorification of military activities") is the West German code of the Periodical Press Association adopted in 1966 (the other code in FRG is the "Press Codex" of the National Press Council). Jamaican and Nigerian codes condemn incitement to violence in general—in accordance with international human rights instruments—but this concerns more the internal order of a country than aggression in international relations. War propaganda as conceived in international law (cf., Chapter 6) is covered, in addition to the West German code, only in the principles declared in 1936 by the International Union of Press Associations, IUPA (an international code)[6] and in the code of ethics adopted in 1979 by the Federation of Latin American Journalists, FELAP (a regional code).[7]

The IUPA list of ten principles to be followed by "a journalist worthy of the name" concludes with these three:

---

[5]J. B. Whitton & A. Larson, *Propaganda; Towards Disarmament in the War of Worlds*, Dobbs Ferry, New York: Oceana Publications, 1964, p. 253.

[6]The principles of IUPA (founded in 1892 and active until World War II) were adopted by a congress in Prague in 1936. They are reproduced in full as Appendix VII to Bruun, op. cit., pp. 103–104.

[7]The FELAP code was adopted in Caracas (Venezuela) in July 1979 by the second Congress of the Federation, founded in Mexico City in 1976 and widely representative of professional journalists in Central and South America, excluding those working for Fascist regimes such as Argentine, Chile, and Uruguay (the democratic journalists of these countries belong to FELAP). The code was drafted in Spanish, but an English translation was published in *Journalists' Affairs* (Bulletin of the International Organization of Journalists, Prague), 1979.

8. To abstain from anything that might be regarded as inculcating the spirit of violence or as giving preference to brutal force over justice and equity or as a preparation for attack on another state.

9. To fight everywhere against the mistaken idea that there are disputes in the world capable of solution otherwise than by war and hence that war is inevitable, for such war would, with the progress of modern science, be an equal threat to the aggressor and the attacked.

10. To spread everywhere the faith that the vast majority of nations wish to live in peace and concord, and that it is also in their power to safeguard and perpetuate peace through an international organization which, with the co-operation of all, will guarantee to all the security of law against violence.

The FELAP code prescribes in Article 2:

Journalism must contribute to the strengthening of peace, peaceful coexistence, self-determination of peoples, disarmament, international détente and mutual understanding among peoples of the world; fight for the equality of human beings without distinction of race, opinion, origin, language, religion or nationality. It is the lofty duty of Latin American journalists to contribute to the economic, political and cultural independence of our nations and peoples, to the establishment of a new International Economic Order and to decolonization of information.

Article 3, listing the fundamental duties of a journalist, includes the following:

—To fight for a new information order in accordance with the interests of the peoples, replacing the one that prevails in the majority of Latin American countries which distorts their reality.

—To reject propaganda for the inevitability of war and the threat or actual use of force in international conflicts.

These codes prove that it is indeed possible to arrive at clearly defined principles, formulated and adopted by the profession itself, but strictly in keeping with the standards of international law.

Concerning the aspect of *objectivity,* etc., the only national code which treats this subject in general, and also from the point of view of international relations, is the Greek "Code of Deontology" (Article 12 of the Press Statute of 1961):

8. Reporting and commenting on foreign affairs shall be allowed to those journalists only who have sufficient knowledge of the country, enabling them to report and comment accurately and objectively.

The same idea is formulated more specifically in the principles of IUPA, and is even extended to an obligation to rectify and to respect diversity in the world:

1. To check conscientiously the truthfulness and authenticity of every news item, particularly such as may be likely to provoke prejudice, mistrust, hatred, or contempt for other nations, or may convey a false impression of their internal value and of their strength.

2. To rectify willingly any news of this nature which may subsequently be found not to be authentic or accurate.

3. To insist on his own right and acknowledge the right of others to report objectively on all internal events and on all questions of interest to other states, to compare their internal situation with that of other countries and to criticize it freely.

4. To bear in mind, however, that the great diversity of historical, physical, and moral conditions naturally implies a similar diversity in the political and social development of the various nations and states, and an equally great diversity in political regimes.

5. To refrain scrupulously from all superficial and nonobjective criticism, and particularly from abusing and casting discredit on other nations and states, including the heads of States and other eminent persons.

The UN draft international code[8] also includes an article (IV) to the same effect, but stated briefly without elaboration:

It is the duty of those who describe and comment upon events relating to a foreign country to acquire the necessary knowledge of such country which will enable them to report and comment accurately and fairly thereon.

This obligation is an international amplification of the overriding call for objectivity contained in Article I of the UN draft code:

The personnel of the press and of all other media of information should do all in their power to ensure that the information the public receives is factually accurate. They should check all items of information to the best of their ability. No fact should be wilfully distorted and no essential fact should be deliberately suppressed.

---

[8]The UN draft code is reproduced in full as Appendix II to Bruun, op. cit., pp. 94–95.

In general, the UN draft code of ethics is a poor reflection of the professionl standards emanating from international instruments. In the early 1950s the collection of instruments was not very extensive, which explains why, when this "model code" was drafted, the aspect of race is missing. But there is no excuse for a UN statement to completely disregard such fundamental aspects of international relations as war propaganda, friendship, and cooperation between nations—standards which had been established by the League of Nations and are contained in the UN Charter, as well as several General Assembly resolutions.

Obviously the UN draft code was a product of a Western orientation under Cold War conditions. Thus it served as an instrument emphasizing the "free flow" doctrine of the time, rather than reminding journalists of their obligations towards the international community. Although the UN text was never formally adopted,[9] it has exercised considerable influence in the preparation of various national codes—contributing to a neglect rather than an observance of journalists' international obligations. Nevertheless, it is true that even such a modest instrument, "if adopted and respected, would make the task of the propagandist or the purveyor of false news extremely difficult," as stated by Whitton and Larson.[10]

Beyond the above-quoted passages from the UN, FELAP, and IUPA codes, there is little in the 50 codes included in this inventory that can serve as a resource for updating the professional codes towards adequate international standards. Our comparative study shows that the *universal values of the international community as expressed by the international in-*

[9]By Resolution 838 (IX) of 17 December 1954, the UN General Assembly decided "to take no further action at the present time" on the proposed international professional conference to prepare the final text of an "international Code of Ethics for the use of information personnel." The UN Secretary-General was only requested to transmit the text of the draft code prepared so far (mainly within ECOSOC's Sub-Commission on Freedom of Information and of the Press), i.e., the "UN draft code" discussed here, to various mass media agencies and journalistic organizations all over the world "for their information and for such action as they may deem proper." The Secretary-General had already been in touch with these "information enterprises and national and international professional associations," requesting their opinions about the proposed conference, and he had received substantive replies from some one hundred of them. The basis for Resolution 838 was a report of the Secretary-General on these consultations (General Assembly, Official Records, IX session, 1954, UN documents A/2691 and Add. 1 and 2). At the end of this report the Secretary-General requested "the General Assembly itself to decide whether it wishes him to co-operate with enterprises and associations which have expressed themselves as in favour of organizing the proposed international professional conference for the purpose of preparing the final text of the code and measures for its implementation." He added, however, that he "would not conceal his feeling that wide and preponderantly favourable professional opinion is necessary if the conference is to achieve practical results and that, at present, there is no clear evidence of such preponderantly favourable opinion." (UN document A/2691, p. 4 paragraph 11). The fact is that over 50 replies supported the conference, less than 30 were against, and over 30 were "non-committal," while some 300 had not responded at all. As in the cases of the Mass Media Declaration 25 years later, the issue was divisive, but even so, a significant majority of the expressed opinion was in support of the project.

[10]Op. cit., p. 250.

struments are poorly reflected in professional ethics as expressed by the codes of ethics. For guidance on how to understand the various aspects of international responsibility in professional ethics—and on how to formulate them in codes of ethics—we have to resort mostly to the international instruments themselves. And these instruments, as shown by the preceding chapters, constitute an abundant resource for the development of professional codes, not only on such "old" questions as promoting peace and international understanding or combating propaganda for war, racialism, etc., but also on such "new" questions as promotion of disarmament, the New International Economic Order, and the respect of cultural diversity.

Why is the profession of journalism so under-developed in terms of international affairs, and why has the tradition of communication research and education similarly neglected a proper consideration of the international responsibility of journalism? Obviously this is not a historically and philosophically insignificant aspect of the profession of journalism—as if international standards were simply "forgotten" by chance. Rather, this is only one manifestation of a more fundamental tendency in the dominant Western tradition of journalism to understand professionalism in narrow technocratic terms, without notable reference to socio-political realities—national any more than international.

However, it would be unfair to the tradition of journalism education and research to blame it indiscriminately for overlooking international concerns. There are some notable exceptions in the Western mainstream: individual scholars and journalists, and even "schools," advocating socially oriented professional ethics that would include a commitment to international responsibility. Moreover, there is the radically different tradition of "Marxist-Leninist" journalism of the socialist countries, with its well-known orientation towards internationalism. Developing countries are largely influenced by the dominant Western tradition, but the movement towards a new international information order has exposed the neo-colonial nature of this situation and has led to a search for "another" orientation. The following is an inventory of various ideas and proposals which can serve as an additional resource in developing codes of ethics aimed at a more adequate concept of international responsibility.

SUGGESTION TO FOSTER INTERNATIONAL RESPONSIBILITY

Few concrete proposals exist on the precise formulation of professional codes in matters of international relevance. The present author knows of only two outstanding examples: "A Code of Ethics for International Communicators" proposed by Whitton and Larson in their *Propaganda:*

Towards Disarmament in the War of Words of 1964, and the "Mexico Declaration," issued by the international and regional organizations of journalists in 1980. There are, however, several other less specific proposals that introduce an approach and a mechanism for raising the standards of journalism (in the international sphere, among others), which should be recalled, even if they may not provide us with all of the elements needed for codes of ethics.

The Hutchins Commission

A "classic" attempt to foster responsible performance in the mass media was the Commission on Freedom of the Press, created in the United States in the middle of the 1940s under a grant by Time, Inc. to the University of Chicago, and composed of 13 distinguished academic and public figures under the chairmanship of Chancellor Robert M. Hutchins.[11] One of the special studies, supplementing the general report of the Commission, was on international communication prepared by two members of the Commission staff, Llewellyn White and Robert D. Leigh, and published as a book entitled *Peoples Speaking to Peoples.*[12]

Among the proposals suggested by White and Leigh were measures intended "to secure the progressive removal of political barriers and the lessening of economic restrictions which impede the free flow of information across national borders." Among these, the following were listed:

> a) There be incorporated, within the framework of United Nations agreements, a multilateral covenant stating that the signatory nations believe in, and will do their utmost to bring about, the fullest possible flow across national borders of true information concerning all events and peoples.

> b) Specific sections of such a covenant include the following provisions:

>> (1) Guaranty of equality of access to the sources of information as between co-nationals and foreigners;

>> (2) The organization in all principal news centers of the world of foreign correspondents' corps with strict, self-administered codes of ethics; the requirement that all newspaper, magazine, and radio reporters and all authors and photographers

---

[11]For background, see, e.g., M. A. Blanchard, *The Hutchins Commission, the Press and the Responsibility Concept,* Journalism Monographs No. 49, May 1977. The main report of the Commission, *A Free and Responsible Press,* was published in 1947 (Chicago: University of Chicago Press).

[12]Like the rest of the Commission's studies, this volume was published by the University of Chicago Press (1946). A reprint edition was prepared in 1972 by Arno Press Inc. (International Propaganda and Communications series).

(including newsreel cameramen) be members of these corps and bound by their codes; specific authority for the corps to handle all disputes among members or with host-governments, with right of appeal to a unit of the United Nations Economic and Social Council previously described . . . .

(9) The creation of an autonomous unit in the United Nations Economic and Social Council, and co-ordinated closely with the United Nation's Educational, Scientific, and Cultural Organization (U.N.E.S.C.O.) or with the Commission on Human Rights, to promote the free flow of true information and the removal of artificial barriers restricting such free flow. This unit, among other things, (a) to scrutinize the observance of the provisions of the multilateral treaty described above, to suggest changes in it from time to time, and to publish its findings and recommendations for the information of the United Nations Assembly; (b) to assist in the formation of professional foreign correspondents' corps as described above; (c) to receive, to consider carefully, and to report on individual or collective violations of the multilateral treaty; and (d) to investigate (by aid of monitoring of broadcasts, examination of printed material, and pictures) areas in which distortion of facts and fomenting of international discord are being carried on, and to report to the Assembly on such dangers to peace and understanding.[13]

Even if the "self-administered codes of ethics" were not defined in greater detail, it is obvious from the context—considering also the overall philosophy of the Commission—that the main function of the codes was to ensure the highest possible truthfulness in reporting of international affairs, including in-depth treatment of the context for instant news events. Accordingly, this approach to professional ethics does not aim at bypassing a consideration of the content of communication. In addition, it is an approach whereby "the continuing struggle to establish a stable, peaceful world society"[14] is understood as an essential part of professional ethics.

Such a balanced approach to international communication was confirmed with the full authority of the Commission in the "Statement by the Commission" issued as an introduction to the study by White and Leigh:

Recent improvements in the machinery and methods of international communication have made possible, for the first time in history, direct communication across national boundaries to the masses of the people of the world. These mechanical improvements offer at once a new hope and a new danger. The choice is not between the

---

[13]White & Leigh, op. cit., pp. 107–110.
[14]Ibid., p. 7.

use or the neglect of these new instruments of communication. The instruments exist and will be used in any case. The choice is between their full, purposeful, and responsible use to enlarge the mutual comprehension of peoples, on the one hand, and, on the other, their incomplete, undirected, and irresponsible use, with the risk of an increase in international hatred and suspicion as a consequence.

If they are used to the limits of their potentialities to increase the nations' knowledge of one another's character and purposes, they will enlarge the area of international understanding and enhance the hope of peace. If they are not so used, these innovations will merely serve to give wider international currency and more rapid dissemination to reports which may increase the distortion and misrepresentation of national conduct, character, and purpose, which have bread wars in the past.

We believe that attempts to suppress the presentation of evils and sources of conflict would be self-defeating. We believe that the cure for distorted information is more information, not less, because we believe the elements of common decency, humanity, and good will are strong enough to outweigh opposing elements if included in a comprehensive and representative picture.

In the opinion of the Commission, it is essential to the realization of our generation's hope for peace that prompt action be taken by governments and those responsible for the management of the international communication industries, to insure the full and considered use of these improved instruments of mass communication for enlarging the area of mutual comprehension between the peoples of the world. Such action would include:

(a) The improvement of physical facilities and operating mechanisms so as to bring about the communication of words and images across national borders as abundantly, as cheaply, as quickly, as efficiently, and over as wide an area as possible;

(b) The progressive removal of political barriers and the lessening of economic restrictions which impede the free flow of information across national borders; and

(c) The improvement of the accuracy, representative character, and quality of the words and images transmitted in international communication.[15]

Such an approach is little different from the "new order" movement which 30 years later became manifested at Unesco in landmarks such as the Mass Media Declaration, the MacBride Report, and the IPDC. In any case, codes of ethics as an integral part of a comprehensive national

---

[15] Ibid., pp. v–vi.

communication policy are not Unesco's invention on the road towards a new order (cf., Chapters 1 and 2); rather they are an invention of the U.S. brand of Western mass media philosophy from the period when there was a transition from a simple "libertarian" tradition to one of "social responsibility" (cf., Chapter 10).

The proposals of the Hutchins Commission were never put into practice—in international communication any more than in other areas of journalism—mainly because of a fierce opposition by the newspaper publishers and other business-related circles in the U.S. Incidentally, the campaign launched by them against the Commission's report was not so different from the later, worldwide campaign against Unesco and the new order. Under these circumstances, the contribution of the Commission to the field of journalism was limited to academic "brainstorming" —innovations at the level of ideas. In this respect, however, the Hutchins Commission has had a permanent and significant impact on the Western tradition of journalism, mainly through the "social responsibility theory" of the press. As far as the international responsibility of journalism is concerned, the movement towards a new order in the 1970s has called forth a kind of rehabilitation of Hutchins.[16]

In fact, the above-quoted idea of White and Leigh was reborn in the post-Declaration debate at Unesco as a proposal to set up a *"World Press Institute."* The proposal was made in December 1978 by *D. R. Mankekar,* a veteran journalist from India and Chairman of the Non-Aligned News Pool.[17] The aims of the Institute would be, according to Mankekar, "to foster highest standards of journalism, both print and audiovisual, in the international arena, and to promote world peace and understanding, and combat racialism, apartheid, colonialism and neo-colonialism," and among the tasks of the Institute would be to "oversee the performance of the media and evolve a code of conduct and ethics for foreign correspondents."[18]

Mankekar's proposal did not catch on, and after four years it has not led to any more concrete steps than were taken based on the proposal by White and Leigh. Obviously, Mankekar's proposal was hit by the mounting controversy on the protection of journalists. However, the idea of a world press institute as a "fully autonomous professional organization"

---

[16]See, e.g., D. R. Mankekar, *Whose Freedom? Whose Order? A Plea for a New International Information Order by Third World,* Delhi: Clarion Books, 1981.

[17]Mankekar explains his idea in his book *Media and the Third World,* New Delhi: Indian Institute of Mass Communication, 1979, pp. 59-62. For a report of the meeting in which the proposal was made, see note 54 below.

[18]Ibid., p. 61. Mankekar's proposal is reproduced as Appendix to the Unesco report referred to in note 3 above (pp. 137-140).

representative of all the three main "worlds" (capitalist, socialist, developing) has received significant support. Unesco's Intergovernmental Conference in Kuala Lumpur (February 1979) recommended a feasibility study,[19] and the International Seminar of Journalists in Tashkent (September 1979) seconded the setting up of such a "representative professional body" which would promote a code of ethics, "monitoring its implementation and functioning as a self-regulating institution for raising the standards of international journalism."[20]

The code in question was defined in Tashkent as follows:

> The participants stressed the need to evolve an international code of ethics and conduct which will foster socially responsible journalism and make the mass media accountable to the international community. Such a code should contain professional principles shared in different parts of the world and should be based on the standards laid down by relevant instruments of international law and especially by the Unesco Mass Media Declaration and by the Final Act of the Conference on Security and Co-operation in Europe. The Seminar welcomed the proposal to elaborate such a code through collaboration between international and regional organizations of journalists.[21]

Indeed, the consultative meetings between international and regional organizations of journalists, held since 1978 under the auspices of Unesco, do constitute a nucleus for what was suggested by Mankekar—and by White and Leigh 30 years earlier. These organizations together represent all the significant "worlds" and the profession of journalism far better than any other organizational group such as the IPI or the World Press Freedom Committee (i.e., those behind the attack against Unesco and the new order movement discussed in Chapter 1). In the first consultative meeting in April 1978 at Unesco (Paris), the organizations agreed "to examine possible common grounds for a definition of basic ethical principles of the journalistic profession."[22] The "Mexico Declaration," adopted in the second meeting in April 1980, proved that although the consultative framework was loose it still managed to deliver

---

[19]Recommendation No. 48; see *Final Report* of the Conference, Unesco document CC/MD/42. Reproduced also as Appendix to the Unesco report referred to in note 3 (p. 142).

[20]*Journalists' Affairs*, No. 21-22, 1979, pp. 18-19. (The full proceedings were published in *International Seminar of Journalists in Tashkent*, Moscow: Novosti Press Agency Publishing House, 1980. This is a translation from the Russian and, therefore, the statement given by the Seminar has somewhat different wording from the original English, published in *Journalists' Affairs*.)

[21]Ibid.

[22]See *Bruun*, op. cit. in note 1 above, p. 10 (The full protocol adopted by the consultative meeting is published in French in *Organizations Internationales et Regionales de Journalistes*, Prague: IOJ, 1980, pp. 87-88.)

historicaly significant ideas and proposals. The third consultative meeting, in Baghdad in Feburary 1982, discussed the perspective of a permanent basis for collaboration along the lines of the Mankekar proposal.[23]

The Whitton and Larson Draft Code

Whitton and Larson characterized their work in 1964 as a "study of law and remedies bearing upon international propaganda."[24] It falls within the same U.S. academic streamline that had produced the Hutchins Commission 20 years earlier. Building on a Western libertarian tradition, it is socially and ethically committed, and commands an undisputable expertise in matters of communication philosophy and law. While this landmark book on international communication is devoted mainly to "a legal analysis of the rules, principles and remedies available to control propaganda of a kind that threatens the peace,"[25] the authors assign great importance to professional self-regulation in journalism:

> There is little doubt that private associations of journalists, broadcasters, cameramen, etc., could become under appropriate circumstances an excellent influence in preventing the dissemination of materials dangerous to good international relations . . . the effort to curb pernicious international communciation would be greatly facilitated by the development throughout the world of a corps of newsmen inspired by high ideals of professional conduct . . . .
>
> It is to be hoped that the efforts to evolve and perfect codes of ethics and to create appropriate tribunals of honor to administer them will be further pursued by responsible associations. To help toward this end, a suggested draft of a code of ethics is attempted in the next chapter.[26]

The "Code of Ethics for International Communicators," suggested in Chapter XVI of the book introduces a system of ethical rules, with the authors submtitting that "if these rules were respected by those in management or control of mass media throughout the world, both governmental and non-governmental, the greater part of the hostile propaganda which today poisons the international atmosphere would be eliminated."[27] The authors' overall approach is given in these "general propositions":

---

[23]See the "Baghdad Declaration" reproduced in *IOJ Newsletter,* No. 5, March 1982. Under point 2 of the Declaration, the participating organizations, among other things, "envisage forming a working group that will strive to prepare studies for and the programmes of future periodical consultative meetings."

[24]Op cit. in note 5 above, p. v (Preface).

[25]Ibid.

[26]Ibid., pp. 254–255.

[27]Ibid., p. 256.

The essential duty of every communicator, whether governmental or non-governmental and whether his message is addressed to the home population or to some foreign country, is to be truthful—to search for and stick to the truth in reporting, explaining and interpreting facts. He should be prepared to furnish accurate information, whatever the consequences. But it is also his duty, so far as it is reasonably possible, to "protect and uphold the dignity and brotherhood of all mankind," by avoiding messages of a nature to cause ill-will and hatred, especially by the systematic diffusion of false or distorted news which undermines friendly relations between nations. For while freedom to communicate, as asserted by the United Nations General Assembly, is a sacred human right, it is a right burdened with important duties. In the words of the General Assembly, "Freedom of information requires as an indispensable element the willingness and capacity to employ its privileges without abuse. It requires as a basic discipline the moral obligation to seek the facts without prejudice and to spread knowledge without malicious intent." Thus the communicator must refrain from sending forth messages which constitute a clear and present danger to peaceful international relations. Defamation, subversion and war-mongering, hate propaganda and false reports, are to be condemned. He should do his best to respect the rights and sensitivities of all peoples.[28]

The suggested draft code which follows is subdivided into five parts, including a definition of rights of the communicator and of the public as well as a list of remedies "in the event of a violation by a communicator of any of the principles set forth in this code." The following are the code's "special prescriptions for the communicator":

1) INTEGRITY

Every one engaged in the process of mass communication is endowed with a high public trust. Hence he is under a duty not to seek any personal advantage through the promotion of a selfish private interest, or any other unworthy purpose contrary to the general welfare of the international community. While naturally sensitive to the demands of a legitimate patriotism, he should not forget his responsibility toward the cause of international good will and world comradeship.

2) KNOWLEDGE AND TRAINING

It is the duty of the communicator (and of him who prepares his material), if he undertakes to comment on or present facts relating to a foreign country, to acquire a degree of knowledge and understanding of such country reasonably adequate to enable his reports thereon to be unbiased, accurate and fair.[29]

[28] Ibid., p. 258.
[29] Ibid., pp. 258–259.

Another part of the code goes in greater detail in laying down "pre-scriptions as to the content":

1) FAIRNESS

In his references to a foreign country, notably concerning its history, culture, institutions, prominent personalities, people, and foreign and domestic problems and policies, the communicator should en-deavor to limit himself to verified facts, presenting them fairly and free from bias. When commentary, opinion or news analysis are of-fered, they should be clearly identified as such. If a given report is based on rumor, it should be so stated. When an issue is controversial, and materially affects the welfare of nations and the cause of world peace, the communicator should endeavor to present or discuss the issue without bias, prejudice or distortion.

2) ACCURACY

It is the duty of the communicator to do all in his power to ensure that the information he is disseminating to the public, either at home or abroad, is factually accurate, in short as near an approximation to the truth as is humanly possible . . . . Those in charge of mass media should endeavor to stop without delay the diffusion of any material, the inaccuracy of which is known, especially if it is of a nature to harm the cause of good international understanding. If such material has already been published or broadcast, the communicator should be prepared to offer appropriate reparation, as indicated below . . . .

3) DEFAMATION

It is the duty of every communicator to refrain from wilfully libellous or slanderous attacks and unfounded accusations against prominent foreign personalities, especially heads of states, governmental leaders, and diplomatic agents. This precept is based, first, on the re-spect which nations mutually owe to each other and to their repre-sentatives, and, secondly, on the fact that such attacks cause resent-ment and constitute a danger to peaceful international relations. Also, and mainly for the second reason just mentioned, the commu-nicator should avoid the diffusion of material tending to hold up to derision or obloquy any foreign people, or any group or minority thereof, because of race, color, creed or national origin, thus causing bigotry or hatred, with the consequent danger of violence. Particu-larly important in this connection is the avoidance of the use of epi-thets, in the form of slang or other expressions which tend to create or perpetuate stereotype images of a disparaging, insulting or de-grading nature, thus causing misunderstanding, resentment, and in-ternational tension. The truth of such attacks is no defense if the ob-ject of the communication is to weaken the loyalty of a given people vis-a-vis its government or to urge one nation to engage in aggression against another, or is otherwise malicious.

Criticism of the policies and aims of a foreign government is permissible if based on the truth, is non-malicious, and is in the best interests of the international community. Fair, unbiased criticism of aggressive policies of a foreign government, if founded on accurate information and not inspired by malice, can be a service to the cause of security and peace.

4) SUBVERSIVE PROPAGANDA

It is the duty of the communicator to refrain from disseminating material, whether true or false, which is designed or is of a nature to disrupt peaceful relations existing between a friendly foreign government and its citizenry, or to foment a rebellion against the government by the use of force. With respect to radio broadcasting, the agency in control of the station in question must prohibit, and, if occasion arises, stop without delay the broadcasting to a foreign country of any transmission which to the detriment of good international understanding is of such a character as to incite the population to acts incompatible with the internal order or the security of such foreign state.

This article does not purport to prohibit popular manifestations of mere moral support on the soil of one state favoring an insurrectionary movement in another state, provided that the communicator is not disseminating propaganda in direct connection with the commission of an overt act of support to such insurrection, notably the preparation of armed bands which are planning to cross the frontier to give active armed aid to the movement. Radio broadcasts beamed or directed to persons in a foreign country urging them to rebel against their government are particularly harmful to good international relations and a real danger to peace.

5) WAR-MONGERING

It is the duty of communicators to avoid the dissemination of any material which is of a nature, whether so designed or not, to incite or provoke the decision-makers of a given state, or the people therein, to threats or acts of aggression against another state with whom it is at peace. This includes the use of words, signs, symbols or any visible or audible representations which are likely to promote feelings of enmity or hatred, or promote a war-spirit, between different peoples. Incitement to threats or acts of aggression is not the less reprehensible if it fails of its object. It is immaterial that such war-mongering propaganda employs argument based on fact, if the motive be malicious.

It is particularly dangerous to international peace for a commentator to make false charges of aggression alleged to have been prepared or committed by a foreign government or its people.

6) COMMUNICATION IN TIME OF CRISIS

In time of grave international tension, particularly when an international crisis occurs during which peace is seriously endangered, communicators should be especially careful not to diffuse unsubstantiated reports or inflammatory comment of a nature to cause alarm or panic either among governmental leaders or their citizenry. At such times, particular care should be taken to verify the sources of all news stories and reports, and also to avoid publicizing matter based on unfounded rumor. At the very least, rumor should be clearly identified as such.[30]

No doubt this draft code is unique and has retained its importance over the years. However, while Whitton and Larson have made by far the most extensive proposal, they were by no means the only outstanding U.S. scholars in the 1960s who demanded that the international responsibility of the mass media should be taken more seriously. An interesting proposal to this effect in the area of disarmament was made at that time by *Karl W. Deutsch* (a distinguished political scientist).[31] He advocated a system of "inspecting" the climate of opinion concerning armament by not only monitoring the content of the mass media, but even finding "an agreement of putting quotas on the amount of space which the mass media in each country might devote to particular controversies or disputes."[32] Moreover, Deutsch suggested "an agreement to make illegitimate to advocate violations of the [arms limitation] agreement or to conceal them," and another agreement "providing not only for the absence of objectionable material from the mass media of communication in the participating countries but also providing for the presence of material agreed on as helpful to their implementation."[33]

More recently, *Hamid Mowlana* (a scholar on international communication) followed the same path in proposing "to create and promote a set of principles or code of ethics that is not culture-bound but universal, strives for the dignity and potential of human beings, and prevents the world from a catastrophic war and destruction."[34] Addressed to professional media organizations, his proposal contains four basic principles of an international code of media ethics: (1) Prevention of war and promotion of peace; (2) Respect for culture, tradition, and values; (3) Promotion of human rights and dignity; (4) Preservation of the home, human association, family, and community. The first of these is based on the reasoning

[30] Ibid., pp. 260–262.

[31] K. W. Deutsch, "Communications, Arms Inspection, and National Security," in J. K. Zawodny (Ed.), *Man and International Relations; Contributions of the Social Sciences to the Study of Conflict and Integration,* (Vol. II), San Francisco: Chandler Publishing Co., 1967, pp. 848-858.

[32] Ibid., p. 851.

[33] Ibid., p. 853.

[34] H. Mowlana, "Communication, World Order, and the Human Potential: Toward an Ethical Framework," paper presented at "1981 World Media Conference" in New York, 1-4 October 1981; published in the Conference Proceedings, New York: News World Communications, Inc., 1981 (quote on pp. 152-153).

that "if, as so often demonstrated, international media can mobilize for war and exacerbate tensions, why can they not do the reverse?" He lists the following points: International media should:

>—Increase the amount of information available on peaceful solutions to conflict.
>
>—Breakdown stereotypes that de-humanize opposing populations.
>
>—Be aware of hidden biases of coverage on controversial issues.
>
>—Serve as early warning devices to bring attention to potential flash points.
>
>—Remind opponents of peaceful solutions to conflicts.
>
>—Confer prestige on the peacemaker.
>
>—Help create a public mood conducive to the spirit of reconciliation.
>
>—Put peacemakers on opposite sides in touch with one another.[35]

It is not difficult to see that such proposals by academic experts are no less "radical" than those by advocates of the new information order. For example, the various drafts for the Mass Media Declaration (cf., Chapter 2 and Appendices 4–18) contain little that goes beyond these positions of U.S. experts. To be sure, these are "liberal" positions, which have been practically overlooked by the political and industrial establishment responsible for the dominant Western "hard line" with regard to the new order. On the other hand, they cannot be discredited as "anti-Western" positions which would run against the constitutional guarantees for free speech and free enterprise. Like the Hutchins Commission, these academic experts aimed at strengthening, rather than eroding, the political and economic system known as "Western democracy" or "capitalism."

In other words, there is room for an enlightened Western opinion in support of codes of ethics that are in line with the new international information order. In fact, it is misleading to characterize this opinion as "radical" since it does not challenge the basic structure of the predominantly non-governmental and private enterprise system of the mass media. Rather, it is a reformist opinion, looking for remedies to obvious defects in the system, to insure that the mass media do not depart from the standards of good international behavior.

It is interesting to note that, by and large, the same approach is taken by those (like Mankekar and the Tashkent seminar participants) who have suggested codes of ethics as an integral part of the establish-

---

[35] Ibid., p. 154.

ment of the new order. As shown by the following overview of proposals made in the socialist countries, the opinion of the communists is also reformist rather than revolutionary.

Proposals from Socialist Countries

The Yugoslavian member of the MacBride Commission, *Bogdan Osolnik* (Emeritus Professor of Journalism and Member of Parliament) has been a leading advocate for journalistic ethics in general (in matters of truth, privacy, public order and morals, and professional honesty) and for higher ethical standards concerning international relations in particular:

> With the demand for a New International Information Order, the need arises for the adoption of a special international code of professional ethics, which should result from the cooperation of the journalists' organiztions themselves on the basis of respect for general human values and interests. An international code of professional journalistic ethics should promote consciousness of journalists' responsiblity to contribute towards understanding and rapprochement among nations, towards the democratization and transformation of international relations and towards the liberation of all mankind.[36]

Osolnik does not suggest any particular formulation for such a code. Instead, he points out that a journalist is bound to "international responsibilities, defined by the obligations of journalism to the international community and the principles of international law deriving from United Nations documents."[37] For him, the Mass Media Declaration already stands for a universal code:

> Its principles derive from the U.N. Charter and the international legal system accepted by the United Nations members states as the cornerstone of their peaceful cooperation. Therefore, its formulation should be considered to represent the application of international law in the communication sphere and the pertinent consequences be derived therefrom for the implementation of the Declaration . . . [38]
>
> . . . The ideals of peace, justice, freedom, respect for human rights and the equality of rights of all nations highlighted by the Dec-

[36]B. Osolnik, "Professional Ethics in Mass Communication," document No. 90bis prepared for the MacBride Commission, Paris: Unesco, 1979, p. 3.

[37]B. Osolnik, *The New International Information and Communication Order*, Belgrade: Jugoslovenska Stvarnost, 1980, p. 80.

[38]Ibid., p. 96.

laration belong to the whole of mankind and must be made the cornerstone of the value structure of the new international order.[39]

While such a concept of journalistic ethics is firmly based on relevant international (UN and Unesco) instruments, the code foreseen to crystallize and enforce it is a matter of professional self-regulation, rather than governmental jurisdiction. Other experts from socialist countries of Eastern Europe take the same overall approach, notably *Spartak Beglov* (USSR)[40] and *Wolfgang Kleinwaechter* (GDR).[41] None of these advocate a governmental code or an all-embracing professional code which would set universal standards for journalistic activity in matters of international as well as national relevance. They point out that journalistic work simply does not lend itself to general international regulation. As stated by Kleinwaechter and Kubach: "In the last instance the class-bound conditions of this work doom such an attempt to remain a utopia."[42] Within these specific limits, however, there is, according to this view, both room and need for an international professional code to reflect the common responsibility of journalists regardless of their class positions and respective socio-economic systems.

Like Osolnik, who represents the views prevailing in a Non-Aligned socialist country, experts from the Soviet Union and its allied countries count heavily on the Mass Media Declaration and other documents manifestating the common will of the international community. Among these is the Final Act of the Conference on Security and Co-operation in Europe (the "Helsinki Accords"), quoted as another recent landmark consensus linking together the formal rights of journalists and their obligations with regard to the contents of the mass media. Based on such international instruments "as expression of a will for détente and of an intention for the democratization of international relations in the spirit of peaceful coexistence," Kleinwaechter and Kubach proposed, in 1980, new efforts to formulate an international code of journalistic ethics:

> Such a code would deal with reporting and commenting for and about other countries as well as processes and events of international importance. It should include above all the following elements:

---

[39] Ibid., p. 79.

[40] See Beglov's contribution in Bruun, op. cit. in note 1 above (pp. 57-63), and in the proceedings of the Orivesi symposium in November 1978 referred to in Chapter 1, note 62.

[41] See, e.g., W. Kleinwaechter, "Unesco Declaration on the Role of Mass Communication Media," *The Democratic Journalist*, No. 7-8, 1979, pp. 2-6, and W. Kleinwaechter & H. Kubach, "Journalismus und Verantwortung in den internationalen Beziehungen" (Journalism and Responsibility in International Relations, in German), *Theorie und Praxis des sozialistischen Journalismus*, No. 3, 1980, pp. 201-219.

[42] Kleinwaechter & Kubach, op. cit., p. 205.

—The foundations of journalistic activity (respect for international and national norms as well as the moral and ethical principles of the profession).

—The aim of journalistic activity (promotion of peace and international understanding, contribution to disarmament, détente and international cooperation).

—The content of journalistic activity (comprehensive, truthful, objective and balanced reporting, adequately reflecting various aspects of life in other countries resp. of international processes and events).

—Forms and conditions of journalistic activity (questions of training, working conditions, cooperation between journalists and their associations, social and other questions).[43]

The authors do not provide a concrete elaboration of these elements in the form of a proposal for such an "international code of journalistic activity for peace, détente and international understanding." They only point out that the time is ripe for it and that it should be at the non-governmental level: a coding process in which all significant international professional organizations should be involved and which would both foster "the moral-political obligations of journalistic activity" and facilitate "an implementation mechanism usually adapted to nationally specific circumstances."[44] The authors see this as a constructive way of supporting international cooperation and efforts by the states to arrive at internationally binding norms concerning the mass media, while at the same time recognizing the fact that journalists are not proper subjects of international law.

Another relevant proposal from the socialist camp was made by *Vladimir Lomeiko,* commentator with the influential Soviet weekly *Literaturnaja Gazeta,* at a Finnish-Soviet seminar on mass media cooperation in 1979. His contribution was based on the Final Act of Helsinki and concluded with an idea to codify the generally accepted principles of peaceful coexistence for the guidance of journalistic practice:

> The more there is mutual understanding and confidence between peoples, the greater significance is attached to the principle that journalists are responsible not only for their own readers but also for each other and the audiences of other countries. The experience of those countries, like the Soviet Union and Finland, which have achieved a higher level of cooperation and confidence in all fields

---

[43] Ibid.
[44] Ibid., p. 214.

including information, may in due course help to bring about a code of journalists' conscience, aiming at information that would be full of responsibility, honesty and humanism. It could be based on the following principles:

—To recognize differences, but also to strive for a mutual consciousness about them.

—To remain faithful to own principles, but to strive for understanding also the others.

—To attempt at proving to be right, but to have respect also for the opponent.

—To argue by means of reasoning and example; not by means of defiance and violence.

—To promote manifestations of nobleness, humanism and international solidarity, but to condemn all forms of national hatred, misanthropy and racialism.[45]

The proposal (with the principles listed) was unanimously endorsed by the seminar which was attended, in addition to half a dozen Soviet participants, by 100 Finnish journalists and media decision-makers from across the political spectrum (from Communists to Conservatives). Similarly, there was wide support for basically the same idea in Helsinki in 1976 from a panel of journalists from the Baltic countries (Finland and other Scandinavian countries, as well as the Soviet Union, Poland, and the two Germanies):

> The principles incorporated in the Helsinki Final Act should be included in the "codes of ethics," voluntarily adopted by journalist unions, specifying thereby what is meant in practice by responsible journalism in the spirit of the Conference on Security and Co-operation in Europe. Such clearly expressed principles for the use of the mass media, as well as codes of journalistic ethics, which support peace and universal social progress based on democracy and equality, serve as a guarantee for freedom of information—not as an obstacle to it.[46]

Unesco

Despite a clear mandate to help professionals in developing the codes of ethics, Unesco has not been particularly instrumental in these efforts (cf., Chapter 2). Its role has been quite passive, obviously due to the para-

---

[45] V. B. Lomeiko, "Responsibility and Freedom of Information" (translated from Finnish, original in Russian), in proceedings of the seminar organized by the Finnish-Soviet Friendship Society in Espoo (Finland), 11-12 September 1979.

[46] See Bruun, op. cit. in note 1 above, p. 11.

lyzing effect of the controversy around the Mass Media Declaration since 1975, but no doubt also due to a lack of capacity and even interest on the part of the Secretariat. Unesco has convened only one meeting on the specific question of journalistic codes,[47] and it has published just one monograph devoted to this topic.[48] All of these focused on general questions of truthfulness, access to sources, etc.—salient aspects of prevailing professional ethics, practically disregarding the aspect of international responsibility. However, beyond this primary Unesco project on the journalistic codes of ethics, there are a number of other Unesco contributions which merit recall.

In May 1977, the Philosophy Division of Unesco's Sector for Social Sciences organized the *Meeting of Experts on Contribution to an Ethic of Communication* in Ottawa (Canada)—an indication of an overall intellectual interest in communication problems at the time when the new information order was being articulated. Although the meeting did not consider codes of ethics specifically, the idea of a universal code was clearly encouraged:

> An ethic of communication for the modern world should be based upon such values as peace, freedom and mutual respect which are common to all mankind and at the same time should take into account the great cultural and political diversity so evident in the world today.[49]

Moreover, a recommendation of the meeting was to "encourage the development of national and international standards concerning

> (a) the principles of freedom of expression and freedom of information;
>
> (b) the right to protection against any abuses in communication that might be detrimental to human dignity and to socio-cultural values;
>
> (c) respect for the cultural identity of groups and communities, and for the principles which are corollary to its acceptance;
>
> (d) mutual respect between different cultures and reciprocity in the exchange of information both within and between countries;
>
> (e) the use of the mass media for raising the cultural level of the people.[50]

---

[47]"Collective Consultations on Codes of Ethics for the Mass Media." Unesco House, 12-13 November 1973. A preliminary report of the meeting is reproduced as Appendix to Bruun as well as to Jones, op. cit. in note 1.

[48]Jones, op. cit.

[49]Unesco document SS-77/CONF./603.17 (Paris, 13 June 1977), p. 1 (paragraph 1 of the Final Report).

[50]Ibid., p. 5 (from Recommendations, point 7).

Another relevant Unesco meeting, the *International Colloquium on the Free and Balanced Flow of Information Between Developed and Developing Countries,* was organized in April 1977 in Florence (by the Office of Public Information in collaboration with Italian authorities) as an unofficial forum to bring together government and media representatives from various camps of the new order debate for a stock-taking exercise after Nairobi. One of the three commissions of the meeting discussed "the status and responsibilities of information personnel and the protection of journalists in the exercise of their profession" on the basis of a working paper prepared by the Secretariat.[51] This working paper outlines, among other things, "the main responsibilities set out in the codes of professional ethics"–a list more comprehensive in terms of the international aspects of the codes than any other Unesco document apart from the Mass Media Declaration:

> *Objective picture of the developing countries*–Journalists have a responsibility towards their own country when informing the public about the developing countries. There is often a tendency to present the most negative aspects of the Third World countries and to ridicule this or that leader of the developing countries. The Third World countries are often victims of a distortion of their image as it is presented by some of the media of the developed countries. Some of the big news agencies lay too much stress on tension or violence in the Third World countries. On the other hand, these agencies often pass over events of a constructive nature which occur increasingly in the same countries. There is a tendency to present the public with a hastily sketched caricature of the daily news. This gives people an absolutely false picture of the problems of the developing countries.
>
> *Respect for national cultures*–Journalists, in the context of the established system in some of the developed countries, are inclined to underestimate the culture of the developing countries, thus contributing to a kind of cultural domination, which is tending to become consolidated because the mass communication media disseminate knowledge and values which are foreign to the developing countries. But, in the context of a new international order, journalists have a certain responsibility in the safeguarding of national cultures. The right to culture is closely linked with the right to communication.
>
> *International understanding and contribution to the strengthening of peace*–Journalists have a great responsibility in the broadening of cooperation between nations and in the preservation of world peace. They must campaign against the use of force and the threat of force in relations between States, for the stability of existing frontiers, and

[51]Unesco document OPO-77/WS/3 (Paris, 6 April 1977).

for security on all continents. Any appeal to national, racial or religious hatred, which incites people to discrimination, hostility or violence, must be avoided. Journalists should endeavor not to disturb relations between nations, to work towards the political settlement of conflicts, to promote better mutual knowledge and understanding between peoples and the organization of peace between States. They should refuse to participate in any propaganda involving racial, warmongering or national hatred, in any defence of genocide, in any appeal to recourse to violence for the settlement of international disputes.[52]

Obviously, such an outspoken text did not appeal to the Western representatives at the meeting (including the leadership of the World Press Freedom Committee), as hinted by a statement in the Commission's Final Report: "journalists from socialist countries, as well as those from the Third World, appreciated in the main the working paper prepared by the Unesco Secretariat."[53] Among the points enumerated in the Final Report as "ideas expressed during the debate" were the following:

—Journalists should carry out their function in a spirit of understanding and of respect for the social and cultural values of each country.

—In the exercise of the profession, particular attention should be paid to the objective image of developing countries and to their national culture and sovereignty.

—The authorities should guarantee to journalists the rights and the means to practice their profession efficiently.

—In information exchanges, the journalist should serve as honestly as possible the cause of peace and understanding and of international cooperation.

Immediately after the adoption of the Mass Media Declaration in 1978, the Unesco Secretariat convened a small but widely representative *Meeting of Consultants on the Free and Balanced Flow of Information in a New Communication Order*.[54] The meeting proposed several measures to follow-up the Declaration and other relevant decisions of the 20th session

[52] Ibid., p. 4.

[53] Since the proceedings of the colloquium are not published, the Final Report is available only as copy of the original document kept at Unesco (e.g., Mass Communication Documentation Centre in the Paris headquarters).

[54] The meeting on 18-21 December 1978 was attended by 14 consultants representing academic and professional, as well as political, expertise, among them MacBride, Mankekar, Masmoudi, Pastecka and Zassoursky (cf. Chapter 1). The U.S. participant was Roger Tatarian from California State University, formerly Editor-in-Chief of UPI. The report of the meeting was issued as Unesco document CC-79/WS/83 (Paris, 26 June 1979).

of the General Conference. Great attention was paid to inserting the principles of the Declaration in journalists' codes of ethics:

> . . . Encourage the adoption of national or regional codes of professional ethics drawn up by journalists themselves or by news agency personnel.
>
> Assess the feasibility of establishing an international code of ethics which would be adopted by journalists possesing a "universal" sense of mission, that is to say transcending their national origin in the defence of peace and fraternity . . .
>
> . . . Draw up, with the co-operation of peace organizations, a model code of conduct for the treatment of information relating to foreign affairs, taking account, in particular, of the tensions that may arise as the results of the distorted reporting of certain events . . . .
>
> . . . Set up a "World Press Council" to help ensure the truthfulness and objectivity of information, in the event of it proving impossible to devise and adopt an "international code of ethics."
>
> Establish a "World Press Institute" that would organize seminars, training courses and consultations on the rights of the press. It would serve as an international "conscience" and as a "forum" for the profession . . . .

These proposals are, by and large, in line with the recommendations in the *MacBride Report,* which took it for granted that codes of ethics at the national and, in some cases, at the regional level are desirable, "provided that such codes are prepared and adopted by the profession itself—without governmental interference."[55] Beyond this, the Report included the question of codes in its list of "issues requiring further study":

> Studies should be undertaken to identify, if possible, principles generally recognized by the profession of journalism and which take into account the public interest. This could also encompass further consideration, by journalists' organizations themselves, of the concept of international code of ethics. Some fundamental elements for this code might be found in the Unesco Declaration on the mass media, as well as in provisions common to the majority of existing national and regional codes.[56]

Although these are moderate—far from revolutionary—recommendations, they imply a critical assessment of the past and present performance of the mass media: "Such values as truthfulness, accuracy and respect for human rights are not universally applied at

[55]*Many Voices, One World,* Paris: Unesco, 1980, p. 262 (Recommendation 43).
[56]Ibid., p. 274 (point 6).

present."[57] Moreover, the principal stand of the MacBride Commission on "professional integrity and standards" poses a direct challenge to the Western "free flow" position: "For the journalist, freedom and responsibility are indivisible."[58]

While the linkage between freedom and responsibility is spelled out by the MacBride Commission in exceptionally clear terms (and unanimously), it should be noted that it is the same philosophical approach that is the essence of the Mass Media Declaration. Thus the Commission just confirmed the position of principle achieved, as a matter of international consensus, in the process of preparing the Declaration. There have been no further steps to promote the ethics of journalism at Unesco since 1978.

This situation also exists on deliberations concerning *protection of journalists*. As noted in Chapter 1, the issue was raised by the MacBride Commission[59] and then carried on by the Unesco Secretariat until it was paralyzed in February 1981 by Western opposition. The idea of protecting journalists in the legitimate excercise of their profession was unanimously accepted as a part of the conceptual and political "package" for which the Declaration stands. The MacBride Commission endorsed this balanced view—without subscribing to the Chairman's proposal to proceed towards a special status and protection of journalists, comparable to that of diplomats.[60]

The parallel Unesco project, based on the unanimously adopted Programme and Budget for 1979–1980, included case studies and consultations "in cooperation with the professional organizations concerned, in order to collect information on the status, rights and responsibilities of journalists, with a view to suggesting ways of improving the status of journalists and information specialists and giving them the necessary protection for the exercise of their profession in the best possible conditions of accuracy and objectivity."[61] The outcome of this project is a publication of background documents,[62] a proposal for the establishment of an international (non-governmental) commission, and a periodical international conference for the protection of journalists,[63] as well as conflicting

[57] Ibid., p. 262 (Recommendation 41).

[58] Ibid., p. 262. It is noteworthy that no reservations were expressed on this point of principle. Earlier, in the descriptive part of the study, in the chapter on "norms of professional conduct," Elie Abel and Betty Zimmerman put on record their displeasure with "planetary" and "international" codes of ethics (pp. 244-245).

[59] See S. MacBride, "The Protection of Journalists," document No. 90 prepared for the Commission in 1979.

[60] See Recommendations 50-51 on pp. 264-265 of the Report (see note 55).

[61] Unesco document 20 C/5, paragraph 4483.

[62] Op. cit. in note 3 above.

[63] The working paper by Professor Pierre Gaborit was issued as Unesco document CC-80/WS/53 (Paris, 17 November 1980).

reports of a consultative meeting held in Paris in February 1981.[64] None of these elaborated a concrete proposal for an international code, let alone suggested that one should be prepared and enforced by governments. But all parties, except for the "gang of four" which was aggressive against the whole project, endorsed the fundamental position that a proper journalist is always "exercising his or her profession in compliance with the ethical principles and customs laid down by profession itself"[65] and that any mechanisms towards better protection of journalists should include "encouraging the search for joint solutions in the field of deontology and professional ethics."[66]

Consequently, Unesco has never suggested a governmentally controlled code—an accusation directed against it by the "Talloires offensive" (cf., Chapter 1). On the contrary, Unesco can be criticized for exercising a kind of passive resistance to the idea of promoting journalistic codes of ethics as instruments for higher professional standards, particularly with regard to journalists' international responsibility.

On the other hand, Unesco has served as a forum for intellectual and political exchanges concerning questions of the role and status of journalists, their rights and responsibilities. This is precisely the function foreseen for this UN agency in the fields of education, science, culture, and communication. But it has not been a completely neutral forum, since it has advocated certain universal values, such as peace and decolonization, which have been unanimously or overwhelmingly recognized by the international community. Again this is in harmony with the letter and spirit of Unesco's Constitution (drawn up mainly by Western countries in 1945—cf., Chapter 1).

An illuminating reading of *Unesco's overall approach in the communication field* is provided by the Director-General in one of his contributions to the General Conference in Belgrade.[67] After reviewing the concept and means of communication, he defined the role of communication as an essential factor in development, hampered in today's world by quantitative and qualitative imbalances. He pointed out that the main issue of the debate on communication has been "the adoption of a standard-setting instrument which, without being legally binding, would, nevertheless,

[64]As described in Chapter 1, the meeting could not agree on any final statement, leaving the international and regional organizations of professional journalists (those involved in the consultative meetings in Paris, Mexico, and Baghdad) on one side, and the "gang of four" on the other. As usual, the international media coverage of the event was dominated by the position of the latter party representing the owners and managers of Western news media.

[65]From the definition of a journalist tentatively adopted at a consultative meeting between representatives of IOJ and IFJ at Unesco in January 1980. See Unesco document referred to in note 3 above, p. 13.

[66]From Gaborit's working paper (see note 63), p. 3.

[67]"Preliminary Report of the Director-General on the Medium-Term Plan for 1984-1989," Unesco document 21 C/4 (General Conference, 21st session, Belgrade 1980, 25 August 1980).

bring together a set of principles forming the basis of an ethical system for the world community in the information sector."[68] The Director-General, reflecting the dominant opinion among Unesco's membership (i.e., practically all independent nations), went on to specify:

> Transcending the natural divergences within the international community, the desire for understanding and the spirit of co-operation asserted both during this Conference and when the Declaration on the media was adopted, have enabled a body of principles to be found which may henceforth provide both food for thought and practical guidance.
>
> This body of principles rests on the recognition that communication among individuals, peoples and nations plays an increasing part both for progress in all walks of life—and especially for the development of the poorest countries—and also for the pursuit of a number of objectives shared by all mankind: the safeguarding of national sovereignty and cultural identity, the establishment of a new international economic order, the strengthening of mutual understanding and international peace, the promotion of universal respect for human rights, and the struggle against racialism, apartheid and colonialism.[69]

The Mexico Declaration

While Unesco, as an intergovernmental agency, kept reminding that ethics—and in general, the question of values—is central in any consideration of human communication, it was "the profession itself" that went beyond an overall conceptualization by beginning to prepare an international code of journalistic ethics. As described in Chapter 1, a decisive step was taken in Mexico City in April 1980, at the second consultative meeting between international and regional organizations of journalists—a loose coalition of non-governmental organizations which together represent some 300,000 professional journalists from all continents. The meeting was organized by FELAP, with some assistance from Unesco and the Government of Mexico.[70] The main outcome of this forum was the "Mexico Declaration" reproduced as Appendix 25.

To appreciate the significance of this document, one has to consider the nature of the organizations that signed it (through their respective leading representatives). First, they stand for the *workers of the mass media,*

---

[68] Ibid., p. 58 (paragraph 332).
[69] Ibid., p. 58 (paragraphs 336-337).
[70] See *IOJ Newsletter,* special issue 1980.

rather than for the employers and managers whose interests have dominated such Western media lobbies as the International Press Institute and the World Press Freedom Committee (as shown in Chapter 1). Their national affiliates are typically journalists' trade unions or such professional associations which unite all socially and politically active journalists of the country. These may or may not be at odds with the media managers and authorities of the country, depending on the media system and political situation in question. In any case, they represent the rank and file "working journalists" and, thus, usually have a clear majority among the journalistic community of a country (which does not necessarily mean a leading role in determining the mass media policies). One of the organizations, the Catholic Union of the Press, is different in that its members are both journalists and media managers working for religiously based (Catholic) media enterprises in various countries.

Second, in terms of geographical and political representation, the signatories to the Mexico Declaration cover *all continents and geopolitical regions* (with the exception of China, which, since the Cultural Revolution, has not participated in international cooperation among journalists). Best represented are the socialist and developing countries, while Western Europe and North America are covered by the scattered members of UCIP and IOJ. The International Federation of Journalists (IFJ), which includes most of the Western Journalist trade unions, did not attend the Mexico meeting, but two years later, at the third consultative meeting of this "professional front" in Baghdad, the IFJ representative joined others in declaring: "We are firmly devoted to the principles of the Mexico Declaration."[71]

Consequently, it can be said (as stated in Chapter 1) that the document has the support of the overwhelming majority of the organized journalists of the world (i.e., those who belong to national trade unions or professional associations, totalling perhaps 400,000 world-wide). Politically, this means that it is supported by various ideological and philosophical orientations extending from communists to Christian democrats. Yet it is obvious that it enjoys little or no support on the political right, particularly among those who sympathize with "tyrannic regimes" (cf., Principle VIII) in Latin America and elsewhere.

The document itself has a political orientation which might simply be called *democratic*. It is a manifestation of the same line of universal values advocated by Unesco in the debate on the new information order (cf., in particular, the "set of principles" spelled out by the Director-

---

[71]From the "Baghdad Declaration" (point 1), see note 23 above.

General in Belgrade). It is logical, then, that the Mexico Declaration spells out the professional journalists' support of Unesco, and their commitment to its Mass Media Declaration, as well as their "respect for other relevant instruments of the international community designed to promote peaceful and democratic relations in the field of information" (preambular paragraphs 1—3). Moreover, the formulation of the principles (especially VII—IX) brings the Mexico Declaration virtually in line with the official position of the Non-Aligned Movement (cf., Chapter 1). To be precise, it is not quite as "radical" as the Non-Aligned position, since it does not use phrases such as "imperialism" and "zionism." At the same time, it is in line with the position advocated by experts from the socialist countries as reviewed above.

Such a *dedication to the values and principles of the international community* is a significant step for a profession with a strong tradition to remain independent and, in particular, free from governmental interference. After all, in practice the international community is made up of governments, although, in theory, the concept ultimately refers to the peoples of the world. However, nothing in the Mexico Declaration suggests that the professionals concerned would welcome governments to assume a greater role in mass communication. It does mean that "the profession itself" is dedicated to the same universal values and principles that are reflected in the UN system and in international law. This was confirmed in the subsequent Baghdad meeting of the organizations concerned, which declared that "while understanding that the new order should be based on respect for the international laws contained in the United Nations Charter, we are convinced that the new information and communication order is in no way aimed at the establishment of government censorship."[72]

A revealing detail in this respect is the formulation of Principle VI. The draft text prepared for the meeting by experts of FELAP and IOJ spoke about "due respect for national security, public order and public morals"—a reference to the generally accepted standards of international law applying to national interests (cf., Chapter 8). However, the meeting found this a risky formulation which could easily be misused by regimes, such as Latin American military dictatorships, to suppress journalists against a democratic course. Accordingly, all references to national security and public order were dropped, and the final text prescribes only "due respect for democratic institutions and public morals."

From a philosophical point of view, the Mexico Declaration (see especially Principles I and X) follows the same orientation as that in the Kuala Lumpur Declaration of Unesco (see Chapter 1). Thus *the journalist*

---

[72] Ibid.

is seen as an instrument to materialize the people's right to true information—the truth understood as objective reality to be discovered and communicated to the public as accurately and comprehensively as possible. This modern appreciation of the concept of objectivity[73] rejects the naive trust in man's (also the journalist's) capacity for acquiring a truthful picture of the world from the pieces of true and false information circulatinag on the "free marketplace of ideas." But it also rejects the epistemological scepticism whereby no objectivity is possible in a world where everything is relative. Naturally, it furthermore rejects the vulgar view that objective truth is equal to whatever is determined by a political or religious authority.

It is interesting to note that this concept of objectivity invites the same kind of *contextualization* in journalism as was advocated by the Hutchins Commission. The "proper context" in which facts should be reported, according to Principle X, compares well with the Commission's credo for "truthful, comprehensive, and intelligent account of the day's events in a context which gives them meaning."[74] On the other hand, unlike the Hutchins Commission, the Mexico Declaration does not emphasize the distinction between fact and opinion. It is also noteworthy that Principle X stresses *journalistic creativity,* thus avoiding a mechanistic concept of journalism as simple transmission information, suggesting instead that journalism may be seen as a type of literature.

As far as the social role of the journalist is concerned, Principles II—IV reconfirm a number of points which belong to the *conventional Western notion of good journalism:* public accountability, "conscience clause," fighting bribery, supporting the right of reply, etc. But these Principles "not only represent common grounds of existing national and regional codes of journalistic ethics" (as in the preambular paragraph 6); they also introduce important *new elements reflecting the movement towards a new information order.* Such an innovation is already "information understood as social need and not commodity" (Principle II).

Significant in this respect is the definition of the *journalist's social responsibility* contained in Principle II. The responsibility in question is not just a hollow phrase, referring to an abstract society to which the journalist is accountable. In specifying that the public at large includes "various social interests," it recognizes that there are several conflicting socio-economic-political interests—with a corresponding class structure—thus suggesting a delicate analysis of the interests served by the journalist in each case. But this concept of responsibility relates the journalist not only to the social interests represented among the public. It also makes the im-

---

[73]For a concise review and analysis of various notions of objectivity, see P. Hemánus, "Objectivity in Mass Communication," *The Democratic Journalist,* No. 10, 1979, pp. 7-11.

[74]*A Free and Responsible Press,* Chicago: The University of Chicago Press, 1947, p. 21.

portant point—often forgotten by advocates of social responsibility in journalism—that the journalist is usually accountable to "those controlling the media," i.e. the owners and managers of the mass media enterprises. In other words, the Mexico Declaration makes the same point as the MacBride Commission did in suggesting that "a distinction may have to be drawn between media institutions, owners and managers on the one hand, and journalists on the other."[75]

Related to this realistic appraisal of the social relations which determine the journalist's position is "the right to participate in the decision-making of the media in which the journalist is employed" (Principle III). This is a justification for demands for what is often referred to as *editorial democracy*—a form of workers' involvement in determining the policy of production. Parallel to this is another demand, challenging especially commercially run private media, concerning *public access and participation* (Principle IV). "The nature of the profession" which promotes such objectives is quite different from a profession viewing itself as a distinct and technocratic entity—a typical view held by journalists who, at least in the Western hemisphere, have a tendency to present themselves as the army of the "fourth branch of government."

As a matter of fact, advocacy of public access and participation implies a paradox: a profession of communication specialists to do away with the monopoly of professional communicators! This is only logical, given a philosophy in which professionalism is understood as a means of democratization rather than an end in itself.

Consequently, the Mexico Declaration stands for a concept of professionalism which, while building on the established (predominantly Western) tradition of journalism, makes *the journalist committed to certain universal values.* This does not mean that the profession would, objectively speaking, be less independent than under a doctrine which has made the libertarian notion of freedom into its value foundation. Journalism is always bound to be dependent on certain social interests and values, whether openly recognized or accepted as "hidden ideology." In this respect the Mexico Declaration has an important function as an instrument to stimulate critical appraisal of "the profession itself"—just as the Unesco Declaration has stimulated critical appraisal of the performance of the mass media.

In fact, the Mexico Declaration was designed to be *a source of inspiration rather than a final product.* The ten Principles are there to be studied by journalists' organizations "for their eventual inclusion in their respective codes of ethics with the ultimate objective of preparing a draft international code of journalistic ethics" (preambular paragraph 6). This is obvi-

---

[75]From Recommendation 41 on p. 262 of the Report (see note 55).

ously a slow process. The first two years after the adoption of the Mexico Declaration have not produced a more advanced "draft international code," although the international and regional organizations concerned have kept the idea alive, confirming it in their third consultative meeting in Baghdad. Despite vocal opposition to the idea—mainly expressed by the Talloires "voices of freedom"—the Mexico Declaration has become the more relevant and timely, the less promising the international situation has turned out to be in the early 1980s.

10

Journalism as a Profession: A Discussion

The Mexico Declaration deserves our attention not only because it is a widely representative and up-to-date call for an international code of journalistic ethics. Its main significance lies in the *kind of ethics* and the *kind of professionalism* which is being advocated. We shall focus on this question after examining the arguments of those who are against any international code of journalistic ethics.

THE DECLARATION OF TALLOIRES

As documented in Chapter 1, the declaration adopted by "leaders of independent news media" at their "Voices of Freedom" conference in Talloires (France) in May 1981 is probably the most representative statement of those who oppose the movement towards a new international information order. This "Magna Carta of the free press" is reproduced as Appendix 26.

As summarized by the organizers of the conference, the Talloires participants "urged to abandon attempts to regulate global information and strive instead for practical solutions to Third World media advancement."[1] Seen in the perspective of the "great media debate" of the 1970s, this means, first, to turn attention *away from a normative considera-tion* of the content of communication and the socio-political objectives which the media are supposed to serve and, second, to invite the media of the developing countries to *cooperate with the private sector* of the industrial-ized West in setting up, training, and maintaining their media infrastructure and personnel; in other words, "trading ideology against cooperation."[2]

Thus Talloires was not a frontal attack against everything put forward by the new order movement. Rather, it was an updated version of the "Marshall Plan" approach which the Western powers employed at

[1]"The Declaration of Talloires. A Statement of Principles to Which an Independent News Media Sub-scribes, and On Which It Never Will Compromise," booklet published by the World Press Freedom Committee's Rex Rand Fund, Leonard H. Marks, Treasurer (quote on p. 1).

[2]R. Righter, "Lessons From Belgrade . . . The Bankruptcy of Consensus," in *Voices of Freedom* (Working Papers of the Talloires Conference), Medford, Mass.: The Edward R. Murrow Center of Public Diplo-macy in cooperation with the World Press Freedom Committee, 1981, p. 20.

Unesco from 1976 to 1980. It was logical, therefore, that among the Talloires participants there were some coming from the developing countries (notably such "moderates" as Jamaica, Egypt, and Malaysia).

An integral part of the Talloires credo is *opposition to governmental involvement,* at the national as well as international level, in the process of mass communication (see especially points 5 and 10 of the Declaration). The concept of government implied by the Declaration follows a *typical libertarian reasoning,* whereby undefined "government interests" are viewed as separate from, or opposed to, "those of the individual" (the individual interests being equally abstract and undefined). Part and parcel of the same reasoning is the belief that it is the government (as an abstract notion) and an "official control" that constitutes the main or sole threat to press freedom. Thus: "To legislate or otherwise mandate responsibilities for the press is to destroy its independence" (point 9). As stated by Leonard Marks, Secretary-Treasurer of the World Press Freedom Committee, "the issue is relatively simple—shall there be media subjected to government control or a free press?"[3]

Accordingly, the official sphere of government, legislation, the state, etc., in this doctrine constitutes the basis for the definition of journalistic freedom—the more there is independence from this sphere, the greater the freedom. However, the Declaration of Talloires also spells out another, albeit less central, criterion for press freedom: *advertising,* which on the one hand provides "financial support for a strong and self-sustaining press," thus serving as a guarantee for press freedom, but which on the other hand gives rise to "the principle that editorial decisions must be free of advertising influence" (point 7).

By and large, philosophically and politically speaking, *the notion of press freedom in the Talloires doctrine is virtually identical with the classic notion of free enterprise.* No wonder then that the post-Talloires campaign has capitalized on the combination of these two forms of libertarianism (cf., the Smith-Kline advertisement quoted in Chapter 1). Likewise, it is natural that the Talloires participants were "leaders of independent news media"—mostly owners or managers of private media enterprises and leading journalists working for them, i.e., representatives of *proprietors' interests,* rather than professional journalists' interests.[4]

---

[3]"The New World Information Order—What Does It Mean?" Paper presented by Marks to the 1981 annual Conference of the International Institute of Communications at Palais de l'Europe, Strassbourg (France), 7-10 May 1981 (quote on p. 1).

[4]Most of the organizations which were represented in Talloires (from the World Press Freedom Committee to the International Press Institute) are well known to stand for the proprietors' interests. No proper professional organizations or trade unions of working journalists were represented (not even the North American Newspaper Guild or its Western umbrella organization, the International Federation of Journalists).

In this overall perspective, it is not difficult to see what is meant by the statement that, in any society, "public interest is best served by a variety of independent news media" (point 6), or that "journalistic freedoms should apply equally to the print and broadcast media" (point 9). Obviously, the target is not private media monopolies and their commercially determined coverage of the world, which hardly meets the standards of pluralism, accuracy, etc. (set by the libertarian doctrine itself); the moral is rather to legitimize the principle of private enterprise in the communication field, including new electronic media (cable, satellite, cassette), and to impose on public media monopolies (broadcasting organizations) influence from the private sector.

Similarly, it is not difficult to see why the Talloires participants stated that "the free flow of information and ideas is essential for mutual understanding and world peace," and declared "restraints on the movement of news and information to be contrary to the interests of international understanding" (point 2). Without doubt, the approach here is far from that of the Mass Media Declaration of Unesco, although the words used are nearly identical. The Declaration of Talloires simply reconfirms the Western political philosophy whereby it is "free flow" that leads to peace and security, instead of a policy which would guide the content of communication toward harmony with that objective (cf., Chapter 7).

The Declaration of Talloires ends with a statement which exposes the overall bias of the document: "Press freedom is a basic human right." This is simply not true, as is evident in the light of Part 2 of this book. First, it is individuals ("everyone") and not the media ("press") that enjoy under international law the "right to freedom of opinion and expression" (not "freedom of information"). Second, the human right in question "carries with it duties and responsibilities" and in no case can it be exercised contrary to the vital interests of the international community, above all the preservation of peace and security.

Such a critical analysis of the Declaration of Talloires does not suggest that the document implies a doctrine which is altogether different from that advocated by the Mexico Declaration. It should be noted, first of all, that *the new order movement has never suggested governmental control as a universal model for the management of the media*. As shown in Chapter 1, the objective has been to achieve a decolonization and democratization of information—internationally as well as nationally—and to establish an order in the field of information that would be in line with international law. It is true that in practice the program for the new order has often led to a bias against private enterprise and for public service, but this has followed from the conditions of colonialism and democracy, or from the general principles of international law, and not from a political intention to legitimize governmental authority in the field of information.

Yet, the Western doctrine as expressed by the Declaration of Talloires takes the new order largely as a program for governmental control. Obviously, this misunderstanding is due in part to ignorance of the objectives of the movement and to the nature of international law and order. But perhaps the main reason is the *difference in philosophical approaches to the question of press freedom*. As demonstrated by the declarations of Mexico and Talloires, the two doctrines are incompatible in their relation to government-media. But it is important to understand that they are not totally opposed to each other in this respect. After all, the Mexico Declaration does not advocate governmental control of the media; it simply does not consider the whole issue of government involvement to be central to the definition of journalistic freedom.

However far apart the two doctrines are philosophically, they do include *some crucial elements in common*. There is agreement in the two documents in their definition of professional dedication. While, in the Mexico Declaration, the journalist's foremost responsibility is to serve the right of people and individuals to "true and authentic information" (Principle II) and to pursue "an honest dedication to objective reality" (Principle X), the Talloires version states: "The press's professional responsibility is the pursuit of truth" (point 9). Although the latter concept of truth remains undefined, and obviously differs in some respects from the epistemological model provided by the Mexico Declaration, it is significant that there is an overall *shared orientation towards truthfulness in journalism*.[5]

This is not a trivial matter, since there also exists a brand of libertarian doctrine which considers dedication to truth to be detrimental to freedom; such a doctrine regards the spreading of lies as a minor risk compared with what follows from obligations to keep to the truth.[6] On closer inspection, the Talloires text is ambiguous in this respect; the pursuit of truth is guaranteed by the "free exchange of ideas," and may even be destroyed if "legislated or otherwise mandated" (point 9). Thus, truth and freedom are conditioned by each other, and a journalist is seen to be dedicated to "the freest, most accurate and impartial information that is within our professional capacity to produce and distribute" (point 10). Yet this statement fits quite well within the doctrine advocated by the Mexico Declaration, the only notable difference being that the Talloires Declaration demands impartiality—even in regard to those universal values which the journalists in Mexico declared they supported.

---

[5] For a lucid discussion of the Western concept of journalistic truth, see A. Gauhar, "Free Flow of Information: Myths and Shibboleths," *Third World Quarterly*, No. 3, July 1979, pp. 61-67.

[6] This doctrine has grown mainly out of the tradition provided by John Milton, John Stuart Mill, and others. A lucid discussion of the doctrine is provided by John Calhoun Merrill (formerly with the University of Missouri, now with Louisiana State University); see his *Imperative of Freedom: A Philosophy of Journalistic Autonomy*, New York: Hastings House, 1974.

However, the beginning of the Declaration of Talloires leads us to question whether this doctrine, after all, requires a journalist to remain impartial and independent with regard to the universal values and principles held by the international community. The first point of the Talloires text is an affirmation of commitment to the principles contained in four international instruments of great importance: the Universal Declaration of Human Rights, the Constitution of Unesco, the UN Charter, and the Final Act of the Conference on Security and Cooperation in Europe. The particular extracts quoted from these instruments in the Talloires document carry a clear bias towards a "free flow" position, and it is interesting to note that the Mass Media Declaration of Unesco is not included in the collection of those documents to which "all international bodies and nations" are called upon to adhere. However, such a bias does not change the true nature of the instruments in question, which, as seen in Part 2 of this book, suggest quite a balanced concept of freedom in the field of information. It is far from the Western "free flow" concept, which, as such, is seen to contribute to mutual understanding and world peace.

It appears that the Talloires participants were not informed about the international law of communications—a paradox, given the fact that one of the organizers was an academic institution that specializes in law and diplomacy. This led them to "affirm our commitment to these principles," although in fact the principles of those international instruments—part and parcel of the fundamental principles of international law discussed in Chapter 4—stand for something other than was advocated by the rest of the Declaration of Talloires.

Notwithstanding this discrepancy, it is of crucial importance that the *Talloires Declaration recognized international instruments as a legitimate foundation for setting the standards of journalism*. This point of departure is clearly shared by the Mexico Declaration and, moreover, it can be seen as the essence of the Mass Media Declaration of Unesco (cf., Chapter 3). Again, it is obvious that the true meaning of the Declaration of Talloires is not to advocate a transformation of international law into national legislation or other types of official mandate. However, this reservation does not do away with the fact that the principles of journalism are conceived and justified in terms of central instruments of international law and politics.

Consequently, the Declaration of Talloires is not only an outspoken demonstration in defence of private enterprise interests and of Western "free flow" values, designed to mobilize a conservative professional and political opposition to the new information order movement. It is also, given a number of internal contradictions, a dedication to principles which make possible a substantial common ground with the advocates of the new order.

What is said here applies to the Declaration of Talloires in broad philosophical terms. The details of the text give rise to less reconciliatory perspectives. For example the Declaration states: "There can be no international code of journalistic ethics; the plurality of views make this impossible" (point 9). This appears to be a position in total opposition to the Mexico Declaration. But considering the commitment to principles enunciated in international instruments, the position becomes less persuasive. Moreover, there is empirical evidence (as shown in Chapter 9 but perhaps not known to the Talloires participants) which proves that, despite the diversity of political systems and professional doctrines across nations, many common elements can be identified in professional ethics around the world.

Accordingly, those who look only at the manifest points that can be read in the Talloires text may come to quite different conclusions from those suggested above. In fact, some of the Talloires participants have since taken positions which no longer show respect for international law and order but which, instead, represent an extreme libertarian doctrine. For example, Robert L. Stevenson (School of Journalism, University of North Carolina), discussing the responsibilities of the news media in issues of peace and disarmament, did not hesitate "to stand up and say that the role of the mass media is not to strengthen peace and understanding, not to promote human rights, not to counter racism and incitement to war."[7] Instead, this journalism scholar and educator defined the role of the media to be more modestly "to maintain surveillance of the institutions which do have the responsibility for international affairs and to force those institutions to operate in the antiseptic glare of informed public opinion."[8]

We might ask which is the real voice of Talloires—the elaborations by Marks, Stevenson, etc., or the Declaration as a whole as we have analyzed it here. There is no doubt that the neo-conservative "hard liners" (with activists such as Marks, Righter, and Sussman) have made great use of the Talloires document in their *political struggle* against the new order movement, getting even the U.S. President and Congress to subscribe to it (cf., Chapter 1). Incidentally, the fact that the leading government of the West emerges as a militant supporter of a declaration which is designed to miminize government interference is a paradox ("the Talloires paradox"), which illustrates well the political and conceptual contradictions prevailing in the field of information.

---

[7]"The Responsibilities of the News Media in Issues of Peace and Disarmament," paper presented at a conference on education for peace and disarmament, International Institute for Peace, Baden (Austria), September 1981 (quote on p. 13).

[8]Ibid. (p. 2).

But beyond politics, Talloires has provided little that advances a neo-conservative cause. From the point of view of *professional philosophy*, it is a conventional statement of a libertarian doctrine. In terms of conceptualization and reasoning, it is an apologetic statement, with no innovations for serious elaboration of any professional doctrines—neither the libertarian, nor the "social responsibility" doctrine. The Declaration of Talloires is intellectually as defensive and obscure as it is politically offensive and sharp.

In this respect, the Mexico Declaration constitutes a kind of antithesis to Talloires; instead of providing a politically conservative defence of the established (Western) tradition, it advocates a new professionalism which could be universally acceptable. As indicated by its broad geopolitical support, the Mexico Declaration has no particular political target—for or against—other than an overall defence of the UN system. It is a professional application of the Mass Media Declaration of Unesco, based on the 1978 consensus and reflecting further progress towards a widely recognized new international information order.

NEW PROFESSIONAL ETHICS

As stated by the Mexico Declaration, journalism is a *socially committed* profession. The commitment originates from the people's right to acquire a truthful picture of objective reality, on the one hand, and from the universal values of humanism on the other. The commitment to truth is, in principle, the same as that held within the libertarian mainstream of journalism (including Talloires), although there are obvious differences between traditions as to the nature of truth. But the commitment to the universal values as established by the international community means a significant departure from the typical Western tradition and a move towards the notion of professionalism as generally understood in the socialist and developing countries.

Accordingly, "a true journalist," as defined by the Mexico Declaration, is not neutral with regard to the universal values of "peace, democracy, human rights, social progress and national liberation" (Principle VII). Neither is a journalist neutral with regard to violations of humanity such as "justification for or incitement to wars of aggression and arms race, especially in nuclear weapons, and other forms of violence, hatred or of national, racial or religious discrimination, oppression by tyrannic regimes, as well as all forms of colonialism and neo-colonialism" (Principle VIII).

In fact, such an ethics of journalism implies two significant steps beyond what is typically held by the libertarian tradition with its passion to remain free from any socio-political obligations other than the pursuit of truth (in a ultra-libertarian doctrine, not even that). First, there is an invitation for a journalist—as a proper citizen—to support a number of universally recognized ideals and to fight corresponding evils. This is a *general social commitment,* applying to all citizens in the same way. But beyond this, it includes a *particular professional commitment,* whereby the universal values in question are understood as vital constituents of the profession of journalism, along with the commitment to truth and all other conventional characteristics of professionalism (integrity, etc.).

Thus, it becomes the professional role of all journalists to pursue, not only truth in general, but the universal values of humanism as well. In other words, the definition of *professionalism* takes a great leap forward from the libertarian notion of a journalist, whose task is to transmit facts and opinions by remaining independent and neutral with regard to various sociopolitical interests and values—supposedly leading to "objectivity."[9] This typical libertarian doctrine of professionalism appears quite technocratic when compared with the socially committed doctrine advocated by the Mexico Declaration. The latter is highly *ethical* in its commitment, not only to decent procedures in the pursuit of truth, but also to certain genuinely *moral values.*[10] Contrary to such a value-orientation, the libertarian doctrine denies that a professional journalist should be committed to general socio-political values. In fact, given such a value nihilism, the doctrine hardly deserves to be called "professional ethics."

An illustration of the new universal doctrine of professional ethics is provided by the positions adopted by journalists in support of the "peace movement," which has gained momentum in the Western hemisphere in the early 1980s. This is how the Helsinki chapter of the Union of Journalists in Finland put the matter at its convention in February 1982:

> The journalists' instrument is the word. This instrument can be used only under conditions of peace; therefore promotion of peace is the most effective way of defending freedom of speech. Every journalist can through his or her own work strengthen the structures of peace in society in influencing public opinion and decision making. It is the duty of a journalist to transmit truthful information about questions of peace and war, armament and national defence. . . .[11]

[9]For the development of the Western concept of objectivity, see, e.g., D. Schiller, *Objectivity and the News,* Philadelphia: Temple University Press, 1981. For a discussion of various concepts of objectivity, see, e.g., P. Hemánus, "Objectivity in Mass Communication," *The Democratic Journalist,* No. 10, 1979, pp. 7-11.

[10]For a basic conceptualization of the sphere of ethics, see, e.g., W. K. Frankena, *Ethics,* Englewood Cliffs, N.J.: Prentice-Hall, 1963.

[11]From a declaration on peace, adopted unanimously by the annual convention of the Helsinki Society of Journalists, which unites over one thousand professionals from all press media, including all political orientations. Published (in Finnish) in *Sanomalehtimies-Journalisten* (Journal of the Union of Journalists in Finland), No. 5, 1982, p. 4. The same kind of resolution was passed in early 1982 by most significant chapters of the Union.

Obviously, not all journalists who stand behind such statements have really made this two-step social commitment an integral part of their professional ethics. For many, what is involved is no doubt as much fashionable lip service as a fundamental reorientation—especially with regard to the second type of commitment, which brings universal values to the heart of professionalism. For example, the initiatives of the Finnish journalists' organizations in support of peace[12] have given rise to critical observations from those who, while not opposing a commitment to peace, warn against the idea that journalists should be involved in different types of social movements.[13] According to this libertarian reasoning, a social commitment in journalism leads easily to a loss of credibility; and it is the public trust (perceived credibility) that matters in this brand of professional ethics, more than any universal values.[14] Moreover, there is scepticism about how to choose the universal values to which a journalist should be committed—the road appears slippery, leading towards censorship.

Such reservations should not be taken as undermining the significance of the new, socially committed professional ethics. After all, the Mexico Declaration does not suggest that all of the 300,000 professionals represented by the organizations concerned have accepted or put into practice the ethics advocated by the document. Rather, it is an indication of a trend among professional journalists around the world—a signal of an historical development taking place along with the movement towards a new international information order. As was shown in Chapter 1, it is a significant trend, supported by an overwhelming majority of the international community. Obviously, a good deal of this support—especially among professional journalists—has been poorly articulated thus far and is a process which is only beginning to shape. But there is little doubt that a thorough consideration of the foundations of journalism, through rational analysis and critical appraisal of professional doctrines, will lead toward the kind of professional ethics advocated by the Mexico Declaration.

---

[12]In March 1982, the Union of Journalists in Finland joined the Society of the Editors-in-chief and various politically oriented professional associations of journalists in setting up the Journalists' Peace Committee. The Committee is charged with the task of mobilizing support for pacifist activities among journalists—among other things, by providing information about the danger of nuclear war. A similar peace movement among journalists surfaced in Sweden in May 1982, and in England it had already led in 1981 to the setting up of an organization, "JANE": Journalists Against Nuclear Extermination. (See *IOJ Newsletter*, No. 9, 1982.)

[13]See, e.g., E. Appel, "Journalisterna och trovärdigheten" (Journalists and Credibility, in Swedish), *Sanomalehtimies-Journalisten*, No. 6, 1982, p. 4.

[14]Gauhar argues that since the Western media "can purvey only a plausible and acceptable form of truth, the claim that their agents are engaged in an unrestricted pursuit of objective truth is, at best, an overstatement" (see op. cit. in note 5 above, p. 65).

For example, those professionals who, under the influence of a libertarian way of thinking, are afraid of the problems created by various sociopolitical values, will find out—through studies such as those reported by this book—that the journalist is not expected to follow a haphazard collection of values, but that a specific set of values emanate from universal ethical standards which have gradually evolved in the international community. There is little ground for fear or reluctance, once a person has realized that, instead of being "politicized" in an unspecified way, he or she is invited to a commitment to those and only those values that have a legitimate status in international law and politics. A commitment to such internationally accepted values can be seen as a mature stage in the professional education of the journalist. As stated by the Mexico Declaration, "it belongs to the ethics of the profession that the journalist be aware of relevant provisions contained by international conventions, declarations and resolutions" (Principle VIII).

Given this awareness, one is able to see that the concepts of peace and war, democracy and tyranny, national liberation and colonialism or neo-colonialism, etc., are not simply political slogans subject to virtually any interpretation (according to tactical needs). Most of these concepts have a specific meaning under international law, and in cases such as war propaganda (cf., Chapter 6) there are extensive applications to journalism. Naturally, there is room for interpretation and political conflict around these universal values and principles, but this is the case with any concepts that embrace human nature and behavior. Scepticism regarding the validity of universal values typically is based on ignorance of the issues involved.

In this perspective, the new "committed" professional ethics appears to be a less remarkable leap forward than was suggested above. After all, *the journalist does no more than to become openly committed to the values which constitute the foundation of international law and order.* If this seems to be a radical step, it shows only how poorly the universal values have been recognized, often due to the dominance of nationally generated values which stand in opposition to those held by the international community. For example, if commitment to peace is perceived as a politically radical position, it exposes a disregard of the universal values of peace, rather than proving that those dedicated to peace represent political extremism.

Thus, the new professional ethics in journalism does not bring any particular "politization" into the field of information; it only provides a safeguard against policies which depart from the universally recognized values of peace, democracy, etc. It goes without saying that journalism is and will continue to be a highly political field—overtly or covertly. In such a situation, any choice of professional ethics—including those proposed at Talloires and Mexico—represents a direct or indirect political position. The question is not which is political and which is apolitical; the question is what is the political orientation being advocated. In this respect, the new professional ethics has as "impartial" a foundation as can be imagined: the universal values of the international community.

Consequently, there are no major *political obstacles* to prevent a gradual recognition and worldwide adoption of the new professional ethics as advocated by the Mexico Declaration. The real obstacles will obviously be *philosophical,* especially among those who have acquired a stereotype libertarian doctrine of journalism. But even in this respect, we can state that the leap forward is not all that great; *much of the new ethics can be found in earlier statements of professional philosophy.*

FROM CONTRADICTIONS TO CHALLENGE

As demonstrated in Chapter 9, the libertarian tradition has several variations, some of which come quite close to the contemporary ideas of the new order movement. In the 1940s, the Hutchins Commission suggested professional responsibility as a safeguard for press freedom, based on private enterprise under conditions of ever stronger commercialization and concentration of the mass media. At the same time, the Commission introduced elements of professional philosophy which, in terms of universal values and theories of knowledge, are strikingly similar to those advocated by the new order movement (and, equally, strikingly different from the Talloires doctrine):

> With the means of self-destruction that are now at their disposal, men must live, if they are to live at all, by self-restraint, moderation, and mutual understanding. They get their picture of one another through the press. The press can be inflammatory, sensational, and irresponsible. If it is, it and its freedom will go down in the universal catastrophe. On the other hand, the press can do its duty by the new world that is struggling to be born. It can help create a world community by giving men everywhere knowledge of the world and of one another, by promoting comprehension and appreciation of the goals of a free society that shall embrace all men.[15]
>
> The surest antidote for ignorance and deceit is the widest possible exchange of objectively realistic information—*true* information, not merely *more,* information; *true* information, not merely, as those who would have us simply write the First Amendment into international law seem to suggest, the *unhindered flow* of information! There is evidence that a mere quantitative increase in the flow of

[15]*A Free and Responsible Press,* Chicago: The University of Chicago Press, 1947, p. 4.

words and images across national borders may replace ignorance with prejudice and distortion rather than with understanding. . . .

The problem, then, is twofold. It is that of bringing the physical facilities for transmitting words and images across national boundaries within the reach of all; of lowering and, wherever possible, removing the barriers erected at those boundaries. It is also that of achieving a degree of quality, accuracy, and total balance calculated to give a fair picture of the life of each country to all the world. And we cannot assume that achievement of the first automatically will produce the second.[16]

The proposals of Whitton and Larson, as well as those of many others since the 1960s concerning the standards of international communication (cf., Chapter 9), fall logically within this framework of social responsibility. They have contributed much in terms of legal and political instruments, while the fundamental paradigm has changed little since the days of the Hutchins Commission. But even that Commission was building on earlier tradition; it did not invent the doctrine of social responsibility, but rather gave shape to something that had existed for a long time. For example, Nelson A. Crawford (Department of Industrial Journalism, Kansas State Agricultural College) articulated, as early as 1924, the ethics of journalism "to further the best interests of society."[17] In setting professional standards, Crawford did not hesitate to propose legal measures, including "compulsory veracity,"[18] and the role foreseen for professional organizations contained most of the elements in the "modern" protection controversy:

An organization embracing practically all working journalists could fix high standards of entrance into the profession, could establish a sound and workable code of ethics, and could insure adequate salaries in the profession. In all of these, of course, it would need public sympathy and cooperation. From the work of such an organization might develop eventually laws for examining and licensing journalists. There would also be a tendency toward the elimination of one of the most unfortunate features of the press, editorial control of newspapers by men who have had no professional training or experience in journalism and who consider journalism merely a business.[19]

That the very roots of the libertarian doctrine are far from clear and uniform is indicated by the position of Thomas Jefferson. Commenting to Madison on the draft Bill of Rights in 1789, Jefferson stated:

[16]L. White & R. D. Leigh, *Peoples Speaking to Peoples*, Chicago: The University of Chicago Press, 1946, pp. 2-3.

[17]N. A. Crawford, *The Ethics of Journalism*, New York: Greenwood Press, 1924, p. vii.

[18]Ibid., p. 134.

[19]Ibid., p. 154.

> The people shall not be deprived of their right to speak, to write,
> or otherwise to publish anything but false facts affecting injuriously
> the life, liberty, property or reputation of others, or affecting the
> peace of the confederacy with foreign nations.[20]

The concept of freedom of expression and of the press advocated here contains, not only limitations concerning the rights of others, but also extends the conditions of freedom to the sphere of international relations. In principle, this is the pattern of the contemporary concept of freedom of information as defined by the 1966 International Covenant on Civil and Political Rights. We may say that Jefferson, in 1789, held a more modern concept of freedom of information than those who in 1948 formulated Article 19 of the Universal Declaration of Human Rights, with its unconditional notion of freedom—as well as those who met in Talloires in 1981. Thus Jefferson deserves to be quoted in connection with the Mass Media Declaration of Unesco—not only to emphasize that "we must tolerate error so long as truth exists to combat it" (cf., the U.S. intervention after the adoption of the Declaration, Appendix 20), but also to emphasize that the media should not counter peaceful international relations.

The tradition of liberalism—in journalism as well as in other fields—is full of contradictions, and the libertarian doctrine of journalism has undergone politico-philosophical changes throughout its history.[21] Today it is once more in crisis, largely but not completely caused by the new order movement. In the present situation it has little power—other than as a political force, as demonstrated by the Talloires offensive—to work against the movement for change.

A significant indication of the changes taking place in professional philosophies are changes of view such as those of John Merrill (School of Journalism, Louisiana State University) who, in 1980, became an advocate of "basic universal ethical standards," whereas, in the 1970s, he had been known as an uncomprising supporter of an ultra-libertarian doctrine of journalistic autonomy which left no room for social responsibility, or even for such ideas as the "people's right to know."[22] It is true that, with this change in view, Merrill does not seem to suscribe to a full set of universal values (as the Mexico Declaration does), but it is important that for him "the ethical journalist is one who desires and tries to promote international harmony and cooperation." For this journalist, he proposes "a kind of existentialist demeanor in ethics":

---

[20]S. K. Padover (Ed.), *Thomas Jefferson on Democracy*, New York: D. Appleton-Century Company, 1953, p. 48.

[21]See e.g. G. Boyce, J. Curran & P. Wingate (Eds.), *Newspaper History: From the 17th Century to the Present Day*, London/Beverly Hills: Constable/Sage, 1978.

[22]Op. cit. in note 6 above.

> Treat the people of other nations not as objects to be moved, used, changed, or managed, but as subjects with basic personal dignity: subjects with their own minds and values, capable of decision and action. But also recognize them as members of humanity who can sense a universality in morality—not just ethno-centric whims.[23]

It is interesting to note that this variation of an old Kantian theme, suggested by a liberal-turned-into-existentialist,[24] is strikingly similar to the proposals made in developing and socialist countries for a code of ethics in support of cultural sovereignty and peaceful coexistence (cf., Chapter 9). Merrill provides another proof of the fact that *despite all the controversy around the new order, there is common ground for universal ethics in journalism.*

On the other hand, Merrill makes the point that there is "an ethics vacuum in American journalism," and that its "basic philosophical foundation stones are not very solid and the mortar holding them together is rapidly turning to powder."[25] In this view, "there is really no consistent and logical philosophy of journalism or press-government symbiosis in the United States—all the high phrases of Thomas Jefferson and others notwithstanding."[26] Merrill hits "the old libertarian mystique about truth winning out in a free encounter with falsehood," about press and government as adversaries, and about the press as an instrument of the people's right to know: "I always thought that the government officials were the representatives of the people, and the press people were profit-making collaborators with the capitalistic system and not representatives of anybody, really, except publishers and other media owners and managers who contend in the the World of Big Business."[27]

Such observations, it should be noted, do not emanate from an anti-Western source hostile to liberalism as a whole. Rather, Merrill is known as a true libertarian—a protestant advocating reformation of the established journalistic "church"—whose criticism exposes the intellectual poverty and ideological bias of the dominant Western doctrine of journalism. In this respect Merrill stands quite close to the advocates of the new order who, it should be recalled, also challenge a number of libertarian myths (above all, "free flow"), but who at the same time count on values which constitute an essential part of the libertarian tradition (just-

---

[23]J. C. Merrill, "Ethics: A Worldview for the Journalist," in A. van der Meiden (Ed.), *Ethics and Mass Communication,* Utrecht, The Netherlands: State University of Utrecht, 1980, p. 118.

[24]See J. C. Merrill, *Existential Journalism,* New York: Hastings House, 1977.

[25]J. C. Merrill, "The Press, the Government, and the Ethics Vacuum," *Communication* (New York: Gordon and Breach), Vol. 6, No. 2, 1981 (issue on "Ethics in Communication," ed. R. L. Johannesen), p. 185.

[26]Ibid., pp. 181-182.

[27]Ibid., pp. 182, 184.

ice, equality, balance, etc.). For example, the present author views Western journalists as "captives of a particular ideology of liberalism which is not the true brand of original idea but rather the particular brand of late capitalism."[28] This reasoning leads to *a call for reformation*—not a revolution but "a reorientation from Madison Avenue to Constitution Avenue":

> Indeed, we should go back to examine the whole theory of democracy and government as well as the theory of the press. I have tried to do some of this homework, and I have been surprised to learn what really was the origin of a libertarian theory of government and public opinion. It is not at all that sort of "free flow" dogmatism heard to day from circles defending free media enterprise. Rather, it was something very deeply and genuinely democratic and popular. In fact, the first notion of government during the rise of bourgeois revolution was based on the philosophy that all power emanates from the people, i.e., the sovereignty of the people. The doctrine of different branches of government—legislative, executive, judiciary, and the press—was developed only at a later stage. This happened after the bourgeoisie had won control of government and when the democracy proclaimed by the bourgeois revolution began to turn against the interests of the new class of rulers and owners because of the working class, which had been brought into the picture by the industrial revolution. The working class threatened to become the majority in the electorate and began to think in different terms and departed from the interests of the owners of capital.[29]

Considering the original pillars of liberalism—the sovereignty of the people and a rational pursuit of truth—it is the advocates of the new order, rather than the opposing "voices of freedom," who deserve to be taken as true descendants of the revolution which once abolished feudalism and its authoritarian rule over the press. In a historical perspective it is fundamentally misleading to regard any limitation of "free flow" as contrary to libertarian principles. Likewise it is an ideological position rather than an adequate reflection of the original aspirations of liberalism to understand that government—any government in all conditions—is anathema to press freedom. In this respect, Marks, Stevenson, and other advocates of Talloires are not more faithful to the philosophy of liberalism than is, for example, the Director of Information Services of the Tanzanian government:

---

[28]K. Nordenstreng, "The Media: Backstopping Official Policy?" in S. M. Murphy, L. E. Atwood & S. J. Bullion (Eds.), *International Perspectives on News*, Carbondale: Southern Illinois University Press, 1982, p. 156.

[29]Ibid., p. 153.

> Where a government is committed to the development of all the
> people . . . media take-over by the government is an act of liberation
> and emancipation. On the other hand, where the party and govern-
> ment are oppressive, media take-over is to enhance the oppression of
> the people. . . .
>
> Therefore what is crucial and important is whether the media
> are used for liberation or oppression of the popular masses in devel-
> oping countries, and not the out-dated and theoretical freedom of
> the media, which the Western countries preach to their neo-colonies
> in order to enhance their oppression over the masses.[30]

Thus, instead of speaking in abstract terms of "government" and
"press," we should ask *what kind of government* and *what kind of media*—the
questions fundamental to any scientific "theories of the press."[31] Such an
analytical approach leads, among other things, to expose the symbiotic
relationship whereby the "free press" quite often serves as an instrument
of official policy. In Great Britain, for example, an awareness is growing
among academic and professional circles:

> . . . that the media generally accepts the legitimacy of the judge-
> ments of the ruling class and, by implication, the accuracy of White-
> hall press releases. The very uniformity of approach to foreign re-
> porting is an indication of the success of the Foreign and
> Commonwealth Office in ordering our responses to world events.
> Iran, Zimbabwe, Afghanistan, France—the FCO has a view which is
> consistently reproduced by Fleet Street, the BBC and ITN. In that
> sense the UK has, literally, a state controlled press.[32]

It is in this overall context that we should view the profession of
journalism, its rights and responsibilities:

> This approach is based on the sociological fact that journalism
> like all other forms of social communication is fulfilling specific tasks
> in society, tasks conditioned by the role and function of the mass me-
> dia in terms of fundamental social structures. Thus no matter
> whether the prevailing journalistic ideology perceives and accepts it
> or not, journalism is always serving certain fundamental social inter-

[30]N. Ng'wanakilala, *Mass Communication and Development of Socialism in Tanzania*, Dar es Salaam: Tanzania Publishing House, 1981, p. 50.

[31]The "classic" *Four Theories of the Press* by F. S. Siebert, T. Peterson, and W. Schramm (Urbana: University of Illinois Press, 1956) largely misses these questions. However, the sociological point of departure of their study, as stated in the Preface, seems quite adequate: "The thesis of this volume is that the press always takes on the form and coloration of the social and political structures within which it operates. Especially, it reflects the system of social control whereby the relations of individual and institutions are adjusted. We believe that an understanding of these aspects of society is basic to any systematic understanding of the press."

[32]N. Cross, "Not the News" (a review of *The Geopolitics of Information* by Anthony Smith and *More Bad News* by the Glasgow University Media Group), *New Statesman*, 6 June 1980.

ests, including class interests. The profession of journalism is bound to be tied with fundamental social forces and it cannot step outside the social structures—except for generating an illusory conception of absolute independence.

In a serious scientific approach the social tasks performed by journalism lead to a natural articulation of the social objectives and to corresponding social responsibilities. In this context journalistic responsibility is of a fundamental nature and it conceptually precedes journalistic rights since the latter are seen as preconditions for the profession in order to fulfill its tasks. . . .

The unity of rights and responsibilities is well reflected in what is known as professional ethics in journalism. It is not difficult to see that the roots of journalistic ethics are not in more or less mechanistically defined professional practices but in the overall objectives which journalism is supposed to serve. Thus journalistic ethics is not composed of a set of distinct rules in terms of rights and responsibilities but in a fundamental sense it is a reflection of certain social objectives advocated by the profession.[33]

We do not suggest that this is an easy approach, leading to simple answers. Obviously, the appproach carries with it an anti-establishment bias, and the new order movement can be seen as "a vehicle for liberating Western journalism from its ideological captivity."[34] After all, as stated by Anthony Smith, an honest, liberal British observer, "it is the super-structure of Western beliefs and values in the field of information which is principally in crisis."[35] However, as Smith points out, "it is unlikely that the press of the West will become less 'free' as a result of the fracas. Rather the reverse. It may force a revaluation of the condition of freedom alongside a reconsideration of press ethics."[36]

But it is not only Western journalism that is placed under challenge. There are a number of hard problems to be settled among the ranks of the new order movement itself, through self-criticism in the developing and socialist countries. The hardest of these may be the fact that, despite all the anti-Western rhetoric, media professionalism in many (most?) developing countries amounts to a neo-colonial transfer of Western ideology.[37] A parallel dilemma is what Smith calls "double standards of freedom" (using India as an example): "Where they are communicating within the élite they perceive the direct relevance of the Western media

[33] K. Nordenstreng, "Status, Rights and Responsibilities of Journalists," in *Protection of Journalists*, Paris: Unesco series New Communication Order, No. 4, 1980, pp. 119-120.

[34] Op. cit. in note 28.

[35] A. Smith, *The Geopolitics of Information; How Western Culture Dominates the World*, London and Boston: Faber & Faber, 1980, p. 172.

[36] Ibid., p. 16.

[37] See, e.g., P. Golding, "Media Professionalism in the Third World: The Transfer of an Ideology," in op. cit. in note 21, pp. 291-308.

models through which they have been trained . . . but in looking at the rest of their own society they perceive an overriding compulsion towards other standards. Creative staff switch from the autonomous intellectual to that of bureaucrat as they switch audience."[38]

Indeed, bureaucracy, corruption, and even tyranny remain a bitter reality in many countries, posing serious problems for those striving towards a new information order. These problems cannot be denied or undermined by any honest observer—just as one has to reject the Western fabrication of the new order movement as a more or less subtle Orwellian design. Altaf Gauhar, Editor of *South* and *Third World Quarterly* puts it bluntly: "The whole information debate and the theme of decolonization of the mind become irrelevant if the creative energies of the people are suppressed."[39]

Consequently, the crisis and the dilemmas which are shaking the profession of journalism provide a welcome *challenge for all*. In fact, the "ethics vacuum" deplored by Merrill can be seen as a promising symptom of change in Western philosophy of journalism, toward the kind of new professional ethics discussed above. There is good reason to speak about an "ethics boom" in contemporary journalism, stimulated by the internal contradictions of liberalism, on the one hand, and by the global forces of the new order, on the other. Merrill himself, as an academic scholar, has been in the avantgarde of what appears in the early 1980s as a *renaissance of a philosophical and ethical approach to communication.*[40]

Internationally, it is the Mass Media Declaration that has played perhaps the major role in bringing social ethics on the agenda of the "great media debate." The Declaration had little to offer in terms of the concrete substance of this ethics; neither did the MacBride Report make a great contribution to the elaboration of professional philosophies. This, however, is not important. What is crucial in an historical perspective is the fact that normative considerations have survived as a matter of highest priority and that a bridge was built between the profession and the international community. It is the task of the profession—and journalism education and research along with it—to meet the challenge.

---

[38]Op. cit. in note 35, p. 162.

[39]From an interview which Gauhar did with Amadou-Mahtar M'Bow on "North-South Dialogue," *Third World Quarterly*, April 1982 (Vol. 4, No. 2), p. 219. See also feature of this interview in *South*, November 1981, pp. 10-11.

[40]See, e.g., the volumes referred to in notes 23 and 25. Particularly active in contributing to the theme of "Media Ethics" have been the Christian organizations and institutions; see, e.g., *WACC Journal*, No. 4, 1979, and *Communication Research Trends* (A Quarterly Information Service from Centre for the Study of Communication and Culture, London), Spring 1980. For a historical review of the U. S. Tradition, see C. G. Christians, "Fifty Years of Scholarship in Media Ethics," *Journal of Communication*, Autumn 1977, pp. 19-29. Another indication of the new attention to ethics in North American schools of communication: C. G. Christians and C. L. Covert, *Teaching Ethics in Journalism Education*, New York: The Hastings Center, 1980.

Appendices

Appendices

APPENDIX 1

Declaration on Fundamental Principles concerning the Contribution of the Mass Media to Strengthening Peace and International Understanding, to the Promotion of Human Rights and to Countering Racialism, Apartheid and Incitement to War

Final text adopted at the 20th session of the General Conference, Paris, October–November 1978
(Unesco document 20C/20 Rev., 21 November 1978)

PREAMBLE

The General Conference,

Recalling that by virtue of its Constitution the purpose of Unesco is to 'contribute to peace and security by promoting collaboration among the nations through education, science and culture in order to further universal respect for justice, for the rule of law and for the human rights and fundamental freedoms' (Art. I, 1), and that to realize this purpose the Organization will strive 'to promote the free flow of ideas by word and image' (Art. I, 2),

Further recalling that under the Constitution the Member States of Unesco, 'believing in full and equal opportunities for education for all, in the unrestricted pursuit of objective truth, and in the free exchange of ideas and knowledge, are agreed and determined to develop and to increase the means of communication between their peoples and to employ these means for the purposes of mutual understanding and a truer and more perfect knowledge of each other's lives' (sixth preambular paragraph),

Recalling the purposes and principles of the United Nations, as specified in its Charter,

Recalling the Universal Declaration of Human Rights, adopted by the General Assembly of the United Nations in 1948 and particularly Article 19 thereof, which provides that 'everyone has the right to freedom of opinion and expression; this right includes freedom to hold opinions without interference and to seek, receive and impart information and ideas through any media and regardless of frontiers'; and the International Covenant on Civil and Political Rights, adopted by the General Assembly of the United Nations in 1966, Article 19 of which proclaims the same principles and Article 20 of which condemns incitement to war, the advocacy of national, racial or religious hatred and any form of discrimination, hostility or violence.

Recalling Article 4 of the International Convention on the Elimination of all Forms of Racial Discrimination, adopted by the General Assembly of the United Nations in 1965, and the International Convention on the Suppression and Punishment of the Crime of Apartheid, adopted by the General Assembly of the United Nations in 1973, whereby the States acceding to these Conventions undertook to adopt immediate and positive measures designed to eradicate all incitement to, or acts of, racial discrimination, and agreed to prevent any encouragement of the crime of apartheid and similar segregationist policies or their manifestations,

Recalling the Declaration on the Promotion among Youth of the Ideals of Peace, Mutual Respect and Understanding between Peoples, adopted by the General Assembly of the United Nations in 1965,

Recalling the declarations and resolutions adopted by the various organs of the United Nations concerning the establishment of a new international economic order and the role Unesco is called upon to play in this respect,

Recalling the Declaration of the Principles of International Cultural Co-operation, adopted by the General Conference of Unesco in 1966,

Recalling Resolution 59(I) of the General Assembly of the United Nations, adopted in 1946 and declaring:

'Freedom of information is a fundamental human right and is the touchstone of all the freedoms to which the United Nations is consecrated;

. . . .

Freedom of information requires as an indispensable element the willingness and capacity to employ its privileges without abuse. It requires as a basic discipline the moral obligation to seek the facts without prejudice and to spread knowledge without malicious intent;

. . . .

Recalling Resolution 110(II) of the General Assembly of the United Nations, adopted in 1947, condemning all forms of propaganda which are designed or likely to provoke or encourage any threat to the peace, breach of the peace, or act of aggression,

Recalling resolution 127(II), also adopted by the General Assembly in 1947, which invites Member States to take measures, within the limits of constitutional procedures, to combat the diffusion of false or distorted reports likely to injure friendly relations between States, as well as the other resolutions of the General Assembly concerning the mass media and their contribution to strengthening peace, trust and friendly relations among States,

Recalling resolution 9.12 adopted by the General Conference of Unesco in 1968, reiterating Unesco's objective to help to eradicate colonialism and racialism, and resolution 12.1 adopted by the General Conference in 1976, which proclaims that colonialism, neo-colonialism and racialism in all its forms and manifestations are incompatible with the fundamental aims of Unesco,

Recalling resolution 4.301 adopted in 1970 by the General Conference of Unesco on the contribution of the information media to furthering international understanding and co-operation in the interests of peace and human welfare, and to countering propaganda on behalf of war, racialism, apartheid and hatred among nations, and *aware* of the fundamental contribution that mass media can make to the realizations of these objectives,

Recalling the Declaration on Race and Racial Prejudice adopted by the General Conference of Unesco at its twentieth session,

Conscious of the complexity of the problems of information in modern society, of the diversity of solutions which have been offered to them, as evidenced in particular by the consideration given to them within Unesco, and of the legitimate desire of all parties concerned that their aspirations, points of view and cultural identity be taken into due consideration,

Conscious of the aspirations of the developing countries for the establishment of a new, more just and more effective world information and communication order,

Proclaims on this twenty-eighth day of November 1978 this Declaration on Fundamental Principles concerning the Contribution of the Mass Media to strengthening Peace and International Understanding, to the Promotion of Human Rights and to Countering Racialism, Apartheid and Incitement to War.

Article I

The strengthening of peace and international understanding, the promotion of human rights and the countering of racialism, apartheid and incitement to war demand a free flow and a wider and better balanced dissemination of information. To this end, the mass media have a leading contribution to make. This contribution will be the more effective to the extent that the information reflects the different aspects of the subject dealt with.

Article II

1. The exercise of freedom of opinion, expression and information, recognized as an integral part of human rights and fundamental freedoms, is a vital factor in the strengthening of peace and international understanding.

2. Access by the public to information should be guaranteed by the diversity of the sources and means of information available to it, thus enabling each individual to check the accuracy of facts and to appraise events objectively. To this end, journalists must have freedom to report and the fullest possible facilities of access to information. Similarly, it is important that the mass media be responsive to concerns of peoples and individuals, thus promoting the participation of the public in the elaboration of information.

3. With a view to the strengthening of peace and international understanding, to promoting human rights and to countering racialism, apartheid and incitement to war, the mass media throughout the world, by reason of their role, contribute to promoting human rights, in particular by giving expression to oppressed peoples who struggle against colonialism, neo-colonialism, foreign occupation and all forms of racial discrimination and oppression and who are unable to make their voices heard within their own territories.

4. If the mass media are to be in a position to promote the principles of this Declaration in their activities, it is essential that journalists and other agents of the mass media, in their own country or abroad, be assured of protection guaranteeing them the best conditions for the exercise of their profession.

Article III

1. The mass media have an important contribution to make to the strengthening of peace and international understanding and in countering racialism, apartheid and incitement to war.

2. In countering aggressive war, racialism, apartheid and other violations of human rights which are *inter alia* spawned by prejudice and ignorance, the mass media, by disseminating information on the aims, aspirations, cultures and needs of all peoples, contribute to eliminate ignorance and misunderstanding between peoples, to make nationals of a country sensitive to the needs and desires of others, to ensure the respect of the rights and dignity of all nations, all peoples and all individuals without distinction of race, sex, language, religion or nationality and to draw attention to the great evils which afflict humanity, such as poverty, malnutrition and diseases, thereby promoting the formulation by States of the policies best able to promote the reduction of international tension and the peaceful and equitable settlement of international disputes.

Article IV

The mass media have an essential part to play in the education of young people in a spirit of peace, justice, freedom, mutual respect and understanding, in order to promote human rights, equality of rights as between all human beings and all nations, and economic and social progress. Equally, they have an important role to play in making known the views and aspirations of the younger generation.

Article V

In order to respect freedom of opinion, expression and information and in order that information may reflect all points of view, it is important that the points of view presented by those who consider that the information published or disseminated about them has seriously prejudiced their effort to strengthen peace and international understanding, to promote human rights or to counter racialism, apartheid and incitement to war be disseminated.

Article VI

For the establishment of a new equilibrium and greater reciprocity in the flow of information, which will be conducive to the institution of a just and lasting peace and to the economic and political independence of the developing countries, it is necessary to correct the inequalities in the flow of information to and from developing countries, and between those countries. To this end, it is essential that their mass media should have conditions and resources enabling them to gain strength and expand, and to co-operate both among themselves and with the mass media in developed countries.

Article VII

By disseminating more widely all of the information concerning the universally accepted objectives and principles which are the bases of the resolutions adopted by the different organs of the United Nations, the mass media contribute effectively to the strengthening of peace and international understanding, to the promotion of human rights, and to the establishment of a more just and equitable international economic order.

Article VIII

Professional organizations, and people who participate in the professional training of journalists and other agents of the mass media and who assist them in performing their functions in a responsible manner should attach special importance to the principles of this Declaration when drawing up and ensuring application of their codes of ethics.

Article IX

In the spirit of this Declaration, it is for the international community to contribute to the creation of the conditions for a free flow and wider and more balanced dissemination of information, and of the conditions for the protection, in the exercise of their functions, of journalists and other agents of the mass media. Unesco is well placed to make a valuable contribution in this respect.

Article X

1. With due respect for constitutional provisions designed to guarantee freedom of information and for the applicable international instruments and agreements, it is indispensable to create and maintain throughout the world the conditions which make it possible for the organizations and persons professionally involved in the dissemination of information to achieve the objectives of this Declaration.

2. It is important that a free flow and wider and better balanced dissemination of information be encouraged.

3. To this end, it is necessary that States facilitate the procurement by the mass media in the developing countries of adequate conditions and resources enabling them to gain strength and expand, and that they support co-operation by the latter both among themselves and with the mass media in developed countries.

4. Similarly, on a basis of equality of rights, mutual advantage and respect for the diversity of the cultures which go to make up the common heritage of mankind, it is essential that bilateral and multilateral exchanges of information among all States, and in particular between those which have different economic and social systems, be encouraged and developed.

Article XI

For this declaration to be fully effective it is necessary, with due respect for the legislative and administrative provisions and the other obligations of Member States, to guarantee the existence of favourable conditions for the operation of the mass media, in conformity with the provisions of the Universal Declaration of Human Rights and with the corresponding principles proclaimed in the International Covenant on Civil and Political Rights adopted by the General Assembly of the United Nations in 1966.

APPENDIX 2

Statement of Amadou-Mahtar M'Bow, Director-General of Unesco

From speech at the close of the 20th session of the General Conference, Paris, 29 November 1978
(Unesco publication of the Declaration, Paris 1979)

It seems to me that the spirit of co-operation and the will to reach a consensus, which have gradually increased over the past two years, have emerged strengthened from the twentieth session of the General Conference and have even acquired greater significance. Any misgivings about the difficulties to which one item of the agenda seemed liable to give rise have now been dispelled. They have been effaced by one of the most striking events of this session: the prolonged, standing ovation of an assembly which adopted by acclamation the Declaration on Fundamental Principles concerning the Contribution of the Mass Media to Strengthening Peace and International Understanding, to the Promotion of Human Rights and to Countering Racialism, Apartheid and Incitement to War.

By virtue of the prominence given to it in the debates of the General Conference and in consultations between delegates, the strong emotions and great zeal shown during its final drafting and the interest which it aroused among the mass media, this Declaration was undoubtedly a central feature of the twentieth session of the General Conference.

I must confess that the ovation with which the Declaration was adopted will most certainly remain in my mind as one of the most intensely moving moments which I have experienced as Director-General of Unesco.

For eight years, delegates to the General Conference, experts and specialists from all regions and all countries have held meetings, consultations and discussions, have accumulated projects, counter-projects and amendments, without the international community being able to agree upon a text.

That agreement was reached during the present session of the General Conference. This happy outcome is even more remarkable in that the probabilities of failure seemed great. It is indeed an example of the triumph of patient efforts to achieve conciliation which have never flagged even when faced with the formidable obstacles. It symbolizes the pre-eminence which should be given to the worldwide approach which, while still taking account of specific circumstances, gives pride of place to the common interests of mankind.

The delegates who spoke in the comission in regard to their subscribing to a consensus that some have not hesitated to describe as historic were so kind as to refer to myself and my colleagues—as other delegates have done this evening—in terms that affected me deeply. I should like to thank them here, as I should like to thank all those who, by their acumen, enabled the General Conference to surmount the obstacles, to understand and thus to ensure the triumph of reason.

I should like now, on the basis of so promising a past, to outline the prospects that the adoption of this Declaration adumbrates for our Organization. In my speech at the closure or the general policy debate I stressed how essential it was to define taking into account the variety and development of communication systems, a new set of moral principles which all creators and distributors of information would be able to endorse. Now that this Declaration has been adopted, this has to a certain extent been achieved. It is a fact of major importance that, for the first time, the international community has at its disposal a body of principles and ideals such as can provide guidance for the action and practice of all those whose hearts are set on justice and peace.

As for the Organization itself, the Declaration further underpins its efforts to create the necessary conditions for a freer, broader and more balanced flow of information and to protect journalists and news reporters in the exercise of their functions.

Encouraged by the extreme attention you have given during this General Conference to the problems of communication and by the leading importance you have assigned to the Declaration, the Organization will pursue its efforts in the field of studies and practical measures.

The fact that the Declaration was adopted unanimously seems to betoken an intensification of the desire for co-operation, but also of the ethical role of the Organization.

But we must not overlook other important decisions that were taken, which also have an ethical bearing, thus confirming the Organization's mission in this sphere.

Mention should be made first of all of the adoption, again by acclamation, of the Declaration on Race and Racial Prejudice.

For the first time in the United Nations system, and even in the history of the protracted efforts of mankind to banish racialism and racial prejudice, the international community will have at its disposal a text that, without being legally binding, represents a moral and ethical undertaking encompassing *all* aspects of a problem that, sad to say, is still very much with us. Thus the biological, sociological, cultural, economic and political aspects of the problem are covered in this instrument which we would like to see give rise to as many hope and practical measures as the Universal Declaration of Human Rights, the thirtieth anniversary of which we celebrated yesterday evening.

Nothing better illustrates the vitality of our Organization; nothing bears greater witness to the desire of its Member States to achieve harmony than the adoption of such a Declaration, which now belongs to all mankind.

APPENDIX 3

Report of Existing Legislation and Measures Taken by Member States to Encourage the Use of Mass Media Against Propaganda on Behalf of War, Racialism and Hatred Among Nations

Presented by the Director-General to the 17th session of the General Conference, Paris, October–November 1972
(Unesco document 17C/77, 15 September 1972)

SUMMARY

This report provides a synthesis of the information supplied to the Director-General by Member States in response to Resolution 4.301 adopted by the General Conference at its sixteenth session.

1. INTRODUCTION

The General Conference adopted at its sixteenth session resolution 4.301 of which operative paragraphs 2 and 3 read as follows:

" 2. *Invites* all States to take the necessary steps, including legislative measures, to encourage the use of information media against propaganda on behalf of war, racialism and hatred among nations, and to provide Unesco with information on the subject;

3. *Invites* the Director-General to submit to the General Conference, at its seventeenth session, a report based on the replies of Member States on existing legislation and measures taken by them to encourage the use of information media against propaganda on behalf of war, racialism and hatred among nations."

On 16 November 1971, the Director-General sent to Member States a circular letter (CL/2173) to which the text of resolution 4.301 was attached. Member States were asked to provide the information requested by 31 March 1972. At the beginning of May 1972, a reminder letter was sent to those Member States which had not answered.

Replies from the following 43 Member States were received by 23 June 1972:

Algeria, Argentina, Austria, Barbados, Belgium, Brazil, Bulgaria, Byelorussian SSR, Canada, Central African Republic, Cyprus, Czechoslovakia, Dahomey, El Salvador, Federal Republic of Germany, Greece, Guatemala, Hungary, India, Ivory Coast, Khmer Republic, Kuwait, Laos, Mali, Malta, Netherlands, Nicaragua, Norway, Panama, Philippines, Poland, Romania, Singapore, Somalia, Spain, Sweden, Switzerland, Syrian Arab Republic, Tanzania, Turkey, Ukrainian SSR, United Kingdom of Great Britain and Northern Ireland, and Yugoslavia.

Of these, Guatemala, Panama and Tanzania acknowledged receipt of circular letter CL/2173, but did not provide information.

The information received has been classified as follows in the present report:

(a) Positive measures, including existing or proposed legislation, which are in accordance with the terms of resolution 4.301; the pertinent passages of the replies are quoted (Section 2).

(b) Information regarding policies governing the mass communication media which are relevant to the subject of the inquiry (Section 3).

(c) Constitutional provisions and legislative measures eliminating or prohibiting propaganda in favour of war and/or racial discrimination (Section 4).

(d) The list of Member States which have reported an absence of legislation specifically applicable to the mass communication media in this field; three comments in this respect are quoted (Section 5).

The replies of some Member States appear under more than one of these sub-headings where different measures may be applicable to war propaganda, hate propaganda and racial discrimination.

2. POSITIVE MEASURES

Paragraph 2 of resolution 4.301 specifies that Unesco should be provided with information on existing legislation and measures taken to encourage the use of information media against propaganda on behalf of war, racialism and hatred among nations. Such positive measures or legislation (or proposals for future legislation) are reported by:

Argentina: "The regulations relating to the broadcasting law in force in the country, approved by Decree No. 5490/65, require that transmissions shall respect national and foreign symbols, authorities and institutions and that respect be shown towards persons, events and ideas which may be the subject of comment or criticism, as well as towards the opinions of others."

Argentina also gave information on proposed legislative measures:

". . . A draft national telecommunications bill is nearing completion. One of the articles of the bill lays down that the broadcasting service shall have a 'formative and informative' character and requires that broadcasting shall respect ethical principles, the dignity of the human person and of the family. As regards the formative, or educational function of the broadcasting service, the article provides that it shall strengthen democratic convictions and international friendship and cooperation. This will enable the responsible authority to require broadcasting stations to take positive action to this end."

Austria: "Federal Law No. 195 of 1966 dealing with the Statutes of the Austrian Radio and Television Broadcasting Company (ORF), requires it to provide the general public with objective information concerning all news and educational, scientific and cultural questions, having due regard to the legal provisions (including the laws prohibiting propaganda on behalf of war, racialism and hatred among nations)."

Dahomey: "Necessary steps to encourage the use of information media against propaganda on behalf of war, racialism and hatred among nations will be taken without delay."

Federal Republic of Germany: In the Federal Republic prizes are awarded for good films which respect the principles of international understanding and the peaceful coexistence of States, races and ideologies.

Furthermore, the Federal Centre for Civic Education (a public law institution) fosters written publications and television shows conducive to international understanding and the peaceful co-existence of States, races and ideologies.

Romania: "Decree No. 307 of 15 September 1971 relating to the organization of the State Committee for Romanian Radio and Television Broadcasting states, *inter alia*, that this Committee shall endeavour to make an active contribution to the implementation of a State policy on behalf of friendship and brotherhood among all workers, irrespective of their nationality."

Sweden: The agreement between the State and the Swedish Broadcasting Corporation refers to the International Convention concerning the use of broadcasting in the cause of peace, signed at Geneva on 23 September 1936, and registered with the Secretariat of the League of Nations.

Syrian Arab Republic: "The Ministry of Information in the Syrian Arab Republic has just drafted a new bill, the aim of which is to encourage the use of the information media against propaganda on behalf of war and hatred among nations."

Ukrainian SSR: "Measures exist for encouraging the most active members of peace movements, including writers, journalists and other workers in the mass media. A large number of them have been awarded certificates of honour by the Praesidium of the Supreme Soviet of the Ukrainian SSR or by the Ukrainian Peace Committee or have been awarded T. G. Shevchenko State prizes."

United Kingdom: "Measures taken in the United Kingdom have concentrated on the positive aspects of encouraging racial harmony. For this purpose, the Race Relations Act (1965) has established the Community Relations Commission which has the duty, *inter alia*, of encouraging and assisting others to secure the establishment of harmonious community relations and to co-ordinate on a national basis the measures adopted for that purpose. To the extent that Government funds are expended on the promotion of racial harmony on a national basis, the Government can be said to be encouraging the use of the information media for the promotion of racial harmony, but no obligation is placed on the information media as such to publicize material produced by the Community Relations Commission."

In addition, Belgium, El Salvador, the Federal Republic of Germany, Romania, Spain, Turkey and the Ukrainian SSR reported that their educational systems were in accordance with the principles recalled in resolution 4.301, and/or described the positive measures adopted in this respect; while Canada, Hungary and India described activities undertaken by their information media during 1971, in support of the International Year for Action to combat Racism and Racial Discrimination, proclaimed by the General Assembly of the United

Nations. Finally, Algeria, Hungary, the Khmer Republic, Somalia, the Ukrainian SSR and Yugoslavia reiterated in their replies their adherence to the principles of the Charter of the United Nations.

3. POLICIES GOVERNING THE MASS COMMUNICATION MEDIA

A certain number of Member States referred to the guiding principles which govern the operation of their mass communication media in relation to the subject of the inquiry:

Algeria: ". . . Algeria is naturally engaged in the propaganda campaign against war, racialism and hatred among nations. . . The Algerian press works towards this end, in accordance with the national policies adopted in regard to information. Because of these policy decisions, it is natural that the Algerian press should unremittingly denounce war, racialism and hatred among nations and support national liberation movements."

Byelorussian Soviet Socialist Republic: ". . . The country's newspapers, magazines, television, radio and news agencies do much to throw effective light on those current problems of domestic and international affairs which are of real concern to the Soviet people.

One of the basic topics of the Republic's mass media is the fight against the aggressive policy of imperialism and the struggle for the peace and security of nations and for social progress."

Czechoslovakia: ". . . In its programme declarations as well as in practical policy in the field of mass communication media, particularly the press, radio and television, the Government of the Czechoslovak Socialist Republic has pursued and intends further to pursue, by all means and instruments, such policy that would make it impossible for those media to be misused for the propaganda of war, racism or hate among nations and would, on the contrary, ensure that they contribute to the strengthening of peaceful international co-operation and security, especially of the European continent."

Federal Republic of Germany: ". . . None of the mass media, press, cinema, radio and television, which in the Federal Republic of Germany are all independent of the Government will tolerate any warmongering or racial discrimination. The statutes and programme directives of radio and television corporations exclude any such propaganda from radio and television programmes. The principles adopted by the voluntary self-censorship board of the film industry do not have the quality of law, but are regulations agreed upon by film producers, film distributors, cinema owners and cinetechnical workshops who are united in the top organization of the film industry. Under Section 2 of these principles, which provide the foundation for voluntary self-censorship on a self-governing basis, it is borne in mind that no film should be allowed to disturb the peaceful relations between nations or to further imperialistic and militaristic tendencies or gloss over the horrors of war. One of the board's principles says, *inter alia*: 'No films likely to further racist tendencies shall be produced, distributed or publicly shown'.

. . . According to the directives of the Illustrated Magazines Board of Self-Censorship, it is not allowed to disparage or debase other races or nations or to glorify war or play down the effects of military conflicts. Any such offences are—irrespective of their liability to prosecution—dealt with by the German Press Council, a voluntary association of journalists and publishers."

Hungary: ". . . On the basis of a policy governed by the principle of peaceful coexistence, Hungary is striving to establish harmonious relations with all States, irrespective of their social systems, and the communication media unreservedly support the Government in this line of action by all means at their disposal."

India: ". . .Although the problem of racial discrimination does not exist in India, yet there are groups of people with different religions, social and economic background and the information media were extensively used to promote harmony and national integration among people."

Ivory Coast: ". . . As most of the information media are concentrated at the Government and Party level, they are of course mobilized in support of these peaceful objectives and are thus instrumental in opposing all propaganda on behalf of war, racialism or hatred."

Kuwait: ". . . The information media in our State serve, actualize and correspond to the general policy of the State which is based on furthering cooperation with the family of nations, on the basis of mutual interests and respect and non-interference in the domestic affairs of other countries."

Singapore: "Singapore is a multiracial, multilingual and multireligious society.

. . . Radio and television in Singapore is part of the Ministry of Culture which is acutely conscious of the social milieu in which it operates and of the impact radio and television transmissions may have not only on Singapore citizens, but also on other nations who listen to them or view them.

. . . In its radio and television programming, the broadcasting station is, in fact, guided by the policy that all programme material should be free of propaganda on behalf of racialism, hatred among nations and war."

Yugoslavia: ". . . Yugoslavia seeks, *inter alia*, to encourage freedom of mutual information, particularly if this serves to strengthen peace, mutual respect and friendship among peoples and States.

Freedom of the press and other information media is guaranteed by the relevant law. It is, however, laid down that this freedom is limited, i.e. it must not be directed towards the suppression of international co-operation or used to endanger peace or contribute to the stirring up of national, racial or religious hatred, or to support propaganda or incitement to aggression."

4. CONSTITUTIONAL PROVISIONS

Neutrality and respect for the national sovereignty of other countries, as part of their national constitutional provisions *prohibiting* progaganda on behalf of war, racialism, and hatred among nations were reported by the following Member States:

Austria: All racial discrimination is prohibited by Austrian constitutional legislation and, in particular, by Article 6 of the Austrian State Treaty of 1955 and Article 14 of the European Convention for the Protection of Human Rights and Fundamental Freedoms, which was ratified by Austria in 1958.

Under its constitutional law of 26 October 1955 Austria has, of its own free will, proclaimed its permanent neutrality and undertaken to defend it by all means in its power. This law necessarily entails the prohibition of all propaganda on behalf of war and hatred among nations.

Brazil: The Brazilian Constitution, at the end of paragraph 8, in Article 153 of Chapter IV (Individual Rights and Guarantees), states that: "propaganda for war, subversion of order, religious, racial or class prejudice and publications or acts that are contrary to ethics and normal procedure shall not be tolerated."

Furthermore, paragraphs 1, 5 and 6 of the same Article prohibit all discrimination in regard to sex, race, occupation, religious beliefs and political convictions.

Bulgaria: The Constitution of the People's Republic of Bulgaria (adopted by referendum in 1971) provides, in Article 35, paragraph IV, that all propaganda on behalf of hatred or the humiliation of men and women on account of their race, country or religion, is prohibited and punishable.

Byelorussian SSR: Legislation in force in the Byelorussian SSR forbids the use of the information media for propaganda on behalf of war, racialism and hatred among nations. The Constitution of the Byelorussian SSR (Article 98) provides as follows: "Equality of rights of all citizens of the Byelorussian SSR, irrespective of their nationality or race, in all spheres of economic, government, cultural, social and political activity is an indefeasible law.

Any direct or indirect restriction of the rights of, or, conversely, the establishment of any direct or indirect privileges for, citizens on account of their race or nationality, as well as any advocacy of racial or national exclusiveness or hatred and contempt, are punishable by law".

Federal Republic of Germany: The Constitution of the Federal Republic of Germany ensures that any propaganda on behalf of war, racialism and hatred among nations is disapproved of under the constitutional and statutory law of the country and made liable to prosecution.

Article 1 of the Basic Law for the Federal Republic of Germany contains an affirmation of "inviolable and inalienable human rights as the basis of every community, of peace and justice in the world", and provides: "The dignity of man shall be inviolable. To respect and protect it shall be the duty of all State authority." This provision is followed by a catalogue of basic rights which according to Article 1, paragraph 3, of the Basic Law "shall bind the legislature, the executive and the judiciary as directly enforceable law" in the Federal Republic, and in which Article 3 provides that no one may be prejudiced or favoured because of his sex, his parentage, his race, his language, his homeland and his origin, while Article 9 prohibits associations whose purposes or activities are directed against the concept of international understanding, Article 25 of the Basic Law says:

"The general rules of public international law shall be an integral part of federal law. They shall take procedence over the laws and shall directly create rights and duties for the inhabitants of the federal territory." And finally, Article 26 declares "acts tending to and undertaken with the intent to disturb peaceful relations between nations, especially to prepare for aggressive war" to be unconstitutional.

Greece: "Greece, which is the embodiment of a peaceful nation, does not 'deal' separately with racial discrimination or propaganda on behalf of war, but precludes them by virtue of the existing constitution."

India: "The Constitution of India prohibits all forms of racial discimination and the problem of racial hatred as such does not exist in India. The information media were, however, used to create an awareness among the Indian people about the problem of racialism in the world."

Laos: "The Government of National Union of Laos, outcome of the 1962 Geneva Agreements signed by 14 nations, can automatically be assumed, by its internationally recognized neutral status, to be opposed to any form of propaganda on behalf of war and hatred among nations."

Poland: The Constitution of the Polish People's Republic lays down for the Polish people and the national authorities, as the ultimate objective of their efforts, the strengthening of freindship and international co-operation and the struggle against aggression.

More specifically, Article 69, paragraphs 1 and 2, of the Constitution prohibit the spreading of hatred, contumely and discrimination, each person enjoying all rights irrespective of race, religion and national origin.

Romania: "The Constitution of the Socialist Republic of Romania provides in Article 14, paragraph 1, that 'the Socialist Republic of Romania is active in international organizations with a view to ensuring peace and understanding among the peoples', while paragraph 2 of this Articles states: 'The foreign relations of the Socialist Republic of Romania are based on the principles of observance of sovereignty and national independence, equal rights and mutual advantages, non-interference in internal affairs'."

Article 17 of the Constitution states that "the citizens of the Socialist Republic of Romania, irrespective of nationality, race, sex or religion have equal rights in all fields of economic, political, juridical, social and cultural life" and that "the State guarantees the equal rights of citizens. No restriction of these rights and no difference in their exercise on the grounds of nationality, sex or religion are permitted. Any expression aiming to establish such restrictions, nationalist-chauvinist propaganda, the fanning of racial or national hatred are punished by law".

Yugoslavia: Section VII of the Constitution states that international relations of the country are based on respect for national sovereignty and equality, non-interference in the internal affairs of other countries and the peaceful settlement of international disputes.

The following countries have indicated legislative acts, penal or criminal codes which enable actions to be taken against those responsible for propaganda advocating war, racialism and hatred among nations: Brazil, Bulgaria, Byelorussian SSR, Canada, Cyprus, Czechoslovakia, Federal Republic of Germany, Greece, Nicaragua, Poland, Romania, Switzerland, Ukrainian SSR and the United Kingdom.

5. ABSENCE OF LEGISLATION

The following Member States informed Unesco that they have no legislative measures *encouraging* the use of information media against propaganda on behalf of war, racialism and hatred among nations: Barbados, Belgium, Central African Republic, Cyprus, Greece, Hungary, Kuwait, Laos, Mali, Malta, Netherlands, Norway, Philippines, Somalia, Sweden, Switzerland and the United Kingdom.

Norway, Sweden and the United Kingdom provided the following comments in this context:

Norway: "In Norway there is no legislation which encourages the use of information media against propaganda on behalf of war, racialism and hatred among nations.

The Norwegian Government is in fact reluctant to influence national information media in any direction or to put obstacles in the way of their entire freedom. Freedom of information is in itself considered as a defence of peace, democracy and human rights. In the Norwegian view and according to Norwegian experience, the guarantee against misuse is the control exercised by the free public opinion of a democratic society. The written and unwritten ethical rules practised by Norwegian press and broadcasting and which in the Norwegian society constitute a defence against propaganda on behalf of war, racialism and hatred among nations, are created and constantly supervised by an alert and active public opinion."

Sweden: "If the object in view is to persuade the information media to actively oppose propaganda on behalf of war, etc., neither legislative nor other measures are taken or planned in Sweden, such measures being contrary to the principle of the freedom of information media.

The resolution could, however, also imply measures to be taken to prevent the information media from pursuing propaganda on behalf of war, racialism and hatred among nations. The question of legislation against war propaganda was recently discussed in Sweden in connexion with the ratification of the United Nations Covenant on Civil and Political Rights. Article 20(1) of the said Covenant prescribes that all propaganda on behalf of war shall be prohibited in law. Having analysed the matter, the Swedish Government found it necessary, however, to refrain from implementing the Article by legislation, mainly due to the difficulties in delimiting the punishable acts and also taking into consideration the negative consequences of such a legislation on the free public debate."

United Kingdom: "In a democracy such as the United Kingdom certain rights are regarded as essential for the maintenance of a democratic society and foremost among those rights is freedom of expression. Since in any society the ideas of governments about what may be desirable will frequently not coincide with the wishes of the people and may at times run directly counter to the best interests of the people, it is inappropriate to enact legislation designed to direct the information media in specific directions. Any legislation of the kind envisaged in operative paragraph 2 of resolution 4.301 would in fact conflict directly with Article 19 of the Universal Declaration of Human Rights which states 'everyone has the right to freedom of opinion and expression; this right includes freedom to hold opinions without interference and to seek, receive and impart information and ideas through any media. . .'. Her Majesty's Government have not therefore enacted, nor do they propose to enact, any legislation which would have the effect of *encouraging* the use of information media towards specific ends.

. . . While Her Majesty's Government have taken measures to make incitement to racial hatred an offence and to promote racial harmony, they have not taken steps to outlaw propaganda on behalf of war. In the current world situation, in which agreement has not been reached on complete disarmament under effective international guarantees, it is necessary for States to maintain armed forces for their collective or individual self-defence. Since measures necessary for the recruitment, training and deployment of armed forces may be said to constitute propaganda on behalf of war, the proposals in resolution 4.301 cannot be applied. . . . Similarly, measures to encourage the use of information media against propaganda on behalf of war would, at the present time, restrict the ability of the information media to discuss the possible use of armed force in Southern Africa. They might even, for example, prohibit dissemination through the information media of certain resolutions adopted by the General Assembly and other bodies in the United Nations family or organizations regarding the provision of assistance to liberation movements which seek to attain their aims by the use of violence."

ADDENDUM

This Addendum provides a short summary, in alphabetical order, of replies received from Member States between 23 June (date of preparation of the main report) and 31 August 1972. The number of replies received thus now totals fifty-seven.

Burundi (letter received on 31 July 1972) The Charter of the UPRONA (Party of Unity and National Progress) condemns all racial or religious discrimination. The Burundi press, as well as the President of the Republic condemn hatred among nations. Adherence to the principles of the Charter of the United Nations is reiterated.

Federal Republic of Cameroon (letter received on 28 June 1972) Cameroon has banished from its mass media all "hate propaganda". Through personal action of the Head of State, the lives of the population of the Federal Republic are oriented towards international understanding. The press and broadcasting follow the same principles.

Denmark (letter received on 9 August 1972) The authorities have not considered it necessary to take special steps to encourage the use of information media against propaganda on behalf of war, racialism and hatred among nations, since this is already the prevailing attitude among mass media.

A special Act of Parliament in 1971 forbids discrimination in commerce and public affairs and the Penal Code enables action to be taken against those responsible for racist propaganda.

Honduras (letter received on 17 August 1972) The Constitution and existing legislation of the Republic confirm the Universal Delcaration of Human Rights, Resolution 110 of the United Nations General Assembly of 3 November 1947, condemning all forms of propaganda encouraging threats to the peace, and the International Convention on the Elimination of all Forms of Racial Discrimination.

The Government, while respecting the freedom of the press and the right of expression, consistently stimulates the use of information media to combat propaganda in favor of war, racialism and hatred among peoples.

Iraq (letter received on 31 August 1972) The Iraqi Republic's Interim Constitution bans all sectarian or racialistic propaganda. The Iraqi Ministry of Information works towards the realization of the ideals expressed in international laws and the United Nations Charter, and uses all available information media for this purpose.

Republic of Korea (letter received on 27 June 1972) The mass media of the Republic are regulated in accordance with pertinent legislative acts, such as Broadcasting Acts, Motion Picture Acts, Performing Acts, and others. There is no necessity for any additional legislation to encourage the use of information media for propaganda against war, racialism and hatred among nations.

Luxembourg (letter received on 17 July 1972) There is no specific legislation applicable to the mass communication media.

New Zealand (letter received on 18 August 1972) Section 25 of the Race Relation Act, which came into force on 1 April 1972, makes it a punishable offence to publish or broadcast words exciting racial hostility. The Broadcasting Act of 1968 ensures that news given in programmes is presented with due accuracy and impartiality and with due regard to the public interest.

Nigeria (letter received on 29 August 1972) There is no legislation that has any direct bearing on the matter.

The activities undertaken by the "National Committee for the dissemination of information on the evils and dangerous implications for international relations of the existence of Apartheid" are described.

Thailand (letter received on 29 June 1972) No legislative measures have been taken by the Government to encourage the use of information media against propaganda on behalf of war, racialism and hatred among nations.

Union of Soviet Socialist Republics (letter received on 25 July 1972) Legislation in force in the USSR forbids the use of information media for propaganda on behalf of war, racialism and hatred among nations. The Constitution of the USSR (Article 123) provides for equality of rights for all citizens, regardless of their nationality and race, and the Law for Defence of Peace (1951) excludes the possibility of such propaganda.

The newspapers, reviews, television and radio broadcasting are never used for such propaganda, but carry out systematic action in promotion of universal peace and European security.

United States of America (letter received on 21 August 1972) A report on Public Information and Promotion of International Understanding has been prepared in implementation of resolution 4.301. It contains the outline of policies guiding information media. The policy is not to regulate or censor for any purpose, but to encourage positive expression through methods of persuasion, education and example. The right of freedom of speech ensures for all citizens maximum liberty and minimizes the influence of government over the expression of ideas by a citizen or group.

In the field of legislation, the Radio Act of 1927 and the Communications Act of 1934 are described.

Under general principles or standards for boradcasting, the Fairness Doctrine ensures the discussion of controversial issues, and every licensee should afford reasonable opportunity for the presentation of contrasting viewpoints. The presentation of controversial issues should present basic facts as completely and impartially as possible.

Programmes which touch upon religion, race or national background enjoy the protection of the constitutional guarantees of free speech.

Venezuela (letter received on 8 August 1972) The national Constitution stresses co-operation with all nations and forbids war propaganda. The Regulation on Radio Communications prohibits broadcasts dealing with political, social or religious matters in a way which might offend part of the listening audience.

A draft of a new Radio Broadcasting Act which will be issued shortly adds to the above that broadcasting stations should strengthen democratic convictions, national unity and international friendship and co-operation.

People's Democratic Republic of Yemen (letter received on 23 August 1972) Activities of the mass media are in accordance with the general principles of the Charter of the People's Party and the Constitution of the People's Democratic Republic, which states adherence to the principles of the United Nations Charter and the Universal Declaration of Human Rights and declares that the State will not employ its armed forces against the liberty of any other people.

APPENDIX 4
Draft Declaration of Fundamental Principles Governing the Use of the Mass Media
First draft prepared by Hilding Eek
(Unesco document COM-74/CONF.616/3, 23 January 1974)

Recalling that by its Constitution Unesco is charged with contributing to peace and security by promoting collaboration among the nations through education, science and culture, and that, to realize this purpose, the Organization will collaborate in the work of advancing the mutual knowledge and understanding of peoples through all means of mass communication and to that end recommend such international agreements as may be necessary to promote the free flow of ideas by word and image,

Recalling the objective enunciated in the Charter of the United Nations to develop friendly relations among nations based on respect for the principle of equal rights, the non-interference in matters within the domestic jurisdiction of any State, the achievement of international co-operation and the respect for human rights and fundamental freedoms,

Considering that freedom of expression, information and opinions are fundamental human rights and that the free interchange of accurate, objective and comprehensive information and of opinions, both in the national and in the international spheres, is essential to the cause of peace and the achievement of political, social, cultural and economic progress,

Considering further that the exercise of the right to freedom of information carries with it duties and responsibilities, so as to ensure the free flow of true and honest information to all peoples,

Endorsing the resolution of the second General Assembly of the United Nations opposing propaganda which is designed or likely to provoke or encourage any threat to the peace, breach of the peace, or act of aggression, and on the spreading of false and distorted reports,

Confirming resolution 11 adopted by the General Conference on 15 November 1968 reiterating Unesco's objective to help to eradicate colonialism and racialism.

Taking account of article 4 of the International Convention on the Elimination of All Forms of Racial Discrimination, whereby State Parties to the Convention condemn all propaganda and all organizations which are based on ideas or theories of superiority of one race or group of persons of one colour or ethnic origin, or which attempt to justify or promote racial hatred and discrimination in any form, (and undertake to adopt immediate and positive measures designed to eradicate all incitement to, or acts of, such discrimination),

Bearing in mind the Declaration of the Principles of International Cultural Co-operation adopted by the General Conference of Unesco, at its fourteenth session, and the Declaration of Guiding Principles on the Use of Satellite Broadcasting for the Free Flow of Information, the Spread of Education and Greater Cultural Exchange, adopted by the General Conference of Unesco, at its seventeenth session,

Noting the rapid development of the mass media which constitute one of the key elements in modern scientific and technological progress, and play an ever-increasing role in the intellectual life of society and the shaping of public opinion,

Proclaims this Declaration concerning the fundamental principles governing the use of the mass media with a view to strengthening peace and international understanding and combating war propaganda, racialism and apartheid.

Article I

Each State is internationally responsible for the conduct of its governmental information services and their activities beyond its own borders as well as for its national legislation relating to the performance of mass media within its own territory. International responsibility is based on the principles and rules of international law, in particular the Charter of the United Nations.

Article II

All possible measures should be taken to ensure that governmental media, which are disseminating information and opinion abroad, do so in a manner which is compatible with the mutual respect of the rights and dignity of States and peoples.

Article III

The right to seek and transmit information should be assured in order to enable the public to ascertain facts and appraise events, bearing always in mind the principle of respect for the sovereignty, equality and territorial integrity of States and of non-intervention in the internal affairs of foreign countries. For that purpose, the widest possible facilities should be afforded for access to foreign news sources. A concomitant to this is the right of States and information media in each country to diffuse reports of national events to others beyond their borders, since the two-way flow of news is fundamental to the strengthening of peace and international understanding.

Article IV

By comprehending and reporting the aims, aspirations, cultures and needs of foreign nations, mass media can help promote the broadening of international co-operation, the reduction of tensions and the settlement of differences and disputes between States by peaceful means.

Article V

The dissemination of false reports harmful to friendly relations among nations or inciting to war or to national, racial or religious hatred should be avoided. To this end legislative action might be envisaged which, nevertheless, should protect freedom of information as defined in international instruments and agreements.

Article VI

Ideas upon hatred of races are contrary to international engagements and the United Nations Declarations of Human Rights; mass media should, therefore, adopt appropriate measures to avoid incitement to racial discrimination, acts of violence or encouragement of such acts against any race or group of persons of another colour or ethnic origin.

Article VII

The right of correction should be accorded foreign governments in cases where they contend that erroneous news reports, diffused by media, injure their relations with other States or their national prestige or dignity.

Article VIII

States can encourage the development of responsible national mass media to ensure that they serve the needs of the people and promote international understanding. They can protect, by international agreements and national legislation, the economic and social independence of information personnel.

Article IX

Professional organizations in the field of the mass media contribute to awareness of journalistic responsibility. Efforts should be made to encourage high ethical standards and to improve the professional training of media personnel both on the national and international level to encourage the use of the media to spread ideas of peace, friendship and mutual understanding among nations.

Article X

The principles of this Declaration shall be applied with due regard for human rights and fundamental freedoms.

APPENDIX 5

Draft Declaration of Fundamental Principles concerning the Strengthening of Peace and International Understanding by the Mass Media
Prepared by meeting of experts, Paris, 11–15 March 1974
(Unesco document COM–74/CONF.616/4 Annex I, 15 March 1974)

The General Conference of the United Nations Educational, Scientific and Cultural Organization,

Recalling that by its Constitution, Unesco is charged with contributing to peace and security by promoting collaboration among the nations through education, science and culture, and that, to realize this purpose, the Organization will collaborate in the work of advancing the mutual knowledge and understanding of peoples through all means of mass communication and to that end recommend such international agreements as may be necessary to promote the free flow of ideas by word and image,

Recalling the purposes and principles of the United Nations, as specified in the Charter,

Recalling Articles 19 and 26 of the Universal Declaration of Human Rights adopted by the General Assembly of the United Nations in 1948, and Articles 19 and 20 of the International Covenant on Civil and Political Rights, adopted by the General Assembly in 1966,

Recalling resolution 110(II) of the General Assembly of the United Nations condemning all forms of propaganda which are designed or likely to provoke or encourage any threat to the peace, breach of the peace, or act of aggression and resolution 3068 (XXVIII) of the General Assembly adopting the International Convention on the Suppression and Punishment of the Crime of Apartheid,

Confirming resolution 9.12 adopted by the General Conference on 15 November 1968 reiterating Unesco's objective to help to eradicate colonialism and racialism,

Taking account of Article 4 of the International Convention on the Elimination of All Forms of Racial Discrimination, whereby States Parties to the Convention condemn all propaganda and all organizations which are based on ideas or theories of superiority of one race or group of persons of one colour or ethnic origin, or which attempt to justify or promote racial hatred and discrimination in any form, and undertake to adopt immediate and positive measures designed to eradicate all incitement to, or acts of, such discrimination,

Bearing in mind the Declaration of the Principles of International Cultural Co-operation adopted by the General Conference of Unesco, at its fourteenth session, and the Declaration of Guiding Principles on the Use of Satellite Broadcasting for the Free Flow of Information the Spread of Education and Greater Cultural Exchange, adopted by the General Conference of Unesco, at its seventeenth session,

Considering that freedom of expression, information and opinion are fundamental human rights and that the free interchange of information and opinions, both in the national and in the international spheres, is essential to the cause of peace and achievement of political, social and economic progress,

Considering further that the exercise of the right to freedom of information entails special responsibilities and duties for persons who disseminate information to strive in good faith to ensure the fullness and accuracy of the facts reported and to respect the rights and the dignity of nations, and of groups and individuals without distinction as to race, sex, nationality or creed,

Considering further that full account must be taken of the needs and rights of audiences and the right of all countries and peoples to protect and preserve their cultures as part of the common heritage of mankind,

Noting the rapid development of the mass media which constitute one of the key elements in modern scientific and technological progress, and play an ever-increasing role in the intellectual level of society and the shaping of public opinion,

Proclaims this Declaration of Fundamental Principles on the role of the Mass Media in Strengthening Peace and International Understanding and in Combating War Propaganda, Racism and Apartheid.

Article I

1. Mass Media in disseminating information and opinion should take all possible measures to do so in a manner which is compatible with the mutual respect of the rights and dignity of States and peoples, and in accord with the principles set out in the Universal Declaration of Human Rights.

2. Subject to adequate protection for the principles of freedom of speech and freedom of the press, States should exert their influence to encourage mass media within their jurisdiction to act in conformity with the principles and standards of the Charter of the United Nations for the purpose of strengthening peace and international understanding and combating war propaganda, racism and apartheid.

Article II

1. The right to seek, receive and transmit information should be assured in order to enable the public to ascertain facts and appraise events, bearing in mind the principles contained in the Charter of the United Nations and the Universal Declaration of Human Rights.

2. For the above purpose, the widest possible facilities should be afforded for access by the public to news sources.

3. States and information media in each country should have the right to diffuse reports of national events to others beyond their borders, since the two-way flow of news is fundamental to the strengthening of peace and international understanding.

Article III

Mass Media should help promote the broadening of international co-operation, understanding and mutual respect, the reduction of tensions and the settlement of differences and disputes between States by peaceful means, by ensuring that the aims, aspirations, needs and culture of their country are reported to other nations, and conversely that those of other nations are made known to their own people.

Article IV

Mass media should promote greater knowledge on the part of the peoples of the world of the evils attendant upon war, violence, apartheid and other forms of national, racial or religious hatred. Conversely, the dissemination of reports conducive to these evils is condemned.

Article V

Racism, racial discrimination and apartheid are contrary to international engagements and the Universal Declaration of Human Rights; mass media should, therefore, adopt appropriate measures to avoid incitement to racial discrimination, acts of violence or encouragement of such acts against any group of persons because of their race, colour or ethnic origin. For this purpose, legislative action might be envisaged which, nevertheless, should protect freedom of information as defined in international instruments and agreements.

Article VI

Mass media have a special responsibility to youth. Consonant with Article 26 of the Universal Declaration of Human Rights they should seek to promote the full development of the human personality and strengthen respect for human rights and fundamental freedoms. They should also promote among youth a spirit of understanding, tolerance and friendship among all nations, racial or religious groups.

Article VII

A right of correction should be accorded in cases where States contend that erroneous news reports have seriously injured their relations with other States or their national prestige or dignity.

Article VIII

States should encourage the development of responsible national mass media and the fostering of their technological independence to ensure that they reflect the needs, aims and aspirations of the people and promote international understanding. They should foster by international agreements and national legislation, the economic and social independence of information personnel, and help ensure that the media have the technical facilities required to carry out their role. Mass media in all countries should also be encouraged to provide access for the voices of those unable to express temselves within their own territory because of the repression brought about by apartheid.

Article IX

Efforts should be made to create and strengthen professional organizations in the field of the mass media to ensure that such media contribute to the achievement of the objectives of this declaration. In particular, these organizations can, on a national, regional, and international level, encourage high ethical standards and improve the professional training of media personnel.

Article X

The responsibility of a State in the international sphere for the activities of mass media under its jurisdiction is governed by customary international law and relevant international agreements.

Article XI

The principles of this declaration shall be applied with due regard for human rights and fundamental freedoms.

APPENDIX 6

Draft Declaration of Fundamental Principles on the Role of the Mass Media in Strengthening Peace and International Understanding and in Combating War Propaganda, Racism and Apartheid

Presented by the Director-General to the 18th session of the General Conference, Paris, October–November 1974
(Unesco document 18C/35, 12 July 1974)

The General Conference of the United Nations Educational, Scientific and Cultural Organization meeting in Paris at its eighteenth session in 1974,

Recalling that by its Constitution Unesco is charged with contributing to peace and security by promoting collaboration among the nations through education, science and culture, and that, to realize this purpose, the Organization will collaborate in the work of advancing the mutual knowledge and understanding of peoples through all means of mass communication and to that end recommend such international agreements as may be necessary to promote the free flow of ideas by word and image,

Recalling the purposes and principles of the United Nations, as specified in the Charter,

Recalling Articles 19 and 26 of the Universal Declaration of Human Rights, adopted by the General Assembly of the United Nations in 1948, and Articles 19 and 20 of the International Covenant on Civil and Political Rights, adopted by the General Assembly in 1966,

Recalling resolution 110(II) of the General Assembly of the United Nations condemining all forms of propaganda which are designed or likely to provoke or encourage any threat to the peace, breach of the peace, or act of aggression and resolution 3068 (XXVIII) of the General Assembly adopting the International Convention on the Suppression and Punishment of the Crime of Apartheid,

Recalling resolution 9.12 adopted by the General Conference at its fifteenth session reiterating Unesco's objective to help to eradicate colonialism and racialism,

Taking account of Article 4 of the International Convention on the Elimination of All Forms of Racial Discrimination, whereby States Parties to the Convention condemn all propaganda and all organizations which are based on ideas or theories of superiority of one race or group of persons of one colour or ethnic origin, or which attempt to justify or promote racial hatred and discrimination in any form, and undertake to adopt immediate and positive measures designed to eradicate all incitements to, or acts of, such discrimination,

Bearing in mind the Declaration of the Principles of International Cultural Co-operation, adopted by the General Conference of Unesco at its fourteenth session, and the Declaration of Guiding Principles on the Use of Satellite Broadcasting for the Free Flow of Information, the Spread of Education and Greater Cultural Exchange, adopted by the General Conference of Unesco at its seventeenth session,

Considering that freedom of expression, information and opinion are fundamental human rights and that the free interchange of information and opinions, both in the national and in the international spheres, is essential to the cause of peace and achievement of political, social, cultural and economic progress,

Considering also that the exercise of the right to freedom of information entails special responsibilities and duties for persons who disseminate information to strive in good faith to ensure the fullness and accuracy of the facts reported and to respect the rights and the dignity of nations, and of groups and individuals without distinction as to race, sex, nationality or creed,

Considering further that full account must be taken of the needs and rights of audiences and the right of all countries and peoples to protect and preserve their cultures as part of the common heritage of mankind,

Noting the rapid development of the mass media which constitute one of the key elements in modern scientific and technological progress, and play an ever-increasing role in the intellectual life of society and the shaping of public opinion,

Proclaims on this day of 1974 this Declaration of Fundamental Principles on the Role of the Mass Media in Strengthening Peace and International Understanding and in Combating War Propaganda, Racism and Apartheid.

Article I

1. The mass media in disseminating information and opinion have a responsibility to do so in a manner which is compatible with the mutual respect of the rights and dignity of States and peoples, and in accord with the principles set out in the Universal Declaration of Human Rights.

2. Subject to adequate protection for the principles of freedom of speech and freedom of the press, it is incumbent upon States to encourage mass media to act in conformity with the principles and standards of the Charter of the United Nations and the Universal Declaration of Human Rights so as to strengthen peace and international understanding and combat war propaganda, racism and apartheid.

Article II

In order to enable the public to ascertain facts and appraise events, the right to seek, receive and transmit information should be assured, and the widest possible facilities afforded, bearing in mind the principles contained in the Charter of the United Nations and the Universal Declaration of Human Rights.

Article III

Since the two-way flow of news is fundamental to the strengthening of peace and international understanding, States and information media in each country have the right to diffuse reports of national events to others beyond their borders. By ensuring that the aims, aspirations, needs and culture of each country are reported to others, mass media promote the broadening of international cooperation, understanding and mutual respect, the reduction of tensions and the settlement of differences and disputes between States by peaceful means.

Article IV

1. It is a responsibility of the mass media to promote greater knowledge on the part of the peoples of the world of the evils attendant upon war, violence, apartheid and other forms of national, racial or religious hatred.
2. The dissemination of reports conducive to these evils is condemned.

Article V

1. Any incitement to racial discrimination, acts of violence or encouragement of such acts against any group of persons because of their race, colour or ethnic origin is to be shunned. For this purpose, legislative action might be envisaged without however infringing upon freedom of information as defined in international instruments and agreements.
2. The voices of those unable to be heard within their own territory because of the repression brought about apartheid should be given expression through the mass media.

Article VI

The mass media have a special responsibility to youth and for the dissemination of their views. It is consonant with Article 26 of the Universal Declaration of Human Rights for the media to promote, particularly among youth, the full development of the human personality, the strengthening of respect for human rights and fundamental freedoms and a spirit of understanding, tolerance and friendship among all nations, racial or religious groups.

Article VII

A right of correction applies in cases where States contend that erroneous news reports have seriously injured their relations with other States or their national prestige or dignity.

Article VIII

In order to encourage the development of responsible national mass media and foster their technological independence, it is incumbent upon States to promote, by international agreements and national legislation, the economic and social independence of information personnel, and help ensure that the media have the technical facilities required to carry out their role.

Article IX

The creation and strengthening of professional organizations in the field of the mass media can help to ensure that the media contribute effectively to the achievement of the objectives of this Declaration. In particular, these organizations can, on a national, regional and international level, encourage high ethical standards and improve the professional training of media personnel.

Article X

The responsibility of States in the international sphere for the activities of mass media under their jurisdiction is governed by customary international law and relevant international agreements.

Article XI

The principles of this Declaration shall be applied with due regard for human rights and fundamental freedoms.

APPENDIX 7
Letter from the Delegation of the United States
To the Chairman of Intergovernmental Meeting of Experts held at
Unesco, Paris, 15–22 December 1975
(dated 18 December 1975)

Dear Mr. Chairman:

The United States Delegation strongly objects to both the substance of the amendment approved yesterday and to the procedures which this meeting adopted. I explained yesterday the views of the United States regarding the Yugoslavian amendment. Yesterday's vote in no way modifies those views, and in no way changes the fact that Zionism is not racism. That vote simply imposes a debilitating handicap on those delegations which were trying to maintain the credibility and intellectual integrity of these deliberations.

The extremely sensitive substance of this meeting, namely international consideration of the rôle of the mass media, and the wide differences among States regarding the proper definition of that rôle, demanded the consensus approval procedures which we adopted at the beginning of these discussions.

There are fundamental differences which separate those who believe in an independent mass media essentially free from government control, from those who believe that the mass media should be a tool of the State. Those differences cannot be eliminated or reconciled here. The most we could have done would have been to discover and clarify whether there were any common points where our different views converge. It now appears that we have lost even that opportunity.

The rejection yesterday of the consensus procedure was not just a procedural move. It was an assertion that international standards can be promulgated by blatant disregard of the views of a substantial number of States. Such a procedure is unrealistic and destructive of the very international co-operation and understanding to which the Organization is dedicated. It is futile in light of the fact that nothing this meeting says or does will change the basic views of States regarding the respective rôles of the government and of the mass media.

The United States Delegation, therefore, believes that there is no constructive purpose to be served by our continued participation in these discussions of the draft declaration. We reserve the right to present additional views on any final drafts produced by this meeting. I would also request that you read this letter to the plenary session of the Experts Meeting and that it be incorporated in full to any final report of that meeting.

Please accept, Sir, the assurance of my highest consideration.

Respectfully submitted

(sgnd.)   Ronald F. Stowe
Chairman,
United States Delegation

APPENDIX 8

Draft Declaration on Fundamental Principles Governing the Use of the Mass Media in Strengthening Peace and International Understanding and in Combating War Propaganda, Racism and Apartheid

Prepared by Intergovernmental Meeting of Experts held at Unesco, Paris, 15–22 December 1975, and presented by the Director-General to the 19th session of the General Conference, Nairobi, October–November 1976
(Unesco document 19C/91, 1 July 1976)

The General Conference of the United Nations Educational, Scientific and Cultural Organization meeting in Nairobi at its nineteenth session in 1976,

1. *Recalling* that by its Constitution Unesco is charged with contributing to peace and security by promoting collaboration among the nations through education, science and culture, and that, to realize this purpose, the Organization will collaborate in the work of advancing the mutual knowledge and understanding of peoples through all means of mass communication and to that end recommend such international agreements as may be necessary to promote the freer and wider exchange of information by word and image on both a multilateral and bilateral basis, the sovereignty of States being fully respected,

2. *Recalling* the purposes and principles of the United Nations, as specified in the Charter, as well as other documents of the Organization,

3. *Recalling* the Universal Declaration of Human Rights, adopted by the General Assembly of the United Nations in 1948, and the International Covenant on Civil and Political Rights, adopted by the General Assembly of the United Nations in 1966,

4. *Recalling* resolution 110(II) of the General Assembly of the United Nations Adoptedin 1947 condemning all forms of propaganda which are designed or likely to provoke or encourage any threat to the peace, breach of the peace, or act of aggression and the International Convention on the Suppression and Punishment of the Crime of Apartheid adopted by the General Assembly of the United Nations in 1973,

5. *Recalling* all the resolutions of the United Nations General Assembly, and more particularly resolutions 1904, 3151 and 3379 on the elimination of all forms of racialisms and racial discrimination,

6. *Recalling* the Declaration and the Programme of Action on the Establishment of a New International Economic Order (resolutions 3201 (S-VI) and 3202 (S-VI) of the General Assembly), and the Charter of Economic Rights and Duties of States (resolution 3281 (XXIX) of the General Assembly), as regards a new international economic order, through which it is hoped to create a new system of international economic relations based upon equity, sovereign equality, common interest and co-operation among all States, which may help to strengthen decisively peace and international understanding,

7. *Recalling* resolution 9.12 adopted by the General Conference at its fifteenth

session reiterating Unesco's objective to help to eradicate colonialsm and racialism,

8. *Taking account* of Article 4 of the International Convention on the Elimination of all Forms of Racial Discrimination, whereby States Parties to the Convention condemn all propaganda and all organizations which are based on ideas or theories of superiority of one race or group of persons of one colour or ethnic origin, or which attempt to justify or promote racial hatred and discrimination in any form and undertake to adopt immediate and positive measures designed to eradicate all incitement to, or acts of, such discrimination,

9. *Bearing in mind* the Declaration of the Principles of International Cultural Co-operation, adopted by the General Conference of Unesco at its fourteenth session,

10. *Noting with satisfaction* the positive results achieved in the area of international détente and, in particular, the contribution to this process made by the Conference on Security and Co-operation in Europe,

11. *Considering* that the mass media are of great importance and have the responsibility for creating an atmosphere of international confidence and mutual respect in conformity with the obligation to abstain from incitement to aggressive wars or any use or threat of force incompatible with the aims of the United Nations, in the interests of strengthening peace and mutual understanding between peoples and contributing to international détente and the spiritual enrichment of the human personality without distinction as to race, sex, language or religion,

12. *Considering* that freedom of expression, information and opinion are fundamental human rights and that the free interchange of information and opinions, both in the national and in the international spheres, is essential to the cause of peace and achievement of political, social, cultural and economic progress,

13. *Considering* the importance of utilizing all means of mass communication for the support and reinforcement of international peace and for the development of friendly relations between States, irrespective of their political, economic or social systems, in the spirit of respect for human rights and fundamental freedoms,

14. *Considering* also that the international exchange of information places special responsibilities on persons and institutions who disseminate information as well as on their professional organizations to strive to ensure the fullness and accuracy of the facts reported and to respect the rights and the dignity of nations and of groups and individuals without distinction as to race, sex, nationality or creed and entails also the responsibility and duty of the States to use all their constitutional means to encourage the mass media to act in accordance with the aims and principles of the United Nations Charter so as to maintain and strengthen peace and international understanding and to combat war propaganda, racialism and apartheid,

15. *Considering* further the right of countries and peoples to protect and preserve their cultures as well as the differences existing among those cultures as part of the common heritage of mankind,

16. *Noting* the rapid development of the mass media which constitute one of the key elements in modern scientific and technological progress, and play an ever-increasing role in the intellectual life of society and the shaping of public opinion,

17. *Proclaims* on this day of 1976 this Declaration on Fundamental Principles

Governing the Use of the Mass Media in Strengthening Peace and International Understanding and in Combating War Propaganda, Racism and Apartheid.

Article I

1. States should encourage the freer and wider dissemination of information through the mass media for the purposes of strengthening peace and international understanding and combating war propaganda, racism and apartheid, acting in a spirit of mutual respect for the rights and dignity of other States, peoples and individuals, in full accord with the principles of international law, including the United Nations Charter.

2. Subject to adequate Constitutional protection of the principle of freedom of information, the mass media, both public and private, and those responsible for dissemination of information, in particular the international news agencies, should act in conformity with the principles of the Charter of the United Nations and of this Declaration.

Article II

1. States shall encourage and develop both multilateral and bilateral exchanges concerning the use of the mass media in the fields of culture, science and education on the basis of equality of rights, mutual advantage and non-interference in each other's affairs, in accordance with the Constitution and other laws and regulations in force in each country, and taking into account their customs and traditions, with the aim of developing feelings of friendship and mutual respect among nations and with a view to the spiritual enhancement of man, without regard for race, sex, language or religion.

2. In order to enable the public to ascertain facts and to appraise events objectively, it is necessary to encourage co-operation with other countries in the field of communication and to improve the conditions in which journalists of one State exercise their profession in another State, on the basis of reciprocity, bearing in mind the principles set forth in this Declaration.

Article III

Since the international exchange of information is fundamental to the strengthening of peace and international understanding, States and information media have the right to diffuse reports of national events beyond their borders. Exchange between countries of information concerning the aims, aspirations, needs and culture for each nation promotes the broadening of international co-operation and understanding, the reduction of tension in international relations and the settlement of disputes by peaceful means.

Article IV

Special support should be given, on the basis of appropriate agreements, to the establishment and furthering of national mass media in the developing countries and to the training of their personnel, so as to correct the existing disequilibrium in the circulation of information from these countries and to make a balanced exchange of information a reality for the whole of the international community.

Article V

It is a responsibility of the mass media to avoid any justification or encouragement of the evils of war, violence, apartheid and other forms of national, racial or religious hatred.

Article VI

Any incitement to racial discrimination which may lead to threats or acts of violence or encouragement of such acts against any group of persons because of their race, colour or ethnic origin is to be shunned. For this purpose, legislative action might be envisaged consistent with the respective Constitutional systems of States and with relevant international instruments and agreements.

Article VII

Similarly, as a means of contributing effectively to the strengthening of peace and international understanding, the mass media have a duty to make widely known among the peoples of the world the objectives of equity, sovereign equality, interdependence, common interest and co-operation among all States, on which, in accordance with the resolutions adopted by the United Nations General Assembly, the foundations of a new international economic order are based.

Article VIII

The voices of those struggling against apartheid and other forms of racial discrimination, colonialism, neo-colonialism and foreign occupation by aggression, and unable to be heard within their own territory, should be given expression through the mass media of other countries with due respect for the sovereignty of the host countries.

Article IX

It is specially important to ensure that the mass media are used for the education of young people in conformity with the Declaration on the Promotion among Youth of the Ideals of Peace, Mutual Respect and Understanding between Peoples, it being incumbent upon States to encourage among young people a spirit of peace, justice, freedom, mutual respect and understanding.

Article X

States, institutions or groups which consider that the circulation of erroneous news reports has seriously impaired their action with a view to the strengthening of peace and international understanding, and their efforts to combat war propaganda, racism and apartheid, should be able to rectify such news reports through the mass media.

Article XI

It is the duty of professional organizations in the field of mass communication to define and promote standards of professional ethics on a national and international level and to support their members in the responsible exercise of their profession.

Article XII

States are responsible for the activities in the international sphere of all mass media under their jurisdiction.

Article XIII

The principles of this Declaration on Fundamental Principles Governing the Use of the Mass Media in Strengthening Peace and International Understanding and in Combating War Propaganda, Racism and Apartheid shall be applied with due regard for human rights and fundamental freedom.

APPENDIX 9

Summary of Interventions Made in Programme Commission III
At the 19th session of the General Conference, Nairobi, November 1976
(Unesco document CC.77/WS/21, April 1977)

In presenting to the Commission Agenda Item 69—Draft Declaration on Fundamental Principles Governing the Use of the Mass Media in Strengthening Peace and International Understanding and in Combating War Propaganda, Racism and Apartheid (Document 19 C/19) the Assistant Director-General for Culture and Communication recalled that the text of the draft Declaration before the Commission had been prepared by an intergovernmental meeting of experts held at Unesco House, Paris, from 15 to 22 December 1975. That meeting had been convened pursuant to Resolution 4.111 adopted by the General Conference at its eighteenth session. He further recalled that the proposal to prepare such a Declaration originated at the seventeenth session of the General Conference in Resolution 4.113 in compliance with which the Director-General had prepared a first draft on the basis of suggestions made by a meeting of experts from 12 countries participating in their private capacity, held at Unesco House in March 1974. At its eighteenth session, the General Conference had considered that draft which was contained in Document 18 C/35 as well as various amendments to it submitted by Member States and had considered that these texts needed a study in depth. It had consequently authorized the convening of the 1975 intergovernmental meeting which prepared the draft Declaration now before the Commission. The meeting had been attended by governmental experts from 85 Member States with the right to vote and by observers from four other Member States. However, a number of delegations had not participated throughout the discussion. The text established by the meeting had been adopted by 41 votes in favour, 8 against and 3 abstentions.

The Assistant Director-General then observed that, as noted by the Director-General in his introduction to the General Policy Debate at the present session of the General Conference, the intergovernmental meeting had brought to light serious divergencies between Member States due to the different conceptions they had on the role of the mass media in society and in particular on the nature and the form of responsibilities incumbent upon these media themselves on the one hand and the State on the other. The Director-General had also referred to the fact that in an Organization such as Unesco which grouped States having different social systems, it was not surprising that certain debates led to the adoption of different positions. The Director-General at the same time had underlined his concern at noting that at least one of the Articles of the draft Declaration could be considered by some as contrary to texts which were recognized by the whole international community, notably Article I of Unesco's Constitution and Article 19 of the Universal Declaration of Human Rights. As he had stated, the Director-General hoped that the General Conference would examine the problem with all due attention keeping in mind that it would be highly prejudicial for Unesco to appear to go in any way against principles which were universally recognized in the field of Human Rights.

The Assistant Director-General concluded by saying that the Director-General and the Secretariat stood ready at the General Conference and in the following biennium to arrange and assist in all measures which the Conference may recommend concerning the role, rights and responsibilities of the mass media.

INTERVENTIONS

Netherlands

The delegate of the Netherlands, speaking on behalf of the Governments of the nine member countries of the European Economic Community—Belgium, Denmark, France, Federal Republic of Germany, Ireland, Italy, Luxembourg, Netherlands and the United Kingdom—said that certain amendments to the draft Declaration introduced at the intergovernmental meeting of experts in 1975 had constrained the nine governments to cease participating in the meeting. Above all, however, the draft Declaration contained concepts that were totally unacceptable to the Governments and public opinion of these countries. In particular, it endorsed state control of the mass media, which was contrary to their deepest convictions concerning human dignity and freedom and the free circulation of information. In conformity with the statement made at the 1975 meeting, the delegations of the nine countries would not contribute to a discussion of the substance of the draft Declaration, though they were ready to join the other delegations in seeking a procedure that would make it possible to find a solution satisfactory to all.

Since 1975 ideas had evolved and it had now become clearer that the fundamental interests of the Third World in matters of information and communication called for an additional effort. It had also been noted that the professional organizations concerned had not been consulted at any time in the preparation of the document.

In his opening address the Director-General had pointed out that at least one article of the draft Declaration could be regarded by some as contrary to Article I of Unesco's Constitution and Article 19 of the Universal Declaration of Human Rights, and had said that it would be highly prejudicial to the Organization if it were to embark on a course that might seem contrary to universally recognized principles in the field of human rights. It was therefore clear that the present text was not sufficiently prepared and that many more studies and consultations would be needed before a text capable of obtaining a general consensus could be presented to the General Conference.

Many of the non-aligned countries appreciated that their only immediate interest was to develop as rapidly as possible mass media in keeping with their own personality and cultural identity. The nine E.E.C. countries were in sympathy with these ideas, which were at the basis of the draft Declaration, and in the general debate their heads of delegations had stressed that it was an urgent duty of the international community to help remedy the inadequacies from which many countries suffered and had expressed their readiness to contribute to that purpose. She therefore hoped that Commission II, when discussing Part IV of 19C/5, would give special and constructive attention to the resolution tabled by a number of non-aligned countries.

Norway

The delegate of Norway, representing the five Nordic countries—Denmark, Finland, Iceland, Norway and Sweden—said the draft Declaration touched upon only one of a series of problems relating to the role of the mass media, isolating it in a way that could be detrimental to the broader context of the Organization's overall mass media policy. Since the decision to prepare a Declaration had been taken in 1972 the situation had changed considerably and both with Unesco and elsewhere attention was not centered on the need and demand of the developing world for a just and equal participation in the global communication structure.

He recalled in this respect such examples as the Colombo Conference of heads of State of the non-aligned countries, which had stressed the need for improving media technologies, forms and institutions and had decided to establish a press agency pool of the non-aligned countries; the request submitted to the United Nations by the ASEAN countries to consider a plan for improving mass communications for social progress and development; the recommendation of the Costa Rica conference concerning the formulation of national and regional communication policies; and the new and challenging concept of the right to communicate now being discussed in the Unesco Secretariat and the Nordic National Commissions.

The draft Declaration was, in fact, no longer relevant, since it defined principles for only one aspect of the problem and did not take into consideration the whole. It did not take into account the fundamental problems of structure and distribution which were at the centre of the debate in many developing countries as well as in the Nordic countries; it practically ignored the specific basic communication needs in different societies and the ever-widening gap between the Northern and Southern hemispheres in regard to information and communication resources; and it overlooked the many different functions of the mass media in today's highly complex world.

The text also contained a few far-reaching principles of references that were unacceptable or even unconstitutional in several Member States. Its adoption would seriously compromise the formulation of a coherent and development-oriented policy for the media which, for the Nordic countries, represented one of Unesco's most challenging and important tasks. The problem it evoked would be better reconsidered in the broader context of an overall Unesco policy for the media and for the actions, normative or other, that could lead to better mutual understanding and respect and the elimination of injustice and discrimination. Such a reexamination would also make it possible to consult the professional groups and media institutions.

Pending such reconsideration it would be better to revise the proposed programmes in Section 4.14 and 4.15 in order to achieve a better and fairer sharing of information at the international level. Efforts should be concentrated on providing extra funds for the execution of such a revised programme in 1977–1978 and the Nordic countries were ready to contribute their share to this.

Colombia

The delegate of Colombia said that the moral force of such a draft Declaration of principles as that contained in document 19C/91 depended upon the number of States which supported it. A declaration adopted by general consensus of the Member States would be an expression of the world conscience. Since there were differing conceptions on the rôle of the mass media and the responsibility of the State, it would be wiser to avoid any debate on the merits and drawbacks of the different systems and instead to concentrate on reaching agreement on those major principles which were acceptable to all or the great majority of Member States.

A starting point for this process could be the fundamental principle, on which agreement must be assumed, that the Declaration should contain no concept that would restrict the free flow of ideas. That principle was enshrined in the U.N. Charter, the Universal Declaration of Human Rights and Unesco's Constitution as a prerequisite for all the other rights and as fundamental for peace and international understanding. A draft Declaration on the use of the mass media should therefore contain a stronger and more energetic call to Member States to guarantee and facilitate freedom of thought and expression and the circulation of ideas, both at national level and across frontiers, since only the unrestricted circulation of ideas would dispel the distorted picture which the peoples of the world had of each other. He recalled in this respect the classical fable, which said: "In the distance I saw a monstrous beast; I drew near and discovered that it was a man; I went nearer still and recognized my own brother".

All States were agreed on the major objectives of the draft Declaration, i.e. strengthening peace and international understanding and combating war propaganda, racism and apartheid. The differences arose when it came to the references, as in Article XII, to the responsibility of the State for the mass media. In Colombia freedom of the press and the other media was guaranteed by the Constitution, which meant that the State could assume no responsibility for the activities of the media, provided they complied with the law. Moreover the wording of Article XII was vague and incoherent; if mass media under the jurisdiction of the State meant all the mass media it was unacceptable; if it applied only to the official media it was superfluous.

There were other provisions of the draft Declaration which were prejudicial for international understanding, or which should be expanded and updated to take account of the desires of the developing countries and technical progress in communication. The Colombian delegation therefore proposed that consideration of document 19C/91 be postponed and that the Director-General be asked to prepare, in consultation with Member States and with the necessary technical and legal advice, a new text likely to obtain the widest possible consensus for submission to the next session of the General Conference.

Canada

The delegate of Canada shared the view of the spokesmen for the nine European Community countries and the five Nordic countries that the Commission was not a suitable forum in which to prepare a document of such importance as the draft Declaration and he would not therefore participate in any substantive discussion of the text. However, he wished to draw attention to the fact that only 41 Member States at the 1975 intergovernmental meeting of experts had approved the text; of the remaining 99 Member States of Unesco, more than 50 were not even present at that meeting, while the remainder either did not vote or voted against it. It could not, therefore, be said that the draft Declaration had gained broad support at that meeting.

The draft Declaration in its present form was simply not acceptable to Canada, both because of its philosophical approach, which favored state control, and such specific elements as preambular paragraph 5, with its reference to U.N. resolution 3379 (XXX), and Articles VIII, X and XII. Article VIII was excessively restrictive in that it did not extend the same rights to be heard to victims of persecution on political and religious grounds, or to any people in states which did not fall in the category of being under foreign occupation or aggression. In Articles X and XII, particularly the latter, it was the implications of state control which were quite unacceptable.

Senegal

The delegate of Senegal said that the draft Declaration was an extremely important document as it established a code of ethics of the highest interest for the mass media and for the professional journalists whose task it was to defend freedom and truth through their pens and the spoken word. Its adoption should therefore be an obligation for all States. However, this in turn called for the broadest possible agreement on the principles set forth in it, and it was clear from the discussions that this was not the case with the present text, which caused very great problems. The delegation of Senegal was therefore in favour of referring the question to the Drafting and Negotiating Group.

Cuba

The delegate of Cuba considered that the Commission should examine the draft Declaration paragraph by paragraph. He did not see how it could affect the interests of either States or private enterprise. Article XII, over which there seemed to be most disagreement, in no way implied State control of the mass media. What it did reflect was the ethical function of the State, whose duty it was to protect society against deliberate distortion of the truth by the mass media, just as it protected the individual citizen and his property from attack by criminals. This was a particularly important point, because tendentious campaigns were often conducted by transnational interests over which the State concerned had no jurisdiction. What was needed was to ensure that the information media stuck to the truth. Article XII, in his view, was designed to ensure this by guiding the media towards the objectives of the Declaration, namely the strengthening of peace and international understanding and elimination of war propaganda, racism and apartheid.

In conclusion, the Cuban delegation considered that if the disparity in mass media between the developed and developing countries was to be eliminated a plan of action would have to be implemented by Unesco. Special attention should therefore be given to the draft resolution submitted by Iraq and the USSR.

Union of Soviet Socialist Republics

The delegate of the USSR said that, to understand the urgency of the problems involved, it had to be remembered that there were now some 800 million radio receivers in the world and that about 2 billion people watched television programmes every day; the newspapers numbered many thousands and millions of copies were printed; and statistics showed that in the three hours which had been spent on procedural discussion on the previous day, 200 book titles had been published. All the time the mass media were bringing some kind of news and ideas to the people, were influencing their minds. The Soviet delegation therefore welcomed the fact that Unesco, which was more concerned with spiritual life than any other international organization, had undertaken the preparation of the first international declaration on the mass media.

It was not true, as had been alleged in the press, that the draft Declaration would place the mass media under state control or that it would be a threat to freedom of speech and information. It was concerned with other matters. It would place a moral obligation on the State to protect the media in order to ensure that they served the cause of peace. The fact that in the Soviet Union war propaganda, racism and apartheid were banned by law, might be dubbed by some as an infringement of freedom of information, but they considered it humanitarian.

In the case of the international exchange of information, other laws came into play. The mass media were concentrated in the hands of private enterprise in a few leading countries and hundreds of millions of people in the developing world had to be satisfied with the information they received from foreign press agencies and radio stations. It was well known that the stream of information going from the West to the developing world was a thousand times heavier than from the developing world to the West.

Hence the draft Declaration contained very important provisions aimed at ensuring a balanced approach to the international dissemination of information. It advocated special support for the development of national mass media in the developing countries and it contained a reference to the new international economic order, all of which was in the interests of the majority of States present at the General Conference.

As concerned freedom of information, the draft Declaration not merely did not curtail, but specifically upheld that freedom. Paragraph 3 of the Preamble referred to two of the most important documents on human rights, the Universal Declaration of Human Rights and the International Covenant on Civil and Political Rights, while paragraph 12 specifically stated that freedom of expression, information and opinion were fundamental human rights. Finally, Article I laid down that States should encourage the freer and wider dissemination of information. It could not therefore be said that the draft Declaration would impede the free flow of information.

Some speakers had asserted that Article XII of the draft Declaration would mean State control of all the mass media. This was not the Soviet delegation's interpretation of the Article. Their view of the responsibility of the State for the international activities of the mass media applied solely to the media which were already under State jurisdiction, such as government information services, state telegraph agencies and state radio stations. It was possible that the Article was not worded clearly enough and the Soviet delegation was prepared to participate in the task of clarifying and improving the text.

The draft Declaration was solely concerned with two basic issues. First, it was the moral responsibility of the State to protect and strengthen the mass media so that they would support peace and the fight against war propaganda, racism and apartheid. And secondly, it was the duty of all to help the developing countries to establish and develop their own mass media. It was thus fully in keeping with the decisions taken at the international meetings on information held in 1977 in Tunis, New Delhi, Colombo and San Jose. As the Prime Minister of India had said, a new international order with regard to information was at least as important as a new international economic order.

Finally, it had been said that the draft Declaration could not be regarded as authoritative because only 41 Member States had voted for it at the 1975 intergovernmental meeting of experts. In fact, while 41 had voted for it only 8 delegations had voted against it.

United States of America

The delegate of the United States of America noted that there was a conflict of ideologies in respect to the mass media which could not be resolved in the Commission. The draft Declaration in document 19C/91 reflected the view that the mass media should serve the interests of the State not those of the citizen as an individual, and that they must therefore be under the control of the State. This view was rejected by other nations, which considered, and frequently established constitutionally, that the press and other media must be free from interference by the State as they represented a counterbalancing force which helped to prevent any abuse of power by the State and gave to the citizens the information about their own community and the world which they needed as the holders of ultimate power in their Governments. They also acted as an early warning device to Governments that changes might be needed and as a safety valve permitting the ventilation of protest before it became destructive. However, the United States of America did not intend to try to impose its own free mass media system on the rest of the world, although they believed it would help to improve the conduct of world affairs, as that would be contrary to the spirit of tolerance and pluralism that should always guide Unesco.

It was true that the developing countries had special problems that called for attention from communication experts. The United States of America was ready to help solve these problems. But this required calm and rational examination as a first step, and it was not in the interests of the developing countries to press for immediate acceptance of one or other of the opposing ideologies.

At the intergovernmental meeting of experts in Paris in December 1975, the present draft Declaration had been adopted by less than half of the nations represented there, which was a very narrow base for a universal declaration. Such normative actions, if they were to be effective in guiding the behaviour of States within the international community, must be acceptable to a high proportion of the States with respect to the direction to be followed. The argument that the draft Declaration was of little importance because it would not have the force of law was to be rejected. To accept it would be to put the moral sanction of Unesco on the side of the controlled media. Since this was contrary to Unesco's Constitution and to the Universal Declaration of Human Rights, the proposers of the draft should in all logic first propose nullifying those to texts before discussing the Declaration. Since a radical change in Unesco's basic philosophy was proposed it should first be subjected to long and thoughtful consideration by experts working in an atmosphere of tranquility.

Freedom of expression and freedom of the news media were fundamental to all other freedoms. If they were lost, or shackled by Unesco's moral sanction, the next to go might well be academic freedom, freedom of scientific enquiry, freedom to enjoy cultural diversity. These subjects were too important to be disposed of in impromptu debate, and called for deliberate and prolonged study. The United States delegation therefore supported the Brazilian proposal to send the matter to the Drafting and Negotiating Group.

Liberia

The delegate of Liberia said that his country's position was, in keeping with its Constitution and laws, that the mass media should be free and independent of State-control. For Unesco to sanction State-control of the media by adopting the present draft Declaration, would be to violate the Universal Declaration of Human Rights which it had pledged to support.

The Liberian delegation accordingly recommended that in Article IV, which spoke of the establishment and furthering of national mass media in the developing countries, the word "national" should be deleted; this would make it clear that the establishment of State-controlled media was not intended. Article VIII also needed clarification, as it was ambiguous and might encourage belligerency between States in its present form. The Liberian delegation supported the Brazilian amendment to this Article, as it made it more specific as well as the proposal to transmit the draft Declaration to the Drafting and Negotiating Group.

Uruguay

For the delegate of Uruguay the draft Declaration was quite unacceptable. It represented the ideological and philosophical approach of one group of nations which was entirely contrary to that of another equally large group of countries. Article XII constituted a direct attack on freedom of information; by making

States responsible for the activities of the mass media in the international sphere, it would encourage them to take control of the media, since no government would accept responsibility for something it could not control.

Another objectionable feature of the draft Declaration was that in several articles it attempted to dictate to States what they should do in regard to their own mass media. This was directly contrary to the principle, shared by many delegations and clearly expressed by the Director-General when opening the Costa Rica Conference, that States had an inalienable right to establish their own policies in this respect.

He could not, therefore, support the draft Declaration in its present wording. However, he hoped that negotiation would lead to agreement on a text that would reconcile the different views expressed and could be adopted by consensus. He therefore supported the proposal that the draft Declaration be referred to the Drafting and Negotiating Group.

In conclusion the delegate of Uruguay wished to point out that, despite the suggestions made by some earlier speakers and the reference contained in the draft resolution submitted by Iraq and the Soviet Union, there was no connexion between the draft Declaration in document 19C/91 and the resolution adopted unanimously at the Costa Rica Conference. Both concerned the mass media but they approached the problem from very different points of view. Whereas the Costa Rica resolution and San Jose declaration were based primarily on the right of States to establish their own national policies, on the plurality of the media and on acceptance of the existence of both private and public channels of communication, nothing was said about these points in the draft Declaration.

China

The delegate of China said that any Declaration issued by Unesco should fully reflect the situation regarding a particular problem and should provide approaches and solutions in line with the interests of the peoples of the world.

That was not the case with the draft Declaration in document 19C/91, which did not meet those requirements. While it rightly supported opposition to racism and apartheid and referred to the new international economic order and the right of countries and peoples to protect and preserve their cultures, it did not take into account such fundamental principles as opposition to imperialism, colonialism, zionism and big-power hegemonism. The Chinese delegation had made clear at the eighteenth session of the General Conference that the draft Declaration lacked the basis for discussion and that was still its view.

Bulgaria

The delegate of Bulgaria considered that the draft Declaration was of particular significance because of the role played by the mass media in informing the public and shaping public opinion and because of their great importance as a positive or negative factor in international relations. Her Government felt that the Declaration was in conformity with the principles of the United Nations and Unesco which all Member States accepted and which had first brought them together thirty years ago. It fitted into the Organization's regular normative activities, and efforts made by the media of some countries to create prejudice against it merely underscored its need and timeliness.

It seemed to the Bulgarian Government that the text as a whole was a good one. There could, for instance, be no disagreement in regard to preambular paragraphs 1, 3, 6, 7, 8, 12, 13 and 16, which stressed that the sovereignty of States must be respected, recalled the Universal Declaration of Human Rights, affirmed the importance and responsibility of the mass media in creating an atmosphere of international confidence and mutual respect, and emphasized the urgent need for the Third World countries to develop their own mass media and a two-way flow of objective information.

As concerned Article XII, which appeared to raise difficulties for some States, the delegate of Bulgaria believed that a broad consensus could be found by taking as a basis the principles enshrined in the second part of paragraph 14 of the Preamble, which read:

> "[the international exchange of information] . . . entails also the responsibility and duty of the States to use all their constitutional means to encourage the mass media to act in accordance with the aims and principles of the United Nations Charter so as to maintain and strengthen peace and international understanding and to combat war propaganda, racialism and apartheid".

The Bulgarian delegation was ready to co-operate in seeking acceptable solutions for this article and for the other few articles, paragraphs or phrases which posed difficulties. But it would be totally unjustified to reject a carefully-worded text, which in general reflected adequately the basic principles of Unesco, merely because of some delegations' reservations concerning a few words, notions and phrases—reservations which, in her view, boiled down to objections to one article and a few words.

She hoped that the General Conference would adopt the draft Declaration at its nineteenth session as all the preliminary stages had been completed. The statements of some delegations that they would not participate in a substantive discussion of the text showed scant respect for the democratic procedure. A much more constructive approach would be to present amendments to it.

German Democratic Republic

The delegate of the German Democratic Republic said that freedom of the press was not the subject of the draft Declaration, as might be thought from some interventions. Nor was the question one of reducing, but rather of expanding the scale of information, which his country considered as basic for the strengthening of peace and understanding among peoples. The great advantage of the draft Declaration was that it proposed ethical norms and positive ideas for the responsible use of the mass media and condemned their use for encouraging war, racism or apartheid. It was thus fully in accord with the principles upheld by his country in regard to the development of cultural co-operation and exchanges of information, which formed an essential element of the policy of peaceful co-existence among States with different social systems. It was also in tune with the national Constitution, Article 6 of which laid down that war propaganda and the spreading of hatred against peoples, races and nations were punishable offences. Finally, it was in conformity with the Final Act of the Helsinki Conference since it afforded a valuable framework for expanding mutually advantageous co-operation among all States.

A careful study of the decisions and recommendations taken at the recent meetings on communication held in Tunis, New Delhi, Colombo and San Jose showed that the draft Declaration also gave expression to the aspirations of the developing countries. In particular, it reflected their desire to set up national and regional communication systems corresponding to their information needs and cultural values. It would thus also support Unesco's contribution to the establishment of a new economic and social order.

The delegation of the German Democratic Republic considered that the draft Declaration took into account the views of all the different Member States. No doubt the text could be improved in places, but that was a task for the Commission, which he hoped would be able to reach agreement on a text that could be accepted by consensus.

Jordan

The delegate of Jordan found the Preamble to the draft Declaration well-balanced and firmly based on the United Nations Charter, the Universal Declaration of Human Rights and the various United Nations and Unesco resolutions concerning racial discrimination. However, he felt it should also contain a clear and unequivocal definition of racial discrimination based on the resolutions adopted by the United Nations General Assembly in 1975.

The draft Declaration rightly took into consideration the diversity of regimes among Member States as well as the need to provide the small states with protection against the information campaigns of the great powers, whose monopoly of the mass media was a constant source of anxiety to the smaller countries.

The delegation of Jordan hoped that the interests of the oppressed peoples would be given full consideration when the text of the draft Declaration was finalized. Article VIII and the Brazilian amendment to it (19C/PRG.III/DR.2) were of particular importance in this respect.

Vietnam

The delegate of Vietnam, after noting that his country has only recently regained its independence after thirty years of war during which it had both profited from correct reporting and suffered from inaccurate and tendentious information, expressed his satisfaction with the principles set forth in the draft Declaration. Those principles were that the mass media must strive to promote peace and international understanding on the basis of the independence of peoples; that they must combat war propaganda, racism, apartheid, colonialism and neo-colonialism; that they must make known the truth about events at home and abroad;

that they must help people to fight for their independence, for democracy, for social progress and for the protection and development of their national culture and cultural identity. For all these reasons the draft Declaration, though possibly incomplete, represented a definite step forward.

Freedom of information was one of the fundamental human rights—the right of the individual to be correctly informed. Accuracy, fidelity to the facts, must be recognized as the principal quality demanded of information and the information media. Freedom of information must therefore be accompanied by responsibility. For that reason his delegation had no difficulty in accepting Article XII. However since it caused problems for other delegations they should try to reformulate it so that it would be acceptable to all.

The delegation of Vietnam also welcomed Article IV with its call for support for the development of the national media of the developing countries.

Some delegations had expressed concern that the draft Declaration might constitute a threat to freedom of information. In fact, the right to freedom of information was specifically upheld in numerous paragraphs of the Preamble, as well as in Articles I and II among others. However, they should all work together on the text in order to remove any misunderstandings, and obtain a draft Declaration that could be adopted by the General Conference by consensus.

Poland

The delegate of Poland said that it was entirely incorrect to interpret the draft Declaration as an attempt to impose State-control over all the media. In fact, it dealt in a very thoughtful way with the problem of the apparent contradiction between freedom of information and responsibility for its content. As previous speakers had already noted the Preamble, particularly paragraphs 3 and 12, recalled various universally-recognized human rights, while in paragraph 14 the only moral restrictions placed on freedom of information related to war propaganda, racism and apartheid.

As a journalist himself he could not share the United States delegate's views that the draft Declaration was a threat to freedom of speech and opinion and the free circulation of ideas. It stressed that the mass media should serve the causes to which the United Nations and Unesco were devoted—peace, international understanding and mutual knowledge and respect among the peoples of the world— and which were aimed at bringing to an end the prejudice and mistrust which still existed today. It was because friendship among all peoples and peaceful co-existence were essential that the draft Declaration drew attention to the responsibilities of the State, which were precisely those responsibilities which led them to participate in the work of Unesco.

Article IV, which was very similar to a resolution adopted by the non-aligned States a few months earlier at the Colombo Conference, was particularly important. At present nearly all the information disseminated in the world went out from a few specific points, and this lack of equilibrium did not serve the cause of peace and was harmful to the vital interests of the developing countries.

He was therefore opposed to the proposal that the draft Declaration should be referred to the Drafting and Negotiating Group. He was convinced that if the Commission examined the text paragraph by paragraph, any disagreements could easily be ironed out in a spirit of compromise.

As concerned the draft resolution tabled by Iraq and the USSR, while it was fully in accord with the spirit of the draft Declaration, he believed that it would lose its relevance once the Commission undertook a detailed study of the Declaration.

Switzerland

The delegate of Switzerland said that the text of the draft Declaration was quite unacceptable to his country, as it ran counter to its constitution and laws, as well as to the principles of freedom of the press and non-interference in the affairs of the mass media.

They had been asked to propose amendments to the text, but at the intergovernmental meeting of experts in December 1975 he had submitted many amendments and all had been rejected. He therefore hesitated to do so now, though he reserved the right to do so. In any case, there were only two articles which he could accept as they stood, even the title raised problems for his delegation.

The Director-General had already pointed out in his introduction to the General Debate that the text of the draft Declaration was at variance with Unesco's Constitution and the Universal Declaration of Human Rights. To adopt the text as it now stood would therefore be a catastrophe for the Organization.

His country had, however, derived some fruitful lessons from the Paris meeting and in particular from the Costa Rica conference and the meeting of non-aligned countries in Colombo. It had become aware, for instance, that there was in fact an imbalance in the exchange of information which was similar to the imbalances in such other Unesco fields as education and science. However, this imbalance would not be corrected through the adoption of a controversial Declaration that would create more problems than it solved, but by more positive action on the part of Unesco through the provision of more assistance to the developing countries in building up their mass media—which was the substance of Article IV of the draft Declaration. His country therefore agreed with the various proposals which had been put forward for strengthening substantially Unesco's work in helping to develop the infrastructure of the mass media in the developing countries and it accepted the consequent financial implications. But they would have difficulty in explaining this to the Swiss taxpayer if the Organization were to adopt a Declaration which ran counter to the many principles on which their action was based.

It was clear from the various interventions that there were wide differences in interpretation of the text and that a great deal more work had to be done on it. He therefore joined with those who were attempting to find a procedure for preparing a new text that would be acceptable to all. What was important was not the adoption of a Declaration at the present or even the next session of the General Conference, but that they should do their best to develop an effective programme of action for Unesco.

Algeria

The delegate of Algeria said that the fact that a group of countries which enjoyed a dominant position in the use of the mass media was endeavouring to preserve its monopoly showed clearly that a new international order in the field of information was needed as urgently as in all other fields. Unesco's normative action in this respect, as represented by the present draft Declaration, was fully justified by the need to protect the weaker from the dominance of the strongest. Moreover, it was doubtful whether there was anywhere in the world where total freedom of information existed, where a journalist could write or say anything; legislation relating to national security and the like would effectively prevent that. There were thus precedents for the formulation of standards to govern matters of information.

The draft Declaration in fact recalled clearly and forcefully the rights of those responsible for information; but, since there could be no freedom without responsibility, it also pointed out their duties. Several speakers had referred to the disadvantages of State interference in information, but he had heard no condemnation of the interference of the power of money in this field. The draft Declaration was in fact an attempt to warn those responsible for the media against the kind of propaganda solemnly condemned by the entire international community, i.e. war propaganda, racism and apartheid.

He had listened with interest to the delegate of Switzerland, who had spoken of the lessons his country had learned from the Colombo and New Delhi meetings concerning the imbalances in information between the developed and developing countries. But he could not agree with his conclusion that it would be better to shelve the draft Declaration and instead to develop cooperation with a view to reducing the technological gap in information media. His suggestion, in fact, was an additional argument in favour of the adoption of the Declaration. For if cooperation in the field of information was to be developed, and this was to be desired, it should be developed within the framework of a proper code of conduct as formulated in the draft Declaration.

Nigeria

The delegate of Nigeria believed that at the present time a Declaration on the mass media was peripheral to the real and urgent needs of overall national development in most developing countries.

Honduras

The delegate of Honduras noted that the draft Declaration, although centred around problems that were of interest to all countries of the world, did not cover certain problems that were of particular interest to some of the developing countries. It reflected some of the points included in the Declaration and resolutions adopted at the Costa Rica conference, one of these on which there had been unanimous agreement at Costa Rica and which was covered by Article IV, being the need to develop the media of the developing countries so that the latter could make their voices heard on the world scene in a more balanced way. But other points, such as the right of international reply, were not included.

In Honduras they were particularly concerned with the role of the mass media in national development, especially in education and culture, and they were at present studying social communication legislation in some of the more developed countries where, although there was no State control of the media, norms had been established to ensure that freedom of the press was exercised in line with the national interest. There was, in fact, no such thing as absolute freedom of the press or indeed of any freedom; true freedom consisted of conforming to the rule of law, wise laws adjusted to the needs of the society concerned. At the national level, this was a matter for the government of each country. However, on the international plane, there also had to be some rules of an ethical nature which, without affecting the freedom of the press, would guarantee a certain degree of responsibility on the part of the media.

The Government of Honduras therefore considered that there should be an international instrument which defined the rights and duties of the mass media as well as the rights and duties of the States and peoples. However, some of the concepts and principles set forth in the draft Declaration were not in conformity with the legal and economic systems of Honduras. Since such a statement of principles had to be based on the broadest possible consensus, the draft Declaration should clearly be subjected to a much closer and calmer analysis than was possible in the Commission. He therefore supported the proposal to refer the matter to the Drafting and Negotiating Group.

Byelorussia

The delegate of Byelorussia noted that the ideas set forth in the draft Declaration had received widespread international support, notably at the Colombo and San José Conferences. Its principal objective was to reduce international tension by furthering political, economic and cultural cooperation among States with different social systems and its adoption would be in accord with the Final Act of the Helsinki Conference, which had been signed by 30 countries of Europe as well as by the United States of America and Canada—countries which owned the larger part of the mass media in the world.

The media today carried a great responsibility in the field of international relations and it was essential that this responsibility should be firmly based on international legal instruments. The Byelorussian delegation noted with satisfaction that the draft Declaration provided for this by recognizing the responsibility not only of the mass media themselves but also of the States and governments on whose territories and under whose control the media came.

He noted that some countries which had the most powerful mass media in the world had spoken in favour of absolute freedom for those media, even in the international sphere. This was understandable in light of the admission by some of their representatives that the media's activities were closely linked to military and commercial policies. He had listened with interest when the United States delegate had said that the mass media in his country controlled the activities of the United States Government. He did not know if this was true, but the mass media of the United States of America certainly tried to control the military, commercial and cultural policies of other governments.

Some speakers had said they would not take part in a substantive discussion of the text of the draft Declaration. However, they had said nothing about the campaign of intellectual blackmail against Unesco, about which the Director-General had spoken. Nor had they said anything about what their governments intended to do to put an end to the intellectual genocide being conducted by the mass media of some countries in the so-called free world against the developing countries through the dissemination of propaganda for violence and pornography.

The Byelorussian delegation found the draft Declaration acceptable and hoped it would be adopted at the present session.

Sudan

The delegate of Sudan said that the question under discussion was first and foremost of concern to the peoples of the deveoping countries, who had always been the victims of the information media, which distorted their regional and national problems in order to prove their underdevelopment and were used by outside powers to encourage intrigue and divergencies. The developing countries needed stronger mass media in order to make known the truth and counter such distortions. The delegates of some countries had spoken of the principles that prevented their governments from interfering in the mass media, but they should remember that as members of the international community they also had the moral obligation of ensuring respect for the basic principles of that community, above all the preservation of peace. He hoped that a way would be found of reconciling the conflicting demands of national sovereignty and international obligations.

In his view the draft Declaration should not be submitted to the Drafting and Negotiating Group, but should be dealt with by the Commission. He firmly supported the draft, because it did not deny the existence of different constitutions and legislations, but took them into account.

Yugoslavia

The delegate of Yugoslavia said that his delegation had come prepared to co-operate in seeking solutions to problems which, despite some differences, were common to all. He therefore regretted that so many speakers had thought fit to approach the debate as if the only things involved were the establishment of State control over the mass media and the exclusion by the developing and non-aligned countries of foreign media from their territories. It was wrong to divide the world into those who were for absolute freedom and those who were for absolute control. Things were not as simple as that, since there were other ways of thinking, other approaches to the problems of information and the role of the mass media in strengthening international co-operation.

There had been much talk about freedom of information and the free flow of information, but little had been said about the responsibilities that went with every freedom. It was therefore interesting to note that in the international convention dealing with the use of broadcasting in the name of peace that was concluded under the auspices of the League of Nations in 1936, the signatory countries had accepted the obligation to refrain from radio broadcasts that would endanger peace and the security of other countries. They had also accepted an obligation both to control such broadcasts from their territories and not to allow on their territories any warlike or provocative propaganda.

The aim of freedom of information, of the free international exchange of information, was to enable man to exercise his right to be informed correctly on what was happening, so that he could participate properly in national and international life. It did not mean endorsing the right of the stronger to interfere in other peoples' lives and affairs, to use their superiority to impose their values and way of life on others, to justify systems of foreign domination where they prevailed. It did not mean that, in the name of freedom of information, efforts should be made to destabilize the situation in other countries.

It was interesting to note that speakers who had quoted various official texts in support of freedom of information had omitted to quote other passages from the same documents which placed a limitation on that freedom. For example, Article 19 of the Universal Declaration of Human Rights concerning the right to freedom of information had been quoted, but not Article 29 which stated that none of the freedoms should be exercized in a way that was contrary to the purposes and principles of the United Nations. Similarly, no mention had been made of Article 20 of the International Covenant on Civil and Political Rights, which stated that propaganda for war and the advocacy of national, racial or religious hatred that constituted incitement to discrimination, hostility or violence should be prohibited by law.

It was not true, as had been alleged by some speakers, that the non-aligned countries wished to exclude the Western media from their territories. They only wanted to cease being purely passive receivers of information conceived and transmitted to them from abroad. They wanted their struggle for political and economic emancipation, their process of decolonization in the fields of information, education and culture, to be presented correctly and objectively to outside public opinion. They wanted the world to know about them. As stated in the declaration adopted by the meeting in New Delhi, the present global information flows were marked by serious inadequacy and imbalance, since the means of communicating information were concentrated in a few hands. This dependence in the field of information not only perpetuated the colonial era by confining judgements and decisions on what should be known about the developing and non-aligned countries to the hands of a few, but also retarded the achievement of political and economic growth. In such a monopoly situation, freedom of information really came to mean freedom for the few to disseminate information in any way they wished and the virtual denial to everyone else of the right to inform and be informed accurately and objectively.

As the delegate of Switzerland had pointed out, the heads of State of the non-aligned countries meeting in Colombo had expressed concern at the vast and ever-growing gap between the communication capacities of their countries and of the advanced countries. The developing and non-aligned countries welcomed the proposal that they be helped to develop their own mass media, but only provided this did not mean equipping them the better to receive the kind of information now disseminated. This was not what they wanted. They wanted the principle of responsible, correct information to be disseminated to their countries and about their countries to other parts of the world. Until some way had been found to ensure that countries only disseminated correct information about each other, the developing and non-aligned countries could not be blamed for taking steps to protect their cultural identity, their interests and their development.

In conclusion, he proposed that the Commission appoint a small drafting group to try and find solutions that would be acceptable to all.

Czechoslovakia

The delegate of Czechoslovakia considered that the draft Declaration was fully in conformity with the principles on which Unesco was based. Despite the allegations made by certain speakers, none of those who supported the document wished in any way to impose their ideology on the others. He supported the Declaration because it was based on humanitarian aims and because it was essential that the press should work for peace, equality and international understanding. All was not in order with the mass media, some sections of which were acting against the principles and resolutions of the United Nations and other UN organizations. There were radio stations and newspapers which violated all principles of mutual understanding and cooperation among peoples and deliberately tried to mislead public opinion. For example, on the frontiers of his own country were two radio stations which set out to destroy order in the country. One of the aims of the draft Declaration, therefore, was to draw the attention of States to the fact that on their territory there might be radio or television stations which attempted to disorient public opinion in other countries. Surely, the press and radio should have as their objectives peace and equality among peoples, it was important to draw the attention of public opinion to this question.

It was not true that the draft Declaration constituted an attack on freedom of the press. The text spoke of many principles that guaranteed freedom of expression, the free exchange of information and so on. But the media were not always objective in their reporting. Only a week earlier when a man who had committed five criminal acts and had killed his brother, had hijacked an aeroplane and landed in the West, it had been reported in the world press and radio that he had sought political asylum. That was misinformation, not information.

One important aspect of the draft Declaration was the stress it laid on the need to help the developing countries to put an end to the existing monopoly in the dissemination of news which had always been to the detriment of the Third World.

The Declaration also made clear that responsibility of the journalist. Some delegates had said that journalists must have complete freedom, that they could be responsible only to their conscience. This had never been the case, however, since every journalist was responsible to his editor among others and many Western journalists had been dismissed by their newspapers because they had not followed the editor's instructions. Moreover, the concept of responsibility to one's own conscience was a very wide one, since everyone had their own conscience and their own criteria. He therefore welcomed the fact that Article XI dealt with the problem of the professional ethics of journalists. Indeed, it might be useful for Unesco to try to work out an agreed code of ethics for journalists.

Article XII, which concerned the responsibilities of the State for the activities of their mass media in the international sphere, had been attacked more bitterly than any other. It was his experience, however, that in any country the mass media were called to order if they went beyond the frontiers of the national interests. No doubt a better wording of the Article that would make it acceptable to all could be found, but the essential thing was to ensure that the mass media were used to further the cause of peace, mutual cooperation and international understanding.

Ukraine

The delegate of Ukraine felt that there had been considerable confusion regarding the subject of their debate. Much had been said about freedom of information and expression, but in fact they were dealing with only a narrow, though important, area of information, namely the fundamental principles which should govern the use of the mass media in strengthening peace and international understanding and in combating war propaganda, racism and apartheid. The issue was purely one of Member States encouraging the use of the mass media for those purposes.

The delegation of Ukraine was very much in favour of information, but it had to be responsible information. As other speakers had pointed out, nearly all the mass media and means of information in the world were concentrated in a few hands, and this could sometimes be prejudicial to the cause of peace and international cooperation because of the one-sided view presented. It would be interesting, for example, to see how the liberation struggle in Kenya had been presented to the world. The developing countries needed their own strong national mass media—and his delegation fully supported Unesco's efforts to help them in this matter—not only in order to make known their own viewpoints but also in order to protect their national culture and traditions from the possible harmful effects of a massive one-way flow of information.

He failed to understand how some delegation could see in the draft Declaration an attempt to impose State control over the media, since a reading of the text, and particularly paragraph 12 of the preamble, made clear that all the fundamental freedoms were to be maintained. To say that those who supported it were in favour of State control was equivalent to saying that those who were against it were in favour of war propaganda, racism and apartheid. The Declaration, in fact, left it to each country to apply the principles in accordance with its own constitution. It offered no stereotype but merely put forward in very general terms the view that it was necessary to stimulate and encourage the use of the mass media for the cause of peace and international understanding. He hoped that the Commission would continue to work on and improve the draft Declaration and he supported the Yugoslav proposal that a drafting group be appointed for that purpose.

Cyprus

The delegate of Cyprus said his country was in full sympathy with and subscribed to the aims of the draft Declaration, since the mass media had an important role to play in strengthening peace, international understanding and the struggle against racism and war. But it was in favour of a Declaration that could and would be implemented. A common complaint made at Unesco meetings was that similar declarations and international instruments, which were sorely needed in order to change the hearts and minds of men and societies for the better, were not being implemented. The present draft Declaration was of such significance that every care must be taken to ensure that it would be acted upon. It must be precise, so that there could be no differences of interpretation. It must be consistent throughout as well as consistent with other declarations and normative instruments. And it should if possible, be universally acceptable.

As regards the basic concepts of the draft Declaration, Cyprus had always supported the concept of free flow of information, but as a two-way process. He therefore noted with satisfaction that it was now almost generally recognized that a one-way flow was not really a free flow and that the idea was gaining ground that assistance should be given to those countries which were unable to contribute adequately to that communication flow. But the developing countries must also help themselves, and it was for that reason that Cyprus was using the non-aligned countries' news agency pool. They did not regard that pool as being in conflict with the existing international news agencies, but as supplementing them in a unique and significant way. It would not only provide an additional source of information, but would also help to correct the present imbalance in the information field since in future they would no longer just be receiving information but would be transmitting it as well.

As concerned relations between the State and the mass media, Cyprus was in favour of a regulatory role being played by the State as such, but was strongly against any control of the media by the government of the day. They had come to the belief that the coup staged against their government two and a half years earlier by the junta of one country and which had offered the pretext to another to invade their island, might have been averted if the mass media had not been tools of the junta but agents of public scrutiny.

Benin

The delegate of Benin considered that the draft Declaration, if it was to have the impact it deserved, must be the result of a consensus. However, the controversy surrounding the present text showed that it was not yet perfect and his delegation therefore proposed that it be sent for further study either to the Drafting and Negotiating Group or, even better, to another meeting of governmental experts.

Portugal

The delegate of Portugal said her delegation would view with great apprehension the adoption of any Declaration not proclaimed by the largest possible consensus. Precedence must therefore be given to the achievement of that goal, rather than to speed.

All Member States were undoubtedly committed to helping the mass media in respect to the aims outlined in the draft Declaration, but she was doubtful whether that purpose could be achieved through moralizing statements of the kind contained in it. That was why her delegation felt that a new and much broader study was needed that would take into account what had happened during the previous twelve months in different regions of the world, as proposed earlier by the delegate of Norway. This need had in fact been underscored by the delegate of the USSR when he quoted figures that showed clearly the dramatic increase in the volume of mass media operations everywhere.

Such a quantitative increase raised the question of a qualitative change in the methods of dealing with the matter at issue. Other factors than the purely numerical growth of the media and their consumers had to be taken into account. There were, for example, new modes of forming the individual's thinking and opinions: "The medium is the message" as a widely-accepted formula put it. There were new forms of interrelations between persons and groups reading about, listening to or viewing the same events from different places. There were new forms of interaction between nations, with imbalances, gaps and distortions in the information received and transmitted.

The qualitative changes in the mass media were seen by some scientific circles as the emergence of a new power. They were in any case bringing about a revolution as drastic in its effects on the lives of individuals and nations as the industrial revolution. The problem of the latter had first been formulated in terms of the role of economic power in the context of political power, but it was soon seen that the manipulation of men by economic forces could not be regulated by moralizing statements of good intentions. So new mechanisms and sometimes totally new structures had had to be devised.

In the case of the mass media they were facing a power of a completely new and different nature, so the rules applying to relations between economic and political power could not be used to analyze this new power, which permeated our daily lives and shaped our opinions. Account must also be taken of the fact that the power of the mass media was not necessarily a centralized power. Power had many facets and those who had recently lived through a revolution knew how diffused and decentralized was the character of power which, at more stable times, seemed firmly implanted at the top of the pyramid.

Very little was yet known about this new power resulting from modern technology. But the changes that had occurred in the past 30 years were so far-reaching in scope that it was useless to pretend that they had not changed our lives and that we could continue with the same values and criteria as before. It was therefore as immigrants discovering a new land that we should approach the role of the mass media and their contribution to peace. Very little had been done to analyze the new power scientifically and on a broad scale. Here then was a whole new field for research, inter-disciplinary analysis and psycho-sociological interpretation. The Portuguese delegation wondered whether Unesco should proclaim a declaration on the role of the mass media before such a study had been made, ignoring the complexity of the nature and role of the media but preaching certain norms of behaviour which it felt the media should adopt.

Her delegation considered that Unesco should pioneer a study of the power of the media. This alone would be an activity worthy of the Organization's role in dealing with key issues of culture and could be its specific contribution to the establishment of a new international economic and social order in the field of the mass media.

In the meantime some steps could be taken to ensure that a declaration on the role of the mass media in relation to peace, international cooperation and the struggle against war and racism was attuned to reality. They were outlined in various draft resolutions, including 19C/DR.19 co-sponsored by Portugal and Tunisia.

On the other hand, if there were pressure for the early adoption of a declaration on the role of the mass media, her delegation would wish to ask questions regarding points not covered by the present text. For instance, was it harmless for peace to have mass media which, in all regions of the world, gave priority to the capacity to have and to possess rather than to be and to live? Was it harmless for international understanding to continue, in a planetary era, with mass media which confined the mentalities of people to their own particular corner of the world? Was it harmless for the struggle against war propaganda to continue to exhibit, in all parts of the world, television films on past wars? Was it harmless for the eradication of racism to have mass media which ignored the marginal people, the voiceless members of their societies? Such questions, which were merely the most obvious ones, were not dealt with in the existing draft Declaration and showed that an entirely new approach to the matter was required.

The Portuguese delegation considered that the draft Declaration did not fulfill the purpose for which it was designed and therefore proposed that its discussion and adoption be adjourned until a later session of the General Conference. It also proposed that the Director-General be requested to carry out a more up-to-date analysis of the role of the mass media, taking into account substantive arguments put forward in the Commission's debate.

India

The delegate of India considered that the draft Declaration had become a subject of dissension because of the publicity given to it and because of misunderstandings about its scope. There was certainly no disagreement regarding the need to strengthen peace and international understanding and to combat war propaganda, racism and apartheid. The question was how the mass media could contribute to these objectives. International understanding required a balanced flow of information, which had so far been lacking. As the heads of State of the non-aligned countries had noted in their Colombo declaration: "a new international order in the field of information and mass communications is as vital as a new international economic order."

In July 1976 at the New Delhi Conference of Ministers, the non-aligned countries had taken the first major step in organizing continuing exchanges of news among themselves by setting up their own press agency pool. Since then the Indian press agency had already arranged to exchange news with news agencies from 21 non-aligned countries. Also at New Delhi it had been decided to set up a committee of experts to study the technical question of tariffs, since the lack of cheap, speedy and effective facilities for transmitting news placed the developing countries at a great disadvantage vis-à-vis the developed countries. Finally, the Colombo summit Conference had decided to establish a coordinating council to organize cooperation in such other communication fields as radio, television and films. These examples showed the efforts being made by the developing countries themselves to redress the imbalance in the information flow.

As regards the draft Declaration, the Indian delegation would have various suggestions to make in order to reflect better the needs of the developing countries. For the time being he wished only to propose the addition to Article IV of the words "and the promotion of their mutual cooperation on a bilateral or multi-lateral basis". The article would then read: "Special support should be given, on the basis of appropriate agreements, to the establishment and furthering of national mass media in the developing countries, to the training of their personnel *and the promotion of their mutual cooperation on a bi-lateral or multi-lateral basis,* so as to correct the existing disequilibrium in the circulation of information from these countries and to make a balanced exchange of information a reality for the whole of the international community."

Since it was only if the draft Declaration was adopted by the broadest possible consensus, which was lacking at present, that Unesco would be able to mobilize the necessary political will in Member States to give effect to it, the delegation of India supported the proposal that the question be referred to the Drafting and Negotiating Group.

New Zealand

The delegate of New Zealand said his country would find it difficult to subscribe to the Declaration as now drafted. They had much sympathy with many of its aspects but could not accept any instrument that attempted to vest control of information and the dissemination of news in the State. He did not believe the necessary amendments could be made by the Commission and he therefore supported the proposal to refer the matter to the Drafting and Negotiating Group.

Togo

The delegate of Togo, a country which was in favour of freedom of information, considered that the information media today were so important and powerful that a code of ethics to guide their behaviour was urgently needed. This was the basic problem and he welcomed Unesco's attempt to deal with it. However, no code of ethics would be truly effective unless it had the support of an overwhelming majority of Member States. As this was clearly not the case with the draft Declaration as it stood, he supported the Brazilian proposal to refer the question to the Drafting and Negotiating Group.

Hungary

The delegate of Hungary said there could be no effective work for peace and international understanding without an internationally-accepted set of principles for guiding the mass media because of the enormous power which the media wielded today. The true purpose of the draft Declaration was to influence the media to work in the common interest of humanity.

His delegation welcomed the attention given in the text to the needs of the

developing countries, particularly Article IV which set out to correct the disequilibrium between the communication networks of the developing and developed
countries.

If we wanted to create a new international economic and social order, the
field of information must not be neglected, since information was power and the
basis of all decision-making. But information could never be separated from
interests of a general or special nature, and there was therefore a potential danger
that wrong information would be circulated which could seriously affect decisions
in the field of peace and international understanding.

There were different ways and philosophies for handling the mass media,
but there was one overriding common interest for all countries, namely our life on
our common globe. We had to reduce inequalities and recognize our most important common values. The State should be responsible for the activities of the mass
media in the international field for the sake of the common interest. Freedom of
expression, opinion and information were real values, but they should not be set
up against the most basic values of humanity: peace, mutual understanding and
growing equality.

In conclusion, the delegate of Hungary supported the Yugoslav proposal
that the Commission set up a drafting group to work on the Declaration.

France

The delegate of France noted that in the past 12 months, as pointed out by the
delegate of Switzerland, a new set of problems had emerged of which they had not
been aware before but which they now recognized as being of importance for the
developing countries. France, for its part, was ready to help in finding solutions to
these problems.

In the meantime, he did not feel that the Commission was the right forum
for ironing out divergencies in regard to a draft Declaration concerning which
even the Director-General had expressed grave doubts. He therefore supported
the proposal to refer it to the Drafting and Negotiating Group.

Japan

The delegate of Japan said that the draft Declaration in its present form was
totally unacceptable to his government, as it contained elements that it would be
impossible to put into effect in Japan. Nor did he believe that the differences of
view could be resolved in the Commission, as they were rooted in completely
different social systems and ideologies. He therefore supported the proposal to
send the draft Declaration to the Drafting and Negotiating Group to discuss not
only the contents but also the procedure for dealing with it again.

Ethiopia

The delegate of Ethiopia observed that the mass media, when properly used,
constituted a powerful instrument for promoting social, economic, political and
educational development. Unesco's efforts to lay down basic minimum standards

for the media, which too often disseminated lies and malicious propaganda as news, therefore deserved the support of all Member States. At present the mass media at international level were the monopoly of a few developed countries and the gap must be narrowed if they were to help the cause of peace and international understanding. He accordingly welcomed the attempt being made to establish an international standard that would help to promote an objective and balanced flow of information.

He also wished to stress that the Third World needed Unesco's assistance in developing their mass media, though each country must also do its utmost to develop the necessary institutions for ensuring a balanced flow of information, both internally and externally.

Ethiopia supported the objectives and spirit of the draft Declaration because it believed that the mass media must be used to combat racism, colonialism, apartheid and other forms of international evils; that they must present balanced and objective information about events in sovereign states; and that States, through their commitment to peaceful co-existence, must play a major rôle in influencing the quality and objectivity of information transmitted through their media.

The Ethiopian delegation also believed that the Commission must reach agreement on the meaning of "free and balanced flow of information". For them "free" meant not to be subjected to cultural, political and economic domination; and there could only be a balanced flow of information when the developing countries were in a position to influence in the international information market on an equal footing with the developed countries.

Finally, they believed that such a declaration must be adopted by consensus and that the present text required further study if it were to reflect the wishes of all concerned.

United Kingdom

The delegate of the United Kingdom said that the draft Declaration had been prepared by a group of governmental experts without the advice of the organizations representing the journalists, broadcasters, newspapers and publishers who knew the technicalities of the business and it was therefore too simplistic in its approach to an exceptionally complex industry. The present debate had made amply clear that a great deal more work had to be done on it before it could be accepted by all the countries present. Although a declaration was not binding on Member States, it laid down guidelines to which Unesco gave moral sanction. Therefore, if the General Conference were to adopt a text to which up to half of the Member States could not subscribe it might give the impression that Unesco's moral sanction was worth nothing.

He therefore felt that it would be better to take time to give Unesco really meaningful moral sanctions against the misuse of the media and to allow the framework of the declaration to emerge, as it must do, from the far-reaching programme of communication development for the coming years which was to be discussed in Commission II. The United Kingdom accordingly supported the proposal to refer the question to the Drafting and Negotiating Group, possibly with the suggestion that the draft Declaration should not be presented again until there had been proper consultations and until a consensus had been reached through discussions among States.

Mongolia

The delegate of Mongolia said his country attached great significance to the draft Declaration. The mass media were playing an increasingly important rôle in the formation of public opinion and it was therefore essential to ensure that they were used in a responsible manner when conveying information on major issues of the day. However, while they favoured adoption of the draft Declaration at the present session of the General Conference, they agreed that further work on it was needed in order that a consensus might be reached.

Australia

The delegate of Australia found the draft Declaration unacceptable for many reasons. Firstly, it had been adopted by a minority at the December 1975 meeting and the basic conflicts still persisted. Secondly, it was penetrated by a conception of the authority of the State and of the rôle of the media that could not be reconciled with the Australian Constitution and way of life. Thirdly, by opening the way to state control of the media and to restrictions on the free flow of information and ideas, it infringed Article I of Unesco's Constitution, Article 19 of the Universal Declaration of Human Rights and Article 19 of the Covenant on Civil and Political Rights. Fourthly, the text was ambiguous, vague and full of inconsistencies. Fifthly, it was premature given the present incomplete state of our knowledge of all the complex problems involved. Finally, it was an inadequate vehicle for meeting the aspirations of the developing countries, which Australia support, to build up their mass media. Much more still had to be done in defining those needs and studying ways and means of meeting them.

The Australian delegation therefore considered that the whole matter, including the question of concrete action to assist the developing countries should be referred to the Drafting and Negotiating Group.

Austria

The delegate of Austria, repeating the statement made in plenary by the Foreign Minister on 1 November, said that his country attached great importance to the right of everyone to freedom of information, which included the freedom to seek, receive and impart information and ideas of all kinds regardless of frontiers. However, the exercise of this right carried with it certain responsibilities. Freedom of information imposed on States the obligation to protect information media from outside interference; but the State had an equal obligation to protect its society against the misuse of this basic right. All measures in this sphere must be taken with great circumspection and in a manner compatible with the essence of freedom of information. A great diversity of sources of information would in itself not guarantee this freedom, if manipulated by public authority. The Austrian delegation could not concur with the view that freedom of information had to remain subject to the concept of state sovereignty. Any consensus reached would have to safeguard the free flow of information and the right to seek and to receive and impart information on the one hand, and the right of States, on the other hand, to impose such restrictions and only such restrictions as were necessary to protect the rights, freedoms and interests of other persons and which are provided for by law. The draft Declaration did not satisfy those requirements, as the prevailing ideas were based on the concept of state-control. This was contrary to fundamental provisions of the Austrian constitution and in contradiction, *inter alia*, with the International Covenant on Civil and Political Rights. The Austrian delegation could not therefore support the draft Declaration in its present form.

Adding to the Foreign Minister's statement the delegate of Austria said his country was aware that information was a prerequisite to advancement in many fields and it believed that more must be done to meet the needs of the developing countries. They also agreed with speakers who had stressed the need for responsibility on the part of the mass media and, in this respect, they welcomed the fact that the journalistic profession was evidently becoming increasingly aware of its ethical obligations, as evidenced by the establishment of press councils in many countries.

As it seemed unlikely that a consensus on the draft Declaration would be reached in the Commission, he supported the proposal to refer it to a more appropriate body.

Egypt

The delegate of Egypt noted that, although there was no consensus on the draft Declaration, there was a consensus that Unesco should prepare an international instrument that set out ethical principles to guide the mass media. These were badly needed, particularly in view of the rapid technological developments and their present unequal distribution. He fully agreed with the delegates of Yugoslavia and India when they stressed the importance for the developing and non-aligned countries of establishing a new international information order as part of the new international economic order.

He believed that the Commission should make every attempt to improve the text of the draft Declaration with a view to obtaining a consensus. He therefore proposed, on behalf of the delegations of Bulgaria and India as well as of Egypt, that the Commission should set up for that purpose a working group consisting of Norway, USSR, USA, China, India, Yugoslavia, Nigeria, Algeria and Colombia.

Guyana

The delegate of Guyana said that freedom of the press had often meant in practice freedom for the developed countries to dominate and exploit other peoples, to project their own culture and life style, to secure their markets and to control resources. He accordingly believed that the creation of a mass media system that would serve the aspirations of the developing countries and permit meaningful exchanges among them should not be left to chance or to foreign profit-oriented interests. Such a system was possible only on the basis of government initiatives, ownership and direction. In Guyana the communication media were regarded as a vital national resource, to be used, like other national resources, to promote the country's interest. As the essential development agency the State had a responsibility for ensuring that the media became an instructive link between government and people and were used to mobilize the citizens for the development of the country.

As concerned the international communication network, the world had often been given a distorted view of life and conditions in the developing countries that served only the interests of the developed countries. It was to correct this imbalance that Guyana had joined with other non-aligned countries in calling for the establishment of a news pool.

The delegation of Guyana supported the idea of a declaration setting forth fundamental principles for the media, but it must be one which could be adopted by general consensus. It therefore favoured any procedure that would help to produce such a document.

Italy

The delegate of Italy said the draft Declaration was unacceptable to his country both in form and substance, as had already been made clear by the delegate of the Netherlands. He also fully agreed with the delegate of Nigeria that it was peripheral to the needs of the developing countries. He did not believe the Commission, or a working party, could improve the text and he therefore supported the proposal to refer it to the Drafting and Negotiating Group.

Federal Republic of Germany

The delegate of the Federal Republic of Germany said the nine E.E.C. countries recognized that there was a disequilibrium in the technological basis for an effective exchange of information between the developed and developing countries and were willing to help remedy the situation.

The Germans had learned from recent bitter experience what it was like when the State controlled the media, determined the information to be disseminated and decided what was true or was not true. The Constitution of the Federal Republic of Germany therefore guaranteed freedom of opinion and information and prohibited all censorship. Nor was the dignity of the State in any way impaired by the fact that the media were free of all State influence and could, and did, criticize the government whenever they wished. On the contrary, in their view the State enhanced its dignity by allowing and promoting the greatest possible measure of individual freedom—a principle which applied to all States and all individuals.

All members of Unesco were bound by the principle of freedom of information embodied in Article I of the Constitution. Moreover, the free flow of information and expression provided the best means for any nation to present itself and its cultural identity to the outside world and for all citizens to learn and form their own opinions. It thus served to promote the dignity of the individual and mutual understanding among nations. The draft Declaration, on the other hand, would encourage abuse of the control it envisaged. The references to the Universal Declaration of Human Rights and the freedoms it embodied were empty words when viewed in the context of the essential part of the text, which was ambiguous and therefore dangerous. As his delegation saw no chance of improving the present text, it believed that another attempt should be made, after due reflexion, to define the rôle of the mass media in the fight against the evils of the world.

Belgium

The delegate of Belgium considered that a resolution or declaration had real moral weight only if it were adopted by an overwhelming majority, in other words by consensus. It was noteworthy in this respect that from the beginning of the Conference on Security and Co-operation in Europe, which had culminated in the Helsinki Final Act, the principle of consensus had been adopted as the golden rule.

There was, however, clearly no consensus for the present draft Declaration, which was unacceptable to the delegation of Belgium. It was not in conformity with the Constitution of Unesco, the Universal Declaration of Human Rights or the International Covenant on Civil and Political Rights, and its adoption would therefore seriously prejudice the Organization's credibility. It did not take into consideration the ideals to which many Member States were firmly attached. The free flow of information, which was the fundamental guarantee for the circulation of ideas and the right to be informed, was essential not only for any serious international co-operation but above all for the establishment of a new international economic order.

He also wished to point out that the Executive Board, at its 99th session, had unanimously expressed its concern at the growing number of resolutions and international instruments adopted by Unesco. He therefore supported the Brazilian proposal to refer the question to the Drafting and Negotiating Group.

Niger

The delegate of Niger considered that the mass media should be mobilized and co-ordinated in order to educate and inform the peoples of the under-informed countries, who urgently needed to revitalize their national cultures and identities, and in order to promote co-operation among peoples.

It was their experience that the news sent out 24 hours a day by the media, particularly the news agencies, was never objective, regardless of the source, and that it seldom respected the sovereignty of States. That was why the non-aligned countries had recommended the creation of national news agencies.

In this respect, unity of views with the recommendations of the New Delhi and Colombo meetings was needed as an aid to the formulation and implementation of national communication policies. The draft Declaration met this legitimate need and he therefore favoured an in-depth examination of it by the Commission.

The head of the delegation of Niger then took the floor to remark that the freedom invoked by so many delegations were purely unilateral. The voice of America, the BBC and so on broadcast 24 hours a day the information they wanted to send in the way they wanted, and the poor countries did not have the means to react against this permanent cultural aggression. Much had been said during the discussion about human rights, but only those who had the means could enjoy them.

Some delegations had also said that their governments could accept no responsibility for their mass media, since that would be an infringement of freedom of the press, information and so on. He found this rather difficult to accept, in view of the well-known close links between powerful private interests and the States in those countries.

Kenya

The delegate of Kenya said that the intergovernmental meeting of experts had done commendable work by bringing out in the draft Declaration many important points that had to be borne in mind if the mass media were to contribute effectively to the strengthening of peace and international understanding. The media were an essential ingredient of the modern world, and their development in the different countries reflected both the traditional, cultural and economic differences and the needs and values of each society.

Kenya was fully in accord with the spirit of the draft Declaration. However, it could not accept Article VIII without modification, as it allowed for the possibility of dissidents from one Member State who had fled to another to launch subversive propaganda against their country of origin. This was in violation of the principle on which Unesco was based—that of contributing to peace and security by promoting collaboration among nations through education, science and culture.

As concerned Article XII, the Kenyan delegation appreciated what it was trying to express but feared that it was inappropriately worded, as it would infringe the constitutions of many states including Kenya, whose constitution guaranteed freedom of information and expression in so far as it was not inconsistent with the interests of the Republic. It should therefore be deleted.

Argentina

The delegate of Argentina considered that the draft Declaration had in large part succeeded in achieving a balance between such opposites as freedom of information and the arbitrariness to which that freedom could lead, between the power of the State and the independence of the news agencies, between objectivity and propaganda. However, that balance was lacking in Articles 3, 8, and 12, which tended to establish the primacy of the State over the independence of the privately-owned media. The draft Declaration was right to warn us against propaganda in favour of racism, colonialism and apartheid but it did not warn us against such other forms of propaganda as the projection of ideologies contrary to a State's constitutional principles, ideologies spread among a people on the pretext of freeing them from supposed economic or social oppression but which were contrary to their way of life. Such penetration of one State by another was more pernicious than the manipulation of news by the international agencies.

Argentina considered that the possible excesses arising from freedom of information and private ownership of the media were preferable to the excesses arising from state domination of the media. The individual could correct the excesses of freedom, but he was always powerless to control the excesses of the State. The faults of freedom were to be preferred to the faults of excessive State power. He therefore considered that the draft Declaration should be sent to the Drafting and Negotiating Group for further study.

Bolivia

The delegate of Bolivia felt that the draft Declaration was very debatable from the point of view of communication policy. At San Jose they had established a general framework for communication policies, but the present draft Declaration strayed from that framework by basing the general on the particular. The use of the mass media to strengthen peace and international understanding and to combat war propaganda, racism and apartheid was only one of their many functions and was peripheral to the overall question of national communication policies.

Bolivia did not consider that the only choices available were either complete government control of the media or total freedom of information. It believed that a midway point could be found by allowing for a certain amount of planning and at the same time establishing principles and rules that would make it possible to counteract the limitations and distortions inherent in both extremes. But this would require taking an overall view of the problem and going from the general to the particular.

Bolivia, therefore, though very much in sympathy with the fundamental spirit of the draft Declaration, considered that it required a great deal more study and reflexion, and supported the proposal to refer it to the Drafting and Negotiating Group.

Iraq

The delegate of Iraq considered that the draft Declaration because of its universal nature and importance, should transcend all ideological and philosophical differences. In this respect he was glad to note that it firmly linked freedom of information with responsibility, since freedom was sometimes abused in the field of information.

Article IV, calling for support for the development of national mass media in the developing countries, was in line with the decisions of the Colombo Conference of Non-Aligned Countries aimed at breaking the present monopoly in the sphere of information. Article II could in no way be regarded as constituting interferences in the domestic affairs of Member States, since it specifically emphasized the need to respect national sovereignty. As for Article XII, it could not be taken as implying government-control of the media, but merely as underlining the moral obligations incumbent upon States. If necessary, however, it could be redrafted to make it clearer and more explicit. Finally, he welcomed the inclusion in paragraph 5 of the Preamble of the reference to resolution 3379 of the United Nations General Assembly concerning zionism.

The delegation of Iraq considered that the Commission should examine the draft Declaration in detail with a view to ironing out points of disagreement and obtaining the broadest possible measure of agreement. It supported the Yugoslav proposal that a small drafting group representing all the different tendencies should be appointed by the Commission for that purpose.

Syria

The delegate of Syria said that the mass media played a fundamental role in forming human behaviour and it was therefore essential to ensure that they were used only for the dissemination of truth. By and large this was the case, but occasionally they were used to distort or conceal the truth, as had happened during the eighteenth session of the General Conference. This was a problem which Unesco must deal with and the draft Declaration, though satisfactory in itself, did not go far enough in that direction. It was a first step which should be followed by others designed to ensure that the media worked in the interests of mankind.

As regards the text itself, he noted that in the first sentence of Article VI the strength of the auxiliary verb varied according to the different language versions ("il convient" in French, "is to be" in English, "must" in Arabic). For the sake of uniformity he proposed that the words "it is necessary" should be used in all language versions.

In paragraph 12 of the Preamble, after the words "considering that freedom of expression, information and opinion" he would suggest adding the words "with a view to spreading the truth and disseminating accurate information", since there could be no real freedom unless it was used to make known the truth. He would also propose adding at the end of Article XII: "Each State should also do its utmost to ensure that the mass media not under its direct jurisdiction operate in accordance with the objectives of the Declaration".

In conclusion, the delegation of Syria, though ready to accept the draft Declaration as it stood, agreed with the Yugoslav proposal that the Commission should set up a small drafting group to try and reconcile the differences of view on it.

Congo

The delegate of the Congo said that what had mainly emerged from the discussions was a sense of the selfishness of the great powers. This had led to a misinterpretation of the draft Declaration, which was intended principally as an appeal to governments to contribute more effectively to the consolidation of world peace.

The Third World, and Africa in particular, objected to the fact that the flow of information was almost entirely one-way, from Europe to Africa. The capitalist countries even had transmitters in Africa which broadcast throughout the day, diverting the attention of people from the problems with which they should be concerned, instilling in them needs and appetites which could not be satisfied within the present economic and social structures, and imposing foreign cultures on them at the expense of the African culture, which was denigrated. Like the press agencies, these transmitters were apt to confuse people. The information given often contradicted the facts and the sensational was stressed at the expense of the objective, which was to the detriment of mutual understanding. As one who had worked in journalism for ten years, she knew that journalists could not always be left to themselves. That was why in press services there were always people responsible for ensuring that standards were respected. In the Congo, which had opted for socialism but where there were also private media, the government issued guidelines to journalists in line with the country's domestic and foreign policy, and all were instructed to present the news objectively, particularly when it concerned foreign countries.

One aspect of the draft Declaration which had evoked concern was the abuse that might be made of it by the universally condemned regimes of Vorster and Ian Smith in order to prevent people from knowing exactly what was going on in Azania, Namibia or Zimbabwe.

Nevertheless the draft Declaration should be taken as a starting point for the major task, in which all must participate, of finalizing a text that would be binding upon States, journalists, radio and television producers, writers and directors and would ensure that their activities contribute to peace, international solidarity and mutual understanding. She proposed that the Commission decide by vote whether to send the draft Declaration to the Drafting and Negotiating Group or to a drafting group of its own appointment.

Ghana

The delegate of Ghana said that a draft Declaration on such an important issue as the establishment of guidelines for the mass media, if it were to be effective, must represent the views of a large majority of Unesco's Member States. To accept it on the technical grounds that it had been agreed by the majority of States present and voting at the Paris meeting would further tarnish Unesco's image.

Since it was clear that there was no general acceptance of the draft Declaration in its present form, his delegation supported the view that it should be sent for further study to the Drafting and Negotiating Group. The latter should be empowered to consult journalists and other media specialists and should also give serious consideration to the withdrawal of Article XII. The draft Declaration should then be resubmitted to the twentieth session of the General Conference.

Guinea

The delegate of Guinea felt that the debate on the draft Declaration in the Commission had been most valuable. It was not surprising that there had been considerable divergencies of view because an important new collective action like this, if it were to be effective, required the marshalling and channelling of all currents of opinion towards the common aim of universal respect for justice, law, human rights and fundamental freedoms for all regardless of race, sex, language or religion. Africa, which was a land of wisdom rather than intellectualism, regarded the antagonistic confrontations as a sign of sincerity and the prelude to agreement.

As concerned the subject of the draft Declaration, it should be recognized that a certain control of information by each State was necessary. In the case of peoples under foreign domination, or suffering from any form of racial segregation or threatened by possible re-colonization, the legitimacy of alerting world opinion with a view to overcoming the forces of evil through armed struggle should also be recognized. He welcomed Article X of the draft Declaration, but was concerned by Article V as it seemed to condemn even wars of liberation waged by oppressed peoples.

He agreed with the proposal that the draft Declaration should be referred to the Drafting and Negotiating Group for further study.

Philippines

The delegate of the Philippines said his country considered freedom of the press and the free flow of information as necessary for individual and national growth. However, when the press abused this freedom by indulging in untruths and defamation the situation had to be reconsidered. Such a review had taken place after the proclamation of the New Society of the Philippines and four years ago the government had begun the reorientation by setting up a Bureau of Standards for the Mass Media. It now treated the communication problem as a problem of the whole society and all the communication systems, government and private, broadcast and print media, had been endowed with their own associations responsible for policing themselves.

At this point in the history of the Philippines the mass media must reinforce the work of government and the idea of nation and nationality. They must inculcate values that helped development, injecting the ethic of work and achievement into the fabric of national life. This suggested that the communications message needed to be achievement-oriented, not power-oriented. Guidelines and standards for the mass media were needed for the development of communication in the present restructuring of Philippines society.

All this demonstrated the need of the developing countries for their own independent systems of communication which would reflect correctly their political, cultural and ideological goals and aspirations, instead of relying on outsiders to interpret them. Above all they must edit themselves as much as they were being edited by others.

The Philippines delegation supported the proposal to submit the draft Declaration to the Drafting and Negotiating Group.

The Chairman of Programme Commission III

The Chairman of Programme Commission III, summing up the discussions, congratulated all those who had contributed to an historical debate that reflected the universal dimensions of Unesco. They had heard the views of those who wanted total freedom of the press, of others who saw that freedom in terms of responsibility, and of others who had pointed out the duties incumbent upon States in regard to the media. They had heard the Third World's appeal regarding the imbalance between the developed and developing countries in the ownership and capacity to use all the means of mass communication, and they had heard the generous offer of a group of countries to provide technical and financial assistance in developing the media of the Third World countries.

A synthesis of all these points of view should take into account the views of all concerned: journalists and other workers in the press, television, radio and other mass media, government officials with responsibility for communication, and the users of the media. For there had been a general consensus that the communication media could become the finest instrument for achieving both Unesco's objective of raising the moral, intellectual, social and economic level of the human race, and that universal unity which was at the very basis of the new international economic order.

At the conclusion of its discussions Programme Commission III decided—by 78 votes in favour, 15 against and 6 abstentions—to send the draft Declaration contained in document 19C/91, together with the draft resolutions presented during the debate (19C/PRG.III/DR.2 and 19C/PRG.III/DR.3) and a summary of the discussions, to the Drafting and Negotiating Group for further study and with a view to seeking a consensus.

APPENDIX 10

Draft Declaration of Fundamental Principles on the Role of the Mass Media in Strengthening Peace and International Understanding and in Combating War Propaganda, Racism and Apartheid

Working document prepared by Gunnar Garbo for the Drafting and Negotiating Group of the 19th session of the General Conference, Nairobi, November 1976
(Unesco document 19C/INF.21, 27 November 1976)

PREAMBLE

The General Conference of the United Nations Educational, Scientific and Cultural Organization meeting in Nairobi at its nineteenth session in 1976,

I

1. *Recalling* that by its Constitution Unesco is charged with contributing to peace and security by promoting collaboration among the nations through education, science and culture, and that, to realize this purpose, the Organization will collaborate in the work of advancing the mutual knowledge and understanding of peoples through all means of mass communication and to that end recommend such international agreements as may be necessary to promote the freer and wider exchange of information by word and image on both a multilateral and bilateral basis, the sovereignty of States being fully respected,

2. *Recalling* the purposes and principles of the United Nations, as specified in the Charter, as well as other documents of the Organization,

3. *Recalling* the Universal Declaration of Human Rights, adopted by the General Assembly of the United Nations in 1948, and the International Covenant on Civil and Political Rights, adopted by the General Assembly of the United Nations in 1966,

4. *Recalling* resolution 110 (II) of the General Assembly of the United Nations adopted in 1947 condemning all forms of propaganda which are designed or likely to provoke or encourage any threat to the peace, breach of the peace, or act of aggression and the International Convention on the Suppression and Punishment of the Crime of Apartheid adopted by the General Assembly of the United Nations in 1973.

5. *Recalling* resolution 9.12 adopted by the General Conference at its fifteenth session reiterating Unesco's objective to help to eradicate colonialism and racialism,

6. *Taking account* of Article 4 of the International Convention on the Elimination of all Forms of Racial Discrimination, whereby States Parties to the Convention condemn all propaganda and all organizations which are based on ideas or theories of superiority of one race or group of persons of one colour or ethnic origin,

341

or which attempt to justify or promote racial hatred and discrimination to eradicate all incitement to, or acts of, such discrimination,

7. *Bearing in mind* the Declaration of the Principles of International Cultural Co-operation, adopted by the General Conference of Unesco at its fourteenth session,

8. *Recalling* the Declaration and the Programme of Action on the Establishment of a New International Economic Order (resolutions 3201 (S-VI) and 3202 (S-VI) of the General Assembly), and the Charter of Economic Rights and Duties of States (resolution 3281 (XXIX) of the General Assembly), as regards a new international order, through which it is hoped to create a new system of international economic relations based upon equity, sovereign equality, common interest and co-operation among all States, which may help to strengthen decisively peace and international understanding,

II

9. *Considering* that it is the task of Member States to secure the development of media structures which correspond to certain basic functions in every society, such as promotion of active participation in the decision-making process, preserving of national cultural identity, dissemination of relevant two-way information and scrutiny of economic and political power,

10. *Being aware* of the fact that the means of communicating information are today concentrated in a few countries and that the great majority of countries are reduced to passive recipients of information which is disseminated from a few centres,

11. *Considering* that freedom of information, in a situation where many nations are deprived of means of communication, may perpetuate relations of domination and dependence, unless decisive steps are taken to create a more equal access to and participation in the process of communication,

12. *Finding* therefore that, just as States internally should promote the right of weaker social groups to communicate, the international community and its institutions should make it an important aim to achieve a more just and effective sharing of information on the international level,

["*Stressing* the importance of decisions of the Fifth Conference of Heads of State and Government of Non-Aligned Countries (Colombo, 1976), concerning the liquidation of the colonial heritage in the field of mass media and 'establishing a balanced and equitable distribution of news and information to the peoples of the world', and also the importance of the decisions and recommendations of the meetings of non-aligned countries held in Tunis, New Delhi and San José."] (Byelorussian Amendment).

III

13. *Noting with satisfaction* the positive results achieved in the area of international détente and, in particular, the contributions to this process made by the Conference on Security and Co-operation in Europe,

14. *Considering* that the mass media can effectively help in combating incitement to aggressive wars or any use or threat of force incompatible with the aims of the United Nations, in *strengthening* peace and mutual understanding between peoples and in contributing to international détente and the spiritual enrichment of the human personality without distinction as to race, sex, language or religion,

15. *Considering* further *the desirability* to preserve and protect the cultures of countries and peoples and the difference existing among those cultures as part of the common heritage of mankind,

16. *Noting* the rapid development of the mass media which constitutes one of the key elements in modern scientific and technological progress, and play an ever-increasing rôle in the intellectual life of society and the shaping of public opinion,

17. *Considering* that freedom of expression, information and opinion are fundamental human rights and that the free interchange of information and opinions, both in the national and in the international spheres, is essential to the cause of peace and achievement of political, social, cultural and economic progress,

18. *Considering* also that the exercise of the right to freedom of information entails special responsibilities and duties for persons who disseminate information to strive in good faith to ensure the fullness and accuracy of the facts reported and to respect the rights and the dignity of nations, and of groups and individuals without distinction as to race, sex, nationality or creed (18 C/35),

19. *Proclaims* on this day of 1976 this Declaration on Fundamental Principles Governing the *Rôle* of the Mass Media in Strengthening Peace and International Understanding and in Combating War Propaganda, Racism and Apartheid,

Article I

1. The mass media in disseminating information and opinion *should* do so in a manner which is compatible with the mutual respect of the rights and dignity of States and peoples, and in accord with the principles set out in the Universal Declaration of Human Rights.

2. Subject to adequate protection for the principles of freedom of the press, *States should make it their aim* to encourage mass media to act in conformity with the principles and standards of the Charter of the United Nations and the Universal Declaration of Human Rights so as to strengthen peace and international understanding and combat war propaganda, racism and apartheid.

(18 C/35)

Article II

1. *To meet the basic communication needs of individuals and of groups and to bridge the information gap between different parts of the world, concerted efforts should be made by the international community to contribute to the creation of adequate mass media structures, especially in the developing countries.*

2. Special support should be given, on the basis of appropriate agreements, to the establishment and furthering of national mass media in the developing countries, to the training of their personnel *and to the promotion of their mutual co-*

operation on a bilateral or a multilateral basis, so as to correct the existing disequilibrium in the circulation of information from these countries and to make a
balanced exchange of information a reality for the whole of the international
community.

(Indian Amendment)

3. *Policies should be formulated for preferential treatment of the poorer nations in the field
of information and communication and for implementations of surveys, research, planning
and development of national and international infrastructures aimed at meeting basic
communication needs in different societies,*

Article III

1. States should encourage and develop both multilateral and bilateral exchanges concerning the rôle of mass media in the fields of culture, science and
education on the basis of equality of rights, mutual advantage and noninter-
ference in each other's affairs, in accordance with the Constitution and other laws
and regulations in force in each country, and taking into account their customs
and traditions, with the aim of developing feelings of friendship and mutual
respect among nations and with a view to the spiritual enhancement of man,
without regard for race, sex, language or religion.

2. In order to enable the public to ascertain facts and appraise events, *it is necessary to assure the right to seek, receive and transmit information to afford the widest possible
facilities for this,* to encourage co-operation with other countries in the field of
communication and to improve the conditions in which journalists of one State
exercise their profession in another State, on the basis of reciprocity, bearing in
mind the principles set forth in this Declaration.

(18 C/35 Art. II)

Article IV

Since the international exchange of information is fundamental to the strengthening of peace and international understanding, States and information media
have the right to diffuse reports of national events beyond their borders. Exchange between countries of information concerning the aims, aspirations, needs
and culture of each nation promotes the broadening of international co-
operation and understanding, the reduction of tension in international relations
and the settlement of disputes by peaceful means.

(18 C/35)

Article V

1. The mass media should promote greater knowledge on the part of the peoples of the world of the evils attendant upon war, violence, apartheid and other
forms of national, racial or religious hatred.

2. The dissemination of reports conducive to these evils should be avoided.

(18 C/35 Art. IV)

Article VI

Any incitement to racial discrimination which may lead to threats or acts of violence or encouragement of such acts against any group of persons because of their race, colour, religion or ethnic origin should be shunned. For this purpose legislative action might be envisaged consistent with the respective Constitutional systems of States and with relevant international instruments and agreements.

(Jordanian amendment)

Article VII

Similarly, as a means of contributing effectively to the strengthening of peace and international understanding, the mass media should make widely known among the peoples of the world the objectives of equity, sovereign equality, interdependence, common interest and co-operation among all States, on which, in accordance with the resolutions adopted by the United Nations General Assembly, the foundations of a new international economic order are based.

Article VIII

The voices of those struggling against apartheid and other forms of racial discrimination, colonialism, neo-colonialism and foreign occupation by aggression, *or who are* unable to be heard within their own territory *because of repression brought about by political, racial or religious persecution*, should be given expression through the mass media of other countries with due respect for the sovereignty of the host countries.

(French amendment to 18 C/35 paragraph 5)
("... their legal system and the relevant domestic laws and regulations."
Brazilian amendment 19 C/PRG.III/DR.2))

Article IX

The mass media should have a special concern for youth and for the dissemination of their views; it is consonant with Article 26 of the Universal Declaration of Human Rights for the media to promote, particularly among youth, the full development of the human personality, the strengthening of respect for human rights and fundamental freedoms and a spirit of understanding, tolerance and friendship among all nations, racial or religious groups.

(18 C/35 Art. VI as amended by the United States of America)

Article X

The creation and strengthening of professional organizations in the field of the mass media can help to ensure that the media contribute effectively to the achievement of the objectives of this Declaration. In particular, these organizations can, on a national, regional and inter-

national level, define and promote standards of professional ethics, *improve the professional training of media personnel* and support their members in the responsible exercise of their profession.

(18 C/35 Art. IX)

Article XI

In order to encourage the development of responsible national mass media and foster their technological independence, States should promote, by international agreements and national legislation, the economic and social independence of information personnel, and help ensure that the media have the technical facilities required to carry out their rôle.

(18 C/35 Art. VIII)

Article XII

The principles of this Declaration on Fundamental Principles Governing the Rôle of the Mass Media in Strengthening Peace and International Understanding and in Combating War Propaganda, Racism and Apartheid shall be applied with due regard for human and fundamental freedom.

APPENDIX 11

Draft Declaration on Fundamental Principles Governing the Use of the Mass Media in Strengthening Peace and International Understanding and in Combating War Propaganda, Racism and Apartheid

Proposal for a revised text of the Declaration with an "Aide Memoire" prepared by a group of consultants in July-September 1977
(Unofficial Unesco document, September 1977)

PREAMBLE

1. *Recalling* that the States parties to the Constitution of Unesco, believing in the unrestricted pursuit of objective truth and in the free exchange of ideas and knowledge, are agreed and determined to develop and to increase the means of communication between their peoples and to employ these means for the purposes of mutual understanding and a truer and more perfect knowledge of each other's lives; and further recalling that by its Constitution Unesco is charged with contributing to peace and security, and that to realize this purpose the Organization will promote the free flow of ideas by word and image,

2. *Recalling* the purposes and principles of the United Nations, as specified in the Charter,

3. *Recalling* the Universal Declaration of Human Rights, adopted by the General Assembly of the United Nations in 1948, and the International Covenant on Civil and Political Rights, adopted by the general Assembly of the United Nations in 1966,

4. *Recalling* the Convention concerning the Use of Broadcasting in the Cause of Peace, adopted by the League of Nations in 1936 and still in force,

5. *Taking account* of Article 4 of the International Convention on the Elimination of all Forms of Racial Discrimination, adopted by the General Assembly of the United Nations in 1965, whereby States Parties to the Convention condemn all propaganda and all organizations which are based on ideas or theories of superiority of one race or group of persons of one colour or ethnic origin, or which attempt to justify or promote racial hatred and discrimination in any form and undertake to adopt immediate and positive measures designed to eradicate all incitement to, or acts of, such discrimination,

6. *Recalling* the International Convention on the Suppression and Punishment of Apartheid, adopted by the General Assembly of the United Nations in 1973.

7. *Recalling* the Declaration and the Programme of Action on the Establishment of a New International Economic Order and the Charter of Economic Rights and Duties of States, adopted by the General Assembly of the United Nations in 1974, as regards a new international economic order through which it is hoped to create a new system of international economic relations which may help to strengthen decisively peace and international understanding,

8. *Recalling* the Declaration of the Principles of International Cultural Cooperation, adopted by the General Conference of Unesco in 1966,

9. *Recalling* resolution 110 (II) of the General Assembly of the United Nations adopted in 1947, condemning all forms of propaganda which are designed or likely to provoke or encourage any threat to the peace, breach of the peace, or act of aggression, and requesting Member States to promote by all means of publicity and propaganda available to them, friendly relations among nations based upon the purposes and principles of the Charter,

10. *Recalling* the resolutions of the General Assembly of the United Nations on the elimination of all forms of racialism and racial discrimination,

11. *Recalling* resolution 9.12 adopted by the General Conference of Unesco in 1968, reiterating the Organization's objective to help to eradicate colonialism and racialism,

12. *Recalling* resolution 4.301 adopted by the General Conference of Unesco in 1970, deeming that the mass media should play an important part in furthering international understanding and co-operation in the interest of peace and human welfare, and inviting all Member States to take the necessary steps, including legislative measures, to encourage the use of the mass media against propaganda on behalf of war, racialism and hatred among nations,

13. *Noting* the results achieved in international détente and, in particular, the contribution to this process made by the Conference on Security and Co-operation in Europe,

14. *Proclaims* on this day of . . . this Declaration on Fundamental Principles Governing the Use of the Mass Media in Strengthening Peace and International Understanding and in Combating War Propaganda, Racism and Apartheid.

Article I

1. It being recognized that freedom of expression, information and opinions are fundamental human rights, peace and international understanding demand that information freely interchanged be accurate, comprehensive and objective.

2. The exercise of freedom of information carries with it the duty and the responsibility to ensure the flow of true and honest information to all peoples and, in order to enable the people to ascertain facts and appraise events objectively, public access to sources of information and participation in its wider dissemination.

Article II

1. The mass media have an important role in contributing to the established principles guiding relations between States, irrespective of their political, economic or social systems, which provide for the promotion of a climate of confidence and respect among peoples, consonant with their duty to refrain from propaganda for wars of aggression or for any threat or use of force inconsistent with the purposes of the United Nations.

2. A special responsibility therefore rests upon the mass media for supporting and reinforcing peace and international understanding and for striving to ensure

the fullness and accuracy of the facts reported, while at the same time respecting the rights and the dignity of nations and of groups and individuals without distinction as to race, sex, language, nationality, religion or philosophical conviction.

Article III

1. It is the responsibility of the mass media to avoid any justification, incitement or encouragement of war, violence, apartheid and other forms of national, racial or religious hatred or discrimination, and to condemn all forms of propaganda for these evils.

2. Legislative action might be envisaged, consistent with the respective Constitutional systems of States and with relevant international instruments and agreements, in order to ensure that this responsibility is carried out.

Article IV

It is incumbent upon all States, subject to adequate Constitutional protection of the principle of freedom of information, to encourage the mass media under their jurisdiction to act in conformity with the principles of this Declaration, so as to strengthen peace and international understanding and combat war propaganda, racism and apartheid, in a spirit of mutual respect for the rights and dignity of other States, peoples and individuals.

Article V

As a means of contributing effectively to the strengthening of peace and international understanding, the mass media need to make widely known among the peoples of the world the principles and objectives of equity, sovereign equality, interdependence, common interest and co-operation among all States, which, in accordance with the resolutions adopted by the United Nations General Assembly, constitute the basis of a new international economic order.

Article VI

1. Since the international exchange of information is fundamental to the strengthening of peace and international understanding, it is essential to correct the existing imbalance in the flow of information to, from and between the developing countries and to make a balanced exchange of information a reality for the whole of the international community. For this purpose, special support is demanded for the establishment and furthering of national mass media in the developing countries and for the promotion of mutual cooperation between them.

2. Among all countries, it is similarly essential to promote and develop both bilateral and multilateral exchanges by the mass media in the fields of culture, science and education on the basis of equality of rights, mutual advantage and non-interference in each other's affairs. These exchanges should take into account the right of countries and peoples to protect and preserve their cultures as

well as the differences existing among those cultures as part of the common heritage of mankind.

Article VII

The international nature of the activities of news and press agencies places upon them a special responsibility to act in the spirit of this Declaration.

Article VIII

The voices of those struggling against apartheid and other forms of racial discrimination, colonialism, neo-colonialism and foreign occupation by aggression, and unable to be heard within their own territory, should be given expression through the mass media of other countries with due respect for the sovereignty of the host countries, their legal system and the relevant domestic laws and regulations.

Article IX

It is specially important to ensure that the mass media contribute to the education of young people in conformity with the Declaration on the Promotion among Youth of the Ideals of Peace, Mutual Respect and Understanding between Peoples, it being incumbent upon States to encourage among young people a spirit of peace, justice, freedom, mutual respect and understanding.

Article X

1. Journalists and other creative media practitioners as well as their professional organizations have a particular social responsibility. Emphasis should therefore be placed, in professional codes of conduct and training on the due respect for the principles of this Declaration. In assuming such a responsibility, all media practitioners and their professional organizations can help ensure that the mass media themselves observe the aforesaid principles.
2. In this context, it is incumbent upon States to see to it that journalists and other creative media practitioners, working in their own countries or abroad, are given a status which protects them from any reprisals and provides them the best possible conditions for the exercise of their profession.

Article XI

States, institutions or groups which consider that the mass media, by publication of reports which they deem erroneous, have seriously impaired their action with a view to the strengthening of peace and international understanding, and their efforts to combat war propaganda, racism and apartheid, should be given the opportunity to correct such reports, or make known their version thereof, through the mass media.

AIDE MEMOIRE

Background

The General Conference of Unesco adopted at its sixteenth session (1970) resolution 4.301, "deeming that information media should play an important part in furthering international understanding and co-operation in the interests of peace and human welfare", it affirmed "the inadmissibility of using information media for propaganda on behalf of war, racialism and hatred among nations" and invited "all States to take the necessary steps, including legislative measures, to encourage the use of information media against propaganda on behalf of war, racialism and hatred among nations, and to provide Unesco with information on the subject."

At its seventeenth session (1972), the General Conference adopted resolution 4.113 which called for the preparation of a "draft declaration concerning the fundamental principles governing the use of the mass media with a view to strengthening peace and international understanding and combating war propaganda, racialism and apartheid".

In conformity with this resolution, a meeting of experts (category VI) was convened at Unesco House in March 1974 to advise the Director-General on a text for submission to the eighteenth session of the General Conference. This meeting had before it, as a basis for discussion, an initial text of a draft declaration established for the Secretariat by a consultant, Prof. Hilding Eek, from Sweden (document COM-74/CONF.616/3). In the course of a detailed examination of this draft, the meeting made a considerable number of suggestions which were embodied in a report to the Director-General.

In the light of the suggestions made by the experts, a second text of a draft declaration was prepared. This text was submitted to the General Conference at its eighteenth session (document 18C/35). The General Conference examined this text and various amendments to it proposed by Member States (18C/COM/Drs 1 to 11). It decided that the question needed a study in depth and consequently adopted resolution 18C/4.111 which called for the convening of an intergovernmental meeting of experts (category II) to prepare a revised draft.

In pursuance of this resolution, the intergovernmental meeting was convened and it took place at Unesco House in December 1975. The meeting had before it notably the draft declaration which was contained in doc. 18C/35 and the proposed amendments to that draft which appeared in 18C/COM/DRs 1 to 11, as well as a number of proposed amendments submitted in the course of its proceedings (COM-75/CONF.201/DRs 1 to 26). The meeting prepared a new draft for submission to the General Conference at its nineteenth session.

After its consideration of this last draft (document 19C/91), the General Conference again decided to call for the preparation of a revised text. It adopted resolution 19C/4.143 which "invites the Director-General to hold further broad consultations with experts with a view to preparing a final Draft Declaration. . .which could meet with the largest possible measure of agreement, as well as to proposing any other action which may be called for in the light of these consultations". This resolution also calls for the submission of such a draft and any other proposal to Member States at the end of 1977 or the beginning of 1978. In the resolution, the General Conference finally decided to include the question in the agenda of its twentieth session.

The present new draft has been prepared by the Director-General with a view to meeting the mandate given by the General Conference in the above-mentioned resolution and thus to serve as a revised text for a final Draft Declaration to be considered by the twentieth General Conference.

General Characteristics of the new draft

The *overall substance* of the present new Draft Declaration (Preamble and Articles taken together) is derived from the three earlier draft texts. This is still a draft declaration primarily concerning the use of the mass media in *strengthening peace* and *international understanding* and in *combating war propaganda, racism and apartheid,* as was indeed supposed by the resolution of the nineteenth General Conference. Other pertinent aspects related to Unesco's role in the field of the mass media—in particular with regards to the establishment of a New International Information Order—have not been given more emphasis in the new draft than they already had in the previous draft (19 C/91).

It is considered that the substance of the present Draft Declaration still today stands on its own merit, despite the rapid developments which have occurred during the last few years in the area of national and international communication policies. A declaration to cover properly also the latter aspects would obviously be at this stage premature. On the other hand, the Director-General has launched a major effort to study all the fundamental problems related to Unesco's role in the field of mass communication and is thereby preparing with the aid of a special committee comprehensive material for a separate consideration of the General Conference at a later stage. To emphasize this effort it is proposed that a *separate resolution* will be passed in the twentieth session of the General Conference, in addition to the adoption of the present Draft Declaration, outlining the ongoing efforts of Unesco to contribute to the establishment of a New International Information Order (first draft of this resolution enclosed).

Although the present draft largely coincides with the earlier texts (particularly the previous draft 19C/91), the elements of the common substance have been to a considerable extent *reorganized* and the text has been notably *reformulated.* Moreover, the following essential elements which were included in the previous draft are *missing from the new draft:*

(a) an explicit reference to the controversial resolution 3379 of the United Nations General Assembly, included in the preambular paragraph 5 of the text 19C/91;

(b) an ambiguous formulation concerning the state responsibility for the activities of the mass media, contained by Article XII of the text 19C/91, which has given rise to a considerable controversy around this Draft Declaration;

(c) a tendency to formulate the principles in terms of "use of the mass media" or other similarly "strong" way open to interpretations that the Draft

Declaration attempts to impose direct State directions upon the mass media.

On the other hand, the following essential elements, not appearing in the two preceding drafts, have been *added to the new draft*:

(a) the qualifiers "accurate", "comprehensive", "objective", "true" and "honest" to characterize the information to be "freely interchanged" or "flown", in Article I of the new draft;

(b) the aspect of public access and participation as another relevant factor to the principle of freedom of information, singled out in Article I of the new draft;

(c) reference in the Preamble (paragraph 12 of the new draft) to the resolution 4.301 of the sixteenth session of the General Conference (1970), constituting a background for the process of drafting this Declaration;

(d) reference in the Preamble (paragraph 4 of the new draft) to the Convention concerning the Use of Broadcasting in the Cause of Peace, which is the only existing convention directly relevant in its entirety to the present Draft Declaration.

Generally speaking, the new draft text has been designed to retain the objective spelled out in the mandate given by the General Conference (as appearing in the title of the Draft Declaration) while at the same time removing from the text those aspects which have turned into major political obstacles. In particular, the responsibility of States for the activities of the mass media under their jurisdiction (Article XII in the previous draft) has been formulated in a clearcut way leaving no room for ambiguity (Article IV in the new draft). Throughout the new draft, as compared with the previous one, there is a tendency to avoid an imposition of direct State directives to the mass media and instead to emphasize, in conformity with the different Constitutional systems of States, the professional, moral and social responsibility of the mass media, particularly with a view to fullness and accuracy or objectivity of the information transmitted. Finally the new draft attempts to bring the scattered elements of the previous drafts into a more systematic and logical order.

Detailed explanatory notes on the new draft

Preamble

Paragraph 1 Reference to Unesco's Constitution reproduces part of the corresponding paragraph in the three earlier drafts (based on Article I of the Constitution) but the bulk of the present text has been taken from another passage of the Constitution (its Preambular Declaration, last paragraph). The latter, appearing as the first part of the new paragraph 1, includes some vital elements directly relevant to the present Draft Declaration: firstly it clearly spells out Unesco's commitment (i) to the pursuit of *objective truth*, (ii) to the *free exchange* of ideas and knowledge, (iii) to the purposes of *mutual understanding between peoples* and a *truer and more perfect knowledge of each other's lives*, as well as (iv) to the *development of the mass media; secondly this passage leaves no doubt that in this context it is perfectly in conformity with the Unesco Constitution for the States to employ the mass media*, thus providing a justification to retain the word "use" in the title of the Draft Declaration.

The extract from Article I of the Constitution is limited in the present draft to stating the overall purpose of the Organization, along with the particular means of realizing this purpose which reads in the Constitution "the free flow of ideas by word and image" (reference to international agreements is irrelevant in connection with a Declaration, and reference to the mutual knowledge and understanding of peoples is already included in the preceding text). Thus the new formulation of this particular passage is considerably abbreviated from the earlier draft texts, and as compared particularly with the preceding draft (19 C/91) it also keeps with the original wording of the Constitution and lacks reference to the respect of State sovereignty (based on paragraph 3 of Article I of the Constitution but formulated in that draft without original wording).

Paragraph 2 Reference to the purposes and principles of the United Nations reproduces the formulation of the two preceding drafts deleting however reference to "other documents of the Organization" which was included in the draft 19 C/91.

Paragraph 3 Reference to the Universal Declaration of Human Rights and the International Covenant of Civil and Political Rights is identical with the draft 19 C/91.

Paragraph 4 Introduces new reference to the Convention concerning the Use of Broadcasting in the Cause of Peace, missing from the earlier drafts but considered highly relevant to the present Draft Declaration. This Convention was adopted by the League of Nations on 23 September 1936, it entered into force on 2 April 1938, and is now deposited with the United Nations (having over 20 ratifications).

Paragraph 5 Reproduces the corresponding text of all earlier drafts.

Paragraph 6 Reproduces the reference included in the two preceding drafts.

Paragraph 7 Reproduces, with minor editing, the corresponding text of third draft 19 C/91.

Paragraph 8 Reproduces the reference included in all earlier drafts, except for "recalling" instead of "bearing in mind".

Paragraph 9 Reproduces the reference included in all earlier drafts but adds to it an extended quotation of the same resolution. This resolution (adopted unanimously) is both highly relevant to the present Draft Declaration and enjoys a special status since reference to it has been made ("taking account of") in the preamble of the Outer Space Treaty adopted (unanimously) by the General Assembly of the United Nations in 1966 (in force since 1967).

Paragraph 10 Reproduces the reference included in the draft 19 C/91 without however singling out particular resolutions by numbers.

Paragraph 11 Reproduces the reference included in all earlier drafts.

Paragraph 12 Introduces new reference to the resolution of the General Conference of Unesco which as such is highly relevant to the present Draft Declaration and may also be seen to constitute the first step in the process of focusing Unesco's commitment to the preparation of the present Draft Declaration.

Paragraph 13 Reproduces, with minor editing, the reference included in the draft 19 C/91.

Paragraph 14 Reproduces the title of the Draft Declaration as appeared in the draft 19 C/91.

Articles:

Article 1 The elements contained in this Article are for the most part to be found in the first draft text prepared by Prof. Eek, in his Preambular paragraphs 3 and 4, of which the former was partly reproduced in the draft 19 C/91 as Preambular paragraph 12. This formulation originates verbatim from the texts prepared for the Draft Convention on Freedom of Information under the auspices of the United Nations. The first version of the relevant text was produced by the United Nations Conference on Freedom of Information in 1948, adopting a Draft Convention (based on a proposal by the Delegation of the United Kingdom) which in its Preamble considered that "the free interchange of information and opinions, both in the national and in the international sphere, is a fundamental human right and essential to the cause of peace ... ". Later on the Third Committee of the General Assembly, at its fourteenth session in 1959, adopted the final wording for the Preamble to the Draft Convention on Freedom of Information, considering that "freedom of expression, information and opinions are fundamental human rights" and that "the free interchange of accurate, objective and comprehensive information and of opinions, both in the national and in the international spheres, is essential to the causes of democracy and peace and for the achievement of political, social, cultural and economic progress". The qualifiers *accurate, objective* and *comprehensive* were added to the earlier draft text by the Third Committee following the proposal submitted by India, Liberia, Mexico, Philippines, Saudi Arabia, United Arab Republic and Venezuela.

The first paragraph of the present Article has been based on these elements without including the aspects of democracy and socio-cultural-economic progress but with adding the aspect of international understanding to accompany that of peace. The term *comprehensive* means in this context that the (accurate) information does not neglect such aspects which are essential to derive at an extensive and in-depth understanding of the events or states of affairs referred to in the information. The term *objective* is used here in a general philosophical sense, as in the Constitution, whereby it is supposed to cover both the aspect of accuracy and of comprehensiveness.

The second paragraph of Article I deals with the principles of freedom of information at the same *general level* as the first paragraph does, without particularly referring to the mass media. This paragraph stresses the duties and responsibilities which according to a widely accepted notion are always accompanying the exercise of the right to freedom of information (see e.g. the above mentioned Draft Convention and the International Covenant on Civil and Political Rights). The principle of responsibility as a concomitant to the principle of right to freedom of information is in the present text defined in most general terms by referring to the aspect of truthfulness and honesty of information, which already in the first paragraph has been singled out to be of vital importance in this context. Thus the notion of duties and responsibilities does not in the present text get extended to the kind of detailed aspects that are customary in this connection (the beforementioned Draft Convention as adopted by the United Nations Conference on Freedom of Information contained altogether ten such provisions).

On the other hand, the present text does extend the notion of duties and responsibilities to cover the aspect of *public access and participation* in the informational processes (sources and dissemination) which is a new element in this draft as compared with earlier relevant documents. The formulation of this paragraph combines the demand for truthfulness with that of public access not only by speaking of true and honest information *to all peoples* but also by referring to the need to *enable the people to ascertain facts and appraise events objectively,* which latter wording is taken from the draft 19 C/91 (Article II, beginning of paragraph 2). Also the phrase *wider dissemination* appears in the draft 19 c/91 (Article I, beginning of paragraph 1) although there in a context which does not explicitly refer to public access and participation.

Article II The first paragraph is based on elements contained for the most part in the Preambular paragraph 11 of the draft 19 C/91. However, the new text has been formulated so that it only refers to the *important role of the mass media,* i.e. their *relevance,* with a view to creating a climate of confidence and respect among nations, etc. Also the present formulation does not directly connect the mass media with the provision of such a climate but just relates them to *the established principles guiding relations between States* (which for their part include the provision for the promotion of a climate, etc.), these principles being those defined by the United Nations Charter and other relevant documents such as the Final Act of the Conference on Security and Co-operation in Europe. The wording of the latter part of the present paragraph ("promotion of a climate. . .") has been taken from this Final Act (from the passage listing matters related to giving effect to the principles guiding relations between States).

The second paragraph introduces the notion of *responsibility of the mass media* in the present context. The formulation is based on elements contained in the Preambular paragraphs 13 and 14 of the draft 19 C/91, without however reproducing reference to "persons and institutions who disseminate information as well as on their professional organizations."

Article III The first paragraph is based on Article V of the draft 19 C/91 with the following additional elements: (i) *incitement* has been added to complement justification and encouragement, (ii) *discrimination* has been added to complement hatred, and (iii) *condemnation of propaganda* for all of the evils listed has been added at the end of the sentence. Aspects (i) and (ii) are derived from the first sentence of Article VI of the draft 19 C/91, in which however they were limited to racial discrimination only. Aspect (iii) states in other terms, consistent with the wording of the draft 18 C/35 and Article 4 of the International Convention on the Elimination of all Forms of Racial Discrimination (referred to in the Preambular paragraph 5), what in all earlier drafts has been the spirit of this Article.

The second paragraph reproduces the second sentence of Article VI of the draft 19 C/91 by removing reference to the preceding paragraph from the beginning of the sentence ("For this purpose") at the end of the sentence ("in order to ensure. . ."). Here again the earlier drafts have only referred to racial discrimination while in the present text this paragraph relates to all forms of evils listed in the first paragraph. This does not however mean an essential deviation from the earlier drafts which have been on this point quite determined in their spirit of condemnation (using even the wording "is to be shunned"). It is also to be noted that such an instrument as the American Convention on Human Rights (which the United States is currently in the process of joining) has been formulated on this point in a 'strong' manner: "Any propaganda for war and any advocacy of national, racial, or religious hatred that constitute incitements to lawless violence . . . shall be considered as offences punishable by law." (Article 13, paragraph 5).

Consequently, the present draft is keeping with the spirit of the corresponding Articles of the previous drafts but is introducing a more compact formulation, whereby a separate Article concerning racial discrimination (VI of the draft 19 C/91) becomes obsolete.

Article IV The elements contained or implied in this Article have been pooled together from Articles I and XII of the draft 19 C/91 and the corresponding Articles of the two other earlier drafts. The Article has been designed to bring clarity to the controversial issue of State responsibility over the mass media by avoiding an elaboration of this issue altogether. The Article simply refers to the overall obligation of States to encourage all mass media—without violating the status of the media as determined by respective Constitutional systems—to act in conformity with the principles of this Declaration.

The Article is based on Article I of the draft 19 C/91 and in fact is reproducing most of its text, with the exception of reference to the "freer and wider dissemination of information through the mass media" in its first paragraph and reference to the "mass media, both public and private, and those responsible for dissemination of information, in particular the international news agencies" in its second paragraph. Also Article I of the draft 18 C/35 is very close to the wording of the present Article. It should be noted that the present Article is only stating the obvious: it just confirms and endorses what is universally understood and legally instituted to be the responsibility relationship between States and the mass media.

Article V This Article is reproducing, with minor editing, Article VII of the draft 19 C/91.

Article VI The first paragraph is reproducing Article IV of the draft 19 C/91 by omitting special reference to the training of media personnel and adding in its reformulation the aspect of mutual cooperation between the developing countries.

The second paragraph of this Article is reproducing the text of the first part of Article II (paragraph 1) and the whole of Preambular paragraph 15 of the draft 19 C/91.

Article VII This Article has its basis in the reference to international news agencies included in Article I (paragraph 2) of the draft 19 C/91. Although the agencies were not in that draft singled out in a separate Article, reference to them was made in a "stronger" way than in the present text which is only repeating that the same responsibility that in the preceding Articles has been stated in terms of the mass media in general applies also in a special manner to these particular forms of the media.

Article VIII This Article reproduces the same Article of the draft 19 C/91 with the amendment proposed in Nairobi by the delegation of Brazil, adding at the end of the Article a provision to the legal systems and the relevant domestic laws and regulations.

Article IX This article reproduces the same Article of the draft 19 C/91, replacing however the phrase "mass media *are used for*" by the formulation "mass media *contribute to.*"

Article X The first paragraph is based on elements contained in Article XI and Preambular paragraph 14 of the draft 19 C/91, with the additional aspect of professional training (contained in Article IV of that draft and not reproduced elsewhere in the present text). While the earlier drafts are speaking in general terms about professionals and their organizations in the field of mass communication, the present draft is explicitly focusing on journalists and other creative media practitioners as well as their professional organizations, considered to be most relevant in the present context. The third sentence of this paragraph is introducing an aspect, appearing in the first two drafts but not clear in the draft 19 C/91, whereby it is because of their protential contribution to the performance of the mass media that a particular emphasis on the professionals and their organizations is justified in the present context.

The second paragraph of this Article is reproducing the idea contained in the second paragraph of Article II (latter part of the sentence) of the draft 19 C/91. However, the present formulation is 'stronger' in terms of calling upon States to guarantee adequate professional working conditions for media practitioners.

Article XI This Article is reproducing Article X of the draft 19 C/91, with minor clarifying reformulations attempting to replace a possible impression of a legal stipulation by that of a moral and professional appeal.

In this connection it should be noted that there is a legally valid Convention on the International Right of Correction, adopted by the General Assembly of the United Nations in 1952 and entered into force in 1962. Although it has been ratified so far by only about ten countries, this Convention constitutes a significant step in reaching for international agreements concerning the topic of the present Article.

The succession of the Articles in the present draft may seem to be logical in the beginning of the operative part, from Article I through IV. From Article V on, the ordering is somewhat arbitrary, due to the varied nature of Articles V through XI. An alternative way to group these Articles, based on another logic, would be the following:

- *new Article V*—present Article VI (support and cooperation)
- *new Article VI*—present Article V (new economic order as a particular topic)

- *new Article VII*—present Article IX (youth as particular target)
- *new Article VIII*—present Article VII (news agencies)
- *new Article IX*—present Article X (journalists)
- *new Article X*—present Article XI (a "right to correction")
- *new Article XI*—present Article VIII (a particular "right to correction")

APPENDIX 12
Draft Declaration on Fundamental Principles concerning the Contribution of the Mass Media to Strengthening Peace and International Understanding and to Combating War Propaganda, Racism and Apartheid
Proposal for a revised text of the Declaration, prepared by consultants in December 1977
(Unofficial Unesco document, December 1977)

The General Conference,

1. *Recalling* that by its Constitution the purpose of Unesco is "to contribute to peace and security by promoting collaboration among the nations through education, science and culture," (Art. I, 1) and that, to realize this purpose, the Organization will "promote the free flow of ideas by word and image," (Art. I, 2),

2. *Recalling* further that States Parties to the Constitution of Unesco, "believing in full and equal opportunities for education for all, in the unrestricted pursuit of objective truth, and in the free exchange of ideas and knowledge, are agreed and determined to develop and to increase the means of communications between their peoples and to employ these means for the purposes of mutual understanding and a truer and more perfect knowledge of each other's lives," (Preamble, 6th paragraph),

3. *Recalling* the purposes and principles of the United Nations, as specified in the Charter,

4. *Recalling* the Universal Declaration of Human Rights, adopted by the General Assembly of the United Nations in 1948, and the International Covenant on Civil and Political Rights, adopted by the General Assembly of the United Nations in 1966,

5. *Recalling* the Convention concerning the Use of Broadcasting in the Cause of Peace, adopted by the League of Nations in 1936 and still in force, whereby the States Parties to this Convention agreed to refrain from the Broadcasting of transmissions which endanger international peace and security,

6. *Recalling* Article 4 of the International Convention on the Elimination of all Forms of Racial Discrimination, adopted by the General Assembly of the United Nations in 1965, whereby States Parties to the Convention condemn all propaganda and all organizations which are based on ideas or theories of superiority of one race or group of persons of one colour or ethnic origin, or which attempt to justify or promote racial hatred and discrimination in any form, and undertake to adopt immediate and positive measures designed to eradicate all incitement to, or acts of such discrimination,

7. *Recalling* the International Convention on the Suppression and Punishment of Apartheid, adopted by the General Assembly of the United Nations in 1973, whereby the States Parties to this Convention agreed to prevent any encouragement of apartheid and similar segregationist policies or their manifestations and to punish persons guilty of that crime,

8. *Recalling* the Declaration on the Promotion among Youth of the Ideals of Peace, Mutual Respect and Understanding between Peoples, adopted by the Gen-

eral Assembly of the United Nations in 1965, emphasizing that young people play an important part in every field of human endeavour and that they are destined to guide the fortunes of mankind,

9. *Recalling* the Declaration and a Programme of Action on the Establishment of a New International Economic Order and the Charter of Economic Rights and Duties of States, adopted by the General Assembly of the United Nations in 1974, as regards a new international economic order, through which it is hoped to create a new system of international economic relations which may help to strengthen decisively peace and international understanding,

10. *Recalling* the Declaration of the Principles of International Cultural Co-operation, adopted by the General Conference of Unesco in 1966,

11. *Recalling* resolution 110(II) of the General Assembly of the United Nations adopted in 1947, condemning all forms of propaganda which are designed or likely to provoke or encourage any threat to the peace, breach of the peace, or act of aggressions, as well as resolution 127(II) of the same Assembly, requesting the Member States to combat, within the limits of constitutional procedures, the diffusion of false or distorted reports likely to injure friendly relations between States.

12. *Recalling* the resolutions of the General Assembly of the United Nations on the elimination of all forms of racialism and racial discrimination,

13. *Recalling* resolution 32/154 of the General Assembly of the United Nations adopted in 1977, which recognizes the need for dissemination of objective information about the developments in the political, social, economic, cultural and other fields of all countries and the role and responsibility of the mass media in this respect, thus contributing to the strengthening of trust and friendly relations among States,

14. *Recalling* resolution 9.12 adopted by the General Conference of Unesco in 1968, reiterating the Organization's objective to help to eradicate colonialism and racialism, as well as resolution 12.1 adopted by the General Conference of Unesco in 1976, stating that colonialism, neo-colonialism and racism in any form and of any type are incompatible with the fundamental objectives of Unesco,

15. *Recalling* resolution 4.301 adopted by the General Conference of Unesco in 1970, deeming that the mass media should play an important part in furthering international understanding and co-operation in the interest of peace and human welfare, and inviting all Member States to take the necessary steps to encourage the mass media to combat propaganda on behalf of war, racism and hatred among nations,

16. *Noting* the results achieved in international détente and, in particular, the contribution to this process made by the Conference on Security and Co-operation in Europe,

17. *Proclaims* on this day of....1978 this Declaration on Fundamental Principles concerning the Contribution of the Mass Media to Strengthening Peace and International Understanding and to Combating War Propaganda, Racism and Apartheid.

Article 1

1. The mass media have an important rôle in reinforcing peace by contributing to the realization of the principles guiding relations between States, irrespective of

their political, economic or social systems, thereby fostering a climate of confidence and respect among peoples, consonant with the duty of the States to refrain from propaganda for wars of aggression or for any threat or use of force inconsistent with the purposes of the United Nations.

2. A particular responsibility therefore rests upon the mass media for supporting peace and reinforcing international understanding, acting in full accord with the principles of international law and in a spirit of respect for the rights and dignity of all States, peoples and individuals without distinction as to race, sex, language, nationality, religion or philosophical conviction.

3. It is also the responsibility of the mass media to avoid any justification or encouragement of war, violence, apartheid and other forms of national, racial or religious hatred or discrimination, as well as all forms of colonialism and neo-colonialism, and to expose propaganda for these evils thus contributing to their elimination.

Article II

1. It being recognized that freedom of opinion, expression and information belong to human rights and fundamental freedoms, the strengthening of peace and international understanding requires that there be free and balanced interchange of accurate, comprehensive and objective information through the mass media.

2. The exercise of freedom of information places a duty and a responsibility upon those who determine the policies of the mass media to ensure the flow of true and honest information to all peoples. Furthermore, in order to enable the people to ascertain facts and appraise events objectively, there needs to be public access to sources of information and participation by the public in its wider dissemination.

Article III

As a means of contributing effectively to the strengthening of peace and international understanding, it is important that the mass media make widely known the objectives and principles which, in accordance with the resolution adopted by the General Assembly of the United Nations, constitute the basis of a new international economic order.

Article IV

1. To create the necessary conditions for just and lasting peace and for political and economic independence, it is essential to correct imbalances, quantitative and qualitative, in the flow of information to, from and between the developing countries and to make the balanced exchange of information a reality for the whole of the international community. For this purpose, the international community has a duty to encourage the establishment and furthering of the mass media including news and press agencies in the developing countries and in so doing promote cooperation among them, and between them and the developed countries.

2. Among all countries, particularly between those having different political, economic and social systems, it is similarly essential that States encourage bilateral and multilateral exchanges among the mass media, on the basis of equality of rights, mutual advantage, non-interference in each other's affairs, and respect for national sovereignty including the rights of countries and peoples to protect and preserve their national cultures, with due regard for the differences existing among those cultures as a part of the common heritage of mankind.

Article V

The international nature of the activities of news and press agencies as well as of radio and television organizations, whether privately or governmentally owned, places upon them a particular responsibility to act in conformity with the principles of this Declaration.

Article VI

It is important that the mass media contribute to the education of young people in the spirit of peace, justice, freedom, mutual respect and understanding in order to promote equal rights for all human beings and all nations, economic and social progress, disarmament and the maintenance of international peace and security. It is also important that the mass media ensure that the views and aspirations of young people are given adequate expression.

Article VII

The voices of those struggling against apartheid and other forms of racial discrimination, colonialism, neo-colonialism and foreign occupation, and unable to be heard within their own territory, need to be given expression through the mass media of other countries, with due respect for the sovereignty of the host countries, their legal systems, and relevant domestic laws and regulations.

Article VIII

Whenever States, institutions or individuals consider that the publication or dissemination of information has seriously damaged their efforts to strengthen peace and international understanding or to combat war propaganda, violence, apartheid and other forms of national, racial or religious hatred or discrimination, as well as all forms of colonialism and neo-colonialism, they ought to be given the opportunity to rectify erroneous information or the possibility of making their own version known through the mass media.

Article IX

1. Journalists and other creative media practitioners, their professional organizations, as well as all who are involved in their professional training, in order to fulfill their particular social responsibility, have a duty to help to ensure that the

mass media observe the principles of this Declaration. For that purpose, special emphasis should be placed on these principles in codes of conduct drawn up by the professional organizations.

2. It is incumbent upon States to ensure that, subject to the laws and regulations of the country, journalists and other creative media practitioners, working in conformity with the principles of this Declaration whether in their own countries or abroad, are given a status which provides them with the best possible working conditions and protects them in the exercise of their profession according to internationally accepted norms.

Article X

It is incumbent upon States, subject to adequate constitutional protection of the principles of freedom of information, and consistent with the relevant international instruments and agreements, to facilitate the observance of the principles of this Declaration by the mass media, so as to encourage the freer and wider dissemination of information to strengthen peace and international understanding and to combat war propaganda, racism and apartheid.

AIDE MEMOIRE

Background

The General Conference of Unesco adopted at its sixteenth session (1970) resolution 4.302, "deeming that information media should play an important part in furthering international understanding and co-operation in the interests of peace and human welfare", it affirmed "the inadmissibility of using information media for propaganda on behalf of war, racialism and hatred among nations" and invited "all States to take the necessary steps, including legislative measures, to encourage the use of information media against propaganda on behalf of war, racialism and hatred among nations, and to provide Unesco with information on the subject."

At its seventeenth session (1972), the General Conference adopted resolution 4.113 which called for the preparation of a "draft declaration concerning the fundamental principles governing the use of the mass media with a view to strengthening peace and international understanding and combating war propaganda, racialism and apartheid".

In conformity with this resolution, a meeting of experts (category VI) was convened at Unesco House in March 1974 to advise the Director-General on a text for submission to the eighteenth session of the General Conference. This meeting had before it, as a basis for discussion, an initial text of a draft declaration established for the Secretariat by a consultant, Prof. Hilding Eek, from Sweden (document COM-74/CONF.616/3). In the course of a detailed examination of this draft, the meeting made a considerable number of suggestions which were embodied in a report to the Director-General.

In the light of the suggestions made by the experts, a second text of a draft declaration was prepared. This text was submitted to the General Conference at its eighteenth session (document 18C/35). The General Conference examined this text and various amendments to it proposed by Member States (18C/COM/DRs 1 to 11). It decided that the question needed a study in depth and consequently adopted resolution 18C/4.111 which called for the convening of an intergovernmental meeting of experts (category II) to prepare a revised draft.

In pursuance of this resolution the intergovernmental meeting was convened and it took place at Unesco House in December, 1975. The meeting had before it notably the draft declaration which was contained in doc. 18C/35 and the proposed amendments to that draft which appeared in 18C/COM/DRs 1 to 11, as well as a number of proposed amendments submitted in the course of its proceedings (COM-75/CONF.201/DRs 1 to 26). The meeting prepared a new draft for submission to the General Conference at its nineteenth session.

After its consideration of this draft (document 19 C/91), the General Conference again decided to call for the preparation of a revised text. It adopted resolution 190/4.143 which "invites the Director-General to hold further broad consultations with experts with a view to preparing a final Draft Declaration. . .which could meet with the largest possible measure of agreement, as well as to proposing any other action which may be called for in the light of these consultations". This resolution also calls for the submission of such a draft and any other proposal to Member States at the end of 1977 or the beginning of 1978. In the resolution, the General Conference finally decided to include the question in the agenda of its twentieth session.

The present new draft has been prepared by the Director-General with a view to meeting the mandate given by the General Conference in the above-mentioned resolution and thus to serve as a revised text for a final Draft Declaration to be considered by the twentieth General Conference.

General Characteristics of the New Draft

The overall substance of the present new Draft Declaration (Preamble and Articles taken together) is derived from the three earlier draft texts. This is still a draft declaration primarily concerning the use of the mass media in *strengthening peace* and *international understanding* and in *combating war propaganda, racism and apartheid,* as was supposed by the resolution of the nineteenth General Conference. Other pertinent aspects related to Unesco's role in the field of the mass media—in particular with regards to the establishment of a New International Information Order—have not been given essentially more emphasis in the new draft than they already had in the previous draft (19 C/91).

It is considered that the substance of the present Draft Declaration still today stands on its own merit, despite the rapid developments which have occurred during the last few years in the area of national and international commuinication policies. A declaration to cover properly also the latter aspects would obviously be at this stage premature, particularly as the Director-General has launched a major effort to consider all the fundamental questions related to Unesco's role in the field of mass communication. The International Commission for the Study of

Communication Problems is thereby preparing comprehensive material for a separate consideration of the General Conference at a later stage.

Although the present draft largely coincides with the earlier texts (particularly the previous draft 19 C/91), the elements of the common substance have been to a considerable extent *reorganized* and the text has been notably *reformulated*. Moreover, the following essential elements which were included in the previous draft are *missing from the new draft:*

(a) an *explicit* reference to the controversial resolution 3379 of the United Nations General Assembly, included in the preambular paragraph 5 of the text 19C/91; however, the new formulation of the corresponding paragraph (No. 12 in the present draft) does imply all the relevant resolutions of the UNGA:

(b) an ambiguous formulation concerning the state responsibility for the activities of the mass media, contained by Article XII of the text 19C/91, which has given rise to a considerable controversy around this Draft Declaration;

(c) the formulation of the title and some principles in terms of *"use* of the mass media" or to refer to *"legislative* measures" thus facilitating interpretations that the Draft Declaration attempts to impose direct State directions upon the mass media.

On the other hand, the following essential elements, not appearing in the two preceding drafts, have been *added to the new draft:*

(a) the qualifiers "accurate", "comprehensive", "objective", "true", and "honest" to characterize the information the interchange of which is furthermore supposed to be "free and balanced" (Article II).

(b) the aspect of public access and participation as another relevant factor to the principle of freedom of information, singled out in Article II of the new draft.

(c) reference in the Preamble to some additional conventions, declarations and resolutions, constituting relevant instruments of international law (including the Convention concerning the Use of Broadcasting in the Cause of Peace, which is the only existing convention directly relevant in its entirety to the present Draft Declaration).

Generally speaking, the new draft text has been designed to retain the objective spelled out in the mandate given by the General Conference while at the same time removing from the text those aspects which have turned into major political obstacles. In particular, the responsibility of States for the activities of the mass media under their jurisdiction (Article XII in the previous draft) has been formulated in a clearcut way leaving no room for ambiguity (Article X in the new draft). Throughout the new draft, as compared with the previous one, there is a tendency towards clarity by emphasizing, in conformity with the different Constitutional systems of States, the professional, moral and social responsibility of the mass media, particularly with a view to fullness and accuracy or objectivity of the information transmitted. Finally the new draft attempts to bring the scattered elements of the previous drafts into a more systematic and logical order.

Detailed Explanatory Notes on the New Draft Articles

Article I The first paragraph of this Article is based on elements contained for the most part in the Preambular paragraph II of the draft 19 C/91. However, the new text has been formulated so that it only refers to the *important role of the mass media*, i.e. their *relevance*, with a view to fostering a climate of confidence and respect among peoples, etc. Hence the present formulation just relates the mass media to *the established principles guiding relations between States* (which for their part include the provision for the promotion of a climate, etc.), these principles being those defined by the United Nations Charter and other relevant documents such as the Final Act of the Conference on Security and Cooperation in Europe. The wording of the latter part of the present paragraph ("fostering of a climate. . . .") has been taken from this Final Act (from the passage listing matters related to giving effect to the principles guiding relations between States).

The second paragraph introduces the notion of *responsibility of the mass media* in the present context. The formulation is mainly based on elements contained in the first paragraph of Article I of the draft 19 C/91.

The third paragraph is based on Article V of the draft 19 C/91 with the following additional elements: (i) *discrimination* has been added to complement hatred, (ii) *all forms of colonialism and neo-colonialism* have been added in the list of evils the justification or encouragement of which is defined here, and (iii) *condemnation of propaganda* for all of the evils listed has been added at the end of the sentence. Aspect (i) has been derived from the first sentence of Article VI of the draft 19 C/91, in which however it was limited to racial discrimination only. Aspect (ii) is a new element in this context but has been included in the draft 19 C/91 under another Article (VIII). Aspect (iii) states in other terms, consistent with the wording of the draft 18 C/35 and Article 4 of the International Convention on the Elimination of all Forms of Racial Discrimination (referred to in the Preambular paragraph 6), what in all earlier drafts has been the spirit of this Article.

The second sentence of Article VI of the draft 19 C/91 has been deleted altogether from this context and its elements are incorporated in another Article (X). Consequently, the present draft is in keeping with the spirit of the corresponding Articles of previous drafts but is introducing a more compact formulation, whereby a separate Article concerning racial discrimination (VI of the draft 19 C/91) becomes obsolete.

Article II The elements contained in this Article are for the most part to be found in the first draft text prepared by Prof. Eek, in his Preambular paragraphs 3 and 4, of which the former was partly reproduced in the draft 19 C/91 as Preambular paragraph 12. This formulation originates verbatim from the texts prepared for the Draft Convention on Freedom of Information under the auspices of the United Nations. The first version of the relevant text was produced by the United Nations Conference on Freedom of Information in 1948, adopting a Draft Convention (based on a proposal by the Delegation of the United Kindgom) which in its Preamble considered that "the free interchange of information and opinions, both in the national and in the international sphere, is a fundamental human right and essential to the cause of peace. . . " Later on the Third Committee of the General Assembly, at its fourteenth session in 1959, adopted the final wording for the Preamble to the Draft Convention on Freedom of Information, considering that "freedom of expression, information and opinions are fundamental human rights" and that "the free interchange of accurate, objective and comprehensive information and of opinions, both in the national and in the international spheres, is essential to the causes of democracy and peace and for the achievement of political, social, cultural and economic progress." The qualifiers *accurate, objective* and *comprehensive* were added to the earlier draft text by the Third Committee following the proposal submitted by India, Liberia, Mexico, Philippines, Saudi Arabia, United Arab Republic and Venezuela.

The first paragraph of the present Article has been based on these elements without including the aspects of democracy and socio-cultural-economic progress but with adding the aspect of international understanding to accompany that of peace. The term *comprehensive* means in this context that the (accurate) information does not neglect such aspects which are essential to arrive at an extensive and in-depth understanding of the events or states of affairs referred to in the information. The term *objective* is used here in a general philosophical sense, as in the Constitution of Unesco, whereby it is supposed to cover both the aspect of accuracy and of comprehensiveness. The phrase *free and balanced* (in the context of information) has been taken from the wording of relevant objectives adopted for Unesco by the 18th and 19th General Conferences.

The second paragraph of Article II stresses the duties and responsibilities which according to a widely accepted notion are always accompanying the exercise of the right to freedom of information (see e.g. The above-mentioned Draft Convention and the International Covenant on Civil and Political Rights). The principle of responsibility as a concomitant to the principle of right to freedom of information is in the present text focused upon those (persons and institutions) who ultimately determine the policies of the mass media, i.e. The owners and controllers of the media; another Article (IX) focuses upon media workers such as journalists. Furthermore, the notion of duties and responsibilities concentrates here on the aspect of truthfulness and honesty of information and does not in the present text get extended to the kind of detailed aspects that are customary in this connection (the before-mentioned Draft Convention as adopted by the United Nations Conference on Freedom of Information contained altogether ten such provisions).

On the other hand, the present text does extend the notion of duties and responsibilities to cover the aspect of *public access and participation* in the informational processes (sources and dissemination) which is a new element in this draft as compared with earlier relevant documents. The formulation of this paragraph combines the demand for truthfulness with that of public access not only by speaking of true and honest information *to all peoples* but also by referring to the need to *enable the people to ascertain facts and appraise events objectively*, which latter wording is taken from the draft 19 C/91 (Article II, beginning of paragraph 2). Also the phrase *wider dissemination* appears in the draft 19 C/91 (Article I, beginning of paragraph 1) although there is a context which does not explicitly refer to public access and participation.

Article III This Article reproduces, with minor editing, Article VII of the draft 19 C/91.

Article IV The first paragraph of this Article is reproducing Article IV of the draft 19 C/91 by omitting special reference to the training of media personnel and adding in its reformulation the following elements: (i) a general motivation in terms of just and lasting peace and of political and economic independence, (ii) the aspect of mutual cooperation among the developing countries, and between them and the developed countries; and (iii) the news and press agencies as a particular category of the mass media. The second paragraph of this Article is based on Article II (paragraph 1) and Preambular paragraph 15 of the draft 19 C/91.

Article V This Article has its basis in the reference to international news agencies included in Article I (paragraph 2) of the draft 19 C/91. Radio and television organizations have been added as a new element altogether. The present text is merely repeating that the same responsibility that in the preceding Articles has been stated in terms of the mass media in general applies also in a special manner to these particular media which are especially international by their nature. (Note that releveant Article III of the draft 19 C/91 has been deleted altogether from the present draft.)

Article VI The first sentence of this Article reproduces the first Principle of the relevant Declaration (see Preambular paragraph 8) which was referred to in Article IX of the draft 19 C/91. The second sentence of the present Article introduces a new element missing from the previous draft.

Article VII This Article reproduces the same Article of the draft 19 C/91 (however deleting the word "*foreign* occupation") with the amendment proposed in Nairobi by the delegation of Brazil, adding at the end of the Article a provision to the legal systems and the relevant domestic laws and regulations.

Article VIII This Article is reproducing Article X of the draft 19 C/91, with minor clarifying reformulations attempting to replace a possible impression of a legal stipulation by that of a moral and professional appeal.

In this connection it should be noted that there is a legally valid Convention on the International Right of Correction, adopted by the General Assembly of the United Nations in 1952 and entered into force in 1962. Although it has been ratified so far by only about ten countries, this Convention constitutes a significant step in reaching for international agreements concerning the topic of the present Article.

Article IX The first paragraph is based on elements contained in Article XI and Preambular paragraph 14 of the draft 19 C/91, with the additional aspect of professional training (contained in Article IV of that draft and not reproduced elsewhere in the present text). While the earlier drafts are speaking in general terms about professionals and their organizations in the field of mass communication, the present draft is explicitly focusing on journalists and other creative media practitioners as well as their professional organizations, which are considered to be most relevant in the present context. The first sentence of this paragraph introduces an aspect, appearing in the first two drafts but not clear in the draft 19 C/91, whereby it is because of their potential contribution to the performance of the mass media that a particular emphasis on the professionals and their organizations is justified in the present context.

The second paragraph of this Article reproduces the idea contained in the second paragraph of Article II (latter part of the sentence) of the draft 19 C/91. However, the present formulation is 'stronger' in terms of calling upon States to ensure best possible working conditions for media practitioners and to protect them in the exercise of their profession (according to internationally accepted norms).

Article X The elements contained or implied in this Article have been pooled together from Articles I, VI and XII of the draft 19 C/91 and corresponding Articles of the two other earlier drafts. The Article has been designed to bring clarity to the controversial issue of State responsibility over the mass media by simply referring to the overall obligation of States to encourage and invite all mass media—without violating the status of the media as determined by respective Constitutional systems—to act in conformity with the principles of this Declaration.

The Article is largely based on Article I of the draft 19 C/91. Also Article I of the draft 18 C/35 is very close to the wording of the present Article. It should be noted that the present Article is only stating the obvious: it just confirms and endorses what is universally understood and legally instituted to be the responsibility relationship between States and the mass media.

APPENDIX 13

Report of the Director-General and Resolution by the Executive Board concerning a Final Draft Declaration

At the 104th session of the Executive Board, Paris, April–June 1978
(Unesco document 104 EX/28, 20 April 1978, and 104 EX/DR.21, 8 June 1978)

SUMMARY

This document, which concerns the consultations held with experts with a view to preparing a final draft declaration, is submitted in order to request the Executive Board's advice on measures to be taken to implement resolution 4.143, adopted by the General Conference at its nineteenth session.

1. After considering the draft declaration submitted to it in document 19 C/91, the General Conference, at its nineteenth session in Nairobi, adopted resolution 4.143, in which it invited the Director-General "to hold further broad consultations with experts with a view to preparing a final Draft Declaration . . . which could meet with the largest possible measure of agreement, as well as to proposing any other action which may be called for in the light of these consultations." In the same resolution, the General Conference requested the Director-General to submit such a Draft Declaration to Member States at the end of 1977 or in early 1978, as well as any other proposal he might formulate," and decided to include this item on the agenda of its twentieth session.

2. In pursuance of this resolution, the Secretariat, with the assistance of experts revised the text in the light of the comments made or objections raised during discussion in Nairobi. The revised version, intended to be used in the preparation of a final draft, was completed in the middle of 1977.

3. In October 1977, the Director-General held fresh consultations which he made as broad as possible given the time and resources available. About 100 persons were consulted, including: (i) the members of delegations who had participated in the work of the Drafting and Negotiation Group set up by the General Conference; (ii) leading specialists chosen from all different regions of the world, so as to reflect not only varying disciplines and professional interests but also varying cultures and ideologies; and (iii) representatives of professional organizations and national and international institutions which specialize in information and communication.

4. These consultations revealed a wide range of reactions and views regarding the draft declaration. Without either over-simplifying, or failing to reflect the originality of the points of view expressed, the opinions expressed can be grouped into five categories:

   a) *The revised text is satisfactory.* This first category includes the opinions of those who consider that the revised text constitutes a satisfactory compromise, better balanced and less controversial than that submitted in Nairobi, and that it might well produce the desired consensus, subject to minor changes as necessary. Some experts nevertheless consider that the draft contains concessions which represent the limit of what is acceptable.

b) *The revised text constitutes an acceptable basis for discussion, subject to improvements at a later date.* The opinions which fall into the second category consist of reservations on alleged points of ambiguity, gaps in the text and the fact that it does not take sufficient account of the amendments proposed by various delegations during the discussion in Nairobi. It should also be noted that the changes proposed go in opposite directions: on the one hand, a softening down of the language (for example, the "role" of the mass media instead of their "use," abandoning the idea of including government guidelines in legislation in this field); and on the other, the provision of additional details (on current imbalance in information flow on human rights, or on the correlation between the information situation and the aftermath of colonialism, or neo-colonialist manifestations, etc.).

c) *The revised text is not the kind of document which was expected.* Into this third category fall the views of those who favour a completely rewritten draft to take greater account of the problems of Third World countries and prepare the way for a "new international information order." It is argued that communication problems have been brought to the attention of the world community sufficiently for it to be possible to proceed beyond a declaration which would be limited to one small part of a much more complex whole.

d) *A draft declaration is not advisable at the present time.* This fourth category contains the opinions of those who consider it preferable to postpone preparation of a final draft declaration until completion of the work of the International Commission for the Study of Communication Problems, whose final report is to be considered by the General Conference at its twenty-first session. Once the report of the Commission has been completed and submitted to the General Conference, it is argued that governments, professional circles and public opinion would have additional information enabling decisions to be taken on a firmer basis.

e) *There is no point in any draft declaration.* To this fifth and last category belong the view of those who state that they are opposed both to any kind of declaration and to any kind of standard-setting action in this field. These views are generally based on the conviction that any governmental action—whether it consists of enacting legislation, applying regulations, introducing supervision, establishing guidelines or merely making an effort at persuasion—might either constitute a violation of the freedom of information or be used as a pretext for undesirable interpretations or as a justification for restrictive and arbitrary action.

5. This brief synopsis of very varying, and sometimes contradictory opinions obtained by the Director-General from the most authoritative specialists and personalities, makes it possible to judge just how difficult the task is which the General Conference assigned to him in requesting him to prepare a final draft declaration "which could meet with the largest possible measure of agreement." One might possibly answer some criticism by so recasting the text as to lay greater

stress on the special responsibilities which Unesco should assume in its own fields of competence to ensure that information, while contributing towards the progress of education, science and culture, can be used more efficiently in the cause of peace and international understanding. This however, would seem to go beyond the framework originally laid down by the General Conference in resolution 4.143. Moreover, the incompatibility of the varying points of view—in some respects irreducible—as confirmed by the consultation, leaves few illusions as to the likelihood of Member States reaching any kind of consensus at this stage.

6. Accordingly, given the divergent opinions and the difficulties raised at this stage by the preparation and submission of a final draft declaration to the General Conference, as specified in resolution 4.143, the Director-General, while stressing the importance of the Organization's standard-setting action in the field of information, considers that he should request the advice of the Executive Board on the measures to be taken.

DRAFT RESOLUTION

Submitted by the Working Group composed of Mr. Luis Echeverria (Mexico), Chairman, and his deputy Miss María de los Angeles López Ortega, Mr. Reginald Agiobu-Kemmer (Nigeria) and his deputies Mr. Augustine A. Ibegbulam and Mr. Mohamed M. Musa, Mr. Gunnar Garbo (Norway), Mr. Esteban Torres and Mr. Constantine Warvariv, deputies for Mr. Henry E. Kerry (United States of America), Mr. Leonid N. Kutakov (Union of Soviet Socialist Republics) and his deputy Mr. V. A. Karpoushin, Mr. Hassan Muraywid (Syrian Arab Republic), Mr. Majid Rahnema (Iran) and his deputy Mrs. Safoura Asfia-Clement.

Adopted by the Executive Board as decision 5.5.4.

The Executive Board,

Referring to resolution 4.143 adopted by the General Conference at its nineteenth session, which,

> (i) *Invites* the Director-General to hold further broad consultations with experts with a view to preparing a final draft Declaration on 'Fundamental Principles Governing the Use of the Mass Media in Strengthening Peace and International Understanding and in Combating War Propaganda, Racialism and Apartheid', which could meet with the largest possible measure of agreement, as well as to proposing any other action which may be called for in the light of these consultations;
>
> (ii) *Requests* the Director-General to submit such a Draft Declaration to Member States at the end of 1977 or early in 1978, as well as any other proposal he might formulate;
>
> (iii) *Decides* to include this item in the agenda of its twentieth session,"

Taking into account the information with regard to mass communication contained in the oral report of the Director-General addressed to the 104th session of the Executive Board on 24 April 1978, and concerning the activities of the Organization since its 103rd session.

Taking note of the report of the Director-General on the implementation of

19 C/Resolution 4.143 (104 EX/28), which reflects the divergent opinions obtained and the difficulties raised at this stage of the broad consultations,

Taking into consideration the recommendation adopted at the Intergovernmental Conference on Communication Policies in Latin America and the Caribbean held at San José (Costa Rica) and referred to in the above-mentioned report of the Director-General,

Affirming the possibility of drafting a final Declaration which, given the good will in the search for a common ground, could meet with the largest possible measure of agreement, as specified in 19 C/Resolution 4.143,

Referring to document 104 EX/32 (Provisional Agenda of the twentieth session of the General Conference),

1. *Highly appreciates* the intensive efforts undertaken by the Director-General since the nineteenth session of the General Conference in fulfillment of the mandate given him in 19 C/Resolution 4.143, by consulting numerous experts, leading specialists from different regions of the world, representatives of professional organizations and other personalities, with a view to elaborating a final draft, which could reflect the largest possible measure of agreement, and, thus constitute a step forward towards the establishment of a new international order of information;

2. *Invites* the Director-General to continue his efforts with a view to producing and forwarding to Member States before the twentieth session of the General Conference a final Draft Declaration as defined in 19 C/Resolution 4.143 and, failing which, to submit to the twentieth session of the General Conference a full report on the matter with such other proposals as he may deem necessary;

3. *Expresses* its satisfaction on the various other activities developed in the field of information and communication within the framework of the biennial programme 1977-1978 and other relevant decisions of the nineteenth session of the General Conference;

4. *Invites* the Director-General to further increase the activities of the Organization in the field of questions of information and communication.

APPENDIX 14

Draft Declaration on Fundamental Principles Governing the Contribution of the Mass Media to Strengthening Peace and International Understanding and to Combating War Propaganda, Racialism and Apartheid

Presented by the Director-General to the 20th session of the General Conference with explanatory notes, Paris, October–November 1978
(Unesco document 20C/20, 6 September 1978)

PREAMBLE

The General Conference,

1. *Recalling* that by its Constitution the purpose of Unesco is "to contribute to peace and security by promoting collaboration among the nations through education, science and culture" (Article I, 1), and that to realize this purpose the Organization will strive to "promote the free flow of ideas by word and image" (Article I, 2),

2. Further *recalling* that under the Constitution the Member States of Unesco, "believing in full and equal opportunities for education for all, in the unrestricted pursuit of objective truth, and in the free exchange of ideas and knowledge, are agreed and determined to develop and to increase the means of communication between their peoples and to employ these means for the purposes of mutual understanding and a truer and more perfect knowledge of each other's lives" (sixth preambular paragraph),

3. *Recalling* the purposes and principles of the United Nations, as specified in the Charter,

4. *Recalling* the Universal Declaration of Human Rights, adopted by the General Assembly of the United Nations in 1948, and the International Covenant on Civil and Political Rights, adopted by the General Assembly of the United Nations in 1966,

5. *Recalling* the Convention concerning the Use of Broadcasting in the cause of Peace, adopted by the League of Nations in 1936, and which is still in force,

6. *Recalling* Article 4 of the International Convention on the Elimination of all Forms of Racial Discrimination adopted by the General Assembly of the United Nations in 1965, and the International Convention on the Suppression and Punishment of the Crime of Apartheid adopted by the General Assembly of the United Nations in 1973, whereby the States adhering to these Conventions undertook to adopt immediate and positive measures designed to eradicate all incitement to, or acts of, racial discrimination, and agreed to prevent any encouragement of the crime of apartheid and similar segregationist policies or their manifestations.

7. *Recalling* the Declaration on the Promotion among Youth of the Ideals of Peace, Mutual Respect and Understanding between Peoples, adopted by the General Assembly of the United Nations in 1965,

8. *Recalling* the Declaration and Programme of Action on the Establishment of a

New International Economic Order, and the Charter of Economic Rights and Duties of States, adopted by the General Assembly of the United Nations in 1974,

9. *Recalling* the Declaration of the Principles of International Cultural Co-operation, adopted by the General Conference of Unesco in 1966,

10. *Recalling* resolution 110 (II) of the General Assembly of the United Nations adopted in 1947 condemning all forms of propaganda which are designed or likely to provoke or encourage any threat to the peace, breach of the peace, or act of aggression,

11. *Recalling* resolution 127 (II), also adopted by the General Assembly in 1947, which invites Member States to take measures, within the limits of constitutional procedures, to combat the diffusion of false or distorted reports likely to injure friendly relations between States, and resolution 32/154, adopted by the General Assembly of the United Nations in 1977, which recognizes the need for objective dissemination of information and the role and responsibility of the mass media in this respect, thus contributing to the growth of trust and friendly relations among States,

12. *Recalling* resolution 9.12 adopted by the General Conference of Unesco in 1968 reiterating Unesco's objective to help to eradicate colonialism and racialism, and resolution 12.1 adopted by the General Conference of Unesco in 1976 which proclaims that colonialism, neo-colonialism and racialism in all its forms and manifestations are incompatible with the fundamental aims of Unesco.

13. *Recalling* resolution 4.301 adopted in 1970 by the General Conference of Unesco, in which the Conference, deeming that information media should play an important part in furthering international understanding and co-operation in the interests of peace and human welfare, invites all Member States to take the necessary steps to encourage the use of information media against propaganda on behalf of war, racialism and hatred among nations,

14. *Recalling* the resolutions of the General Assembly of the United Nations on the eradication of all forms of racialism and racial discrimination,

15. *Proclaims* on this   day of   1978 this Declaration on Fundamental Principles governing the Contribution of the Mass Media to Strengthening Peace and International Understanding and to Combating War Propaganda, Racialism and Apartheid.

Article I

The strengthening of peace and international understanding and the combating of war propaganda, racialism and apartheid necessitate a free, reciprocal and balanced flow of accurate, complete and objective information, to which the mass media have the duty and responsibility of contributing. To this end, journalists and other agents of the mass media should enjoy a status which ensures that they are adequately protected.

Article II

1. The exercise of freedom of opinion, expression and information, recognized as an integral part of human rights and fundamental freedoms, is a vital factor in

the strengthening of peace and international understanding. It confers special responsibilities and duties on the mass media.

2. Access by the public to information should be guaranteed by the diversity of the information media available to it, thus enabling each individual to check the accuracy of facts and to appraise events objectively. Similarly it is important that the mass media should express the concerns of peoples and individuals, thus promoting the participation of the public in the elaboration of information.

3. With a view to the strengthening of peace and international understanding and to combating war propaganda, racialism and apartheid, it is essential that the mass media should contribute to promoting human rights, in particular by giving expression to those who combat colonialism, neo-colonialism and foreign occupation, apartheid and other forms of racial discrimination, and who are unable to make their voices heard within their own territories. This should be done with due respect for the sovereignty and legislation of the countries in which these media are located.

4. If the mass media are to be in a position to promote the principles of this Declaration in their activities, it is essential that journalists and other agents of the mass media exercising their activities in accordance with the principles of the present Declaration, in their own country or abroad, should enjoy professional status and be assured of protection guaranteeing them the best possible conditions for the exercise of their profession with conscientiousness and impartiality.

Article III

1. The mass media have an important part to play in the strengthening of peace and international understanding and in combating war propaganda, racialism and apartheid.

2. It is therefore incumbent on them to respect the rights and dignity of all nations, peoples and individuals, without distinction of race, sex, language, nationality or philosophical conviction. It is likewise incumbent on them to avoid any justification of or incitement to war-mongering, violence, apartheid and other forms of hatred or of national, racial or religious discrimination, as well as all forms of colonialism and neo-colonialism. As a contribution towards the total eradication of these evils, they should also denounce all forms of related propaganda, in particular propaganda on behalf of wars of aggression, and any threat or use of force incompatible with the aims of the United Nations.

3. By applying these principles, which are in conformity with those governing relations between States, the mass media will thus promote the establishment of a climate of confidence, mutual respect and tolerance between men and peoples of different origins and cultures.

Article IV

It is important that the mass media take part in the education of young people in a spirit of peace, justice, freedom, mutual respect and understanding, in order to promote human rights, equality of rights as between all human beings and all nations, and economic and social progress. It is also important that they should make known the views and aspirations of the younger generation.

Article V

In order that freedom of opinion, expression and information may be respected and that information may be more impartial, the mass media should make known the versions of facts presented by States, institutions and individuals who consider that the information published or disseminated about them has done serious harm to their efforts to strengthen peace and international understanding or to combat war propaganda, violence, apartheid and other forms of national, racial or religious discrimination, as well as all forms of colonialism and neo-colonialism.

Article VI

For the establishment of a new equilibrium and greater reciprocity in the flow of information, which will be conducive to the institution of a just and lasting peace and to the economic and political independence of the developing countries, it is necessary to correct the quantitative and qualitative inequality in the flow of information to and from developing countries, and between those countries. To this end, it is essential that their mass media should have adequate resources enabling them to gain strength and expand, and to co-operate both among themselves and with the mass media in developed countries.

Article VII

By making widely known the objectives and principles which, under the resolutions adopted by the General Assembly of the United Nations, form the basis of a new international economic order, the mass media make an effective contribution to the strengthening of peace and international understanding.

Article VIII

It is particularly incumbent on the mass media, owing to extensive international coverage, to act in accordance with the principles proclaimed in the present Declaration.

Article IX

It is the duty of journalists and other agents of the mass media, their professional organizations, and all those who participate in their professional training, to act in such a way that the mass media apply the principles stated in the present Declaration, thus assuming the responsibilities inherent in their role. To this end, professional organizations should lay particular emphasis on these principles in drawing up professional codes of ethics.

Article X

Action by the international community, and more especially by Unesco, is regarded as essential for the application of the present Declaration. In particular, it is the responsibility of the international community to endeavour to create a freer and more balanced flow of information, promote a professional status for journalists and other agents of the mass media, and give expression to those who, in their struggle against colonialism, neo-colonialism, foreign occupation, apartheid and other forms of racial discrimination, are unable to make their voices heard within their own territories.

Article XI

1. In compliance with the constitutional provisions designed to guarantee freedom of information and with the relevant international instruments and agreements, it is the duty of States to facilitate the application of the present Declaration, and to ensure that the mass media coming directly under their jurisdiction act in conformity therewith.

2. It is important that States should encourage a freer, wider and better balanced flow of accurate, complete and impartial information.

3. To this end, it is necessary that States should facilitate the procurement, by the mass media in the developing countries, of adequate resources enabling them to gain strength and expand, and that they should promote co-operation by the latter both among themselves and with the mass media in developed countries.

4. Similarly, on a basis of equality of rights, mutual advantage, non-interference in domestic affairs and respect for national sovereignty, including respect for the diversity of cultures which go to make up the common heritage of mankind, it is essential that States should encourage and develop bilateral and multilateral exchanges between the mass media in all countries, and in particular between those of countries having different economic and social systems.

5. For this Declaration to be fully effective, it is also incumbent on States, with due respect for the legislative and administrative provisions of each country, to help to promote a professional status for journalists and other agents of the mass media, and to seek internationally acceptable standards which would enable them to exercise their profession with conscientiousness and impartiality.

EXPLANATORY NOTES

While derived from the three preceding versions, this new draft declaration (in both the preamble and the articles) takes account of the opinions expressed since the inception of work on its preparation, and of the desire stated by the General Conference at its nineteenth session that it should "meet with the largest possible measure of agreement".

In accordance with resolution 4.113, and notwithstanding the comments expressed by some of the persons consulted, this draft maintains the same objective for the declaration, without extending it, namely the strengthening of peace and international understanding and the combating of war propaganda, racialism and apartheid.

National and international communication policies and practice have changed very rapidly over the last few years. However, the Director-General considered that he should entrust to a special commission, the International Commission for the Study of Communication Problems, the preparation of a complete document which would later be the subject of separate consideration by the General Conference. Accordingly, even if the field covered by the present draft in relation to the contribution by the mass media is limited, this declaration is in accordance with the wishes expressed by the Executive Board at its 104th session in inviting "the Director-General to continue his efforts with a view to producing . . . a final draft declaration as defined in 19 C/Resolution 4.143"; it marks progress in Unesco's action in the domain of the mass media, and constitutes a step forward towards the establishment of a new international information order. The declaration thus incorporates the material added to the three preceding versions.

However, so that the draft may "meet with the largest possible measure of agreement", in view of the invitation to propose "any other action which may be called for in the light of these consultations", and taking advantage of the consensus which emerged during the preparation of the Declaration on Race and Racial Prejudice, it was both necessary and possible to *recast, reformulate* and *rearrange* the material common to all the preceding versions of the present declaration.

The greatest obstacle to a formulation which could meet with the largest possible measure of agreement stemmed, in the earlier drafts, from their inherent ambiguousness as to the role devolving on the mass media in relation to other entities (States) or individuals (journalists, professional organizations) in achieving the objectives stated in the title. This ambiguousness might have given grounds for a univocal interpretation of the relations between the mass media and the public authorities, whereby the declaration might be used to impose control over the former by the latter. The culmination of this ambiguousness was expressed in Article XII of the draft in document 19 C/91 ("States are *responsible* for the activities in the international sphere of all mass media under their jurisdiction") and Article VI (". . . *legislative* action might be envisaged consistent with the respective constitutional systems of States and with relevant international instruments and agreements"). However, this was probably inevitable given the wording of the title of the declaration, which referred explicitly to "the use" of the mass media.

The most important alterations made by comparison with the earlier drafts, in particular with the version in document 19 C/91, are designed to remove this obstacle by eliminating all traces of ambiguousness. To this end:

> The present text contains no reference whatsoever to the responsibility of the State *vis-à-vis* the activities of the mass media or to any invitation to implement legislative action;
>
> the title of the declaration has been altered: "Declaration on fundamental principles governing the *contribution* (instead of 'the use') of the mass media . . .".

The somewhat different logical approach made it necessary, therefore, to rearrange the text. Whereas in the earlier drafts, the most active role devolved primarily on States, with the mass media acting as *intermediaries* in achieving the stated objectives, it became necessary in the new text to make the mass media the primary *actors*. The new draft therefore refers more directly to the moral, social and professional responsibilities of the mass media, on the basis of the universally recognized principles of freedom of expression, information and opinion, and the firmly stated role played by the media in achieving the objectives of the declaration. The role of States has been reformulated with the same purpose in mind, and is presented in a single article which sets out very clearly how the task incumbent upon States is differentiated according to the status of the mass media, which varies from one country to another.

In the light of the experience acquired in the preparation of the Declaration on Race and Racial Prejudice, the new text recalls the resolutions on the eradication of all forms of racialism and racial discrimination.

Furthermore, in addition to the inclusion in the preamble of a reference to a number of declarations, conventions and resolutions (including the Convention concerning the Use of Broadcasting in the Cause of Peace, which is the only existing convention directly linked to the present declaration), new ideas have been introduced:

> the adjectives "accurate", "complete" and "objective" are used to define the quality of the information to be disseminated, while the flow of information should be "free, reciprocal and balanced";
>
> reference is made to the channels through which the public can have access to information and participate in its elaboration; and also to
>
> the notion that journalists and other agents of the mass media should enjoy professional status and be assured of protection, essential if the mass media are to assume the duties and responsibilities ascribed to them by the declaration, and accordingly make it operative.

Lastly, in order to avoid any ambiguous wording which might give rise to a certain guardedness with respect to the declaration, a systematic effort has been made at *clarification*.

APPENDIX 15

Letter from the Union of Journalists in Finland with proposal for a "Professional Alternative" text of the Declaration and explanatory notes

Presented to international and regional organizations of journalists and to the Director-General of Unesco (dated Helsinki, 27 September 1978)

Dear Colleagues,

You certainly are aware of the latest Draft Declaration on the mass media, which Unesco's Dirctor-General has issued earlier this month for the adoption of the forthcoming 20th session of the General Conference of Unesco (according to the preliminary time table the matter will be on the Agenda in November 13th to 16th).

The Congress of the International Federation of Journalists meeting in Nice last week declared its standpoint i.e. as follows:

> The IFJ-Congress instructs the Bureau to take, in due time all effective measures to prevent adoption of such unacceptable provisions in any Unesco Declaration, notably by means of discussing such measures with other professional journalists' organizations, both on an international and national level, in order to influence in a positive way a revision of the present Draft Declaration.
>
> The IFJ Congress equally appeals to all member unions to act on their own national level in accordance with this Resolution.

We understand, after consulting a number of delegations at the Congress and after hearing the discussions and discussing the matter among the Nordic Unions that the Draft Declaration, now issued by the Director-General is considerably better for professional journalists than the version debated in Nairobi two years ago. It seems to us that this latest draft will no more be as controversial an issue as the earlier version did and that it can form a constructive basis "which could be met with the largest possible measure of agreement" (as was the wish of the 19th General Conference in Nairobi, when it adopted the resolution postponing the matter until next session).

However, the latest Draft does not appear to be quite finalized at least from the point of view of professional journalists, because it still contains some unnecessarily ambiguous wordings and repetitions and because the subdivision into Articles does not provide for an obvious and clear structure. Consequently there is a need for further refining of the Director-Generals draft without undermining his efforts in preparation of this Draft. In fact the issue this time is the form rather than the substance.

It seems to us that the most natural source for such a refined draft would be the common voice of the international and regional as well as national organizations of journalists and thus bringing together the different social and ideological standpoints which exist among journalists in various parts of the world. If presented as their joint initiative this "professional alternative" might in this connection well capture a consensus support of the delegations of the Member States—the political side, thus saving us from any serious harm caused by premature wordings with unpredictable voting at the General Conference.

In this situation the Union of Journalists in Finland has wanted to expedite the preparation of such a Draft, taking into consideration its role as a member of the IFJ as well as its contacts with the IOJ. Enclosed you will find our proposal for the text of the Declaration and accompanying explanatory notes.

This letter with its annexes has been sent to all member unions of the IFJ, as well as to the offices of all those organizations which were invited to attend the consultative meeting organized by Unesco in April 1978, namely International Federation of Journalists, International Organization of Journalists, International Federation of ASEAN Journalists, Federation of Latin American Journalists, Union of African Journalists and Federation of Arab Journalists and also to the Director-General Amadou-Mahtar M'Bow.

We suggest that the offices of the above mentioned organizations, first and foremost IFJ and IOJ, should soon get in touch as pointed out at the IFJ Congress in order to agree upon a joint proposal before the General Conference.

> Yours sincerely,
> UNION OF JOURNALISTS
> IN FINLAND
> Antero Laine   Eila Hyppönen
> President   General Secretary

PREAMBLE

The General Conference,

1. *Recalling* that by its Constitution the purpose of Unesco is "to contribute to peace and security by promoting collaboration among the nations through education, science and culture" (Article I, 1), and that to realize this purpose the Organization will strive to "promote the free flow of ideas by word and image" (Article I, 2),

2. *Further recalling* that under the Constitution the Member States of Unesco "believing in full and equal opportunities for education for all, in the unrestricted pursuit of objective truth, and in the free exchange of ideas and knowledge, are agreed and determined to develop and to increase the means of communication between their peoples and to employ these means for the purposes of mutual understanding and a truer and more perfect knowledge of each other's lives" (sixth preambular paragraph),

3. *Recalling* the purposes and principles of the United Nations, as specified in the Charter,

4. *Recalling* the Universal Declaration of Human Rights, adopted by the General Assembly of the United Nations in 1948, and the International Covenant on Civil and Political Rights, adopted by the General Assembly of the United Nations in 1966,

5. *Recalling* the Convention concerning the Use of Broadcasting in the Cause of Peace, adopted by the League of Nations in 1936, and which is still in force,

6. *Recalling* Article 4 of the International Convention on the Elimination of all Forms of Racial Discrimination adopted by the General Assembly of the United Nations in 1965, and the International Convention on the Suppression and Punishment of the Crime of Apartheid adopted by the General Assembly of the United Nations in 1973, whereby the States acceding to these Conventions undertook to adopt immediate and positive measures designed to eradicate all incitement to, or acts of, racial discrimination, and agreed to prevent any encouragement of the crime of apartheid and similar segregationist policies or their manifestations,

7. *Recalling* the Declaration on the Promotion among Youth of the Ideals of Peace, Mutual Respect and Understanding between Peoples, adopted by the General Assembly of the United Nations in 1965,

8. *Recalling* the Declaration and Programme of Action on the Establishment of a New International Economic Order, and the Charter of Economic Rights and Duties of States, adopted by the General Assembly of the United Nations in 1974,

9. *Recalling* the Declaration of the Principles of International Cultural Cooperation, adopted by the General Conference of Unesco in 1966,

10. *Recalling* resolution 110(II) of the General Assembly of the United Nations adopted in 1947 condemning all forms of propaganda which are designed or likely to provoke or encourage any threat to the peace, breach of the peace, or act of aggression,

11. *Recalling* resolution 127(II), also adopted by the General Assembly in 1947, which invites Member States to take measures, within the limits of constitutional procedures, to combat the diffusion of false or distorted reports likely to injure friendly relations between States, and resolution 32/154, adopted by the General Assembly of the United Nations in 1977 which recognizes the need for objective dissemination of information and the role and responsibility of the mass media in this respect, thus contributing to the growth of trust and friendly relations among States,

12. *Recalling* resolution 9.12 adopted by the General Conference of Unesco in 1968, reiterating Unesco's objective to help to eradicate colonialism and racialism, and resolution 12.1 adopted by the General Conference of Unesco in 1976 which proclaims that colonialism, neo-colonialism and racialism in all its forms and manifestations are incompatible with the fundamental aims of Unesco,

13. *Recalling* resolution 4.301 adopted in 1970 by the General Conference of Unesco, in which the Conference, deeming that information media should play an important part in furthering international understanding and co-operation in the interests of peace and human welfare, invites all Member States to take the necessary steps to encourage the use of information media against propaganda on behalf of war, racialism and hatred among nations,

14. *Recalling* the resolutions of the General Assembly of the United Nations on the eradication of all forms of racialism and racial discrimination,

15. *Proclaims* on this   day of   1978 this Declaration on Fundamental Principles governing the Contribution of the Mass Media to Strengthening Peace and International Understanding and to Combating War Propaganda, Racialism and Apartheid.

Article I

1. The mass media have an important part to play in the strengthening of peace and international understanding and in combating war propaganda, racialism and apartheid.

2. A particular responsibility therefore rests upon the mass media for supporting peace and reinforcing international understanding, acting in full accord with the principles of international law and in a spirit of respect for the rights and dignity of all nations, peoples and individuals without distinction as to race, sex, language, nationality, religion or philosophical conviction. It is incumbent on them to avoid any justification of or incitement to war-mongering, violence, apartheid and other forms of hatred or of national, racial or religious discrimination, as well as all forms of colonialism and neo-colonialism. As a contribution towards the total eradication of these evils, they should also denounce all forms of related propaganda, in particular propaganda on behalf of wars of aggression, and any threat or use of force incompatible with the aims of the United Nations.

3. By applying these principles, which are in conformity with those governing relations between States, the mass media will thus promote the establishment of a climate of confidence, mutual respect and tolerance between men and peoples of different origins and cultures.

Article II

1. The exercise of freedom of opinion, expression and information, recognized as an integral part of human rights and fundamental freedoms, is a vital factor in the strengthening of peace and international understanding and in the combating of war propaganda, racialism and apartheid. It confers special duties and responsibilities on the mass media to facilitate a free, reciprocal and balanced flow of accurate, comprehensive and objective information. To this end, journalists and other agents of the mass media should enjoy a status which ensures that they are adequately protected.

2. Access by the public to information should be guaranteed by the diversity of the information media available to it, thus assisting each individual to check the accuracy of facts and to appraise events objectively. Similarly it is important that the mass media should express the concerns of peoples and individuals, thus promoting the participation of the public in the elaboration of information.

3. In order that freedom of opinion, expression and information may be respected and that information may be more balanced, the mass media should make known the versions of facts presented by States, institutions and individuals who consider that the information published or disseminated about them has done serious harm to their efforts to strengthen peace and international understanding or to combat war propaganda, violence, apartheid and other forms of national, racial or religious discrimination, as well as all forms of colonialism and neo-colonialism.

Article III

With a view to the strengthening of peace and international understanding and to combating war propaganda, racialism and apartheid, it is essential that the mass media should contribute to promoting human rights, in particular by giving expression to those who combat colonialism, neo-colonialism and foreign occupation, apartheid and other forms of racial discrimination, and who are unable to make their voices heard within their own territories. This should be done with due respect for the sovereignty and legislation of the countries in which these media are located.

Article IV

It is important that the mass media take part in the education of young people in a spirit of peace, justice, freedom, mutual respect and understanding, in order to promote equal rights for all human beings and all nations, economic and social progress, disarmament and the maintenance of international peace and security. It is also important that they should make known the views and aspirations of the younger generation.

Article V

By making widely known the objectives and principles which, under the resolutions adopted by the General assembly of the United Nations, form the basis of a new international economic order, the mass media make an effective contribution to the strengthening of peace and international understanding.

Article VI

The international nature of the activities of news and press agencies as well as of radio and television organizations, whether privately or governmentally owned, places upon them a particular responsibility to act in conformity with the principles of this Declaration.

Article VII

1. It is the duty of journalists and other agents of the mass media, their professional organizations, and all those who participate in their professional training, to act in such a way that the mass media apply the principles stated in the present. Declaration, thus assuming the responsibilities inherent in their role. To this end, professional organizations should lay particular emphasis on these principles in drawing up professional codes of ethics.

2. For this Declaration to be fully effective, it is essential that journalists and other agents of the mass media exercising their activities in accordance with the principles of the present Declaration, in their own country or abroad, should enjoy professional status and be assured of protection guaranteeing them the best possible conditions for the exercise of their profession.

Article VIII

1. For the establishment of a new equilibrium and greater reciprocity in the flow of information, which will be conducive to the institution of a just and lasting peace and to the economic and political independence of the developing coun-

tries, it is necessary to correct the quantitative and qualitative imbalances in the flow of information to and from developing countries, and between those countries. To this end, it is necessary that States should facilitate the procurement, by the mass media in the developing countries, of adequate resources enabling them to gain strength and expand, and that they should promote co-operation by the latter both among themselves and with the mass media in developed countries.

2. Similarly, on a basis of equality of rights, mutual advantage, non-interference in domestic affairs and respect for national sovereignty, including respect for the diversity of cultures which go to make up the common heritage of mankind, it is essential that States should encourage and develop bilateral and multilateral exchanges between the mass media in all countries, and in particular between those of countries having different economic and social systems.

Article IX

It is incumbent upon States, subject to adequate constitutional protection of the principles of freedom of information, and consistent with the relevant international instruments and agreements, to facilitate the observance of the principles of this Declaration by the mass media.

Article X

Action by the international community, and more especially by Unesco, is regarded as essential for the application of the present Declaration. In particular, it is the responsibility of the international community to endeavour to promote a professional status for journalists and other agents of the mass media, so as to encourage the freer and wider dissemination of accurate, comprehensive and objective information to strengthen peace and international understanding and to combat war propaganda, racialism and apartheid.

EXPLANATORY NOTES

The draft submitted by the Director-General to the 20th session of the General Conference (see annex to Unesco document 20 C/20), has been designed so that "a systematic effort has been made at *clarification*" (as pointed out in the Explanatory Note attached to the Director-General's draft). Yet the professional journalists' organizations, while appreciating the effort made by the Director-General in preparing this new draft, cannot help an impression that this draft still contains some ambiguous wordings and unnecessary repetitions; furthermore, there appears to be a lack of obvious logic in its structure.

The further refined text has been prepared to overcome these drawbacks, but it still mainly rests on wordings of the Director-General's draft. At the same time it aims at bringing together, as a kind of common base, the different social and ideological points of view which exist among journalists in various parts of the world.

Title. No change has been made in the title of the Declaration, as presented in the Director-General's draft.

Preamble. No changes have been made in the preamble of the Declaration, as presented in the Director-General's draft. Yet it may be observed that some international instruments are merely listed whereas for others more detailed descriptive references are given; in this respect the style is somewhat unsystematic. Also it deserves to be noted that a paragraph on international détente has been deleted. (it was included in the Nairobi draft and subsequent working drafts in 1977); one is led to ask why it has been deleted.

Article I In order to create a logical structure in the Declaration the principles expressed in the *Article III* of the draft 20 C/20 have been placed as Article I of the present refined draft, thus pointing out the overall role and responsibility which the mass media have in matters listed in the title. The wording of paras 1 and 3 has been retained unchanged, but the first sentence of para 2 has been somewhat elaborated by giving prominence to the responsibility which rests upon the mass media, instead of implying a direct imposition upon them ("incumbent . . . to respect").

Article II This "new" Article has been drafted on the basis of *Art. I, II/1, II/2 and V* of the draft 20 C/20. The aim is to pool together all aspects of freedom of information appearing in this Declaration and to construct such a "package" that it would be both rich in terms of substance and balanced in terms of various ideological positions.

Para II/1 is a combination of *Art. I and II/1* of the draft 20 C/20. In the phrase "accurate, comprehensive and objective information" the qualifier "complete" has been replaced by "comprehensive" in order not to make it professionally too demanding (in fact it would hardly be possible to be absolutely complete even with the best intentions and facilities). Furthermore, the three qualifiers used in the present refined version have an established status in the international community after being included in the Preamble of the UN Draft Convention on Freedom of Information, adopted by the Third Committee of the UN General Assembly at its 14th session (1959). It should also be noted that the same phrase has been established as a norm for the U.S. Overseas broadcasting of the Voice of America (VOA).—The term *comprehensive* means in this context that the (accurate) information does not neglect such aspects which are essential to arrive at an extensive and in-depth understanding of the events or states of affairs referred to in the information. The term *objective* is used here in a general philosophical sense, as in the Constitution of Unesco, whereby it is supposed to cover both the aspect of accuracy and of comprehensiveness.

Para II/2 equals to the same para (Art. *II/2*) of the draft 20 C/20 with the exception of the word "enabling" which has been changed to "assisting", thus stressing the role of the mass media in securing objective information for each individual—but not necessarily as the only means available for the individual in this respect.

Para II/3 is identical with *Art. V* of the draft 20 C/20 with the exception of the word "balanced" which is used here instead of "impartial"; there is no need to introduce new words and definitions but to use expressions consistent with the wording of other Articles and with the established phraseology of current debate around international communications (including Unesco documents). The fact that a separate Article (V) has been "lowered" here into a subpara of another overall Article is a reflection of a particular position (predominantly "western") which is reluctant to accept rectification and "the right to reply" as an international norm.

Article III Considering the vital relevance of the principles expressed in *Art. II/3* of the draft 20 C/20 in this connection, the paragraph in question has been given a status of a separate Article. The wording remains unchanged.

Article IV This Article corresponds to *Art. IV* of the draft 20 C/20. The latter part of the first sentence has been slightly changed to bring it in conformity with the wording of Principle I of the Declaration on the Promotion among Youth of the Ideals of Peace, Mutual Respect and Understanding between Peoples, recalled in Preambular para 7.

Article V This Article equals to *Art. VII* of the draft 20 C/20.

Article VI This Article has been elaborated from *Art. VIII* of the draft 20 C/20 with the intention to avoid ambiguity and diluting; particularly the wording "which enjoy extensive international coverage" invites difficulties in the interpretation. The present text is merely repeating that the same responsibility that in the preceding Articles has been stated in terms of the mass media in general applies also in a special manner to these particular media which are especially international by their nature.

Article VII This Article is a combination from *Art. IX and II/4* of the draft 20 C/20 so that para VII/1 of the present draft equals to the above-mentioned Art. IX and para VII/2 to Art. II/4, respectively. However, the beginning of the latter has been shortened (using the wording of Art. XI/4 of the draft 20 C/20) and the last words ("with conscientiousness and impartiality") have been deleted in order to again reduce possible difficulties in interpretation and to give the Article a more concise form of expression.

With the second para of the present Article, the related para Art. XI/4 of the draft 20 C/20 is considered redundant or even dubious because it calls for a direct action on behalf of the States with regards to journalists. Relevant State action (in terms of protection of journalists) will be sufficiently taken into account by the proposed new Art. IX below.

Article VIII This Article is a combination of *Art. VI, XI/3 and XI/4* of the draft 20 C/20, thus combining the general principles of the "new international information order" and related action on behalf of the States.

Para VIII/1 reproduces *Art. VI* of the draft 20 C/20, however replacing the last sentence by the text in *Art. XI/3* corresponding to exactly the same idea. Furthermore, the word "inequality" has been replaced by the word "imbalances" for reasons mentioned above in the note on Art. II/3.

Para VIII/2 corresponds to *Art. XI/4*

Article IX This Article has been elaborated from *Art. XI/1 and XI/2* of the draft 20 C/20. While Art. I and II of the present draft expresses the duties and responsibilities of the mass media, this Article reminds of the obligations of the States to act in a way which ensures that the mass media can fulfill their contribution according to the Declaration—without, however, interfering in the prevailing system of freedoms and controls of the mass media in each country. Consequently, the present Article is only stating the obvious: it just confirms and endorses what is universally understood and legally instituted to be the responsibility relationship between States and the mass media.

Article X This Article corresponds to *Art. X* of the draft 20 C/20. However, the last part of the second sentence has been deleted, because its content has been expressed above in Art. III. Furthermore, this sentence has been reformulated so that the promotion of the professional status of journalists etc. remains as the prime operative target and that also the framework of the present Declaration is made more explicit in this connection. (Already in terms of pure form it may be convenient to finish the Declaration with the phrasing that appears in the title.) The phrase "freer and wider dissemination" is taken from the "third basket" of the Final Act of Helsinki, and it also appeared as an uncontroversial element in the Nairobi draft (Art. I/1 of the draft 19 C/91). As to the phrase qualifying information, see above notes on Art. II/1.

APPENDIX 16

Proposal for a "Western Alternative" text of the Declaration
Amendments submitted by the Federal Republic of Germany, Belgium, Canada, France, Greece, Ireland, Luxembourg, Netherlands, Switzerland, United States of America
(Unesco document 20C/PRG.IV/DR.7, 17 November 1978)

TITLE

"Declaration on fundamental principles concerning the contribution of the mass media to strengthening human rights, freedom of information, peace and international understanding and countering racialism and apartheid"

PREAMBLE

1. *Considering* that by its Constitution the purpose of Unesco is to contribute to peace and security by promoting collaboration among the nations through education, science and culture in order to further universal respect for justice, for the rule of law and for the human rights and fundamental freedoms and that to realize this purpose the Organization will strive to promote the free flow of ideas by word and image.

2. *Further recalling* that under the Constitution the Member States of Unesco, "believing in full and equal opportunities for education for all, in the unrestricted pursuit of objective truth, and in the free exchange of ideas and knowledge, are agreed and determined to develop and to increase the means of communication between their peoples and to employ these means for the purposes of mutual understanding and a truer and more perfect knowledge of each other's lives",

3. *Recalling* the purposes and principles of the United Nations, as specified in the Charter,

4. *Recalling* the Universal Declaration of Human Rights, adopted by the General Assembly of the United Nations in 1948, and particularly Article 19 which provides that everyone has the right to freedom of opinion and expression; this right includes freedom to hold opinions without interference and to seek, receive and impart information through any media and regardless of frontiers, and the International Covenant on Civil and Political Rights, adopted by the General Assembly of the United Nations in 1966,

5. *Delete.*

6. *Delete.*

7. *Recalling* the Declaration on the Promotion among Youth of the Ideals of Peace, Mutual Respect and Understanding between Peoples adopted by the General Assembly of the United Nations in 1965,

8. *Confirming* the role that Unesco is called upon to play, in the fields of its competence, in the establishment of a new international economic order,

9. *Recalling* the Declaration of the Principles of International Cultural Co-operation, adopted by the General Conference of Unesco in 1966,

9 bis. *Recalling* resolution 59(1) of the General Assembly of the United Nations, adopted in 1946 and declaring that freedom of information is a fundamental human right and is the touchstone of all the freedoms to which the United Nations is consecrated,

10. *Recalling* resolution 110(II) of the General Assembly of the United Nations adopted in 1947 condemning all forms of propaganda which are designed or likely to provoke or encourage any threat to the peace, breach of the peace or act of aggression,

11. *Recalling* resolution 127(II), also adopted by the General Assembly in 1947, which invites Member States to take measures, within the limits of constitutional procedures, to combat the diffusion of false or distroted reports likely to injure friendly relations between States, ans well as the other resolutions of the General Assembly concerning the mass media and their contribution to strengthening peace, thus contributing to the growth of trust and friendly relations among States,

12. *Recalling* resolution 9.12 adopted by the General Conference of Unesco in 1968 reiterating Unesco's objective to help to eradicate colonialism and racialism, and resolution 12.1 adopted by the General Conference of Unesco in 1976 which proclaims that colonialism, neo-colonialism and racialism in all its forms and manifestations are incompatible with the fundamental aims of Unesco,

13. *Conscious* of the important contribution which the mass media can make in actions in favor of international understanding and co-operation, in the interests of peace and human welfare,

14. *Recalling* the Declaration on Race and Racial prejudice adopted by the General Conference of Unesco at the present,

14 bis. *Conscious* of the complexity of the problems of information in modern society, of the diversity of solutions which have been offered, as evidenced in particular by consideration given to them within Unesco as well as of the legitimate desire of all parties concerned that their aspirations, points of view and cultural identity be taken into due consideration,

15. *Proclaims* on this day of 1978 this Declaration on Fundamental Principles concerning the Contribution of the Mass Media to Strengthening Human Rights, Freedom of Information, Peace and International Understanding and Countering Racialism and Apartheid.

Article I

1. Freedom of opinion, expression and information are internationally recognized human rights and fundamental freedoms.

2. These rights include the right of all people to access to sources of information and to unfettered participation in the dissemination of information.

3. The strengthening of peace and international understanding, the furthering of human rights as well as the encouragement of co-operation among peoples in all fields of human endeavour and particularly in education, science and culture demand a free flow and better balanced exchange of informaton. The mass media have an important contribution to make in achieving this end.

Article II

1. *Delete.*
2. Access by the public to information from a diversity of sources of information are essential to enable each individual to check the accuracy of facts and objectively to form his opinion on events. It is important that the mass media should take account of the diversity of ways of life and the concerns of peoples and individuals, thus promoting the participation of the public in the dissemination of information.
3. *Delete.*
4. To enable the mass media to promote the principles of this Declaration, it is important that journalists in their own country or abroad, should enjoy the best possible conditions in their work.

Article III

1. The mass media have an important part to play in strengthening human rights, freedom of information, peace and international understanding and countering racialism and apartheid.
2. Since aggressive war and other violations of international law and of human rights often spring from prejudice and ignorance, the mass media, by disseminating information on the aims, aspirations, cultures and needs of all people, can help them eliminate ignorance and misunderstanding between peoples, to make nationals of a country sensitive to the needs and desires of others, thereby facilitating the formulation by states of policies best able to promote the reduction of international tension and the peaceful and equitable settlement of international disputes.
3. By the unfettered dissemination of information, the mass media can promote the establishment of a climate of confidence, mutual respect and tolerance between men and peoples of different origins and cultures.

Artcle IV

It is desirable that the mass media contribute to the education of young people in a spirit of peace, justice, freedom, mutual respect and understanding, in order to promote human rights, equality of rights between human beings and all nations, and economic and social progress. It is also desirable that they should make known the views and aspirations of the younger generation.

Article V

Delete.

Article VI

In order to contribute to a free flow and better balanced exchange of information, and to promote economic and political independence of the developing countries as well as to strive for an improvement in the flow of information to and from developing countries, and between those countries, it is essential that their mass media have adequate resources enabling them to gain strength and expand, and co-operate both among themselves and with the mass media in developed countries.

Article VII

By making more widely known the objectives and universally accepted principles which are the bases of the resolutions adopted by the United Nations General assembly, the mass media can make an effective contribution to the strengthening of peace and international understanding as well as to the establishment of a more just and equitable international economic order.

Article VIII

Delete.

Article IX

It is desirable that professional organizations in the field of the mass media should lay particular emphasis on the principles stated in this Declaration in drawing up codes of ethics.

Article X

Delete.

Article XI

1. The free and open dissemination of information, internationally, nationally and locally, through the mass media, should be encouraged in order to enhance international understanding and to strengthen international peace by the widest possible flow of information. For this purpose, in particular, States should:
• facilitate the granting of visas, including multiple entry and exit visas, to journalists;
• minimize and seek to eliminate, travel restrictions;
• promote opportunities for free communications with citizens and officials;
• grant the right to import any necessary technical equipment and enable media personnel to communicate, nationally and internationally, completely and rapidly the results of their professional activities without censorship or any interferences of any kind.
2. Furthermore the procurement, by the mass media, in the developing countries, of adequate resources enabling them to gain strength and expand should be facilitated. Co-operation between the mass media in developing and developed countries should be promoted in a spirit of partnership.
3. Bilateral and multilateral exchanges between the mass media in all countries

should be encouraged, in particular, among countries having different economic and social systems.

4. The organizations and persons responsible for the dissemination of information in every State should, in conformity, with its national legislation, administrative system and journalistic tradition, encourage the achievement of the goals of the present Declaration.

* This proposal was received by the Secretariat on 15 November 1978.

APPENDIX 17

Proposal for a "Socialist Alternative" text of the Declaration
Amendments submitted by the Byelorussian SSR, the People's Republic of Bulgaria, the Socialist Republic of Czechoslovakia, the German Democratic Republic, the Hungarian People's Republic, the Mongolian People's Republic, the Polish People's Republic, the USSR and the Ukrainan SSR, Viet Nam, Afghanistan, Mozambique, Ethiopia (Unesco document 20C/PRG.IV/DR.8, 17 November 1978)

AMENDMENTS

to the Draft Declaration on Fundamental Principles Governing the Contribution of the Mass Media in Strengthening Peace and International Understanding and in Combating War Propaganda, Racialism and Apartheid (document 20 C/20).

TITLE

Unchanged

PREAMBLE

Paragraph 1: Unchanged
Paragraph 2: Unchanged
Paragraph 3: Unchanged
Paragraph 4: Add the following words at the end of the paragraph: which declare in Article 20 that "any propaganda for war shall be prohibited by law" and "any advocacy of national, racial or religious hatred that constitutes incitement to discrimination, hostility or violence shall be prohibited by law".
Paragraph 5: Unchanged
Paragraph 6: Unchanged
Paragraph 7: Unchanged
Paragraph 8: Unchanged
Paragraph 9: Unchanged

Add a new paragraph to read as follows:

Recalling resolution 59(I) of the General Assembly of the United Nations adopted in 1946, which declares that "Freedom of information requires as an indispensable element the willingness and capacity to employ its privileges without abuse. It requires as a basic discipline the moral obligation to see the facts without prejudice and to spread knowledge without malicious intent."

Add a further new paragraph to read as follows:

Noting the results achieved in international détente, and in particular the contribution to this process made by the Conference on Security and Co-operation in Europe,

(Note: text verbally quoted from the Nairobi Draft 19 C/91)

Paragraph 10: Unchanged
Paragraph 11: Unchanged
Paragraph 12: Unchanged
Paragraph 13: Unchanged
Paragraph 14: Unchanged

Add a new paragraph to read as follows:

Recalling resolution 13.1 adopted by the General Conference in 1976 which orientates to generate a climate of public opinion conducive to the halting of the arms race and the transition to disarmament,

Add a new paragraph to read as follows:

Bearing in mind the aspirations of the developing countries for a new international order of information and communication,

Paragraph 15: Unchanged

Article I

To replace by the unchanged text of Article III of document 20 C/20.

Article II

"The strengthening of peace and international understanding and the combating of war propaganda, racialism and apartheid are inseparable from a free, reciprocal and balanced flow of accurate, comprehensive and objective information, it being recognized that the exercise of freedom of opinion, expression and information is an integral part of human rights and fundamental freedoms, it confers special duties and responsibilities on the mass media."

Note: Redrafted on the bases of Articles I and II, paragraph I, of document 20 C/20.

Article III

To replace by Article II, paragraph 3, document 20 C/20, unchanged.

Article IV

Unchanged

Article V

Unchanged

Article VI

The implementation of the new international order of information and communication, which implies *inter alia* the development of national systems of communication, the establishment of a new equilibrium and better reciprocity in the flow of information, which are the favourable conditions for the achievement of a just and lasting peace and the economic and political independence of developing countries, demands the correction of the quantitative and qualitative inequality in the flow of information to and from the developing countries as well as among themselves. To this end it is essential that the mass media in the developing countries have the capacity to transmit and receive news by word, image and sound over international telecommunication systems under favourable conditions.

Note: (as proposed in the unofficial draft of the non-aligned countries and group 77.)

Article VII

By disseminating more widely all of the information concerning the objectives and principles universally accepted which are the bases of the resolutions adopted by the different organs of the United Nations, the mass media contribute effectively to the strengthening of peace and international understanding, to the promotion of human rights, as well as to the establishment of a more just and equitable international economic order.

Note: (as proposed in the unofficial draft of the non-aligned countries and group 77.)

Article VIII

To be redrafted to read as follows: The international nature of the activities of news and press agencies as well as of radio and television organizations, whether privately or governmentally owned, places upon them a particular responsibility to act in conformity with the principles of this Declaration.

Article IX

Unchanged

Article X

Unchanged

Article XI

Paragraph 1: unchanged
Paragraph 2: unchanged
Paragraph 3: unchanged
Paragraph 4: unchanged
Paragraph 5: delete

* This proposal was received by the Secretariat on 17 November 1978.

APPENDIX 18
Proposal for a "Non-Aligned Alternative" text of the Declaration
Amendments submitted by the Member States of Unesco belonging to the Group of Non-Aligned Countries and to the Group of 77 (Unesco document 20C/PRG.IV/DR.9, 20 November 1978)

PREAMBLE

The General Conference,

1. *Considering* that by its Constitution the purpose of Unesco is to "contribute to peace and security, collaboration among the nations in order to further universal respect for justice, law and fundamental freedoms" (Article I,1), and that to realize this purpose the Organization will strive "to promote the free flow of ideas by word and image" (Article I,2),

2. *Further recalling* that under the Constitution the Member States of Unesco, "believing in full and equal opportunities for education for all, in the unrestricted pursuit of objective truth, and in the free exchange of ideas and knowledge, are agreed and determined to develop and to increase the means of communication between their peoples and to employ these means for the purposes of mutual understanding and a truer and more perfect knowledge of each other's lives" (sixth preambular paragraph),

3. *Recalling* the purposes and principles of the United Nations, as specified in the Charter,

4. *Recalling* the Universal Declaration of Human Rights, adopted by the General Assembly of the United Nations in 1948 and the International Covenant on Civil and Political Rights, adopted by the General Assembly of the United Nations in 1966,

5. *Recalling* Article 4 of the International Convention on the Elimination of all Forms of Racial Discrimination adopted by the General Assembly of the United Nations in 1965, and the International Convention on the Suppression and Punishment of the Crime of Apartheid adopted by the General Assembly of the United Nations in 1973, whereby the States adhering to these Conventions undertook to adopt immediate and positive measures designed to eradicate all incitement to racial discrimination, and agreed to prevent any encouragement of the crime of apartheid and similar segregationist policies or their manifestations,

6. *Recalling* the Declaration on the Promotion among Youth of the Ideals of Peace, Mutual Respect and Understanding between Peoples, adopted by the General Assembly of the United Nations in 1965,

7. *Recalling* the declarations and resolutions adopted by the various organs of the United Nations concerning the establishment of a New International Economic Order and the role that Unesco is called upon to fulfil in this field,

8. *Recalling* the Declaration of the Principles of International Cultural Co-operation, adopted by the General Conference of Unesco in 1966,

9. *Recalling* resolution 110(II) of the General Assembly of the United Nations

adopted in 1947 condemning all forms of propaganda which are designed to provoke or encourage any threat to the peace, breach of the peace, or act of aggression,

10. *Recalling* resolution 127(II), also adopted by the General Assembly in 1947, which invites Member States to take measures, within the limits of constitutional procedures, to combat the diffusion of false or distorted reports likely to injure friendly relations between States, as well as the other resolutions of the General Assembly concerning the mass media and their contribution to strengthening trust and friendly relations among States,

11. *Recalling* resolution 9.12 adopted by the General Conference of Unesco in 1968 reiterating Unesco's objective to help to eradicate colonialism and racialism, and resolution 12.1 adopted by the General Conference of Unesco in 1976 which proclaims that colonialism, neo-colonialism and racialism in all its forms and manifestations are incompatible with the fundamental aims of Unesco,

12. *Recalling* the Declaration on Race and Racial Prejudice adopted by the General Conference of Unesco at its twentieth session,

13. *Recalling* resolution 4.301 adopted in 1970 by the General Conference of Unesco on the contribution of the information media to furthering international understanding and co-operation in the interests of peace and human welfare, and to countering propaganda on behalf of war, racialism, apartheid and hatred among nations, and conscious of the fundamental role that the mass media can play in these fields,

14. *Conscious* of the complexity of the problems of information in modern society, of the diversity of solutions which have been offered to them, as evidenced in particular by the consideration given to them within Unesco, and especially of the legitimate desire of all parties concerned that their aspirations, points of view and cultural identity be taken into due consideration.

15. *Bearing in mind* the aspirations of the developing countries for the establishment of a new world order of information and communication,

16. Proclaims on this   day of   1978 this Declaration on Fundamental Principles concerning the Contribution of the Mass Media to Strengthening Peace and International Understanding and to Countering Racialism, Apartheid and Incitement to War.

Article I

1. The mass media have an important part to play in the strengthening of peace and international understanding and in countering racialism, apartheid, and incitement to war,

2. In the struggle against aggressive war, racialism, apartheid, and other violations of human rights, the mass media, by disseminating information on the ideals, aspirations, cultures and needs of all peoples, contribute to eliminating ignorance, prejudice and misunderstanding between peoples, to making nationals of a country sensitive to the needs and desires of others, and to ensuring respect for the rights and dignity of all nations, peoples, and individuals, without distinction of race, religion, sex, language, or nationality, and to drawing attention to the great problems which afflict mankind such as poverty, malnutrition, igno-

rance, and disease. In so doing, the mass media assist States in the formulation of policies best able to promote the reduction of international tension and the peaceful and equitable settlement of international disputes.

Article II

The strengthening of peace and international understanding and the countering of racialism, apartheid, incitement to war and all other violations of human rights demand a free, wider, and better balanced flow of information. To this end, the mass media have a leading role to play. The role will be the more effective to the extent that the information is accurate, comprehensive and objective.

Article III

1. The exercise of freedom of opinion, expression and information, recognized as an integral part of human rights and fundamental freedom, is a vital factor in the strengthening of peace and international understanding.

2. Access by the public to information should be guaranteed by the diversity of the sources and media of information available to it, thus enabling each individual to check the accuracy of facts and to appraise events objectively. Similarly, it is important that the mass media be responsive to concerns of peoples and individuals, thus promoting the participation of the public in the preparation of information.

3. With a view to the strengthening of peace and international understanding and to countering racialism, apartheid, incitement to war and all other violations of human rights, the mass media throughout the world, by reason of their role, contribute to promoting human rights, in particular by giving expression to oppressed peoples, who are unable to make their voices heard within their own territories.

4. So that the mass media can fulfil their professional tasks in a responsible manner and be in a position to promote the principles of this Declaration in their activities, it is essential that journalists and other agents of the mass media, in their own country or abroad, be assured of protection guaranteeing them the best conditions for the exercise of their profession.

Article IV

The mass media have an essential part to play in the education of young people in a spirit of peace, justice, freedom, mutual respect and understanding, in order to promote human rights, equality of rights as between all human beings and all nations, and economic and social progress. Equally they have an important role to play in making known the views and aspirations of the younger generation.

Article V

In order that freedom of opinion, expression and information may be respected and that information may be more impartial, it is important that the mass media make known the versions of the facts presented by States, institutions and individuals who consider that the information published or disseminated about them has seriously prejudiced their efforts to strengthen peace and international understanding or to counter racialism, apartheid, incitement to war, and all other violations of human rights.

Article VI

The establishment of a new world order of information and communication, which implies *inter alia* the development of national systems of communication, and the securing of a new equilibrium and greater reciprocity in the flow of information, which are the favourable conditions for the achievement of a just and lasting peace and for the economic and political independence of developing countries, demand the correction of the quantitative and qualitative inequalities in the flow of information to and from the developing countries as well as among themselves. To this end, it is essential that the mass media in the developing countries should have the capacity to transmit and receive news by word, image and sound over international telecommunication systems under the best possible technical and financial conditions.

Article VII

By disseminating more widely all information concerning the objectives and principles universally accepted which are the bases of the resolutions adopted by the different organs of the United Nations, the mass media contribute effectively to the strengthening of peace and international understanding, to the promotion of human rights, as well as to the establishment of a more just and equitable international economic order.

Article VIII

In the field of the mass media, professional organizations should support their members so that the latter can fulfil their professional tasks in a responsible manner; they should also define and promote codes of professional ethics at the national and international levels. In so doing they are invited to emphasize the principles enunciated in this Declaration.

Article IX

It is the responsibility of the international community, and more especially of Unesco, to endeavour to create the conditions for a free, wider, and more balanced flow of information, and for the protection, in the exercise of their functions, of journalists and other agents of the mass media, and for affording expresssion to those who, in their struggle against colonialism, neo-colonialism, foreign occupation, apartheid, and other forms of racial discrimination and oppression, are unable to make their voices heard within their own territories.

Article X

1. With due respect for constitutional provisions designed to guarantee freedom of information and for the applicable international instruments and agreements, it is indispensable to create and maintain throughout the world the conditions which will make it possible for the organizations and persons involved in the dissemination of information to achieve the objectives of this Declaration.

2. It is important that a free, wider and better balanced flow of information be encouraged.

3. To this end, it is necessary that States should facilitate the procurement, by the mass media in the developing countries, of adequate resources enabling them to gain strength and expand, and that they should support co-operation by the latter both among themselves and with the mass media in developed countries.

4. Similarly, on a basis of equality of rights, mutual advantage, and respect for the diversity of cultures which go to make up the common heritage of mankind, it is essential that bilateral and multilateral exchanges of information among all States, in particular between those which have different economic and social systems, be encouraged and developed.

5. For this Declaration to be fully effective it is the duty of States, with due respect for their legislative and administrative provisions, to guarantee the existence of favourable conditions for the operation of the mass media, in conformity with the provisions of the Universal Declaration of Human Rights.

Article XI

For this Declaration to be fully effective it is necessary with due respect for legislative and administrative provisions and the principle of non-intervention in the affairs of sovereign States and other obligations of Member States, to guarantee the existence of favourable conditions for the operation of the mass media, in conformity with the provisions of the Universal Declaration of Human Rights.

* This proposal was received by the Secretariat on 18 November 1978.

APPENDIX 19
Coverage of the debate on the Declaration in *Time* magazine
20 November and 5 December 1978

THIRD WORLD vs. FOURTH ESTATE

Showdown in Paris over a bid to curb the free flow of news

In his 1942 autobiography, *Barriers Down,* former Associated Press Chief Kent Cooper described how a cartel of European press agencies controlled all the news that flowed into and out of the U.S. until well into the 1930s. "It told the world about the Indians on the warpath in the West, lynchings in the South and bizarre crimes in the North . . . nothing creditable to America ever was sent," Cooper complained.

A similar complaint is being heard today. This time it is the developing nations of the Third World that claim to be the victims of biased and inadequate news coverage. And this time one of the accused is Cooper's own A.P., along with other Western-based news agencies that keep reporters abroad. These organizations, say Third World officials, monopolize the flow of news in much the same way that Western industrial firms dominate markets. So Third World countries are demanding U.N. endorsement of a "new world information order" to correct imbalances in the distribution of news.

This week they will try to do something drastic about it at the biennial general conference of the 146-nation United Nations Educational, Scientific and Cultural Organization in Paris. Third World delegates are pushing for adoption of a draft declaration on the mass media that many Western diplomats and journalists consider a grave threat to press freedom. The document is based on a similar resolution proposed at UNESCO's 1970 meeting by the Soviets and rewritten since then to eliminate some of its more heinous features. Yet the present 1,500-word version still contains several provisions with chillingly Orwellian overtones. One would endorse government licensing of journalists. Another would compel news organizations to print official replies to stories a government deems unfair.

By far the most troubling of the declaration's eleven articles is the last: "It is the duty of states . . . to ensure that the mass media coming directly under their jurisdiction act in conformity" with the declaration. To Western critics, that means nothing less than government control of the press. Warns Roger Tatarian, a longtime United Press International executive now teaching journalism at California State (Fresno): "It would in effect be putting UNESCO's badge of approval on government meddling with the news."

A number of major U.S. journalists' and publishers' associations have hotly denounced the declaration. Some have also urged that the U.S., which pays 25% of UNESCO's budget ($303 million this year), withdraw from the body if the declaration is adopted. In a letter to Secretary of State Cyrus Vance, New York's Senator Daniel Moynihan last month called on the U.S. to "thunder our contempt for this contemptible document." In Paris, the 38-member U.S. delegation has been lobbying quietly to water down the declaration. But the *Wall Street Journal* and the New York *Times* last week editorialized against compromise. Demanded the *Times:* "What on earth have *Pravda* and the New York *Times* to bargain about in the definition of news?"

The heart of the conflict is a fundamental, perhaps irreconcilable disagreement over the role of the press. To the West, the press is the independent Fourth Estate, watchdog of the other three, and profit-making servant of an informed electorate. To the Communist world, the press is an apparatus of the state charged primarily with educating the masses about state policies. Third World leaders may prefer the Western model, but believe they need a controlled press to promote economic development, accentuate the positive and eliminate the negative. Observes Chicago *Tribune* Editor Clayton Kirkpatrick: "I hear the same complaints from the Third World as I do from Highland Park, Ill., where people think we should cover the opening of a new civic center."

The Third World's brief against the Western press contains two principal complaints:

▶ Western coverage of developing nations is shot through with colonial stereotypes; just as Europe's cartel once painted the U.S. as a land of scalpings, lynchings and ax murders, the Western press allegedly sees the Third World as a slough of coups, corruption and natural catastrophes.

▶ Western news organizations have so tight a strangle hold on international communications that the Third World simply cannot make itself heard, an imbalance that also purportedly perpetuates Western cultural dominations.

Says Columbia Journalism Dean Elie Abel: "On the whole, the major media do an incredibly bad job of covering the Third World." To be sure, the West's press does devote considerably more ink and airtime to the likes of Uganda's Idi Amin than to more responsible leaders, and usually pays more attention to scandals and disasters than to complex social and economic stories. Yet those complaints can also be made about the West's coverage of its own affairs. If Western reporting about the developing world is thin, that may be because news follows the realities of world power; Washingto and Moscow are more newsworthy capitals than, say, Lagos and Lima, especially to Western readers. Indeed, Third World news outlets are as parochial as their Western counterparts: a 1975 State Department study of Latin American newspapers showed that they carried little news of other developing countries.

Many Third World governments do not exactly encourage better coverage. The London-based International Press Institute, a watchdog group that monitors press freedom, reported in 1976 that 15 developing nations had expelled or refused entry to foreign correspondents in the previous year, and the rate has probably increased since then. Nigeria has booted out nearly all resident foreign journalists; the last Reuters man there was put into a dugout canoe with his wife and eight-year-old daughter and advised to start rowing toward neighboring Benin.

Perhaps the Third World's most accurate complaint is that the West dominates the world flow of communications, principally through the hegemony of the so-called Big Four (A.P., U.P.I., Reuters and Agence France Press). A study this year of 14 Asian newspapers made for the Edward R. Murrow Center at Tufts University showed the Big Four accounted for 76% of Third World news in those papers. Western dominance, however, is more a matter of economics than conscious conspiracy. International cable rates discriminate against small national news agencies and other low-volume users.

That imbalance may change. With UNESCO's blessing and the facilities of Yugoslavia's Tanjug news agency, ten nations in 1975 formed their own international news cooperative. The Non-Aligned News Agencies Pool, as it is called, now has 50 member nations, and exchanges lightly edited government press releases among subscribers. Roger Tatarian has proposed a joint multinational news agency that would concentrate on national-development stories. A task force of the New York-based 20th Century Fund including Third World journalists has endorsed the idea. The World Press Freedom Committee, a group of 32 international publishers and broadcasters, has raised about half of the $1 million it plans to spend training Third World journalists and technicians. American UNESCO Delegation Chief John Reinhardt, who heads the Government's International Communications Agency, this month promised the nonaligned nations a package of U.S. technical assistance and hardware, presumably as an incentive to water down or table the UNESCO mass media declaration.

With debate on the declaration scheduled to begin this week, there seemed to be a chance that a let's-be-friends approach might prevail. The Soviets, more concerned with keeping SALT on the right track than with making trouble for Western reporters, appeared to be growing bored with the whole issue. UNESCO Director-General Amadou Mahtar M'Bow of Senegal, whose ambition is to succeed Kurt Waldheim as U.N. Secretary-General, is staking his prestige on passage of a mass media declaration, preferably by consensus. To that end, delegates from Western and nonaligned nations were caucusing last week to come up with a compromise acceptable to the U.S. Some American opponents of the declaration seem ready to go along. They note that it is not binding, and that Third World governments hardly need the permission of UNESCO to harass journalists.

Even if the measure is watered down or pigeonholed, the issue will come up again next year when a UNESCO commission of "wise men" led by former Irish Foreign Minister Sean MacBride completes an exhaustive study on the subject. In addition, the International Telecommunications Union will meet next fall to consider the first redistribution of world radio frequencies in 20 years. The frequencies are now dominated by the West and the Soviets. Third World nations are agitating for a better slice of the spectrum and for the right to block direct satellite broadcasting across national borders.

Whatever happens next in the newsflow dispute, the Third World countries have already achieved some major goals. They have made the West aware of their displeasure with slapdash coverage of their affairs. They have pried pledges of equipment and training from the West. Perhaps most important, and most disturbing, they have realized that they can, in the words of one specialist, "pull the plugs anywhere" in the international communications system.

What the West has yet to make clear to them is that press freedom need not be incompatible with national development, that government-dictated news is no more believable in the Third World than elsewhere and that any "new world information order" should be blessed with fewer government curbs on the flow of news, not more. As the 20th Century Fund's task force concluded: "The practices of a free press may be erratic, even in the West, but the aspirations of freedom should ultimately serve to unite the West and the Third World."

TRUCE IN PARIS

UNESCO delegates drop a threat to curb the news.

For a time it seemed as if the biennial general conference of the 146-nation United Nations Educational, Scientific and Cultural Organization in Paris would be remembered for adopting Soviet-style curbs on press freedom. But last week, applauding delegates passed by acclamation a U.S.-supported compromise, lifting at least temporarily a threat that has been hanging over the West since 1970.

Leading the conference to a middle ground was UNESCO's director general, Amadou Mahtar M'Bow, of Senegal. He steered his Third World colleagues away from a declaration, originally sponsored by M'Bow himself, intended to counter what they perceive as distorted and inadequate coverage of their affairs (TIME, Nov. 20). The first draft, which sanctioned state control of the press and called for news organizations to publish official replies to "harmful" stories, was replaced by a version ostensibly affirming Western-style press freedoms. Though U.S. delegates would have preferred no declaration, they found the weakened version acceptable. Observed *Newsday* President William Attwood, a U.S. media representative on the American delgation: "If there's a reptile in the house, far better to have it a garter snake than a rattlesnake." Third World delegates also praised the compromise that M'Bow, as one of their own, had put together, but they continued to call for a "new world information order" more favorable to developing nations than the existing one.

APPENDIX 20
Selected Interventions in Programme Commission IV (Culture and Communication)
At the 20th session of the General Conference, Paris, November 1978 (Unesco document 20C/135)

The Delegate of the United States of America:

This revised Declaration, as approved by the Commission, is a triumph of the spirit of goodwill and international co-operation that can and should animate the United Nations in general, and Unesco in particular. I congratulate all those who participated in the deliberations that produced it, and especially the Director-General, whose patience and perseverance encouraged those of us who felt at one point that a document satisfactory to all might be too much to expect.

There is not only a diversity of cultures represented in this Conference, but a broad spectrum of differing social, economic and political systems. In some of our Member States the role of the press is seen as being totally supportive of government policy. In others, such as the United States, the absolute freedom of the press from coercion or restraint is a deeply held article of faith. This freedom is sometimes abused but, as Thomas Jefferson said in the early days of our young and revolutionary Republic, "we must tolerate error so long as truth exists to combat it". In our own generation, a distinguished American clergyman, the Rev. A. Powell Davies, spoke of this issue in terms even more relevant to the times in which we live. "The world", he said, "has become too small for anything less than brotherhood and too dangerous for anything less than the truth".

I am not so naive as to think that we have yet attained the age-old ideal of brotherhood. But I do believe that the paths to that goal will be easier if the peoples of this ever smaller and more interdependent world know more of the truth about each other. And that can be achieved only if all of the barriers to the free flow of information between nations are eliminated. Not everyone, I am sure, is fully satisfied with every word or phrase this Declaration contains. But it does express ideals to which we can all subscribe while imposing no ideological or mandatory constraints on the way each of us conceives to be the role of the press in our society. This is why I call it a triumph of goodwill and, may I add, of commonsense, that can only serve to strengthen Unesco and the cause of international understanding. Thank you, Mr. Chairman.

The Delegate of France:

(Translation from the French) I should like to express the satisfaction felt by the French delegation at the result we have just achieved. This result marks the combination of lengthy efforts and I should like to congratulate all those who participated in this effort—the President of the General Conference, who understood that agreement on this item was a precondition for the success of this session of the General Conference; the Director-General, who must have felt in the ac-

clamation he heard this morning a feeling of gratitude towards him, and under-standing—and, as he said, friendship—from those who presented the text which we have just approved; Mr. Boissier-Palun, his representative in Nairobi, contrib-uted as Chairman of the drafting negotiations approved to permit progress in this matter—even if our efforts were not crowned with total success—he also played a role in arriving at compromise; Ambassador Carducci who spoke on behalf of countries to whom the previous text had caused concern; I would also mention Mr. Masmoudi, who enabled us to benefit from his knowledge and concern for the non-aligned countries in this field.

Mr. Chairman, the difficulties we had to overcome were considerable. The French delegation, perhaps more than any other, was aware of the preoccupa-tions of the Third World countries. We believe that they do not have sufficient share in the facilities of the mass media and we realize the importance of this dec-laration and respect it. One of our major obstacles was to arrive at a text which could apply to the whole international community, that is countries which have different traditions, views and legislation in this field.

As far as we are concerned, we are profoundly attached to freedom and truth of information. The declaration in this respect should not have given any cause for misunderstanding. And it was necessary for this to be understood by those who provide information and who accomplish the noble and difficult task which is theirs with different convictions, but with the same selflessness and good will. The text at which we arrived is not perfect, sometimes its style reflects the difficult circumstances of its birth, but it is a good text to the extent that there is no victory of one ideology over another, and it expresses ideas and feelings to which all of us can unreservingly subscribe. The French delegation in this organization will continue to facilitate solutions through conciliation, and therefore we fully support the efforts of the Director General and are particularly pleased with the success of his efforts.

The Delegate of Egypt:

(Translation from the Arabic) Mr. Chairman, on behalf of Egypt I should like to welcome the declaration which we have just approved in an impressive and indeed historic consensus. I should also like to associate myself with the remarks of pre-vious speakers regarding the significant role played by the Director-General of Unesco in bringing that consensus about. As we all remember, he had been striv-ing ever since the eighteenth session of the General Conference to produce a draft that could command the support of a majority of delegations. The eventual out-come was the draft submitted to the present session and, I am sorry to say, widely misrepresented in the press.

I have kept many of the comments published on the declaration contained in document 20 C/20 Rev., and have noted with regret and concern that they are unfair, being based on inaccurate information and perhaps in some cases on passages of the draft declaration as set out in document 20 C/20 in its unrevised form. Such incidents open our eyes, day after day, to the significance of the role played by the information media.

In any event, we have now succeeded, thanks to the efforts of the Director-

General and the co-operation of the various States, in arriving at a new draft described in the document submitted to us as a compromise draft text. I am not
quite in agreement with this description. In fact the revised draft does not relin-
quish any of the fundamental principles embodied in the earlier version. It simply
takes into consideration the diversity of political and social systems necessarily reflected in the information systems of different States. I would therefore describe
the declaration we have approved today not as a compromise version, but as a reasonable one.

I believe that this declaration is not less important than the Universal Declaration of Human Rights, being a specific application thereof in a certain domain
namely the domain of information, inasmuch as war-mongering and the propa-
gation for racialism are man's arch-enemies. And I believe that the concrete proposals that could be arrived at by the International Commission for the Study of
Communication Problems, of which I have the honour of being a member, with a
view to ensuring a balanced exchange and a just flow of information between the
developing and the developed countries—and indeed among all countries,
whether developing or developed—could represent a further contribution to the
strengthening of peace.

All this, Mr. Chairman, gives Unesco a significant role to play in the
strengthening of peace and deomcracy. The most urgent task of each of us, now
that we have approved this declaration by such an impressive consensus should be
to return to his own country in order to give it the widest possible publicity and to
ensure that it is taught to young people alongside the principles which are taught
in connection with human rights, in accordance with the conclusions of the Conference convened by Unesco last September.

I do not propose at this time to embark on an analysis of the admirable declaration that we have unanimously approved, but I do believe that we need a large
number of analytical studies and articles designed to explain its principles to public opinion and impress it upon the minds of young people, and indeed of citizens
in general, for the strengthening of peace, liberty and democracy. Thank you,
Mr. Chairman.

The Delegate of China:

(Translation from the Chinese) Mr. Chairman, we approve of document 20 C/20
Rev., and I would like to make some remarks in this regard.

We have noted that quite a few Member States, especially the developing
countries, have expressed their hope that some guiding principles for the use of
the mass media should be established in the world. We fully understand this
justified demand of theirs. We have also noted that, to meet their demand, the
Director-General and his colleagues have made great efforts to prepare a new
draft Declartion acceptable as far as possible to all the parties concerned. The new
text stresses that bilateral and multilateral exchanges of information among all
States should be based on "equality of rights, mutual advantage and respect for
the diversity of cultures". It also advocates that the mass media should contribute
to the struggle against "colonialism, neo-colonialism, foreign occupation and all
forms of racial discrimination and oppression". These views embody some of the

basic principles to be followed in international press activities, and conform to the interests of the Member States. We hereby express our support for them.

At the same time, we should also like to point out that this draft Declaration still contains some ambiguous features. Here are two examples.

First, in the draft Declaration, the expression "freedom of information" occurs quite a number of times, but its meaning is not made sufficiently clear. We uphold the citizen's freedom of speech and the freedom of the press, which are clearly stipulated in our Constitution. But what we uphold is not sham but genuine freedom of the press, which conforms to the interests of the majority of nations and peoples in the world. We maintain that freedom and equality are inseparable. When men are not equal in respect of their social status, economic conditions and cultural levels, and when the views and press policies of one nation are imposed on other nations through powerful material means without showing any respect for their sovereignty, national and economic independence and cultural identity, this is inequality in itself, hindering the free flow and dissemination of information among peoples and nations.

Second, the wording "countering incitement to war" in the draft Declaration can be misleading. We love peace and have always been safeguarding world peace and fighting against wars of aggression. But there are just and unjust wars. We are resolutely opposed to unjust wars launched by war maniacs in order to control and plunder other countries, but we give our full support to the just war waged by the oppressed peoples to safeguard their national independence and win national liberation. It has been our consistent stand to oppose the hegemonists' propaganda for the arms race, war preparation and expansion. But when peace-loving forces, in the light of the characteristics of the present international situation, point out the obviously increasing danger of war, expose the war instigators' plots and machinations and help people to see where threats of war originate and keep vigilant and forearmed against them, this information is conducive to putting off the outbreak of a new world war and contributes, in a dynamic way, to the safeguarding of world peace. The dissemination of information of this kind should, therefore, be greatly encouraged and advocated.

There are in the draft Declaration some other ambiguous formulations which give rise to differing interpretations. However, I will not elaborate on them here.

Furthermore, most of the conventions, declarations and resolutions mentioned in the preamble to the draft Declaration were adopted without our participation. We will have to examine them carefully before determining our attitude.

The Delegate of the Socialist Republic of Viet Nam:

(Translation from the French) Mr. Chairman, Mr. Director-General. Like all other delegations, we have entirely supported the Director-General's proposal. In order to contribute to the success of the Conference and with a spirit of large cooperation and solidarity, the delegation of the Socialist Republic of Vietnam has accepted the compromise text submitted by the Director-General to whom we wish to pay a great tribute for the goodwill and perseverance he has shown in the search of a solution acceptable to all of us.

For our part, we consider that the text we have just adopted takes into account—to a certain extent—our main preoccupations. We have therefore accepted this text as a solution, acceptable to all delegations, to the problem before us at this stage of our negotiations.

Now, please allow us to make some reflexions which are not meant for the Director-General whose stand we appreciate very much, but for certain delegations whose attitude during the negotiations we still keep in mind. Firstly, human rights figure in the title itself, and we fully agree with that, but we would like that the rights of the peoples be more forcefully stressed by all the delegations as human rights and the rights of the peoples are as you know closely connected with each other. In many cases, if not always, the respect of the rights of the peoples is the *sine qua non* condition of the exercise of human-rights. A great many countries represented here have suffered too much from colonialism and neocolonialism not to be aware of it.

Secondly, there has been an enormous emphasis on the free flow of information and on the freedom of expression. It's all very good, but the responsibility of the journalists and information agencies are not enough emphasized. All of us repeat over and over again that there must be more justice in the world, more justice in the field of information. Justice is often presented in the form of a balance. We completely agree if you put freedom on one of the scales. We have fought thirty years, and in fact we have fought almost all along our history, for freedom, so how can we refuse now to put freedom of expression on one of the scales. But then on the other scale we must put the responsibility of the journalists and of the information agencies. We are living in an era when science and technology are making tremendous progress, but "science without conscience is but ruin of the soul". It is not anachronistic to recall this beautiful and wise thought when information techniques have become marvels but some times have become also horrible things. The more science makes progress, the more techniques in the field of information wield power, and the more we must put soul in it, the more we must have a sense of responsibility in making use of science and techniques, for freedom makes no sense if it is not accompanied by a sense of responsibility from the men who are enjoying it.

Human rights and the rights of the peoples, freedom and responsibility must be balanced if we really want to have a free and balanced flow of information, if we want to have a new international information order, more just and more efficient, which all of us are hoping for.

We avail ourselves of this opportunity to express our sincere thanks and deep gratitude to those of the journalists, information workers, information agencies, writers and artists who have reported with objectivity and responsibility on our long struggle for independence and freedom and who have thus contributed to the victory of our just cause.

Mr. Chairman, Mr. Director-General, dear colleagues,

By adopting this compromise text, the apt title of which has been the meritorious work of the Director-General, we have made a step forward. Let us hope that at the 21st and subsequent sessions, we shall make more steps forward together, thus fully assuming the responsibilities which are ours.

Thank you, Mr. Chairman.

The Delegate of the Philippines:

Mr. Chairman, fellow delegates and friends, I do not wish to introduce a sour note into the euphoria of what many of us in this room have rightly described as an historic moment. I merely wish to express certain reservations corresponding both to my personal conviction and to the policy of my Government on this important issue.

May I first thank the Director-General for his praiseworthy efforts in elaborating the draft Declaration just approved by acclamation by this honourable body. I can appreciate the pressures to which he has been subjected during the past few days, especially from forces which sought a confrontation among Member States and calculated that confrontation would surely negate any effort at writing such a Declaration; we are all aware now of this problem. We are sensitive to the Director-General's expression of gratitude for the friendship addressed to him, but let us remind him that this friendship is the direct result of the friendship and warmth that he himself has from the outset and consistently extended to us all.

Mr. Chairman, although we would have voted in favour of the draft just approved if there had been a vote on it, we wish to place on record our reservations concerning the following parts of the Declaration, namely: paragraph 11 of the preamble; paragraphs 1 and 4 of Article II; paragraph 2 of Article III; part of Article IV; Article IX; paragraphs 2 and 4 of Article X.

Mr. Chairman, I am sincerly perplexed that a number of ideas and sentiments embodied in the initial draft in document 20 C/20 have been deliberately removed from the paragraphs and Articles to which I have just referred. Thus, the final sentence in the original draft of paragraph 1 of Article II, which read "It [the exercise of freedom of opinion, expression and information] confers special responsibilities and duties on the mass media" has disappeared. The modifying phrase in reference to the exercise of the profession of journalists and other agents of the mass media, which read "with conscientiousness and impartiality" has disappeared from paragraph 4 of the same Article. The important requirements expressed in the phrase "accurate, complete and impartial information" in paragraph 2 of what was initially Article XI have been completely discarded from the present Article X.

I have tried to examine in my mind the reason for, and reasonableness of, the decision to dispense with all these phrases, which spell out quite objectively the duties, and the simple principles of the responsibilites, that mass media practitioners, like all other elements of society, should assume and exercise in the international community. Why are mass media practitioners and the decision-makers that deploy their forces exempted from any definition of duties? I share the belief that journalists are important and that they fulfil useful functions in society; but are they a special class of men and institutions above and beyond the purview of laws and international covenants? If this is the case, then what is it that placed them in such an exalted position? Is it their superior intellect or wisdom? Is it their superior moral qualifications? Is it a special mandate from heaven? What is it? I am honestly lost for an answer.

Perhaps, this is neither the time nor place to press for a reply to these questions, but in the spirit of free inquiry which the Declaration just approved enshrines, permit me to say they must be asked at any time, at any place and of anyone, including mass media practitioners. Thank you very much, Mr. Chairman.

The Delegate of Australia:

Thank you, Mr. Chairman. It is a matter of great satisfaction to my delegation that we in this Commission have succeeded to-day in adopting by acclamation the text of the draft Declaration on the Mass Media. This is a step of major importance for our Organization, and we welcome it in the true spirit of consensus. In the process, each of us has had to ascertain that our basic principles and objectives were respected in the final wording, while at the same time being prepared to acknowledge provisions regarded as essential by others. Australia's Foreign Minister put our position clearly in a formal statement which he made to Parliament on 8 November; and he has encouraged us to work with other delegations in developing an acceptable text at this session of the General Conference.

For us, Mr. Chairman, it was essential to obtain a text which encouraged the free flow of information from a diversity of sources and from which all implications of government control of the media had been removed. We also sought provisions which would ensure to journalists the best possible conditions for the exercise of their profession. Furthermore, we have strongly supported the inclusion of clauses recognizing that the mass media of developing countries should have conditions and resources which would permit them to gain strength and expand and to co-operate both between themselves and with the media of developed countries. We are very pleased that the final text does contain such provisions, and we have noted with satisfaction during this debate that other delegations are equally satisfied with the contents. In the interests of Unesco too, Mr. Chairman, we are pleased that the Declaration has obtained such wide support.

One of Unesco's constitutional objectives is to promote the free flow of ideas by word and image: this Declaration marks a significant step in that direction. With the Declaration now adopted, Mr. Chairman, we look forward to continuing our participation in efforts to develop the information and communication infrastructures in Member States and particularly in developing countries. The work plan already adopted by this Commission and the new initiatives adopted early this morning provide a framework for practical co-operation in the future. Australia stands ready to assist where it can in this important work. Thank you, Mr. Chairman.

The Delegate of Yugoslavia:

Mr. Chairman, Mr. Director-General, ladies and gentlemen, during the days that preceded the adoption of this Declaration, the Yugoslav delegation, together with representatives of other non-aligned and developing countries, took part in many discussions on the subject, and strove for an agreement which would make it possible to adopt the documents by consensus. In so doing, we were convinced that the moral and political authority of the Declaration would be so much the greater if it were largely accepted as a result of general will and agreement.

We are glad that we have achieved this result, and I would like to join in the expressions of congratulation to the Director-General, who personally entered into action to help in the search for a consensus. I should like to take the opportunity of reiterating my expression of recognition to Mr. Masmoudi, the distinguished delegate of Tunisia, the country which is now assuming the role of co-ordinator in the field of information among the non-aligned countries. On behalf of the Group of 77, he made an enormous contribution to the negotiations and was a tireless interpreter of our views.

Mr. Chairman, we are well aware that the preparation of this Declaration was no easy undertaking. It was rendered even more difficult by the fact that conflicting issues from other domains of international life could not be set aside and often diverted our discussion away from the essence of the problem. I will not return to dwell upon the negative influences of all kinds which made their appearance and which often created in world opinion a distorted impression of what was being done and what was aimed at, but merely express the hope that this Declaration, after being adopted by such an impressive consensus, will now receive sufficient publicity for the public at large and especially those who are most concerned—the journalists—to obtain a correct idea of its intentions and its content.

Mr. Chairman, the United Nations General Assembly will shortly be starting its own discussion on the subject of information. We hope that the adoption of this Declaration will stimulate more efficient action by the United Nations in this field, particularly with regard to the establishment of new international information order, the idea of which has been so strongly supported by a great number of delegations at this General Conference. As we have already stated in the debate on the programme, this objective represents an essential element of the struggle for new, more equal and democratic international relations and for new, more just human relations in our society.

Mr. Chairman, I have been authorized to state, on behalf of the Yugoslav delegation, that we shall strive for full implementation of the principles of this Declaration in our country, and for the general achievement of its goals. Thank you, Mr. Chairman.

The Delegate of Cuba:

(Translation from the Spanish) Mr. Chairman, we should like to acknowledge the remarkable work of exchange, dissemination and mobilization which is behind the draft declaration and the new international information order, brought to a successful conclusion with signal courage and determination by Unesco and its Director-General, Mr. Amadou-Mahtar M'Bow.

We should like particularly to underline the major role of the Director-General who, with thoroughly exemplary and inspiring strength of purpose, made it perfectly clear to us how important this declaration was for development and showed what an uncertain future a world linked not by self-governing countries but rather by supranational firms could have in store for education, science and culture.

To have made this fundamental topic the centre of international debate, to have faced up to the incomprehension and hostility of the huge interests involved in this sector and helped to find acceptable solutions is worthy of a place in history whose importance we cannot yet gauge.

Never before has it been so necessary for underprivileged and developing countries to be able to count on a future guaranteeing their freedom of expression and the identity of their own cultures.

The interdisciplinary and intersectoral nature of information today highlights the large number of nations which still have neither the appropriate infrastructure for disseminating information nor co-ordinated policies on information, education and culture.

Never in the history of Unesco and the United Nations system has any projected declaration been subject to so much misrepresentation and misunderstanding from the outset. Even this Organization's constant drive to explain its objectives did not save it from a campaign warned against by the Deputy Prime Minister of Cuba, Dr. Carlos Rafael Rodriguez, during the second session of the Intergovernmental Council of the Non-Aligned Countries for Co-ordination of Information.

We should like to point out that, on that occasion, the movement of non-aligned countries, considering it to be a favourable step towards the establishment of the new international information order and the new international economic order, unanimously agreed to endorse a declaration of principles on the mass media that would embody their aspirations for understanding and mutual respect, in the context of a balanced, objective circulation of news and messages among all the nations of the world.

It is worth noting that this consensus among nearly 100 countries, achieved in April of this year, was ratified immediately afterwards at the Conferences of Foreign Ministers held in Belgrade and Havana, in accordance with the founding principles of the movement.

For these reasons we acknowledge the efforts made by the Director-General and our distinguished colleagues to focus attention on mankind's higher destiny and, setting aside political prejudice, to investigate ways of ensuring that communication—now rapidly being overtaken by tele-informatics—serves as a means of liberating man and not as an obstacle to his solidarity.

Its role and function are laid down in the principles of universality enshrined in the United Nations Charter and the Constitution of Unesco. We do not deny the right to make use of an indispensable technology— already applicable to every activity and requirement of society—but we do point out that it would be appropriate to explore and apply it in full knowledge of its general short-term and long-term implication i.e., with an advance assessment of the effects it could have on the social context in situations of dependence.

The impact of the new technology is doing away once and for all with the traditional restrictive concepts of frontier and nation. For this very reason, there is a need to search for and revitalize individual identity and to preserve all that is best in our various traditions and ways of life. Let us never permit these mass media, capable as they are of broadening and liberating man's outlook, to be used to strengthen mercantilist policies which further loosen the ties between man and senselessly increase personal property. The essential task of communication is not to transmit bare facts without context or content but rather to spread enlightening knowledge that can fuel rapprochement and development.

Above and beyond the differences which may exist in what is often termed a pluralist world, let this twentieth session of the General Conference be a milestone for understanding and mutual respect among countries with different systems of society and government. Let us reassure an increasingly computer-dominated world that for this representative conclave men are more important than computers. The implacable development of technology applied mainly for mercantilist purposes shows that the time left to us for analysis and preventive action is short.

Mr. Chairman, we wish to pay tribute to the self-denial, devotion, courage and intelligence with which the Director-General has struggled to make it understood that a document of this sort expresses the fundamental aspirations for peace and understanding of the greatest part of humanity. This achievement, in spite of the limitations which may exist in a text approved by so highly diverse a community, is of a magnitude which the immediate future can be expected to reveal. And it is the personal achievement of the Director-General, Mr. M'Bow, whose action merits a place not merely in the history of communication, but in that of the people themselves and of their quest for a better way of life in an atmosphere of peace and understanding. Thank you, Mr. Chairman.

The Delegate of Algeria:

(*Translation from the French*) Mr. Chairman, the discussion on international communication, especially since the Conference of Heads of States and Governments of the Non-Aligned Countries, has permitted a better understanding of all the problems that arise in this field. Unesco for its part, under the high authority of its Director-General, has more than largely contributed to the realization of this objective by extending studies on this topic and by making efforts in order to promote a new world information order based on consensus, in spite of difficulties of the task and of manifold unjustified attacks whose object it had become. My delegation is pleased to stress this point, for Algeria, as she has proved, is eager to give her support to the actions of Unesco and her help in favor of peace and understanding in the world—a world that we should like to free from all its defects—and to join forces very closely with the efforts of the developing and all progressive countries for the promotion of a new, more just and better balanced economic order. That is why our delegation, although it had come here with quite exact proposals, has joined the appearing consensus and adopted all the initiatives conformable to the ideals that inspire the policy of our country.

In order to clearly explain its attitude the Algerian delegation would like once more to stress the importance of certain aspects of international communication, those that are of particular concern for the developing countries. To be sure, at issue are specific functions of the communication, on the one hand, and weak capacities of production and diffusion of the products of communication, on the other. The misunderstanding of these aspects by the developed countries which are dominating the market, a fact that has to be admitted, their refusal to take them into consideration, as well as the weakness or the absence of development assistance prove inevitably harmful to an effective implementation of any declaration or decision and, accordingly, slow down any planned action.

In our countries the mass media have a more complex function than that of spreading information. In addition to their traditional functions they have to assume another task, which is equally or even more important, that of participating and assuring the participation of people and peoples in the struggle for their right to independence in both political and economic fields and for development. Hence, the role of information in our countries is much larger than we think. It should facilitate the transition from the traditional to the modern society, which is a task to whose fulfilment the Governments dedicate themselves with sincerity and determination when technological and financial conditions allow that. It is not easy to provide for good financial conditions, Mr. Chairman, since owing to the international economic order, the existing system of international relations, and a certain ideological and cultural imperialism as its inevitable outcome, leads to an obvious lack of balance in the world as to the level of supports and means of information and, on the one hand, and of the understanding of the activities linked with assembling, treating and diffusing information.

As far as the means are concerned—which could be called "containers"—in spite of the efforts made by the developing countries for their own liberation from their dependence and for a betterment of their economic situation, it seems that the lack of equilibrium of information, to say nothing about the international communication, is inclined to grow worse in view of the tremendous progress of technology in the advanced countries. For this very reason we demand that urgent, global, coherent and suitably adapted measures be taken that would not be profitable only to those who, as a matter of fact, do not need it.

Now let's discuss the "contents" of information, on which so much doubt is thrown by representatives of certain countries who bring forward arguments that are in our view mostly unacceptable, as well as deliberately false interpretations that are at least inconvenient, when we know the history or a part of history of many of these countries, which in fact, unfortunately, have neither a real knowledge nor—which is more serious—a conscience for the problems of development. What are essentially these contents? The matter is the freedom of information and the free flow of information. It is very important for us to inquire about such concepts, taking, to be sure, as our basis the above-mentioned considerations,for we have an impression that, as said more or less in the same words by the outstanding economist Alfred Sauvy, the ideas of the Western developed countries concerning freedom flow perhaps even more than their currencies. First of all it would be necessary to admit that these concepts are highly political, because in spite of their undeniable universality they are profoundly stigmatized with differences of political systems and with related activities. In the interest of peace and international understanding, we should not allow ourselves here to judge their value.

We for our part esteem that the basic liberties and the free flow of information are noble and generous principles, which we have been always trying to implement, yesterday during the colonial period as much as nowadays during the period of the national construction, and for which we have to endeavour to find a concrete, quick and total translation. There cannot be a consequential reapproachement among the peoples without a greater extent of liberties and a free flow of information. But at the same time, we think that the society is sometimes obliged, within an exact constitutional, legislative and prescriptional framework based on national consensus, to set precise limits to liberties in order to prevent individuals from doing harm to others or to the society itself. For a stronger reason it is necessary to regulate the liberties we are speaking about. In this context we are pleased to quote the philosopher Simone Weil who admits that the freedom of information is not boundless and of whatever kind.

A great many have said before us: essential is the meaning we give to freedom and especially the use that is made of it every day. Very often, indeed, one purposely speaks of these liberties in a partial and equivocal way; this is true mainly for the countries exporting information. In most cases blindfolded by the quantitative development of their capacities and by the interest and their economic, political and ideological profits which they draw from this source either directly or by means of interposed persons or institutions, they are in fact prisoners of their strive for power that is difficult to understand, so great are the interests at stake. We all know that many relevant accusations, justified warnings and enlightened appeals have been pronounced by outstanding personalties on the basis of the above-mentioned considerations. We may quote here Jaques Kaiser who in his remarkable work "Death of Freedom" rightfully stressed the often woeful consequences of a bad understanding and of an erroneous implementation of these concepts. The always topical appeal by him who was a great French journalist and also a reputable specialist in problems of communication illustrates these trends unbearable for both individuals and peoples, the trends that have asserted themselves and developed through the recent years. Hence a belief should be avoided that the problems of communication could be solved just by proclaiming one's attachment to freedom of information and to the free flow of information throughout the countries. We are deeply convinced that there will be no real freedom in the matter of information as long as the lack of equilibrium of means and exchanges persists and as long as the world remains devided into countries that produce and export information and those that import and consume the same. Nothing delays and threatens the employment of the liberties so much as the present-day lack of a state of balance, whose gravity dangerously increases as the time goes ahead.

On the other hand, if we held it important to elucidate more precisely certain concepts, we think it is also necessary to mention the problem of the effects of international information. We think that the great extent of damage that may be caused by big media of information should urge us not only to adopt norms and regulations of conduct, but also and especially to prevent their violating. This is the whole problem of the responsibility of the institutions entrusted with information and of all those who have the mandate to put it in due form and to spread it. In our opinion, this should not be a matter of mere moral responsibility dictated only by everyone's conscience; it would be convenient to introduce mechanisms of sanctions, even moral ones, and rectifications of damage caused by violating the international obligations in the field of communication. It is of little importance whether the responsible is a moral or physical person. The importance of information, in particular in the developing countries, and the woeful effects that may be and really are provoked by certain information call for such a regulation, or at least, at the first stage, for a deeper deliberation. Unesco seems to us to be an ideal objective framework for such deliberation.

In conclusion, Mr. Chairman, ladies and gentlemen, Mr. Director-General, allow me to turn to honourable delegates of the developed countries, especially the Western ones, and also to honourable representatives of certain specialized organizations. By approving unanimously the Draft Declaration presented today, as well as by a unanimous approval, to which we have spontaneously adhered, of certain draft resolutions presented here tonight on the world information order, the Non-Aligned Countries, the Group of 77, have wished to give a concrete proof of their eagerness to carry on the dialogue on the world problems concerning the whole international community. By doing so they have wished to act in favour of peace, international understanding and a rapprochement among the peoples. Thank you, Mr. Chairman.

The Delegate of Denmark:

Thank you, Mr. Chairman. I would like to add the voice of the Danish delegation to those which have congratulated the Director-General on the consensus that has been reached. Our admiration for his efforts is very great indeed, and I believe that it is obvious that he increasingly personifies the very concept of consensus in international organizations. The fact that in this matter the tenacious efforts of some very skilled diplomats in our midst have also played an important role in no way detracts from his merit.

Mr. Chairman, my Government did not wish to oppose a consensus on a matter that has proved to be so important for Unesco and its deliberations over the past few years. However, it was not wholeheartedly that we took part in this particular consensus. May I recall the remarks made by a member of the Danish delegation the other day, who stated in this Commission that at the core this Declaration is a kind of international code of ethics for the mass media, and who expressed our belief that if such a code were to be made at all the task should be left to organizations of journalists, editors and publishers, and not to governments.

We recognize, of course, that the Declaration now adopted emphasizes the importance of freedom of opinion, expression and information, but we note with regret that these references are qualified and certainly fall short of the statement made in the general policy debate by our Minister of Education, who observed that "the independence of the mass media with regard to the Government and their entire freedom of opinion and expression are cornerstones in our democracy."

The Minister also said in the same debate that the Danish Government was, and may I again quote, "prepared to make its contribution to bring about a result which respects the freedom of the press and which meets the technical requirements of so many countries, especially in the Third World, which are faced with communication problems that call for immediate action of a practical nature". We would have wished to see the need to solve the practical media problems of the Third World accorded greater emphasis in the Declaration. There exists today a profound inequality between countries in respect of national news media structures, broadcasting facilties, number of radio and television receivers, national news agencies, newspaper printing and distribution possibilities and the like. We consider concrete measures to remedy these deep inequalities to be much more important for the development of communication than any number of lofty declarations.

Finally, Mr. Chairman, since Article 20 of the International Covenant on Civil and Political Rights is mentioned in the preamble of this Declaration, I have to draw your attention to the fact that Denmark expressed reservations in regard to paragraph 1 of that Article when Denmark was ratifying the Covenant, because we feared that its provisions might not be in complete accordance with the principles of freedom of expression. Thank you, Mr. Chairman.

The Delegate of the United Kingdom of Great Britain and Northern Ireland:

Mr. Chairman, this is a great day for Unesco, a kind of coming of age; the achievement of a new maturity which is due partly to the patient work behind the scenes of the Chairman of our Commission, but especially to the unstinting efforts of the Director-General in finding a consensus among us. My delegation welcomes this consensus, and hopes that it may prove a precedent for the future.

The Declaration on the Mass Media, important as it is for all of us, has been crucial for Unesco. Had the original draft been put to the vote, the United Kingdom and many of the Western democracies would have had to oppose it, because it implied State control of editorial content. Had that draft been accepted by a simple majority, it is Unesco which would have suffered most. Western public opinion would have been aroused against it, and some of those practical projects which are dear to us all could have suffered.

Happily, this is not the case, for the Director-General, at the very last moment, came to our rescue with a solution which we could all accept, with—may I suggest, remembering the story by Guy de Maupassant—a child whose parentage each of us can accept.

Of course, each of us may look at the child and think sometimes how much better it would be if its image were more like our own; there may be parts we positively dislike. We in the United Kingdom, for example, need to enter a reservation on preambular paragraph 5, which refers to the International Convention on the Suppression and Punishment of the Crime of Apartheid. We are totally opposed to apartheid, which is a flagrant violation of human rights, but we have been unable on legal grounds to subscribe to this Convention.

Personally, I also mourn the crime against the English language which has been committed in some parts of the text. But do not think Mr. Chairman, that we are complaining. The child may be less beautiful than we dreamed of, but it is ours and we welcome it.

No consensus can be perfect. It seeks only to define—if I may now speak in arithmetic terms—the highest common factor between all our views. As the distinguished delegate from Egypt has said, this text is not a compromise. None of us has compromised our principles. For example, the Declaration meets our major concerns. It places no hint of State control on the freedom for information to flow, nor on the freedom for journalists to have access to information. These are the freedoms which, in our view, make democracy work. They are an essential part, indeed the basis of the social and cultural structure of the whole Western world. They are the only true safeguards against the very kinds of extreme nationalistic behaviour to which this Declaration addresses itself.

A State without the means of change, wrote Edmund Burke about the French Revolution, is without the means of its conservation. That, Sir, is still true today. The mass media, free to criticize their own governments, may sometimes be a nuisance or even an embarrassment; but they are the means of ensuring evolutionary rather than revolutionary change. This text is a reaffirmation of principles in defense of freedom of the press.

So, the new baby is born, Mr. Chairman, but let us not believe that this happy event marks the end of the road. It is only the beginning. We in the United Kingdom welcome the views which many delegations have expressed so eloquently, and which our Minister for Overseas Development made very strongly in her address to the General Conference, on the need to assist the developing countries in building up their national media resources. Let us now clothe our new baby, Mr. Chairman, in a series of practical measures to assist the developing countries among our Member States to develop their mass media. Thank you.

The Delegate of Argentina:

(Translation from the Spanish) Mr. Chairman, my delegation congratulates the Director-General on having helped to draw up a text which is worthy of the consensus of the General Conference. I am sure that this individual effort so worthily undertaken by the Director-General is also the expression of collective endeavour by the permanent delegations, the regional groups, the Secretariat and the distinguished consultants: in short, Unesco's endeavour. It is to Unesco, Mr. Chairman—this assembly of individual viewpoints working in collaboration and harmony in spite of their differences—that I should like to pay tribute at this time.

I am gratified to see that this declaration on mass media legitimate principles are affirmed and beneficial recommendations made. There is ungrudging affirmation of the principle of freedom, to the extent that it fully satisfies the most zealous of its defenders: freedom of opinion, freedom of expression, freedom to seek and to receive information without limitation of frontiers, freedom to disseminate ideas through word and image; freedom to ascertain facts, freedom of access to sources of news and freedom for the public to take part in its preparation and rectification.

Mr. Chairman, all this is praiseworthy; but it is also interesting to note that this declaration displays an awareness of the risks implied in the excesses of freedom. Thus, it clearly states that those enjoying freedom of information should not abuse their privileges or yield to prejudice, but show self-discipline and rigour. My delegation joins in this call for responsible information. We also agree with the warning that information should not be identified with the spirit of tendentious propaganda: it is vital not to encourage its use to further hate, racial discrimination and violence. Above all, we are in full agreement with the recommendation which appears in preambular paragraph 11, whereby no false reports should be diffused with the aim of injuring friendly relations between States. Indeed, the dissemination of news persistently detrimental to the image of a neighbouring country, to the extent of constituting a systematic campaign, is an illegitimate and reprehensible use of freedom of information.

The Declaration also affirms the pluralism of information and the importance of its being open to the aspirations of the young stresses the need to correct the inequalities of information between developing and developed countries; and calls for recognition of the diversity of cultures and of the salutary effect of exchanges between countries with different economic and social systems.

My delegation is pleased to state its agreement with all those principles, but above all the Argentine delegation would like to point out that the declaration contains a praiseworthy effort to harmonize the spirit of free circulation of news on the one hand, and responsibility in information on the other. I repeat: in our opinion, the greatest merit of this declaration lies in the desire to harmonize freedom on one side and self-discipline in information on the other. Thank you.

The Delegate of Jamaica:

Thank you, Mr. Chairman. The delegation of Jamaica has accepted the compromise text contained in the revised draft Declaration on the Mass Media submitted to us by the Director-General but, quite frankly, it has done so somewhat reluctantly. We have accepted this compromise primarily because of our desire to maintain the solidarity of the Group of 77 and the Non-Aligned Group—an objective to which my Government attaches great importance—rather than because of real satisfaction with the text of the Declaration.

During the period of his attendance at this Conference, our Minister of Information and Culture made it clear that Jamaica considered a consensus decision on a Declaration on the Mass Media to be a highly desirable objective, provided that it could be obtained on the basis of what seemed to us certain minimum conditions.

Mr. Chairman, my delegation wishes to join with previous speakers in paying a very sincere tribute to the Director-General and other negotiators, in particular to Mr. Masmoudi, the spokesman for the Non-Aligned Group, for all the intensive efforts which they have put into the almost soul-destroying task of trying to reach a formulation acceptable to all. We are genuinely grateful to them. We would be less than honest, however, if we did not admit that we are profoundly disappointed that such monumental efforts of skill, time, physical and metal energy and above all of goodwill should have resulted in a document which, in order to secure a consensus, has in our opinion become so enfeebled.

Distinguished delegates will perhaps appreciate the position of my delegation when I say that my Government would have been able to accept the original document 20 C/20 without difficulty. Indeed, we had felt that this document was already a compromise reflecting existing needs and possibilities. Thus, the Declaration which has been adopted indicates further concessions which, in our view, almost calls in question the usefulness of the document. My delegation does not consider it appropriate to comment in detail here on our various reservations. Suffice it to say that in our opinion there is, for example, a totally inadequate reference to the responsibility of journalists and an almost unrecognizable reference to the right of reply. I would point out in this regard, Mr. Chairman, that these are matters of concern to us precisely because in my country there is a very free press; believe me, Sir, when I say that anyone who has read the newspapers in Jamaica will confirm this. We cannot but feel, therefore, that the Declaration as adopted fails to deal with a number of problems of the existing world information order which we ourselves have recognized, and which have indeed been recognized in the interim report of the MacBride Commission.

Having said this, Mr. Chairman, I should nevertheless like to end by expressing my delegation's sincere hope that the Declaration which has been adopted by acclamation will be regarded as a mere beginning, as a bare minimum upon which Unesco will be able to build, so that by the time of the next General Conference there will be clear evidence of a significant advance towards the establishment of a new international information order. Indeed, my delegation would request the Director-General to be kind enough to prepare and submit to the next General Conference an evaluation of the practical measures taken towards implementation of the principles and goals set out in the Declaration. Thank you, Mr. Chairman.

The Delegate of the Union of Soviet Socialist Republics:

(Translation from the Russian) Thank you, Mr. Chairman. The Soviet delegation played an active role in the drafting of the Declaration that we today adopted by consensus, and we were witness to the intense, literally titanic, efforts made by a number of delegations, by the Director-General personally and his associates to achieve a consensus. It is, therefore, with a feeling of special satisfaction that we congratulate the Director-General, and the entire General Conference on this historic event.

We realize, Mr. Chairman, that the text of the Declaration as adopted represents the best available compromise under present circumstances. Some provisions of this document could be better, and we also feel that the previous version 20 C/20 was by and large superior, but a compromise is a compromise—everyone has to give a little to make it possible. We consider it more expedient today to speak of the fundamental importance implicit in the adoption of the Declaration than to express reservations, although it is the right of every delegation to do so. What, then, does the Soviet delegation feel to be the major importance of the adoption of the Declaration?

First of all, for the first time in many decades—perhaps for the first time in history—an authoritative international document has been adopted which proclaims that the mass media have a contribution to make to the cause of peace and international understanding, to the furtherance of human rights and to the combat against racialism, apartheid and warmongering. Secondly, we see the importance of the Declaration in the fact that it clearly confirms the necessity of combining the concept of freedom of information, which we all advocate, with the concept of the responsibility of the mass media and journalists, responsibility which derives from the special nature of their activities and which has a strong influence on the international climate. Thirdly, we see the importance of the Declaration in the fact that it calls unequivocally for the reorganization of international relations in the field of information—relations which were the outgrowth of colonialism and imperalism. It calls for the reorganization of those relations on the basis of present-day standards of equity, with due regard for the right of developing countries to have their own voice, to have their own mass media. This is an important step in the decolonizing of information, which the Soviet Union has always advocated both in word and deed.

It was not my intention, Mr. Chairman, to touch on the philosophy underlying the communication policies of the various societies which we represent here. But, unfortunately, we have heard today a great deal of moralizing about which countries enjoy a free press and those which do not. We feel that this subject is out of place today. Obviously, the majority of those present in this hall have a completely different concept of what constitutes freedom of information from, say, Lord Thomson, Mr. Hearst or Mr. Springer, etc. As regards that type of press freedom, the last word has been said by a famous French journalist—Servan-Schreiber, I believe—who, in his book *Le pouvoir d'informer* wrote that in the West every citizen has as much right to publish his own newspaper as to launch his own earth satellite. I feel, therefore, that this isn't the place to lecture one another on what press freedom is and, in so doing, detract from the significance of the Declaration that has been adopted.

In a lighter vein, I would not myself be inclined to compare our Declaration with a child born of an unknown father. But if we pursue that thought of Guy de Maupassant, we might imagine the following picture: one member of a ship's crew did not have the kind of relations with a woman that would make her pregnant. Moreover, he suggested that she postpone the date of the baby's birth to a later time, whereupon he put in his name as one of the fathers so as to be considered as a real man and not some queer bird. I don't think Unesco is the kind of place where there can be any doubt as to the paternity of something. I hope nobody will take offense at this note of humour. We know very well, Mr. Chairman, who suggested that this Declaration be drafted, we know who advocated its adoption, and we know who opposed it. And the Soviet Union, which worked hard for the adoption of the Declaration, officially states today that it will do everything in its power to realize the lofty ideals and aims which the Declaration embodies. Thank you, Mr. Chairman.

The Delegate of Zambia:

Thank you, Mr. Chairman. The delegation of Zambia joins you and other speakers who have paid tribute to the Director-General for the tireless efforts which have resulted in the draft on which we reached consensus this morning. My delegation participated in the consultations on the draft in its capacity as Chairman of the Group of 77 and for us it is a matter of great satisfaction that we have achieved this consensus.

Permit me to place on record our understanding of the step we have taken this morning. For us in the developing countries, it marks the beginning of a new international information order which must of necessity evolve in parallel with the new international economic order towards which we are working. All these efforts are appreciated within the framework of decolonization. Zambia believes that the democratization of international relations that would result from a new order of things will take us closer to a more equitable order, and thus towards world peace. We are working for the creation of new attitudes which will make it possible for all members of the international community to forsake the exploitation of one country by another and to abandon war propaganda, racism and apartheid. In fact, Mr. Chairman, there is a crying need for every one of us—even those who advocate them—to forsake these evils, which are the certain causes of war. The acclamation with which we welcomed this Declaration is a sign that we mean business. Let us not turn back.

Finally, Mr. Chairman, permit me to express my delegation's appreciation to those Western delegations which have made a positive contribution to the consensus we have achieved today, despite pressures in their own countries against agreement to the draft, or to any draft at all. I should like to single out for particular mention, Mrs. Judith Hart, the head of the United Kingdom delegation, who worked with us on this issue and who gave us hope that we could work together in Unesco for the good of all its members. Thank you, Mr. Chairman.

The Delegate of Poland:

Thank you, Mr. Chairman. In congratulating the Director-General on his long-term efforts and in congratulating Unesco and ourselves on the adoption of the Declaration, my delegation is fully aware that the text is not ideal; nor does it bear comparison with the original draft of document 20 C/20, which was already a compromise text. But from the outset, my delegation and my country have fully supported the Director-General; we continue to do so, notwithstanding certain reservations with regard to the text we have adopted.

Mr. Chairman, we understand that to reach consensus on such a controversial issue always requires considerable concessions on every side. Besides, one should, at certain moments, view things in a broader perspective, and where what I described this morning as historical decisions are concerned, minor points should be disregarded, and attention focused on the essence of the problem.

From this point of view, we may consider the mere act of the adoption of the Declaration as a victory, victory for everybody, for the whole international community, and for our Organization in particular: victory for all those reasonable and responsible people—although I have recently noticed an especially irrational phobia with regard to our objective—I repeat for the responsible people in our international community who look ahead, who see the world in a wider sense and who see the need to introduce more just and equal and more advantageous relations in the field of information, both for the developing countries and for many other countries as well.

Whatever we may think of the Declaration as it stands, it is the first full document to confer certain obligations on the mass media and to define their role and contribution in support of such worthy causes as the strengthening of peace and international understanding and the promotion of human rights and the combating of such negative phenomena as racialism, apartheid and incitement to war. I said "the first *full* document", because it would be wrong to suggest that the sphere of information has up to now been an empty one. This is not at all the case. A mere look at the preamble of the Declaration shows how many resolutions, conventions and declarations have already in one way or another concerned this important field in its international aspects and dimensions, containing as they do certain norms, principles and ethical standards for those powerful instruments of information which shape and influence our minds and hearts, our views and our emotions, our value systems and our knowledge.

Mr. Chairman, the Declaration constitutes a moral obligation, but an obligation none the less, whether or not we use the word itself in the text. In all United Nations and Unesco documents, in all bilateral agreements, in the ethical codes of the vast majority of journalists' associations themselves throughout the world, Western countries included, freedom of information is accompanied by social responsibility. As the Director-General stated in his inaugural address to the first session of the MacBride Commission, "Those who exercise a freedom to which they are rightly attached must take its significance to heart, that is to say, its effects on others, and the responsibilities which it entails, for does it need to be recalled that freedom without responsibility is not freedom but licence". Journalists all over the world are not happy-go-lucky, irresponsible free agents; they are social agents, they are servants of their own society and of all mankind, whose problems and joys are the very object of their work. That is why I hope that the journalists and mass media practitioners the world over will themselves accept and apply the Declaration with all seriousness and sincerity. As for my country, I can assure you, Mr. Chairman and Mr. Director-General, that the journalists and the mass media of Poland will do their utmost to fulfil the Declaration both in letter and in spirit in the best possible way.

Permit me, Mr. Chairman, before the end of my intervention, to extend my personal thanks to all my friends, to all the members of the various groups, macro-, micro-and mini- alike, to all the representatives of the Secretariat and many other people from Nordic countries and from Western countries, our host French delegation included, with whom I have had the pleasure of working on this consensus. I am particularly grateful for their real contribution, for their actual contribution, it might be better to say, or at least for their moral support—moral support which in the given circumstances and atmosphere, especially at the beginning, was so much needed and appreciated by me personally. May I conclude by adding a word to our discussion on the parentage of our child, the Declaration. I am the veteran—and perhaps the only one of them in this room today—among those who were present at its conception, March 1974. And even then, we reached consensus. So perhaps I am the mother, after all! Thank you, Mr. Chairman.

The Delegate of Indonesia:

Thank you Mr. Chairman. We asked for the floor because we feel duty bound to explain our attitude to the adoption of this Declaration by consensus. In principle, we support the aims and spirit of the Declaration and we did not want to stand in the way of its adoption by consensus. But before giving our explanation,

Mr. Chairman, we want to express our deep appreciation to the Director-General and his staff and to all the delegates of the Member States for their untiring efforts during the last few days to produce a compromise text which would be acceptable to all and which has now been adopted. We realize the difficulties that had to be surmounted to produce a text which would enjoy the general support of all Member States. We also realize that what we have agreed upon today is the maximum that we could achieve under the present circumstances.

Nevertheless, after having studied all the relevant documents, the Indonesian delegation feels that there are several principles contained in the previous documents which could have been retained in the adopted Declaration.

Let me first of all refer to the principle of non-interference in internal affairs and respect for national sovereignty. This principle was adequately formulated in certain documents I have referred to. We feel that this principle is only partly reflected in Article XI of the adopted Declaration which specifies only respect for the legislative and administrative provisions of Member States.

Secondly, we believe in the principle of a free and responsible press. According to our understanding, the freedom it enjoys should be coupled in its application with a sense of responsibility for the improvement of law and order, for the general well-being of the people as well as for the effective implementation of the democratic process. In this connection, we hold the view that Article VIII would have to be interpreted in the spirit embodied in paragraph 9 of the preamble.

Last but not least, Mr. Chairman, we regret and consider it as very unfortunate that the concept of a new international information order has been very much watered down, as the establishment of the new international information order would bring the unsatisfactory situation in the field of communication and information to an end and start a new era in information.

Mr. Chairman, it is against this background that we would like to put on record the standpoint of the Indonesian delegation on this Declaration. Let me conclude, Mr. Chairman, by saying that we accept this Declaration with the foregoing explanation. I thank you.

The Delegate of Netherlands:

Thank you Mr. Chairman. I shall be brief in my comment on our adoption by consensus of the draft Declaration. The Netherlands delegation expresses its satisfaction that, owing to the tenacious efforts of the Director-General, of the President of the Conference, of the Chairman of this Commission and of many others, it was possible finally to reach a consensus on a text for the draft Declaration on fundamental principles concerning the contribution that the mass media can make to the causes mentioned in the title of that draft Declaration, 20 C/20 Rev. The Netherlands delegation congratulates Unesco, its Member States, its Director-General and its Secretariat on this result.

Having said this, Mr. Chairman, the Netherlands delegation, if it had had its own interests solely in mind, would never have felt the need for an international instrument of this kind. This statement is in conformity with the views expressed by the Netherlands delegation in all the discussions that have taken place in the years during which this draft Declaration was under preparation.

But, Mr. Chairman, in the perspective of the plurality of Unesco, the Netherlands delegation accepts the fact that other delegations are sincerely convinced of the desirability of adopting a Declaration of this kind and respects their conviction. In this spirit of compromise, we have co-operated in the efforts to adapt the text of document 20 C/20 in order to achieve a consensus. In supporting the consensus on the adoption of this draft Declaration, the Netherlands delegation was exclusively concerned with the need to comply with the legitimate wishes of the developing countries.

However, Mr. Chairman, I regret to have to state that the reference in the draft Declaration to the aspiration of the developing countries for the establishment of a new, more just and more effective world information and communication order gives rise to certain doubts in our minds. If these aspirations are directed towards diminishing the disparities in mass media infrastructures between developed and developing countries, we are more than willing to accept this concept. But, if, in the future, this concept of a new, more just and more effective world information and communication order is modified and eventually replaced by the concept of a new international information order, that would be a source of considerable concern for the Netherlands. Our reservation on the concept of a new international information order stems from the fact that the meaning and implications of this concept have nowhere been clearly defined as yet. If this concept means that the legitimate interests and developing countries are to be recognized, we want to co-operate fully, both bilaterally and multilaterally, as we have shown already by the offer of assistance we made in earlier discussions in this Commission. If, however, this Declaration is a first step towards restriction in the future of freedom of information, expression of opinion and fundamental human rights through governmental control on editorial content, a fear expressed by several speakers earlier in our discussions, we shall not be willing to accept this. Both the Constitution of Unesco and the Constitution of my country would forbid us to do so. Thank you, Mr. Chairman.

The Delegate of Hungary:

Mr. Chairman, the Hungarian delegation wholeheartedly welcomes the decision taken this morning to adopt unanimously document 20 C/20 Rev. presented to us by the Director-General. We interpret this historic moment for Unesco as the ending of one period of its work in the realm of communications and the beginning of a new one.

My delegation, Mr. Chairman, has always favoured the elaboration of guiding principles designed to facilitate the work of the mass media in strengthening peace and international understanding; in promoting the rights of individuals, societies and nations; and in helping the means of modern communication to combat racialism, apartheid and war propaganda.

As a matter of fact, since 1972, when at the request of our distinguished Soviet colleagues this idea was introduced into the working processes of Unesco, we

have endeavoured to contribute actively in outlining these principles and in helping the Director-General in his efforts to draw up an appropriate document. We
did so in the profound conviction that this international body had to face up to the
hard realities of the world today in the sphere of communication as well as in
other fields. We did so in the belief that—as we attempted to point out in the debates of the last General Conference—the principles of classical liberalism do not
work any more, or if they do, it is in the sense of sustaining the existing
imbalances, inequalities and injustices of the world communication system.

We believe, Mr. Chairman, that the Declaration which we have adopted reveals that more and more nations are conscious of this, and that more and more
societies are envisaging the new possibilities and duties of the mass media, the
new avenues of action and the new responsibilities of all the actors and agents of
mass communication in our world. Can we be content with the result of our deliberations and actions, as they are embodied in the Declaration? The Hungarian
delegation's answer is: yes. We are convinced that it marks a victory for all those
forces in the world which wish communication to serve the historical development of mankind. It is on this point, Mr. Chairman, that I should like to express
our gratitude to the Director-General, who, with his efforts, insight, understanding and empathy, has succeeded in creating a field of compromise for all these
forces. And so we can, and I believe we must, be jubilant in this victory.

At the same time, however, we should not forget that, having closed one
definite period in the history of international communication, we have opened a
new one, in which the tasks, duties and obligations that lie ahead will be no less
difficult than the preceding ones. This is not only because the Declaration, like
every compromise text, may be subject to different interpretations on certain crucial points, but also because the principles which it enshrines should be put into
practice by Member States, by the mass media institutions, by professional organizations and by the communicators themselves. And this will not be an easy process. It will be full of contradictions and daily confrontations; but in the long run,
Mr. Chairman, I am convinced that it will bear fruit. Let us not forget that our
own generation has learnt only how to live with the mass media. Our children's
generation has already learnt how to use the mass media. With this Declaration, I
hope, Mr. Chairman, that we are giving our children a key to understanding how
they may profit from the immense possibilities of the mass media, in their own
long-term interests. Thank you very much, Mr. Chairman.

The Delegate of the Syrian Arab Republic:

(Translation from the Arabic) Mr. Chairman, I should like, on behalf of the delegation of the Syrian Arab Republic, to congratulate the Director-General on having
brought his earlier and much appreciated efforts to such a successful conclusion
by presenting us with a draft declaration which has been unanimously approved
by all parties. At the same time, I should like to state that the delegation of the
Syrian Arab Republic approved this draft as a first step towards its eventual
expansion to reflect the aspirations of the developing nations in their entirety.

The peoples of the Third World, determined to exercise to the full their
freedom of thought and behaviour and the right to shape for themselves the new

life to which they aspire, reject the established information models with their one-sided presentation of issues in the form selected by the media of the dominating powers in an attempt to control the perceptions, thinking, mentality and behaviour of the developing nations.

They are striving to change these models, which have their roots in long centuries of oppression during which dependence, injustice and class inequality were imposed upon peoples. That is why we attach such importance to the establishment of responsibility on the part of the media for honest and objective presentation of the aspirations, problems and struggles of our peoples, on an equal footing with their presentation of issues which concern the developed societies; to the achievement of an exchange of information between the peoples of the developing world and the peoples of the developed world which is free and balanced as regards content, volume and intensity; and to the elimination of all practices resulting from prejudice or one-sided reporting, while approving the present draft, we still do not regard it as reflecting the interest of the developing countries in their entirety; our acceptance of it is motivated by a sense of collective responsibility towards the international community, the Non-Aligned Group and the Group of 77, and by the fact that we see it as an important first step inasmuch as it imposes a duty to contribute to strengthening peace and international understanding, to the promotion of human rights and to countering racialism, apartheid and incitement of war. Perhaps this draft will in due course and as a result of further endeavours—possibly at the twenty-first session of the General Conference—be expanded to call for the mass media to be encouraged to support the liberation struggles and legitimate rights of the peoples of the Third World and the developing countries. Only then, perhaps, will some at least of the more powerful mass media abandon their historic partiality and constant distortion of the truth, and instead of bewailing the fate of the world's aggressors—foremost among whom are the Zionist aggressors in the occupied Arab territories—support the cause of a people subjected to every form of torture, persecution, slaughter, suppression of freedoms and violation of rights, including the right to determine its own destiny in the land of its ancestors.

As regards the concept and practice of press freedom, we have nothing to add to the eloquent and detailed remarks of the delegate of Algeria. While we are grateful to the Director-General for all the effort he put into the preparation of his draft, we feel sure that he will understand the aspirations of the developing countries and of the peoples that are struggling for liberation. This is a field in which, unfortunately, much still remains to be done; we would mention specifically in this connection the establishment of a new international information order, and the study of all the other measures necessary for the establishment of such an order. This will entail a number of changes in national, regional and international information arrangements, taking into consideration the various charters, conventions, resolutions and decisions which have attempted to bring about improvements in this field as regards the safeguarding human rights on the one hand, and of the principle of justice, equilibrium, the protection of the peoples' freedoms and independence, respect for their cultural and civilizational values and the protection of their wealth, on the other hand. This also calls for the laying down of a new code of ethics for the transfer of information technology, within the framework of a new international order for the ethics of technology transfers in general, which encourages and facilitates the transfer of new information technology to the countries of the Third World. Unesco has a role to play in organizing all this, and so too have the developed countries, which can help, in co-operation with the various international and regional organizations, by providing assistance for the training of the necessary technical and other personnel to a standard at which they will be able and qualified to make sound choices, to process information and to contribute thereby to the service of their society and the realization of its aspirations, in harmony with national values and with the development of the Third World as a whole.

We reiterate our thanks to the Director-General, who has proved that he is a faithful and devoted son of the Third World; we greet in his person the determination of Unesco and its understanding of the aspirations of these peoples, and we remain confident that Unesco will continue its untiring efforts on behalf of justice and defence of the rights of peoples and their indigenous civilization and values. Thank you, Mr. Chairman.

The Delegate of Nigeria:

The delegation of Nigeria is very pleased indeed to participate in this exciting process of achieving acceptance and legitmacy for this very important Declaration. The experience of the past couple of weeks has reinforced our confidence in the ability of men of reason and goodwill to find acceptable and even dignified solutions to difficult and sensitive questions, if they are willing to commit themselves to the process of dialogue in a spirit of equality and mutual respect. It is not easy, but it can be done and has been done: it provides an important lesson to us all.

Mr. Chairman, we, in Africa, realize only too well the frustrations and the spiritual violence which can explode when human beings are prevented from speaking to one another as equals. We know that when the lines of human communication are entangled in a web of partial truths, accumulated prejudices and negative images, everyone is the loser and nobody can truly be the winner. For this reason, Mr. Chairman, we, in Nigeria, are spending a lot of our human and economic resources in building up a national capacity for involving our own people in the realities of their nation and of the world in which we live, so that we can participate as equals in the international dialogue in which we are all involved.

We are devoting a good deal of thought and energy to ensuring that we can provide an accurate and comprehensive record of our own activities and aspirations for the information of all people of goodwill who wish to know our view of the world. But other countries and other institutions will have to be willing both to listen to what we wish to say and to use the accurate information and true knowledge of us that we provide to them.

We recognize that the mass media are now the most potent means of cross-cultural communication, but we see that they are in danger of providing smoke screens through which we may see ourselves and our neighbours fleetingly and imperfectly as fragmented images. The cause of peace and progress cannot be fostered unless we resolve together to let the warm sunshine of reason and compassion pierce the fog of ignorance, suspicion, racism and apartheid which threatens humanity.

In accepting by acclamation with other members of Unesco the Declaration on the Mass Media, we, in Nigeria, are convinced that it is possible for more equal, more just and more creative relationships to emerge among peoples and among the media institutions and systems of the world. We see the need for change in the present understanding of the meaning of media ownership and control. It is clear that we and other so called developing countries should continue to expand our capacity for self-expression and self-projection on the international scene. We shall continue to insist on participating in the international dissemination of information, but as equals, and will engage in action to bring about the conditions that guarantee and sustain our equality. If the Member States of Unesco follow up the agreement reached on the Declaration with concrete activity in the spirit of co-operation and respect for the rights and dignity of others, it should be possible for all of us to become winners rather than losers.

We are deeply concerned that journalists and other agents of the mass media should show a sense of responsibility at all times, but especially when they attempt to report on other cultures. We wonder if those who so strenuously object to the mention of the responsibility of journalists would advocate irresponsibility. While we intend to use our resources and energies to support wider and freer distribution of information and ideas, we shall continue to insist that license and irresponsibility are not promoted in the name of absolute freedom.

Mr. Chairman, all that remains for me is to join all our colleagues in saluting the great experience which we have shared and to congratulate the Director-General and his colleagues of the Secretariat for assisting and promoting this laudable objective. Thank you, Mr. Chairman.

The observer for the International Organization of Journalists:

(Presented by its President, Professor Kaarle Nordenstreng) Mr. Chairman, distinguished delegates, I am speaking in the name of 150,000 journalists of over 110 countries from all parts of the world, representing various socio-economic conditions and political outlooks within an overall progressive and democratic orientation. These mass media professionals are hereby expressing their delight over the fact that on this historical occasion Unesco has achieved a landmark—small but clearly visible—along the road towards a more just and peaceful world.

The International Organization of Journalists has always supported Unesco in its endeavours to fulfil its primary mandate—that is: the promotion of international peace and security as well as a full realization of human rights—not only by means of education, science and culture but also through the means of mass communication. Professional journalists, namely those employed by the media as creative labour force and usually organized into national unions of journalists, thus representing the interests of wide strata of the people and not just the typically commercial interests of the media owners—these professionals have seldom questioned the right of the United Nations, Unesco and their Member States to pass resolutions and stipulations within the general framework of international law. Certainly, we are not inviting State control of journalism—on the contrary, we are very much concerned about it particularly in many Latin American countries and in Southern Africa—but we do understand that the mass media and journalists alike do not operate in a vacuum but are always bound to a framework of national tradition and legislation, and what's more, to a framework of international law.

In this respect, it seems to us that those distinguished delegates who have been so worried about the States with respect to the mass media are less faithful to the international law and order, and indeed to the United Nations system. Would it not be a bad idea to organize to the benefit of all of us a rehearsal course in elementaries to international law?

To be sure, the declaration adopted here is as such a useful piece of learning material: it serves as a pedagogical vehicle to remind us— media professionals, politicians as well as the general public—that freedom of information, which we all naturally very much respect, is already today, without any new media resolutions in Unesco or elsewhere, conditioned by several considerations, whereby the exercise of this freedom "carries with it special duties and responsibilities", to use the words of the International Covenant on Civil and Political Rights. Already the Constitution of Unesco, as recalled in the first two paragraphs of the present declaration, carefully places the well-known phrase of "free flow" into a framework where the utmost factors are peace and security. Responsible journalists welcome this goal and are not afraid, not only to place themselves in the service of profit-making enterprises, but also "to employ these means for the purposes of mutual understanding and a truer and more perfect knowledge of each other's lives". Indeed, it would be irresponsible and unethical to forget about these perspectives of Unesco's Constitution at the present time of arms race and constant risk for a nuclear war.

In fact, the declaration appears to be quite mild and vague—in any case less definite than the Constitution—in such crucial matters of mankind as the question of war and peace. Obviously the diluted text reflects the political compromises made in order to achieve consensus. Professional journalists understand this and although we are sensitive to conceptual and linguistic obscurities, we make our best in indicating a proper interpretation even to such formulations as "journalists and other agents of the mass media". At the same time, however, we want to point out that professionals need more than you have just adopted—we need a clear and honest, intellectually and morally unmasked approach to our profession and to the crucial questions of the time that we are facing. If it has been difficult for you as politicians to agree upon a moral and ethical emphasis to complement liberty, you may be sure that it will be no obstacle for us in the profession: we are people with moral and ethical standards.

The fact that journalists tend to think in uncompromised terms also helps us not to be mislead by the contemporary tactical cross currents in the global communication policies whereby a tendency is more and more clearly to be noticed that so-called "help to poor countries" and "action programmes" are being introduced as a means to prevent analyses and changes of a principal and structural nature and at the same time to turn attention away from the contents and the performance of the media almost exclusively into the more or less technical infrastructures of the media. It has been very instructive indeed to observe at this session how the genuine call by the developing countries for a new international information order, designed originally against colonial, neo-colonial and imperialist structures which have dominated the cultural and information field of these countries—how this call has now been formulated in a number of documents, including the declaration, in a way that points at a significantly different kind of an order which after all may not be very far from the existing one.

Development aid from the former colonial powers is naturally a reasonable compensation to the accumulation of welfare over a few centuries at the expense of present-day developing countries, but at the same-time we—at least we professional journalists—shall not sell our freedom to think and change the structures so as to ensure not only a "more effective world order" but an international order which supports peace, promotes justice and helps to materialize human rights.

Mr. Chairman, permit me to conlcude by repeating what I said two years ago in Nairobi:

> "The International Organization of Journalists represents those forces that stand firmly behind the New International Information Order and the objective of freer and more balanced flow of information within and between countries. The world's largest journalists' organization is willing to continue its co-operation with Unesco in its ever more important tasks in the field of mass communication. The new and more universal approach taken by Unesco means relinquishing the 'distinctly Western character' that the organization took in the past, to use an expression by Mr. M'Bow. We are all for such a reorientation and promise our active support to it against attacks and attempts to water down—in ways illustrated by the case of the draft declaration."

Thank you, Mr. Chairman.

And hereafter, Mr. Chairman, I shall go over to another statement which I have been authorized to read on this occasion. It is by the *Federation of Latin American Journalists, FELAP,* which unfortunately was deprived from attending this General Conference, unlike some other and less representative media bodies.

> The Latin-American Federation of Journalists is hereby ratifying its unbreakable and firm support to the actions towards the creation of a New International Information Order, with a view to achieving a more fair and balanced circulation of news.

> FELAP has publicly expressed itself in favour of this policy since its creation in 1976 Congress in Mexico, and in consequence with this determination, it organized a Seminar in Caracas on the flow of information in Latin America, and it also convened a meeting of Journalists from the Andean Area, in order to study the flow of news in the region. It also held a seminar in Havana with this same purpose.

> During the past month of October, the Directive Board of FELAP approved a declaration supporting Unesco's purpose towards defining a set of general principles about the role and the responsibility of the press regarding the new international information order, and also regarding the professional practice of journalism.

> During the past month of October, the Directive Board of FELAP approved a declaration supporting Unesco's purpose towards defining a set of

general principles about the role and the responsibility of the press regarding the new international information order, and also regarding the professional practice of journalism.

Both the President and the Secretary General of FELAP were formally consulted about the draft document to be considered by the 20th General Conference of Unesco, and both of them gave their views on it. Now FELAP wishes to ratify its support to this draft document and of course to the right that assists Unesco in providing this formulation, which is a right that has been pretendedly denied by some international organisations of newspaper owners and businessmen such as IAPA and by some Governments like the U.S.A.

We Latin American journalists have been requesting the right to participate and to give our opinion that such institutions as Unesco, are studying problems related with journalism and with mass communication in general. We are thus restating our opinion that those matters cannot be adequately examined without organized professional journalists being present, which is the case of FELAP in Latin America.

FELAP is an organization defintely in favour for the creation of a New International Information Order, which should gradually stop the domination of the transnational in the field of information and news flow, and which should also establish a more balanced flow of informational messages towards the settlement of a New International Economic Order.

FELAP is hereby expressing its wishes for the success of the 20th General Conference of Unesco and is specially supporting the Draft Declaration on the Mass Media.

FELAP's viewpoints on this draft were forwarded to the Director-General, thus giving their basic agreement with it, but also including some clarifications which are expressing the opinion of Latin American professional journalists and of their authentically representative organizations as well. These opinions are also coincident with those of international organizations such as International Organization of Journalists and some others.

> FOR FREE JOURNALISM IN A
> FREE COUNTRY!
> ELEAZAR DIAZ RANGEL
> President
> GENARO CARNERO CHECA
> General Secretary

Thank you, Mr. Chairman.

The Observer for the International Federation of Journalists:

(Presented by its President, Mr. Paul Parisot; translation from the French) Mr. Chairman, at the time of its last congress in September, the International Federation of Journalists, which represents 88,000 free journalists in the whole world, greeted the spirit of the Draft Declaration as an important contribution to the improvement of international understanding of the functions and problems of the mass media. At the same time we found it indispensable to reject certain tendencies of the earlier proposal which might have lead to intervention of the states into the

ethics of journalism or to constraints on their professional status. Since then we have noticed that the new text presented by the Director-General, to whom we pay homage, and now adopted by consensus, contains some perceptible improvements. We welcome, for example, more frequent references to human rights, although, I must point it out, the French version of the text in paragraph 1 of the preamble seems to have forgotten to quote them in reference to Unesco's Constitution.

Of course this text does not correspond entirely to our wishes. We confine ourselves to two examples. We would have preferred that political discimination be mentioned explicitly among all forms of oppression referred to in Article II, paragraph 3. We are also concerned about the use likely to be made of the obligation for the mass media to respect the dignity of nations. If nations are fully respectable, we equally insist on protecting the right of criticism for the opposition to political regimes which speak on their behalf. These regimes can sometimes behave in a way that does not deserve respect. There are situations in which journalists have the right and even the duty to follow their critical judgement rather than a sense of respect.

Having said this we appeal to all states to make easier the task of us information professionals, that is to protect and promote free information which, in our opinion, must be pluralist. Fulfilling their mission with professional conscience and meeting fully the responsibilities facing them, journalists will be able to serve the main intentions of the Declaration in accordance with codes of ethics worked out by themselves and to which they freely subscribed.

APPENDIX 21

"Unesco Declaration—Best of Bad Alternatives" by Leonard R. Sussman

From *Freedom at Issue* (New York), January–February 1979, Number 49, pp. 16–17. Reprinted with the permission of the author.

UNESCO's declaration on the mass news media—unanimously approved in November by 146 countries—was the least objectionable of a series of bad alternatives. American and allied rejection of this text would assuredly have produced a far more restrictive declaration. Government censors, of course, can *distort* this as any text to justify their mischief. Advocates of press freedom must remain alert to such possibilities. Yet the approved version is highly significant for (1) its positive support of government-free news media, (2) the omission of earlier press-control proposals, and (3) the implicit promise to improve Western reporting of the developing countries and bolster their communications capabilities.

Most important in the long term, the Third World and the West have shown they can avoid ideological dogma and negotiate improvements in their relationships.

The Soviet bloc's statist control of information was rejected as a universal standard. But the Third World's valid complaints of Western news coverage remain to be answered by improvements in the style and content of world-news reporting.

The Issues

Before the Soviets proposed the state-control drafts in 1972, some Third World countries had complained that Western journalists either distorted or ignored events in their countries. Third World spokesmen also pleaded for modern transmission equipment, lower press tariffs, and help in training their own communications people. For the past six years, while the Soviets increasingly tried to exploit Third World dissatisfaction with Western journalism, the developing countries resisted supporting the USSR's approach through UNESCO. Black African countries voted with the West at Nairobi in 1976 to defer the Soviet Union's most blatant press-control draft.

The past two years, many drafts prepared by the UNESCO secretariat under the 1976 biennial's authority favored governmental regulation of the news media, and would have required the media to grant governments the right of reply when the latter believed their views were misrepresented or even underreported. The "final" draft sent to member states in August for consideration at the October-November conference still carried strong government-control clauses.

Extensive preparatory negotiations were held in several capitals prior to the Paris conference. These preparatory meetings included Third World representatives, and spokesmen of Western governments and independent journalists. The Third World delegates recognized increasingly that the Soviet draft had been prepared mainly to advance the political and ideological interests of the Soviet Union, and not essentially to assist Third World communications development.

Some hardline spokesmen from developing countries demanded, in return for defeating the Soviet approach, a declaration announcing the creation of a New World Information Order. This would parallel and assist the UN-promised New International Economic Order. The information "order," in the view of the hardline Third World spokesmen, would be linked to the intricate negotiations later this year at the International Telecommunications Union. The ITU's World Administrative Radio Conference (WARC) will consider the assignments of all domestic and international broadcast, radio, and satellite communications. To tie this to a UNESCO declaration on the mass news media would open, in advance of the WARC, an immensely complex series of critical security and trade as well as news-media issues.

The Western negotiators at Paris, therefore, had the delicate objective of securing Third World support to defeat the press-control elements of the draft declaration, while not yielding to the hardline effort to link WARC issues under the rubric of the New World Information Order.

The Declaration

The solution was an honorable one. The declaration as approved stands clearly on the side of the independent journalist and "free flow," while properly calling for "a wider and better balanced dissemination of information." The declaration—again properly, and distinct from earlier drafts—leaves entirely to the media themselves, the determination of how to improve the balance. Indeed, safeguards are recommended for the security of the news media at home and abroad. Journalists "must have freedom to report and the fullest possible facilities of access and information." This would provide a check on governments, in order to assure the public's right to a diversity of "sources and means of information available to it." This principle runs directly counter to the collectivist assertion that the state is the only entity capable of determining what the people shall see or hear. Journalists were urged in the same article to be "responsive to concerns of peoples and individuals, thus promoting the participation of the public in the elaboration of information." The declaration thus urges greater access by the public to the news media, while denying governmental control to assure such access.

In the context of extolling the value of the news media in strengthening peaceful objectives, the journalists are also expected to give expression to those "who are unable to make their voices heard within their own territories." This would apply not only to blacks in South Africa but dissenters within the Soviet Union and elsewhere in Eastern Europe.

The "contribution" of the mass media, described in detail in Article III, no longer calls for governmental assurance that the media perform as stipulated. While it may be argued that the determination of press or broadcast content should not become the concern of governments through intergovernmental declarations such as this, the tallying of media contributions in Article III may be regarded as a statement of principle solely for the guidance of journalists.

In the same vein, the plea in Article V for the dissemination of views opposing those already published, should be seen as a proper objective, properly left to journalists themselves to fulfill.

The declaration avoids earlier demands for an international code of journalistic ethics.

Article X, which had earlier carried the harshest press-control stipulations, was significantly tempered. It now calls for maintaining "throughout the world the conditions which make it possible for the organizations and persons professionally involved in the dissemination of information to achieve the objectives of this declaration." That is linked to the improvement of mass communications facilities and resources in developing countries.

The Challenge

The declaration represents an act of faith on the part of the Third World delegates. They clearly understood and rejected the self-serving implications in the Soviet Union's approach. The developing countries also recognized that they had touched a sensitive nerve in challenging the Western world-news media. That challenge, in turn, is understood by Western governments, especially the United States. Our delegation, early in the UNESCO conference, announced a $24 million program to assist Third World communicators. This government would make available for free Third World use, a satellite that could carry information to and between developing countries. The United States also offered to help create regional journalist-training centers on several continents.

Most of the world-wide information flow directed by Americans is not controlled by the government. The independent world-news services, commercial and educational broadcasting systems, and major newspapers and news magazines convey the news and views which Third World critics would change. Improving that flow may be seen in the Third World as part of the bargain struck at Paris with passage of the mass media declaration in its final form.

The challenge, therefore, remains: Western journalists will be expected to cover the Third World with greater understanding of the long-term implications of events, and less emphasis on *today's* dramatic crisis. Most important, the government-free news media must be seen to use their freedom to report more sensitively the great "human need" stories in the Third World.

APPENDIX 22

"Declaration and Its Falsifiers" by Yuri Kashlev

From *Soviet Mass Media: Aims and Organization, Past and Present*,
Moscow: Novosti Press Agency Publishing House, 1979, pp. 49–55.
Reprinted with the permission of the author.

One only has to read the full title of the Declaration (Declaration on Fundamental Principles Concerning the Contribution of the Mass Media to Strengthening Peace and International Understanding, to the Promotion of Human Rights and to Countering Racialism, Apartheid and Incitement to War) to appreciate its uniqueness. This is the first instrument in the history of international relations which clearly and directly draws the attention of the mass media to their responsibilities for peace and friendship and the independence of peoples. "The mass media", says Article III, have an important contribution to make to the strengthening of peace and international understanding and in countering racialism, apartheid and incitement to war." It further states that the media are called upon to contribute "to eliminate ignorance and misunderstanding between peoples, to make nationals of a country sensitive to the needs and desires of others, to ensure the respect of the rights and dignity of all nations, all peoples and all individuals". Article IV stresses that "the mass media have an essential part to play in the education of young people in a spirit of peace, justice, freedom, mutual respect and understanding. . ." The Declaration's preamble contains references to many international instruments, including the Charter of the United Nations and the Constitution of UNESCO, which deal with the tasks of strengthening world peace and international security. It is important that the content of these instruments has been linked with the tasks of information activities in the international arena. Of fundamental importance, for instance, is the citing of Resolution 110 (II) of the General Assembly of the United Nations condemning all forms of propaganda which are designed or likely to provoke or encourage any threat to the peace, breach of the peace, or act of aggression. That resolution, which was adopted as far back as 1947 despite the opposition of the imperialist powers, has thus been given new life.

Another point which emerges strongly in the Declaration, both in its title and in many of its articles, is struggle against neocolonialism, racialism and apartheid. The Western countries bitterly opposed any mention of such acts as the International Convention on the Elimination of All Forms of Racial Discrimination, the International Convention on the Suppression and Punishment of the Crime of Apartheid. (Western "champions of human rights" still refuse to ratify these very important instruments which are of particular significance for the developing countries.) Both these conventions are, nevertheless, cited in the Declaration. Some articles refer to colonialism, racialism and apartheid as constituting gross violations of human rights. Against these phenomena the mass media should fight, promoting human rights, "in particular by giving expression to oppressed peoples who struggle against colonialism, neo-colonialism, foreign occupation and all forms of racial discrimination and oppression and who are unable to make their voices heard within their own territories." (Article II).

For the first time ever an international instrument at such a level clearly declares the need "to correct the inequalities in the flow of information to and from developing countries" (Article VI) and asks that "States facilitate the procurement by the mass media in the developing countries of adequate conditions and resources enabling them to gain strength and expand." (Article X).

In a number of cases the Declaration is addressed to workers in the mass media and journalists. Article VIII, for example, reads: "Professional organisations, and people who participate in the professional training of journalists and other agents of the mass media and who will assist them in performing their functions in a responsible manner should attach special importance to the principles of this Declaration when drawing up and ensuring application of their codes of ethics." Of fundamental importance is the stipulation that journalists who have freedom to report and the fullest possible facilities of access to information must act "with due respect for the legislative and administrative provisions and the other obligations of Member States." (Article XI). This accords with the relevant provisions of the Final Act of the Conference on Security and Cooperation in Europe.

And, finally, the Declaration recalls the international covenants on human rights some of whose articles directly bear on information issues (condemning incitement to war, the advocacy of national or racial hatred, stipulating measures against the abuses of freedom of information, and so on).

It would be naive to expect that now, since the Declaration has been adopted, all the information media of the West will immediately begin to act in its spirit. At first the West tried to present as a victory for itself the adoption of the Declaration which it had been opposing for so many years. Very soon, however, influential Western press organs hastened to express their negative attitude and to dissociate themselves from the authoritative instrument adopted by practically all states. *The New York Times* of November 29, 1978, commented that for the Americans there could be no question of freedom of speech or balanced information until those who were for racism and apartheid and for war were also given freedom of speech.

One wonders whether *The New York Times* is indeed expressing the true opinion of American journalists, the public at large and state bodies? Can the allocation of newspaper space or broadcasting time to the advocates of war and racialism really be a condition for freedom of speech? For we are dealing not with a gathering of anarchists, but with an international community guided by international law, numerous conventions and the Charter of the United Nations whose purpose is the strengthening of peace and good-neighbourly relations between nations.

As for claims that the Declaration is incompatible with the principle of unlimited freedom of information which allegedly flourishes in capitalist society, on this score opinions differ. As one influential French journalist put it, a citizen in the West is as free to publish his own newspaper as to launch his own earth satellite.

On the question of freedom of speech, the following incident comes to mind. It happened in Paris last year in late November, a few days before the end of the session of the General Conference. On the day after the adoption of the

Declaration the Soviet delegation held a news conference. Asked what criteria, if any, existed by which to judge whether information was biased or not, the author of these lines produced a fresh issue of the *International Herald Tribune*, a US newspaper published in Paris, with a lengthy comment on the Declaration and the claim that its adoption had been a victory for Western diplomacy. But the most surprising thing about the article was that it did not once give the title of the Declaration, nor did it even once mention the words *peace, international understanding, racialism, apartheid* or *incitement to war,* concepts which lie at the very heart of the Declaration. In my turn I asked western newsmen how could one adequately inform readers without mentioning the title of the Declaration and without saying a word about its substance, but, on the contrary, totally distorting it? This was precisely a case of the highly irresponsible attitude of a reporter being masked by demagogical talk about freedom of the press.

The following day *International Herald Tribune*, which had been caught in a gross distortion, had to report the incident very briefly, saying that the Soviet delegate accused the Western press of bias. But here again, it did not name the Declaration or give its substance and the essence of my criticism. A very instructive example of freedom of information—or rather political manipulation.

In the course of arguing about the Declaration many people asked: Is it realistic in the present situation to seek the adoption and observance of such understandings on the principles governing international information activities which states with different social systems could accept? Understandings which would meet the conditions of détente and take account of the legitimate interests of the developing world? It must be admitted that this is indeed a very difficult task. For it concerns the most deep-seated ideological interests of the opposing social systems, states and classes.

Notwithstanding the difficulties, a solution of this task must be found and as soon as possible. Just as political détente cannot develop for ever side by side with the arms race, so mutual understanding and trust cannot grow stronger in conditions of continuing subversion and "psychological warfare". The developing countries' striving for complete independence and their efforts to rid themselves of traces of colonialism will fail, if an end is not put to the "imperialist domination of information". Joint action by the socialist and developing countries, by sober-minded political leaders in the West and by progressive journalists and their organisations should help the mass media to get rid of the cold war inertia and of colonialist attitudes. It is in this context that the UNESCO Declaration should be viewed. Journalists and lawyers will most certainly be analysing and commenting on the Declaration time and again. But already the first assessments show that an exceptionally important instrument has been evolved, one which is beneficial to the cause of peace and understanding between peoples. UNESCO's achievement can be an example for other forums considering the problems of information. For the Declaration is but a first promising sign that international information activities will be pursued in accordance with the recognized principles of the peaceful coexistence and independence of nations.

APPENDIX 23

"All's Well That Ends Well" by D. R. Mankekar

From *Media and the Third World*, New Delhi: Indian Institute of Mass Communication, 1979, pp. 74–81. Reprinted with the permission of the author.

The dark clouds that lowered over the twentieth General Conference of Unesco in Paris proved to be dark toy balloons that burst at the first touch of reality. Once distrust was replaced by goodwill an agreed Draft Declaration emerged, which had eluded the grasp for two years. Looking back, it all seemed like much ado about nothing.

Loudly-trumpeted Western apprehensions and insinuations about the sinister motives of developing countries proved misplaced. Developing countries' fears about the West's seeming obduracy and stone-walling opposition to the Draft Declaration also turned out to be unjustified. A spirit of give-and-take and much semantic jugglery did the trick.

Trust begot trust. The sense of accommodation displayed by Tunisia's Mustapha Masmoudi and his team of negotiators dissipated Western distrust and evoked like response from the latter. The West came to realise that developing countries—and certainly those with whom they were negotiating—were not actuated, as they had earlier suspected, by any ulterior motive of shielding authoritarian regimes from external media but were genuinely concerned about their legitimate needs and grievances in the sphere of international media. The willingness of negotiators of developing countries to drop from the Draft the objected references to the state and its responsibilities and duties towards the media demonstrated their good faith.

Throughout, the Soviet role was that of friendly co-operation, solely aimed at ensuring that the Draft Declaration was adopted by Unesco during the current twentieth General Conference.

Nevertheless, while they lasted, the hectic two-week, behind-the-scene negotiations involved much nervous tension, many anxious moments and ups and downs and fluctuations between hope and despair, with one or other of the three parties—the West, developing countries and the socialist group—raising a hurdle just about the moment the negotiators thought they had achieved the feat of consensus on their latest draft.

On 20 November the agreed draft emerged at last but it was discussed in whispered tones, lest there be, even at that stage, a slip between the cup and the lip. On 21 November the final draft was released. Still, not everyone was sure of its ultimate passage.

On 22 November, Director-General of Unesco moved the Draft Declaration in the Commission. The unanimity and standing acclamation with which it was adopted at once demonstrated the sense of relief as well as rejoicing from all sections of Unesco.

And then it was suddenly realised all round that much of the preliminary lightning and thunder of threats and counter-threats from either side seemed out of place and meaningless.

If anyone deserves the Nobel Peace Prize for 1979, for averting a disastrous media confrontation on a global scale between developed and developing countries, it is Ahmadou Mahtar M'Bow the Unesco Director-General. For we owe this happy consummation largely to his genius: he was at once determined and tactful, firm and yet accommodating where necessary. Mr. M'Bow's firm grasp of the fundamentals made it easy for him to decide when to give in. He refused to be browbeaten, and kept his cool throughout.

The next prize for patience and perseverance unanimously goes to Tunisia's Permanent Representative at Unesco, Mr. Mustapha Masmoudi, and the third prize to Mr. Esmond Wikramasinghe of Sri Lanka, who laboured day and night alongside Mr. Masmoudi, now wooing the British delegation, next humouring the American, and then pacifying the Soviet, and then convincing their own colleagues from developing countries about the wisdom of the concessions made to the West. It was a nerve-racking task.

Just about the time they thought they had at last found the right formula, the negotiators were faced, to their chagrin, with Dr. Yuri Kashlev loudly complaining that the Soviet bloc had been taken for granted by the non-aligned group and ignored in all the prolonged parleys. Mr. Masmoudi and Mr. Wikramasinghe went into a huddle with the Soviet delegate. Dr. Kashlev seemed furious at the insertion of the Declaration of Human Rights not only into the title of the Draft Declaration, but in quite a few other places in the text. He was ultimately appeased with substitution of the word "promotion" in place of "violation" of Human Rights and a few other semantic changes.

Then Mr. Masmoudi and Mr. Wikramasinghe found that the final draft, as presented by the Director-General, had dropped the reference to "The New World Information Order" in the preamble, which was so dear to the hearts of Mr. Masmoudi himself and the non-aligned group. Mr. M'Bow cajoled them into acquiescing in the changed phrasing: "the establishment of a new, more just and more effective world information and communication order". This of course was not the same as "The New World Information Order" of the developing countries' concept, which had taken on its own distinctive connotation. But they bowed to Mr. M'Bow.

Mr. M'Bow's plea seemed legitimate to my mind, as, in any case, Unesco was seized of the question and the New World Information Order was part of Unesco's 1978–79 Programme, apart from the fact that the MacBride Commission's interim report had dilated upon the subject at some length. Irrespective of whether the Draft Declaration mentioned it or not, Unesco was therefore committed to pursue the question on its own.

The insinuation of the West that through the Draft Declaration developing countries were seeking to shield misuse of the media by authoritarian regimes was exploded the moment the negotiators of developing countries readily accepted the Western amendment deleting all references that could be construed as authorising the state to interfere with the media. All mention of the "states" was deleted from the Declaration except for one innocuous reference in Article X para 3 and 4 which spoke of "states facilitating the procurement by the mass media in the developing countries, of adequate conditions and resources enabling them to gain strength and expand. . . ." The fact remains however, that in many developing countries, whether the term "states" is mentioned in the Declaration or not, the Government has to fill the vacuum and get the provisions of the Declaration implemented by its media.

Indeed, the leading negotiators from among developing countries, like Sri Lanka, India and Tunisia would not care less. Nor did the negotiators of developing countries object to Article XI guaranteeing "the existence of favourable conditions for the operation of the mass media in conformity with the provisions of the universal declaration of human rights".

Similarly, if the sprinkling of the phrase "human rights" all over the Draft Declaration could please the West and enlist their support, the negotiators did not at all grudge them the concession—only however to be further amended at the behest of the Soviet delegate into "promotion" instead of "violation" of human rights. In addition, a couple of other Soviet amendments were also accommodated in the final version.

While the credit for intensive labours and initiatives at negotiation table and readiness to accommodate the other viewpoint should go to Mr. Masmoudi and Mr. Wikramasinghe and their team, bouquets are also merited by the Soviet delegation for their consistenly co-operative and helpful attitude during the negotiations, by the British delegation for their friendly co-operation and by the U.S. delegates for the unexpectedly flexible attitude brought to bear by them at the long-drawn out parleys, after their earlier obduracy. It was indeed reported that the U.S. delegation's new accommodating posture stemmed from fresh instructions received from Washington, following consultations from Paris.

What is the balance-sheet of this great debate that turned out to be no debate at all?

It can be justly claimed that the greatest beneficiaries from the Draft Declaration are the developing countries. Their demand for a free and balanced flow of information has been reaffirmed in more than one article of the Declaration. Article III specifically emphasises the important contribution the mass media have to make to the strengthening of peace and international understanding and in countering racialism, apartheid and incitement to war—all subjects after their heart.

Paragraph 2 of this article further stresses that the mass media, by disseminating information on the aims, aspirations, cultures and needs of all peoples, contribute to eliminate ignorance and misunderstanding between peoples, to make nationals of a country sensitive to the needs and desires of others, to ensure the respect of the rights and dignity of all nations, etc.

As for the highly controversial Article V, while the phraseology has been changed and made circumlocutory, the right of reply or rectification, as originally contemplated in the article, has been conceded in a round-about way—to which right the developing countries attached high importance.

Article VI underlines the necessity to correct the inequalities in the flow of information to and from developing countries, and between these countries: "It is essential that their mass media should have conditions and resources enabling them to gain strength and expand and to co-operate among themselves and with the mass media in developed countries."

Similarly, Article VII seeks the establishment of a more just and equitable international economic order, and Article VIII recognises the need for codes of ethics for journalists and accepts the concept of "responsibility" of media men (one of the points of Western objection earlier).

Article IX speaks of the "international community" contributing to the creation of the conditions for a free and more balanced dissemination of information (the West had hitherto betrayed an allergy to the phrase "international community").

Article X, paragraph 2, reiterates "that a free flow and better balanced dissemination of information be encouraged" (even though developing countries preferred the original phrase "free and balanced flow"). Paragraph 3 requires that states (the only reference to "states" in the Declaration) should facilitate the procurement, by the mass media in developing countries, of adequate conditions and resources enabling them to gain strength and expand. Paragraph 4 declares, "On a basis of equality of rights, mutual advantage and respect for the diversity of cultures which go to make up the common heritage of mankind, it is essential that bilateral and international exchanges of information among all states, and in particular between those which have different economic and social systems, be encouraged and developed."

The West had their gains too. They ensured that the state did not interfere with or control media under any pretext and freedom of information was guaranteed. They successfully got deleted all references to states and their duties and obligations to media; introduced the Declaration of Human Rights into the title and the text; ensured to journalists freedom to report, the fullest possible access to information and the best possible conditions for the exercise of their profession. They also succeeded in diluting the controversial Article V, though not in altogether eliminating it.

They further accepted the commitment of the media to make important contribution to the strengthening of peace and international understanding and in countering racialism, apartheid and incitement to war—a responsibility and duty which many Western media men had refused to accept and considered that the exclusive obligation of the state.

The Soviet bloc, which generally backed the non-aligned draft or the Director-General's version of it, gained the insertion in the preamble of the provision that "freedom of information requires as an indispensable element the willingness and capacity to employ its privileges without abuse. It requires as a basic discipline the moral obligation to seek the facts without prejudice and to spread knowledge without malicious intent."

Yet another provision the Soviet delegation got incorporated in the preamble recalled the resolution of the General Assembly of the U.N., adopted in 1947, condemning "all forms of propaganda which are designed or likely to provoke or encourage any threat to the peace, breach of the peace or act of aggression"—a "provision after the Soviet heart. Besides, as stated earlier, the Soviets also managed to change the word "violation" to "promotion" of the declaration of human rights in the title of the Draft Declaration as also in the text.

By adopting the Declaration on media at Unesco, the world has laid the foundations and ground rules for orderly international operations of the media in consonance with modern conditions created by the electronic revolution. The world has thus taken a big step towards the establishment of the New World Information Order, for which the developing countries have been agitating, and given recognition to the latter's grievances and demands in the sphere of media.

The Declaration, however, carries no sanctions behind it, apart from its moral impact on the world community. So that Idi Amin of Uganda or the White regime of South Africa can ignore it with impunity; but even they will feel the constraints induced by the Declaration and the universal censure implied when they violate human rights. At least, that is the hope!

A reality that a responsible and representative international body like Unesco cannot but take into account is the fact that there exist three different and distinct concepts of the role of the media, dictated by the respective needs and ideologies of the three blocs comprising that international body. The Stockholm Press Seminar's report defines the three concepts of the role of media as follows:

In Western countries, they are "concerned essentially to record facts, events and situations in terms of market requirements".

In the Socialist countries, the "media lay the emphasis first and foremost on the major problems besetting mankind and on educational and cultural needs". Indeed, Lenin prescribed a positive and distinctive role for the media in the building up of a socialist society.

In the Third World, "the media are seen as instruments of development," and therefore the Press, while functioning as the public's watch-dog, has also to share the burden with the Government of nation-building. That is the reason why several of the senior Indian editors and journalists objected to the inclusion in the joint I.P.I.-India declaration of last winter the attribution of an automatic "adversary role" for the Indian Press.

In formulating the Draft Declaration on the use of mass media, an international body like Unesco has perforce to strive to synthesise the fundamentals of all the three viewpoints. The time is past when the Western concepts and definitions on the freedom and role of the Press could be imposed upon international forums like the U.N. and Unesco.

Today, with the developing countries enjoying a significant majority both at the U.N. and Unesco, their demands, based upon their own realities and needs, cannot be ignored by either Unesco or the U.N. Nor would they dare overlook the socialist viewpoint.

APPENDIX 24
International Instruments concerning Journalism and Mass Communication

XXX = the instrument as a whole relates directly to the mass media
XX = the instrument contains parts relating directly to the mass media
X = the instrument relates to the mass media indirectly through a broader concept ("information", "propaganda", "public opinion" etc.)
0 = the instrument does not include standards concerning information, but it has been quoted in relevant instruments

CONVENTIONS AND CHARTERS

1. The International Convention Concerning the Use of Broadcasting in the Cause of Peace   XXX
League of Nations
Geneva 23.9.1936, entered into force 2.4.1938

2. United Nations Charter   O
San Francisco 26.6.1945

3. Charter of the International Military Tribunal (Nuremberg)   X
London 8.8.1945

4. Constitution of Unesco   XX
London 16.11.1945

5. Convention on the Prevention and Punishment of the Crime of Genocide   X
UN General Assembly Resolution 260 (III)
New York 9.12.1948, entered into force 12.1.1951

6. Convention on the International Right of Correction   XXX
UN General Assembly Resolution 630 (VII)
New York 16.12.1952, entered into force 24.8.1962

7. International Convention on the Elimination of All Forms of Racial Discrimination   XX
UN General Assembly Resolution 2106 (XX)
New York 21.12.1965, entered into force 4.1.1969

8. International Convention on Civil and Political Rights   XX
UN General Assembly Resolution 2200 (XXI)
New York 16.12.1966, entered into force 23.3.1976

9. Treaty on Principles Governing the Activities of States in the Exploration and Use of Outer Space, Including the Moon and other Celestial Bodies   X
UN General Assembly Resolution 2222 (XXI)
Moscow, London and Washington 27.1.1967, entered into force 10.10.1967

10. International Convention on the Suppression and Punishment of the Crime of Apartheid   X

UN General Assembly Resolution 3068 (XXVIII)
New York 30.11.1973, entered into force 18.7.1976
11. Draft Convention on Freedom of Information XXX
UN Third Committee
New York 1959–1961
12. Convention for the Protection of Human Rights and Fun- XX
damental Freedoms
Council of Europe
Rome 4.11.1950
13. American Convention on Human Rights XX
Inter-American Specialised Conference on Human Rights
San José, Costa Rica 22.11.1969

DECLARATIONS

14. Universal Declaration of Human Rights XX
UN General Assembly
New York 10.12.1948
15. Declaration on the Granting of Independence to Colonial O
Countries and Peoples
UN General Assembly Resolution 1514 (XV)
New York 14.12.1960
16. Declaration of the Disarmament Conference XX
The eighteen nation Disarmament Committee
Geneva 25.5.1962
17. Declaration on the Promotion among Youth of the Ideals X
of Peace, Mutual Respect and Understanding between Peoples
UN General Assembly
New York 7.12.1965
18. Declaration of the Principles of International Cultural XX
Cooperation
Unesco General Conference
Paris 4.11.1966
19. Declaration on Principles of International Law Concern- X
ing Friendly Relations and Co-operation among States in Ac-
cordance with the Charter of the United Nations
UN General Assembly Resolution 2625 (XXV)
New York 24.10.1970
20. Declaration on the Strengthening of International Security O
UN General Assembly Resolution 2734 (XXV)
New York 16.12.1970
21. Declaration of Guiding Principles on the Use of Satellite XXX
Broadcasting for the Free Flow of Information, the Spread of
Education and Greater Cultural Exchange
Unesco General Conference
Paris 15.11.1972

22. Declaration on the Establishment of a New International   O
Economic Order
UN General Assembly Resolution 3201 (S–VI)
New York 1.5.1974

23. Recommendation Concerning Education for Interna-   X
tional Understanding, Co-operation and Peace and Education
relating to Human Rights and Fundamental Freedoms
Unesco General Conference
Paris 19.11.1974

24. Definition of Aggression   O
UN General Assembly Resolution 3314 (XXIX)
New York 14.12.1974

25. Final Document of the Tenth Special Session of the Gen-   X
eral Assembly (on Disarmament, UN S–10/2)
New York 30.6.1978

26. Declaration on Race and Racial Prejudice   XX
Unesco General Conference
Paris 27.11.1978

27. Declaration on Fundamental Principles Concerning the   XXX
Contribution of the Mass Media to Strengthening Peace and
International Understanding, to the Promotion of Human
Rights and to Countering Racialism, Apartheid and Incitement
to War
Unesco General Conference
Paris 28.11.1978

28. Declaration on the Preparation of Societies for Life in   XX
Peace
UN General Assembly Resolution 33/73
New York 15.12.1978

29. Draft Declaration on Freedom of Information   XXX
UN Economic and Social Council Resolution 756 (XXIX)
New York 21.4.1960

Regional Scope

30. Declaration on Mass Communication Media and Human   XXX
Rights
Council of Europe
Strassbourg 23.1.1970

31. Final Act of the Conference on Security and Co-operation   XX
in Europe
The Conference on Security and Cooperation in Europe
Helsinki 1.8.1975

RESOLUTIONS

32. Calling of an International Conference on Freedom of   XXX
Information

UN General Assembly Resolution 59 (I)
New York 14.12.1946

33. Measures to be Taken against Propaganda and the Inciters   XXX
of a New War
UN General Assembly Resolution 110 (II)
New York 3.11.1947

34. False or Distorted Reports   XXX
UN General Assembly Resolution 127 (II)
New York 15.11.1947

35. Freedom of Information: Interference with Radio Signals   XXX
UN General Assembly Resolution 424 (V)
New York 14.12.1950

36. Question of False or Distorted Information   XXX
UN General Assembly Resolution 634 (VII)
New York 16.12.1952

37. Freedom of Information: B   XXX
UN General Assembly Resolution 1313 (XIII)
New York 12.12.1958

38. Programme of Action for the Full Implementation of the   XX
Declaration on the Granting of Independence to Colonial
Countries and Peoples
UN General Assembly Resolution 2621 (XXV)
New York 13.10.1970

39. Public Information and Promotion of International   XXX
Understanding
Unesco General Conference Resolution 4.301
Paris 14.11.1970

40. Dissemination of Information on Decolonization   XX
UN General Assembly Resolution 2879 (XXVI)
New York 20.12.1971

41. Preparation of an International Convention on Principles   XXX
Governing the Use by States of Artificial Earth Satellites for
Direct Television Broadcasting
UN General Assembly Resolution 2916 (XXVII)
New York 9.11.1972

42. Free Flow of Information and International Exchanges   XXX
Unesco General Conference Resolution 4.113
Paris 15.11.1972

43. European Co-operation   X
Unesco General Conference Resolution 5.61
Paris 16.11.1972

44. Role of Unesco in Generating a Climate of Public Opinion   X
Conducive to the Halting of the Arms Race and the Transition
to Disarmament
Unesco General Conference Resolution 13.1
Nairobi 26.11.1976

45. Unesco's Contribution to Peace and its Tasks with Respect   X
to the promotion of Human Rights and the Elimination of Colonialism and Racialism; Long-Term Programme of Measures
whereby Unesco can Contribute to the Strengthening of Peace
Unesco General Conference Resolution 12.1
Nairobi 29.–30.11.1976

46. Implementation of the Declaration on the Strengthening   XX
of International Security
UN General Assembly Resolution 32/154
New York 19.12.1977

47. Role of Unesco in Generating a Climate of Public Opinion   XX
Conducive to the Halting of the Arms Race and the Transition
to Disarmament
Unesco General Conference Resolution 11.1
Paris 23.11.1978

48. Culture and Communication: General Resolution   XXX
Unesco General Conference Resolution 4/0.1
Paris 28.11.1978

49. Questions Relating to Information B: International Rela-   XXX
tions in the Sphere of Information and Mass Communications
UN General Assembly Resolution 33/115
New York 18.12.1978

APPENDIX 25
Mexico Declaration
Adopted by representatives of international and regional
organizations of professional journalists, Mexico City, 3 April 1980
(Second consultative meeting among international and regional
organizations of journalists under the auspices of Unesco, 1–3 April
1980)

We representatives of international and regional non-governmental organizations, which unite nearly 300.000 professional journalists from all continents, meeting in Mexico City on 1-3 April 1980

1. Declare our support for Unesco, which by its Constitution is entrusted with the task of contributing to international peace and security and to this effect of promoting unrestricted pursuit of objective truth as well as mutual understanding between peoples and a truer and more perfect knowledge of each other's lives;

2. Declare our commitment to the Declaration on Fundamental Principles Concerning the Contribution of the Mass Media to Strengthening Peace and International Understanding, to the Promotion of Human Rights and to Countering Racialism, Apartheid and Incitement to War, adopted by acclamation at the 20th Session of the General Conference of Unesco in 1978;

3. Declare furthermore our respect for other relevant instruments of the international community designed to promote peaceful and democratic relations in the field of information, notably the Final Act of the Conference on Security and Co-operation in Europe, signed in Helsinki in 1975;

4. Declare our willingness to maintain and further develop contacts and co-operation between professional organizations of working journalists, such as the traditional meetings of European journalists in Capri and Jablona as well as the recent Arab-European dialogue of journalists in Baghda the meeting of journalists from the Andean area and the bilateral meetings of journalists' associations in South—East Asia, and in the last instance the consultative meetings among international and regional organizations of journalists convened by Unesco and commenced in Paris in 1978 and now continuing in Mexico, and we recommend that meetings among journalists from neighbouring countries be arranged, it being understood that the relations between organizations of journalists are based on full equality, mutual respect and non-interference in the internal affairs of the organizations concerned;

5. Recognize the recent progress in articulating the professional ethics of journalism, as demonstrated by the adoption of the Latin American Code of Journalistic Ethics in the Second Congress of FELAP in 1979;

6. Propose to all international, regional and national organizations of journalists that they analyze the contents of the following principles, which represent common grounds of existing national and regional codes of jour-

nalistic ethics as well as relevant provisions contained by various international instruments of legal nature, for their eventual inclusion in their respective codes of ethics with the ultimate objective of preparing a draft international code of journalistic ethics:

Principle I: People's Right to True Information

People and individuals have the right to acquire an objective picture of reality by means of accurate and comprehensive information as well as to express themselves freely through the various media of culture and communication.

Principle II: The Journalist's Social Responsibility

The foremost task of the journalist is to serve this right to true and authentic information, information understood as social need and not commodity, which means that the journalist shares responsibility for the information transmitted and is thus accountable not only to those controlling the media but ultimately to the public at large, including various social interests.

Principle III: The Journalist's Professional Integrity

The social role of the journalist demands that the profession maintain high standards of integrity, including the right to refrain from working against the journalist's conviction or from disclosing sources of information as well as the right to participate in the decision-making of the media in which the journalist is employed. The integrity of the profession does not permit the journalist to accept any form of bribe or the promotion of any private interest contrary to the general welfare. Likewise plagiarism constitutes a violation of professional standards.

Principle IV: Public Access and Participation

The nature of the profession demands furthermore that the journalist promote access by the public to information and participation of the public in the media, including a right of correction or rectification and a right of reply.

Principle V: Respect for Privacy and Human Dignity

An integral part of the professional standards of the journalist is the respect for the right of individuals to privacy and human dignity, in conformity with provisions of international and national law concerning protection of the rights and reputations of others, such as libel, calumny, slander and defamation.

Principle VI: Respect for Public Interest

Likewise, the professional standards of the journalist prescribe due respect for democratic institutions and public morals.

Principle VII: Respect for universal values and diversity of cultures

Moreover, a true journalist stands for the universal values of humanism, above all peace, democracy, human rights, social progress and national liberation, while respecting the distinctive character, value and dignity of each culture as well as the right of each people freely to choose and develop its political, social, economic and cultural systems.

Principle VIII: The Struggle Against Violation of Humanity

Consequently, a true journalist assumes a responsibility to fight against any justification for or incitement to wars of aggression and arms race, especially in nuclear weapons, and other forms of violence, hatred or of national, racial or religious discrimination, oppression by tyrannic regimes, as well as all forms of colonialism and neo-colonialism. This fight contributes to a climate of opinion conducive to international détente, disarmament and national development. It belongs to the ethics of the profession that the journalist be aware of relevant provisions contained by international conventions, declarations and resolutions.

Principle IX: Promotion of a New International Order in the Field of Information and Communication

The struggle of the journalist for universally recognized objectives takes place in the contemporary world within the framework of a movement towards news international relations in general and a new international information order in particular. This new order, understood as an integral part of the New International Economic Order, is aimed at the decolonization and democratization of the field of information and communication on the basis of peaceful coexistence between peoples and with full respect for their cultural identity. The journalist has a special obligation to promote this process of democratization of international relations in the field of information, in particular by safeguarding and fostering peaceful and friendly relations between States and peoples.

Principle X: The Journalist's Dedication to Objective Reality

Finally, a true journalist contributes to the Principles listed above through an honest dedication to objective reality whereby facts are reported conscientiously in their proper context, pointing out their essential connections and without causing distortions by improper emphasis, with due deployment of the creative capacity of the journalist, so that the public is provided with adequate material to facilitate the formation of an accurate and comprehensive picture of the world in which the origin, nature and essence of events, processes and states of affairs are understood as objectively as possible.

Kaarle Nordenstreng, President; Jiri Kubka, Secretary-General International Organization of Journalists (IOJ)

Marcel Furic, Administrative Secretary; Amador Merino, Secretary International Catholic Union of the Press (UCIP)

Eleazar Diaz Rangel, President; Genaro Carnero Checa, Secretary-General Latin American Federation of Journalists (FELAP)

Mohamed Laarbi Messari, Secretary; Sahib Hussain, Member of Bureau Federation of Arab Journalists (FAJ)

Djafar Assegaff, Secretary Confederation of ASEAN Journalists (CAJ)

Mexico, 3 April 1980

APPENDIX 26
The Declaration of Talloires
Adopted by leaders of independent news organizations at the Voices of Freedom Conference, Talloires (France), 15–17 May 1981

We journalists from many parts of the world, reporters, editors, photographers, publishers and broadcasters, linked by our mutual dedication to a free press.

Meeting in Talloires, France, from May 15 to 17, 1981, to consider means of improving the free flow of information worldwide, and to demonstrate our resolve to resist any encroachment on this free flow,

Determined to uphold the objectives of the Universal Declaration of Human Rights, which in Article 19 states, "Everyone has the right to freedom of opinion and expression; this right includes freedom to hold opinions without interference and to seek, receive and impart information and ideas through any media regardless of frontiers,"

Mindful of the commitment of the constitution of the United Nations Educational, Scientific and Cultural Organization to "promote the free flow of ideas by word and image,"

Conscious also that we share a common faith, as stated in the charter of the United Nations, "in the dignity and worth of the human person, in the equal rights of men and women, and of nations large and small,"

Recalling moreover that the signatories of the final act of the Conference of Security and Cooperation in Europe concluded in 1975 in Helsinki, Finland, pledged themselves to foster "freer flow and wider dissemination of information of all kinds, to encourage cooperation in the field of information and the exchange of information with other countries, and to improve conditions under which journalists from one participating state exercise their profession in another participating state" and expressed their intention in particular to support "the improvement of the circulation of access to, and exchange of information,"

Declare that:

1. We affirm our commitment to these principles and call upon all international bodies and nations to adhere faithfully to them.

2. We believe that the free flow of information and ideas is essential for mutual understanding and world peace. We consider restraints on the movement of news and information to be contrary to the interests of international understanding, in violation of the Universal Declaration of Human Rights, the constitution of UNESCO, and the final act of the Conference on Security and Cooperation in Europe; and inconsistent with the charter of the United Nations.

3. We support the universal human right to be fully informed, which right requires the free circulation of news and opinion. We vigorously oppose any interference with this fundamental right.

4. We insist that free access, by the people and the press, to all sources of information, both official and unofficial, must be assured and reinforced. Denying freedom of the press denies all freedom of the individual.

5. We are aware that governments, in developed and developing countries alike, frequently constrain or otherwise discourage the reporting of information they consider detrimental or embarrassing, and that governments usually invoke the national interest to justify these constraints. We believe, however, that the people's interest, and therefore the interests of the nation, are better served by free and open reporting. From robust public debate grows better understanding of the issues facing a nation and its peoples; and out of understanding greater chances for solutions.

6. We believe in any society that public interest is best served by a variety of independent news media. It is often suggested that some countries cannot support a multiplicity of print journals, radio and television stations because there is said to be a lack of an economic base. Where a variety of independent media is not available for any reason, existing information channels should reflect different points of view.

7. We acknowledge the importance of advertising as a consumer service and in providing financial support for a strong and self-sustaining press. Without financial independence, the press cannot be independent. We adhere to the principle that editorial decisions must be free of advertising influence. We also recognize advertising as an important source of information and opinion.

8. We recognize that new technologies have greatly facilitated the international flow of information and that the news media in many countries have not sufficiently benefited from this progress. We support all efforts by international organizations and other public and private bodies to correct this imbalance and to make this technology available to promote the worldwide advancement of the press and broadcast media and the journalistic profession.

9. We believe that the debate on news and information in modern society that has taken place in UNESCO and other international bodies should now be put to constructive purposes. We reaffirm our views on several specific questions that have arisen in the course of this debate, being convinced that:

- Censorship and other forms of arbitrary control of information and opinion should be eliminated; the people's right to news and information should not be abridged.

- Access by journalists to diverse sources of news and opinion, official or unofficial, should be without restriction. Such access is inseparable from access of the people to information.

- There can be no international code of journalistic ethics; the plurality of views makes this impossible. Codes of journalistic ethics, if adopted within a country, should be formulated by the press itself and should be voluntary in their application. They cannot be formulated, imposed or monitored by governments without becoming an instrument of official control of the press and therefore a denial of press freedom.

- Members of the press should enjoy the full protection of national and international law. We seek no special protection or any special status and oppose any proposals that would control journalists in the name of protecting them.

- There should be no restriction on any person's freedom to practice journalism. Journalists should be free to form organizations to protect their professional interests.
- Licensing of journalists by national or international bodies should not be sanctioned, nor should special requirements be demanded of journalists in lieu of licensing them. Such measures submit journalists to controls and pressures inconsistent with a free press.
- The press's professional responsibility is the pursuit of truth. To legislate or otherwise mandate responsibilities for the press is to destroy its independence. The ultimate guarantor of journalistic responsibility is to the free exchange of ideas.
- All journalistic freedoms should apply equally to the print and broadcast media. Since the broadcast media are the primary purveyors of news and information in many countries, there is particular need for nations to keep their broadcast channels open to the free transmission of news and opinion.

10. We pledge cooperation in all genuine efforts to expand the free flow of information worldwide. We believe the time has come within UNESCO and other intergovernmental bodies to abandon attempts to regulate news content and formulate rules for the press. Efforts should be directed instead to finding practical solutions to the problems before us, such as improving technological progress, increasing professional interchanges and equipment transfers, reducing communication tariffs, producing cheaper newsprint and eliminating other barriers to the development of news media capabilities.

Our interests as members of the press, whether from the developed or developing countries, are essentially the same: Ours is a joint dedication to the freest, most accurate and impartial information that is within our professional capability to produce and distribute. We reject the view of press theoreticians and those national or international officials who claim that while people in some countries are ready for a free press, those in other countries are insufficiently developed to enjoy that freedom.

We are deeply concerned by a growing tendency in many countries and in international bodies to put government interests above those of the individual, particularly in regard to information. We believe that the state exists for the individual and has a duty to uphold individual rights. We believe that the ultimate definition of a free press lies not in the actions of governments or international bodies, but rather in the professionalism, vigor and courage of individual journalists.

Press freedom is a basic human right. We pledge ourselves to concerted action to uphold this right.

APPENDIX 27
Major Events, Statements, and Resolutions of a Worldwide Debate Until 1978

Notes to Chart:

(Documentation on those events extensively covered in Chapter 1 is not reproduced here.)

33 The Conference

Conscious of the imbalance in the dissemination of information which is prejudicial to Africa . . .

Supports efforts being made by non-aligned countries to establish a new international information order in consonance with the interests of Third World countries . . .

32 COUNCIL OF EUROPE: Committee on the Mass Media

(Draft Report —23 September 1977)

. . . the principle of the free flow of information is a universal one. For the member States of the Council of Europe the principle is self-evident.

31 UNITED STATES SENATE, 95th Congress, 1st Session.

Report to the Subcommittee on Internal Operations of the Committee on Foreign Relations United States Senate. (Washington, June 1977.)

For several years, the Russians have been trying in several forums to get written into an international document the precedent that all nations have the right to control information coming into their country and that which goes out . . .

The basic conflicts between open societies dedicated to a free flow of all information and controlled societies in the Second, Third and Fourth Worlds have raised heated debates and actions . . .

UNESCO continues to be the action organization for nations which believe controlled information is the only logical policy . . .

The issues agreed to at this 1977 World Administrative Radio Conference (WARC) were narrowly defined technical questions concerning direct broadcasts from satellites. It is argued that the precedent nonetheless was set for prior consent. If this principle is expanded upon at the 1979 WARC when the entire broadcast spectrum is up for grabs, there could be a seriously damaging blow to the concept of the free flow of information across world borders . . .

30 Art. 22.a) The African Governments should ensure the total decolonization of the mass media . . .

c) African Governments should establish joint cooperation in order to break the monopoly of non-African countries in this field.

26 TARGET FOR 1982

(i) Greater understanding of the world situation concerning international information flows and formulation of strategies likely to achieve a more equitable two-way flow of information particularly between developing and developed countries.

23 Final Act, Helsinki, 1 August 1975.

The participating States, . . .

Make it their aim to facilitate the freer and wider dissemination of information of all kinds, to encourage co-operation in the field of information and the exchange of information with other countries, and to improve the conditions under which journalists from one participating State exercise their profession in another participating State . . .

21 UN Resolution 3201 (S-VI), 1 May 1974

We, the Members of the United Nations, . . .

Solemnly proclaim our united determination to work urgently for THE ESTABLISHMENT OF A NEW

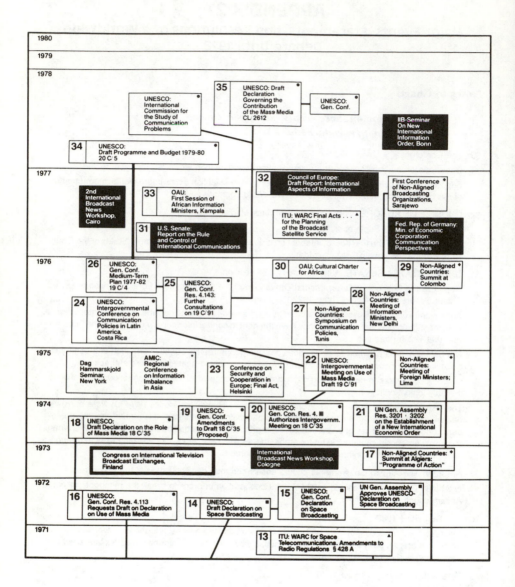

1970 | 12 | UNESCO: Gen. Conf. Res. 4.21: "To Assist in Formulating Mass Communication Policies" • | 11 | UN: Gen Assembly: International Development Strategy, Second Decade ★ | | Non-Aligned Countries: Summit at Lusaka •

1969 | 10 | UNESCO: Intergovernmental Meeting on Space Communication ■

| 9 | UNESCO: Meeting of Broadcast Organizations on Space Communication ■ | 9 | UNESCO: Gen Conf.: Authorizes Intergovernmental Meeting on Space Communication ■ | | UNESCO: Gen. Conf.: Requests "Research on Mass Media" •

1967

1966

1965 | 9 | UNESCO: Expert Meeting on Space Communication ■ | 8 | Intelsat I (Early Bird) ▲

1964 | 9 | UNESCO: Gen. Conf.: Authorizes Expert Meeting on Space Communication ■ | 8 | Intelsat Consortium Founded ▲

1963 | | 8 | Syncom II ▲

1962 | 6 | UN: Gen. Assembly Res. 1802 IV "Communication by Satellite" ■ | 7 | UNESCO: Gen. Conf.: Res., "Consequences of Artificial Satellites" ■ | 8 | Telstar I ▲

1961 | 5 | UN ECOSOC: Res. On Mass Media in Developing Countries

1960

1959 | UN ECOSOC: Requests UNESCO to Conduct World Survey on Mass Media | 4 | ITU: Radio Regulations §423 ▲

1958

1957

1956 | J. Kayser Mort d'une liberté

1955-1949

1948 | 3 | UN: Universal Declaration of Human Rights ★

1947

1946

1945 | 1 | UN: Charter ★ | 2 | UNESCO: Constitution ★

●	UNESCO on the Role of Mass Media	◆	Non-Aligned Coutries on the Role of Information
■	UNESCO on Space Broadcasting		Related Events
▲	Technical Aspects of Space Broadcasting	★	Basic Documents

© Institut fur internationale Begegnungen—Friedrich-Ebert-Stiftung, Dietrich Berwanger, Bonn, Oktober 1978—Grafik: Michael Hagemann

INTERNATIONAL ECONOMIC ORDER based on equity, sovereign equality, interdependence, common interest and cooperation among all States, irrespective of their economic and social systems which shall correct inequalities and redress existing injustices, make it possible to eliminate the widening gap between the developed and the developing countries . . .

15   Adopted, November 1972

Art.II: Satellite broadcasting shall respect the sovereignity and equality of all States. Satellite broadcasting shall be apolitical . . .

Art.V: The objective of satellite broadcasting for the free flow of information is to ensure the widest possible dissemination, among the peoples of the world, of news of all countries, developed and developing alike.

Art.IX, 1: In order to further the objectives set out in the preceding articles, it is necessary that States, taking into account the principle of freedom of information, reach or promote prior agreements concerning direct satellite broadcasting to the population of countries other than the country of origin of the transmission.

Art.IX, 2: With respect to commercial advertising, its transmission shall be subject to specific agreement between the originating and receiving countries.

14   UNESCO: Declaration of Guiding Principles on the use of SPACE BROADCASTING for the Free Flow of Information, the Spread of Education and Greater Cultural Exchange.

Draft, March 1972.

Art.II: In the use of space broadcasting for the free flow of information . . . should respect the sovereignity and equality of States . . .

Art.V: The objectives of space broadcasting . . . are to increase the flow of information . . . to the peoples of the world, bearing in mind the need for a balanced flow of news between all countries developed and developing alike.

Art.IX: States, taking into account the principle of freedom of information, should reach or promote agreement on the procedures to be followed with respect to the notification and acceptance of direct satellite broadcasts to the population of countries not participating in the preparation, production or transmission of the programme.

13   RADIO REGULATIONS

Amendment made by the WARC for Space Telecommunications Geneva 1971

Regulation 428 A: In devising the characteristics of a space station in the broadcasting satellite service, all technical means available shall be used to reduce, to the maximum extent practicable, the radiation over the territory of other countries unless an agreement has been previously reached with such countries.

12   "The Director-General is authorized to assist Member States in formulating their policies with respect to the mass communication media . . ."

11   Action programme of the General Assembly for the Second United Nations Development Decade.

(3) . . . While a part of the world lives in great comfort and even affluence, much of the larger part suffers from abject poverty, and in fact the disparity is continuing to widen . . .

(9) International co-operation for development must be on a scale commensurate with that of the problem itself. Partial, sporadic and half-hearted gestures, howsoever well intentioned, will not suffice.

(849 An essential part of the work during the Decade will consist of the mobilization of public opinion in both developing and developed countries in support of the objectives and policies for the Decade . . .

10   It was felt that the objectives for the future development of communication satellite systems for international broadcasts should include:

(i) making the flow of visual news in the world more balanced, particularly with regard to providing news coverage to and from, as well as between developing areas.

9   At the 1964 General Conference, the Director-General was authorized to convene a meeting of experts to define the principles and main lines of a long-term programme in the space communication field . . .

At this meeting, convened in Paris at the end of 1965, experts from a broad range of disciplines, . . . urged Unesco . . . to undertake a study of the problems posed by space communication for the free flow of information, the spread of education and greater cultural exchange . . .

As a further step in this programme, a Unesco expert meeting, in Paris in 1968, brought together representatives of broadcasting organizations from the various regions . . .

The General Conference at its 1968 session authorized the convening of a meeting of governmental experts on international arrangements in the space communication field. The findings of this meeting were to provide the basis for a Déclaration . . .

The meeting, held at Unesco Headquarters in December 1969, was attended by governmental representatives from 61 countries . . .

8 TELSTAR I, the first commercially built active communication satellite, was launched into a low-altitude elliptical orbit on July 10, 1962 . . .

On February 4, 1963, SYNCOM I achieved the correct synchronous orbit, but it failed within minutes. In July of the same year, SYNCOM II successfully demonstrated the practicality of synchronous communications satellites . . .

In 1964 the International Telecommunications Satellite Consortium (INTELSAT) was formed . . .

INTELSAT I (Early Bird) was orbited over the Atlantic Ocean on April 6, 1965 . . .

7 The General Converence of Unesco in December 1962 authorized a study of "the consequences which the use of new techniques of communication on a world scale, by means of artificial satellites", is likely to have upon the achievement of Unesco's essential objectives . . .

6 Communication by satellite offers great benefits to mankind, as it will permit the expansion of radio, telephone and television transmissions, thus facilitating contact among the peoples of the world.

5 The Economic and Social Council,

. . .

5. Recommends that the governments of the more developed countries co-operate with less developed countries with a view to meeting the urgent needs of the less developed countries in the development of independent national information media, with due regard for the culture of each country; . . .

(VI) Governments of the underdeveloped countries might consider reviewing their tariff and fiscal policies with a view to facilitating the development of the information media and the free flow of information within and between countries.

4 RADIO REGULATIONS

Regulation 423: In principle, except in the frequency band 3900 —4000 kHz broadcasting stations using frequencies below 5060 kHz or above 41 MHz shall not employ power exceeding that necessary to maintain economically an effective national service of good quality within the frontiers of the country concerned.

(Note: In general terms regulation 423 is the basis of International Shortwave Broadcasting, Services as Voice of America, Deutsche Welle, Radio Moscow etc.)

3 Article 19. Everyone has the right to freedom of opinion and expression; this right includes freedom to hold opinions without interference and to seek, receive and impart information and ideas through any media and regardless of frontiers.

2 Article 1,2. . . . the Organization will:

(a) Collaborate in the work of, advancing the mutual knowledge and understanding of peoples, through all means of mass communication and to that end recommend such international agreements as may be necessary to promote the free flow of ideas by word and image;

1 The Purposes of the United Nations are:

. . .

2. To develop friendly relations among nations based on respect for the principle of equal rights and self-determination of peoples, and to take other appropriate measures to strengthen universal peace.

Name Index

A

Abdulgani, R., 115, 117
Abel, E., *39*, 39–40, *40*, 242*n*, 405
Abrams, E., 61*n*, 75
Ago, R., *163*
Akkerman, R. J., *179*
Alanen, A., 154*n*
Amin, I., 448
Anand, R. P., *141*
Anderson, M. H., *3*, 23
Androunas, E., 25
Appel, E., *259*
Arbatov, G., *153*
Asamoah, O. Y., *150*
Asfia-Clement, S., 373
Attwood, W., 407

B

Barron, J., *165*
Bascur, R. S., *103*
Becker, J., 38–39, *39*
Beebe, G., *3*, 5, 15
Beglov, S., 235
Behrstock, J., *14*, *84*
Bishop, W. W., *179*
Blaker, P., 58
Blanchard, M. A., *223*
Boissier-Palun, 110, 124, 409
Bourquin, J., 88
Boyce, G., *263*
Brezhnev, L., 16, 66*n*, 72*n*
Brownlie, I., *148*, *176*, *196*
Bruun, L., *95*, 122*n*, *215*, 219, 220, 227, 237, 238
Buergenthal, T., *209*
Burke, E., 422

C

Capriles, O., 37
Carducci, 409
Carnero Roque, G., 114, 117
Carter, J. E., *18*, 59
Castaneda, J., *150*
Checa, G. C., 436
Christians, C. G., *215*, *268*
Cohen, S., 16–17, *16*, 58
Cooper, K., 404

Covert, C. L., *268*
Crawford, N. A., *262*
Crockett, G. W., 62*n*
Cross, N., *266*
Curran, J., *263*

D

Dahn, G., *164*
Davies, A. P., 408
Davison, W. P., *153*, 165
Deleon, A., 114*n*, 117–18
Deutsch, K. W., *232*
Dohna, B. G. zu, *144*

E

Echeverria, L., 120, 373
Eek, H., *13*, 87–88, 99, *153*, 155, *169*, 289, 355, 364, 367

F

Fascell, D. B., *43*
Fischer, R. M., 95*n*
Frankena, W. K., *258*
Friedman, L., *168*

G

Gaborit, P., *59*, *242*, 243
Garbo, G., 105, 106, 110, 120*n*, 341, 373
Garcia-Mora, M. R., *180*
Gauhar, A., *67*, *254*, 259*n*, 268
Gazeta, L., 236
Gerbner, G., *4*, *12*
Golding, P., *267*
Grachov, A., *66*
Graefrath, B., *163*
Greenshields, R. A. E., *180*
Greenspan, M., *183*
Gross, L., *153*, *208*
Grotius, H., 141

H

Hall, W. E., *141*
Halloran, J. D., *12*, 72*n*
Hamelink, C., 37–38, *37*, 69, 72*n*
Hannikainen, L., 140, 141, 154*n*, 167
Harley, W., *46*

Harris, P., 98, *107*
Hart, J., 426
Havighurst, C. C., *162*
Heacock, R., *98*
Hemanus, P., *195, 247, 258*
Herczegh, G., *144*
Hess, R., 168
Homet, R., *20,* 48
Horton, P., *114*
Hostie, J., *180*
Hurd, D., 62
Hutchins, R. M., 223, 226
Hypponen, E., 383

I

Ibegbulam, A. A., 373
Irani, C., *53,* 57, 122–123*n*

J

Jefferson, T., 262–63, 408
John Paul II, Pope, 35
Jokelin, R., *103*
Jones, J. C., *101,* 113, 117, 119, *215,* 238

K

Kaiser, J., 419
Kandil, H., 115*n,* 117*n*
Karpoushin, V. A., 373
Kashlev, Y., *56,* 72*n,* 130, 441–43, 445
Kekkonen, U., 13*n*
Kerry, H. E., 373
Kirkpatrick, C., 405
Kivisto, K., 26
Kleinwaechter, W., *7,* 69, *153,* 161*n, 235*
Kolossov, Y., *153*
Korey, W., *206*
Krasikov, A., 66
Krieken, P. J. van, *179*
Kroloff, G., 16–17, *16,* 58
Kubach, H., *235*
Kutakov, L. N., 373

L

Laine, A., 383
Larson, A., *153, 169,* 171, *172,* 179,
    180–81, *183, 218,* 221, 228, 232, 262
Lefort, R., 121
Leigh, R. D., 223–24, *224,* 226, 227, *262*
Lewis, P., *58*
Lomeiko, V. B., 236–37, *237*

Long, G., 43–44, *44*
Losev, S., 36, *40*

M

MacBride, S., *34,* 36, 240*n, 242,* 406
McGovern, G., 39–40
McNair, A. D., *164*
McPhail, T., *43*
Maheu, R., 84
Makagiansar, M., 53, 114, 115, 117
Mankekar, D. R., *69,* 72*n,* 119, 131, *226,*
    228, 233, 240*n,* 444
Margan, I., *56*
Marks, L. H., *60, 61,* 67, *251, 252,* 256,
    265
Marques, C., 36
Martin, L. J., *153, 180*
Masmoudi, M., 23–25, *23,* 36, 39–40, 69,
    124, 409, 415, 423, 444, 445, 446
M'Bow, A. M., 2, *6,* 15, 67*n,* 72*n, 75,* 93,
    110, *112, 118,* 119–20, 124, 268*n,*
    276–77, 406, 407, 415, 417, 445
Mehan, J. A., *6 ,* 6–7
Merrill, J. C., *254,* 263–64, *264,* 268
Mill, J. S., 254*n*
Milton, J., 254*n*
Mowlana, H., 61*n,* 76, *232*
Moynihan, D., 404
Muraywid, H., 373
Murty, B. S., *169*
Musa, M. M., 373

N

Naesselund, G., *89,* 108*n,* 113–14, 115*n*
Navaux, P., 115, 117
Nawatz, M. K., *144*
Negulesco, 148
Ng'wanakilala, N., *266*
Nixon, R., 16
Nordenstreng, K., *22, 38, 86,* 95*n,* 108*n,*
    109*n,* 113–14, 115, 117, 119, 140, *153,*
    154*n,* 169, *185, 186,* 187, 190, *208,*
    265, 267, 433–36
Nussbaum, A., *141*

O

Obradovic, K., *172*
O'Brien, W. V., *152,* 171, *172*
O'Connell, D. P., *196*
Oeser, E., *163*

Ornes, G. E., 15
Ortega, M. de los A. L., 373
Osolnik, B., *23*, 23–26, *26*, 39–40, *69*, 76, 88, 97, *234,* 235

P

Padover, S. K., *263*
Pannenborg, C. O., *179*
Parisot, P., 436–37
Pastecka, J., 72*n*, 117, 240*n*
Peterson, T., *87, 266*
Ploman, E., *15*
Power, P. H., *40*
Power, S. G., *54,* 54–56, *56, 59–60*
Prendergast, C., *43*

Q

Quarmyne, A., 115, 117
Quayle, C., 61*n*

R

Rahnema, M., 383
Rangel, E. D., 436
Rashidov, S., 72*n*
Reagan, R., 59, 62
Reinhardt, J. E., 18–19, *19, 21,* 41–42, *42,* 44, 107*n*, 406
Richstad, J., *3,* 23
Righter, R., *5, 16,* 17, *25,* 57–58, *58, 60,* 117*n, 121, 251,* 256
Rivers, W. L., *215*
Roosevelt, F., 64
Rosas, A., *172*

S

Sahovic, M., *144, 179*
Salinas, R., 98, *103*
Sauvy, A., 418
Schiller, D., *258*
Schiller, H. I., *8,* 17–18, 69, *86, 95, 153, 157, 169, 185, 208*
Schlochauer, H., *162*
Schramm, W., *87, 215, 266*
Servan-Schreiber, 425
Siebert, F., *87, 266*
Siefert, M., *4*
Sinclair, I. M., *148*
Small, W. J., 61*n*
Smith, A., *69, 267*
Somavia, J., 36–37, 69

Sorensen, M., *142, 148, 163, 179*
Spasic, A., *9*
Spaulding, S., 62*n*
Steininger, P. A., *163*
Stevenson, R. L., 256, 265
Stone, M., *61*
Stowe, R. F., 300
Streicher, J., 168
Strupp, K., *162*
Sujka, B., *172*
Sussman, L. R., *15,* 16, 24–25, *62,* 123*n,* 130, 256, 438–440

T

Tammes, A. J., *179,* 180
Tatarian, R., 240*n*, 404, 406
Terrou, F., 88
Thirlway, H. W. A., *148*
Topuz, H., *59*
Torres, E., 373
Truman, H., 64
Tunkin, G., *144, 148,* 171, *172*

V

Vance, C., 24, 404
Van Dinh, T., *9,* 69
Varis, T., *103*
von Glahn, G., *142*
Vuckovic, C., *66*

W

Wagner de Reyna, A., 124
Waldheim, K., 406
Waldock, H., *148*
Warren, C., *180*
Warvariv, C., 373
Weil, S., 419
Weinstein, A., *65,* 66
White, L., 223–24, *224,* 226, 227, *262*
Whitton, J. B., *153, 169,* 171, *172,* 179, 180–81, *183, 190,* 196, *218,* 221, 228, 232, 262
Wikramasinghe, E., 445, 446
Wingate, P., *263*
Wright, Q., 171, *172*

Z

Zassoursky, Y., *25, 40,* 72*n,* 95*n,* 240*n*
Zawodny, J. K., *232*
Zimmerman, B., 242*n*

Subject Index

A

Action Program for Economic Cooperation, 9

Algiers Summit, *see,* Summit Conference of the Non-Aligned Countries, Algiers, 1973

American Convention of Human Rights, 202, 206

American Society of Newspaper Editors, 218

B

Baghad Declaration, 1982, 68

C

Code of Ethics for International Communicators (Whitton and Larson), 228–232, 262

Columbo Summit, *see,* Summit Conference of the Non-Aligned Countries, Columbo, 1976, 11, 48, 65, 102

Commission on Freedom of the Press (Hutchins Commission), 223–228, 233, 247, 261–262

Conference on Press Agencies Pool of the Non-Aligned Countries, New Delhi, 1976, 10

Conference on Security and Cooperation in Europe (CSCE), Helsinki, 1975, 16, 77, 94, 170, 185, 235

Conventions, *see under,* United Nations

Cooperation, among states, 189–191

Copyright, 210

Council of Europe, Declaration on the Mass Communication Media and Human Rights, 1970, 194–195, 210

CSCE, *see,* Conference on Security and Cooperation in Europe (CSCE), Helsinki, 1975

D

Declarations, *see under,* Council of Europe,. Unesco, United Nations

Decolonization, 197–199

Détente, 185–187

Disarmament Conference, Geneva, 1962, 183

E

EEC, *see,* European Common Market (EEC)

Environment, obligations of states for protection, 147

Ethics,
codes, 215–249
professional, 211–268
proposals from socialist countries, 234–237

European Common Market (EEC), 26, 98

European Convention on Human Rights, 206

F

Federation of Latin American Journalists (FELAP), 218–219, 221, 244, 246

FIEJ, *see,* International Federation of Newspaper Publishers (FIEJ)

Force,
legal and illegal use of, 174–178
restrictions against use, 145

Free flow of information, 12, 14, 21, 23, 32, 38, 41, 59–65, 67, 92, 104, 113, 134, 157, 212

Freedom House, 24, 130

Friendship, among states, 189–191

G

Genocide, 205–206

H

Havana Summit, *see,* Summit Conference of the Non-Aligned Countries, Havana, 1979

Helsinki Conference, *see,* Conference on Security and Cooperation in Europe (CSCE), Helsinki

Human rights, respect for, 146

Hutchins Commission, *see,* Commission on Freedom of the Press (Hutchins Commission)

I

IAPA, *see,* Inter-American Press Association
IFJ, *see,* International Federation of Journalists (IFJ)
Individuals, rights of, 206–210
Inter-American Press Association (IAPA), 16, 61, 103
Intergovernmental Conference for Cooperation on Activities, Needs and Programmes for Communication Development, 44
Intergovernmental Conference on Communication Policies in Africa, Yaoundé, 1980, 30, 32, 45
Intergovernmental Conference on Communication Policies in Asia and Oceania, Kuala Lumpur, 1979, 29, 30, 32, 45
Intergovernmental Conference on Communication Policies in Latin America and the Carribean, San José, 1976, 45, 102
Intergovernmental Council for the Coordination of Information among Non-Aligned Countries, 65, 69, 119
International Catholic Union of the Press, 35
International Colloquium, *see under,* Unesco
International Commission for the Study of Communication Problems (MacBride Commission), 20, 23, 34, 36–40, 48, 50–51, 55, 117–118, 120, 123, 225, 241–242, 248
International conventions, *see under,* League of Nations, United Nations
International Court of Justice, 179–180
International covenant, *see under,* United Nations
International Federation of Editors-in-Chief, 59
International Federation of Journalists (IFJ), 245
International law, *see,* Law, international
International Organization of Journalists (IOJ), 109, 245–246
International Press Institute (IPI), 16, 53–54, 57, 59, 103, 121, 227, 245
International Programme for the Development of Communication (IPDC), 4, 5, 20, 44–46, 51, 53, 55, 225

International relations, regulation by international law, 141–151
International Seminar of Journalists, Tashkent, 1979, 72–73, 227
International Telecommunication Union (ITU), 209
International Union of Press Associations (IUPA), 218, 221
Inter-Parliamentary Union (IPU), 32, 33
IOJ, *see,* International Organization of Journalists (IOJ)
IPDC, *see,* International Programme for the Development of Communication (IPDC)
IPI, *see,* International Press Institute (IPI)
IPU, *see,* Inter-Parliamentary Union (IPU)
ITU, *see,* International Telecommunication Union (ITU)
IUPA, *see,* International Union of Press Associations (IUPA)

J

Journalism,
    as a profession, 251–268
    codes of ethics, 81–82, 91–92, 101, 211–268

K

Kellogg–Briand Pact, 1928, 167

L

Law, international
    basic principles, 143–148
legal and illegal use of force, 174–178
    objectives, 142–143
    prohibition of war propaganda, 172–174
    responsibility of states, 178–181
    sources, 148–151
League of Nations, International Convention Concerning the Use of Broadcasting in the Cause of Peace, 1936, 155, 168, 188, 190, 196

M

MacBride Commission, *see,* International Commission for the Study of Communication Problems (MacBride Commission)
MacBride Report, *see,* International Commission for the Study of Commu-

nication Problems (MacBride
   Commission)
Mass media,
   international instruments on, 154–161
   relation to international law, 139–199
   responsibility for veracity, 192–195
   responsibility of state for conduct of,
      163–166
Meetings of consultants, *see under,* Unesco
Meetings of experts, *see under,* Unesco
Mexico Declaration, 1980, 2, 34, 59, 68,
      227–228, 244–249, 253, 257–261
Ministerial Conference of the Non-
      Aligned Countries, Lima, 1975, 68
Ministerial Conference on Press Agencies
      Pool, New Delhi, 1976, 69
Movement of Non-Aligned Countries, *see,*
      Non-Aligned Movement

N

Nations, *see,* States
NATO, *see,* North Atlantic Treaty Organi-
      zation (NATO)
New Delhi Declaration, 10–11
New international economic order, 9, 21,
      27, 70, 72, 75, 158, 197–199
New international information order
      (NIIO), 1, 3–77
   concepts, 68–75
New world information and communica-
      tion order, *see,* New international
      information order (NIIO)
NIIO, *see,* New international information
      order (NIIO)
Non-Aligned Movement, 8–11, 15, 22, 23,
      25, 28, 32, 34, 50, 56, 67–69, 72,
      76, 96, 102–103, 105, 113, 118,
      120, 125, 126, 197, 246
Non-Aligned Symposium of Information,
      Tunis, 1976, 10, 102
North Atlantic Treaty Organization
      (NATO), 26
Nuremberg International Military Tri-
      bunal, 168, 171–172, 175, 178

O

Outer Space Treaty, *see,* United Nations,
      Outer Space Treaty

P

Peace, through communication, 187–189
Peaceful coexistence among nations,
      183–199

Pool of Press Agencies of the Non-
      Aligned Countries, 9
Propaganda, subversive, 195–197

R

Racial discrimination, 202–205

S

Security, through communication,
      187–189
Standards,
   international, responsibility of states,
      161–162
   national, 201–210
States,
   legal obligation to fulfill commitments,
      147
   rights of self-defense, 145
   rights and obligations in international
      cooperation, 147
   sovereign equality, 144
   standards relating to communication,
      201–210
Strategic Arms Limitation Treaty, 1972,
      16
Summit Conference of the Non-Aligned
      Countries, Algiers, 1973, 9, 69
Summit Conference of the Non-Aligned
      Countries, Columbo, 1976, 11, 48,
      65, 69, 102
Summit Conference of the Non-Aligned
      Countries, Havana, 1979, 48, 65,
      69

T

Talloires Conference, *see,* Voice of Free-
      dom Conference of Independent
      News Media, Talloires, 1981
Talloires Declaration, *see,* Voices of Free-
      dom Conference of Independent
      News Media, Talloires, 1981
Tunisian Resolution, 108

U

Unesco,
   Declaration of the Principles of Inter-
      national Cultural Cooperation,
      186–187
   Declaration on Direct Satellite Broad-
      casting, 1972, 156

Unesco (*continued*)

Declaration on Race and Racial Prejudice, 1978, 204–205

Declaration on Security and Cooperation in Europe, 158

Declaration on the Preparation of Societies for Life in Peace, 1978, 156

General Conference, 1946, 6

General Conference, 1956, 7

General Conference, 1960, 7

General Conference, 1968, 7

General Conference, 16th, Paris, 1970, 79, 80

General Conference, 17th, Paris, 1972, 79, 82–86

General Conference, 18th, Paris, 1974, 79, 90–94

General Conference, 19th, Nairobi, 1976, 15, 17, 26, 52, 79, 101–113

General Conference, 20th, Paris, 1978, 1, 18–20, 22, 26–27, 32, 45, 52, 79, 122– 28, 185

General Conference, 21st, Belgrade, 1980, 20, 45–57, 243–244

Intergovernmental Meeting of Experts on Draft Resolution, Paris, 1975, 79, 94–101

International Colloquium on the Free and Balanced Flow of Information between Developed and Developing Countries, 1977, 239–240

Mass Media Declaration, 1–199

context, 1–77

history, 79–132

textual examination, 133–138

Meeting of Consultants on the Free and Balanced Flow of Information in a New Communication Order, 1978, 240–241

Meeting of Experts on Communication Policies and Planning, 1972, 12

Meeting of Experts on Contribution to an Ethic of Communication, 1977, 235

Meeting of Experts on Draft Resolution, Paris, 1974, 79, 88

Meeting of Experts on Mass Communication and Society, Montreal, 1969, 12

politization, 13–14

Programme Commission, 90–92, 107, 110, 124, 126–127

Programme Committee on Communication, 81, 83

Proposals for an International Programme of Communication Research, 1971, 12

Regional Conference on Communication Policies, San José, 1976, 68

Universal Declaration of Human Rights, 1948, 156

Union of Journalists in Finland, 122, 258

United Nations,

Charter, 167–168, 171, 174–176

Conference on Freedom of Information, Geneva, 1948, 134

Convention on the International Right of Correction, 192–194, 211, 213

Convention on the Law of the Sea, 207–208

Convention on the Prevention and Punishment of the Crime of Genocide, 205–206

Declaration of Principles of International Law Concerning Friendly Relations and Cooperation among States, 170

Declaration on Principles of International Law, 1970, 164

Declaration on the Granting of Independence to Colonial Countries and Peoples, 197–198

Declaration on the Preparation of Societies for Life in Peace, 171, 191, 198–199

Definition of Aggression, 170, 174

Disarmament Committee, 169

Draft Convention on Freedom of Information, 193

Economic and Social Council, 4, 13

General Assembly, 4, 27, 28, 46, 51, 96, 169, 184

Special Session on Disarmament, 1978, 184

International Convention on the Elimination of All Forms of Racial Discrimination, 1965, 202–204

International Convention on the Suppression and Punishment of the Crime of Apartheid, 1973, 203

International Covenant on Civil and Political Rights, 169, 171, 178, 201–207, 210, 263

International Covenant on Economic,

Social and Cultural Rights, 1966, 210

International Law Commission, 162

Outer Space Treaty, 170, 180

Resolution on Dissemination of Information on Decolonization, 1979, 198

United States, House of Representatives, Committee on Foreign Affairs, 61–62

United States, Senate, Committee on Foreign Relations, 16

V

Venezuelan Resolution, 50

Voice of America, 163–164

Voices of Freedom Conference of Independent News Media, Talloires, 1981, 59–65, 251–257, 265

W

War propaganda, prohibition, 167–181

World Administrative Radio Conference (WARC), Geneva, 1979, 43

World Press Freedom Committee, 59, 227, 245